COMBATING CORRUPTION

ENCOURAGING ETHICS

A SOURCEBOOK
FOR PUBLIC SERVICE ETHICS

EDITED BY
WILLIAM L. RICHTER
FRANCES BURKE
JAMESON W. DOIG

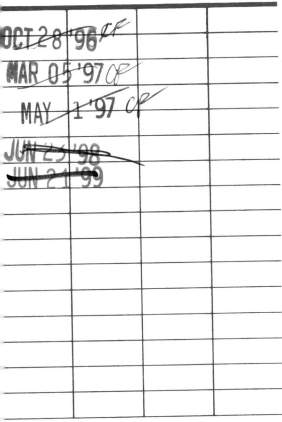

ASPA

Advancing excellence
in public service . . .

The American Society for Public Administration
1120 G Street NW, Suite 500
Washington, DC 20005

International Standard Book Number: 0-936678-14-3

Susan England, Designer

Preface

This volume seeks to address three audiences: (1) public servants at all levels of government, from cities and towns to state and national agencies, who are frequently confronted with ethical issues and ethical choices; (2) students preparing for careers in public service, for whom ethics education is increasingly recognized as essential preparation; and (3) that community of scholars, many of whose works are represented in this book, who in their teaching and writing seek to clarify our understanding of ethical issues and options. We also hope that a wider public might take interest in a work which addresses the urgent tasks of combating corruption and encouraging ethical behavior in public service.

As the title of this volume suggests, the following pages focus primarily upon those ethical problems and topics which are associated with the concept of corruption and its cousins — lying, evasion of accountability, and the abuse of authority. We recognize that there are other dimensions to the field of ethics, but the problems covered here are, we believe, central to the subject and of sufficient public concern to merit this emphasis.

The title of the book also underscores the importance of thinking about the positive as well as the negative side of ethics. Too frequently the public debate is focused on the unethical behavior of individuals and organizations, and on how to "throw the rascals out" and deliver appropriate punishment. Equally or perhaps more important, we need to think carefully about underlying standards of ethical behavior, about political and other pressures that are likely to lead to corrupt practices, and about strategies of prevention — i.e., about ways of establishing and maintaining an ethical climate within organizations and in the broader society. These are central themes throughout the volume, and several readings in each section emphasize the positive side of the corruption-ethics nexus and appropriate strategies for reform.

The issues raised in this collection of readings are complex, and inevitably some of the essays will raise as many questions as they seem to answer. Therefore, while the volume is likely to be useful to an individual reader, it will be considerably more valuable, we believe, if it is also used as a basis for discussion and an active exchange of views — among students, scholars, and practitioners.

The process of reviewing, sorting, and selecting items for inclusion would have been much simpler if we had opted to use only a small number of scholarly articles, but we thought it would be better to draw upon a wide diversity of materials, including newspaper articles, congressional hearings, cases, and a few classics as well as contemporary essays. In selecting and organizing these materials, and in developing the introductory essays, the editors have benefited greatly from the suggestions of a number of knowledgeable and helpful readers: Eileen Siedman, Elaine Sudanowicz, Patrick Dobel, Kathryn Denhardt, and Bayard Catron. Elaine Cinelli, Robert Denhardt, George Frederickson, and Naomi Lynn offered valuable encouragement and occasional prodding. Students in Bill Richter's and Fran Burke's ethics courses read, discussed and evaluated many of the materials, as did participants in Jim Doig's seminars in administrative behavior.

We thank the Daniel and Florence Guggenheim Foundation for providing financial support to ASPA for the preparation of this volume. We also wish to thank the many individuals who submitted cases and other materials to us for possible inclusion. Lengthy though the final product may be, it is still only a small portion of the items we reviewed.

Finally, we wish to acknowledge the valuable administrative and clerical support of the College of Arts and Sciences at Kansas State University, the Suffolk University School of Management, and the Woodrow Wilson School at Princeton. We are especially grateful to the several individuals without whom this volume might never have been completed: to Shirley Wester, David Shingler, Martin Kohout, Sheila McCormick and Sandi England at ASPA; and to Barbara Warren, Delaine Edwards, Heather Resz, Paige Nichols, and Robert Richter, who prepared the text materials for word processing.

In view of the wealth of existing materials on ethics, and the rapidity with which new materials are appearing, we have little confidence that this volume includes everything which ought to be in it. We take some solace in the fact that the volume deals with enduring issues, and we hope that the ideas and approaches it explores will have some enduring qualities as well.

William L. Richter, Kansas State University
Frances Burke, Suffolk University
Jameson W. Doig, Princeton University

Combating Unethical Behavior:
What to Do When the Angels are Missing

I. The Timely, Ambiguous, and Fragile Nature of Ethical Concerns

Introductory Essay

In these closing years of the twentieth century, ethics is a prominent topic of public discourse. The news media are filled with stories concerning unethical behavior and ethical issues in virtually every aspect of public life: in government and politics, business, religion, education, and other arenas.

These problems are by no means limited to the United States. Investigations following the ouster of Ferdinand and Imelda Marcos from the Philippines have revealed graft and other corrupt practices amounting to billions of dollars.[1] Similar stories of abuse of power for personal gain surround the regimes of the Duvaliers in Haiti and Manuel Noriega in Panama. Scandals have shaken the Rajiv Gandhi government of India and led to the political demise of successive governments in Japan. These and other instances suggest that, although moral values and standards may vary somewhat from culture to culture, most contemporary societies are vulnerable to problems of government corruption.[2]

Indeed, human beings from the beginnings of recorded history have been plagued by dishonesty and other forms of unethical activity. Every American presidential administration, from Washington at least through Reagan, has featured one or another form of corruption. Some have been worse than others, of course, with Presidents Grant, Harding, Nixon, and Reagan generally acknowledged to have presided over the administrations most troubled by such problems. Richard Nixon has the distinction of being the only president to be forced to resign from office, but the Reagan administration may hold the record for numbers of high-level individuals involved in ethical cases, including Edwin Meese, who as Reagan's Attorney General served as the chief law enforcement officer of the United States.[3]

It would be difficult to argue, however, that political or administrative behavior is on the whole less ethical at the end of the twentieth century than it was at its beginning. Recall that George Washington Plunkitt, "the sage of Tammany Hall," openly advocated what he called "Honest Graft" and took pride in having taken many of the "opportunities" which had come his way in New York City government.[4]

There is considerable merit in the argument that the prominence of ethics cases in the closing years of the twentieth century has been at least partially a function of increased public awareness, decreased public tolerance for wrong-doing, and more rigorous legal standards. Post-Watergate ethics legislation, more aggressive investigative journalism, and the willingness of greater numbers of governmental and private-sector personnel to "blow the whistle" on cases of graft and malfeasance have all tended to *publicize* ethics, that is, to draw the subject more dramatically to public attention. Rapid technological change — in computers, communications, and life support systems, for example — has raised additional substantive ethical issues. Whatever the causes, ethics has become a topic of high public prominence and concern. Professional journals devote full issues to it. New publications and organizations have been established to promote ethics.[5] States and other governmental units have passed whistle-blower protection laws and other legislation, established ethics commissions, and addressed the subject in other ways.[6]

Within the broad and rather diffuse field of ethics, attention to *public administration* ethics has been no less intense. The American Society for Public Administration (ASPA) promulgated a Code of Ethics in 1984 and later issued guidelines and actively encouraged a national dialogue on the code. National and regional ASPA meetings have featured numerous panels on ethics. A national ethics network — *ETHNET* — has established a quarterly newsletter. The National Association of Schools of Public Affairs and Administration (NASPAA) has added ethics to the list of core subjects which should be covered in accredited MPA programs.

Despite all this activity, administrative ethics remains a subject about which there is much conceptual disagreement. Kathryn Denhardt accurately summarizes the situation:

> Ethics in public administration suffers from the absence of a theoretical framework to supply focus, definition, background, and a common frame of reference for the research

and practice of ethical administration. No paradigm presently exists to provide a shared understanding of what "ethics" means when applied to the field of public administration.[7]

Despite the efforts of Denhardt and others to provide definition and coherence to the field, there still remains a high degree of diversity, frequently described as "chaotic."

Conceptual Ambiguity

Much of the difficulty in discussing administrative ethics derives from the ambiguity surrounding the subject of ethics generally. What is ethical? The readings we have included in this section are organized in relation to four approaches, each of which has a respectable heritage and some degree of currency in discussion of contemporary issues of public service ethics: ethics as *virtue,* as *consequence,* as *principle,* and as *responsibility.*

Ethics as virtue. Although valuable ethical lessons may be gleaned from the writings of Homer and later Greek poets (for example, Sophocles' *Antigone*), as well as from the scriptures of most religions, it is from Plato's dialogues (e.g., *Gorgias, Crito, Meno, Republic*) and Aristotle's treatises that we derive both the term *ethics* and the first systematic discussions of the subject. As the selection we have included in this volume indicates, Aristotle regarded ethics as moral virtues, which could be instilled in individuals through training and practice. In this sense, ethics is more a way of life than a system of rules and principles (deontology) or calculations of outcomes (consequentialism).

While this approach to understanding ethics has been overshadowed in the philosophical literature, we have continued to use much of its language, although often without its original meaning. Recent attempts to revive *virtue* as a key operating concept in understanding administrative ethics, illustrated by the Cooper selection, show the continuing relevance of this perspective.[8]

Ethics as consequence. Historically the second major approach to understanding ethics, and the most radical alternative to the classical virtues of Aristotle and Plato, was that of Niccolò Machiavelli. Machiavelli warned in *The Prince* that good and well-intentioned people often produce bad policy and bad administration. He argued, as the selection included in this volume illustrates, that people needed to learn "how not to be good" and how to "use good and bad" as appropriate for beneficial ends. This approach, based upon the assumption that the ethical merit of an act should be judged by its consequences rather than by the virtue or principles of the actor, is termed *teleological* or *consequentialist* by philosophers.[9]

The best known and most persuasive manifestation of consequentialist thinking concerning ethics is utilitarianism, the doctrine that acts should be judged in terms of providing "the greatest good to the greatest number." Developed in the early nineteenth century by John Stuart Mill (whose writing is included in Part I), as well as by Jeremy Bentham and others, utilitarianism continues to have a major impact on how people think about the ethics of their actions.

Another variant of consequentialism which should be mentioned, if only because it pervades public and private life, is ethical egoism: the notion that a person should do those things which most benefit himself or herself.[10] This "ethic" is probably more widespread in private than in public enterprise. In its more blatant forms, it may be regarded as an important source of *un*ethical behavior in public administration and elsewhere in public life.

In general, consequentialism raises the means-ends question, that is, whether the goal of an action can justify the means undertaken to achieve it. The question becomes particularly poignant in a constitutional democratic society, where the maintenance of certain procedures (means) is important for the survival of the political system, and where administrators may find themselves faced with choices between major programmatic objectives and important procedural values.

Ethics as principle. One of the problems with consequentialist theories of ethics is that one cannot always predict accurately the outcome of one's actions. It is also somewhat absurd to imagine that a malevolent act which turns out to have beneficial effects might be considered more ethical than a benevolent one which fails to do so. Moreover, utilitarian calculations of the good of the majority may not provide much protection for the rights of minorities. For these and other reasons, many ethicists prefer a deontological, or principle-based, theory of ethics.[11]

The Timely, Ambiguous, and Fragile Nature of Ethical Concerns

The most famous deontological theory of ethics was formulated by Immanuel Kant 200 years ago. As illustrated in the selection below, Kant's *categorical imperative* admonishes us to act on the basis of those principles which we might wish everyone to follow. He also required that other people be treated as ends in themselves and not merely as means to an end.

A prominent contemporary exponent of deontological ethics is Harvard philosopher John Rawls. In his *Theory of Justice* (1971), Rawls develops a set of principles based upon a line of reasoning which resembles the seventeenth-century state of nature theories of Thomas Hobbes and John Locke. In brief, he argues that we should follow those principles which we would design for a society if each of us were ignorant of what our individual position might be in that society. His two basic principles are, therefore, that rights ought to be distributed as equally as possible and that any inequalities ought to be arranged for the benefit of the least advantaged.[12]

Although most contemporary philosophers emphasize some variant of a deontological or a utilitarian approach to ethics, few people fit totally into one or the other category. Rather, many individuals act according to some combination of approaches, using one under some circumstances and another under others. For instance, people who generally adhere to the principle that "honesty is the best policy" might tell a "white lie" to make a friend feel good. Similarly, a generally honest person might withhold information or even lie in order to avoid bringing harm to an innocent person.

Ethics as responsibility. When we move beyond the ethical options faced by individuals in general to consider specifically *administrative* ethics, we encounter an added dimension: that of the responsibility of the public official to multiple sources of authority or legitimacy. Operating within any organization imposes upon individuals certain loyalties and obligations, which may sometimes come into conflict with their personal ethical preferences. Loyalties to one's superior, one's agency, one's professional standards, the Constitution, and the less clearly defined "public interest" all may compete for the administrator's attention.[13]

This approach to ethics has been prominent in much of the public-administration literature, from Woodrow Wilson in the late 19th century through the celebrated Friedrich-Finer debate in the 1940s and beyond. John Rohr's recent *Ethics for Bureaucrats,* for instance, argues that administrative officials inevitably confront ethical issues because they have significant administrative discretion, and the guidelines for their ethical choices ought to be derived from the core values of the society, as represented by the letter and spirit of the Constitution.[14] From other perspectives, Terry Cooper and John P. Burke develop full-scale theories of administrative ethics based upon the concepts of responsibility and administrative role.[15] In this volume, we have included excerpts from the writings of several writers who have grappled in important ways with these issues.

This list of approaches, and the accompanying sets of readings and cases, are by no means exhaustive, but they should stimulate the reader to ask some introspective questions:

> Which definition of ethics do I find most acceptable?
>
> What are the conditions under which one approach might be more appropriate than another?
>
> What problems might I expect to encounter in "real life" as a result of my ethical preferences?
>
> Do other people operate on the basis of the same ethical assumptions as my own?

In addition to conceptual complexity, the field of ethics faces additional ambiguities in the definitional boundaries between law and ethics on the one hand and between ethics and corruption on the other. Some analysts focus attention upon legal issues such as conflict of interest, and concentrate their attention on how to avoid running afoul of the law. Although this perspective is valuable, it neglects that broader range of ethical choices which are not fully covered by the law. Other writers, asserting that illegal activities are by definition unethical, place their main emphasis on those situations not covered by legal prohibitions, that is, on behavior which is legal but may nonetheless be unethical. This book incorporates both approaches, treating legal remedies as one among several approaches to addressing ethical problems.

A related definitional question centers upon the relevance of corruption to the study and practice of ethics. As with the law/ethics distinction, there is widespread disagreement among scholars on the corruption/ethics relationship. Some see corruption as the core of ethical concerns,[16] while others argue that corruption, like illegality, is by definition unethical and therefore less important as a focus for sustained analysis than more ambiguous ethical situations.[17]

As the title of this book indicates, we see corruption as both a significant component of ethical concerns and a continuing problem of considerable magnitude in public administration and in public life generally. As many of the readings in Part II of this volume illustrate, it is sometimes difficult to determine whether a specific act *is* unethical. Is a policeman acting unethically when he regularly accepts a free cup of coffee from a restaurant owner while on duty? Is the person who makes photocopies of personal papers at the office without reimbursing the organization engaged in corruption? There is also the problem of awareness: how many administrators unknowingly commit acts which they would regard as wrong if they thought through the implications?

To focus upon the problems of graft, lying, and other aspects of corrupt behavior is not to deny the merit of other types of ethical concerns. It is valuable at this point to recall the distinction made by Amy Gutmann and Dennis Thompson between *policy ethics* and *process ethics*.[18] "Policy ethics" is concerned with questions of distributive justice, the sanctity of life, and other ultimate moral choices, as illustrated by the continuing controversies over welfare policy and abortion. "Process ethics" deals with those problems encountered in the administrative process, regardless of the policy issues involved: secrecy, abuse of authority, graft, etc. It is often difficult to separate these two types of ethical questions. For the most part, however, this volume focuses upon the ethics of process rather than the ethics of policy choices.[19]

Changing Ethical Standards

Finally, some of the ambiguity in administrative ethics derives from changing public perceptions which help to define what is ethical and what is not. Many principles ("one should tell the truth") and practices (lying, bribery) have been part of the terrain of ethics discourse for centuries. Others are of more recent vintage ("one should not engage in sexual harassment," for instance). The history of public administration is replete with traditions and reforms which were regarded as ethical in one era and unethical in another. The practice of rewarding party faithful with public office, defended by Andrew Jackson as a means of providing broader access to governmental positions, later came to be regarded as the "spoils system" and viewed by many as an odious form of political corruption.

The practice of hiring friends and relatives led at one time to nepotism rules which, among other consequences, barred spouses from working in the same institution or agency. More recently, such rules have been perceived as discriminatory against women and have been replaced by other structural arrangements. Inclusion of racial and ethnic information on application forms was eliminated at one point because it was seen as discriminatory, but revived later in order to facilitate affirmative-action programs.

"New occasions teach new duties," James Russell Lowell wrote in the 1840s, in the midst of the deepening crisis over slavery in America. "Time makes ancient good uncouth."[20] Among the major challenges of ethical enquiry, in public administration or elsewhere, is not only to determine what general perspective one should take to ethical issues, but also to apply underlying principles to the exigencies of "new occasions."

The Fragile Nature of Ethical Behavior

The final problem we wish to consider in this introductory section is the *fragile* nature of ethical behavior. Even when a person wishes to be ethical, to do right, it is often difficult. This is a recurrent theme in literature and religion. ("The spirit is willing but the flesh is weak.") Two examples from private industry provide dramatic illustration of this phenomenon: the young broker in the film "Wall Street" who becomes an inside trader despite his knowledge that he is doing wrong, and the author of "The Aircraft Brake Scandal" (reprinted in Part II), who allows himself to be drawn into a maelstrom of deception on a government contract.

There are numerous reasons for this gap between good intentions and actual practice, of which the following is by no means an exhaustive list.

*The Timely, Ambiguous,
and Fragile Nature of
Ethical Concerns*

Ethical imperative versus personal benefit. As Michael Josephson notes: "Perhaps the main reason that people fail to act ethically is that it usually meets immediate self interest to do the unethical or less ethical thing. Simply put, it is easier."[21] Individuals perceive that the benefits to themselves or to friends or relatives, or to causes that they favor, neutralize their ethical principles. The human capacity for rationalization plays an important role here.

Ethical imperative versus personal danger. Sometimes people fail to do what is right because of the anticipated harm such actions might cause to themselves or others. Whistle blowing, a typical example, is considered in Part III.

Ethical imperative versus other responsibilities. What is "right" by one standard may conflict with other obligations. The person who believes that lying is wrong, but who is asked to present false information on behalf of his or her superior, agency, or country faces just this sort of dilemma.

Ethical imperative versus "reasonableness". Many problems arise when a person's ethical standards come into conflict with practices which have become firmly established and now seem natural to most of the community. One is expected to "go along to get along." Several of the cases in Part II ("The New Manager Wants to Shoot Santa Claus," for instance) illustrate this problem.

The "Dirty Hands" Problem. One rationalization for engaging in unethical behavior in public life is the argument that one cannot succeed without getting one's hands dirty. As Machiavelli argues in *The Prince,* good (i.e., ethical) people are likely to "come to grief" among so many who are not good. This argument is particularly seductive when the objective of the unethical activity is not personal gain but benefits for one's agency, program, or operation.[22]

The "Many Hands" Problem. In organizations, particularly large organizations, there is the temptation not to assume personal responsibility for the ethics of one's actions when a person is regarded as only a small part of the overall operation, only a "cog in the wheel." If "many hands" are involved in a decision or set of decisions (such as dropping the atomic bomb in 1945, or the Vietnam War, or the Challenger disaster), can any individuals be held responsible?[23]

Insensitivity to ethical considerations. Perhaps the most insidious and ubiquitous problem is simply the failure to think about the ethical considerations of the many decisions each of us faces in our daily work.

Having noted some of the reasons why we believe people fail to behave ethically, it is perhaps appropriate to raise the opposite question: Why *should* people, particularly public administrators, act ethically? Unfortunately, it is much more difficult to give a straightforward response to this question, since the answer is directly related to how one perceives and defines ethics generally.

One writer has suggested that businesses should improve their ethical behavior in order to gain the "ethics edge."[24] Clearly, there are practical advantages — for the individual, the organization, and the society — in maintaining ethical standards, not the least of which is the greater sense of self-respect which a public or private manager might obtain by doing so. Yet to argue that one should be ethical *because* it is advantageous to do so—however one defines advantage — immediately biases the discussion in the direction of a consequentialist theory of ethics.

Without venturing to provide ultimate justification for ethics, we might at least suggest that there are increasingly strong individual, professional, and societal motivations to strengthen ethics both in public and private organizations. The readings in this section are intended as a starting point for that enterprise.

Endnotes

1. Belinda A. Aquino, *Politics of Plunder: The Philippines Under Marcos* (Manila: University of the Philippines College of Public Administration, 1987).
2. For discussions of public service ethics in several different national settings, see Kenneth Kernaghan and O.P. Dwivedi, eds., *Ethics in the Public Service: Comparative Perspectives* (Brussels: International Institute of Administrative Sciences, 1983); and Special Issue on Bureaucratic Morality, *International Political Science Review,* 9:3 (July 1988), pp. 163-242.
3. The case of Edwin Meese III is discussed in Part II of this volume. For earlier examples, see Joan Joseph, *Political Corruption* (New York: Pocket Books, 1974); and C. Vann Woodward, ed., *Responses of the Presidents to Charges of Misconduct* (New York: Dell Publishing, 1974).
4. William L. Riordon, *Plunkitt of Tammany Hall* (New York: E.P. Dutton, 1963), pp. 3-6.

5. For example, the *Business and Professional Ethics Journal*, sponsored by three universities, began publication in 1981, and the Josephson Institute for the Advancement of Ethics published the first issue of its journal, *Ethics: Easier Said Than Done*, in Winter, 1988.

6. The Council on Governmental Ethics Laws (COGEL) publishes biennially *The Campaign Finance, Ethics and Lobby Law Blue Book* (Lexington, KY: The Council of State Governments) as well as periodic updates on new ethics legislation in the states.

7. Kathryn G. Denhardt, *The Ethics of Public Service: Resolving Moral Dilemmas in Public Organizations* (New York: Greenwood, 1988), p. 1.

8. Cf. Alisdair MacIntyre, *After Virtue* (2nd. ed. Notre Dame: University of Notre Dame Press, 1984); and Alisdair MacIntyre, *A Short History of Ethics* (New York: Collier, 1966).

9. Cf. William K. Frankena, *Ethics* (Englewood Cliffs: Prentice-Hall, 1963). Since "teleology" (the science of the *telos* or end) has other connotations in classic philosophy, we utilize the more cumbersome but less ambigious term *consequentialist*. Philosophers like Frankena also distinguish between sub-categories of these approaches: rule utilitarian, act utilitarian, etc. Discussion of these distinctions is not essential for this essay.

10. See, for example, Robert J. Ringer, *Looking Out for Number One* (New York: Fawcett, 1977); Ayn Rand, *The Fountainhead;* and the film "Wall Street."

11. While consequentialist (or teleological) theories of ethics judge actions in terms of their consequences, "a deontologist contends that it is possible for an action or rule of action to be the morally right or obligatory one even if it does not promote the greatest possible balance of good over evil for self, society, or universe." Frankena, *Ethics*, pp. 77-128.

12. Rawls, *A Theory of Justice* (Cambridge: Harvard University Press, 1971).

13. See, for example, Woodrow Wilson's essay, excerpted in this volume, and Max Weber, "Politics as a Vocation," in H.H. Gerth and C. Wright Mills, *From Max Weber* (New York: Oxford University Press, 1958), pp. 77-128.

14. John A. Rohr, *Ethics for Bureaucrats* (New York: Marcel Dekker, 1978).

15. Terry L. Cooper, *The Responsible Administrator: An Approach to Ethics for the Administrative Role* (Rev. Ed. Port Washington, NY: Associated Faculty Press, 1986); John P. Burke, *Bureaucratic Responsibility* (Baltimore: Johns Hopkins University Press, 1986).

16. See Gerald E. Caiden, "Toward a General Theory of Official Corruption," *Asian Journal of Public Administration* (Summer, 1988), pp. 1-17; George C.S. Benson, *Political Corruption in America* (Lexington, MA: Lexington Books, 1978).

17. Denhardt, *The Ethics of Public Service*, p. ix.

18. Amy Gutmann and Dennis Thompson, *Ethics and Politics* (Chicago: Nelson-Hall, 1984), p. xiii.

19. A valuable starting point, particularly for enquiry into policy ethics, is Peter J. Bergerson, *Ethics and Public Policy: An Annotated Bibliography* (New York and London: Garland, 1988).

20. James Russell Lowell, "The Present Crisis" (1844), in *The Complete Poetical Works of James Russell Lowell* (Boston and New York: Houghton Mifflin, 1897), P. 68.

21. Josephson, *Ethics: Easier Said Than Done*, 1:1, p. 4.

22. See Oliver North's defense of his lying to Congress in the Iran-Contra operation, reprinted in Part II of this volume. The problem of dirty hands is widely discussed in the ethics literature. Cf. Michael Walzer, "Political Action: The Problem of Dirty Hands," *Philosophy and Public Affairs*, 2:2 (Winter, 1973), pp. 160-180; W. Kenneth Howard, "Must Public Hands be Dirty?" *Journal of Value Inquiry*, 11 (Spring 1977), pp. 29-40; and Dennis F. Thompson, *Political Ethics and Public Office* (Cambridge, MA: Harvard University Press, 1987), pp. 11-39.

23. One response to this position, as Debra Stewart argues below, is the assertion that individuals remain morally responsible for their actions regardless of the size and complexity of their organizations. See also Dennis F. Thompson, *Political Ethics and Public Office*, pp. 40-65.

24. Mark Pastin, *The Hard Problems of Management: Gaining the Ethics Edge* (San Francisco: Jossey-Bass, 1986).

1. Ethics As Virtue

Virtue, Habit, and Ethics
Aristotle

. . . Moral virtue comes about as a result of habit, whence also its name *ethike* is one that is formed by a slight variation from the word *ethos* (Habit). From this it is also plain that none of the moral virtues arises in us by nature; for nothing that exists by nature can form a habit contrary to its nature. For instance, the stone which by nature moves downwards cannot be habituated to move upwards, not even if one tries to train it by throwing it up ten thousand times; nor can fire be habituated to move downwards, nor can anything else that by nature behaves in one way be trained to behave in another. Neither by nature, then, nor contrary to nature do the virtues arise in us; rather we are adapted by nature to receive them, and are made perfect by habit.

The Nicomachean Ethics serves as the base point for the systematic consideration of the subject of ethics. In this selection from that work, Aristotle establishes the notion that ethics consists of virtues, which are forms of habits, and therefore learnable.

. . . The things we have to learn before we can do them, we learn by doing them, e.g., men become builders by building and lyre players by playing the lyre, so too we become just by doing just acts, temperate by doing temperate acts, brave by doing brave acts.

This is confirmed by what happens in states; for legislators make the citizens good by forming habits in them, and this is the wish of every legislator, and those who do not effect it miss their mark, and it is in this that a good constitution differs from a bad one.

Again, it is from the same causes and by the same means that every virtue is both produced and destroyed, and similarly every art; for it is from playing the lyre that both good and bad lyre-players are produced. And the corresponding statement is true of builders and of all the rest; men will be good or bad builders as a result of building well or badly. For if this were not so, there would have been no need of a teacher, but all men would have been born good or bad at their craft. This, then, is the case with the virtues also; by doing the acts that we do in our transactions with other men we become just or unjust, and by doing the acts that we do in the presence of danger, and being habituated to feel fear or confidence, we become brave or cowardly. The same is true of appetites and feelings of anger; some men become temperate and good-tempered, others self-indulgent and irascible, by behaving in one way or the other in the appropriate circumstances. Thus, in one word, states of character arise out of like activities. This is why the activities we exhibit must be of a certain kind; it is because the states of character correspond to the differences between these. It makes no small difference, then, whether we form habits of one kind or of another from our very youth; it makes a very great difference, or rather all the difference.

Source: *Introduction to Aristotle*, ed. Richard McKeon (New York: Random House, 1947), pp. 331-332.

Hierarchy, Virtue, and the Practice of Public Administration: A Perspective for Normative Ethics

Terry L. Cooper

Although somewhat out of vogue for some time, the concept of virtue has in recent years gained renewed prominence as a key to ethical behavior. As Terry Cooper notes in this selection, much of the credit for that resurgence is attributable to the influence of contemporary philosopher Alisdair MacIntyre, whose books (especially A Short History of Ethics, 1966, and After Virtue, 1981, 1984) provide a basis for understanding the ways in which virtue has changed in meaning through the centuries. In this selection Cooper applies the concept to the practice of public administration.

A military police officer is instructed by a commander not to issue citations to senior officers for driving while intoxicated. Also, certain specified junior officers and noncommissioned officers whose services and support are needed are to be similarly exempted. However, citations are to be issued strictly to all other personnel and maximum punishment is to be sought. When the officer objects to this order on the grounds of its illegality and unfairness, he is threatened with a poor proficiency rating and removal from his position.

* * *

The design supervisor for a state water project is told by one of her engineers that the initial specifications for one section of water main must be changed. It has recently been discovered that the soil in that area contains toxic wastes which corrode steel pipe and will eventually enter the water supply. Consequently, only concrete-jacketed pipe is safe for this area. The supervisor agrees that the initial design represents a public health hazard and must be changed. Both go to inform the project chief of the necessary change. Upon hearing them out the chief says that it is too late to incorporate these changes due to the significantly higher costs and time delays which would be required to complete the design phase. After leaving the chief's office, the supervisor tells the engineer that they have no other choice but to proceed with the initial specifications.

* * *

The tendency of hierarchical organizations to demand absolute loyalty to superiors and thereby displace other important values, even those associated with the formal goals of the organization, is a well documented phenomenon.[1] Furthermore, it is clearly and overwhelmingly the most frequently occurring problem among the cases written by the more than 200 participants in administrative ethics workshops which I have conducted during the last few years.

An Ethic of Virtue for the Practice of Public Administration

Examination and analysis of this serious problem is not for the purpose of arriving at a set of specific recommendations about what one should do in such risky and painful situations. Nor is the intention to provide a decision-making model for the analysis and evaluation of the various alternatives for action in any particular case. Frameworks exist for those purposes.[2]

Rather, this essay considers the general approach to the development of normative administrative ethics which would be most appropriate for public administration and, more specifically, the *Code of Ethics of the American Society for Public Administration* (ASPA). The concern is to develop a moral identity for the public administrative role which provides a general orientation for action. The specific purpose is to explore an ethic of virtue for public administration which complements and supports ethical analysis of principles and alternatives for conduct by identifying certain desirable predispositions to act.

Source: Terry Cooper, "Hierarchy, Virtue, and the Practice of Public Administration," *Public Administration Review* 47:4 (July/August 1987), pp. 320-328.

Lilla has argued that the analytical approach to administrative ethics amounts to equipping public officials with the means to create self-justifying rationalizations for their conduct.[3] He argues instead for inculcation of a set of virtues derived from a democratic ethos. My position is that the problem of normative ethics should not be approached with the assumption that these are mutually exclusive options. Rather I find myself more in agreement with Frankena's judgment that an ethic of virtue is necessary to identify the predispositions to act which support courses of conduct which one has identified through some analytical process.[4]

Thus a complete normative ethics for public administration must include: (1) an understanding of appropriate ethical principles, (2) an identification of virtues which are supportive of those principles, and (3) analytical techniques which may be employed in specific situations to interpret the principles. The second item concerning "predispositions" or "inclinations," traditionally called virtues, which move an administrator to act upon principle, even in the face of anticipated resistance or punishment, deserve more consideration than they have received recently in the full development of normative administrative ethics.

In both of the case summaries presented above, subordinates confront organizational superiors with concerns which appear to be rooted in general principles derived from a professional ethic. In the first situation the officer is concerned both about obeying the law and maintaining justice in the enforcement of policy. In the second, the obligation of public servants to act in ways which are beneficent for the public and at least to follow the principle of nonmaleficence (do not harm) seem to be the motivating principles.

In neither of these instances is ethical understanding lacking; both individuals perceive a legitimate ethical issue. Also, both are able to identify what needs to be done to act responsibly. Furthermore, both demonstrate inclinations to act on their perceived obligations. However, in both cases, these would-be ethical public officials find their good intentions thwarted by higher executive authority.

Information is insufficient in the case summaries to make possible more than conjecture about reasons why the superiors resist attempts of their subordinates to conduct themselves ethically. However, it is plausible to infer from the information available that, as is often the case, interorganizational politics is a powerful deterrent to ethical conduct in the first case, and costs in time and money are an overriding concern in the second. Managers responsible for the well-being of the organizations seem to allow goods associated with organizational status, position, and power to prevail over the professional ethics of subordinates.

If this problem occurs as frequently as both literature and experience suggest, why might this be so? What virtues support the action needed to maintain one's professional principles, even in the face of resistance and retribution if one is in a subordinate position or, in spite of the pressures to think first of the organization, if one is in an executive role?

Characteristics of a Practice

A useful perspective for analyzing the ethical difficulties inherent in the hierarchical relationships of modern organizations is suggested by the concept of "practices" and their virtues developed by Alasdair MacIntyre.[5] . . .

MacIntyre focuses on "practices" rather than "professions" in dealing with the ethics of groups of people involved in common activities. Practices are forms of activity which possess the following characteristics:

1. They exhibit coherence and complexity.
2. They are socially established.
3. They are carried out through human cooperation.
4. They involve technical skills which are exercised within evolving traditions of value and principles.
5. They are organized to achieve certain standards of excellence.
6. Certain internal goods are produced in the pursuit of excellence.
7. Engaging in the activity increases human power to achieve the standards of excellence and internal goods.
8. Engaging in the activity systematically extends human conceptions of its internal goods.

MacIntyre explains that the skillful throwing of a football is not a practice, but "the game of football is, and so is chess. Bricklaying is not a practice; architecture is. Planting turnips is not a practice; farming is. So are the enquiries of physics, chemistry and biology, and so is the work of the historian, and so are painting and music." He concludes that "the range of practices is wide," including "arts, sciences, games, politics in the Aristotelian sense" and "the making and sustaining of family life."

The concept of practice is more appealing and constructive than that of profession; it is a larger framework within which to develop a normative perspective for public administration. Profession, unfortunately, may connote self protection and self aggrandizement and produce images of paternalistic expertise which are not appropriate for public administration in a democratic society. In addition, practice provides a broader concept which permits escape from often petty and generally class-conscious debate over which occupations are properly understood as professions. Practice includes professions and many other human activities.

This notion of practices is particularly appropriate as a conceptual perspective for understanding ethical problems inherent in organizational hierarchies. It suggests that the work of public administration needs to be understood in terms that transcend employment in a particular public organization. Organizations are unequivocally the *setting* for administrative practice, but the practice must have norms of its own. That is the reason for adopting the ASPA code of ethics.

But more broadly, the eight characteristics of practices represent a normative framework that might be used profitably to guide reflection about the ethical development of the public administrative role. They suggest a working agenda and establish some tentative boundaries for inquiry. This concept calls attention to normative dimensions of public administrative activity which need greater clarity, particularly concerning the fourth, fifth, and sixth characteristics.

Internal Goods of a Practice

The concept of internal goods is essential to understanding the nature of practices. These are goods which can be realized only through participating in a particular practice or one very similar. For example, only through pursuing the practice of painting is one able to cultivate the finest sense of color, tone, texture, perspective, line, and proportion, as well as the skill to employ the relationships among these artistic elements in the pursuit of aesthetic excellence which can enrich the lives of others.

These goods which are internal to practices cannot be purchased, stolen, or acquired through persuasion. They must be gained by engaging in a practice and submitting to its standards of excellence until one is able to go beyond them. It is in the nature of internal goods that although they are produced out of competition to excel, "their achievement is a good for the whole community."[6] The ethical norms for a practice of public administration, therefore, must grow out of an understanding of its internal goods.

Can public administration be understood as a practice? As we consider the viability of conceiving of public administration in this way, *internal good* is clearly one of the central concepts upon which normative thinking needs to focus. Although the field has achieved neither precision nor clarity about its internal goods, public administration practitioners are aware of these in a general way. For example, administrators refer to such normative concepts as the public interest, popular sovereignty, accountability, social order, social justice, citizenship development, political equality, efficiency, and liberty as goods which they are attempting to achieve.

What appears to be needed is further discussion, debate, and consensus-building about the meaning of these concepts and priorities among them. There is a need to consider *how* certain of these values should be understood as supportive of public administration practice and *how* they may subvert it. For example, the practice may require maintaining a certain balance between social order and social justice while organizational goals may well favor social order for the sake of organizational stability, predictability, survival, and control. Without some considered consensus about these goods which are internal to the practice of public administration in a democratic society, public administration practitioners remain vulnerable to organizational definitions of what is good and at the mercy of arbitrary organizational authority.

Furthermore, no intelligible way exists to distinguish the work of *public* administration from that of *business* administration without identifying the internal goods which are the unique ends of each. Without clarity concerning the goods toward which the practice is directed, it is impossible to identify the virtues which public administration practitioners should be expected to embody.

External Goods of a Practice

External goods are those which can be achieved in many ways other than engaging in a particular practice. They are genuine goods in that they are necessary to some extent for the support of members of the practice, but they do not contribute directly to the development of a practice. Typical of these external goods, such as money, prestige, status, position, and power, is that they always become the property of some individual, and, furthermore, the more one person has in a fixed-sum situation, the less there is for others. Consequently, external goods are often objects of competition in which there are winners and losers. This is essentially different from the value accrued through the achievement of internal goods, where the value is shared by the community of practice and the larger community as well.

External goods may become the dominant concerns of either organizations or individual practitioners.[7] It is important at this juncture to remember that organizations should not be confused with practices but that they do coexist in an interdependent relationship. Practices typically require support by organizations, and organizations are, in turn, often dependent upon practices for their very reasons for existence. However, considerable evidence shows that organizations do *tend* to corrupt the practices which they support as a result of their focus on external goods.[8] In the competitive struggle for the scarce resources necessary for survival, organizations "are involved in acquiring money and other material goods; they are structured in terms of power and status, and they distribute money, power and status as rewards." Organizations have goals oriented around achieving and maintaining these external goods; practices should not allow these to have priority over internal goods.

Practices should be primarily oriented toward their internal goods, the tradition which has evolved from the quest for those goods, and a relationship among those currently seeking such goods.[9] However, most practices are dependent upon organizations for resources and work settings. Consequently, the internal goods of a practice are at risk in an organizational environment dominated by the external goods inherent in organizational survival and growth. Thus, a precarious relationship exists. The practice of organizational management can support or corrupt the integrity of practices which function under their purview.[10]

Virtues and Practices

Finally, the concept of virtue is to be considered. Virtue, along with the internal goods of public administrative practice, is one of the two points upon which fundamental normative thinking most needs to be focused. Virtue has been an important word in ethical thought throughout most of western philosophical history.[11] It is rooted in Aristotelian thought. However, when the language of moral philosophy in recent decades is considered, a substantial break is evident in the long and lively intellectual history of the concept of virtue.[12] Nevertheless, a revival of interest in virtue has occurred during the last 15 years.[13]

During this recent period the works of four scholars, in addition to MacIntyre, exemplify the revival of interest in virtue as a significant concept in moral philosophy: Stuart Hampshire, James D. Wallace, R. E. Ewin, and William Frankena.[14] All five reflect a generally Aristotelian perspective, at least in some basic respects. For example, all understand virtues as inclinations or dispositions to act, not just to think or feel in a certain way. They are traits of character, more or less reliable tendencies to conduct oneself in a generally consistent fashion under similar conditions. Furthermore, virtues are not innate and, therefore, must be cultivated. In the work of all four scholars, virtues appear to involve cognitive activity. Virtuous conduct does not amount to merely conditioned reflex behavior; it is not just unthinking habitual response to stimuli, even though the term "habit" is sometimes used to characterize virtues, even by Aristotle. One might say that reason is employed in addressing particular situations, but with a certain preestablished attitude and a conditioned will.

MacIntyre contributes an additional dimension of meaning to the concept of virtue. He understands virtues as the character traits which make it possible for one to engage effectively in a practice by seeking to excel in achieving its internal goods while keeping the external goods of its organizational setting in a position of lesser importance. For example, if beneficence for the citizenry is one of the internal goods of public administration, benevolence on the part of public administrators is an essential virtue. If justice is also an important internal good for public administration practice, then fairmindedness is a necessary attribute for administrators.

Public administrators need to determine which human attributes are most likely to advance the internal goods which are defined as essential to the practice and protect them from organizational pressures, to the extent possible. For example, attributes associated with effective administration and management in the business world, such as competitiveness and profit orientation, may be unsuited to or less appropriate to the interests of a democratic political society. Similarly, virtues such as concern for efficiency which advance organizational goals may not create openness to popular sovereignty if given more than secondary importance. The virtues of the public administrator must be consistent with agreed-upon internal goods of the practice of public administration.

Hierarchy, Virtue, and Normative Ethics

Through the concept of practices, with their standards of excellence, internal goods, and virtues on the one hand, and the analysis of institutions, with their external goods on the other, it is now possible to explore more profoundly the specifically ethical problems of hierarchy and loyalty, as well as the larger question concerning an appropriate perspective for the development of normative ethics for public administration.

Maintaining the Internal Goods and Virtues of a Practice

The most visible ethical, as distinct from tactical, problem which subordinates confront in dealing with superiors can be defined as one of maintaining the internal goods and virtues of their practice in the face of demands for personal or organizational loyalty rooted in external goods. Similarly, executives face the difficulty of maintaining these in order to support the practice(s) under their organizational authority in spite of pressures to place the organization's needs for survival and growth first.

For example, in the first case presented at the beginning of this paper, the problem for the subordinate is to maintain the practice of law enforcement by upholding one of its internal goods — the just treatment of all violators of the law against driving while intoxicated. In all probability this will require a measure of courage on the part of the subordinate, one of the generic virtues of all practices, according to MacIntyre.[15] Indeed, extraordinary courage may be necessary since the commander's orders reflect a primary commitment, not to justice in the practice of law enforcement, but to the external goods of the organizational unit. Those he intends to exempt from the law are perceived as having the ability to provide resources and support for the unit. No doubt the commander's justification, if challenged by his subordinate, will be that he is looking at "the big picture" and acting in such a way that the policy unit will be in a stronger position to carry out its mission. He may even convince the subordinate that this is the case; that he is acting ethically in terms of the larger organizational view.

However, it is clear that if the commander is successful in either persuading or forcing the subordinate to obey the order, the organization may be strengthened, but the practice of law enforcement will be weakened. No order which subverts the practice which the organization is established to support can be assumed to be a legitimate order, even in a strict chain of command such as a military unit. It may be legal and/or consistent with organizational politics, but it is illegitimate in terms of the internal goods of law enforcement practice. One must acknowledge, however, that in the "real world" of public administration circumstances may occur in which such an order may be deemed a necessary compromise between the purity of the practice and the survival of its organizational host. The essential point here is that the justification for each such compromise should receive serious and careful reflection. One instance must not become a precedent for future action.

With the second case the engineer and the design supervisor were apparently attempting to uphold safety, one of the paramount internal goods of engineering practice, and we might reasonably infer that the design supervisor was trying to maintain beneficence for the public which would seem to be one of the central internal goods of public administration practice. The internal goods of engineering and public administration then appear to be congruent in this situation. However, the project chief seems more committed to the economical and efficient completion of the project than to safety and the public good that it represents. Economy and efficiency are goods, to be sure, but in this case they appear to be more associated with the external goods of the organization than the fundamental goods of either public administration or engineering. At most they are secondary internal goods.

Reflecting on the conduct of the engineer and the design supervisor, it seems reasonable to view their acts as motivated by a commitment to the internal goods of their practices and supported by the virtues of courage, honesty, benevolence, and prudence. However, in the face of resistance from the project chief, the design supervisor appears to lack sufficient administrative courage to uphold the internal good of her own practice and that of her engineer subordinate. Both practices may be eroded as a result.

Of course, this case might have unfolded differently. The project chief might have reflected a commitment to public beneficence by engaging in ethical analysis of the situation through which he or she seriously weighed safety over against cost factors without simply dismissing the former for the sake of the latter. However, for the chief to have done so might have required rescheduling of the project and a request for budget augmentation. These actions might have made the project chief vulnerable to criticism from superiors and might have required a greater measure of courage and benevolence, both obvious candidates for a list of essential public administrative virtues.

The NASA Tragedy: A Recent Case in Point

A recent tragic example of the seriousness of this problem of preserving the internal goods of a practice was provided by the events leading to the explosion of the U.S. National Aeronautics and Space Administration (NASA) space shuttle on January 28, 1986.[16] It now appears that four vice presidents of Morton Thiokol overruled 12 of its own engineering experts in their strenuous objections to the safety of the launch. This fateful management decision was made, according to Seymour Melman, professor of engineering at Columbia University, using "criteria unique to management — having to do with profitability, security of contracts, *positions of the managers in the hierarchy. . .but not the strengths of materials or design*" (emphasis added).[17]

Morton Thiokol's decision to ignore engineering standards of excellence through the imposition of management authority seems clearly to have been a response to expectations generated by NASA. During the decade before the shuttle tragedy, NASA had begun to orient itself increasingly to pressures for short turn-around times and frequent and reliable launch schedules.[18] Safety, an internal good for manned space flight engineering, was sacrificed or at the very least devalued. Redundancy, a standard of excellence for achieving safety in this kind of engineering, was set aside. Prudence, one of the virtues of aerospace engineers involved in maintaining safety for human crew members, was rejected. The external goods of contract security, maintenance of schedules, profit, and marketability appear to have ruled the day.[19]

The most significant factor in the dominance of these external goods is alleged to have been the Reagan Administration's decision to "have as many commercial customers as possible use the shuttle to help defray the astronomical cost of operations."[20] On July 4, 1982, President Reagan stated that the first priority of the United States Space Transportation System is "to make the system fully operational and cost-effective in providing routine access to space."[21] George Will has recently noted this pressure for commercialization of the space program by the President in his promotion of the construction of a space station. Will laments President Reagan's promise that such a space station will produce "jobs, technologies and medical breakthroughs beyond anything we ever dreamed possible." He argues to the contrary that such "commercial bonanzas" from space research are not likely to justify their cost, but more importantly, that such expectations are inconsistent with the goals of science and tend to pervert it. In MacIntyre's terms, they are goods which are external to space research. In words which are remarkable for their clear focus on the internal goods of space science, Will asserts:

> The dignity of our species derives from the fact that we value knowing. We value it not merely for utilitarian reasons, but for its own sake. We will have a space program that is both reasonable and inspiriting only when we are sufficiently inspired by the noble quest to know.[22]

Beneath this most visible ethical problem of protecting the internal goods of a practice from displacement by the external goods of an organization lies a deeper generic problem. This is the prior problem of achieving and maintaining clarity among practitioners about the standards of excellence and internal goods of their practice, as well as the virtues they must cultivate to preserve the practice in institutional settings. Without this kind of clarity, external goods are more likely to prevail.

The Practice of Public Administration

To deal with the specific problem of subversion by public organizations of the practices they were created to support, it is first necessary to clarify the nature of that potential practice or set of practices known as public administration. An attempt is required at least, to identify and understand its internal goods and virtues. That is the prior task which must be engaged before particular issues can be addressed adequately or general rules of conduct can be prescribed.

At the outset of this discussion, it is important to address the instrumental orientation of the field. Public administration is an instrumental practice, but only in a particular sense. Its reason for being is to create and sustain institutional and other frameworks within which other practices such as public health, planning, accounting, law enforcement, and education may flourish. The justification for supporting other practices is that they provide goods which a democratic citizenry has determined either directly, or through its representatives, to be in its collective interest. Therefore, public administration should not be understood as instrumental in the sense of the "classical paradigm" with its assumptions about the separation of politics from administration. The practice of public administration involves more than the simple subordination of the administrative role to that of the politician and the dominance of functional rationality as the only legitimate style of thought for the administrator. Rather, the role of the public administrator as a fiduciary for the citizenry gives rise to certain internal goods and virtues associated with carrying out the trust inherent in that role. . . .

Obligation to Pursue the Public Interest

For example, one may reasonably argue that beneficence is the central internal good related to the first of the three realms, the obligation to pursue the public interest. The most fundamental test of conduct and policy then would be the extent to which good is accomplished for the citizenry. Achieving good for the organization or the practitioners of public administration would have to be secondary considerations; no act could be deemed acceptable on the grounds that it strengthened the organization or furthered the interests of practitioners unless it first produced significant public good. Benevolence would be the essential virtue for the achievement of this internal good.

Justice would then seem to be the central internal good which follows from public beneficence. Justice defines the most essential political good; it is the fundamental ordering principle of democratic society from which such goods as political equality, representation of the citizenry, and citizenship development are derived. If that is the case, then fairmindedness,[23] rationality, prudence,[24] and courage are essential virtues for the practice of public administration. To achieve just decisions, rules, policies, and distribution of resources, it is essential that the inescapable exercise of discretion by administrators be guided by the inclination to search for and uphold what is fair or just.

However, this fairminded orientation to decisions and conduct needs to be buttressed by the propensity to deal rationally and prudently with problems, rather than simply determining what is fair according to the way one feels or what seems to be advantageous in the short term. And, of course, administrative courage is required if one is to resist the pressures and temptations to decide and act in response to goods which are external to this aspect of the practice of public administration, such as interest group offers of political support, threats of retribution, or organizational advantage.

Obligation to Authorizing Processes and Procedures

When considering the second realm — a public administrator's obligation to authorizing processes and procedures — popular sovereignty, accountability, and due process are critical internal goods around which a public administration practice should be formed. In that case one might reasonably argue that honesty, respect for law, prudence, self discipline, and civility are essential administrative virtues. If law, including its constitutional foundation, is a reflection of public will, then we might agree that those who implement its provisions should cultivate and maintain respect for the letter and the intent of statutes, while being attentive to their constitutional authority. It may plausibly be maintained also that practitioners should develop their knowledge and appreciation of the role of law and the constitutional tradition in a self-governing society. This implies an avoidance of that cynical attitude which simply sees the law as an opportunity for administrative intervention, reinterpretation, and imposition of one's own views.

Taking the law and legal processes seriously as instruments of popular sovereignty appears to require rational analysis and honesty in seeking to understand the intent of the law where it is vague, ambiguous, or even self contradictory. Prudent judgment is necessary in its execution. Furthermore, the ability to discipline one's own impulses, impatience, and preconceived convictions in order to serve the will of the people rather than one's own will would seem to be another requisite virtue. It may be argued that upholding popular sovereignty and accountability requires, whenever possible, in both the formation and implementation of public policy, effective provision for citizen participation. Civility, then, would predispose practitioners toward solicitation of open, serious, respectful, and rational exchange of views among the citizenry and between the citizenry and themselves.

Obligation to Colleagues

As concerns the third realm, the obligation of public administration practitioners to colleagues, the essential internal good appears to be the continual enhancement of the standards of excellence with which the practice is carried out. Practitioners have a right to expect their colleagues to strive to achieve clearer and more profound insight into the meaning of beneficence, justice, popular sovereignty, and accountability, as well as more effective ways of realizing those goods in public administrative practice. Both of these require the inclination to approach the practice in a responsible manner, bringing reason and honesty to bear to establish relevant factual material as well as the formation of normative judgments about the nature of the practice. Trustworthiness is an essential virtue for colleagues engaged in such tasks.

The *sine qua non* for the fulfillment of this obligation to colleagues would seem to be resistance to the dominance of external goods. The ability to keep the external goods of organizations in proper perspective calls for certain dispositions to act. Qualities of character such as independence, respect for colleagues, prudent judgment, and a sense of responsibility for the practice of public administration, as well as other practices which function within an organization, might be identified as crucial. One might also maintain that colleagues ought to be able to expect each other to exercise sufficient independence of mind to discern the difference between the internal goods of public administrative practice and the externally imposed goods of the organization in which they are employed. Practitioners should also be able to assume enough independence of conduct on the part of their colleagues to be assured that they will not give in to organizational demands which are subversive of the practice.

Furthermore, one might insist that colleagues should feel obligated to treat each other with civility, receiving each other's ideas in an open, rational, and fairminded manner. It may be logically argued that the members of a practice should assume that they are bound to respect each other's views about the development of the practice and the threat of external goods. Honest expression of differences is an expression of this respect. Similarly, it may be suggested that a sense of responsibility for the practice(s) commonly assumed and held in trust among colleagues is an essential character trait for establishing the ground of that bond. It is neither friendship nor propinquity that obligate colleagues to each other as practitioners, but their shared responsibility for preserving and enhancing the practice of public administration. This sense of responsibility for the practice should encourage the redefinition of situations in which the commitment of superiors to external goods threatens the internal goods of the practice of public administration. Resistance to illegitimate organizational demands is not necessarily just a conflict between one individual's personal conscience and the goals of the organization, as is often thought. Rather, it may well represent a threat to certain internal goods of the practice which the entire community of practitioners as colleagues are obligated to confront.

Conclusion

These comments suggest the texture of normative ethical reflection and discussion which flow from the perspective which is advocated here. The specific substantive proposals concerning internal goods and virtues are intended to be suggestive and provocative of a focus for normative deliberation, not as a final prescription. The development of such prescriptions is not the work of individuals but of colleagues devoted to a practice — or in *search* of a practice. For example, such a framework might provide a helpful orientation for deliberations about the *American Society for Public Administration Code of Ethics and*

Implementation Guidelines.[25] It would encourage rooting an ethical code in a combination of experience and moral philosophy rather than relying too heavily on the politics of the committee process within ASPA.[26]

In its present form the ASPA code of ethics is a conglomeration of prescribed virtues and modes of conduct, with some mention of specific goods, most of which have value and relevance when taken individually. However, what is lacking is a coherent ethical identity for public administration. ASPA's code contains no clear and systematic statement of the internal goods from which the particulars are derived and around which practice ought to be formed. The framework discussed here, on the one hand, would ground prescriptions in some understanding of the underlying internal goods of public administration. On the other, it would focus attention on dispositions to act, on character traits which should be mutually cultivated, and qualities of people being recruited into the field.

The development of prescriptions without some understanding of the internal goods which are fundamental leaves public administrative ethics disconnected from the core of the practice; the promulgation of such prescriptions without a collegial commitment to the cultivation of the virtues which support those internal goods is likely to be an exercise in confusion, futility, and collective self deception.

Endnotes

1. Illustrative examples are: David Ewing, *Freedom Inside the Organization: Bringing Civil Liberties to the Workplace* (New York: E.P. Dutton, 1977); Stanley Milgram, *Obedience to Authority: An Experimental View* (New York: Harper & Row, 1974); Alberto G. Ramos, *The New Science of Organizations* (Toronto: Toronto University Press, 1981); William G. Scott and David K. Hart, *Organizational America* (New York: Houghton Mifflin, 1979); William H. Whyte, *The Organization Man* (New York: Simon & Schuster, 1956).

2. John Rohr, *Ethics for Bureaucrats: An Essay on Law and Values* (New York: Marcel Dekker, 1978); Terry L. Cooper, *The Responsible Administrator: An Approach to Ethics for the Administrative Role*, 2d ed. (New York: Associated Faculty Press, 1986).

3. Mark Lilla, "Ethos, 'Ethics,' and Public Service," *Public Interest*, vol. 63 (Spring 1981), pp. 3-17.

4. William K. Frankena, *Ethics* (Englewood Cliffs: Prentice-Hall, 1973).

5. Alasdair MacIntyre, *After Virtue* 2d ed. (Notre Dame: Notre Dame University Press, 1984), pp. 181-225.

6. *Ibid.*, pp. 188-190.

7. With respect to their attraction to internal goods, MacIntyre's distinction between practices and organizations is too simplistic. See endnote eight.

8. This tendency is true also of organizations specifically established to support and develop practices such as professional associations. A practice may be corrupted by the external goods sought by its own professional association. Thus the practice may begin to orient itself more toward the pursuit of money, political power, social status, and protection from its clients than the whole-hearted development of the proactive.

9. *Ibid.*, pp. 193-194.

10. *Ibid.*, pp. 194-196.

11. Philippa Foot, one of the leaders in regenerating philosophical treatment of virtue, argues in *Virtues and Vices and Other Essays in Moral Philosophy* (Berkeley: University of California Press, 1978) that in developing contemporary thinking on the subject it is best to go back to Aristotle. For Aristotle, moral virtues were understood as habits which constitute our "states of character" specifically concerned with choice. They are the inner, although not innate, dispositions which make it possible for people to resist the pleasures that divert conduct from the good ends of human existence and keep them from being intimidated by the pain which may be required for noble acts. They help people to maintain a "mean" in their conduct between extremes and excesses. Virtues drawn from the political community of which one is a member were seen by Aristotle as essential for the fulfillment of its citizenship. Far from being irrelevant to the rough and tumble world of government, Aristotle indicated in *Nicomachean Ethics*, Book II, that the cultivation of these habits of conduct was considered one of the central responsibilities of legislators because without them democratic government would be impossible. According to Richard McKeon in *The Basic Works of Aristotle*, it seems clear that *Politics* and *Nicomachean Ethics* "treat a common field" (New York: Random House, 1941). Politics without attention to the cultivation of virtue was simply thought to reflect a defective understanding of the ends and purposes of political activity.

12. For examples of this tradition more directly related to American thought, see: Adam Smith, *The Theory of Moral Sentiments*, D.D. Raphael and A.L. Mackie, eds. (Oxford: Clarendon Press, 1976), pp. 216, 231; John R. Howe, *The Changing Political Thought of John Adams* (Princeton: Princeton University Press, 1966), pp. 30-32, 87-88.

13. Peter Geach, discussing the resurgence of interest in ethics of virtue in *The Virtues* (Cambridge: Cambridge University Press, 1977), observed that for some time philosophers had neglected virtue as a subject of serious interest and development, but he offered no insight into the reason for this lapse (Geach, 1977: 1). Foot attributed the neglect of the concept of virtue to the dominance of the analytic school of philosophy, but she indicated also that the situation had begun to change during the previous 10 to 15 years.

14. Stuart Hampshire, *Morality and Conflict* (Cambridge: Harvard University Press, 1983); James D. Wallace, *Virtues and Vices* (Ithaca: Cornell University Press, 1978); R.E. Ewin, *Cooperation and Human Values: A Study of Moral Reasoning* (New York: St. Martin's Press, 1981); William Frankena, *Ethics* (Englewood Cliffs: Prentice-Hall, 1973).

15. *Op. cit.*, pp. 191-192.

16. *Report of the Presidential Commission on the Space Shuttle Challenger Accident* (Washington: U.S. Government Printing Office, 1986). See especially chapters V, VI, and VII.

17. William C. Rempel, "Shuttle Puts Spotlight on Engineers," *Los Angeles Times* (March 5, 1986), p. 1; J. Michael Kennedy, "Shuttle Veteran Charges Earlier Safety Lapses," *Los Angeles Times* (March 9, 1986), p. 1.

18. William D. Marbach with Mary Hager, John Barry, and William Burger, "1986: A Space Odyssey," *Newsweek* (March 24, 1986), p. 18.

19. Kathy Sawyer, "NASA Has Fewer People Minding the Store Now," *The Washington Post Weekly Edition* (May 19, 1986), p. 31.

20. William Marbach with Ron Moreau, Richard Sandza, and Daniel Pedersen, "No Cheers for NASA," *Newsweek* (March 24, 1986), p. 18.

21. *Report of the Presidential Commission,* pp. 164-165. See the remainder of chapter VIII for the details of these pressures on the space shuttle program. See also an institutional analysis of the problems of multiple expectations and competing accountability systems within NASA in Barbara S. Romzek and Melvin J. Dubnick, "Accountability in the Public Sector: Lessons from the Challenger Tragedy," *Public Administration Review,* vol. 47 (May/June 1987).

22. George Will, "Who Will Lead the Noble Quest?" *Newsweek* (June 23, 1986), p. 84.

23. "Fairmindedness" is used to indicate the virtue which is directly supportive of achieving and maintaining justice although in the philosophical literature "justice" is typically used both for the principle and the virtue. I find this much too confusing.

24. Since "prudence" seems to have acquired negative connotations of preoccupation with self interest in contemporary discourse, both popular and philosophical, it seems important at least to indicate that this is a relatively recent phenomenon. Through most of the western philosophical tradition, prudence has been understood quite differently and regarded with greater esteem. For Aristotle, prudence (*phronesis*) was an essential human quality for moral conduct, as was true also in the thought of St. Thomas Aquinas as he appropriated and incorporated Aristotelian concepts into his Christian theology. In both of these cases prudence meant "practical wisdom," the ability to achieve good ends through good means. Prudence was understood as the deliberative skills necessary to move from principle to specific action in a concrete situation. For treatments of prudence which are generally consistent with this older tradition, see Adam Smith, *op. cit.*,; R.E. Ewin, *op. cit.*; and Joseph Pieper, *Prudence* (New York: Pantheon Books, 1959). For one recent view which takes a more negative view of the concept see William Frankena, *op. cit.* See also David K. Hart's argument for prudence as one of the essential virtues of public administrators in "The Virtuous Citizen, the Honorable Bureaucrat, and Public Administration," *Public Administration Review,* vol. 44, special issue (March 1984), pp. 116-117.

25. Both documents are obtainable from the American Society for Public Administration, (1120 Gπ Street, NW, Suite 500, Washington, DC 20005). [They are also reprinted in this volume.]

26. See Ralph Chandler's treatment of this problem in "The Problem of Moral Reasoning in American Public Administration: The Case for a Code of Ethics," *Public Administration Review,* vol. 43 (January/February 1983), pp. 32-39.

Case 1: The New City Manager

You have been the assistant manager of a small city for three years. One day, the city manager calls you in for a professional talk about your career. He thinks that you are a highly competent individual and that you have learned about all you are going to learn in the position you now hold. Since he has no plans to retire or move, he advises that for your own career development you should be looking for a more demanding position to develop your executive abilities and achieve career goals. His advice is to seek the management of a small jurisdiction, or become assistant manager of a large suburb or city. In either position you will have new and more responsible duties which would go far in getting you that position you really desire. He asks you to think about it and after you have decided which course you want to take, he will assist you in getting an appropriate assignment. After you inform the manager of your desire to try for a small jurisdiction managership, he assists you by calling other managers, and the International City Management Association (ICMA), informing them that you are a good executive and are available.

The recommendation of your manager and your excellent record result in a number of inquiries. You take several interviews and are then invited to interview for the managership of Sylvan Hills Town, a residential suburb outside a major metropolitan area in another state. Your present manager knows the two former managers of Sylvan Hills. Both went on to bigger cities and both have good reputations in the profession. He agrees to call them; does so; and reports back that with some minor idiosyncrasies in council activities, the manager is generally free to manage and is given the resources to do so. The only problems that the jurisdiction is facing are those of development pressures from the metropolitan area and a rather constant involvement with labor, both internally and with the construction unions.

You have a very successful interview with the five-member town board, like what you see in the community and the region (with the exception of metropolitan news reports about labor troubles and crime syndicate links with a nearby city), and you agree to accept the job. After all, what that city does is no concern of yours. You will be the manager of a nice quiet suburban community that seems to be quite free of professionally inappropriate activities on the part of public officials.

After a week on the job, you note that you are expected to have dinner with the council and the treasurer prior to your first board meeting. You attend, thinking that this is a nice way to get the evening's agenda in order. At dinner, you notice two strangers, who are introduced to you as a prominent labor leader and the other as the president of a local construction company. The board's activities are discussed and most of the board seem to be in agreement on most of the subjects. However, as you begin to talk about the road construction contracts, one of the board members looks your way and asks you what percentage you expect?

The look of surprise on your face is a cue for the board chairman to suggest a break. He draws you aside, saying that he understands your surprise and would like to explain how things like construction contracts work in Sylvan Hills. Most major construction activities are controlled by a big holding company association which has several "independent" construction firms located throughout the state. For years the Sylvan Hills Town board had dealt with this company in exchange for labor peace and other occasional "protective" services. The town board and some of the town executives are given "bonuses" for their cooperation with the company. Since all the bids are from the holding company's firm, they are rigged to give the firms alternating contracts for town work. Generally, ten percent of the contract is returned by the company to those who participate in the decisions.

Source: Leigh Grosenick, Virginia Commonwealth University.

You express astonishment at this process and suggest that it is illegal. The understanding board chairman nods and says that he agrees that it could be thought of in that way, but that they were only doing what brought peace to the town, and on a much smaller scale than what you would find in the older cities in the metropolitan area. People in the area assume that city officials accept private payments for assisting them in various activities — so long as it isn't outrageous and the process does not create undue publicity.

At this point you say that you are not interested in any percentage. That you can do a good job without benefiting financially from this type of operation.

The board chairman, however, says that this is not a good idea. The people who run the company and the unions can be rough and have insisted upon the town manager's participation in this process. The chairman explains to you that you will become a consultant for the company and that the percentage that you receive will be listed as a consulting fee. You are free to consult under the terms of your contract with the board, and thus, no illegalities for tax or other purposes are encountered. He informs you that the last two managers were able to function very well under this system and accomplish much for the community. Both of them gave their fees to local charities, something that you might consider.

2. Ethics as Consequence

The Prince
Niccolò Machiavelli

XV. On Those Things for Which Men, and Particularly Princes, Are Praised or Blamed

. . . There is such a gap between how one lives and how one ought to live that anyone who abandons what is done for what ought to be done learns his ruin rather than his preservation: for a man who wishes to profess goodness at all times will come to ruin among so many who are not good. Hence it is necessary for a prince who wishes to maintain his position to learn how not to be good, and use this knowledge or not according to necessity.

Leaving aside, therefore, the imagined things concerning a prince, and taking into account those that are true, I say that all men, when they are spoken of, and particularly princes, since they are placed on a higher level, are judged by some of these qualities which bring them either blame or praise. And this is why one is considered generous, another miserly (to use a Tuscan word, since 'avaricious' in our language is still used to mean one who wishes to acquire by means of theft; we call 'miserly' one who excessively avoids using what he has); one is considered a giver, the other rapacious; one cruel, another merciful; one treacherous, another faithful; one effeminate and cowardly, another bold and courageous; one humane, another haughty; one lascivious, another chaste; one trustworthy, another frivolous; one religious, another unbelieving; and the like. And I know that everyone will admit that it would be a very praiseworthy thing to find in a prince, of the qualities mentioned above, those that are held to be good; but since it is neither possible to have them nor to observe them all completely, because the human condition does not permit it, a prince must be prudent enough to know how to escape the bad reputation of those vices that would lose the state for him, and must protect himself from those that will not lose it for him, if this is possible; but if he cannot, he need not concern himself unduly if he ignores these less serious vices. And, moreover, he need not worry about incurring the bad reputation of those vices without which it would be difficult to hold his state; since, carefully taking everything into account, he will discover that something which appears to be a virtue, if pursued, will end in destruction; while some other thing which seems to be a vice, if pursued will result in his safety and his well-being.

Niccolò Machiavelli (1462-1527) is regarded by many as a great political philosopher whose writings mark the beginning of modern political thought. Others regard Machiavelli's ideas as so evil that his very name has become an adjective to designate unprincipled and unethical behavior. One of his many major breaks with the classical thought of Plato and Aristotle was his argument that acts should be judged good or bad in relationship to their consequences or results, rather than their intentions or the characteristics of the actor. These two selections from The Prince outline that argument, a foreshadowing of later utilitarian and other consequentialist ethical theories.

Source: Niccolò Machiavelli, *The Prince* (Oxford: Oxford University Press, 1984), ch. 15, 18.

XVIII. How a Prince Should Keep His Word

How praiseworthy it is for a prince to keep his word and to live by integrity and not by deceit everyone knows; nevertheless, one sees from the experience of our times that the princes who have accomplished great deeds are those who have cared little for keeping their promises and who have known how to manipulate the minds of men by shrewdness; and in the end they have surpassed those who laid their foundations upon loyalty.

You must, therefore, know that there are two means of fighting: one according to the laws, the other with force; the first way is proper to man, the second to beasts; but because the first, in many cases, is not sufficient, it becomes necessary to have recourse to the second. Therefore, a prince must know how to use wisely the natures of the beast and the man. . . .

Since, then, a prince must know how to make good use of the nature of the beast, he should choose from among the beasts the fox and the lion; for the lion cannot defend itself from the traps and the fox cannot protect itself from the wolves. It is therefore necessary to be a fox in order to recognize the traps and a lion in order to frighten the wolves. Those who play only the part of the lion do not understand matters. A wise ruler, therefore, cannot and should not keep his word when such an observance of faith would be to his disadvantage and when the reasons which made him promise are removed. And if men were all good, this rule would not be good; but since men are a contemptible lot and will not keep their promises to you, you likewise need not keep yours to them. A prince never lacks legitimate reasons to break his promise. Of this one could cite an endless number of modern examples to show how many pacts, how many promises have been made null and void because of the infidelity of princes; and he who has known best how to use the fox has come to a better end. But it is necessary to know how to disguise this nature well and to be a great hypocrite and a liar; and men are so simple-minded and so controlled by their present needs that one who deceives will always find another who will allow himself to be deceived. . . .

Therefore, it is not necessary for a prince to have all of the above-mentioned qualities, but it is very necessary for him to appear to have them. Furthermore, I shall be so bold to assert this: that having them and practicing them at all times is harmful; and appearing to have them is useful; for instance, to seem merciful, faithful, humane, trustworthy, religious, and to be so; but his mind should be disposed in such a way that should it become necessary not to be so, he will be able and know how to change to the contrary. And it is essential to understand this: that a prince, and especially a new prince, cannot observe all those things for which men are considered good, for in order to maintain the state he is often obliged to act against his promise, against charity, against humanity, and against religion. And therefore, it is necessary that he have a mind ready to turn itself according to the way the winds of fortune and the changeability of affairs require him; and, as I said above, as long as it is possible, he should not stray from the good, but he should know how to enter into evil when necessity commands.

A prince, therefore, must be very careful never to let anything slip from his lips which is not full of the five qualities mentioned above: he should appear, upon seeing and hearing him, to be all mercy, all faithfulness, all integrity, all kindness, all religion. And there is nothing more necessary than to seem to possess this last quality. And men in general judge more by their eyes than their hands; for everyone can see but few can feel. Everyone sees what you seem to be, few touch upon what you are, and those few do not dare to contradict the opinion of the many who have the majesty of the state to defend them; and in the actions of all men, and especially of princes, where there is no impartial arbiter, one must consider the final result. Let a prince therefore act to conquer and to maintain the state; his methods will always be judged honorable and will be praised by all. . . .

Utilitarianism
John Stuart Mill

. . . All action is for the sake of some end, and rules of action, it seems natural to suppose, must take their whole character and color from the end to which they are subservient. When we engage in a pursuit, a clear and precise conception of what we are pursuing would seem to be the first thing we need, instead of the last we are to look forward to. A test of right and wrong must be the means, one would think, of ascertaining what is right or wrong, and not a consequence of having already ascertained it.

John Stuart Mill (1806-1873), like Machiavelli, judged actions on the basis of their consequences. As he argues in this selection, to be good, actions must be "a means to something admitted to be good without proof," such as health or pleasure.

The difficulty is not avoided by having recourse to the popular theory of a natural faculty, a sense of instinct, informing us of right and wrong. For — besides that the existence of such a moral instinct is itself one of the matters in dispute — those believers in it who have any pretensions to philosophy have been obliged to abandon the idea that it discerns what is right or wrong in the particular case in hand, as our other senses discern the sight or sound actually present. Our moral faculty, according to all those of its interpreters who are entitled to the name of thinkers, supplies us only with the general principles of moral judgments; it is a branch of our reason, not of our sensitive faculty, and must be looked to for the abstract doctrines of morality, not for perception of it in the concrete. The intuitive, no less than what may be termed the inductive, school of ethics insists on the necessity of general laws. They both agree that the morality of an individual action is not a question of direct perception, but of the application of a law to an individual case. They recognize also, to a great extent, the same moral laws, but differ as to their evidence and the source from which they derive their authority. According to the one opinion, the principles of morals are evident *a priori,* requiring nothing to command assent except that the meaning of the terms be understood. According to the other doctrine, right and wrong, as well as truth and falsehood, are questions of observation and experience. But both hold equally that morality must be deduced from principles; and the intuitive school affirms as strongly as the inductive that there is a science of morals. Yet they seldom attempt to make out a list of the *a priori* principles which are to serve as the premises of the science; still more rarely do they make any effort to reduce those various principles to one first principle or common ground of obligation. They either assume the ordinary precepts of morals as of *a priori* authority, or they lay down as the common groundwork of those maxims some generality much less obviously authoritative than the maxims themselves, and which has never succeeded in gaining popular acceptance. Yet to support their pretensions there ought either to be some one fundamental principle or law at the root of all morality, or, if there be several, there should be a determinate order of precedence among them; and the one principle, or the rule for deciding between the various principles when they conflict, ought to be self-evident.

To inquire how far the bad effects of this deficiency have been mitigated in practice, or to what extent the moral beliefs of mankind have been vitiated or made uncertain by the absence of any distinct recognition of an ultimate standard, would imply a complete survey and criticism of past and present ethical doctrine. It would, however, be easy to show that whatever steadiness or consistency these moral beliefs have attained has been mainly due to the tacit influence of a standard not recognized. Although the nonexistence of an acknowledged first principle has made ethics not so much a guide as a consecration of men's actual sentiments, still, as men's sentiments, both of favor and of aversion, are greatly influenced by what they suppose to be the effects of things upon their happiness, the principle of utility, or, as Bentham latterly called it, the greatest happiness principle, has had a large share in forming the moral doctrines even of those who most scornfully reject its authority. Nor is there any school of thought which refuses to admit that the influence of actions on happiness is a most material and even predominant consideration in many of the details of morals, however unwilling to acknowledge it as the fundamental principle of morality and the source of moral obligation. I might go much further and say that to all those *a priori* moralists who deem it necessary to argue at all, utilitarian arguments are indispensable. It is not my present purpose to criticize these thinkers; but I cannot help referring, for illustration, to a systematic treatise by one of the most illustrious of them, *The Metaphysics of Ethics* by Kant. This remarkable man, whose system of thought will long remain one of the landmarks in the history of philosophical speculation, does, in the treatise in question, lay down a universal first principle as the origin and ground of moral obligations; it is this: "So act that the rule on which thou actest would admit of being adopted as a law by

Source: John Stuart Mill, *Utilitarianism,* (Indianapolis: Bobbs-Merrill Educational Publishing, 1957. Originally published in 1861.), Ch. 1.

all rational beings." But when he begins to deduce from this precept any of the actual duties of morality, he fails, almost grotesquely, to show that there would be any contradiction, any logical (not to say physical) impossibility, in the adoption by all rational beings of the most outrageously immoral rules of conduct. All he shows is that the consequences of their universal adoption would be such as no one would choose to incur.

On the present occasion, I shall, without further discussion of the other theories, attempt to contribute something toward the understanding and appreciation of the "utilitarian" or "happiness" theory, and toward such proof as it is susceptible of. It is evident that this cannot be proof in the ordinary and popular meaning of the term. Questions of ultimate ends are not amenable to direct proof. Whatever can be proved to be good must be so by being shown to be a means to something admitted to be good without proof. The medical art is proved to be good by its conducing to health; but how is it possible to prove that health is good? The art of music is good, for the reason, among others, that it produces pleasure; but what proof is it possible to give that pleasure is good? If, then, it is asserted that there is a comprehensive formula, including all things which are in themselves good, and that whatever else is good is not so as an end but as a means, the formula may be accepted or rejected, but is not a subject of what is commonly understood by proof. We are not, however, to infer that its acceptance or rejection must depend on blind impulse or arbitrary choice. There is a larger meaning of the word "proof," in which this question is as amenable to it as any other of the disputed questions of philosophy. The subject is within the cognizance of the rational faculty; and neither does that faculty deal with it solely in the way of intuition. Considerations may be presented capable of determining the intellect either to give or withhold its assent to the doctrine; and this is equivalent to proof.

Case 2: Per Diem

The state allows each person so much *per diem* for travel (a bit more for out-of-state). Recently, we were called upon to travel to a work site in the state for several days to work on an emergency, one-time problem. We were authorized to travel and to be gone from the office for more than 24 business hours. Most of us worked so close to our homes that we ate most meals there and spent each night there. Still, "vouchers" were submitted for 3 meals per day and housing each evening. Although it was argued that this is SOP and expected and would cause others problems if not done, it seems unfair (to taxpayers), unethical and dishonest. I am bothered by this practice and feel that we should not claim a travel allowance. Some co-workers disagree. I'm sure that I will lose them as friends if I "squeal." What should I do? Why?

Source: Debra Stewart, North Carolina State University.

3. Ethics as Principle

The Categorical Imperative
Immanuel Kant

Each thing in nature works according to laws. Only a rational being has the faculty to act *according to the conception* of laws, that is according to principles, in other words has a will. Since the deduction of actions from laws requires *reason* the will is nothing but practical reason. . . .

The conception of an objective principle in so far as it is obligatory for the will, is called a command (of reason), and the formula of the command is called an IMPERATIVE. . . .

Now all *imperatives* command either *hypothetically* or *categorically*. The former represents the practical necessity of a possible action as a means to arrive at something else that is willed (or may be willed). The categorical imperative would then be that which represented an action as objectively necessary of itself without relation to another end. . . .

. . . [T]here is only one categorical imperative and it is this: *Act only on that maxim which will enable you at the same time to will that it be a universal law.*

Now if all imperatives of duty can be deduced from this single imperative as from their principle, then, although we here refrain from stating whether what one calls duty may be an empty notion, we shall at least be able to indicate what we understand by it and what the concept means.

Because the universality of the law according to which effects are produced constitutes what we really mean by nature in the most general sense (according to form), that is, the existence of things in so far as it is determined by universal laws, the universal imperative of duty may read thus: *Act as if the maxim of your action by your will were to become a UNIVERSAL LAW OF NATURE.*

We will now enumerate a few duties. . . .

A person who is wearied with life because of a series of misfortunes that has reduced him to despair still possesses sufficient reason to be able to ask himself, whether it may not be contrary to his duty to himself to take his life. Now he asks himself, whether the maxim of his action could possibly be a universal law of nature. But this maxim reads: Out of love of self I make it my principle to shorten my life if its

Immanuel Kant (1724-1804) approached the question of ethics from a very different angle from Machiavelli or Mill. In the following passages he outlines his categorical imperative, the fundamental principle he sees as the ultimate basis of ethical action.

As you read Kant, consider whether your own ethical assumptions are closer to his or to those of Machiavelli. In real-life ethical situations, do you act primarily on the basis of principle or on the basis of expected consequences?

Source: Immanuel Kant, *The Fundamental Principles of the Metaphysic of Ethics* (Trans. Otto Manthey-Zorn. New York: Appleton-Century, 1938), pp. 29-31, 38-42.

continuation threatens more evil than it promises comfort. But he will still ask, whether his principle of self-love is capable of being a universal law of nature. Then he will soon see that a nature, whose law it would be to destroy life by the very feeling which is meant to stimulate the promotion of life, would contradict itself and therefore not persist as nature. Accordingly the maxim cannot possibly function as a universal law of nature, and it consequently completely refutes the supreme principle of all duty.

Another person is in need and finds it necessary to borrow money. He knows very well that he will not be able to repay it, but he also realizes that he will not receive a loan unless he promises solemnly to pay at a definite time. He has a desire to make this promise, but he still has enough conscience to ask himself whether it is not improper and contrary to duty to relieve distress in this manner. If he should nevertheless decide to do so, then the maxim of his action would read thus: When I think that I am in need of money I will borrow and promise to repay, even though I know that I will never do so. Now this principle of my love of self or advantage may perhaps well agree with my whole future well-being; the next question, however, is, whether it is right. Thereby I change the interpretation of self-love into a universal law and arrange my question thus: How would things be if my maxim were a universal law? Then I see at once that it could never count as a universal law of nature and still agree with itself, but must necessarily contradict itself. For the universality of a law, according to which anyone who believed himself in distress could promise anything he pleased with no intention of keeping it, would make promises themselves and any purpose they may have impossible; since nobody would believe that a promise had been made, but everybody would ridicule such statements as vain pretenses.

A third finds that he possesses a gift which with some cultivation could make a useful man of him in all sorts of respects. But he is in comfortable circumstances and prefers to indulge in pleasure rather than trouble himself with the expansion and improvement of his fortunate natural faculties. But he still questions, whether his maxim of neglect of his natural gifts, besides agreeing with his inclination to diversions, also agrees with what is called duty. Then he sees that according to such a universal law a nature could still go on persisting although man, like the South Sea islander, should let his talents rest and his life were intent only on idleness, diversions, propagation, in a word, pleasure; but he cannot possibly will this to be a universal law of nature or be given to us as such by a natural instinct. For as a rational being he necessarily wants all his faculties to develop because they after all are given to him and serve him for all sorts of possible purposes.

Again a *fourth,* who is well off while he sees others struggling with great difficulties (which he could well alleviate), thinks: What concern is it of mine? May each man be as happy as the heavens decree or he can make himself to be; I shall deprive him of nothing and not even envy him. But neither do I care to contribute to his welfare nor offer him help in his distress. Now if such an attitude were to be a universal law of nature the human race could subsist very well, to be sure, and doubtless better than when everybody chatters of sympathy and good will, even endeavors occasionally to exert it, but also takes every chance to deceive and to plunder or otherwise to violate the rights of man. But although it is possible that a universal law of nature could exist by that maxim, it is still impossible to will that such a principle count as a law of nature generally. For by deciding for such a law a will would run counter to itself, inasmuch as many an occasion might arise where a person of such will might need the love and sympathy of others and where he would deprive himself of all hope of the desired assistance because of such a natural law arisen from his own will.

These are then a few of the duties, actual or at least accepted as such by us, whose derivation from the single principle which we have described is at once clear. The canon of the moral judgment of actions generally is this: One must be *able to will* that the maxim of an action be a universal law. . . .

. . . Assuming, however, that there is something, *the existence of which of itself* has an absolute value which, *as in itself,* could be the basis of definite laws; then the possible categorical imperative or practical law would lie in it and in it alone.

Now I say: Man and every rational being anywhere *exists* as end in itself, *not merely as means* for the arbitrary use by this or that will; but in all his actions, whether they are directed upon himself or upon other rational beings, he must at all times be looked upon as an *end.* . . .

If then there is to be a supreme practical principle and in respect to the human will a categorical imperative, then it must be one which, when we conceive what is necessarily an end for everybody because it is the *end in itself,* must constitute an *objective* principle of the will and therefore be able to serve as universal practical law. The basis of this principle is: *Rational nature exists as end in itself.* Man necessarily conceives his own being in this way, and therefore it is thus far a *subjective* principle of human actions. But every other rational being conceives his existence in the same way and on rational grounds identical with my own; therefore it is at the same time an *objective principle* from which as the supreme practical basis all laws of the will must be capable of being deduced. The practical imperative will then read as follows: *Act so that in your own person as well as in the person of every other you are treating mankind also as an end, never merely as a means.* Let us see whether this can be put into practice.

We shall illustrate this by means of our previous examples.

Firstly according to the concept of the necessary duty to oneself. The person who is contemplating suicide will ask himself, whether his act can coexist together with the idea of mankind *as end in itself.* If he destroys himself in order to escape from a burdensome situation he uses a person merely as a *means* to maintain a tolerable condition up to the end of his life. However, man is not a thing and therefore not something that may be used as means only, but in all his actions he must always be considered as end in itself. Consequently I can make no disposition of the man in my own person to manipulate, destroy or kill him. (The more detailed definition of this principle which would avoid all misunderstanding I must omit here, as for example, the question of the amputation of limbs to save life, exposing one's life to danger in order to maintain it, etc. This belongs to ethics proper.)

Secondly in regard to the necessary or bounden duty to others. The person who intends to make a lying promise to others must realize at once that he is about to use some other person as mere means, without the latter at the same time containing the end in himself. For the person whom I am about to use for my purposes by such a promise cannot possibly agree with my conduct toward him, and thus himself contain the end of this action. This conflict with the principle of other men becomes more obvious when examples of attacks upon the freedom and property of others are employed. Then it becomes clear that such a transgressor against the rights of man intends to use the person of others as means without considering that these others as rational beings must always be esteemed also as ends, that is to say as such who also be able to contain in themselves the end of the very same action.

Thirdly in respect to the contingent (meritorious) duties to oneself, it is not enough that the action should not be in conflict with the humanity in one's person as end in itself, it must also harmonize with it. Now there are in mankind faculties for greater perfection which belong to the end which nature possesses in view of the humanity in us as subjects. To neglect these might perhaps be consistent with the *preservation* of mankind as end in itself, but could not agree with *advancement.*

Fourthly in regard to the meritorious duties toward others, the natural end which all men possess is their own happiness. Mankind would indeed be able to persist if no one contributed to another's happiness and did not intentionally deprive the latter's happiness of anything. However, it is only a negative and not a positive agreement with *mankind* as *end in itself* when each person does not also seek to advance the end of others as far as he is able. For the ends of the subject, which is an end in itself, must as far as possible be *my* ends also if the conception of happiness is to be *fully* effective with me.

A Guide to Ethics for Public Servants
Ralph Clark Chandler

Public Administrators in the United States, Ralph Chandler argues, operate on the basis of a variety of principles or precepts. Chandler describes ten of these, noting that they are often mutually contradictory and that several draw upon long historical tradition. His survey provides a rich historical perspective to contemporary debates and codes of ethics. His account also touches upon numerous themes raised elsewhere in this volume, including virtue, responsibility, codes of ethics, and accountability.

. . . Certain ethical precepts have guided American public administrators from the earliest days of the republic. Some are implicit, some are explicit, several are contradictory to each other, and all are subject to differing interpretations. Let us now turn to a description of ten of these precepts, not claiming them to be the new decalogue, and let us consider them in the rough chronological order of their ascendancy. Each has held up over time, and each has been devoutly maintained by professional groups of varying and unknown size.

Ten Ethical Precepts

Demonstrate Fiscal Integrity. The principles that guided the administration of the Massachusetts Bay Colony in the seventeenth century, the establishment of the U.S. General Accounting Office in 1921, and the passage of the Ethics in Government Act of 1978, are very nearly the same. The common denominator is fiscal integrity. An important benchmark of ethical behavior is how one handles money.

The great Puritan migration of 1630 overwhelmed the separatist Pilgrim settlements in New England by sheer numbers and moral fervor. Puritanism established a legacy of values that endures today as the puritan Ethic. It says that hard work begets prosperity and that the proper stewardship of prosperity is the chief end of the state. The related doctrine of "calling" means that everyone is called to take some part in building God's righteous empire. Some are tradesmen, some are fishermen, some are farmers, some are educators, and some are keepers of the hearth, but the highest calling of all is to bear rule.

The magistrates whom the Puritans elected, and the public officials whom the magistrates appointed to manage public property, were called *visible saints* by the people of Massachusetts Bay. The constitutional responsibility of the saints was to enforce the canons of sobriety, piety, and a balanced economy, so that capital could be accumulated. Their professionalism consisted of their ability to add to the common good by avoiding the foul disorders of the commonwealth associated with public assistance to rogues, beggars, and vagabonds. By being thrifty and frugal with tax monies, public officials could use them to increase the wealth of the state and thereby assure all its citizens that they were indeed the elect of God.

The Congress of the United States had the same fiscal integrity precept in mind when it created, in the Budget and Accounting Act of 1921, a comptroller general to investigate all matters related to the receipt, disbursement, and application of public funds. It reiterated this common understanding of ethical behavior both in the Budget and Accounting Procedures Act of 1950 and in the Legislative Reorganization Act of 1970.

Similarly, when Congress could no longer avoid the necessity of explicit ethics legislation for federal officials in the late 1970s, it asked witness after witness what were the essential characteristics of ethical behavior in government. The answers it frequently got and eventually acted on would have warmed the heart of John Winthrop and all those who equate high ethical performance with sound fiscal management. The Ethics in Government Act of 1978 deals extensively and almost exclusively with financial disclosure, as well as with the reporting of potential conflicts of interest among officers and employees of the federal government at the GS-16 level and above. The Puritan Ethic's preoccupation with the material signs of God's grace, later translated into the principles of the Yankee trader, is now and has always been a leading ethical precept in American public administration. When one handles the accounts right, he or she is a moral public servant by definition.

Avoid Moral Abstractions. By the time of the American Revolution, the Puritan Ethic had lost its primary references to the Holy Commonwealth and the City of God. It had gone secular and been translated into a practical utopianism that wished to avoid moral abstractions. Even in Puritan New England, English law had been a sobering influence on the theocrats. The colonists did what they had to do to retain their charters and their land titles, which meant that they kept finding new examples of how the laws of England and the laws of God coincided.

Source: Ralph Clark Chandler, "A Guide to Ethics for Public Servants," in James L. Perry, ed., *Handbook of Public Administration* (San Francisco: Jossey-Bass, 1989), pp. 602-620.

The deists of the Revolutionary period fully subscribed to the injunctions of the Puritan Ethic. No man more methodically industrious than Thomas Jefferson ever lived, but he was hardly a Puritan. Experience had taught the founders that public administrators were not saints after all, and that precautions had to be taken for keeping them virtuous. These precautions could not be based on such moral abstractions as duty or the public good, however. If they were, moral reductionism and indoctrination would carry the nation into the kind of moral tyranny that may have worked in Geneva and other Calvinist strongholds but surely would not work in a land as culturally diverse as the United States. The founders counseled moderation on moral matters. The real danger, they said, was that a self-consciously moral public service would relegate individual rights and all things private were more important than prosperity, although not by much.

Public servants and everyone else would henceforth be coerced by law, not by the sermons of Cotton Mather or any of this progeny, including Jerry Falwell. Moral purists do not understand the ways in which political liberty and economic energy inevitably produce some immorality. The institutions of government will control whatever evil is necessary, without the social consequences of religious sectarianism. The members of the new administrative class will live with immorality moderately, remembering that men and women are not angels. If they were, no government would be necessary. This was the sage advice of that former theology student James Madison.

This serviceable wisdom has been translated by subsequent generations of American civil servants into a legalist position, which equates ethical behavior with obedience to law. The paramount ethical responsibility of public administrators is to follow the legally constituted directives of hierarchical superiors and elected representatives of the people. The strength of this precept lies in its fit with fundamental democratic political values and principles. Its weakness is that it reinforces a technocratic and instrumentalist conception of professional practice, which glosses over the inescapable moral content of real administrative life.

Embrace Moral Abstractions. Standing alongside the founders' advice to be moderate on moral matters was their paradoxical impulse to be passionate about certain moral abstractions. The most common of these was the idea of virtue. By virtue, the founders meant good character, civic concern, a willingness to sacrifice comfort and personal wealth for the public good, and a commitment to the development of the soul of the state. In its Aristotelian context, virtue is related directly to action, and not just to thinking or feeling in a certain way. It involves cognitive activity that is not innate but cultivated.

If virtue is a character trait that can be taught, it follows that ethical behavior may be influenced by a code of ethics that encourages the public administrator to make prescribed choices and judgments and pursue approved actions. In the Athenian oath, for example, virtue included a promise to fight for the ideals and the sacred things of the city. In the *Code of Ethics of the American Society for Public Administration* (ASPA), virtue includes a commitment to demonstrate the highest standards of personal integrity, truthfulness, honesty and fortitude.

Long before 1984, when the ASPA *Code of Ethics* was adopted, such administrative Platonists as Paul H. Appleby and Stephen K. Bailey, both former deans of the Maxwell School of Citizenship and Public Affairs at Syracuse University, described ethical behavior in terms of moral abstractions such as optimism, courage, fairness, and charity. Neither Appleby nor Bailey was very sentimental. Appleby (1952) offered a practical description of the moral administrator that included a sense of responsibility; skills in communication and personnel administration, with special emphasis on recruiting competent assistants, advisers, and specialists; the ability to cultivate and use institutional resources; a willingness to engage in problem solving and to work with others as a team; and enough personal confidence to initiate new ideas. Bailey was equally practical. He argued (1965) for a personal code of ethics for the public administrator because he or she must relate what is specific and private to what is general, public, and moral; because, when ethical codes are absent, the public loses confidence in public processes; and because controversial policy decisions focus inordinate political pressure on administrators. Adherents of Bailey's third precept believe that translating moral abstractions into the marketplace of professional practice makes ethical behavior the predicate of administrative being and thus the appropriate expression of civic virtue.

Affirm Pluralist Theory. The founders devised a political system of countervailing power in which public policy is the product of compromises among competing interests. The American political system is a balance of power among economic, professional, religious, ethnic, and geographical groups whose memberships overlap. Each of these groups seeks to impose its will on public policy, but each is limited in its ability to do so because it must accommodate the demands of the other groups. Pluralism is the expression of this bargaining process. It is the political reality that has displaced the ideals of civic virtue in the American republic. Madison was correct in his prediction that interest would play the role of virtue in American government.

The norms of pluralism define the agencies of government as arenas for the expression of self-interest. Since bureaucracies are representative institutions, they provide access to government for everyone in society. They ensure stability because multiple group pressures on government virtually guarantee that the most important policy questions will eventually be processed and resolved by the public administrators who preside over the bureaucracies. The officials behave ethically to the extent that they fairly moderate the interests brought to them. Theoretically, they serve all interests, but they can serve none exclusively. Therein lies moral public service.

The definition of administrative agencies as representative institutions was the result of the Jacksonian revolution of 1829. From the rise of the spoils system until about 1869, representativeness in administration meant that bureaucracies should reflect the dispersion of citizens demographically, and that administrative personnel should be mirror images of the majority party. There should be an integration of politics and administration. A complete administrative ethic meant that society's plebeian interests were consciously being served.

In the place of majority rule, pluralism recognizes rule by minorities. This fact of American life is given theoretical justification in the works of John C. Calhoun and Alexis de Tocqueville, both of whom argue that majority opinion holds no claim on abstract standards of justice merely because it is the opinion of the majority. The doctrine of rule by minorities is reflected in the checks-and-balances provisions of the Constitution. The ethical quandary associated with pluralism comes at the point of democratic theory. Civil servants are expected, especially by presidents, to be responsive to the leadership of whatever administration has the trust and authority of the American people, as demonstrated at the ballot box. Civil servants are also expected to be efficient. Neither majoritarianism nor efficiency is a value honored by pluralism, however. Representation, service, and accommodation are much more important to the pluralist, which means that traditional techniques of motivating or evaluating employees are not applicable to many public sector operations. When goal ambiguity is the norm, market-based performance measures do not work. If civil servants respond to their environment as pluralist theory asks them to, the results are often at odds with the goals of classical majoritarianism.

According to pluralist ethics, public administrators act responsibly by representing important interests and attitudes that are excluded from Congress and other representative bodies. The principle of representation — or the lack of it for millions of Americans — is one of the most serious defects of the Constitution. The huge career public service helps remedy that defect by interpreting professionalism to include the role of the public administrator as representative citizen.

Believe the Dichotomy. The political efficacy and administrative egalitarianism envisioned by Andrew Jackson had degenerated into crass political opportunism by the 1870s. Public administration came to be viewed as a managerial extension of the political machine. A reform movement arose to redress the incompetence and corruption of the Jacksonian and radical republican eras by proposing administrative models based on professionalism and neutrality. In 1887, Woodrow Wilson posited a major distinction between politics and administration: Politics is the proper activity of legislative bodies and other policymaking groups, he said, and administration is the proper activity of a professional class of public managers who carry out the directives of the policymakers as efficiently as possible (Wilson, 1887). Reformers such as United States Senator George H. Pendleton had said four years earlier that the appointment of these public managers should be based on fitness and merit, rather than on partisanship; hence, the Pendleton Act of 1883.

It was left to Weber (1946), however, to offer the classic justification of the dichotomy. Weber said that the unique attributes of the politician are exactly the opposite of those of the civil servant. The essence of politics, he maintained, is to take a stand, be passionate, exercise conscience, take personal responsibility for policies, and admit the transitory nature of the political role. The public administrator, however, is to execute the orders of the political authority conscientiously, regardless of their compatibility with the administrator's convictions and values. Thus, the morality of the civil servant consists in obedience to higher authority.

It was said that ethical behavior results from administrative neutrality, because public officials are free to apply to government what Frederick Winslow Taylor called the principles of scientific management. Bureaucracy is a rational and legal system designed to attain precision and reliability in serving the needs of mass democracy. The best thing that can be said about government is that it is businesslike in its procedures. Two months before Wilson's (1887) essay appeared, *The Nation* ran an editorial lauding the Secretary of the Treasury Charles S. Fairchild, for establishing "a great business institution." President Grover Cleveland had done the right thing by ensuring "a most notable extension of the system of conducting the affairs of the Government on business principles" ("Government on Business Principles," 1887, p. 288).

When the dichotomy discourages the public administrator from making value judgments, it leaves him or her in a relativist position, which assumes that ethical norms are matters of arbitrary preference and that no objectively valid moral statements can be made. Is this the way administrative life is actually lived? Is moral responsibility possible without administrative discretion? Proponents of the dichotomy precept say that the answer to this question does not matter, because rules are ends in themselves, and the facilitating devices of administration are invested with self-evident moral legitimacy.

Disbelieve the Dichotomy. Lasswell (1930) identified what he considered the real significance of the dichotomy: The internal bureaucrat would be able to exercise power that was informal, unseen, and greatly underestimated by doctrinaire proponents of the dichotomy. The defects of the dichotomy were clearly visible during the presidencies of Franklin D. Roosevelt and Harry S. Truman, when the administrative energies required to overcome the turbulence of global depression and global war fashioned a public administration that combined political effectiveness (the Jacksonian ideal) and administrative efficiency (the Wilsonian ideal) in ingenious ways. The standing of civil servants in American public esteem has never been higher.

The dichotomy must be disbelieved, according to the proponents of this precept, because the sanctions of science claimed for the principles of administration could not be sustained, nor could American government be modeled after the cameralist traditions of Europe or the self-aggrandizing business practices of American capitalism. A constitutional system of divided powers and federal divisions of delegated functions simply cannot absorb the artificial distinction between politics and administration. The rule-making and case-deciding activities of administrative agencies cannot be carried out by legislatures and courts, nor can they be abandoned.

Public administrators have independent standing before the law. There is no doubt that a dichotomy of a particular sort exists, but it is not a dichotomy between decision and execution. Waldo (1987) identifies the real dichotomy as creative tension between the civic culture and imperial traditions of American government. In the civic culture tradition of classical Greece, thinking about government and deciding what it should do are the most important responsibilities of political man. In the imperial tradition of the ancient Middle Eastern and Mediterranean empires, organizing and executing the functions of government are the most important responsibilities of political man. The United States is a blend of these distinct traditions. For Waldo, our politics are Greek, but our administration is Roman. Americans live with an anomaly: Expanded democracy has called forth imperial mechanisms of government.

Not wanting public administrators to assume the dignity of the Roman imperium, political leaders of both parties have tried in recent years to reassert the discredited dichotomy. Public administrators themselves have responded in three distinct ways to these efforts to bring them to heel. One strategy is to reestablish the old claims to technical competence, efficiency, and administrative rationality. Another is to retreat into the techniques of organizational "guerrilla warfare." A third is to search for a theoretical basis of trusteeship — the idea that civil servants are sworn to uphold the Constitution, just as other officers of government are, and that they are competent to define the public good on their own authority. The contest between the proponents of the first and the third positions describes much of the professional discussion in modern public administration. The proponents of the second position mostly keep quiet, because they still believe in the professional ethic described in Simon, Smithberg, and Thompson (1950, pp. 554-555): "The administrator is always to some extent an initiator of values, partly as a representative of some interest group or groups, but also independently, in his own right. He can never be completely governed by others, and, as a matter of fact, he has considerable latitude of choice before the consequences of his decisions will bring reactions that threaten his survival."

Advocate Social Equity. The public service fell on hard times in the mid 1950s, and in some sense it has not yet recovered. Gawthrop (1987, p. 198) identified the reasons for what he called "a steady deterioration of administrative competency" as the insidious psychological destructiveness of McCarthyism, which intermittently revived questions of disloyalty, distrust, and disdain; the decline of the bureau-chief component of the iron triangle of policymaking, occasioned by television's opening up of congressional committee oligarchies; the establishment of the supergrade positions of GS-16, 17, and 18, which drew a distinction between policy careerists and proceduralists and fragmented political and administrative power; the venture of the Eisenhower administration into the implementation of a global containment policy, which extended the competency of the American administrative system beyond its capacity; and the fragmentation of the bureaucracy into a multiplicity of sovereign fiefs buffeted by the centrifugal forces of single-issue politics, the new politics of litigation, and a system of intergovernmental relations that defied administrative control.

While the Balkanization of federal, state, and local bureaucracies was taking place, civil servants were also being asked to meet the needs of greater and greater numbers of citizens. To do so effectively, they had to define people in the aggregate: as clients, cases, and categories, rather than as individual persons in discrete social circumstances. It was said that impersonal transactions actually facilitated expert solutions to social problems, and that compassion is an individual virtue, not an organizational one. The rule of law, it was believed, required that everyone in the same problem category be treated in the same way. Institutional stability was thought to be incompatible with deviations from universal norms.

The result of this subtle reconceptualization of the essence of democracy into terms of the greatest good for the greatest number led a generation of civil servants into a trained incapacity to discern the difference between means and ends, facts and values, and the processes and purposes of government. The career service had neither the time nor the inclination to consider the qualitative consequences of its actions. The qualitative aspects of democracy came to be understood primarily in terms of quantitative measurements.

A counterattack on this understanding of public morality was launched in 1968 at the Minnowbrook conference site of Syracuse University. A gathering of "young Turks" produced the Minnowbrook perspective, which tried to refocus public administration away from the technical and toward the normative, away from administrative science toward social equity. Social equity makes the actual delivery of public services the criterion for judging the value of administrative policy and the ethical behavior of the transfer agent. Is there a fair distribution of services? Are disadvantaged people adequately represented in the policymaking process? Are public administrators working to replace the politics of having and doing with the politics of being?

In the end, say the advocates of the social equity precept, the bureaucracy cannot be neutral. It must be involved with clients as human beings, and it must bend the rules for them and take risks for them, if necessary. Civil servants must actively advance the causes of social justice. At the same time, they must seek increased citizen participation in government and encourage the personal development of individual members of administrative organizations. The "young Turks" of Minnowbrook are now older, and they still face the problem of bringing programmatic fruition to their noble ideas.

Pursue Professional Discourse. One of the most striking characteristics of American public administration in the last decade has been the extent to which practitioners and academics alike have committed themselves to talking about who they are. The conversation began in the late 1970s, when a code of ethics was proposed in the original Professional Standards and Ethics Committee of the American Society for Public Administration. Initially, there was a good deal of resistance to a code for many different reasons. The most compelling one was that the lack of stated public purpose in American society was one of the nation's fundamental strengths. Throughout our history, continuing redefinitions of purpose and compromises of principle have allowed us to make the incremental changes necessary for political stability. Proceduralism must be a terminal value, because in a pluralist system truth, unity, and especially morality can never be forged from a single ideal form. Only from the clash of opposites, contraries, extremes, and poles can come the accommodations that are themselves American public service ethics. In this view, the process of discovery must never be sacrificed to the approved "word"; the "word" is always being spoken.

After years of debate, even proceduralists have come to see the fundamental moral problem of building consensus around an agreement to agree on nothing substantive. Assent was being given not to value but to value default. As the need for shared values in a professional context grew, adversaries who could no longer find in their disagreements a basis for common norms were transformed from adversaries into enemies. Thus, a code of ethics was approved by the National Council of ASPA on April 8, 1984. Next came a set of guidelines to interpret each of the twelve canons of the code. At this time, subcommittees of the Professional Ethics Committee are working on finding appropriate ways to impose sanctions on those who violate the code, as well as to aid members who get into trouble because they follow it.

It is certain that debate about the tenets and tone of the code will continue. There is already a movement to revise certain parts of it. The code of ethics of the International City Management Association (ICMA) has been revised six times since it was first adopted in 1924, and ASPA is no less adaptive an organization than ICMA. The self-correcting system that is now in place keeps the membership of ASPA involved in ethical reflection and committed to the results of ongoing negotiations about ethical norms. Professional discourse reduces the moral confusion that a lack of authority brings, and eventually it turns words into reflective human activity.

Maintain Constitutional Order. The Constitution of the United States implicitly and explicitly assigns a demanding role to public administrators. Historic practice has made administrative institutions the balance wheel of the constitutional order. Capitalism allows individual projects of personal aggrandizement to proceed virtually unchecked, until they are checked by government. Only government compares the designs of private interests to collective needs and social concerns. Thus, public officials are called on to employ the processes of moral reasoning, judgment, and, finally, lawful coercion to affirm the safeguards of constitutional democracy. In applying state power to humane ends, public officials regulate, distribute, and redistribute national resources to promote the general welfare.

Capitalism does not like the regulatory role, of course, and the result is a continuing battle between public and private interests. The size and power of the federal government lead many to believe the struggle is unequal; but when we consider that ten of the twenty-five largest organizations in the world, ranked by revenues, are American corporations, it may surprise us that public administration can hold its own. When General Motors has economic power significantly greater than that of Canada, and when Exxon doubles the receipts of Sweden, we cannot underestimate the power of American economic institutions.

The public sphere has been diminished and denigrated by the preachment that society exists apart from government and is prior to and greater than government. In the ethos of capitalism, life finds its essential meaning in the consumption of goods and services. The balanced interests of constitutionalism become an obstacle to the pursuit of happiness. (When someone asked John D. Rockefeller, Jr., how much money it would take to make him happy, he reportedly answered, "Just a little more.")

In the face of the values of economization, the civil servant is called on to assert the values of the polity. His or her basis for doing so, according to this precept, is the moral imperative of covenant. The public administrator has entered into solemn agreement with the citizens whom he or she serves to honor the promissory note of equal opportunity that the founders signed for all future generations. Public administration is a professed obligation, informed and constrained by constitutional principle, to maintain the public interest against all competing private interests.

Serve the Community. The Preamble to the Constitution is not exactly an ethics text, but it comes as close to that as any piece of writing in American history: "We the people of the United States, in order to form a more perfect union, establish justice, insure domestic tranquillity, provide for the common defense, promote the general welfare, and secure the blessings of liberty to ourselves and our posterity, do ordain and establish this Constitution for the United States of America." Gouverneur Morris, he of the suave manners and wooden leg who actually wrote the Constitution as the amanuensis of the Committee of Style and Arrangement, believed that verbs should count for something, so he let them roll out: form, establish, insure, provide, promote, secure, and ordain.

That is what the profession of public administration does in American life: It forms, establishes, insures, provides, promotes, secures, and ordains. It does so in the interest of the community. Moral behavior in public administration is not just a matter of private preference and personal integrity. Judgments about right and wrong are community decisions, because the community is the final arbiter of what is ethical. The community looks at the nature of an act to decide whether it is moral. Moral vices can be made into relative goods by their context; moral virtue can have patently evil results in particular circumstances. Law is therefore an uncertain guide to ethical behavior. It is possible to obey every law and regulation in the books and still be highly unethical. The profession of public administration operates to mediate the particularistic interests of the civil society while it tries to increase the ability of citizens to comprehend society's total purposes and participate unselfishly in the making of policies to implement them.

The cutting edge of ethical theory and practice today, say devotees of communalism, is that public policy is co-produced by public administrators and affected citizens' groups. Public administrators are social partners, rather than autonomous state agents or pluralist-oriented brokers of competitive interests. Ethical behavior fosters a culture of reciprocity, obligation, and responsibility. Citizen co-producers are treated as colleagues, rather than as clients and supplicants. The model of the future is Habermas's (1981) vision of a communicative ethics, which breaks down the barriers between professionals and laity and reconnects political authority to the vibrant content of civic virtue.

Summary

This chapter has discussed ten ethical precepts that have guided American public administration at one time or another in its history. Obviously, some of these precepts are mutually exclusive and exist tenuously in relationship to one another, but each one does describe a legitimate point of view in the profession, and each one is represented in the profession's codes of ethics. Two of the best known of these codes are those adopted by the American Society for Public Administration, in 1984, and by the International City Management Association, first in 1924, with six revisions through 1987. The American Planning Association has also been a leader in developing ethical standards and guidelines for local government. The ASPA and ICMA codes are representative. . . .

Is there a unifying thread that weaves the precepts and codes together? Obviously, one can pick and choose which of the precepts and which of the tenets of the codes form a coherent personal and professional value system. The thread is not in the combinations one can discern in this variegated quilt. It is in the symbolic power of words. They inspire, they set a tone, and they create expectations. They are rallying points for conceptual clarity. With them, we tell others who we are. Both the precepts and the codes, which try to translate words into habits of action, are images of what professional public administrators think we should live up to. Thus, ethical discourse brings order, direction, and idealism to public service.

References

Appleby, P. H. *Morality and Administration in Democratic Government*. Baton Rouge: Louisiana State University Press, 1952.
Bailey, S. K. "The Relationship Between Ethics and Public Service." In R. C. Martin (ed.), *Public Administration and Democracy: Essays in Honor of Paul Appleby*. Syracuse, N.Y.: Syracuse University Press, 1965.
Gawthrop, L. "Toward an Ethical Convergence of Democratic Theory and Administrative Politics." In R. C. Chandler (ed.), *A Centennial History of the American Administrative State*. New York: Free Press, 1987.
"Government on Business Principles." *The Nation*, Apr. 7, 1887, p. 288.
Habermas, J. *The Theory of Communicative Action*. Vol. 1: *Reason and the Rationalization of Society*. Boston: Beacon Press, 1981.
Lasswell, H. *Psychopathology and Politics*. Chicago: University of Chicago Press, 1930.
Simon, H. A., Smithberg, D., and Thompson, V. *Public Administration*. New York: Knopf, 1950.
Waldo, D. *The Enterprise of Public Administration*. Novato, Calif.: Chandler and Sharp, 1980.
Waldo, D. "Politics and Administration: On Thinking About a Complex Relationship." In R. C. Chandler (ed.), *A Centennial History of the American Administrative State*. New York: Free Press, 1987.
Weber, M. "Politics as a Vocation." In H. H. Gerth and C. W. Mills (eds.), from *Max Weber: Essays in Sociology*. New York: Oxford University Press, 1946. [Originally a speech at Munich University, 1918, and published in 1919.]
Wilson, W. "The Study of Administration." *Political Science Quarterly*, 1887, 2 (2), 197-222.

Case 3:
Free Pencils and
Paper Clips

The situation presented below raises the issue of whether it is ever appropriate to use state equipment or materials for personal purposes.

Characters
Mary Green — Employee, State Bureau of
Standards and Field Services
Ruth Soriano — Employee, State Bureau of Administration
Bill Blake — Employee, State Bureau of Public Relations

Scene
State Office Building Cafeteria. Mary, Ruth,
and Bill are having lunch.

Mary: Well, I'll see you people later. I've got to get back to work a little early this afternoon.

Bill: Why such an eager beaver?

Mary: I'm not actually going back to work. I want to get to the photocopy machine before half the Department is lined up to use it. I have to photocopy two dozen invitations for my daughter's Halloween party.

Ruth: Gee, Mary. Aren't you worried about someone saying something about this to your supervisor? It's against the rules to use the photocopier for anything other than state business.

Bill: What? You've got to be kidding! Everyone uses the photocopier for little personal jobs. It's one of the few, and I do mean few, personal benefits you get for working for the Department. Why, last spring I was standing in line to use the machine and I watched Mary's supervisor copy her income tax form.

Ruth: But it is against Departmental rules so it's wrong.

Bill: Rules, smules. The rules are there to prevent abuses — like if a person turned the privilege into a business by bringing in other people's copying and then charged them for it.

Ruth: Yes, but when we use the copier or any other state equipment for our personal use, aren't we ripping off the taxpayer?

Mary: The way I look at it is that the use of state equipment, as long as we don't abuse the privilege, is one of the little benefits we get that help make up for our low salaries compared to the private sector. We don't get big salaries or Christmas bonuses. The limited personal use of state equipment and materials is part of our compensation for being state employees.

Source: Edward B. Laverty, Northeastern University.

Bill: Mary has a good point. I've seen any number of State Troopers taking their kids to school or picking up the family groceries in their cruisers. Game Wardens take their state assigned snowmobiles ice fishing. The other day, the Deputy Commissioner left work at 9:30 in the morning, took a state car, picked up his son at school, took him to the orthodontist for an appointment, and didn't get back to work until after lunch.

Mary: That's right! You watch the news. The President of the State Senate flew three hundred miles in the state plane just to watch his son play football. All I want to do is make a few photocopies for my kid's party.

Ruth: I don't care. It's against the rules and it's wrong. Just because you're not walking off with the store doesn't justify stealing penny candy.

Bill: Oh, come on Ruth! Aren't you being just a bit extreme and self righteous? The whole time we've been talking you've been doodling on that napkin with a pen and I see two more pens sticking out of your purse. What does it say on the side of those pens? 'Property of the State of'. . . ?

QUESTIONS FOR DISCUSSION

1. Is there an ethical conflict here?

2. Is Ruth being a bit extreme and self-righteous?

3. Is the limited use of state equipment or material a legitimate benefit of state employment?

4. Is the personal use of state equipment or material ever justified?

4. Ethics as Responsibility

The Study of Administration
Woodrow Wilson

The field of administration is a field of business. It is removed from the hurry and strife of politics; it at most points stands apart even from the debatable ground of constitutional study. It is a part of political life only as the methods of the counting-house are a part of the life of society; only as machinery is part of the manufactured product. But it is, at the same time, raised very far above the dull level of mere technical detail by the fact that through its greater principles it is directly connected with the lasting maxims of political wisdom, the permanent truths of political progress.

The object of administrative study is to rescue executive methods from the confusion and costliness of empirical experiment and set them upon foundations laid deep in stable principle.

It is for this reason that we must regard civil-service reform in its present stages as but a prelude to a fuller administrative reform. We are now rectifying methods of appointment; we must go on to adjust executive functions more fitly and to prescribe better methods of executive organization and action. Civil-service reform is thus but a moral preparation for what is to follow. It is clearing the moral atmosphere of official life by establishing the sanctity of public office as a public trust, and, by making the service unpartisan, it is opening the way for making it businesslike. By sweetening its motives it is rendering it capable of improving its methods of work.

Let me expand a little what I have said of the province of administration. Most important to be observed is the truth already so much and so fortunately insisted upon by our civil-service reformers; namely, that administration lies outside the proper sphere of *politics*. Administrative questions are not political questions. Although politics sets the tasks for administration, it should not be suffered to manipulate its offices.

This is distinction of high authority; eminent German writers insist upon it as of course. Bluntschli, for instance, bids us separate administration alike from politics and from law. Politics, he says, is state activity "in things great and universal," while "administration, on the other hand," is "the activity of the state in individual and small things. Politics is thus the special province of the statesman, administration of the technical official." "Policy does nothing without the aid of administration"; but administration is not therefore politics. But we do not require German authority for this position; this discrimination between administration and politics is now, happily, too obvious to need further discussion.

This seminal essay of Woodrow Wilson is widely regarded as a benchmark for the profession of public administration. In the second section of the essay, reprinted here, Wilson emphasizes two types of administrative responsibility: that of civil servants to elected officials and that of civil servants to the public interest.

Source: Woodrow Wilson, "The Study of Administration," *Political Science Quarterly,* 2:2 (June 1887), 209-217. Also available in *The Papers of Woodrow Wilson,* ed. Arthur S. Link (Princeton: Princeton University Press), V, 370-376.

There is another distinction which must be worked into all our conclusions, which, though but another side of that between administration and politics, is not quite so easy to keep sight of: I mean the distinction between *constitutional* and administrative questions, between those governmental adjustments which are essential to constitutional principle and those which are merely instrumental to the possibly changing purposes of a wisely adapting convenience.

One cannot easily make clear to every one just where administration resides in the various departments of any practicable government without entering upon particulars so numerous as to confuse and distinctions so minute as to distract. No lines of demarcation, setting apart administrative from non-administrative functions, can be run between this and that department of government without being run up hill and down dale, over dizzy heights of distinction and through dense jungles of statutory enactment, hither and thither around "ifs" and "buts," "whens" and "howevers," until they become altogether lost to the common eye not accustomed to this sort of surveying, and consequently not acquainted with the use of the theodolite of logical discernment. A great deal of administration goes about *incognito* to most of the world, being confounded now with political "management," and again with constitutional principle.

Perhaps this ease of confusion may explain such utterances as that of Niebuhr's: "Liberty," he says, "depends incomparably more upon administration than upon constitution." At first sight this appears to be largely true. Apparently facility in the actual exercise of liberty does depend more upon administrative arrangements than upon constitutional guarantees; although constitutional guarantees alone secure the existence of liberty. But — upon second thought — is even so much as this true? Liberty no more consists in easy functional movement than intelligence consists in the ease and vigor with which the limbs of a strong man move. The principles that rule within the man, or the constitution, are the vital springs of liberty or servitude. Because independence and subjection are without chains, are lightened by every easy-working device of considerate, paternal government, they are not thereby transformed into liberty. Liberty cannot live apart from constitutional principle; and no administration, however perfect and liberal its methods, can give men more than a poor counterfeit of liberty if it rest upon illiberal principles of government.

A clear view of the difference between the province of constitutional law and the province of administrative function ought to leave no room for misconception; and it is possible to name some roughly definite criteria upon which such a view can be built. Public administration is detailed and systematic execution of public law. Every particular application of general law is an act of administration. The assessment and raising of taxes, for instance, the hanging of a criminal, the transportation and delivery of the mails, the equipment and recruiting of the army, and navy, *etc.*, are all obviously acts of administration; but the general laws which direct these things to be done are as obviously outside of and above administration. The broad plans of governmental action are not administrative; the detailed execution of such plans is administrative. Constitutions, therefore, properly concern themselves only with those instrumentalities of government which are to control general law. Our federal constitution observes this principle in saying nothing of even the greatest of the purely executive offices, and speaking only of that President of the Union who was to share the legislative and policy-making functions of government, only of those judges of highest jurisdiction who were to interpret and guard its principles, and not of those who were merely to give utterance to them.

This is not quite the distinction between Will and answering Deed, because the administrator should have and does have a will of his own in the choice of means for accomplishing his work. He is not and ought not to be a mere passive instrument. The distinction is between general plans and special means.

There is, indeed, one point at which administrative studies trench on constitutional ground — or at least upon what seems constitutional ground. The study of administration, philosophically viewed, is closely connected with the study of the proper distribution of constitutional authority. To be efficient it must discover the simplest arrangements by which responsibility can be unmistakably fixed upon officials; the best way of dividing authority without hampering it, and responsibility without obscuring it. And this question of the distribution of authority, when taken into the sphere of the higher, the originating functions of government, is obviously a central constitutional question. If administrative study can discover the best principles upon which to base such distribution, it will have done constitutional study an invaluable service. Montesquieu did not, I am convinced, say the last word on this head.

To discover the best principle for the distribution of authority is of greater importance, possibly, under a democratic system, where officials serve many masters, than under others where they serve but a few. All sovereigns are suspicious of their servants, and the sovereign people is no exception to the rule; but how is its suspicion to be allayed by *knowledge*? If that suspicion could be clarified into wise vigilance, it would be altogether salutary; if that vigilance could be aided by the unmistakable placing of responsibility, it would be altogether beneficent. Suspicion in itself is never healthful either in the private or in the public mind. *Trust is strength* in all relations of life; and, as it is the office of the constitutional reformer to create conditions of trustfulness, so it is the office of the administrative organizer to fit administration with conditions of clear-cut responsibility which shall insure trustworthiness.

And let me say that large powers and unhampered discretion seem to me the indispensable conditions of responsibility. Public attention must be easily directed, in each case of good or bad administration, to just the man deserving of praise or blame. There is no danger in power, if only it be not irresponsible. If it be divided, dealt out in shares to many, it is obscured; and if it be obscured, it is made irresponsible. But if it be centered in heads of the service and in heads of branches of the service, it is easily watched and brought to book. If to keep his office a man must achieve open and honest success, and if at the same time he feels himself intrusted with large freedom of discretion, the greater his power the less likely is he to abuse it, the more is he nerved and sobered and elevated by it. The less his power, the more safely obscure and unnoticed does he feel his position to be, and the more readily does he relapse into remissness.

Just here we manifestly emerge upon the field of that still larger question, — the proper relations between public opinion and administration.

To whom is official trustworthiness to be disclosed, and by whom is it to be rewarded? Is the official to look to the public for his meed of praise and his push of promotion, or only to his superior in office? Are the people to be called in to settle administrative discipline as they are called in to settle constitutional principles? These questions evidently find their root in what is undoubtedly the fundamental problem of this whole study. That problem is: What part shall public opinion take in the conduct of administration?

The right answer seems to be, that public opinion shall play the part of authoritative critic.

But the *method* by which its authority shall be made to tell? Our peculiar American difficulty in organizing administration is not the danger of losing liberty, but the danger of not being able or willing to separate its essentials from its accidents. Our success is made doubtful by that besetting error of ours, the error of trying to do too much by vote. Self-government does not consist in having a hand in everything, any more than housekeeping consists necessarily in cooking dinner with one's own hands. The cook must be trusted with a large discretion as to the management of the fires and the ovens.

In those countries in which public opinion has yet to be instructed in its privileges, yet to be accustomed to having its own way, this question as to the province of public opinion is much more readily soluble than in this country, where public opinion is wide awake and quite intent upon having its own way anyhow. It is pathetic to see a whole book written by a German professor of political science for the purpose of saying to his countrymen, "Please try to have an opinion about national affairs"; but a public which is so modest may at least be expected to be very docile and acquiescent in learning what things it has *not* a right to think and speak about imperatively. It may be sluggish, but it will not be meddlesome. It will submit to be instructed before it tries to instruct. Its political education will come before its political activity. In trying to instruct our own public opinion, we are dealing with a pupil apt to think itself quite sufficiently instructed beforehand.

The problem is to make public opinion efficient without suffering it to be meddlesome. Directly exercised, in the oversight of the daily details and in the choice of the daily means of government, public criticism is of course a clumsy nuisance, a rustic handling delicate machinery. But as superintending the greater forces of formative policy alike in politics and administration, public criticism is altogether safe and beneficent, altogether indispensable. Let administrative study find the best means for giving public criticism this control and for shutting it out from all other interference.

But is the whole duty of administrative study done when it has taught the people what sort of administration to desire and demand, and how to get what they demand? Ought it not to go on to drill candidates for the public service?

There is an admirable movement towards universal political education now afoot in this country. The time will soon come when no college of respectability can afford to do without a well-filled chair of political science. But the education thus imparted will go but a certain length. It will multiply the number of intelligent critics of government, but it will create no competent body of administrators. It will prepare the way for the development of a sure-footed understanding of the general principles of government, but it will not necessarily foster skill in conducting government. It is an education which will equip legislators, perhaps, but not executive officials. If we are to improve public opinion, which is the motive power of government, we must prepare better officials as the *apparatus* of government. If we are to put in new boilers and to mend the fires which drive our governmental machinery, we must not leave the old wheels and joints and valves and bands to creak and buzz and clatter on as best they may at bidding of the new force. We must put in new running parts wherever there is the least lack of strength or adjustment. It will be necessary to organize democracy by sending up to the competitive examinations for the civil service men definitely prepared for standing liberal tests as to technical knowledge. A technically schooled civil service will presently have become indispensable.

I know that a corps of civil servants prepared by a special schooling and drilled, after appointment, into a perfected organization, with appropriate hierarchy and characteristic discipline, seems to a great many very thoughtful persons to contain elements which might combine to make an offensive official class, — a distinct, semi-corporate body with sympathies divorced from those of a progressive, free-spirited people, and with hearts narrowed to the meanness of a bigoted officialism. Certainly such a class would be altogether hateful and harmful in the United States. Any measures calculated to produce it would for us be measures of reaction and of folly.

But to fear the creation of a domineering, illiberal officialism as a result of the studies I am here proposing is to miss altogether the principle upon which I wish most to insist. That principle is, that administration in the United States must be at all points sensitive to public opinion. A body of thoroughly trained officials serving during good behavior we must have in any case: that is a plain business necessity. But the apprehension that such a body will be anything un-American clears away the moment it is asked, What is to constitute good behavior? For that question obviously carries its own answer on its face. Steady, hearty allegiance to the policy of the government they serve will constitute good behavior. That *policy* will have no taint of officialism about it. It will not be the creation of permanent officials, but of statesmen whose responsibility to public opinion will be direct and inevitable. Bureaucracy can exist only where the whole service of the state is removed from the common political life of the people, its chiefs as well as its rank and file. Its motives, its objects, its policy, its standards, must be bureaucratic. It would be difficult to point out any examples of impudent exclusiveness and arbitrariness on the part of officials doing service under a chief of department who really served the people, as all our chiefs of departments must be made to do. It would be easy, on the other hand, to adduce other instances like that of the influence of Stein in Prussia, where the leadership of one statesman imbued with true public spirit transformed arrogant and perfunctory bureaus into public-spirited instruments of just government.

The ideal for us is a civil service cultured and self-sufficient enough to act with sense and vigor, and yet so intimately connected with the popular thought, by means of elections and constant public counsel, as to find arbitrariness of class spirit quite out of the question.

The Friedrich-Finer Debate

Public Policy and the Nature of Administrative Responsibility

Carl Joachim Friedrich

It has long been customary to distinguish between policymaking and policy execution. Frank J. Goodnow, in his well-known work, *Politics and Administration,* undertook to build an almost absolute distinction upon this functional difference.

> There are, then, in all governmental systems two primary or ultimate functions of government, viz. the expression of the will of the state and the execution of that will. There are also in all states separate organs, each of which is mainly busied with the discharge of one of these functions. These functions are respectively, Politics and Administration.[1]

But while the distinction has a great deal of value as a relative matter of emphasis, it cannot any longer be accepted in this absolute form. Admittedly, this misleading distinction has become a fetish, a stereotype in the minds of theorists and practitioners alike. The result has been a great deal of confusion and argument. The reason for making this distinction an absolute antithesis is probably to be found in building it upon the metaphysical, if not abstruse, idea of a will of the state. This neo-Hegelian (and Fascist) notion is purely speculative. Even if the concept "state" is retained — and I personally see no good ground for it — the idea that this state has a will immediately entangles one in all the difficulties of assuming a group personality or something akin to it.[2] In other words, a problem which is already complicated enough by itself — that is, how a public policy is adopted and carried out — is bogged down by a vast ideological superstructure which contributes little or nothing to its solution. . . .

The concrete patterns of public policy formation and execution reveal that politics and administration are not two mutually exclusive boxes, or absolute distinctions, but that they are two closely linked aspects of the same process. Public policy, to put it flatly, is a continuous process, the formation of which is inseparable from its execution. Public policy is being formed as it is being executed, and it is likewise being executed as it is being formed. Politics and administration play a continuous role in both formation and execution, though there is probably more politics in the formation of policy, more administration in the execution of it. Insofar as particular individuals or groups are gaining or losing power or control in a given area, there is politics; insofar as officials act or propose action in the name of public interest, there is administration. . . .

Several of the issues of responsibility raised by Wilson were echoed half a century later in an interchange of journal articles which has come to be known as the Friedrich-Finer debate. Friedrich's position placed much greater emphasis on the moral responsibility of the public servant, rather than upon accountability to democratically elected leaders. Inseparable from this argument is Friedrich's frontal assault upon the Wilsonian politics/administration dichotomy. Herman Finer argued for a much stricter concept of responsibility.

Some of the issues raised by the Friedrich-Finer debate remain relevant in the contemporary dialogue over structural vs. educational approaches to encouraging ethical behavior. Which is needed more — stiffer laws and enforceable codes of ethics or more virtuous people? These and other approaches are considered in Part III of this volume.

Shall We Enforce or Elicit Responsible Conduct?

Those old-timers who are enamored of strict subserviency undoubtedly will be inclined to argue that the foregoing is all very well, but that it depends entirely for its effectiveness upon the goodwill of the administrator, and that as soon as he is indifferent or hostile to such public reactions he can and will discard them. There is unquestionably some truth in this objection. Responsible conduct of administrative functions is not so much enforced as it is elicited. But it has been the contention all along that responsible conduct is never strictly enforceable, that even under the most tyrannical despot administrative officials will escape effective control — in short, that the problem of how to bring about responsible conduct of the administrative staff of a large organization is, particularly in a democratic society, very largely a question of sound work rules and effective morale. As an able student of great practical experience has put it:

Sources: Carl Joachim Friedrich, "Public Policy and the Nature of Administrative Responsibility," *Public Policy,* 1 (1940), pp. 5-6, 19-20.

The matter of administrative power commensurate with administrative responsibility, or the administrator's freedom from control, is not, under our system of government, anything absolute or complete: it is a question of degree. . . . Nothing which has been said should be construed to mean that preservation of administrative freedom, initiative and resourcefulness is not an important factor to be considered in organization: quite the contrary, it is one of the major factors.[3]

The whole range of activities involving constant direct contact of the administrator with the public and its problems show that our conception of administrative responsibility is undergoing profound change. The emphasis is shifting; instead of subserviency to arbitrary will we require responsiveness to commonly felt needs and wants. The trend of the creative evolution of American democracy from a negative conception to a positive ideal of social service posits such a transformation. As the range of government services expands, we are all becoming each other's servants in the common endeavor of operating our complex industrial society. . . .

Endnotes

1. Frank J. Goodnow, *Politics and Administration* (New York: Macmillan, 1900), p. 22.
2. See Carl J. Friedrich, *Constitutional Government and Politics* (New York: Harpers, 1936), pp. 29ff and elsewhere.
3. Lewis Meriam, *Public Personnel Problems* (Washington: Brookings Institution, 1938), p. 340.

Administrative Responsibility in Democratic Government
Herman Finer

Are the servants of the public to decide their own course, or is their course of action to be decided by a body outside themselves? My answer is that the servants of the public are not to decide their own course; they are to be responsible to the elected representatives of the public, and these are to determine the course of action of the public servants to the most minute degree that is technically feasible. Both of these propositions are important: the main proposition of responsibility, as well as the limitation and auxiliary institutions implied in the phrase, "that is technically feasible." This kind of responsibility is what democracy means; and though there may be other devices which provide "good" government, I cannot yield on the cardinal issue of democratic government. . . .

Never was the political responsibility of officials so momentous a necessity as in our own era. Moral responsibility is likely to operate in direct proportion to the strictness and efficiency of political responsibility, and to fall away into all sorts of perversions when the latter is weakly enforced. While professional standards, duty to the public, and pursuit of technological efficiency are factors in sound administrative operation, they are but ingredients, and not continuously motivating factors, of sound policy, and they require public and political control and direction. . . .

Herman Finer, "Administrative Responsibility in Democratic Government," *Public Administration Review,* 1 (1941) pp. 336, 350.

Contemporary devices to secure closer cooperation of officials with public and legislatures are properly auxiliaries to and not substitutes for political control of public officials through exertion of the sovereign authority of the public. Thus, political responsibility is the major concern of those who work for healthy relationships between the officials and the public, and moral responsibility, although a valuable conception and institutional form, is minor and subsidiary.

Ethics and the Public Service
Stephen K. Bailey

When Dean Appleby was asked to deliver the Edward Douglass White lectures at Louisiana State University in the Spring of 1951, he chose as his topic, *Morality and Administration in Democratic Government*. He preferred the term "morality" because he did not wish to suggest his lectures were "either a treatment in the systematic terms of general philosophy or a 'code of administrative ethics'."[1]

His attempt instead was to cast the light of his uncommon wisdom upon what he considered to be the central ethical and moral issues of the American public service. These issues centered upon the felicitous interaction of moral institutional arrangements and morally ambiguous man.

In some ways *Morality and Administration* is a disconcerting book. The essays are discontinuous. Each one is chocked with insight, but in the collection viewed as a whole, theoretical coherence and structure emerge implicitly rather than explicitly. Some inherently ambiguous terms like "responsibility" are clarified only by context. The final chapter, "The Administrative Pattern," is not the logical fulfillment of the preceding chapters. It stands beside the other essays, not on top of them. Furthermore, in spite of the highly personal connotation of the word "morality," Dean Appleby spent most of his time discussing the effect of the governmental system upon official morality rather than vice versa. He saw in the American governmental system a series of political and organizational devices for promoting ethical choices. The most serious threats to the "good society" came, in his estimation, not from the venality of individuals but from imperfections in institutional arrangements.

Stephen K. Bailey (1916-1982), in this memorial essay on Paul Appleby, suggests "optimism, courage, and fairness tempered by justice" as key ethical qualities. Is this, in effect, an "ethics as virtue" argument posed against Appleby's "ethics as responsibility?" Or does it reassert Friedrich's "personal responsibility" position from the Friedrich-Finer debate?

A Normative Model for Personal Ethics

His normative model ran something as follows: politics and hierarchy force public servants to refer private and special interests to higher and broader public interests. Politics does this through the discipline of the majority ballot which forces both political executives and legislators to insert a majoritarian calculus into the consideration of private claims. Hierarchy does it by placing in the hands of top officials both the responsibility and the necessity of homogenizing and moralizing the special interests inevitably represented by and through the lower echelons of organizational pyramids.[2] Both politics and hierarchy are devices for assuring accountability to the public as a whole. The public makes its will known in a variety of ways and through a variety of channels but its importance is largely in its potential rather than in its concrete expressions. "Its capacity to be, more than its being, is the crux of democratic reality."[3] Politics and hierarchy induce the public servant to search imaginatively for a public will-to-be. In this search, the public servant is often a leader in the creation of a new public will, so he is in part accountable to what he in part creates. But in any case the basic morality of the system is in its forcing of unitary claims into the mill of pluralistic considerations.

The enemies of this normative model, then, are obvious: they are whatever disrupts politics and hierarchy. For whatever disrupts politics and hierarchy permits the settlement of public issues at too low a level of organization — at too private a level, at too specialized a level. As Madison saw in *Federalist #10*, bigness is the friend of freedom. But Appleby saw more clearly than Madison that bigness is freedom's friend only if administrative as well as legislative devices exist to insure that policy decisions emerge out of the complexity of bigness rather than out of the simplicity of its constituent parts. The scatteration of power in the Congress, the virtual autonomy of certain bureaus and even lesser units in the executive branch, an undue encroachment of legal and other professional norms upon administrative discretion, the substitution of the expert for the generalist at the higher levels of general government, the awarding of statutory power at the bureau rather than at the department level, the atomized character of our political parties — these, according to Dean Appleby, are the effective enemies of morality in the governmental system. They are the symptoms of political pathology. "Our poorest governmental performances, both technically and morally," he wrote, "are generally associated with conditions in which a few citizens have very disproportionate influence."[4] ". . . the degradation of democracy is in the failure to organize or in actual disintegration of political responsibility, yielding public interest to special influence."[5]

Source: Stephen K. Bailey, "Ethics and the Public Service," *Public Administration Review*, 24:4 (December 1964), 234-243.

Here, then, is the grand design. Government is moral insofar as it induces public servants to relate the specific to the general, the private to the public, the precise interest to the inchoate moral judgment. Within this context, a moral public decision becomes one in which:

> the action conforms to the processes and symbols thus far developed for the general protection of political freedom as the agent of more general freedom; . . . leaves open the way for modification or reversal by public determination; . . . is taken within a hierarchy of controls in which responsibility for action may be readily identified by the public;. . . and embodies as contributions of leadership the concrete structuring of response to popularly felt needs, and not merely responses to the private and personal needs of leaders.

It is no disparagement of Dean Appleby's contributions to a normative theory of democratic governance to point out that he dealt only intermittently and unsystematically with the moral problems of the individual public servant. The moral system intrigued him far more consistently than the moral actor. All of his books and essays contain brilliant flashes of insight into the moral dilemmas of individual executives, administrators, and legislators, but there emerges no gestalt of personal ethics in government. One can only wish that he had addressed himself to a systematic elaboration of the personal as well as the institutional aspects of public ethics. For the richness of his administrative experience and the sensitivity of his insight might have illuminated uniquely the continuing moral problems of those whose business it is to preserve and improve the American public service.

Perhaps, without undue pretention, this memorial essay can attempt to fashion a prolegomena to a normative theory of personal ethics in the public service — building upon and elaborating some of the fragments which Dean Appleby scattered throughout his writings and teaching.

Dean Appleby's fragments suggest that personal ethics in the public service is compounded of mental attitudes and moral qualities. Both ingredients are essential. Virtue without understanding can be quite as disastrous as understanding without virtue.

The three essential mental attitudes are: (1) a recognition of the moral ambiguity of all men and of all public policies; (2) a recognition of the contextual forces which condition moral priorities in the public service; and (3) a recognition of the paradoxes of procedures.

The essential moral qualities of the ethical public servant are: (1) optimism; (2) courage; and (3) fairness tempered by charity.

These mental attitudes and moral qualities are relevant to all public servants in every branch and at every level of government. They are as germane to judges and legislators as they are to executives and administrators. They are as essential to line officers as to staff officers. They apply to state and local officials as well as to national and international officials. They are needed in military, foreign, and other specialized services quite as much as they are needed in the career civil service and among political executives. They, of course, assume the virtue of probity and the institutional checks upon venality which Dean Appleby has so brilliantly elaborated. They are the generic attitudes and qualities without which big democracy cannot meaningfully survive.

Mental Attitudes

The Moral Ambiguity of Men and Measures

The moral public servant must be aware of the moral ambiguity of all men (including himself) and of all public policies (including those recommended by him). Reinhold Neibuhr once stated this imperative in the following terms: "Man's capacity for justice makes democracy possible, but man's inclination to injustice makes democracy necessary."[6] American public ethics finds its historic roots in the superficially incompatible streams of Calvinism and Deism. The former emphasized a depravity which must be contained; the latter emphasized a goodness which must be discovered and released. The relevance of this moral dualism to modern governance is patent. Any law or any act of administrative discretion based upon the assumption that most men will not seek to maximize their own economic advantage when reporting assets for income tax purposes would be quite unworkable. But so would any law or any act of administrative discretion which assumed that most men would use any and every ruse to avoid paying taxes at all. Similarly, any administrative decision threatening the chances of re-election of a powerfully placed Congressman almost inevitably invokes counter forces which may be serious both for the decision maker and for the program he or his agency espouses. But administrative decisions fashioned totally out of deference to private ambitions and personal interests can negate the very purposes of general government and can induce the righteous reaction of a voting public.

The fact is that there is no way of avoiding the introduction of personal and private interests into the calculus of public decisions. As James Harvey Robinson once wrote,

> In all governmental policy there have been overwhelming elements of personal favoritism and private gain, which were not suitable for publication. This is owing to the fact that all governments are managed by human beings, who remain human beings even if they are called kings, diplomats, ministers, secretaries, or judges, or hold seats in august legislative bodies. No process has been discovered by which promotion to a position of public responsibility will do away with a man's interest in his own welfare, his partialities, race and prejudices. Yet most books on government neglect these conditions; hence their unreality and futility.[7]

The most frequently hidden agenda in the deliberations of public servants is the effect of substantive or procedural decisions upon the personal lives and fortunes of those deliberating. And yet the very call to serve a larger public often evokes a degree of selflessness and nobility on the part of public servants beyond the capacity of cynics to recognize or to believe. Man's feet may wallow in the bog of self-interest, but his eyes and ears are strangely attuned to calls from the mountain top. As moral philosophy has insistently claimed, there is a fundamental moral distinction between the propositions "I want this because it serves my interest," and "I want this because it is right."

The fact that man is as much a rationalizing as a rational animal makes the problem of either proving or disproving disinterestedness a tricky and knotty business. "I support the decision before us because it is good for the public," may emerge as a rationalization of the less elevated but more highly motivational proposition: "I support the decision before us because it will help re-elect me, or help in my chance for promotion, recognition, or increased status." But the latter may have emerged, in turn, from a superordinate proposition: "Only if I am re-elected (or promoted) can I maximize my powers in the interests of the general citizenry." Unfortunately, no calipers exist for measuring the moral purity of human motivations.

But, in any case, few would deny the widespread moral hunger to justify actions on a wider and higher ground than personal self-interest. In fact, the paradox is that man's self-respect is in large part determined by his capacity to make himself and others believe that self is an inadequate referent for decisional morality. This capacity of man to transcend, to sublimate, and to transform narrowly vested compulsions is at the heart of all civilized morality. That this capacity is exercised imperfectly and intermittently is less astounding than the fact that it is exercised at all. A man's capacity for benevolent and disinterested behavior is both a wonder and a challenge to those who work below, beside, and above him. It is in recognition of this moral reality that Dean Appleby wrote in one of his most eloquent statements,

> the manner and means of supporting one's own convictions, including inventiveness in perceiving how high ground may be held, are one measure of skill in the administrative process.[8]

But appeal to high morality is usually insufficient. It is in appreciating the reality of self-interest that public servants find some of the strongest forces for motivating behavior — public and private. Normally speaking, if a public interest is to be orbited, it must have as a part of its propulsive fuel a number of special and particular interests. A large part of the art of public service is in the capacity to harness private and personal interests to public interest causes. Those who will not traffic in personal and private interests (if such interests are themselves within the law) to the point of engaging their support on behalf of causes in which both public and private interests are served are, in terms of moral temperament, unfit for public responsibility.

But there is a necessary moral corollary: a recognition of the morally-ambivalent effect of all public policies. There is no public decision whose moral effect can be gauged in terms of what game theorists refer to as a "zero-sum" result: a total victory for the right and a total defeat for the wrong. This ineluctable fact is not only because "right" and "wrong" are incapable of universally-accepted definition. It is because an adequate response to any social evil contains the seeds of both predictable and unpredictable pathologies. One can, in the framing of laws or decision, attempt to anticipate and partly to mitigate the predictable pathologies (although this is rarely possible in any complete sense). But one mark of moral maturity is in the appreciation of the inevitability of untoward and often malignant effects of benign moral choices. An Egyptian once commented that the two most devastating things to have happened to modern Egypt were the Rockefeller Foundation and the Aswan Dam. By enhancing public health, the Rockefeller Foundation had upset the balance of nature with horrendous consequences for the relationship of population to food supplies; by slowing the Nile, the Aswan Dam had promoted the development of enervating parasites in the river. The consequence of the two factors was that more people lived longer in more misery.

The bittersweet character of all public policy needs little further elaboration: welfare policies may mitigate hunger but promote parasitic dependence; vacationing in forests open for public recreation may destroy fish, wildlife, and through carelessness in the handling of fire, the forests themselves. Unilateral international action may achieve immediate results at the cost of weakening international instruments of conflict resolution. Half a load may be worse than no load at all. It also may be better in the long run but worse in the short run — and vice versa.

Awareness of these dilemmas and paradoxes can immobilize the sensitive policy maker. That is one of the reasons why both optimism and courage are imperative moral qualities in the public service. At best, however, awareness of moral ambiguity creates a spirit of humility in the decision maker and a willingness to defer to the views of others through compromise. Humility and a willingness to compromise are priceless attributes in the lifestyle of the generality of public servants in a free society. For they are the preconditions of those fruitful accommodations which resolve conflict and which allow the new to live tolerably with the old. Humility, however, must not be equated with obsequiousness, nor willingness to compromise with a weak affability. As Harold Nicolson once wrote,

> It would be interesting to analyze how many false decisions, how many fatal misunderstandings have arisen from such pleasant qualities as shyness, consideration, affability or ordinary good manners. It would be those weaknesses of human nature which impede the intelligent conduct of discussion. The difficulties of precise negotiation arise with almost equal frequency from the more amiable qualities of the human heart.[9]

Men and measures, then, are morally ambiguous. Even if this were not a basic truth about the human condition, however, moral judgments in the public service would be made difficult by the shifting sands of context. An awareness of the contextual conditions is an essential mental attitude for the moral public servant.

The moral virtues of the Boy Scout oath are widely accepted in the United States. But, as Boy Scouts get older, they are faced time and again with the disturbing fact that contexts exist within which it is impossible to be both kind and truthful at the same time. Boy Scouts are trustworthy. But what if they are faced with competing and incompatible trusts (e.g. to guard the flag at the base and to succor a distant wounded companion)? Men should be loyal, but what if loyalties conflict?

Winds Above the Timber Line

To the morally-sensitive public servant, the strains of establishing a general value framework for conducting the public business is nothing compared to the strains of re-sorting specific values in the light of changing contexts. The dilemmas here are genuine. If value priorities are shifted with every passing wind, the shifter would suffer from his developing reputation as an opportunist. If value priorities are never adjusted, the saints come marching in and viable democratic politics goes marching out. To be consistent enough to deserve ethical respect from revered colleagues and from oneself; to be pliable enough to survive within an organization and to succeed in effectuating moral purposes — this is the dilemma and the glory of the public service.

In general, the higher a person goes on the rungs of power and authority, the more wobbly the ethical ladder. It is not the function of the junior civil servant in a unit of a branch of a bureau to worry about

Congressional relations — except on specific mandate from above. But a bureau chief, an assistant secretary, under-secretary, or secretary of a department may find himself contextually conditioned to respond frequently to Congressional forces whose effect it is to undermine the integrity of the hierarchical arrangements in the executive branch. The heroic proportions of the Presidency become clear when one recognizes that the winds are fiercest and most variable above the timber line. The very fact that the President has fewer moments in the day than there are critical problems to be solved, and that crises often emerge unheralded, means an unevenness in the application of his time and energies on only a few things. On as many matters as possible he normally yields for the sake of larger concerns.[10] The crucial word is "yields." Put in another way, if the President had more time and staff assistance he would "yield" to far fewer private and petty claims than he presently supports tacitly or openly.

During the Kennedy administration, the President called together a small group of top legislators, cabinet officers, and executive office staff to advise him on whether he should support the extension of price supports for cotton. His staff reminded him of the bonanza which price supports gave to the biggest and wealthiest cotton farmers. Legislative and cabinet leaders reminded him that a Presidential veto on an important agricultural bill could mean forfeiting key and critical legislative support on subsequent domestic and international matters of over-riding importance to the nation's security and welfare. The President agreed not to veto the bill, but the moral torment was there. According to one witness, he stared at the wall and mumbled to himself, "There is something wrong here. We are giving money to those who don't need it. If I am re-elected in 1964, I'm going to turn this government upside down."

President Eisenhower was an honorable chief executive. Yet he publicly lied about the U-2 affair. The context was the crucial determinant.

If the heat in the ethical kitchen grows greater with each level of power, no public servant is immune from some heat — some concern with context. As Dean Appleby has written, " . . . a special favor, in administration even — as by a traffic policeman, to a blind person or a cripple — would be regarded as a political good when it appears an act of equity compensating for underprivilege."[11]

There is not a moral vice which cannot be made into relative good by context. There is not a moral virtue which cannot in peculiar circumstances have patently evil results.

The mental attitude which appreciates this perversity can be led, of course, into a wasteland of ethical relativity. But this is by no means either inevitable or in the American culture even probable. Where this attitude tends to lead the mature public servant is toward a deep respect for the inconstant forces which swirl around public offices, and toward a deeper understanding of the reasons why moral men sometimes appear to make unethical public decisions. An old American Indian proverb is relevant: "Do not scoff at your friend until you have walked three miles in his moccasins." Because it is not easy for any man to place himself empathetically in the arena of moral dilemmas faced by another man, charity is a difficult moral virtue to maintain with any constancy. But as we shall review more fully below, charity is an essential moral quality in the public service of a democracy.

Paradoxes of Procedure

The third mental attitude which the public servant of a free society must cultivate is a recognition of the paradoxes of procedures. Justice Frankfurter once wrote, "The history of American freedom is, in no small measure, the history of procedure."[12] Rules, standards, procedures exist, by and large, to promote fairness, openness, depth of analysis, and accountability in the conduct of the public's business. Those who frequently bypass or short-cut established means are thereby attacking one aspect of that most precious legacy of the past: the rule of law. Official whim is the enemy of a civilized social order. Not only does it sow the seeds of anarchy in organization, it denies to a new idea the tempering which the heat of procedural gauntlets normally provides. John Mill's "market place" is of little utility if an idea is never allowed to enter the town at all.

But, alas, if procedures are the friend of deliberation and order, they are also at times the enemy of progress and dispatch. Furthermore, there are procedures and procedures. There are apt procedures and inept procedures. The only really bitter comments in *Morality and Administration* are reserved for those members of the legal profession who believe that administration should be circumscribed by precise legal norms, and that a series of administrative courts should be the effective arbiters and sanctioners of administrative discretion.[13] And this, of course, is only one aspect of the problem. Juridic procedures aside, both administration and legislation are frequently encumbered by rules and clearances which limit both responsiveness and the accountability they were presumably designed to enhance. The Rules Committee of the House of Representatives is not only the guardian of orderly procedures, it is the graveyard of important social measures. The contract and personnel policies of many agencies, federal, state, and local, have frequently led to what Wallace Sayre has termed "the triumph of technique over purpose." Anyone who has been closely associated with reorganization studies and proposals knows that every shift in organization — in the structural means for accomplishing governmental ends — is pregnant with implications for the ends themselves. Only a two-dimensional mind can possibly entertain seriously the notion that the structural and procedural aspects of government are unrelated to competing philosophies of substantive purpose.

The public servant who cannot recognize the paradoxes of procedures will be trapped by them. For in the case of procedures, he who deviates frequently is subversive; he who never deviates at all is lost; and he who tinkers with procedures without an understanding of substantive consequence is foolish. Of all governmental roles, the administrative role is procedurally the most flexible. But even here procedural flexibility in the public interest is achieved only by the optimistic, the courageous, and the fair.

Moral Qualities

If mental attitudes related to the moral ambiguities, contextual priorities, and procedural paradoxes of public life are necessary prerequisites to ethical behavior on the part of public servants, they are insufficient to such behavior. Attitudes must be supported by moral qualities — by operating virtues. A list of all relevant virtues would be a long one: patience, honesty, loyalty, cheerfulness, courtesy, humility — where does one begin or stop? One begins beyond the obvious and ends where essentiality ends. In the American context, at least, the need for the virtue of honesty is too obvious to need elaboration. Although Dean Appleby has a chapter on "Venality in Government," he properly dismisses the issue with a single sentence: "Crude wrong doing is not a major, general problem of our government." And he continues with the pregnant remark, "Further moral advance turns upon more complicated and elevated concerns."[14]

The three *essential* moral qualities in the public service are optimism, courage, and fairness tempered by charity.

Overcoming Ambiguity and Paradox

Optimism is an inadequate term. It connotes euphoria, and public life deals harshly with the euphoric. But optimism is a better word than realism, for the latter dampens the fires of possibility. Optimism, to paraphrase Emerson, is the capacity to settle with some consistency on the "sunnier side of doubt." It is the quality which enables man to face ambiguity and paradox without becoming immobilized. It is essential to purposive, as distinct from reactive behavior. Hanna Arendt once commented that the essence of politics is natality not mortality. Politics involves creative responses to the shifting conflicts and the gross discomfitures of mankind. Without optimism on the part of the public servants, the political function is incapable of being performed. There is no incentive to create policies to better the condition of mankind if the quality of human life is in fact unviable, and if mankind is in any case unworthy of the trouble.

Optimism has not been the religious, philosophical, or literary mood of the twentieth century. But, in spite of a series of almost cataclysmic absurdities, it has been the prevailing mood of science, education, and politics. It is the mood of the emerging nations; it is the mood of the space technologist; it is the mood of the urban renewer. Government without the leavening of optimistic public servants quickly becomes a cynical game of manipulation, personal aggrandizement, and parasitic security. The ultimate corruption of free government comes not from the hopelessly venal but from the persistently cynical. Institutional decadence has set in when the optimism of leadership becomes a ploy rather than an honest mood and a moral commitment. True optimism is not Mr. Micawber's passive assumption that something will turn up; true optimism is the affirmation of the worth of taking risks. It is not a belief in sure things; it is the capacity to see the possibilities for good in the uncertain, the ambiguous, and the inscrutable.

Organic aging and the disappointments and disaffections of experience often deprive mature individuals of the physical and psychic vitality which in youth is a surrogate for optimism. That is why optimism as a moral virtue — as a lifestyle — is one of the rare treasures sought by all personnel prospectors whose responsibility it is to mine the common lodes for extraordinary leadership talent. This is true in all organizations; it is especially true in the public service. What else do we mean, when we speak disparagingly of "bureaucratic drones," than that they are those who have entered the gates of Dante's Hell and have "abandoned all hope"?

In the midst of World War II when crises were breaking out at every moment and from every quarter, an ancient White House clerk was caught by a frenetic Presidential aide whistling at his work. The aide asked, "My God, man, don't you know what's going on?" The clerk replied, "Young man, you would be terrified if you knew how little I cared." A sprinkling of such in the public service can be tolerated as droll. If a majority, or even a substantial minority of public servants become jaded, however, especially at leadership levels, an ethical rot settles in which ultimately destroys the capacity of a government to function effectively in the public interest.

A Capacity for Impersonality and Decision

The second essential moral quality needed in the public service is courage. Personal and public life are so shot through with ambiguities and paradoxes that timidity and withdrawal are quite natural and normal responses for those confronted with them. The only three friends of courage in the public service are ambition, a sense of duty, and a recognition that inaction may be quite as painful as action.

Courage in government and politics takes many forms. The late President John F. Kennedy sketched a series of profiles of one type of courage — abiding by principle in an unpopular cause. But most calls upon courage are less insistent and more pervasive. In public administration, for example, courage is needed to insure that degree of impersonality without which friendship oozes into inequities and special favors. Dean Appleby relates a relevant story about George Washington. Washington told a friend seeking an appointment: "You are welcome to my house; you are welcome to my heart. . . my personal feelings have nothing to do with the present case. I am not George Washington, but President of the United States. As George Washington, I would do anything in my power for you. As President, I can do nothing."[15] Normally it takes less courage to deal impersonally with identifiable interest groups than with long standing associates and colleagues upon whom one has depended over the years for affection and for professional and personal support. This is true in relationship to those inside as well as those outside the organization. Part of the loneliness of authority comes from the fact, again in the words of Dean Appleby, that "to a distinctly uncomfortable degree [the administrator] must make work relationships impersonal."[16] Appleby was quick to see that impersonality invites the danger of arrogance, but he also saw that the courage to be impersonal in complicated organizational performance is generally valuable as far as the affected public is concerned. "Its tendency is to systematize fair dealing and to avoid whimsy and discrimination — in other words to provide a kind of administrative due process."[17]

The need for this kind of courage on a day-to-day basis is probably greater, and more difficult to conjure, in the legislative than in either the executive or the judicial branches of government.

A second area for consistent courage in the public service is to be found in the relationship of general administrators to experts and specialists. It takes quite as much courage to face down minority expert opinion as it does to face down the majority opinion of a clamoring crowd. In some ways it takes more courage, for relationships with experts are usually intimate in the decisional process, whereas relations with the crowd are often distant and indistinct. Both courage and wisdom are reflected in the words of Sir Winston Churchill: "I knew nothing about science, but I knew something about scientists, and had had much practice as a minister in handling things I did not understand."[18]

Perhaps on no issue of public ethics is Dean Appleby more insistent than on the necessity of experts being kept in their proper place — subordinate to politicians and general administrators. "Perhaps," he wrote, "there is no single problem in public administration of moment equal to the reconciliation of the increasing dependence upon experts with an unending democratic reality."[19] The expert, whether professional, procedural, or programmatic, is essential to the proper functioning of a complex and highly technical social system. But the autonomous or disproportionate power of experts, and of the limited worlds they comprehend, is a constant threat to more general consideration of the public good.

During World War II, a twenty-five-year-old civil servant in the soap division of O.P.A. found himself, because of the temporary absence of superiors, dealing directly with the president and legal staff of Lever Brothers. After a few minutes of confrontation the president of Lever Brothers turned scornfully to the government employee and asked, "Young man, what in hell do you know about soap?" A strong voice replied, "Sir, I don't know much about soap, but I know a hell of a lot about price control."

This is the courage needed by a Budget Bureau examiner dealing with the Pentagon; this is the courage needed by an Assistant Secretary of Health, Education, and Welfare in dealing with the Surgeon General; this is the courage needed by a transient mayor in dealing with a career engineer in the public works department; this is the courage needed by a Congressman faced with appraising the "expert" testimony of an important banker in his district.

Perhaps the most essential courage in the public service is the courage to decide. For if it is true that all policies have bitter-sweet consequences, decisions invariably produce hurt. President Eliot of Harvard once felt constrained to say that the prime requisite of an executive was his willingness to give pain. Much buck-passing in public life is the prudent consequence of the need for multiple clearances in large and complex institutions. But buck-passing which stems from lack of moral courage is the enemy of efficient and responsible government. The inner satisfactions which come from the courage to decide are substantial; but so are the slings and arrows which are invariably let loose by those who are aggrieved by each separate decision. The issues become especially acute in personnel decisions. Courage to fire, to demote, to withhold advancement, or to shift assignments against the wishes of the person involved, is often the courage most needed and the most difficult to raise.

Man's Sense of Injustice

The third and perhaps most essential moral quality needed in the public service is fairness tempered by charity. The courage to be impersonal and disinterested is of no value unless it results in just and charitable actions and attitudes. Government in a free society is the authoritative allocator of values in terms of partly ineffable standards of justice and the public zeal. It requires the approximation of moving targets partly camouflaged by the shadows of an unknowable future. The success or failure of policies bravely conceived to meet particular social evils is more frequently obscured than clarified by the passage of time. As R.G. Collingwood once pointed out, "The only thing that a shrewd and critical Greek like Herodotus would say about the divine power that ordains the course of history is that. . . it rejoices in upsetting and disturbing things."[20]

What remains through the disorder and unpredictability of history is the sense on the part of the public and of working colleagues that power for whatever ends was exercised fairly and compassionately. The deepest strain in our ethical heritage is "man's sense of injustice." The prophetic voices of the Old Testament repaired time and again to this immemorial standard. "Let Justice roll down like waters. . ." Hesiod, speaking for generations of ancient Greeks, wrote, "Fishes and beasts and fowls of the air devour one another. But to men Zeus has given justice. Beside Zeus on his throne Justice has her seat."[21] Justice was the only positive heritage of the Roman World. The establishment of justice follows directly behind the formation of union itself in the Preamble to the American Constitution.

But the moral imperative to be just — to be fair — is a limited virtue without charity. Absolute justice presupposes omniscience and total disinterestedness. Public servants are always faced with making decisions based upon both imperfect information and the inarticulate insinuations of self-interest into the decisional calculus. Charity is the virtue which compensates for inadequate information and for the subtle importunities of self in the making of judgments designed to be fair. Charity is not a soft virtue. To the contrary, it involves the ultimate moral toughness. For its exercise involves the disciplining of self and the sublimation of persistent inner claims for personal recognition, power, and status. It is the principle above principle. In the idiom of the New Testament, it is the losing of self to find self. Its exercise makes of compromise not a sinister barter but a recognition of the dignity of competing claimants. It fortifies the persuasive rather than the coercive arts. It stimulates the visions of the good society without which government becomes a sullen defense of existing patterns of privilege.

The Essential Humanity

The normative systems of politics and organization which Dean Appleby elaborated in his writings are umbilically related to mental attitudes and moral qualities of the individual moral actor in the public service. They nourish these attitudes and qualities. They condition and promote public morality. But the reverse is also true. Without proper mental attitudes and moral qualities on the part of the public servant, Dean Appleby's normative systems could neither exist nor be meaningfully approximated.

Bureaucracy and technology are the pervasive realities of modern civilization. Together they have made possible order, prosperity, and mobility in unprecedented magnitudes. But, unfortunately, they have demonstrated a perverse tendency to drain from man the blood of his essential humanity. The nobility of any society is especially encapsulated and made manifest to the world in the personal example of its public leaders and public servants.

Perhaps, therefore, Dean Appleby's writings about morality and government — no matter how wise and how provocative — were of less importance than the lessons of his example as a public servant. For in selecting the mental attitudes and moral qualities of the moral public servant, I have been guided far more by my memories of Paul Appleby than by my perusal of his writings. Dean Appleby in his public career demonstrated an uncommon understanding of the moral ambiguities, the contextual priorities, and the paradoxes of procedures in ethical governance. Of all men of my acquaintance in public life, he was the most completely endowed in the moral qualities of optimism, courage, and fairness tempered by charity. While his wisdom illuminated everything he observed and experienced, his example shone even more brilliantly than his wisdom.

Endnotes

1. Paul H. Appleby, *Morality and Administration in Democratic Government* (Baton Rouge: Louisiana State University Press, 1952), p. vii.
2. The intellectual as distinct from the moral implications of hierarchy have been suggested by Kenneth Underwood in his contention that "The policy-making executive is to be distinguished from the middle management-supervisor levels most basically in the excessively cognitive, abstract dimensions of his work." See his paper "The New Ethic of Personal and Corporate Responsibility," presented at the Third Centennial Symposium on *The Responsible Individual,* April 8, 1964, University of Denver.
3. Appleby, *op. cit.,* p. 35.
4. *Ibid,* p. 214.
5. *Ibid,* p. 211.
6. *The Children of Light and the Children of Darkness* (New York: Scribners, 1944), p. xi of Foreword.
7. *The Human Comedy* (London: The Bodley Head, 1937), p. 232.
8. *Op. cit.,* p. 222.
9. Quoted by James Reston, in the *New York Times,* April 11, 1957.
10. *Op. cit.,* p. 127.
11. *Op. cit.,* p. 64.
12. Felix Frankfurter, *Malinski v. New York,* 324, U.S. 401, 414, 1945.
13. See especially, *op. cit.,* Chapter 4.
14. *Op. cit.,* p. 56.
15. *Op. cit.,* p. 130.
16. *Op. cit.,* p. 221.
17. *Op. cit.,* p. 149.
18. *Life,* February 28, 1949, p. 61.
19. *Op. cit.,* p. 145.
20. *The Idea of History* (Oxford: Clarendon Press, 1946), p. 22.
21. Quoted in Edith Hamilton, *The Greek Way* (New York: W.W. Norton and Co., Inc., 1930) p. 292.

ASPA Workbook: Responsibility and Accountability

As part of its developing involvement with issues of professional standards and ethics, the American Society for Public Administration published in 1979 a workbook on professional standards and ethics. A second, expanded edition of the workbook was published in 1982. This selection, and others elsewhere in this volume, are drawn from the later edition.

Responsibility and accountability are professional standards applied to administrators in their service to the public. When used as measures of quality and performance, they enable the professional administrator to identify strengths and weaknesses. Such self-diagnosis can be useful in developing a personal program for upgrading performance.

A. Background — Responsibility

The administrator is responsible for performing tasks effectively: for taking care of, managing, and reliably discharging various functions. The administrator is expected to be trustworthy, willing, and able to carry out tasks with competence and conformity to professional standards. Obviously, public managers/administrators must deal with defining their ultimate responsibility to the public.

B. Some Self-Diagnostic Questions Concerning The Administrator's Responsibility

1. How do I assure that I fully comprehend the nature and scope of my assigned tasks?

2. Do I feel personally responsible for the level of performance and effectiveness with which my organization meets public needs?

3. On some issues, do I feel that my input will not matter? Does the fact that no one will ever know the effect that I might have on an outcome influence my professional behavior?

4. How do I deal with conflicting responsibilities to my agency, client groups, profession, and outside interests?

5. Do I take positions on the basis of principles, or of demands and pressures of the immediate situation?

6. Do I seek opposing views on sensitive issues that involve my responsibilities?

7. Do I undertake assigned tasks with which I do not identify as vigorously as others which I favor?

8. Is it important for me to have a reputation as one who can be "counted on" by my agency? How do I view the characteristic of reliability?

C. Background — Accountability

Accountability is based on the idea that the public administrator is answerable first to the public and second to his or her organization for the results of work performed. It also involves generating and providing credible, accurate information that facilitates evaluation of performance by the public, the employing agency, client groups, and the profession. Accountability also call for disclosures that illuminate how responsibilities were assigned, methods adopted to accomplish tasks, tasks executed, and outcome realized.

Source: Herman Mertins, Jr., and Patrick J. Hennigan, *Applying Professional Standards & Ethics in the Eighties: A Workbook & Study Guide for Public Administrators* (Washington, DC: American Society for Public Administration, 1982), pp. 6-7.

D. Some Self-Diagnostic Questions Concerning Accountability

1. Do I undertake tasks in ways that contribute most effectively to achieving the goals of my organization?

2. Do I measure my accountability in terms specific to the values of my organization, e.g., efficiency, effectiveness, productivity, and orderliness? Or do I have another sense of what accountability implies?

3. Do I ever manipulate the requirements of accountability?

4. If my organization suffers a lapse in performance, how do I respond?

5. Am I aware of "rules of the game" in my organization? Do I accept them?

6. Have my administrative acts included, where appropriate, provisions to facilitate public scrutiny?

7. Is the information on my performance that I furnish others accurate, timely, and complete?

8. Do I respond to the "right to know" and the "need to know" requirements of appropriate individuals, authorities, and groups?

9. Do I use clear, understandable language in my communication that contributes to measurement of accountability?

Case 4:
Following Orders

My office provides benefits to welfare recipients, some of whom are not always able to document their needs as fully as they should. In the past, we have generally been accepting a client's assurances if we felt that the person was telling us the truth (that is, if we had no reason to doubt his or her veracity). We have thus far had no instances, as far as we know, of fraud or lying using this procedure.

The new director of our agency, however, has recently urged us to be much more stringent in requiring documentation from possible clients. I suspect that she has done so as part of a general movement in the state to reduce the welfare rolls.

I am concerned that several deserving people are going to be hurt by our imposing stricter requirements. I don't think that confronting my agency director would do any good. I could probably get by doing what we have been doing, if I am careful about it, but I have the feeling I might be running some personal risk in doing so.

Source: Eileen Hoult-berg and William L. Richter, Kansas State University.

What should I do? Do I have an obligation to follow orders even if I think they will have harmful consequences? On the other hand, do I have a right to substitute my notions of justice and fair play for the directions coming to our office from the state government?

II. Ethical Problems: Some Blatant, Some Not So Obvious

Introductory Essay

Public officials confront a wide variety of ethical issues and dilemmas. The problems discussed in this volume — lying and other forms of deception, graft and fraud, harassment of staff members and clients, abuse of authority — form only a part of the total landscape of administrative ethics. It is, however, an important part, for these patterns of behavior (or misbehavior) have long been prominent features of the American political scene, from local police precinct to county courthouse to the White House. In recent years, indeed, they have become matters of public debate not only in the United States but in virtually every country of the world. Problems of corruption and deceptive practices are not limited, certainly, to government officials, but in the mind of the citizen these issues may be more readily associated with the public service, in part because it *is* public.

In thinking about ethical problems of these kinds, we can usefully distinguish among three important perspectives from which a decision — or a pattern of behavior — might be viewed as raising ethical concerns. The first perspective is that of the *individual* government official, who may (for example) be offered a free plane ticket to a business convention. From this point of view, the problem is often that of identifying and clarifying the ethical issue. For example: Are some of my future program decisions likely to help — or harm — the businesses holding this convention? If so, will the free plane ride incline me to view their interests more favorably than I should, in relation to overall program goals? And if, on reflection, I conclude that my objectivity will *not* be contaminated by the gift, would I still risk damage to my personal reputation for objectivity (and to my effectiveness) if that free ride is later reported by the news media? Thus the individual official must be sensitive to the conditions under which one's objectivity may be compromised in reality, and also to the question of whether the person's behavior might reasonably *appear to others* to be unethical.

A second perspective is that of the manager, who is not only responsible for her own behavior but also for that of others within the agency. Here, in addition to her concerns regarding whether she is behaving ethically, the manager must consider whether existing practices and rules encourage ethical behavior — or whether external pressures, together with the "organizational culture" within the agency, encourage behavior that might reasonably be criticized on ethical grounds. For example, the manager might want to ensure that her agency has rules regarding free airplane rides and the acceptance of other gifts, and that the importance of these rules — and "gray areas" that need to be clarified — are *regularly* discussed in meetings of the agency's staff.

The third perspective is that of the public, who have entrusted government officials with a portion of their society's affairs and well-being. Public opinion on an issue — such as conditions under which gifts can be properly received by public officials, or conditions under which deception by government officials is justified — will frequently be unclear, or divided. Even so, there often are fundamental standards that can be applied in judging particular cases. Two important standards, particularly in a democratic society, are the need of the citizenry to be *well informed,* so that officials are accountable to the public in reality as well as in theory, and the need of the citizen to have a *sense of trust* in public officials, based on the citizen's judgment that officials are motivated in their actions by a concern with the broad interests of the local community, or the nation, and not by narrow interests of self aggrandizement, or party advantage.

The purpose of Part II of this volume is to describe a range of problem areas, together with specific examples, in which public officials confront ethical issues — including some where officials have acted in violation of law or against acceptable ethical standards. Our aim is not, however, to provide a display of "public horrors." There would be little benefit if the cases described below merely appalled the reader or lent grim satisfaction to the critic who believes that government must inevitably do more harm than good.

Our primary goals are two: first, to illustrate and analyze pressures which give rise to unethical or questionable behavior; and second, to encourage our readers to exercise both their analytical skills in exploring the sources of ethical lapses, and their own judgment in considering how the officials in the cases should behave — or should have behaved if they had thought systematically and carefully about the issues. Our hope, then, is that by reading these essays and cases, reflecting on them, and debating them with others, our readers might be in a better position to understand the ethical risks and ethical implications of their own behavior, and to make choices that will be defensible in ethical terms.

From the perspective of the manager, some of the articles and cases illustrate the importance of the agency's traditions in encouraging or undermining ethical behavior, as well as suggesting strategies that managers may be able to use in order to improve the ethical climate within their agencies. Finally, the selections in Part II illustrate some of the pressures that can erode public trust in government action, and that can weaken the capacity of the citizenry to be well informed and thus able to carry out its crucial function in a democratic society — holding government officials accountable for their rhetoric and their actions. These examples will also suggest to the reader some steps that might be used to protect these ingredients of the public interest. In Part III, then, we turn explicitly to strategies that can be used to encourage ethical behavior when viewed from the perspective of the individual, the manager, and the broader public.

In the remaining paragraphs of this introductory essay, we suggest some ways of sorting out the range of ethical problems that public officials often confront in the course of their duties.

"Clearly wrong" and "Conditionally wrong" Behavior

It may be useful to divide the kinds of unethical behavior encountered in public life, and in the selections in this volume, into two categories. The first group we might label "clearly wrong." These include those behaviors which are so widely viewed as unethical that few people would attempt to justify them on moral grounds. Some philosophers label these as *prima facie* wrong." Harassment of co-workers and clients, as well as graft, fraud, and other forms of corruption would appear to fit in this category; these behaviors subvert the trust in fair-dealing that is a hallmark of constructive human relationships, and they may also undermine effective accountability in a democratic society.[1] The phrase "fraud, waste and abuse," now widely used in critical assessments of agency programs by the U.S. General Accounting Office and other evaluators, extends across an even wider terrain of misbehavior.

The articles by Kermit Vandivier, Edward Koch and Robert Kenney, for example, illustrate several different patterns of fraudulent behavior; LeRoy Harlow's essay describes a pattern of wasteful behavior which most observers would probably consider "clearly wrong"; and some of the practices described in the Malek Manual, excerpted in Chapter 8, would seem to illustrate the "abuse" of public office.

In the second category, of "conditionally wrong" behaviors, we might place lying and other forms of deception, for example, and some aspects of conflict of interest. As to lying and other behavior in the "conditionally wrong" category, the student of ethics begins by asking, "Under what conditions is [lying] ethically permissible?" The initial challenge, then — for the public official, and for those who would evaluate their activities — is to clarify the conditions that *might* be used to justify such behavior, and then to subject these rationales to close scrutiny, in order to test the persuasiveness of the reason (or excuse). Often that analysis is so challenging and complex that much less attention is given to the questions that must follow: For those categories (of lying and deception, etc.) that are judged unethical, (1) what are the factors that lead to such behavior, and (2) what managerial strategies might be employed to reduce the extent of such unethical behavior in the future?

Although "clearly wrong" and "conditionally wrong" patterns of behavior can be provisionally distinguished, the lines between the two categories are, in fact, not clear. For example, "corruption" — historically branded as clearly unethical — has recently taken on a new life as "conditionally wrong." Thus some observers have looked closely into the corrupt practices found in urban political machines in the United States, and in the political economies of some developing nations, and have pronounced these activities beneficial — at least under certain conditions.[2] And there are times when bribery, harassment, and other widely condemned behaviors might be defended on ethical grounds because they are necessary stratagems to avoid a still greater evil.[3]

Motivations: Helping Yourself, Helping Your Agency, Improving Society

There is a second distinction that might usefully be made among activities that are labelled as unethical, a distinction based on motivation. The dominant motive for exacting a bribe is usually self-interest, narrowly understood: lining one's own pocket with dollars or rubles, or aiding one's family or one's political party. A similar motivation underlies familial or party nepotism.[4] But lying and other forms of deception by public officials are often motivated substantially by other concerns — the desire to advance important program goals; loyalty to co-workers or a desire to keep one's own agency in high public repute; patriotism. Again, lines are blurred: lies in defense of agency goals may be rewarded by promotion and other benefits for the "loyal" official; to harass clients of a welfare program may reduce agency costs and so earn praise for "efficient" staff activities. Still, in thinking about causes of certain kinds of unethical behavior — and especially in thinking about remedies — it may be helpful to sort out motivations in this way.

For example, deception and other unethical behavior at lower staff levels is often motivated by a desire to meet goals set — implicitly or explicitly — by one's superiors; the essay by Richard Halloran provides illustrations on this point, as does the testimony of Oliver North. In such cases, punitive action directed toward lower-level staff members who follow those signals may have very little long-term effect. Penalizing the senior executives, despite their efforts to use "the strategy of deniability," or employing other strategies to change the signals they send down the line may be far more important.[5]

Both of these categories of behavior — lining one's pockets, helping one's organization — place the emphasis on the *active* decision-maker, taking the initiative to uphold or to undermine ethical standards. But often, the situation is otherwise; an individual is required to take little or no action, simply "looking the other way" or "going along" passively while unethical behavior continues. Others may take the initiative; and the organization's "culture" may provide a pervasive environment in which *ethical* behavior is viewed as deviant. What can one do then? Several readings in Part II illustrate this pervasive problem of large organizations, private and public; see in particular the articles by William Riordan, Paul Heisig, and LeRoy Harlow, and the case, "The Five Percent Solution."

Professional Integrity and the Political Environment

Underlying these comments on the problems of ethics that confront public officials is the assumption of "professional integrity" — the expectation that professional expertise and judgment should predominate in shaping and implementing agency programs, and that every agency staff member is expected to adhere to and contribute to this orientation. In a democratic society, other factors must also come into play — accountability to elected officials will sometimes lead to policies that agency professionals would not favor, and accountability to law will at times require bending professional standards to meet the peculiarity of statutes. But these modifications should carry with them the requirement of *openness* — that the policies and orders of elected officials, and the constraints of statutes, be understood by the public and available for critical review by the media and other observers. With openness comes the possibility of self-correction, so that "professional integrity" and democratic accountability can fruitfully co-exist.[6]

While these general standards may seem reasonably clear, they mask some important elements in the environment of public officials which often operate against the grain of ethical behavior. Some of these elements are linked directly to the struggle to achieve popular control over a large and expanding public bureaucracy; others are pressures and problems frequently found in private corporations as well as government agencies. In these final paragraphs, we list some aspects of the environment and direct the reader's attention to selections which illustrate them.

The struggle for political control, and the desire of party leaders to nurture loyal and active party service, will often generate pressures to use government positions and workers on behalf of political-party goals, as the article by Heisig and the excerpts from the Malek Manual illustrate. The search for ways to overcome the red tape and other alleged inefficiencies of government bureaucracy will sometimes lead to corruption, as the article by Gerald and Naomi Caiden demonstrates. The availability of public funds in large amounts — not always carefully supervised — is likely to attract the venal, as honey attracts bees.[7] And there will be gray areas — where a battle to eliminate the *appearance* of conflict of interest may reveal lack of careful ethical standards and thinking ("The New Manager Wants to Shoot Santa Claus"), and where ethical laxity and confusion abound in high places (see the articles on the problems of Edwin Meese).

The environment of the public official also includes crucial factors — that press against professional integrity and ethical behavior generally — which are also widely found in private organizations. These include, for example, a culture of minor fraud, and pressure to cover up professional analyses and findings that senior officials find uncomfortable (illustrated by the case on "Executive Morale"). These cases illustrate the point that no individual can safely yield to superiors or organizational pressures in deciding, "Is this ethical?" We must each remain the keeper of the keys to our own individual conscience.

Even so, the prospects for maintaining ethical behavior throughout an organization depend on more than individual self-reflection. Managers and other senior officials can crucially shape the possibilities for ethical behavior throughout their agencies by their own sensitivity — or insensitivity — to ethical concerns, and by the structure of rewards and other incentives they provide within an organization. These important dimensions of ethical leadership are strongly suggested by Kermit Vandivier's instructive analysis of behavior at the B.F. Goodrich Corporation, by Frank Nebeker's detailed commentary on leadership at the U.S. Department of Justice, and in other cases in Part II. They are illustrated once again, as this volume goes to press, by the evidence of ethical laxity at the U.S. Department of Housing and Urban Development in the 1980s. To the official who headed the Department during the years 1981-88, a pattern of selecting housing developers with close ties to political allies was "a beautiful thing," and top officials apparently devoted little energy to identifying the ethical implications or political risks that might attend this philosophy.[8] When, in the spring of 1989, it became clear that some of those political associates had received large sums of money for little work, and that a range of abuses had occurred in recent years, HUD's Secretary, Jack F. Kemp, attempted to establish a new and different tone. "There was mismanagement . . . and there was political influence," Kemp argued; the new Secretary promised to ensure that under his administration, HUD programs would be operated "on behalf of the needy, not the greedy."[9] The materials in Part III suggest some strategies that he and other officials could use if they want to match performance to rhetoric.

Endnotes

1. "Corruption" is the "perversion or destruction of integrity in the discharge of public duties by bribery or favor" (Oxford English Dictionary). To "harass" someone is to distress, often through repeated verbal attacks. "Sexual harassment" is now defined under federal law, in the context of a working environment, to include "unwelcome sexual advances, requests for sexual favors, and other verbal or physical conduct of a sexual nature" which interfere with an appropriate work atmosphere; for a more complete statement, see the EEOC guidelines below.

2. This issue is critically reviewed in the article by Gerald and Naomi Caiden reprinted below.

3. For example, a bribe to a police official in Nazi Germany, to protect a family guilty only of being Jewish.

4. Nepotism in this context means the appointment of relatives or members of one's political faction to positions providing income or prestige, in preference to the appointment of better qualified individuals. In some cases, of course, appointing members of one's political faction may be a strategy to advance important programmatic goals; then the term "nepotism," as defined here, would not apply.

5. For a recent example of the "deniability" strategy, see the testimony by John Poindexter excerpted in Chapter 8, below. The argument for directing greater attention at organizational leaders, in ways that will pierce the shield of deniability, is developed in J.W. Doig, D. Phillips and T. Manson, "Deterring Illegal Behavior in Complex Organizations," *Criminal Justice Ethics,* vol. 3, no. 1 (Winter/Spring 1984), pp. 39-48.

6. On the tension between these goals, see the selections by Woodrow Wilson, Carl Friedrich and Herman Finer in Part I. For the application of openness as a managerial tool, see Part III. For further exploration, see Sissela Bok, *Secrets,* especially Chapter 12.

7. Several of our cases illustrate this theme: "The New City Manager" (Chapter 1) and "Free Pencils and Paper Clips" (Chapter 3), "Free Lunch?" (Chapter 5) and "The Five Percent Solution" (Chapter 6).

8. "From a developer's point of view, it's money; from a politician's point of view, you get buildings and they're all over the country. You can steer the units toward certain builders. When your election comes around, those builders chip in money for your campaign. It's a beautiful thing." (Former HUD Secretary Samuel R. Pierce, Jr., in an interview in January 1989; quoted in E.J. Dionne, Jr., "Aides and Critics Call Pierce a Loyal but Detached Chief," *New York Times,* June 18, 1989, p. 22).

9. Jack F. Kemp quoted in "Kemp Sees Criminality in HUD Program," *New York Times,* June 18, 1989, p. 22. Referring to political consultants who had profited from housing programs that the Reagan Administration had advocated eliminating, Kemp commented: "It's a flaw in the character of some people. There are lots of folks who on the one hand beat up on the Government and when they got their chance to make some money out of it were willing to do so."

5. Understanding Fraud, Waste, Abuse and Corruption

Administrative Corruption
Gerald E. Caiden and Naomi J. Caiden

The increased visibility of administrative corruption has become a persistent and disturbing feature of our times. Almost every issue of the daily press brings, it seems, fresh examples of allegedly corrupt behavior on the part of responsible public and private figures. This growing prominence of corruption has coincided with increased academic interest in a subject long deemed inappropriate for serious research, and still not regarded as a respectable topic for study in certain circles. Fortunately, obvious objections to research into corruption — problems of measurement, difficulties of access, bias, and evaluation — have been largely attenuated, if not overcome. It is accepted now that it is the responsibility of social scientists to choose for their research subjects which touch on or embrace problems central to human society, and not merely those convenient to the tools they have on hand.

For those interested in corruption as a social phenomenon, the traditional approach, which treated it in a moralistic manner, was inappropriate. Studies of corruption were vague as to definition, condemned it *a priori,* and looked for explanations in individual behavior. Social scientists demanded precise definitions, objectivity, and some relationship between the workings of society and the existence of corruption. Thus was born a "revisionist" approach,[1] which defined corruption in terms of divergence from a specific norm of accepted behavior, explained its existence by reference to social mores and deficiencies in economic and political systems, and enumerated conditions in which it might elicit approval rather than condemnation. Although this approach contains much that is appealing, and has paved the way to more serious study of the problem of administrative corruption by non-revisionists,[2] careful examination of its assumptions and conclusions reveals several misconceptions. These arise mainly because although the revisionists deal with social variables, they still think of corrupt behavior in individual terms without recognizing the existence of systematic corruption.

In the writings on comparative politics and administration, much of the discussion of ethical issues has focused on the concept of corruption. In this essay Gerald and Naomi Caiden review several contending views of corruption, and they direct attention particularly at the view that corrupt behavior is often beneficial to a society. That position, they argue, fails to take account of the pervasive and long-lasting negative effects in any society of widespread corruption. Is their analysis persuasive?

Source: Gerald E. Caiden and Naomi J. Caiden, "Administrative Corruption," *Public Administration Review* 37:3 (May/June, 1977), 301-309.

The Revisionist Approach

Until recently corruption was treated in a moralistic manner. Its cause was seen as the gaining of positions of power and trust by evil and dishonest men. The solution was to "turn the rascals out." Corruption was therefore incidental to the working of society which might be safeguarded by appropriate laws and exhortations. But even as the muckrakers did their work of uncovering graft and corruption in the turn-of-the-century United States, suspicion was growing that these phenomena did not exist in isolation. The arch-muckraker, Lincoln Steffens himself, late in his career drew attention to the role of incentives fostering corruption in the private enterprise society, by providing "ordinary men" with "extraordinary temptations."[3]

A similar disquiet, and concern for corruption as rooted in the mores and institutions of society, stimulated a rejection of moralistic and individualistic explanations by students of comparative administration. As interest grew in non-Western systems of government and in the workings of development programs, those concerned with international aid and development encountered apparent and blatant corrupt administrative practices in poor countries. It was natural to ask, "Why do certain societies at particular times appear especially prone to corruption?" Rejecting the answer of comparative moral virtue as somewhat out of keeping with the premises of the comparative administration movement, the revisionists were led to the view that corruption stemmed from norms of politics and administration which differed from those of the West, and might even fulfill political, administrative, and economic needs better than the public ethic fostered by aid officials. Corruption was not incidental but structural: it could therefore be removed from the realm of the moral (and unspeakable) to the neutral (and researchable).

The first problem was, "What is corruption?" Definitions have been classified into three types:[4] public interest, public duty, and market centered. The first, which has largely been rejected by the revisionists, regards corruption as arising:

> whenever a powerholder. . . i.e., a responsible functionary or office holder, is by monetary or other rewards not legally provided for, induced to take an action which favors whoever provides the rewards, and thereby does damage to the public and its interests.[5]

Such definition pre-judges the result of corruption, is imprecise (as the meaning of public interest is open to different interpretations), and may preclude recognition of corruption until after the event only when the public interest can be clarified and judged.

The second type of definition, public duty, appears more promising. Though a number of variations exist,[6] the basic idea is conveyed by the most often used definition:

> . . . behavior which deviates from the formal duties of a public role because of private-regarding (personal, close family, private clique) pecuniary or status gains; or violates rules against the exercise of certain types of private-regarding influence.[7]

As long as no confusion exists regarding the standard from which corrupt practices diverge, i.e., the nature of public duty, corruption may clearly be defined and recognized. Once, however, the public standard is challenged, or regarded as relative to circumstances, then considerable ambiguity enters. Who sets the standard to say what behavior is acceptable and what corrupt? What is *undue* influence? What is *misuse* of authority? What is public *irresponsibility*? If there is no accepted public standard, or if the standards of public office and public duty are regarded as foreign importations inapplicable in given conditions, is there then innocence of corruption?[8] In short, "Are ideas and theories offered by Western scholars about the state of corruption in the developing nations valid in the light of the divergent social norms that govern the conduct of public office in the West and those in the transitional societies of Asia."[9]

The issue is one of conflict of values. Against the Western, impersonal, and universalistic norms of bureaucracy are set the values of kinship and reciprocity. Are these to be denied validity, and the public servant who fulfills their expectations to be considered as corrupt? After all,

> . . . in a given society, various kinds of norms operate, some congruent, others inconsistent with one another. Legal norms may conflict with moral, religious and cultural norms, so that a sample of behavior defined as illegal may be acceptable using cultural standards.[10]

In retaining a residual definition of corruption, but rejecting the specific substantive standard to which it pertains, the revisionists have dissolved corruption. In their conception, corruption is by definition exceptional, the departure from the normal ways of doing business: corruption cannot itself be the norm. Once

Understanding Fraud, Waste,
Abuse and Corruption

corruption, in other words, becomes sufficiently widespread as to constitute a normal rather than an exceptional mode of behavior, it ceases to exist.

Analysis is taken beyond public ethics by market-oriented types of definition, such as "Corruption involves a shift from a mandatory pricing model to a free-market model"[11], or "Corruption is an extra-legal institution used by individuals or groups to gain influence over the actions of the bureaucracy."[12] Unlike the public duty-type definitions, there is no doubt as to what "public" ways of doing things represent. It is in the former case a "centralized allocative mechanism" and in the latter a stipulated institutionalized decision-making process. But again, the standard is purely relative, since these institutions are regarded as so inadequate to fulfill the demands placed upon them that corruption provides an alternative means of allocation or of access to decision making. Once again corruption is legitimized in terms of its prevalence and of faulty working of Western-style norms and institutions.

These definitions provide the underpinning for explanations of why corruption is allegedly more prevalent in certain places, notably poor countries. The "cultural" explanation starts from the assumption that in "developing" countries there exists a gap between law (as imposed Western and alien standards) and accepted informal social norms (sanctioned by prevailing social ethics), i.e., there is a divergence between the attitudes, aims, and methods of the government of a country and those of the society in which they operate.[13] The individual who assumes a public role is:

> . . . torn between two social forces operating in his world. Because of the rational, impersonal and universalistic norms of the bureaucracy, he must accept that a public office is a public trust, not a personal domain. He must therefore commit himself to serve the national and community's need ahead of his personal and family interests. But there, too, are strong kinship bonds which compel him to look after the needs not only of the immediate members of his family but even those of his extended family system, otherwise he violates a stronger norm which is deeply rooted in the personalistic and familistic outlooks which characterize traditional cultural values. As he imbibes Weberian ideas in school, including possible post-graduate studies abroad, he faces a conflict in regard to his duties to his family and his kin, some of whom may have helped him bear the cost of an expensive education.[14]

In the resulting role conflict, the Weberian, bureaucratic role is only one open to the official, and not necessarily the most compelling.[15] So-called corruption appears to be consistent with customs and traditions, whereas the laws and ethics that make it illegal and immoral are alien, imported, or super-imposed.[16] It is also suggested that traditional values predispose toward corruption, which in turn eases the gap between citizen and government.[17] A variation on this theme is the view that corruption is "dislocated" behavior resulting from a lag in the value system of the community in relation to institutional change.[18]

The "cultural" explanation blurs into considerations of governmental capacity, which have two major emphases. The first of these might be called "economic," since it relates to the government's inability to provide the services demanded of it. The centralized allocative mechanism breaks down because of disequilibrium between supply and demand, and the market reasserts itself.[19] In poor countries the situation is aggravated by cultural factors, rising expectations and demands, the predominance of government as a supplier of resources, and lack of alternatives. Similarly, one can refer to the inability of morally approved structures to fulfill essential social functions.[20]

The "political" aspect of the explanation relates corruption to access to power and political institutionalization. Corruption is seen as primarily related to inadequate political channels, and as such simply a special case of political influence.[21] Again, poor countries are good candidates for corruption because of the disproportionate impact of government on society, bureaucratic dominance, a weak sense of nation with a high value placed on kinship, and a marked gap between citizen and government. There is a heavy burden for political institutions to carry in terms of capacity and legitimacy, and corruption fills the gap. Corruption is the equivalent of pressure group influence in more politically developed countries, but taking place after the passage of legislation rather than prior to its passage because of factors such as erratic administration or public discrimination against minorities.[22] Similarly corruption is regarded as the result of modernization in the absence of political institutionalization.[23] Reference is made to the disruptive effects of changes in values (e.g., ascription to achievement; acceptance of public role), the creation of new sources of wealth and power, the expansion of governmental functions and regulation, and the lack of strong political parties. Corruption has much the same function as violence (and acts as an alternative). Its emergence is inversely related to the degree of social stratification in the society. The lack of opportunities outside government leads to the use of public office to build private fortunes, and foreign business activities tend to encourage local corruption.[24]

As these explanations have strong functional overtones, they stress the positive effects of corruption. Since attention is on "developing" countries, the main issue raised is the probable effect of corruption on economic, political, and, to a lesser extent, administrative, development. On the whole, considerations relating to administrative development are the most pessimistic, for obvious reasons, since corruption undermines bureaucratic norms. Cited are non-achievement of goals, rise in the price of administration, diversion of resources from public purposes, erosion of morale, lowered respect for authority, a poor example enhancing lack of political courage, diversion of energies into lobbying, fiddling, etc., resulting in argument and bitterness, delays, and the use of inappropriate criteria in decisions.[25] On the other hand, corruption is also regarded as a means of surmounting either traditional laws and/or bureaucratic regulation[26] and considered as a means of cutting down uncertainty in decision making.[27] Nepotism may even result in the appointment of more competent bureaucrats.[28]

As far as economic development is concerned, however, corruption is seen as positive in effect, on the assumption that governmental administration acts as a stifling force against private initiative. Thus corruption may impel better choices, increase the allocation of resources to investment, improve the quality of public servants, increase the responsiveness of bureaucracy and through nepotism substitute for a public works system.[29] While admitting that corruption may lead to capital outflow, investment distortions and aid foregone, it may be functional as a source of capital formation, cutting red tape and offering private incentives to entrepreneurs given certain conditions, *viz.*, a tolerant culture and dominant groups, perceived security by elites, and certain societal or institutional restraints. Corruption funnels capital to struggling entrepreneurs, minimizing wastage of resources, wresting control of trade and industry from aliens, and promoting investment through politicians.[30]

Finally, corruption is seen as making a positive contribution to political development, usually viewed in terms of national integration and the strengthening of political parties. Corruption is cited as an acceptable alternative to violence[31] and as aiding national unification and stability, helping integration by bringing in groups otherwise alienated, and increasing participation in public affairs.[32] It is also argued that corruption reduces pressure for policy change and weakens the governmental bureaucracy, both of which are regarded as functional for political institutionalization.[33] Others stress elite integration: the bourgeoisie can buy its way into the elite, and corruption can cement together a conservative coalition, while holding back or cancelling out the effects of growing collective demands and humanizing government for non-elites. Finally, corruption contributes to the strengthening of political parties and will itself be defeated in the long run, since vigilant and strong political parties will tend to reduce opportunities for corruption.[34]

In sum, poor countries for cultural and historical reasons have a propensity toward corruption, seen as a violation of Western norms. To this propensity may be added a breakdown in the allocative mechanisms of society, or economic, political, and administrative reasons, so that corruption steps in to fulfill the missing functions. Corruption is thus legitimized in terms of its prevalence, and of its functionality: indeed, given the inappropriateness of Western norms and inadequacy of Western institutions, corruption does not really exist at all — it is simply a different way of doing business. Before such conceptualization can be accepted, however, we have to ask two questions. First, does corruption really disappear once it becomes normal behavior, or is it a substantive phenomenon, which may exist as normal behavior itself? Second, whereas corruption may arise because a system is failing to achieve its purpose, might not that purpose be better served by reforming the system than acquiescing in corruption?

Administrative Corruption as a Norm

Up to this point, corruption has been treated simply as divergence from an acknowledged standard, whose applicability is now felt in some quarters to be in doubt. It is assumed, therefore, that until this standard came into being in Western Europe at the end of the 18th century, corruption did not exist: corruption was, in effect, the creation of bureaucracy.

Before the clear distinction between public and private standards of behavior which emerged with the ideas of the French Revolution, the argument runs, many practices now regarded as corruption, such as venality and nepotism, were not against the law and were even exploited to their own benefit by rulers. Corruption, in accordance with a public duty definition, did not and could not exist since no concept of public duty existed. Behavior now thought of as corrupt might at most be seen as a special category of "proto-corruption," regarded as normal and legitimate by contemporaries.[35]

It is true that current concepts of corruption date from the ideas of the French Revolution, which swept away private monarchical government and replaced it with representative government.[36] Office became a public trust, and officials servants of the community. Public and private were separated. Privilege and hereditary tenure were replaced by qualification for office. Venality and nepotism were abolished and office holders ceased to have private rights in their office. Officials became full-time, and were paid by salary, not from private profits gained from conducting the government's business. A clear distinction was made between the personal lives of officials and the conduct expected from them in their work by the enforcement of rules. Public accountability entailed continued hierarchical bureaucratic control, as opposed to sporadic, dilatory judicial intervention.[37]

It is also true that before this transformation practices now thought of as corrupt provided the basis of government. Nepotism, venality, exploitation of public function for private profit, were not only usual but also served needs of the crown which could not be fulfilled through more legitimate channels. But even while such practices were commonplace, they were by no means accepted. As long ago as the ancient empires, before even money was in common use, corruption was recognized and vigorous attempts made to combat it, as for example in the bureaucracy of Mauryan India.[38] In the Athenian city-state, a public audit was instituted in order to check corruption and enforce a public role upon officials.[39] In republican Rome, even while provincial officials and others were making their fortunes at the expense of the state and its subjects (the current joke was that a governor needed three years to make his fortune — one to pay off his debts, one to provide a nest-egg for himself, and one to bribe his judges when he returned to Rome[40]) awareness of corruption existed and orators such as Cicero spoke out against it. Machiavelli attempted to analyze corruption in the Italy of his day.[41] The monarchies of Europe all instituted some machinery to combat corruption, even though to serve their own needs, they sometimes acquiesced in its subversion.[42]

Lack of bureaucratic standards, entrenchment and pervasiveness, functionality for the short-run purposes of the regime or participants, did not mean that corruption did not exist. Though widespread and prevalent, the phenomenon of corruption was well recognized and its consequences realized. As a frequent, and sometimes normal, accompaniment of government, it was not an exception from the norm: it was the norm itself, although regarded as wrong.

Administrative Corruption as Functional

That corruption should at times serve certain interests, even those of the state itself, is not surprising: its very *raison d'être* indicates that someone is profiting. The revisionists, however, have made a link between corruption and development, by indicating that where political and administrative systems are deficient, corruption may compensate and prove of general benefit to development.

The problem is to what exactly the revisionists are referring. They link "corruption," defined in residual rather than substantive terms, and "development," a concept which has come to mean all things to all men.[43] Further, the relationship may be far from positive, i.e., rather than "corruption" (whatever it might be) aiding "development" (in mythic terms of whatever one would like it to be), a particular kind of development may tend to be accompanied by corruption. Often there is an uneasy ambivalence regarding which is to be the dependent variable, development (or modernization) or corruption.

Beyond the semantic problem, however, lies the issue of functionality. It is generally accepted that system survival is bound up with a system's ability to adapt and survive, in turn dependent on its ability to absorb and benefit from change. The revisionists handle the problem of change along classic functional lines, i.e., corruption is a dysfunction of the system, which arises because the system cannot accommodate change — it is thus a *functional* dysfunction, whereby the new (and therefore functional) norms it represents replace outmoded norms. Exactly where this fits into the argument regarding cultural norms or propensity to corruption is unclear: for here the new norms are, in fact, the old (pre-development, non-Western) norms. There is a further ambiguity in the "cultural" argument, which does not make it altogether clear whether we are discussing actual traditional norms held by "traditional man" (if he exists) or the breakdown in these norms impacted upon by Western-type development. There is also a missing link in the analysis, which should explain the actual dynamic whereby new norms are evolved, and what kind of norms these will be.

Leaving aside the ambiguities, we have to ask whether the norms of corruption have been able to accommodate the needs of societal change. In the case of the transition to bureaucratic norms and public responsibility in Western countries, they failed to do so. In the end the old ways of conducting state business simply could not cope with the state's needs for increased mobilization of resources, effective and honest disbursement of funds, public trust in government, and control over its activities.[44]

The entrenchment of corruption prevented these changes taking place on an orderly basis. In the most extreme example, that of 18th-century France, corruption helped suppress and funnel opposition to the regime until it reached disastrous proportions, on the analogy of landscape along a fault line which remains unaffected by repeated shocks for a long period and then is completely transformed by a catastrophic earthquake. In other words, the more that corrupt practices approached the dimensions of a norm, or accepted standard of behavior, the more they impeded both administrative and societal changes. The impulse for change had to come not from within, from the continuing development and modification of accepted and corrupt means of administration, but from reformers promoting innovation and new norms. Though corruption might prove functional to the interests of certain individuals and groups, and to the system insofar as it shares those interests, its very functionality is a symptom or indication of the need for reform. Corruption does not disappear when it becomes entrenched and accepted: rather it assumes a different form, that of *systemic* as opposed to *individual* corruption.

Individual and Systemic Corruption

Although revisionists have recognized corruption as a social fact, with structural causes and consequences, it is our contention that they have continued to think of it in individual terms. The definitions they suggest are well suited to individual corruption — the individual who strays from a prevailing norm of official public behavior. Several of the hypotheses they put forward may even be plausible as long as they are thought of in individual terms — informal organizational short-cuts; the occasional accommodation of personal favor; mutual "understandings." These may, according to circumstances, be condonable or reprehensible, but they still bear the vital characteristics of individual corruption — they can be coped with and minimized (though rarely if ever eliminated) within a reasonably effectively control system, and they do not subvert or sabotage organizational purpose.

The conceptions of the revisionists, however, do not appear to stretch to encompass the significance of what they often appear to describe, which is systemic corruption — a situation where wrong-doing has become the norm, and the standard accepted behavior necessary to accomplish organizational goals according to notions of public responsibility and trust has become the exception not the rule. In this situation, corruption has become so regularized and institutionalized that organizational supports back wrong-doing and actually penalize those who live up to the old norms. Such systemic corruption is found today in many countries and jurisdictions, particularly where society prizes organizational loyalty over the public interest, where past standards of public rectitude and personal integrity have been eroded and where notions of public responsibility and trust have been thrust aside with exploitation of public office for private gain. The key is not so much the techniques of organizational method, e.g., bureaucracy, as organizational goals and the qualities necessary to support and maintain them, *viz.,* honest administration and public accountability. The issue only becomes tangled where goals are displaced, so that specific, substantive, and public goals are transposed into, on one level, generalized and hazy development goals, and on another, particularized benefits for privileged individuals or groups.

Systemic corruption has not been subject to much specific research. Examples readily come to mind in many large-scale organizations and at different levels of government. The Watergate affair showed that the White House was not immune. The Fitzgerald revelations indicated that defense contracting was riddled with systemic corruption, and other brave whistle-blowers have questioned law enforcement agencies, regulatory commissions, and public inspection bodies. Systemic corruption occurs whenever the

Understanding Fraud, Waste, Abuse and Corruption

administrative system itself transposes the expected purposes of the organization, forces participants to follow what otherwise would be termed unacceptable ways, and actually punishes those who resist. Deviant conduct is so institutionalized that no individual can be personally faulted organizationally (not morally) for participating, and dysfunction is actually protected. In systemic corruption:

(a) the organization professes an external code of ethics which is contradicted by internal practices;

(b) internal practices encourage, abet, and hide violations of the external code;

(c) non-violators are penalized by foregoing the rewards of violation and offending violators;

(d) violators are protected, and when exposed, treated leniently; their accusers are victimized for exposing organizational hypocrisy, and are treated harshly;

(e) non-violators suffocate in the venal atmosphere; they find no internal relief and much external disbelief;

(f) prospective whistle-blowers are intimidated and terrorized into silence;

(g) courageous whistle-blowers have to be protected from organizational retaliation;

(h) violators become so accustomed to their practices and the protection given them that, on exposure, they evidence surprise and claim innocence and unfair discrimination against them;

(i) collective guilt finds expression in rationalizations of the internal practices and without strong external supports there is no serious intention of ending them;

(j) those formally charged with revealing corruption rarely act and, when forced by external pressure to do so, excuse any incidents as isolated, rare occurrences.

The point to be stressed above all is that few corrupt practices can be conducted without collusion. Few can be kept secret for any length of time. Violations of public norms are known to all.

As we have previously illustrated, some revisionists argue that, moral judgment apart, if public business is conducted according to systemic corruption, that is how things are, that is how public power is exercised, that is the operational norm of public administration, and can no longer be considered corruption. It is merely an extra-legal device to gain influence over public policy, to fill vacuums left by inadequate public laws, to get around unrealistic administrative norms, to bridge lags in the value system of the community in relation to institutional change, to reallocate resources and services when disequilibrium arises between supply and demand, to stabilize the political system and replace violence, to cut down uncertainty in decision making, to cut through bureaucratic red tape, and to increase the responsiveness and sensitivity of public organizations. Systemic corruption may do all these things and more, but when one reduces the term to specific actions, then the dangers are self-evident and its institutionalization is obviously dysfunctional to society. In most cases, the practices constitute theft, bribery, or extortion and probably involve deceit, hypocrisy, and false testimony, and so are indictable offenses, even if they fall into the category of victimless crime.

Individual cases of corruption can be rooted out by the application of organizational sanctions. The wrong-doer is taxed with the evidence, penalized for minor offenses, and dismissed, and possibly prosecuted under the criminal code, for major offenses. The scandal is localized and steps are taken to prevent repetition. Systemic corruption cannot be handled so easily. There is no guarantee that if the most serious offenders are dismissed, or if everyone who is guilty is replaced, corruption will not persist. The old patterns will continue with new players. Further, the scandal will have a reinforcing effect. Successors will make sure they will not be caught so easily by examining where their predecessors went wrong and so reorganizing to make any repetition of exposure much harder. The people may change, but the system persists. Moreover, in the wider society, systemic corruption impedes rather than aids change.

(a) Systemic corruption perpetuates closed politics and restricts access, preventing the reflection of social change in political institutions.

(b) Systemic corruption suppresses opposition contributing to increasing resentment. Thus corruption far from being an alternative to violence is often accompanied by more violence.

(c) Systemic corruption perpetuates and widens class, economic, and social divisions, contributing to societal strain and preventing cohesion.

(d) Systemic corruption prevents policy change, particularly where this works against immediate market considerations. Individual or sectional interests are not the best guide to the public interest.

(e) Systemic corruption blocks administrative reform, and makes deleterious administrative practices profitable, e.g., induced delays.

(f) Systemic corruption diverts public resources and contributes to a situation of private affluence, public squalor, especially serious where affluence is confined to the few.

(g) Systemic corruption contributes to societal anomie in shoring up or transmuting traditional values into inappropriate areas.

(h) The effects of systemic corruption are not limited to a specific case: there is an accumulator effect upon public perceptions and expectations which subverts trust and cooperation far beyond the impact upon the individuals immediately concerned.

(i) Systemic corruption is not confined to poor, developing, or modernizing countries, but found in all organizational societies.

These hypotheses might better form the starting point for serious research into administrative corruption that the historically inaccurate assumptions and often unfounded assertions of the revisionists, who have confused individual and systemic corruption. In contemporary public administration, the issue is not so much individual misconduct in public, serious as that is, as the institutionalized subversion of the public interest through systemic corruption.

Endnotes

1. Ben Dor, G., "Corruption, Institutionalization and Political Development: The Revisionist Theses Revisited," *Comparative Political Studies,* Vol. 7 (April 1974), pp. 63-83.
2. Alatas, S.H., *The Sociology of Corruption: The Nature, Function, Cause and Prevention of Corruption* (Singapore: Donald Moore, 1968); Wraith, R., and E. Simpkins, *Corruption in Developing Countries* (New York: Norton, 1964); Myrdal, G., *Asian Drama: An Inquiry into the Poverty of Nations II* (New York: Twentieth Century, 1968), reproduced in A.J. Heidenheimer, *Political Corruption: Readings in Comparative Analysis* (New York: Holt Rinehart and Winston, 1970); Monteiro, J.B., *Corruption: Control of Maladministration* (Bombay: Manaktalas, 1966).
3. Steffens, L., "Los Angeles and the Apple," in J.A. Gardiner and D.J. Olson (eds.), *Theft of the City: Readings on Corruption in Urban America* (Bloomington: Indiana University Press, 1974).
4. Heidenheimer, A.J., *Political Corruption: Readings in Comparative Analysis* (New York: Holt, Rinehart and Winston, 1970).
5. Friedrich, C.J., "Political Pathology," *Political Quarterly,* Vol. 37 (1966), reproduced in A.J. Heidenheimer, *Political Corruption: Readings in Comparative Analysis* (New York: Holt, Rinehart and Winston, 1970).
6. Alatas, S.H., *The Sociology of Corruption: The Nature, Function, Cause and Prevention of Corruption* (Singapore: Donald Moore, 1968); Bayley, D.H., "The Effects of Corruption in a Developing Nation," *Western Political Quarterly,* Vol. 19 (December 1966), reproduced in A.J. Heidenheimer, *Political Corruption: Readings in Comparative Analysis* (New York: Holt, Rinehart and Winston, 1970); Huntington, S., *Political Order in Changing Societies* (New Haven: Yale University Press), reproduced as "Modernization and Corruption" in A.J. Heidenheimer, *Political Corruption: Readings in Comparative Analysis* (New York: Holt, Rinehart and Winston, 1970); McMullan, M., "A Theory of Corruption," *The Sociological Review* (Keele), Vol. 9 (July 1961), pp. 181-200.
7. Nye, J.S., "Corruption and Political Development: A Cost-Benefit Analysis," *American Political Science Review,* Vol. 61 (June 1967).
8. Heidenheimer, A.J., *Political Corruption: Readings in Comparative Analysis* (New York: Holt, Rinehart and Winston, 1970).
9. Guzman, R.P., et al., "Graft and Corruption: Issues in and Prospects for a Comparative Study of a Specific Type of Bureaucratic Behavior," paper prepared for the IDRC Project Development Meeting on Bureaucratic Behavior and Development, Baguio City, January 26-30, 1975.
10. Guzman, R.P., et al., "Graft and Corruption: Issues in and Prospects for a Comparative Study of a Specific Type of Bureaucratic Behavior," paper prepared for the IDRC Project Development Meeting on Bureaucratic Behavior and Development, Baguio City, January 26-30, 1975.
11. Tilman, R.D., "Emergence of Black-Market Bureaucracy: Administration, Development and Corruption in the New States," *Public Administration Review,* Vol. 28, No. 5 (September/October 1968), pp. 432-444.

*Understanding Fraud, Waste,
Abuse and Corruption*

12. Leff, N., "Economic Development through Bureaucratic Corruption," *American Behavioral Scientist,* Vol. 8 (November 1964), pp. 8-14.

13. McMullan, M., "A Theory of Corruption," *The Sociological Review* (Keele), Vol. 9 (July 1961), pp. 181-200.

14. Guzman, R.P., et al., "Graft and Corruption: Issues in and Prospects for a Comparative Study of a Specific Type of Bureaucratic Behavior," paper prepared for the IDRC Project Development Meeting on Bureaucratic Behavior and Development, Baguio City, January 26-30, 1975.

15. Carino, L.V., "Bureaucratic Behavior and Development: Types of Graft and Corruption in a Developing Country," paper presented at the Conference on the Political Economy of Development, Manila, 17-18 December 1974.

16. Abueva, J., "What Are We in Power For? The Sociology of Graft and Corruption," *Philippine Sociological Review,* Vol. 18 (July-October 1970), pp. 203-210.

17. Scott, J.C., *Comparative Political Corruption* (Englewood Cliffs, N.J.: Prentice Hall, 1972).

18. Van Roy, E., "On the Theory of Corruption," *Economic Development and Cultural Change* (October 1970), pp. 86-100.

19. Tilman, R.D., "Emergence of Black-Market Bureaucracy: Administration, Development and Corruption in the New States," *Public Administration Review,* Vol. 28, No. 5 (September/October 1968), pp. 432-444.

20. Merton, R., *Social Theory and Social Structure* (New York: Free Press, 1957).

21. Scott, J.C., *Comparative Political Corruption* (Englewood Cliffs, N.J.: Prentice Hall, 1972).

22. Scott, J.C., *Comparative Political Corruption* (Englewood Cliffs, N.J.: Prentice Hall, 1972).

23. Huntington, S., *Political Order in Changing Societies* (New Haven: Yale University Press), reproduced as "Modernization and Corruption" in A.J. Heidenheimer, *Political Corruption: Readings in Comparative Analysis,* pp. 492-500.

24. Scott, J.C., *Comparative Political Corruption* (Englewood Cliffs, N.J.: Prentice Hall, 1972).

25. Bayley, D.H., "The Effects of Corruption in a Developing Nation," *Western Political Quarterly,* Vol. 19 (December 1966), reproduced in A.J. Heidenheimer, *Political Corruption: Readings in Comparative Analysis,* pp. 521-533.

26. Huntington, S., *Political Order in Changing Societies* (New Haven: Yale University Press), reproduced as "Modernization and Corruption" in A.J. Heidenheimer, *Political Corruption: Readings in Comparative Analysis,* pp. 492-500.

27. Scott, J.C., *Comparative Political Corruption* (Englewood Cliffs, N.J.: Prentice Hall, 1972).

28. —— "The Contribution of Nepotism, Spoils and Graft to Political Development," *East-West Center Review,* Vol. 3 (June 1966), pp. 45-54, reproduced in A.J. Heidenheimer, *Political Corruption: Readings in Comparative Analysis* (New York: Holt, Rinehart and Winston, 1970).

29. Bayley, D.H., "The Effects of Corruption in a Developing Nation," *Western Political Quarterly,* Vol. 19 (December 1966), reproduced in A.J. Heidenheimer, *Political Corruption: Readings in Comparative Analysis.*

30. —— "The Contribution of Nepotism, Spoils and Graft to Political Development," *East-West Center Review,* Vol. 3 (June 1966), pp. 45-54, reproduced in A.J. Heidenheimer, *Political Corruption: Readings in Comparative Analysis* (New York: Holt, Rinehart and Winston, 1970).

31. Nye, J.S., "Corruption and Political Development: A Cost-Benefit Analysis," *American Political Science Review,* Vol. 61 (June 1967); Huntington, S., *Political Order in Changing Societies* (New Haven: Yale University Press), reproduced as "Modernization and Corruption" in A.J. Heidenheimer, *Political Corruption: Readings in Comparative Analysis* (New York: Holt, Rinehart and Winston, 1970).

32. —— "The Contribution of Nepotism, Spoils and Graft to Political Development," *East-West Center Review,* Vol. 3 (June 1966), pp. 45-54, reproduced in A.J. Heidenheimer, *Political Corruption: Readings in Comparative Analysis* (New York: Holt, Rinehart and Winston, 1970); Huntington, S., *Political Order in Changing Societies* (New Haven: Yale University Press), reproduced as "Modernization and Corruption" in A.J. Heidenheimer, *Political Corruption: Readings in Comparative Analysis* (New York: Holt, Rinehart and Winston, 1970).

33. Huntington, S., *Political Order in Changing Societies* (New Haven: Yale University Press), reproduced as "Modernization and Corruption" in A.J. Heidenheimer, *Political Corruption: Readings in Comparative Analysis* (New York: Holt, Rinehart and Winston, 1970).

34. Huntington, S., *Political Order in Changing Societies* (New Haven: Yale University Press), reproduced as "Modernization and Corruption" in A.J. Heidenheimer, *Political Corruption: Readings in Comparative Analysis* (New York: Holt, Rinehart and Winston, 1970).

35. Scott, J.C., *Comparative Political Corruption* (Englewood Cliffs, N.J.: Prentice Hall, 1972).

36. Bosher, J., *French Financial Administration 1770-1795: From Business to Bureaucracy* (Cambridge: Cambridge University Press, 1970).

37. Caiden, G.E., *The Dynamics of Public Administration* (New York: Holt, Rinehart and Winston, 1971).

38. Gopal, M.H., *Mauryan Public Finance* (London: Allen and Unwin, 1935); *Kaurilya, Arthasastra* (Shamasastry translation) (Mysore: Mysore Printing and Publishing House, 1961).

39. Boeckh, A., *The Public Economy of the Athenians* (London: John Murray, 1828).

40. Arnott, P.D., *The Romans and Their World* (London: St. Martin's Press, 1970).

41. Bonadeo, A., *Corruption, Conflict and Power in the Works and Times of Niccolo Machiavelli* (Berkeley: University of California Press, 1973).

42. Dent, J., "An Aspect of the Crisis of the Seventeenth Century: The Collapse of the Financial Administration of the French Monarchy 1653-61," *Economic History Review* (August 1967); Durand, Y., *Les Fermiers Generaux au xviii Siecle* (Paris: Presses Universitaires de France, 1971); —— *Crisis in France: Crown, Financiers and Society in Seventeenth Century France* (Newton Abbot: David and Charles, 1973); —— "Cambres de Justice in the French Monarchy," in J. Bosher (ed.), *French Government and Society 1500-1850* (London: Athlone, 1973).

43. Caiden, N., and A. Wildavsky, *Planning and Budgeting in Poor Countries* (New York: Wiley, 1974).

44. Bosher, J., *French Financial Administration 1770-1795: From Business to Bureaucracy* (Cambridge: Cambridge University Press, 1970).

Not Easy: Honest Government Possible

James T. Ryan

In this brief essay, a former city mayor in Illinois outlines a set of principles for ethical behavior in local government. Do governments today meet these standards? Are any of the principles undesirable or unrealistic? Would some or all of Ryan's positions be appropriate for state government as well?

A reputation as a no-nonsense, honest municipality is not acquired overnight. It must be earned and maintained. I know of no shortcut to this goal. I can, however, outline the 10 basic principles a community committed to honest government must be willing to meet to ensure that result:

An informed electorate. The people served by the municipality must set the tone of the kind of government they wish to represent them. In order to do this, they must be informed. While the media play a significant part, the local municipality must also play a major role. Informational handouts, specialized informational packets for new residents, periodic municipal newsletters, periodic questionnaires and the like are conduits that a municipality must be willing to utilize.

A participating electorate. A municipal government whose structure permits a high degree of participation by numerous interested individuals provides an opportunity for future elected officials to experience governmental operations firsthand without having to accept the final responsibility for legislative and policy decisions. The more citizens are involved in government, the more likely government is to serve all the people rather than a select few.

An experienced and professional municipal manager. The Law Enforcement Assistance Administration's recent study gives considerable credit to the city manager form of government for our community's exemplary record. There should be no politics in providing basic day-to-day municipal operations.

Policy established by elected officials. All policy decisions must be decided on behalf of the electorate by their elected officials. Once having established policy there must be follow-through and follow-up to ensure that the policy is being implemented. Policy manuals must also be maintained and regularly updated so that administration personnel are provided guidelines in carrying out policy.

Clear lines of demarcation between policy and administration. Once it is established that policy is to be developed by elected officials and administered by municipal employees, constant attention must be focused on this division of responsibility lest policy be changed by the manner in which it is administered or administration be hindered or interfered with by those establishing policy.

Adoption of anti-corruption ordinances and procedures. It is not enough to know what is right and proper, for right and proper may mean one thing to one person and another thing to another person. Elected officials should be prevented by statute from voting on measures that concern them, and financial-disclosure affidavits should be required of all elected and appointed officials as well as of key municipal employees. Ethics ordinances are an additional must, for even the appearance of impropriety must be avoided in order to ensure public trust and confidence.

Municipal meetings. With the exception of personnel matters and litigation, all municipal meetings must be open to the spotlight of public scrutiny as well as the scrutiny of the press. When executive or closed sessions are held, the purpose of the meeting must be clearly indicated and discussion limited to that purpose. An open government is far less likely to result in private benefit than a closed, secretive form of government.

Competitive compensation for municipal employees. Municipal employees pay the same amount of money for goods and services that private individuals do, and as a result they must be compensated accordingly. Individuals who are fairly compensated develop a feeling of their worth as well as receive tangible indication of the community's estimation of their worth. The resulting pride in one's job and one's performance is inimical to payoffs and kick-backs.

Source: James T. Ryan, "Not Easy: Honest Government Possible," *Christian Science Monitor.*

Control of employees' outside employments. A hard and fast rule at certain job levels against outside employment is impractical. However, moonlighting that does take place must be approved by the municipality and monitored and controlled where municipal job performance suffers or is likely to suffer, or where a conflict of interest results or is likely to result.

Understanding Fraud, Waste, Abuse and Corruption

An enforceable "no-gift" policy. Gifts to municipal employees are frequently offered in good faith but just as frequently offered in the hope of obtaining special benefit. In either case, all gifts to municipal employees must be refused.

In the final analysis, it is people who must commit their community to honest government. Constant vigilance is required, but at the same time a reputation, a feeling of honesty, a feeling of equal dealing to developing and this, in and of itself, aids the commitment of the people involved.

People appreciate this kind of government. People stop asking for favorable treatment. They neither offer nor accept favors, and those involved say it becomes an exceptional experience — and exceptional and exciting it is. With a few more examples of how it can work, it might even become the rule.

Corruption in Government: A Rational Approach to Reform
Edward I. Koch

Corruption has, in every age, been a feature of both government and private life. No system and no amount of human energy will ever be sufficient to eradicate corruption. Yet, with an understanding of these limitations, we must be ever vigilant and never tolerate corruption, to any degree. It is a poison that will spread if not constantly checked. On the other hand, exaggerating the presence of corruption can greatly demoralize those in public service, discourage good men and women from entering the public fray, erode institutional standards of fair play, and impede the effective functioning of government.

In the end, the experience of the last two years in the public life of New York City teaches us that systematic, even-handed, fact-oriented inquiry is the only process through which the true character of the problem can emerge and upon which intelligent reform can be predicted. Rhetorical excess, of which there has been much during this period, only obscures and impedes the necessary work of reform. At times, only scant attention was paid to crucial distinctions between criminal conduct on the one hand and poor judgment, lack of vigilance, or insensitivity to appearances on the other. If one chooses in such circumstances to define corruption in other than legal terms and lumps such conduct indiscriminately with that of extortionists and bribe takers, standards of virtue and sin become very confused indeed. This, in turn, can lead to an excess from the opposite point — to hold no one accountable publicly whose misdeeds do not sink to the level of crime. Although public officials must be held to a high standard, what is needed is the measure of balance and fairness that holds each official accountable, but only to the precise limits of the delinquency established.

From the perspective of New York City Mayor Edward Koch, corruption may be divided into three groupings: (1) bureaucratic corruption, which roughly corresponds to what Caiden and Caiden call "systemic" corruption; (2) standards of personal behavior; and (3) the intersection of political influence and governmental decision-making. Is his view that (2) represents a "wholly different problem" from (1) persuasive? Are there powerful groups other than political parties which can have corrupting effects of the kind which Koch describes under his category (3)? Some of the reforms Koch advocates are discussed further in Part III of this volume.

Categories of Corruption

Having said this, I think it useful, first, to address the corruption problem from three very different perspectives: bureaucratic corruption in the agencies, wrongdoing in the personal behavior of individual officials, and the improper peddling of influence in governmental decision making by party officials who seek to capitalize personally on a real or perceived political alliance with persons holding public office. These discrete categories of the corruption problem as it has evolved during the past two years present different administrative and public policy questions.

Source: Edward I. Koch, "Corruption in Government: A Rational Approach to Reform," *City Almanac*, 20:1-2 (1987), pp. 5, 8-9.

The first category, *bureaucratic corruption,* represents the principal and ongoing challenge to governments at all levels. The more complex governmental organization becomes, the more difficult is the task of keeping it corruption free. Problems range from persistent patterns of gratuity and bribe-receiving in, for example, the inspectional services, to sophisticated manipulation for improper advantage of contracting, land use, or franchising procedures.

New York City employs tens of thousands of street enforcement agents and lets billions of dollars in public contracts. The purchasing function of the city government dwarfs that of many countries. The oversight and control mechanisms, therefore, must be equal to the intricate and differentiated power exercised in these bureaucracies. In this respect, we have taken unprecedented reform measures during the last two years to render our anticorruption machinery more powerful, more flexible, and more effective.

The second category, concerning the *standards of personal behavior* for those in office, represents a wholly different problem. The assessment of character, judgment, and, more ambiguously, collateral relationships, as these three considerations relate to the qualifications of potential appointees and those already in office, is extraordinarily difficult. Who among us has not been surprised and disappointed with respect to the conduct of those we have admired and, indeed, even emulated? But it cannot be denied that terrible damage is done to the public's respect for government when it learns that high officials have not paid their income taxes, have created no-show jobs, entered into secret business relationships to profit from government contracts, lied on disclosure documents, intentionally misled the press and the public, or misused their positions in some other way to benefit themselves and their friends.

This aspect of New York City's corruption problem has been dealt with, in the first instance, by the employment of far more effective investigative machinery to detect and expose hidden conflicts and deficiencies. Furthermore, strengthening the penalties for such derelictions will surely have a greater deterrent effect. Most important, legal disclosure requirements have been strengthened and the capacity of the Department of Investigation to achieve comprehensive character assessments of prospective appointees has been enhanced.

The third category, relating to the *nexus of political power and governmental decision making,* has been the most spectacular feature of New York City's corruption problem. The successful prosecution of Stanley Friedman and others in the Parking Violations Bureau case demonstrates the poisons that can overwhelm public business where party influence is put to work, especially when weak investigative systems and poor leadership in the investigative process inadvertently impede its exposure.

An examination of the two principal documents relating to the scandal is instructive in deriving guidance on how this problem ought to be addressed. The first document is the proceedings record of the Friedman trial itself, and the second is the formal report of the Martin Commission, which I appointed to determine why allegations brought to the Department of Investigation in 1982 relating to the integrity of a data and judgment collection contract at the Parking Violations Bureau were not adequately pursued.

These documents demonstrate, beyond any question, that such corruption must be fought through effective, conventional law enforcement techniques. These may include integrity testing, sting operations, electronic eavesdropping, and other forms of surveillance, as well as the granting of immunity to disreputable characters. But in doing so, we must be sensitive to civil liberties and privacy rights. Thus, these often controversial investigative techniques should be resorted to only on a case-specific basis and should be grounded on a sound legal and factual predicate. They are, when competently and professionally carried out, a significant defense against crimes like those of Donald Manes and Stanley Friedman.

Our experiences over the past two years indicate that, regrettably, flaws exist in the structure of government that will inevitably lead some individuals to behave unethically, if not illegally. Although I have seen it in my own administration, and while it has led to great disappointment, fortunately, fact does not meet perception. Since January 1, 1986, six administration officials have been indicted, and four others have resigned, not because of criminal conduct but because of poor judgment, lack of vigilance, or insensitivity to appearances. With only these few individuals from this administration having been indicted or convicted, or having resigned for lesser misdeeds, it would be unfair to impugn the integrity of their 300,000 colleagues in New York City government.

But these instances of corruption have also formed the impetus for some much needed reforms, and the remainder of this article identifies those areas of reform, the changes we have implemented to eradicate the flaws in our system, and additional changes we are working toward.

Major Areas Requiring Reform

The use of public or political party positions for personal enrichment. Illegal profiteering by public or party officials by extortion, the accepting of bribes, or other felonious activity is certainly not a new phenomenon. The paradigm of this in the city's recent experience is the personal greed of Stanley Friedman and Donald Manes in the securing of two major contracts with the Parking Violations Bureau. Yet, to fully understand the meaning of this case, one must look beyond the discrete facts of the contract award process, which we have reformed and continue to reform, and address the intricate web of influence, power, and retainer profits that both Friedman and Manes controlled.

Friedman's law practice was, in practical terms, shaped and enriched exclusively as a result of his powerful party position. His legal practice was devoted almost totally to lobbying politicians and their aides in the city and state governments on behalf of private clients. In 1985, Friedman earned over $900,000 from his "law" practice; however, the scope of any inquiry into the genesis and dimensions of this profiteering should not end with Friedman. Other cases that reveal the form and substance of such corruption include the interrelationship of Donald Manes' public and party positions, his role in contract decisions at the Board of Estimate, and his control over court guardianships and assignments. Also instructive is the case of Richard Rubin, a democratic party official who used his influence in the party to facilitate his dealings with various public officials.

Disclosure laws. Related to the problem discussed above is the issue of how extensive disclosure obligations should be and how to devise adequate bars to conflicts of interest necessary to prevent corruption. Disclosure laws have been promulgated principally to uncover hidden interests of people holding positions of public trust and to deter conflicts of interest. Government officials must be willing to provide information that is rationally related to their ability to perform their public duties in a forthright and unbiased manner.

Ideally, such disclosure, on a confidential basis to professional investigators, should serve to enhance public confidence in government. However, unless the procedures for reviewing the disclosed information are efficient and comprehensive and sanctions for eroding or violating disclosure and conflict of interest rules are enforced, disclosure laws, in practice, will do little more than create cartons of unread documents. We have substantially increased the resources of the Department of Investigation and dealt severely with those who have misled investigators on such matters.

Financial and background disclosure forms serve several functions. First, they are intended to reveal whether a candidate for public employment is qualified for the position he or she seeks to hold. Second, they provide some basis for determining the honesty of the candidate by allowing for independent verification of the information provided. Third, they are designed to bring to light areas in which a candidate's personal relationships of financial involvements conflict with his or her public office. It is in this last regard that disclosure requirements are especially valuable as a tool to prevent corruption.

Sadly, some who recognize that a relationship creates a conflict of interest and seek to hide that fact will always try to devise a method for doing so by, for example, holding property in someone else's name, concealing the true nature of an interest in a dummy corporation, hiding assets in a blind trust, or simply refusing to list a known asset. The Department of Investigation is now committed to and is, in fact, following up the receipt of disclosure documents with proactive, aggressive field work in appropriate cases.

Conflicts of interest. There are, nevertheless, weaknesses in existing enforcement machinery relating to unethical practices. The viability of the statutory and institutional controls in the city and state with respect to conflicts of interest and ethics generally has been a principal focus of the scandal. As the state has recently enacted improved statutory controls, so should the city. Section 2604 of the city charter should be amended to make it clear that a plea of ignorance of the specific provisions of the law will not deflect criminal charges! We must clarify, simplify, and strengthen our conflict-of-interest law so that criminal prosecution is a viable and realistic threat to those public officials whose ethical standards are too low, too loose, and too convenient.

The problem of public officials and political party leaders representing private clients before public agencies is commonly thought by the public to constitute trafficking in office. No elected or public official should personally represent, or indirectly through his or her law firm represent, any private individual or interest before a state agency, public benefit corporation, or public authority, whether or not compensated. The Sovern Commission took a similar position. The State Legislature's recently passed ethics bill does place some restrictions on this practice. However, the interests of the public are best served and the restoration of public confidence in the governmental process will only result with a blanket restriction on this practice by both public officials and those in business with or in professional association with them.

State political party officials should be barred from appearing before or lobbying governmental agencies, and city party officials, now barred from appearing before city agencies, should also be prohibited from appearing before state agencies. The risk that favored treatment will result simply because of the individual's party position is too great to permit this practice.

Selection of judges. The judiciary in New York City has sadly not remained unscathed during the corruption scandal. Two sitting state supreme court justices, Brennan and Smith, both with strong ties to the Queens County Democratic organization, have been convicted of felonies. The case of Justice Brennan involved the misuse of his official position, while the case of Justice Smith concerned the misuse of political connections. Furthermore, the trial and conviction of Stanley Friedman highlighted his action in 1983 by which he blocked the renomination of two qualified sitting supreme court justices so that two more politically connected candidates could be elected to take the incumbent's place.

These are concrete examples of the pernicious effect clubhouse politics can have on the fair and honest selection and conduct of the judiciary. The practice of judges running for election following their nomination by one of the political parties gives great discretion to political leaders, who usually control the nominating process. Such discretion may result in the election of judges who are not of the highest professional or ethical character and who are more loyal to their political benefactors than to their official duties. It is, therefore, imperative that all judges in New York be appointed by the highest officers of the executive branch (such as the governor or mayor) following merit selection of candidates by a nominating commission. The openness of the merit selection process, which allows decisive roles for several disinterested segments of the legal community, as well as the public, ensures that the process is free from the pernicious influence of clubhouse politics.

Public financing of political campaigns. The proposed local law providing for public financing of election campaigns prepared by Corporation Counsel Peter Zimroth and the Department of Law, and introduced in the City Council at my request bears on matters that are critically important in the fight against corruption. The proposed local law would create a system of optional public financing of campaigns for candidates for New York City elective offices. In return for public funding, candidates would agree to limit their receipt of private contributions and their overall expenditures. By providing candidates access to campaign funds, thereby freeing them from reliance on the largesse of wealthy contributors, this bill would reduce the possibility of undue influence on elected officials and reduce the apathy and cynicism of citizens who now perceive that privilege and favoritism play a major role in the city's decision-making process. In addition, public financing of campaigns could open up the political process to persons who do not have access to private money or to the political party apparatus.

Protecting the whistle-blowers. Under Local Law 10 of 1984 and executive Order 78, dated October 5, 1984, city officers and employees are prohibited from taking adverse action against personnel in retaliation for the reporting of information involving corruption, criminal activity, conflict of interest, gross misconduct, or abuse of authority. I strongly believe that government employees should be encouraged to report corruption and be protected when they do.

The Department of Investigation created a special whistle-blower unit in August 1986 to centralize whistle-blower complaints and to ensure that all whistle-blower investigations are given thorough and immediate attention. Investigative conclusions reached in whistle-blower cases are reviewed by the department's general counsel and then by the first deputy commissioner, and if approved, the findings are sent to the appropriate agency head.

The Department of Investigation receives an average of 250 complaints a month from both city employees and the general public, many of them anonymous. It has received up to 650 complaints in some months. Only a very small percentage of these complaints, however, involve assertions by city employees that they have suffered adverse personnel action for reporting corruption. Accordingly, the vast majority of such complainants are not whistle-blowers under the formal terms of Local Law 10. Of course, the department investigates whatever it perceives to be a legitimate complaint even if the source does not fall into the legal whistle-blower category. City employees are a vital and indispensable source of information in the investigation, exposure, and reduction of corruption in government. It is the determined policy of this administration that all city employees participate fully and freely in the campaign against corruption.

Understanding Fraud, Waste, Abuse and Corruption

Conclusion

I have committed an unprecedented amount of resources to the anticorruption effort and authorized the greatest aggregate resource increase, by far, in the 114-year history of the Department of Investigation. Major structural changes in anticorruption techniques and machinery have been accomplished, and others are being designed, including major reorganization of the inspector general system, broad cross-designation with prosecutors and involvement in the grand jury process, and the introduction of computers to better organize and control the investigative case process.

I believe that there is a new awareness among the many able and honest commissioners in the government that to fulfill the duties of one's place, vigilance against the hazards of corruption and against corrupt acts must be utterly uncompromising. Yoking our resolve to this commitment will surely lead to a sounder government for New York.

"Why Should My Conscience Bother Me?"
Kermit Vandivier

The B.F. Goodrich Company is what business magazines like to refer to as "a major American corporation." It has operations in a dozen states and as many foreign countries; and of these far-flung facilities, the Goodrich plant at Troy, Ohio, is not the most imposing. It is a small, one-story building, once used to manufacture airplanes. Set in the grassy flatlands of west-central Ohio, it employs only about six hundred people. Nevertheless, it is one of the three largest manufacturers of aircraft wheels and brakes, a leader in a most profitable industry. Goodrich wheels and brakes support such well-known planes as the F111, the C5A, the Boeing 727, the XB70, and many others. Its customers include almost every aircraft manufacturer in the world.

Contracts for aircraft wheels and brakes often run into millions of dollars, and ordinarily a contract with a total value of less then $70,000, though welcome, would not create any special stir of joy in the hearts of Goodrich sales personnel. But purchase order P-23718, issued on June 18, 1967, by the LTV Aerospace Corporation, and ordering 202 brake assemblies for a new Air Force plane at a total price of $69,417, was received by Goodrich with considerable glee. And there was good reason. Some ten years previously, Goodrich had built a brake for LTV that was, to say the least, considerably less than a rousing success. The brake had not lived up to Goodrich's promises, and after experiencing considerable difficulty, LTV had written off Goodrich as a source of brakes. Since that time, Goodrich salesmen had been unable to sell so much as a shot of brake fluid to LTV. So in 1967, when LTV requested bids on wheels and brakes for the new A7D light attack aircraft it proposed to build for the Air Force, Goodrich submitted a bid that was absurdly low, so low that LTV could not, in all prudence, turn it down.

Goodrich had, in industry parlance, "bought into the business." Not only did the company not expect to make a profit on the deal; it was prepared, if necessary, to lose money. For aircraft brakes are not something that can be ordered off the shelf. They are designed for a particular aircraft, and once an aircraft manufacturer buys a brake, he is forced to purchase all replacement parts from the brake manufacturer. The $70,000 that Goodrich would get for making the brake would be a drop in the bucket when compared with the cost of the linings and other parts the Air Force would have to buy from Goodrich during the lifetime of the aircraft. . . .

This "cautionary tale" is set in a private corporation, but the pressures that undermine integrity as described here are found in public as well as private organizations. Moreover, as a study of government contracting, the case suggests that the interface between the private and public sectors provides a fertile ground for unethical behavior and ineffective management. The recent defense procurement scandals, discussed in later selections below, underscore the continuing relevance of Vandivier's story.

This essay can be converted into a decision-forcing case which will encourage a wide range of student ideas and insights, by adding one or two future-oriented questions. For example: (1) Assume that you are the president of B.F. Goodrich, that you have read Vandivier's account in an early draft and determined (through your own inquiry) that it is essentially accurate, and that the Proxmire hearings are to commence in a few days. What actions would you take? Would you, for example, admit at the hearing that a number of your officials have been engaged in fraud? (2) If you were an Air Force official with responsibility for contracting, and if you concluded that the Vandivier article was essentially accurate, what remedies — oriented to contracting with private corporations generally — would you consider?

There was another factor which had undoubtedly influenced LTV. All aircraft brakes made today are of the disk type, and the bid submitted by Goodrich called for a relatively small brake, one containing four disks and weighing only 106 pounds. The weight of any aircraft part is extremely important: the lighter a part is, the heavier the plane's payload can be. . . .

The brake was designed by one of Goodrich's most capable engineers, John Warren. A tall, lanky blond and a graduate of Purdue, Warren had come from the Chrysler Corporation seven years before and had become adept at aircraft brake design. The happy-go-lucky manner he usually maintained belied a temper that exploded whenever anyone ventured to offer criticism of his work, no matter how small. On these occasions, Warren would turn red in the face, often throwing or slamming something and then stalking from the scene. As his coworkers learned the consequences of criticizing him, they did so less and less readily, and when he submitted his preliminary design for the A7D brake, it was accepted without question.

Warren was named project engineer for the A7D, and he, in turn, assigned the task of producing the final production design to a newcomer to the Goodrich engineering stable, Searle Lawson. Just turned twenty-six, Lawson had been out of the Northrop Institute of Technology only one year when he came to Goodrich in January 1967. . . . At the Troy plant, Lawson had been assigned to various "paper projects" to break him in, and after several months spent reviewing statistics and old brake designs, he was beginning to fret at the lack of challenge. When told he was being assigned to his first "real" project, he was elated and immediately plunged into his work.

The major portion of the design had already been completed by Warren, and major assemblies for the brake had already been ordered from Goodrich suppliers. Naturally, however, before Goodrich could start making the brakes on a production basis, much testing would have to be done. Lawson would have to determine the best materials to use for the linings and discover what minor adjustments in the design would have to be made.

Then, after the preliminary testing and after the brake was judged ready for production, one whole brake assembly would undergo a series of grueling, simulated braking stops and other severe trials called qualifications tests. These tests are required by the military, which gives very detailed specifications on how they are to be conducted, the criteria for failure, and so on. They are performed in the Goodrich plant's test laboratory, where huge machines called dynamometers can simulate the weight and speed of almost any aircraft. . . .

Searle Lawson was well aware that much work had to be done before the A7D brake could go into production, and he knew well that LTV had set the last two weeks in June, 1968, as the starting dates for flight tests. So he decided to begin testing immediately. Goodrich's suppliers had not yet delivered the brake housing and other parts, but the brake disks had arrived, and using the housing from a brake similar in size and weight to the A7D brake, Lawson built a prototype. The prototype was installed in a test wheel and placed on one of the big dynamometers in the plant's test laboratory. The dynamometer was adjusted to simulate the weight of the A7D and Lawson began a series of tests, "landing" the wheel and brake at the A7D's landing speed and braking it to a stop. The main purpose of these preliminary tests was to learn what temperatures would develop within the brake during the simulated stops and to evaluate lining materials tentatively selected for use.

During a normal aircraft landing the temperatures inside the brake may reach 1000 degrees, and occasionally a bit higher. During Lawson's first simulated landings, the temperatures of his prototype brake reached 1500 degrees. The brake glowed a bright cherry-red and threw off incandescent particles of metal and lining material as the temperature reached its peak. After a few such stops, the brake was dismantled and the linings were found to be almost completely disintegrated. Lawson chalked this first failure up to chance and, ordering new lining materials, tried again.

Source: Kermit Vandivier, "Why Should My Conscience Bother Me," in Robert L. Heilbroner, ed., *In the Name of Profit* (Garden City, NY: Doubleday & Company, 1972), pp. 3-31.

The second attempt was a repeat of the first. The brake became extremely hot, causing the lining materials to crumble into dust.

After the third such failure, Lawson, inexperienced though he was, knew that the fault lay not in defective parts or unsuitable lining material but in the basic design of the brake itself. Ignoring Warren's original computations, Lawson made his own, and it didn't take him long to discover where the trouble lay — the brake was too small. There simply was not enough surface area on the disks to stop the aircraft without generating the excessive heat that caused the linings to fail.

The answer to the problem was obvious, but far from simple — the four-disk brake would have to be scrapped, and a new design, using five disks, would have to be developed. The implications were not lost on Lawson. Such a step would require junking the four-disk-brake subassemblies, many of which had now begun to arrive from various suppliers. It would also mean several weeks of preliminary design and testing and many more weeks of waiting while the suppliers made and delivered the new subassemblies.

Yet, several weeks had already gone by since LTV's order had arrived, and the date for the delivery of the first production brakes for flight testing was only a few months away.

Although John Warren had more or less turned the A7D over to Lawson, he knew of the difficulties Lawson had been experiencing. He had assured the young engineer that the problem revolved around getting the right kind of lining material. Once that was found, he said, the difficulties would end.

Despite the evidence of the abortive tests and Lawson's careful computations, Warren rejected the suggestion that the four-disk brake was too light for the job. He knew that his superior had already told LTV, in rather glowing terms, that the preliminary tests on the A7D brake were very successful. Indeed, Warren's superiors weren't aware at this time of the troubles on the brake. It would have been difficult for Warren to admit not only that he had made a serious error in his calculations and original design but that his mistakes had been caught by a green kid, barely out of college.

Warren's reaction to a five-disk brake was not unexpected by Lawson, and, seeing that the four-disk brake was not to be abandoned so easily, he took his calculations and dismal test results one step up the corporate ladder.

At Goodrich, the man who supervises the engineers working on projects slated for production is called, predictably, the projects manager. The job was held by a short, chubby and bald man named Robert Sink. . . . Some fifteen years before, Sink had begun working at Goodrich as a lowly draftsman. Slowly, he worked his way up. Despite his geniality, Sink was neither respected nor liked by the majority of the engineers, and his appointment as their supervisor did not improve their feelings toward him. They thought he had only gone to high school. It quite naturally rankled those who had gone through years of college . . . to be commanded by a man whom they considered their intellectual inferior. But, though Sink had no college training, he had something even more useful: a fine working knowledge of company politics.

Puffing on a Meerschaum pipe, Sink listened gravely as young Lawson confided his fears about the four-disk brake. Then he examined Lawson's calculations and the results of the abortive tests. Despite the fact that he was not a qualified engineer, in the strictest sense of the word, it must certainly have been obvious to Sink that Lawson's calculations were correct and that a four-disk brake would never had worked on the A7D.

But other things of equal importance were also obvious. First, to concede that Lawson's calculations were correct would also mean conceding that Warren's calculations were incorrect. As projects manager, not only was he responsible for Warren's activities, but, in admitting that Warren had erred, he would have to admit that he had erred in trusting Warren's judgment. It also meant that, as projects manager, it would be he who would have to explain the whole messy situation to the Goodrich hierarchy, not only at Troy but possibly on the corporate level at Goodrich's Akron offices. And having taken Warren's judgment of the four-disk brake at face value . . . , he had assured LTV, not once but several times, that about all there was left to do on the brake was pack it in a crate and ship it out the back door.

There's really no problem at all, he told Lawson. After all, Warren was an experienced engineer, and if he said the brake would work, it would work. Just keep on testing and probably, maybe even on the very next try, it'll work out just fine.

Lawson was far from convinced, but without the support of his superiors there was little he could do except keep on testing. By now housings for the four-disk brake had begun to arrive at the plant, and Lawson was able to build a production model of the brake and begin the formal qualification tests demanded by the military.

The first qualification attempts went exactly as the tests on the prototype had. Terrific heat developed within the brakes and, after a few, short, simulated stops, the linings crumbled. A new type of lining material was ordered and once again an attempt to qualify the brake was made. Again, failure.

Experts were called in from lining manufacturers, and new lining "mixes" were tried, always with the same result. Failure.

It was now the last week in March 1968, and flight tests were scheduled to begin in seventy days. Twelve separate attempts had been made to qualify the brake, and all had failed. It was no longer possible for anyone to ignore the glaring truth that the brake was a dismal failure and that nothing short of a major design change could ever make it work.

In the engineering department, panic set in. A glum-faced Lawson prowled the test laboratory dejectedly. Occasionally, Warren would witness some simulated stop on the brake and, after it was completed, troop silently back to his desk. Sink, too, showed an unusual interest in the trials, and he and Warren would converse in low tones while poring over the results of the latest tests. Even the most inexperienced of the lab technicians and the men who operated the testing equipment knew they had a "bad" brake on their hands, and there was some grumbling about "wasting time on a brake that won't work."

New menaces appeared. An engineering team from LTV arrived at the plant to get a good look at the brake in action. Luckily, they stayed only a few days, and Goodrich engineers managed to cover the true situation without too much difficulty.

On April 4, the thirteenth attempt at qualification was begun. This time no attempt was made to conduct the tests by the methods and techniques spelled out in the military specifications. Regardless of how it had to be done, the brake was to be "nursed" through the required fifty simulated stops.

Fans were set up to provide special cooling. Instead of maintaining pressure on the brake until the wheel had come to a complete stop, the pressure was reduced when the wheel had decelerated to around 15 mph, allowing it to "coast" to a stop. After each stop, the brake was disassembled and carefully cleaned, and after some of the stops, internal brake parts were machined in order to remove warp and other disfigurations caused by the high heat.

By these and other methods, all clearly contrary to the techniques established by the military specifications, the brake was coaxed through the fifty stops. But even using these methods, the brake could not meet all the requirements. On one stop the wheel rolled for a distance of 16,000 feet, or over three miles, before the brake could bring it to a stop. The normal distance required for such a stop was around 3500 feet.

On April 11, the day the thirteenth test was completed, I became personally involved in the A7D situation.

I had worked in the Goodrich test laboratory for five years, starting first as an instrumentation engineer, then later becoming a data analyst and technical writer. As part of my duties, I analyzed the reams and reams of instrumentation data that came from the many testing machines in the lab, then transcribed all of it to a more usable form for the engineering department. And when a new-type brake had successfully completed the required qualification tests, I would issue a formal qualification report.

Qualification reports were an accumulation of all the data and test logs compiled during the qualification tests and were documentary proof that a brake had met all the requirements established by the military specifications and was therefore presumed safe for flight testing. Before actual flight tests were conducted on a brake, qualification reports had to be delivered to the customer and to various government officials.

On April 11, I was looking over the data from the latest A7D test, and I noticed that many irregularities in testing methods had been noted on the test logs.

Technically, of course, there was nothing wrong with conducting tests in any manner desired, so long as the test was for research purposes only. But qualification test methods are clearly delineated by the military, and I knew that this test had been a formal qualification attempt. One particular notation on the test logs caught my eye. For some of the stops, the instrument that recorded the brake pressure had been deliberately miscalibrated so that, while the brake pressure used during the stops was recorded as 1000 psi (the maximum pressure that would be available on the A7D aircraft), the pressure had actually been 1100 psi.

I showed the test logs to the test lab supervisor, Ralph Gretzinger, who said he had learned from the technician who had miscalibrated the instrument that he had been asked to do so by Lawson. Lawson, said Gretzinger, readily admitted asking for the miscalibration, saying he had been told to do so by Sink.

I asked Gretzinger why anyone would want to miscalibrate the data-recording instruments.

"Why? I'll tell you why," he snorted. "That brake is a failure. It's way too small for the job, and they're not ever going to get it to work. They're getting desperate and instead of scrapping the damned thing and starting over, they figure they can horse around down here in the lab and qualify it that way."

An expert engineer, Gretzinger had been responsible for several innovations in brake design. It was he who had invented the unique brake system used on the famous XB70. "If you want to find out what's going on," said Gretzinger, "ask Lawson; he'll tell you."

Curious, I did ask Lawson the next time he came into the lab. He seemed eager to discuss the A7D and gave me the history of his months of frustrating efforts to get Warren and Sink to change the brake design. "I just can't believe this is really happening," said Lawson, shaking his head slowly. "This isn't engineering, at least not what I thought it would be. Back in school, I thought that when you were an engineer, you tried to do your best, no matter what it cost. But this is something else."

He sat across the desk from me, his chin propped in his hand. "Just wait," he warned. "You'll get a chance to see what I'm talking about. You're going to get in the act too, because I've already had the word that we're going to make one more attempt to qualify the brake, and that's it. Win or lose, we're going to issue a qualification report!"

I reminded him that a qualification report could be issued only after a brake had successfully met all military requirements, and therefore, unless the next qualification attempt was a success, no report would be issued.

"You'll find out," retorted Lawson. "I was already told that regardless of what the brake does on test, it's going to be qualified." He said he had been told in those exact words at a conference with Sink and Russell Van Horn.

This was the first indication that Sink had brought his boss, Van Horn, into the mess. Although Van Horn, as manager of the design engineering section, was responsible for the entire department, he was not necessarily familiar with all phases of every project, and it was not uncommon for those under him to exercise the what-he-doesn't-know-won't-hurt-him philosophy. If he was aware of the full extent of the A7D situation, it meant that matters had truly reached a desperate stage — that Sink had decided not only to call for help but was looking toward that moment when blame must be borne and, if possible, shared.

Also, if Van Horn had said, "regardless of what the brake does on test, it's going to be qualified," then it could only mean that, if necessary, a false qualification report would be issued! I discussed this possibility with Gretzinger, and he assured me that under no circumstances would such a report ever be issued.

"If they want a qualification report, we'll write them one, but we'll tell it just like it is," he declared emphatically. "No false data or false reports are going to come out of this lab."

On May 2, 1968, the fourteenth and final attempt to qualify the brake was begun. Although the same improper methods used to nurse the brake through the previous tests were employed, it soon became obvious that this too would end in failure.

When the tests were about half completed, Lawson asked if I would start preparing the various engineering curves and graphic displays that were normally incorporated in a qualification report. . . .

I flatly refused to have anything to do with the matter and immediately told Gretzinger what I had been asked to do. He was furious and repeated his previous declaration that under no circumstances would any false data or other matter be issued from the lab.

"I'm going to get this settled right now, once and for all," he declared. "I'm going to see Line [Russell Line, manager of the Goodrich Technical Services Section, of which the test lab was a part] and find out just how far this thing is going to go!" He stormed out of the room.

In about an hour, he returned and called me to his desk. He sat silently for a few moments, then muttered, half to himself, "I wonder what the hell they'd do if I just quit?" I didn't answer and I didn't ask him what he meant. I knew. He had been beaten down. He had reached the point when the decision had to be made. Defy them now while there was still time — or knuckle under, sell out.

"You know," he went on uncertainly, looking down at his desk, "I've been an engineer for a long time, and I've always believed that ethics and integrity were every bit as important as theorems and formulas, and never once has anything happened to change my beliefs. Now this . . . Hell, I've got two sons I've got to put through school and I just. . . ." His voice trailed off.

He sat a few more minutes, then, looking over the top of his glasses, said hoarsely, "Well, it looks like we're licked. The way it stands now, we're to go ahead and prepare the data and other things for the graphic presentation in the report and when we're finished, someone upstairs will actually write the report.

"After all," he continued, "we're just drawing some curves, and what happens to them after they leave here, well, we're not responsible for that.". . .

I wasn't at all satisfied with the situation and decided that I too would discuss the matter with Russell Line, the senior executive in our section.

Tall, powerfully built, his teeth flashing white, his face tanned to a coffee-brown by a daily stint with a sunlamp, Line looked and acted every inch an executive. . . . He had been transferred from the Akron offices some two years previously, and . . . he commanded great respect and had come to be well liked by those of us who worked under him.

He listened sympathetically while I explained how I felt about the A7D situation, and when I had finished, he asked me what I wanted him to do about it. I said that as employees of the Goodrich Company we had a responsibility to protect the company and its reputation if at all possible. I said I was certain that officers on the corporate level would never knowingly allow such tactics as had been employed on the A7D.

"I agree with you," he remarked, "but I still want to know what you want me to do about it."

I suggested that in all probability the chief engineer at the Troy plant, H.C. "Bud" Sunderman, was unaware of the A7D problem and that he, Line, should tell him what was going on.

Line laughed, good-humoredly. "Sure, I could, but I'm not going to. Bud probably already knows about this thing anyway, and if he doesn't, I'm sure not going to be the one to tell him."

"But why?"

"Because it's none of my business, and it's none of yours. I learned a long time ago not to worry about things over which I had no control. I have no control over this."

I wasn't satisfied with this answer, and I asked him if his conscience wouldn't bother him if, say, during the flight tests on the brake, something should happen resulting in death or injury to the test pilot.

"Look," he said, becoming somewhat exasperated, "I just told you I have no control over this thing. Why should my conscience bother me?"

His voice took on a quiet, soothing tone as he continued. "You're just getting all upset over this thing for nothing. I just do as I'm told, and I'd advise you to do the same.". . .

I made no attempt to rationalize what I had been asked to do. It made no difference who would falsify which part of the report or whether the actual falsification would be by misleading numbers or misleading words. Whether by acts of commission or omission all of us who contributed to the fraud would be guilty. The only question left for me to decide was whether or not I would become a party to the fraud.

Before coming to Goodrich in 1963, I had held a variety of jobs, each a little more pleasant, a little more rewarding than the last. At forty-two, with seven children, I had decided that the Goodrich Company would probably be my "home" for the rest of my working life. The job paid well, it was pleasant and challenging, and the future looked reasonably bright. My wife and I had bought a home and we were ready to settle down into a comfortable, middle-age, middle-class rut. If I refused to take a part in the A7D fraud, I would have to either resign or be fired. The report would be written by someone anyway, but I would have the satisfaction of knowing I had had no part in the matter. But bills aren't paid with personal satisfaction, nor house payments with ethical principles. I made my decision. The next morning, I telephoned Lawson and told him I was ready to begin on the qualification report. . . .

I had written dozens of qualification reports and I knew what a "good" one looked like. Resorting to the actual test data only on occasion, Lawson and I proceeded to prepare page after page of elaborate, detailed engineering curves, charts, and test logs, which purported to show what had happened during the formal qualification tests. Where temperatures were too high, we deliberately chopped them down a few hundred degrees, and where they were too low, we raised them to a value that would appear reasonable to the LTV and military engineers. Brake pressure, torque values, distances, times — everything of consequence was tailored to fit the occasion.

Occasionally, we would find that some test either hadn't been performed at all or had been conducted improperly. On those occasions, we "conducted" the test — successfully, of course — on paper.

For nearly a month we worked on the graphic presentation that would be part of the report. Meanwhile, the fourteenth and final qualification attempt had been completed, and the brake, not unexpectedly, had failed again. . . .

We finished our work on the graphic portion of the report around the first of June. Altogether, we had prepared nearly two hundred pages of data, containing dozens of deliberate falsifications and misrepresentations. I delivered the data to Gretzinger, who said he had been instructed to deliver it personally to the chief engineer, Bud Sunderman, who in turn would assign someone in the engineering department to complete the written portion of the report. He gathered the bundle of data and left the office. Within minutes, he was back with the data, his face white with anger.

"That damned Sink's beat me to it," he said furiously. "He's already talked to Bud about this, and now Sunderman says no one in the engineering department has time to write the report. He wants us to do it, and I told him we couldn't."

The words had barely left his mouth when Russell Line burst in the door. "What the hell's all the fuss about this damned report?" he demanded loudly.

Patiently, Gretzinger explained. "There's no fuss. Sunderman just told me that we'd have to write the report down here, and I said we couldn't. Russ," he went on, "I've told you before that we weren't going to write the report. I made my position clear on that a long time ago."

Line shut him up with a wave of his hand and turning to me, bellowed, "I'm getting sick and tired of hearing about this damned report. Now, write the goddamn thing and shut up about it!" He slammed out of the office.

Gretzinger and I just sat a few seconds looking at each other. Then he spoke.

"Well, I guess he's made it pretty clear, hasn't he? We can either write the thing or quit. You know, what we should have done was quit a long time ago. Now, it's too late."

Somehow, I wasn't at all surprised at this turn of events, and it didn't really make that much difference. As far as I was concerned, we were all up to our necks in the thing anyway, and writing the narrative portion of the report couldn't make me any more guilty than I already felt myself to be. . . .

Within two days, I had completed the narrative, or written portion of the report. As a final sop to my own self-respect, in the conclusion of the report I wrote, "The B.F. Goodrich P/N 2-1162-3 brake assembly does not meet the intent or the requirements of the applicable specification documents and therefore is not qualified."

This was a meaningless gesture, since I knew that this would certainly be changed when the report went through the final typing process. Sure enough, when the report was published, the negative conclusion had been made positive.

One final and significant incident occurred just before publication.

Qualification reports always bear the signature of the person who has prepared them. I refused to sign the report, as did Lawson. Warren was later asked to sign the report. He replied that he would "when I receive a signed statement from Bob Sink ordering me to sign it." ·

The engineering secretary who was delegated the responsibility of "dogging" the report through publication told me later that after I, Lawson, and Warren had all refused to sign the report, she asked Sink if he would sign. He replied, "On something of this nature, I don't think a signature is really needed."

On June 5, 1968, the report was officially published and copies were delivered in person to the Air Force and LTV. Within a week flight tests were begun at Edwards Air Force Base in California. Searle Lawson was sent to California as Goodrich's representative. Within approximately two weeks, he returned because some rather unusual incidents during the tests had caused them to be canceled.

His face was grim as he related stories of several near crashes during landings — caused by brake troubles. He told me about one incident in which, upon landing, one brake was literally welded together by the intense heat developed during the test stop. The wheel locked, and the plane skidded for nearly 1500 feet before coming to a halt. The plane was jacked up and the wheel removed. The fused parts within the brake had to be pried apart. . . .

That evening I left work early and went to see my attorney. After I told him the story, he advised that, while I was probably not actually guilty of fraud, I was certainly part of a conspiracy to defraud. He advised me to go to the Federal Bureau of Investigation and offered to arrange an appointment. The following week he took me to the Dayton office of the FBI and after I had been warned that I would not be immune from prosecution, I disclosed the A7D matter to one of the agents. The agent told me to say nothing about the episode to anyone and to report any further incident to him. He said he would forward the story to his superiors in Washington.

A few days later, Lawson returned from a conference with LTV in Dallas and said that the Air Force, which had previously approved the qualification report, had suddenly rescinded that approval and was demanding to see some of the raw test data. I gathered that the FBI had passed the word.

Omitting any reference to the FBI, I told Lawson I had been to an attorney and that we were probably guilty of conspiracy.

"Can you get me an appointment with your attorney?" he asked. Within the week, he had been to the FBI and told them of his part in the mess. He too was advised to say nothing but to keep on the job reporting any new development.

Naturally, with the rescinding of Air Force approval and the demand to see raw test data, Goodrich officials were in a panic. A conference was called for July 27, a Saturday morning affair at which Lawson, Sink, Warren and I were present. We met in a tiny conference room in the deserted engineering department. Lawson and I, by now openly hostile to Warren and Sink, ranged ourselves on one side of the conference table while Warren sat on the other side. Sink, chairing the meeting, paced slowly in front of a blackboard, puffing furiously on a pipe.

The meeting was called, Sink began, "To see where we stand on the A7D." What we were going to do, he said, was to "level" with LTV and tell them the "whole truth" about the A7D. "After all," he said, "they're in this thing with us, and they have the right to know how matters stand."

"In other words," I asked, "we're going to tell them the truth?"

"That's right," he replied. "We're going to level with them and let them handle the ball from there."

"There's one thing I don't quite understand," I interjected. "Isn't it going to be pretty hard for us to admit to them that we've lied?"

"Now, wait a minute," he said angrily. "Let's don't go off half-cocked on this thing. It's not a matter of lying. We've just interpreted the information the way we felt it should be."

"I don't know what you call it," I replied, "but to me it's lying, and it's going to be damned hard to confess to them that we've been lying all along."

He became very agitated at this and repeated his "We're not lying," adding, "I don't like this sort of talk."

I dropped the matter at this point, and he began discussing various discrepancies in the report.

We broke for lunch, and afterward, I came back to the plant to find Sink sitting alone at his desk, waiting to resume the meeting. He called me over and said he wanted to apologize for his outburst that morning. "This thing has kind of gotten me down," he confessed, "and I think you've got the wrong picture. I don't think you really understand everything about this."

Perhaps so, I conceded, but it seemed to me that if we had already told LTV one thing and then had to tell them another, changing our story completely, we would have to admit we were lying.

"No," he explained patiently, "we're not really lying. All we were doing was interpreting the figures the way we knew they should be. We were just exercising engineering license."

During the afternoon session, we marked some forty-three discrepant points in the report: forty-three points that LTV would surely spot as occasions where we had "engineering license."

After Sink listed those points on the blackboard, we discussed each one individually. As each point came up, Sink would explain that it was probably "too minor to bother about," or that perhaps it

Understanding Fraud, Waste,
Abuse and Corruption

"wouldn't be wise to open that can of worms," or that maybe this was a point that "LTV just wouldn't understand." When the meeting was over, it had been decided that only three points were "worth mentioning."

Similar conferences were held during August and September, and the summer was punctuated with frequent treks between Dallas and Troy, and demands by the Air Force to see the raw test data. Tempers were short and matters seemed to grow worse.

Finally, early in October 1968, Lawson submitted his resignation, to take effect on October 25. On October 18, I submitted my own resignation, to take effect on November 1. In my resignation, addressed to Russell Line, I cited the A7D report and stated: "As you are aware, this report contained numerous deliberate and willful misrepresentations which, according to legal counsel, constitute fraud and expose both myself and others to criminal charges of conspiracy to defraud. . . . The events of the past seven months have created an atmosphere of deceit and distrust in which it is impossible to work. . . ."

On October 25, I received a sharp summons to the office of Bud Sunderman. . . . Tall and graying, impeccably dressed at all times, he was capable of producing a dazzling smile or a hearty chuckle or immobilizing his face into marble hardness as the occasion required.

I faced the marble hardness when I reached his office. He motioned me to a chair. "I have your resignation here," he snapped, "and I must say you have made some rather shocking, I might even say irresponsible, charges. This is very serious."

Before I could reply, he was demanding an explanation. "I want to know exactly what the fraud is in connection with the A7D and how you can dare accuse this company of such a thing!"

I started to tell some of the things that had happened during the testing, but he shut me off saying, "There's nothing wrong with anything we've done here. You aren't aware of all the things that have been going on behind the scenes. If you had known the true situation, you would never have made these charges." He said that in view of my apparent "disloyalty" he had decided to accept my resignation "right now," and said it would be better for all concerned if I left the plant immediately. As I got up to leave he asked me if I intended to "carry this thing further."

I answered simply "Yes," to which he replied "Suit yourself." Within twenty minutes, I had cleaned out my desk and left. Forty-eight hours later, the B.F. Goodrich Company recalled the qualification report and the four-disk brake, announcing that it would replace the brake with a new, improved, five-disk brake at no cost to LTV.

Ten months later, on August 13, 1969, I was the chief government witness at a hearing conducted before Senator William Proxmire's Economy in Government Subcommittee. I related the A7D story to the committee, and my testimony was supported by Searle Lawson, who followed me to the witness stand. Air Force officers also testified, as well as a four-man team from the General Accounting Office, which had conducted an investigation of the A7D brake at the request of Senator Proxmire. Both Air Force and GAO investigators declared that the brake was dangerous and had not been tested properly.

Testifying for Goodrich was R.G. Jeter, vice president and general counsel of the company, from the Akron headquarters. Representing the Troy plant was Robert Sink. These two denied any wrongdoing on the part of the Goodrich Company, despite expert testimony to the contrary by Air Force and GAO officials. Sink was quick to deny any connection with the writing of the report or directing of any falsifications, claiming to have been on the West Coast at the time. John Warren was the man who had supervised its writing, said Sink.

As for me, I was dismissed as a high-school graduate with no technical training, while Sink testified that Lawson was a young, inexperienced engineer. "We tried to give him guidance," Sink testified, "but he preferred to have his own convictions."

About changing the data and figures in the report, Sink said: "When you take data from several different sources, you have to rationalize among those data what is the true story. This is part of your engineering know-how." He admitted that changes had been made in the data, "but only to make them more consistent with the overall picture of the data that is available."

Jeter pooh-poohed the suggestion that anything improper occurred saying: "We have thirty-odd engineers at this plant . . . and I say to you that it is incredible that these men would stand idly by and see reports changed or falsified. . . . I mean you just do not have to do that working for anybody. . . . Just nobody does that."

The four-hour hearing adjourned with no real conclusion reached by the subcommittee. But the following day the Department of Defense made sweeping changes in its inspection, testing, and reporting procedures. A spokesman for the DOD said the changes were a result of the Goodrich episode.

The A7D is now in service, sporting a Goodrich-made five-disk brake, a brake that works very well, I'm told. Business at the Goodrich plant is good. Lawson is now an engineer for LTV and has been assigned to the A7D. And I am now a newspaper reporter.

At this writing, those remaining at Goodrich are still secure in the same positions, all except Russell Line and Robert Sink. Line has been rewarded with a promotion to production superintendent, a large step upward on the corporate ladder. As for Sink, he moved up into Line's old job.

Fraud Cases Have Changed Face of Procurement
Robert J. Kenney, Jr.

This essay provides an overview of patterns of procurement fraud in computer contracts and in defense contracting generally. The author is a partner in a Washington, D.C. law firm.

The Reagan administration's campaign against fraud, waste and abuse in federal procurement is entering its sixth year [1986] with no sign of letting up. It has touched in some way every industry that supplies products or services to the federal government, and the computer industry is certainly no exception.

In recent years and months many well-known companies have been formally charged with fraud in connection with federal computer contracts. Some of these companies are threatened with debarment from future federal government business. And some government officials responsible for awarding or administering federal ADP contracts also have been caught up in criminal fraud prosecutions.

Recent Cases

In 1985 alone there were dozens of reported cases of alleged civil or criminal fraud involving federal computer contracts. A list of just a few of these cases is enough to demonstrate the magnitude of the problem:

On Oct. 30, Rockwell International Corp. pleaded guilty to charges that one of its divisions had made false statements to the government regarding an Air Force ADP contract. Rockwell was sentenced to pay $1.2 million in damages and penalties.

On Dec. 12, Paradyne Corp., a Florida-based manufacturer of computer equipment, was indicted on charges of fraud in obtaining a $100 million contract from the Social Security Administration. Indicted along with Paradyne were several of its current or former employees and a former director of SSA's data communications office.

On Oct. 24, another former Social Security official pleaded guilty to soliciting a $280,000 bribe in connection with a $7 million computer software contract.

In August, Intel Corp. settled charges that one of its divisions had submitted false pricing information to GSA in violation of the False Claims Act. As part of the settlement, Intel agreed to repay $560,000 to the government. A few days earlier, the Justice Department announced a $499,999 settlement of similar charges against Codex Corp., a Massachusetts manufacturer of ADP accessories and support equipment.

Source: Robert J. Kenney, Jr., "Fraud Cases Have Changed Face of Procurement," *GCN*, April 25, 1986.

Also in August, the Justice Department obtained more than $1 million from ITT in settlement of civil charges, under the False Claims Act, that ITT Dialcom Inc. and its predecessor company fraudulently overcharged the government in connection with computer time-sharing and communications contracts.

In December, Hybrid Components Inc., a Massachusetts manufacturer of semiconductors and other electronic components, was charged with criminal fraud in connection with the manufacture and testing of products Hybrid supplied under government subcontracts.

The large number of recent procurement fraud cases involving the computer industry is not only disturbing but also a little surprising. Although computer companies are by no means immune from procurement fraud charges, their exposure to such charges is fundamentally different in character and degree from that of the typical defense contractor. In fact, because of the way they normally do business with the federal government, computer companies ordinarily do not encounter some of the most familiar kinds of procurement fraud problems.

Most cases of procurement fraud fall into one of four fairly well-defined categories. The largest of these categories is "mischarging" cases — cases in which a contractor that is required to keep track of its costs on individual contracts intentionally charges labor or other costs to the wrong contract or accounting category.

The most common and obvious example of mischarging is a case in which a contractor facing an overrun on a cost-plus contract instructs employees to charge future work relating to that contract to some other contract for which funding is still available or to an overhead account.

The mischarging problem is unlikely to arise in the case of a computer company that sells commercially available hardware or software to the federal government on a firm, fixed-price basis. Such sales are usually made competitively, without reference to the contractor's costs, so that the contractor's cost-accounting practices are irrelevant to the price the government pays.

Defective Pricing

For similar reasons, most computer companies do not frequently encounter the second major source of procurement fraud problems: defective pricing. Defective pricing fraud cases typically arise when a contractor required to submit internal cost data to the government in connection with negotiations on a particular contract intentionally submits data that is not accurate, current and complete. The number of defective pricing cases is rapidly growing and may soon outstrip mischarging as the principal source of procurement fraud problems for contractors in general.

Computer companies selling hardware or software to the federal government on a commercial basis are unlikely to encounter defective pricing problems because the Federal Acquisition Regulations specifically provide that cost or pricing data is not required in the case of commercial products — especially commercial products acquired with adequate competition. There is a closely related problem, however, that does significantly affect many computer companies.

Each year the federal government purchases billions of dollars worth of commercially available hardware and software under multiple-award Federal Supply Schedule contracts. The General Services Administration, which negotiates these contracts, requires each contractor to disclose during contract negotiations the best price offered by the contractor to any other customer on items the contract covers. This requirement has been a major source of difficulty for computer companies because of the complex nature of their pricing and the administrative difficulty of keeping track of all prices offered to other customers.

Contractors who fail to make accurate disclosure of such "most-favored customer" pricing are subject to retroactive contract price reductions, and contractors who intentionally make inaccurate disclosure are subject to criminal or civil prosecution under the False Statements Act, the False Claims Act and other criminal statutes.

Several companies in the computer industry have encountered difficulties with this requirement in recent years. As noted previously, last year both Intel and Codex Corp. were caught up in fraud charges under the False Claims Act in connection with overcharges allegedly resulting from submission of false or misleading data to GSA regarding commercial discounts.

In 1984, the government settled similar charges against Digital Equipment Corp. and Lanier Business Products; those settlements required repayments of $3.2 million and $1 million, respectively. And just this month, it was reported that Cullinet Software Inc. had agreed to pay the government $615,000 to settle a dispute concerning the accuracy of its discount disclosures to GSA.

Inferior Products

The third major category of procurement fraud cases involves substitution of inferior materials, fraudulent testing or other fraudulent acts by which a contractor intentionally delivers inferior products to the government. There have been a number of notorious cases in this category outside the ADP context, including one case in which a subcontractor intentionally supplied defective wing bolts for use on military aircraft.

Cases of this sort have been relatively rare in the computer industry. In 1984 an intensive investigation of fraudulent testing of microcircuits in the semiconductor industry culminated in the indictment and conviction of National Semiconductor Corp., which paid a $1.8 million fine. The recent indictment of a Massachusetts semiconductor manufacturer on similar charges indicates that the government is still focusing attention on this area. But in general, fraudulent testing and product substitution have not been major sources of fraud problems for the computer industry.

Fraudulent Marketing

The last major category of procurement fraud — fraudulent marketing practices — is by far the most significant source of exposure for the typical computer vendor. The very factors that tend to reduce the exposure of computer companies to other categories of procurement fraud may actually increase their exposure in the marketing practices area. For example, the existence of intense competition in the industry, though it often relieves computer companies of the requirement to submit cost or pricing data, may also put pressure on some companies or individuals to engage in questionable marketing practices to secure a large contract award.

There have been a number of cases in recent years involving charges of fraudulent or otherwise questionable marketing practices by companies selling ADP products to the federal government. One of the most widely reported in this category is the case of Paradyne Corp., which was indicted in December on charges that it had fraudulently obtained a large contract to supply computer equipment to the Social Security Administration. Among the specific charges in the indictment is an allegation that Paradyne rigged an operational capability demonstration to conceal that the equipment it had proposed in its response to the agency's request for proposals did not in fact exist at the time of the proposal.

Marketing Practice Cases

The Paradyne case is by no means the only recent case involving charges of illegal marketing practices in the computer industry. Last July, two former government officials and three contractor employees were indicted on charges of bribery, bid-rigging and illegal information-sharing in connection with $2 billion worth of potential Postal Service and Small Business Administration computer contracts.

In separate incidents, two former officials of the Social Security Administration have been convicted within the past year of soliciting or accepting bribes to influence the award of SSA computer contracts.

In other cases less widely reported, computer companies have recently been caught up in allegations of conflict of interest, illegal gratuities, undue influence, illegal access to information and other forms of illegal or unethical marketing behavior.

Some of the allegations of fraud and bribery referred to in this article have not yet been proven. Some of them may never be proven. But the fact that such charges are becoming so common in federal ADP procurement and the fact that federal investigators and prosecutors are pursuing them so vigorously should suggest to those involved in ADP procurement that a potentially serious problem exists. It is a problem, moreover, that no federal ADP contractor can afford to ignore.

Pentagon Procurement Probe:
Individual Improprieties, or Systemic Sickness?
David Riley

When FBI agents raided more than 35 offices in a dozen states last June [1988], gathering information for the current defense procurement investigation, outraged Members of Congress across the political spectrum erupted. "The system is sick," declared conservative Rep. Denny Smith, R-Ore. "We have an epidemic of corruption," intoned Rep. Larry Hopkins, R-Ky. "I'm shook to the shoes," announced Sen. John Warner, R-Va., and Sen. David Pryor, D-Ark., said he was ashamed that Senators were not "standing on our desktops. . . demanding some public hangings. . . . "

Yet for all the outrage, there is also a strong sense of "deja vu all over again," to use Yogi Berra's phrase. Procurement abuse periodically outrages people, but it never seems to go away. One of the most important vehicles for ferreting out fraud in use today, the False Claims Act, was enacted in 1863 after President Lincoln got tired of Union troops receiving ammunition boxes filled with sawdust.

Since the Hoover Commission in 1949, there have been more than 30 major studies of defense procurement problems, according to the Aerospace Industries Association. But "you can study this problem at length, and still not understand it," says Jim Colvard, a former assistant director of the Office of Personnel Management who has many years' experience as a Navy procurement official.

Why is defense procurement such an intractable mess? Partly because it is a huge enterprise. The Pentagon buys about $120 billion worth of goods and services every year, including weapons, research, and consultant services. Defense acquisition provides part- or full-time employment for three million people in 170,000 companies. The Pentagon approves 61,000 contracts every day.

Competition vs. Regulation

But perhaps the most basic reason for the procurement mess is the anomalous position of the defense industry. The government can't decide whether defense companies are private businesses or public utilities. They contain aspects of both, and the government vacillates between encouraging competition as if the contractors were businesses and strictly regulating them as if they were utilities. Defense contractors don't have a monopoly on goods and services in the same way most utilities do, but they often have a near monopoly, since only two or three companies are equipped to build bombers, another two or three to build submarines, and so on.

The government aims to use competition and regulation in tandem, tailoring both to the special circumstances of defense procurement, hoping that competition will cut costs while regulation curbs profiteering. That would be the best of both worlds, but some observers, such as former undersecretary of the Navy James Woolsey, say the United States has ended up with the worst of both worlds: competition that produces instability for the industry and regulation that inhibits creativity.

The timing of the current imbroglio is unfortunate for defense industries. With former Defense Secretary Caspar Weinberger out of the picture — and Herblock cartoons picturing him with a $600 toilet seat around his neck out of the newspapers — the public's memory of the spare-parts scandal has been receding. Defense industries have had some success in getting Congress to ease up on further regulation and adopt a wait-and-see attitude.

But the latest investigation has changed all that, and the tide of regulation is coming in again. The Senate has passed, by voice vote, two amendments regulating the consultant business, with the House

David Riley's analysis of recent investigations in the field of defense contracting identifies several problems that make it difficult to design a system which meets high standards of probity and efficiency. For example, close working relationships between government and corporate officials may be essential in building modern weapons, but those patterns may interfere with objective evaluation of the performance of the tanks and other weapons that are produced. Also, in the search for greater efficiency, more emphasis is now being placed on competition among contractors; this effort "has cut costs'" Riley argues, "but it has also increased companies' reliance on industrial espionage to give them that extra competitive edge." As Riley's essay suggests, any complex social system will often respond in unexpected ways to reform efforts, and the reformer needs a clear understanding of the incentives that shape the behavior of the major actors if a reform strategy is to be effective.

Source: David Riley, "Pentagon Procurement Probe: Individual Improprieties, or Systemic Sickness?" *Government Executive,* October, 1988, pp. 65-68.

expected to follow suit. Many other bills are pending, particularly in the House, including some that would remove procurement management from the military altogether and place it in a separate agency.

Largest White-Collar Probe

Defense industries will have trouble forging a more positive public image in the face of the unprecedented scale of the investigation being presented to a grand jury in northern Virginia; it involves 270 subpoenas and may lead to as many as 100 indictments. It focuses on three principal kinds of illegal activity: collusion among competing contractors in submitting bids, defense officials leaking inside information to contractors about competing bids, and officials changing contract specifications to improve a particular company's chance of winning a contract. Some of these transactions allegedly involve bribery. *Business Week* has called the inquiry "the largest white-collar crime investigation ever."

The inquiry began in September 1986 when a former Navy official working for a defense contractor told Navy investigators that a consultant had offered to sell him confidential information. The former official, and later the consultant, agreed to cooperate with the investigation, allowing their conversations to be recorded. The investigation spread until it now encompasses at least 15 defense contractors — including such major ones as McDonnell Douglas, Northrop, Unisys, and United Technologies — and 25 individuals, including five company officials, 15 consultants, and five current Pentagon officials, three of them with the Navy. Several Members of Congress have been implicated as well.

The two people who initially cooperated with the investigation have not been identified, but many others have. The highest-ranking individual identified as a target of the investigation thus far is former assistant secretary of the Navy Melvyn Paisley, who worked closely with former Navy Secretary John Lehman to streamline naval procurement policies. Affidavits that have been released allege that Paisley gave McDonnell Douglas inside information obtained from government officials pertaining to the Navy's plans for developing jet fighters. Another former Navy official working as a consultant allegedly bought inside information from his successor at the Space and Naval Warfare Systems Command.

The FBI's search warrant for United Technologies alleges that its subsidiary Pratt & Whitney, obtained copies of General Electric's competing bid to build jet engines for Navy fighter planes. The two companies have been arch-rivals in competing for jet engine contracts. If proven, such allegations would taint the contracts involved, and could result in the offending company having its progress payments suspended, its security clearance removed, or its eligibility for future contracts jeopardized. Defense Secretary Frank Carlucci temporarily suspended payments to nine implicated contractors for three weeks in July, declaring his intention to take tough action if companies are found guilty in forthcoming trials.

Indictments Delayed

But just how forthcoming those trials will be is not yet clear. When the story first broke, then-Attorney General Edwin Meese boasted that the inquiry would lead to indictments in 60 to 90 days. But indictments are now considered several months away, says the U.S. Attorney's office in charge of the investigation.

Set against a background of arcane procurement regulations covering highly technical weapons systems, defense procurement cases are difficult to prosecute because of their complexity, their reliance on classified material, and their milieu: the murky relationship between industry and government. Legally, the two entities are supposed to remain at arm's length from each other. But practically, they must work closely together in order to build modern weapons systems. Their personnel sometimes switch from one side to the other, parading through a "revolving door." Military procurement officers reaching retirement age, and others looking to raise their salaries, keep an eye out for private sector jobs; many end up working for the same companies they oversaw as government officials.

Given the difficulties of procurement prosecution, the government's case would be greatly strengthened if more targets of the investigation would turn state's witness in exchange for leniency. But such deals have been slow in coming. There are other problems, too: the political sensitivity of the inquiry in a presidential election year, less direction from the Justice Department since former criminal division chief William Weld resigned, and reported turf battles over control of the investigation between the Justice Department and U.S. Attorney's offices in Virginia and in Brooklyn, N.Y.

A recent General Accounting Office (GAO) report criticized the Justice Department for being under-staffed, hampered by turnover, and not aggressive enough in prosecuting defense procurement cases in general. Sens. Charles Grassley, R-Iowa, and William Proxmire, D-Wis., have decried the Department's "lackadaisical, careless" work in this area. Justice Department officials, blaming insufficient funding for the lack of staff, have expressed concern about Virginia U.S. Attorney Henry Hudson's handling of the investigation, particularly the failure of his office to prevent the release of three affidavits containing information of possible use to targets of the investigation.

Congress Responds

The deferral of the indictments has not kept either the Pentagon or Congress from responding to procurement fraud allegations. In addition to Carlucci's temporary suspension of progress payments for nine contractors, a specially appointed Pentagon task force has issued guidelines for future suspensions and other punitive actions it might take should any of the 85 contracts currently related to the investigation turn out to be tainted. The Pentagon is also asking the 16 companies whose offices were searched in June to certify that they have not used inside information in bidding for defense contracts.

In recent congressional appearances, Carlucci and other Pentagon officials have urged Congress not to pass new legislation in response to the investigation. With several thousand procurement-related laws and regulations already on the books, virtually everyone agrees that procurement procedures need to be simplified, not complicated further. The scope of the pending investigation indicates that the government has its work cut out for it in trying to enforce laws currently on the books. Sweeping legislative changes are unlikely, at least until the investigation unfolds further.

But Congress is alert to plugging loopholes in existing procurement laws, and the Senate has passed two amendments sponsored principally by Sen. Pryor. One reduces by 15 percent federal funds available to pay outside consultants; the other requires defense consultants to register with the agencies hiring them, listing their other clients and describing the work they have been hired to do. The definition of a consultant is by no means clear; the GAO has said that DoD spent anywhere between $2.87 billion and $18.8 billion in fiscal 1987 for consulting services. Pryor's amendment would require the Pentagon to cut consulting fees by $420 million, or 15 percent of the lower figure.

Pryor hopes his amendment will discourage officials from paying consultants for work they can do themselves. Although not directly related to the current probe — Pryor has been proposing similar measures for years — the current success of Pryor's legislation to cut funds for consultants can probably be attributed to all the publicity about the Navy procurement investigation. "The time is right," Pryor said in August. The Senate has attached the amendment reducing funding for consultants to nine out of the 13 appropriations bills that will fund the government for fiscal 1989; the House is also expected to approve the amendments, which limit most consulting funds to 85 percent (and research and development consulting funds to 95 percent) of fiscal 1987 levels. The Senate attached the consultant registration amendment to the defense appropriations bill for fiscal 1989; Pryor has also introduced a similar bill that would apply government-wide.

The Pentagon, with the encouragement of Congress, has been moving away from no-bid contracts and toward competitive bidding. DoD claims, for example, that 56.5 percent of the Air Force's procurement budget in 1987 was awarded in competitive bidding procedures, up from 32.4 percent in 1983. Critics argue that most of what the Pentagon claims as competitive bidding is actually negotiated bidding with a few selected contractors.

Congress has also encouraged a move away from sole-source contracting, instead giving part of a job to the losing company in a competitive bid, and allowing that company to re-bid when the contract comes up for renewal. The Pentagon has also moved away from cost-plus contracts, where the government absorbs unanticipated costs, toward fixed-price contracts, where the company does so. The first have sometimes led to huge cost overruns, the second to serious financial problems for companies.

Also at the Pentagon, the Defense Contract Audit Agency has begun a review of the 12 largest defense firms to determine how much they have charged the government for consultants' fees, and whether these charges were legitimate. Legitimate charges include consultants who contribute to the production of the weapons system — for example, technical experts. But the audit is expected to reveal that the government is also paying illegitimate costs: consultants who — either through knowledge of Pentagon regulations or access to military contracting officials — help the company win the contract in the first place.

Competition Pressure Cooker

More competition in contracting has cut costs, but it has also increased companies' reliance on industrial espionage to give them that extra competitive edge. Recent defense budget cuts have added to the pressure-cooker atmosphere. "People respond to the economic motivation we create for them," says Colvard, who sees a misplaced emphasis on the bottom-line dollar figure in final bid decisions, which again puts a premium on obtaining inside information.

If such decisions were based on a combination of cost and quality factors, says Colvard, the government's assessment of a bid would be more complicated, involving the evaluation of many factors by many people. But the result, he says, would be both a better product and an evaluation process that is more difficult for industrial spies to penetrate.

Colvard would also like to see the government adopt a middle ground between cost-plus and fixed-price contracts. Unanticipated expenses are inevitable on contracts to build complex weapons systems involving new, constantly evolving technologies. Colvard's solution, which he says has worked successfully in cases he's been involved in, is cost-plus contracts with an award fee arrangement under which a board of government officials reviews contracts quarterly and decides which additional costs should be awarded to the contractor.

This arrangement requires that procurement officials have the expertise to make technical, as well as accounting, judgments. Colvard believes that by overemphasizing the role of accountants and lawyers, the government has abdicated its responsibility to be a knowledgeable buyer of military equipment. "Acquisition has got to be conceived of as a hell of a lot more than just writing a contract," says Colvard. "There's a difference between a good contract and a good product. We've fallen in love with abstraction. We've substituted it for experience."

The most far-reaching proposal to gain momentum in the wake of the procurement fraud investigation is the idea of an independent professional corps of civilian procurement officials. One bill, introduced by Rep. Dennis Hertel, D-Mich., and endorsed by 65 co-sponsors, would create the Defense Acquisition Agency within the Pentagon; another, sponsored by Rep. Barbara Boxer, D-Calif., would place such an agency outside the Pentagon. The proposal would reverse the trend under the Reagan Administration toward decentralizing procurement and giving more authority to the military services.

Procurement experts and former top-level defense officials such as Ronald Fox, James Wade, and Edward Luttwak all support the idea of an independent procurement corps as a way of reducing costs, duplication, and interservice rivalry. Major American allies — England, France, West Germany, Canada, and Sweden—have adopted a centralized approach to military procurement. But some experts, such as former defense official Woolsey, are concerned that removing the military from procurement management would isolate weapons developers from their users, leading to less useful weapons.

A civilian procurement corps would address the problem of military procurement officers being forced into retirement — or private industry — by the military's combat-oriented age limits, just at the time when their experience is most valuable to the government.

Defense Secretary Carlucci, undersecretary for acquisition Robert Costello, and defense industry officials emphasize that the current investigation is a matter of the misdeeds and excessive greed of a few individuals, not the fault of a procurement system in need of overhauling. Others emphatically take the view that the government needs to both prosecute offenders and drastically change the procurement system. For the moment, Congress has pushed the pause button, waiting to see if legal developments fizzle out or rekindle public outrage and the political pressure for major change.

If the predicted barrage of indictments should materialize and convictions follow, there may well be a major overhaul of the procurement system under the next administration. For now, there are clear signs of at least the potential for a broad constituency for change when a notably conservative congressman like Rep. Denny Smith writes in the *Washington Post* that, "The problem is not that there is fraud in defense procurement. The problem is that defense procurement is a fraud."

Groups Pay for Trips by Top HUD Officials

WASHINGTON- Senior officials at the Department of Housing and Urban Development took two dozen trips last year to places such as Milan, Italy, in which their air fare or hotel costs were paid by groups of real estate agents, builders and city and county officials.

HUD Undersecretary Donald L. Hovde, for example, spent two days in Puerto Rico in September as a guest of the Pennsylvania Association of Realtors, according to department records. The group paid for his stay at the Cerromar Beach Hotel, where single rooms start at $105 a night. Mr. Hoyde also took a six-day $3,000 trip to Italy, where his plane fare, hotel bill and some meals were paid for by the Italian chapter of the International Real Estate Federation.

Do you agree with Donald Hovde's view of travel and hotel costs? Is he sufficiently sensitive, in your view, to questions of appearance as well as the reality of potential favoritism? How do the Hovde guidelines compare with those of government organizations in your state and locality?

Builders, realtors and cities and counties all receive money from HUD and are affected by a variety of department decisions. The travel financed by these groups is in addition to numerous trips to London, Paris, Athens, Geneva, and elsewhere that senior department officials took last year at government expense.

HUD policy prohibits employees from accepting free trips from specific companies that are regulated by or do business with the department. But, in a memo last May that largely continued what had been Carter administration policy, Mr. Hovde encouraged senior employees to accept free travel from trade associations, "regardless of whether the industry or group is regulated by HUD or the members of the association have business dealings with the department."

"Current fiscal realities make it appropriate that such offers be not only accepted but encouraged," Mr. Hovde wrote, "even to the extent that the organization's willingness to reimburse expenses will be taken into account in the department's determination of whether to approve the travel."

Mr. Hovde added, however, that free travel should be discouraged in some circumstances because it "may tend to create a public impression that the offer is made to influence the department's official actions or to obtain preferential treatment."

Asked this week about his own travel, Mr. Hovde said his eight expense-paid trips were "just part of the invitation. I've checked with the general counsel's office and it's perfectly legitimate."

Mr. Hovde said he went to Milan for a conference of Italian officials and real estate executives. He said he met with a number of housing and municipal officials on his six-day trip to the Virgin Islands and Puerto Rico.

Stephen Bollinger, HUD's assistant secretary for community planning and development, had some expenses paid on 10 trips last year.

"The test I have is . . . am I being brought there to be manipulated?" He added that such trips "provide an opportunity to communicate the kind of information they need . . . and not have the expense borne by the taxpayers."

Source: "Groups Pay for Trips by Top HUD Officials," *Kansas City Times,* January 7, 1983, p. A-2.

Case 5: Free Lunch?

This scenario depicts a relationship between a state administrator and a businessman. Don't become too involved in the small details of the scenario — they are only props. What we wish to study are the larger questions concerning their relationship, the idea of mixing business and pleasure, the direct costs and hidden costs involved.

Characters
Charles Rodriguez — Director, Bureau of Administrative Services
Harry Jones — Business Executive

Scene
Lunch hour in a fancy restaurant. Harry is new in town; at the suggestion of the state Chamber of Commerce, he has called Charles and invited him to lunch.

Harry: I'm sure glad that you accepted my invitation for lunch. You don't know how hard it is to get started in a new area. My wife and I were pretty settled out West and she really balked at moving here.

Charles: How did you come to pick our state?

Harry: I was really impressed, Charles, with the young and progressive attitude of the people in this section of the country. Right down the line — businesspeople, government, all top-notch — I think I made a smart move.

Charles: I see you bought out "The Duckworth Paper Company," have you always been in that line?

Harry: Yes, paper, that's my whole life. We handle everything from confetti to newsprint. What do people do around here for recreation anyway?

Charles: Fantastic fishing — 15 miles out of Dana Point, you can't pull them in fast enough. Last week I caught 14 haddock. Thought my arm would fall off. And sports — this is a great area. Minor league baseball, university football, ice hockey.

Harry: Sounds great. I'm thinking of buying a 40 footer and sure would like to know where that fishing hole is. (motions for check) Check please, (to Charles) everything on this card is tax deductible. Sure was a pleasure talking to you Charles. Thanks for the tip on the fishing hole. That was just the excuse I needed to buy that boat.

TWO MONTHS LATER (phone rings in Charles' office)

Harry: Charlie? This is Harry. Guess what I did? I bought that 40 footer. It's a magnificent boat, twin diesels, the whole works. When can you break free and lead me to that fishing hole?

Charles: Well, I'm pretty tied up right now, let me see my calendar. Oh, I'm free next Saturday. How does that sound?

Source: Edward B. Laverty, Northeastern University.

Harry: Just great — don't bring a thing. I have poles and all. How about if I pick you up at 7:30 Saturday morning?

Charles: Okay, it's a deal. See you then.

Understanding Fraud, Waste, Abuse and Corruption

ONE MONTH LATER (phone rings in Charles' office)

Harry: Hi Charlie, how you doing? That was some fishing trip wasn't it? What a spot, I'm still pulling them out by the dozen. Say, I got a couple box seats for the Red Sox game tonight. I can't get rid of them and was coming by the state office building. I wondered if you knew anyone who could use them?

Charles: Hey — they're playing Baltimore tonight and Ryan's pitching. I'm sure I can find someone who'd put them to good use.

TWO WEEKS LATER (phone rings in Charles' office)

Harry: Hi ol' buddy. Just been down in purchasing and saw where the state put a bid out for 27,000 rolls of Perfecto carbon paper for your automatic billing machines in the Bureau of Taxation. I wondered if the Bureau could possibly use our Excel brand — a competitive product to Perfecto. The price is right and it would do the job — mind you Charles, I'm not asking for any special favors, but I think the state could save a few bucks.

Charles: (What do I say to this?)

QUESTIONS TO START THE DISCUSSION

1. Has Charles done anything unethical yet?

2. What if Charles calls the purchasing agent and mentions the Excel brand? Would this be unethical?

3. Is there ever a free lunch?

6. Graft, Bribery and Conflict of Interest

Honest Graft and Dishonest Graft
William L. Riordon

Everybody is talkin' these days about Tammany men growin' rich on graft, but nobody thinks of drawin' the distinction between honest graft and dishonest graft. There's all the difference in the world between the two. Yes, many of our men have grown rich in politics. I have myself. I've made a big fortune out of the game, and I'm gettin' richer every day, but I've not gone in for dishonest graft — blackmailin' gamblers, saloonkeepers, disorderly people, etc. — and neither has any of the men who have made big fortunes in politics.

There's an honest graft, and I'm an example of how it works. I might sum up the whole thing by sayin': "I seen my opportunities and I took 'em."

Just let me explain by examples. My party's in power in the city, and it's goin' to undertake a lot of public improvements. Well, I'm tipped off, say, that they're going to lay out a new park at a certain place.

I see my opportunity and I take it. I go to that place and I buy up all the land I can in the neighborhood. Then the board of this or that makes its plan public, and there is a rush to get my land, which nobody cared particular for before.

Ain't it perfectly honest to charge a good price and make a profit on my investment and foresight? Of course it is. Well, that's honest graft.

Or supposin' it's a new bridge they're goin' to build. I get tipped off and I buy as much property as I can that has to be taken for approaches. I sell at my own price later on and drop some more money in the bank.

Wouldn't you? It's just like lookin' ahead in Wall Street or in the coffee or cotton market. It's honest graft, and I'm lookin' for it every day in the year. I will tell you frankly that I've got a good lot of it, too.

I'll tell you of one case. They were goin' to fix up a big park, no matter where. I got on to it, and went lookin' about for land in that neighborhood.

I could get nothin' at a bargain but a big piece of swamp, but I took it fast enough and held on to it. What turned out was just what I counted on. They couldn't make the park complete without Plunkitt's swamp, and they had to pay a good price for it. Anything dishonest in that?

Behind George Washington Plunkitt's homespun philosophy in support of "honest graft" and against the "evils" of civil-service reform lie some serious questions. Are all of Plunkitt's cases illustrations of "graft," or can we distinguish among the ethical problems raised by the various examples? Is it possible to make a plausible argument in favor of Plunkitt's distinction between "honest graft" and "dishonest graft"?

Source: William L. Riordon, *Plunkitt of Tammany Hall*, (New York: E. P. Dutton & Co., 1963), Ch. 1.

Up in the watershed I made some money, too. I bought up several bits of land there some years ago and made a pretty good guess that they would be bought up for water purposes later by the city.

Somehow, I always guessed about right, and shouldn't I enjoy the profit of my foresight? It was rather amusin' when the condemnation commissioners came along and found piece after piece of the land in the name of George Plunkitt of the fifteenth Assembly District, New York City. They wondered how I knew just what to buy. The answer is — I seen my opportunity and I took it. I haven't confined myself to land; anything that pays is in my line.

For instance, the city is repavin' a street and has several hundred thousand old granite blocks to sell. I am on hand to buy, and I know just what they are worth.

How? Never mind that. I had a sort of monopoly of this business for a while, but once a newspaper tried to do me. It got some outside men to come over from Brooklyn and New Jersey to bid against me.

Was I done? Not much. I went to each of the men and said: "How many of these 250,000 stones do you want?" One said 20,000, and another wanted 15,000, and other wanted 10,000. I said: "All right, let me bid for the lot, and I'll give each of you all you want for nothin'."

They agreed, of course. Then the auctioneer yelled: "How much am I bid for these 250,000 fine pavin' stones?"

"Two dollars and fifty cents," says I.

"Two dollars and fifty cents!" screamed the auctioneer. "Oh, that's a joke! Give me a real bid."

He found the bid was real enough. My rivals stood silent. I got the lot for $2.50 and gave them their share. That's how the attempt to do Plunkitt ended, and that's how all such attempts end.

I've told you how I got rich by honest graft. Now, let me tell you that most politicians who are accused of robbin' the city get rich the same way.

They didn't steal a dollar from the city treasury. They just seen their opportunities and took them. That is why, when a reform administration comes in and spends a half a million dollars in tryin' to find the public robberies they talked about in the campaign, they don't find them.

The books are always all right. The money in the city treasury is all right. Everything is all right. All they can show is that the Tammany heads of departments looked after their friends, within the law, and gave them what opportunities they could to make honest graft. Now, let me tell you that's never goin' to hurt Tammany with the people. Every good man looks after his friends, and any man who doesn't isn't likely to be popular. If I have a good thing to hand out in private life, I give it to a friend. Why shouldn't I do the same in public life?

Another kind of honest graft. Tammany has raised a good many salaries. There was an awful howl by the reformers, but don't you know that Tammany gains ten votes for every one it lost by salary raisin'?

The Wall Street banker thinks it shameful to raise a department clerk's salary from $1500 to $1800 a year, but every man who draws a salary himself says: "That's all right. I wish it was me." And he feels very much like votin' the Tammany ticket on election day, just out of sympathy.

Tammany was beat in 1901 because the people were deceived into believin' that it worked dishonest graft. They didn't draw a distinction between dishonest and honest graft, but they saw that some Tammany men grew rich, and supposed they had been robbin' the city treasury or levyin' blackmail on disorderly houses, or workin' in with the gamblers and lawbreakers.

As a matter of policy, if nothing else, why should the Tammany leaders go into such dirty business, when there is so much honest graft lyin' around when they are in power? Did you ever consider that?

Now, in conclusion, I want to say that I don't own a dishonest dollar. If my worst enemy was given the job of writin' my epitaph when I'm gone, he couldn't do more than write:

"George W. Plunkitt. He Seen His Opportunities, and He Took 'Em."

Oklahoma: Where the Graft Comes Sweepin' Down the Plain
Paul Marshall Heisig

Cast of Characters

Hoss Dobbin, a newly elected Tushumtaha (Ta-SHUM-ta-ha) County commissioner;

Purvis Slattery, a former member of the Tushumtaha Board of County Commissioners, currently a self-employed materiel supplier;

Mary Frances Lane, a long-time self-employed materiel supplier;

David T. Robinson, a sales representative for a large heavy road equipment manufacturer;

This selection describes an actual recent case, with names and some details altered. The situation is not unusual in rural America — and in parts of suburban and urban America too. Some questions are appended to the end of the case.

Others

Mildred Dobbin, Hoss' wife;

Elmo ("Gob") Fiero and **Johnnie Ray Lighthorse,** Dobbin's fellow Board members;

Jerry Rock, editor and publisher of The Tushumtaha County Chronicle;

Billy Ed Smith, the Tushumtaha County/District Attorney;

J. T. ("Chief") Stoole, the Tushumtaha County sheriff;

Mrs. LuAnn Scribner, the Tushumtaha County Clerk;

John Marner, the Tushumtaha County Treasurer;

Frank Jones, Jr. and **Will Herbert,** Tushumtaha County's State Representative and State Senator, respectively;

Mike Carter, the state's Attorney General;

Ben Yale, the state's Auditor and Inspector General;

Marvin ("Wimp") Casper, the state's Governor; and

James T. Craig, Oklahoma City-based U. S. Attorney.

Hoss Dobbin, by everybody's account, was a real good ol' boy. Hoss and his family had lived on the same smallish ranch in rural southern Tushumtaha County since shortly after statehood. There, they had survived the Crash and the Dust Bowl, the dry wells and the crop failures, the foreclosures and the bank failures, and had never asked nobody for nothin'.

Everybody in their part of the county liked the Dobbins, especially Hoss. Through hard work, shrewdness and a little luck, Hoss had seen to it that the ranch stayed Dobbins' property. Along the way, he had also managed to graduate from high school and had even taken a few extension courses through the state university after having served in the Pacific for several months at the end of World War II. Like his daddy before him, Hoss was a deacon in the little Baptist church down to the crossroads and, also like his daddy, he didn't take it too seriously.

Times had been tough, and still were, but Hoss and his wife Mildred and the rest of the Dobbins, well, they just managed to make do — and also managed to help out a lot of folks, too. Crop harvests, fence mendings, barn raisings and birthings for neighbors all 'round. The Dobbins were good people and now that things didn't look so bad, Hoss has had the time to seek, successfully, the 3rd District seat on the county Board of Commissioners.

Source: Paul Marshall Heisig, "Oklahoma: Where the Graft Comes Sweepin' Down the Plain," paper presented at annual meeting of the American Society for Public Administration, 1986.

You couldn't say that Hoss had just fallen off the turnip truck, but you really couldn't call him a politician either. Sure, he had helped talk it up down to the sale barn in town when his daddy ran for sheriff several years ago and, as a lifelong yellow dog Democrat, he had supported the county Party and its candidates and had even given a few bucks, when he could, to the campaign kitties of Tushumtaha's longtime state legislators, Frank Jones and Will Herbert, but mostly he was just a hard-working small rancher.

When "Big Jim," the former District 3 commissioner, died suddenly after 30 years at the helm, a bunch of the folks down at the courthouse thought Hoss would make a pretty good commissioner and encouraged him to throw his hat in the ring. Characteristically, though, Hoss hesitated some. He'd heard some pretty outlandish stories about how Big Jim had operated, about those quarterly statewide commissioners' workshops in the City. Workshops? With the booze and the women and those suppliers' hospitality suites — in a pig's eye! Hoss knew about Big Jim's big spread that got much bigger, his big cars, his many trips to the races (and Heaven only knows what else!) in Hot Springs. Hoss, and everybody else, knew that Big Jim didn't make enough on his commissioner's salary to afford those kinds of things. Everybody also knew that Big Jim took the dime.

Hell, folks knew that all of 'em did: the commissioners took it; the state legislators they supported took it; a governor had been shown to take it; even the state Supreme Court judges had been shown to take it! The folks tolerated Big Jim's shady deals because, well, all of 'em took it, and he was such a good friend and would help anybody, well, anybody but those damn Franklins, anytime. He'd help put people to work when they needed a job; he'd help folks with groceries if they'd been goin' without; he'd help folks out if they needed a crop loan or had a busted tractor. He had even seen to it that his county road crew graded and paved the church lot regularly.

Hoss had always helped folks out, too, and figured he could do a better job of it as commissioner. He knew that good roads were necessary to the county folks' well-being and was confident that he could keep them up all right. But he decided to go ahead and run mostly because Mildred, his wife, wanted him to take his "rightful" place in the community. She hadn't been feeling too well lately but she felt that between her and her daddy, who lived with them, they could keep the ranch operating in the black. So, with Mildred's support and with the help of Big Jim's old friends in the courthouse and out in the precincts, a healthy financial contribution to his campaign from Purvis Slattery, a former commissioner and now self-employed materiel salesman, and another from Mary Frances Lane, another supplier from the next county, Hoss won handily.

Well, it didn't take ol' Hoss too long to realize that he'd struck the mother lode. After the swearing in ceremony, at which the judge mumbled something about the public trust and not for private gain — Hoss was too excited to pay much attention — he got to visiting with the courthouse regulars: "Chief" Stoole, the sheriff; LuAnn Scribner, the county's clerk; and Mr. Marner, the treasurer; as well as his fellow board members "Gob" Fiero and Johnnie Ray Lighthorse; and found out how vast his new powers really were.

Hoss could find county jobs for most of his friends and supporters, some in the courthouse, some on the road crews and some, through his old friend Senator Herbert, with the state. Hoss had his own district barn and he could buy supplies and equipment for it and his road crews pretty much as he liked. Hoss was his own personnel officer and his own purchasing and receiving agent; getting the state-required approval of the other two board members was just bothersome red tape: as long as he approved their appointments and purchases, they approved his — he scratched their backs, they scratched his.

From a box of ten penny nails to a box culvert, from a grader blade to an $80,000 grader itself, if he wanted it, he could get it. Hoss once thought about what his high school civics teacher had said many years before about there being checks and balances in government. Here in Tushumtaha County, he realized, only his innate sense of proportion kept him balanced and in check. Without that, he could've run amok.

Together, Gob and Johnnie Ray and Hoss controlled a lot of the county voters as well as the county's budget and, thus, in large measure, its officers, including Billy Ed Smith, the county/district attorney. Not that he ever would, but if Billy Ed dared to give the commissioners any serious lip, they could take fully half his money away and, further, withdraw their support at re-election time. Between the three of them, they knew all the voters in the county by their first names and were thus in a position to help elect — or unelect — Billy Ed, Chief Stoole, LuAnn, Mr. Marner, and Frank and even Will. Their own county officers' organizations could assist politicians in statewide campaigns: Ben Yale, the state auditor, Mike

Carter, the attorney general, and "Wimp" Casper, the governor. Not only in Tushumtaha County but around the state, what the commissioners wanted, the commissioners seemed to get.

By the time Hoss got into office, the commissioners were getting an awful lot of their money from the state. The county lobby in the state capitol had the stroke to obtain appropriations for their people in the courthouses and with few, if any, strings attached. Just that much less the commissioners had to raise at home. Didn't have to take the heat themselves, could blame tax increases on the state politicians and those damn bureaucrats. All the commissioners got to do was spend what wasn't really their folks' money but rather money from people way 'cross the state, from people they didn't know, from people they didn't really much care about. While not entirely sure, Hoss thought this was a pretty cushy set-up. No wonder Big Jim did OK. It wasn't too long before some of Big Jim's road equipment started to wear a bit and Hoss decided he ought to repair or replace it. Mr. Slattery and that Mary Frances woman had been by his barn a couple of times already to see how he was doing and if he needed anything and all. So had a fella in a suit from the heavy equipment manufacturer in the city, card said David T. Robinson, Sales Representative.

Well, Hoss hadn't needed anything then but he did now. So in walked Mary Frances Lane and she said she's got nails and gravel and oil and lumber and grader blades and she can even lay her hands on some used road machinery if Hoss needed it. Hoss told her what he needed and asked, "What'll it cost?" Mary Frances toted it up and said, "Well, with your ten percent, that comes to. . . ." Hoss' back got up a little and he said, "I don't want no ten percent. I deal square. You got to know that right off." Mary Frances protested that Big Jim had always taken his share and so had Purvis Slattery when he was a commissioner. Then she said, "Hoss, in my thirty years in this business, I have met only three people who didn't take the dime. You're gonna be the fourth, huh?" Next in came Mr. Slattery and with the same deal: a ten percent markup on the price of goods delivered to Hoss. Again, Hoss said no thanks. Purvis, shaking his head, left the barn thinking to himself, we'll see, we'll see, we'll just wait and see. Then, as Hoss was, after all, in the market for a new grader, Mr. Robinson showed up and, after a few preliminaries, said, "As an inducement to purchase from our firm, my sales manager has authorized me to offer to you 1.875 per cent of the total price of our grader, or about $1,500." "Jeez, Louise," Hoss whistled incredulously, "fifteen hundred bucks!?" He thought about it for a minute, then said, "No thanks. I need a grader, but I don't need your money." And so it went for a few months: them offering; Hoss saying no thanks.

When the campaign dust had finally settled and Hoss had pretty much moved in down to the courthouse, he decided to accept Purvis' offer of a trip to the City to attend one of the commissioners' quarterly workshop meetings. Hoss hadn't really believed the stories that Big Jim had told about these meetings and figured he really could use some help with budgetary matters and such. After attending a couple of workshops the first morning, Purvis thought he'd show Hoss around, have him meet some of the other commissioners and suppliers. To Hoss' surprise, folks were kinda stand-offish, didn't take too kindly to him for some reason.

"It's 'cause you don't take the dime," Purvis told him straight out. "Everybody else takes it. It's tradition, been doin' it since statehood. They want to know why you don't. Right now, they think you're just uppity, not one of us at all." Hoss just stood there with his mouth hanging open not knowing what to say. Finally, he said "My daddy didn't raise me that way. You don't take what ain't yours, what you don't earn. And besides, the preacher's always goin' on about sinnin' and corruption leadin' to eternal hellfire and damnation, and I kinda think that way, too."

"Well," Purvis replied, "nothin' against your daddy, Hoss, but everybody knows that the preacher's got a little hideaway across the state line and he ain't usin' it for no tent revival neither! And besides, no one's ever going to find out. No one has yet. Nobody snoops, surely not ol' Jerry down to the *Chronicle*. He knows better. You and Gob and Johnnie Ray send an awful lot of business his way, what with your public notices and all. He'd have to fold his tent if it wasn't for the advertising revenue from the county, your county. Same all over the state. The Oklahoma Press Association knows which side of the toast their butter's on."

"Besides," Purvis continued, "even if somebody did get an inkling, state's got no balls, no enforcement power even if it did have some. Feds neither, not even that Craig creep. Billy Ed? He don't want to make no trouble for the A. G. Carter wants to be governor and needs our votes. And Wimp wants to be a U.S. Senator and needs our votes, too. Ditto for Frank and Will. Who do you think got them elected and reelected all these years?"

"All them badges and guns and lawyers and no way to make folks talk," laughed Purvis. "Hoss, you talk to Mary Frances. A couple of years ago, in another county where she does business, the grand jury tried to subpoena her as a witness against a couple of commissioners. She just said no, state law says I don't have to — and didn't!"

"Hell's fire, boy," he went on, "nobody'd squeal to the feds 'cause we all do business the same way. You can't sell to commissioners if you don't. Took Mary Frances herself a couple of years of rejected bids before she asked and LuAnn set her straight. Figure it out, boy. LuAnn and Mr. Marner aren't goin' to say anything. They're in this up to their eyeballs, too. Who do you think's been signin' off on all them vouchers all these years? I'm tellin' ya, they'll play along, always have. Smartin' up, Hoss, smartin' up." Hoss thought in silence on the way home about the way he'd been treated by his fellow commissioners and about all what Purvis had told him.

Not too long after Hoss' first statewide commissioner meeting and his talk with Purvis, Mildred got sicker, too sick to mind the ranch properly. First, it was her gall bladder that had to be removed, then a hernia operation. Sure, Daddy was still there but he hadn't been able to help much since his stroke a few months back. Between the two of them, the doctor and hospital bills were piling up and Hoss was into the local druggist for four figures a month. And then the damn feds quarantined his herd because it hadn't been properly vaccinated and tested for Bung's disease since his election. "Good Lord, what next?" muttered Hoss.

Well, around came Mary Frances Lane again. Mary Frances knew what Hoss was going through and wanted to help out however she could. In addition to the standard ten percent on a few odds and ends, Mary Frances now offered Hoss a deal that seemed too good (or too bad) to be true. She'd write out an invoice for, say, a used tractor; Hoss would get it approved like he always did, but instead of delivering the tractor, Hoss and Mary Frances would split the face value of the invoice right down the middle, 50-50. A quick fifteen thousand dollars for each of them. "That'd go a long way toward getting Mildred and her daddy on their feet again, wouldn't it, Hoss? Might even get the feds off your back."

QUESTIONS TO START THE DISCUSSION

1. Should Hoss take the kickback and consummate the 50-50?

2. If he does not, should he continue to remain silent or should he blow the whistle on Mary Frances?

3. To whom? What alternative steps might he consider?

4. Suppose you were an aspiring young reporter for a daily newspaper in a nearby city and heard rumors of the patterns described in this case. What strategies might you consider in order to get a "good story"?

Without Fear or Favor
LeRoy F. Harlow

Competition Is Great . . . but Count Me Out

My experience tells me there are essentially three ways local officials can save taxpayers money:

1. Systematize work procedures and methods for maximum efficiency of production;

2. Guide and help employees perform at greater efficiency through directing them, training them, facilitating their work, and providing inspiration and incentives;

3. Manage the purchase, control, and use of goods and contract services.

I have observed that, paradoxically, although number 3 provides the most precise measure of how much is saved and where, it also generates the greatest resistance. I want to describe my Fargo [North Dakota] experience because it illustrates the kinds of pressure that can converge on a lone official trying to protect the people's pocket book.

First, let me put the situation in perspective. Municipalities buy cars, trucks, parts, tires, gasoline, grease, and oil. They buy uniforms and work clothes. They need food and medical supplies. They pay for heat, power, and insurance. They spend millions for asphalt, cement, gravel, steel, lumber, and other construction materials. And they are continually in the market for desks, chairs, files, paper, ink, printed materials, and other office supplies. From cranes and construction projects to paper clips and toilet paper, local governments are among America's largest consumers of goods and services.

Studies show that in most situations, centralizing the purchase of these goods and services will save 10 to 15 percent of their costs. In Fargo our total expenditures for these items ran about $350,000 a year. Conservatively, by investing $5,000 a year for centralized purchasing, we could make a net saving of $30,000 to $35,000 a year — one mill on the tax rate. This saving was possible simply because, although our division and department heads were specialists in water treatment, police and fire protection, airport management, laboratory analyses, and engineering, they were not specialists in purchasing. They could not keep track of new products coming on the market, of seasonal changes in supplies and prices, or of the opportunities for discounts and tax exemptions available to local governments. They could not know what the other departments were buying that might be pooled with their own needs for quantity discounts — or what the other departments had on hand that they might use instead of buying. Moreover, it was a waste of their time to listen to the stream of salesmen wanting to sell their wares to the city.

With these benefits for the city in mind, I recommended to the city commission that we set up within the finance department a central purchasing division under a purchasing agent. The division would prepare specifications in cooperation with the using departments and would buy all supplies, materials, and equipment for all city departments. Also, the purchasing agent would handle contracts for services and would inventory and manage the land and buildings the city owned. The commission approved unanimously.

I appointed a longtime assistant to the city auditor as our first purchasing agent. Unfortunately, almost immediately thereafter the city auditor died unexpectedly. The new purchasing agent was the logical successor to this important position; so I appointed him city auditor, and he was confirmed by the city commission as required by the city manager plan law. This left vacant the purchasing agent's position. I was unable to fill the vacancy for several months.

By November I had located a Fargo resident with experience in governmental purchasing. Donald E. Bloese went to work for us on December 14. He began writing the operating procedure for the centralized purchasing system, setting up a small office with necessary forms and files. In addition, I had him

Source: LeRoy F. Harlow, *Without Fear or Favor: Oddysey of a City Manager* (Brigham Young University Press, 1977), pp. 178-184.

visit several cities in the Midwest to observe their central purchasing operations. He spent two days in Milwaukee, Wisconsin, where he received special and useful counsel from city purchasing agent Nicholson, then president of the National Institute of Governmental Purchasing. On February 1 we put central purchasing into operation.

The new program was not entirely free from problems. At a staff meeting of department heads and their assistants a week before we planned to get underway, Police Chief Jester took the floor and declared that the plan spelled out in detail by the purchasing agent was a "Rube Goldberg" invention and one which he, the chief, found impossible to understand.

It was not long after that that an irate individual presented himself at my office door and demanded to know, "What in hell's going on around here?" He said he was the district sales manager for one of the chemical companies that supplied chemicals for our water purification plant. He wanted to know how come the last order for a certain chemical had not gone to his firm. He had driven up from Minneapolis to find out. I replied that we were buying on a bid basis and perhaps his company had not submitted the lowest bid.

"Wha'd ya mean, bid?" he asked. "We've got a deal. I made it with Fred Hagen. We were to get all the business."

"Commissioner Hagen is no longer the water commissioner," I said. "The city has changed to the council-manager form of government, and I now have responsibility for that department."

"I don't give a damn what you've done. All I know is we had a deal, and I'm going to find out about this." With this he left.   That wasn't the only flak I ran into while Don Bloese was with us. For instance, the mayor and I were walking back to our offices from a service club luncheon one day. The mayor had been sitting next to his good friend, Larry Hamm, head of the largest office supply and equipment firm in both Fargo and the state and chairman of Fargo's fire and police Civil Service Commission. "Larry tells me the city's now buying paper from some cheap New York outfit," the mayor said.

I didn't comment. I knew the purchasing agent had advertised for bids on paper, specifying both quality and quantity, and that a representative of a firm across the street from City Hall had come over to ask if we really meant that we wanted bids — that he had never been able to get any city business before. I also knew that Larry Hamm's firm had not submitted the low bid and had not been given our order. As I recall, the "cheap New York outfit" that got the order was the Burroughs Corporation, almost a household name in American business since the turn of the century.

The mayor's comment alerted me that sooner or later I'd have to fight for our policy of seeking the best price we could get on city purchases, even after we had met the legal requirements for giving preference to local vendors.

State law gave a preference to residents over nonresidents. Cities were required to purchase goods and accept bids from North Dakota resident bidders if the resident bidder's proposal was not more than 5 percent above the lowest bid of an out-of-state firm. We went further than that; we added more than a 5 percent differential on the assumption that we would get better service from local merchants, although that was not always the case.

But even our strict compliance with state law plus additional preference did not satisfy some gasoline vendors, and it didn't satisfy Larry Hamm. The gasoline vendors argued that if a company had its headquarters out of state, even if its service stations were in Fargo, they were non-residents; therefore we should not buy from them on a competitive basis.

Larry Hamm telephoned to make a bitter complaint because we had given our order for two files to someone else. He wanted to know why his firm didn't get the order. The purchasing agent had talked to me about this, so I had the facts in mind.

"Larry," I said, "we invited bids on those files. The bids came in. For the identical file — same manufacturer, same catalog number, same color — everything the same — there was a 30 percent spread between your price and the other man's." Then I gave him the exact figures.

He said,"You're forcing me to give a larger discount than I think I ought to. You're chiseling."

"Larry, we can't force you to do anything. We simply ask for bids, and we accept the lowest one for equal quality goods," I replied.

"This is taxpayers' money, and they don't want you to spend it this way. They want you to pass the business around," he said.

"I'm not sure the taxpayers would want it passed around if they knew the facts," I said. "I made an analysis of our purchases over a period of a year. We know that only 20 percent of the businesses in town — I'm not talking professional people or anything like that; I'm talking about the fellows in the merchandising business — only 20 percent of them received from the city of Fargo more than twenty dollars last year. In other words, for all practical purposes 80 percent of the merchants in town don't get a penny from the city. Why? Because they happen to be in the type of business we don't use. For example, George Hoenck has a fur store. We never buy fur coats. And the ladies' ready-to-wear stores. We never buy ladies' ready-to-wear. But we happen to have to buy office equipment, trucks and tractors, and so on.

"It seems to me that the 80 percent of the merchants and all the other taxpayers are entitled to know that when they put a dollar down here in city tax money, we're going to get the most we can get for a dollar."

"Look," Larry said, "I've been in business here for forty years, and I've seen them come and go. If you give business to that fellow who is willing to undersell, he's going to go broke in a little while. He'll soon be out of business."

"That's a very interesting statement," I said. "I know you are for the American free enterprise system — free competition. You are opposed to paternalistic government; I've heard the speeches you give on the subject. Yet now you're telling me that when one of your competitors is willing to sell for less — because of better merchandising or for whatever reason — I should say to him, 'Joe, if you offer your item at this price, and we buy price, and we buy from you, you'll soon be broke. Therefore, I'm not going to accept your bid.'"

"Well," Larry said, "I see I'm not getting anyplace with my argument."

"I guess I'm not getting anyplace with mine either," I replied, and we hung up.

I kept in close touch with Bloese, to be helpful where I could and to encourage him, knowing the change would be difficult. He was a conscientious and agreeable young man who did everything possible to cater to the needs and wishes of the department heads. They responded in kind, except for the police chief. Despite my specific request that insofar as possible the departments consolidate their monthly supply requirements, the chief sent three and four officers at a time to the purchasing agent, each with a requisition for a single roll of Scotch tape, a box of paper clips, and other small items. He gave several salesmen orders for merchandise, then sent them to the purchasing agent for confirmation of the order.

Despite these difficulties, Don Bloese was making progress. We were catching up on the payment of bills, had eliminated duplicate payments (made previously because of inadequate record keeping), and were realizing some substantial savings. Because we had no system for servicing vehicles, except in the fire department and street division, each department took its vehicles to be serviced wherever and whenever they wished. The purchasing agent was negotiating for a standardized preventive maintenance program that promised substantial savings as well as better service.

Then one day in early April, Bloese did not come to work. I asked Dwight Ink, our budget and personnel officer and my principal assistant, to check. Dwight called Mrs. Bloese, who reported she thought Don had gone to the office.

When we didn't hear from Don in an hour or so, I called Mrs. Bloese. By this time she was very upset. She had heard nothing from Don and had no idea where he was. When I asked if she could explain his actions, she said, "Mr. Harlow, has Don told you the problems he's been having with the police department?"

I replied I knew he was having some problems.

She said, "Every night this week he has walked the floor most of the night, saying over and over again, 'I've got to work it out with Jester; I've just got to get it worked out with Jester.' Don has worried me, he's been so nervous and tired."

I tried to reassure her, telling her we would start a search for Don, and I would call her back.

I asked Dwight to do everything he could to locate Don — find out who some of his friends were, where he might be.

At noon Dwight called in to say he had not located Don but thought he was on his trail. He had seen some people who had seen Don around.

Later that afternoon Dwight called again. He was at the bus station. He had arrived there in time to see Don leaving, but too late to speak to him.

We kept in touch with Mrs. Bloese but didn't hear of Don for several weeks. Finally we got word. Don had reenlisted in the army. He was at Fort Riley, Kansas.

I immediately began a search for a successor to Don Bloese. After interviewing several candidates, I appointed Harold Conway, a disabled World War II paratrooper retrained by the army for purchasing work, who was living in a nearby small town. He was an exceptionally fine and able man. He knew purchasing procedures and markets and had the ability to get along with department heads, vendors, and the public.

He moved his family to Fargo and went right to work. Although we had lost some time due to Don Bloese's sudden departure, it looked as though we were finally on our way with the purchasing program. But Bloese's troubles had not all been inside City Hall, and neither were Conway's to be.

Harold Conway started work as purchasing agent in late June. The following July 13, during the city commission's budget hearings, the commission had a lengthy discussion about the function and need for centralized purchasing. Finally, on a 3-2 vote, they decided to continue it a year to determine whether the savings made it a profitable operation.

On July 27, after the budget passed the Board of Budget Review and the last person had been heard, with no protest or comment of any kind on the central purchasing program, the commissioner alignment changed, and by a 2-3 vote the city commission cut out all funds for the purchasing office.

This was a blow. Although we had had only three months of actual operation, we had realized the following savings:

- On office supplies, a 10 percent discount on some items, and on carbon paper and typewriter ribbons, 40 percent;

- Office equipment, a 10 percent discount, standard to government offices, if requested;

- By purchasing chlorine for the water department in carload lots, for which we had plenty of storage space, instead of month-by-month, we dropped the price from 14¢ a pound to 10 $1/2$¢ a pound. The saving: $980 per year;

- The purchasing agent had negotiated a new price for sand, from $2.25 per yard to $2.00 per yard, for a saving of $200 in one month;

- He obtained a 25+10 percent and a 20+10 percent discount on tires and tubes;

- The estimated savings on printing was 20 percent;

- A 26 percent discount was obtained on electric lamps.

In total, during July the city spent $13,000 at a saving of $2,100 or about 14 percent. And that was only the start; but it was also the finish of the central purchasing program.

QUESTIONS TO START THE DISCUSSION

1. As the introductory essay for Part II suggests, "fraud, waste and abuse" is a phrase now used to cover a wide range of undesirable practices; could the problems described in this case be sorted out in terms of these three standards?

2. How successful was Harlow in this case? Are there steps he might have taken before late July to save the central purchasing program?

Case 6: The Five Percent Solution

In all organizations, travel vouchers provide a significant challenge to individual morality and, in the absence of careful controls, they provide a risk as well that the broader ethical culture of the organization may be eroded. In the agency described below, a pattern of corruption has infected a central unit charged with preventing fraud in the wider organization; one interesting question is whether the infection is likely to spread, and if so in what directions. Specific questions on the case are appended at the end of the selection.

Six months ago you were hired as an internal auditor for a federal agency which has the responsibility for auditing the accounts of other units within a department of the executive branch.

Your job requires almost daily travel, either individually or as a team member, over a wide geographical area. Typically, in any one week you will incur expenses of $250-$400. Since you are reimbursed for everything, including the use of your automobile, record keeping becomes an important part of your job. Initially, you calculated your expenses on an actual basis and submitted the appropriate vouchers. Soon, however, it becomes common knowledge that your vouchers are consistently lower than those of others who accompanied you on the same trip, or who had submitted expense vouchers for similar trips in the past.

One day a team partner takes you aside and explains to you that everyone in the unit adds five percent to each weekly expense voucher. This is accomplished through various means which are not easily verifiable. Some of the auditors pick up blank meal receipt stubs from chain restaurant and hotel eating facilities; some expand on tips and gratuities, adding some that were never given or inflating the tips that were provided. Most, however, simply added extra mileage to the voucher. As your friend tells it, almost everyone feels this is justifiable because they are not able to claim certain expenses — bar bills — or because they have lost certain required receipts. One employee felt he was compensating for a deserved promotion which he did not get. Some others felt that they were not being paid enough for what they were doing.

Your friend explains to you that you are making the rest of the unit look bad by not claiming an extra five percent, and that you would really be doing everyone on the team a big favor by engaging in this practice. You consider this, and then decide to go along with your colleagues. On your next two vouchers, you inflate your mileage to approximately five percent of your expenses. You do not feel good about this, however, and decide not to do it any more. From then on, you feel yourself becoming more and more isolated from the social and conversational activities of your colleagues. One of the auditors even requests that the unit manager not assign you to any of his team activities.

Finally, you feel like an agency pariah and decide to do something about it. Your remaining friend advises that the only thing he thinks you can do is to utilize the five percent solution. You consider this again, but decide against it. You now decide to talk to your supervisor. Before you can make an appointment to see him, you receive a written evaluation of your first six months of employment. Since this is a probationary period, you may be subject to dismissal if your evaluation is poor. To your dismay, you find that your supervisor has dedicated a major part of the evaluation to your inability to get along with your fellow workers. He states that a decision about continued employment will hinge on the required interview. You are required to respond in writing to this evaluation before the interview.

QUESTIONS TO START THE DISCUSSION

1. How would you respond? What other steps should you consider taking?

2. If you were a recently-hired senior officer of the agency, and heard rumors of the "five percent solution," what steps would you consider taking?

Source: Leigh Grosenick, Virginia Commonwealth University.

A Guide to Ethics
Commonwealth of Massachusetts

The Conflict of Interest Law
Chapter 268A

In many states, "conflict of interest" laws have been enacted or strengthened in the past decade. The following selection, drawn from a guide to ethics distributed to state legislators in Massachusetts, describes the purposes of these statutes in that state and the specific acts prohibited by law. Questions: Do other states include the same range of prohibitions as Massachusetts? Specifically, does the "appearance or impression" of a conflict of interest violate the law? Do you think such a standard is desirable, or does it suggest an "overreach" of the law? If the Massachusetts standards were applied to the HUD case (earlier in this section), would they suggest that Hovde and his aides need to alter their guidelines?

Introduction

Chapter 268A, the so-called Conflict of Interest Law, governs the conduct of elected and appointed state, county, and municipal officials and employees. In general, the law is intended to assure that the conduct of these public officials and employees, in the execution of their public obligations, is not jaded by their personal interests. The law is constructed in such a manner so as to curtail conduct which intimates even the appearance or potential of conflict.

Section 2 — Corrupt gifts, offers or promises to influence official acts; corruption of witnesses

Section 2 prohibits legislators from corruptly seeking or receiving gifts, promises, bribes or anything else of value in exchange for being influenced in the performance of their official acts or duties. Under this section, penalties are levied upon both the legislator soliciting or accepting the gifts or bribes, as well as private parties offering them.

Specifically, legislators may not solicit or receive anything of value in exchange for:

1. Being influenced in the performance of any official act;

2. Being influenced to commit, collude, or allow the opportunity for the perpetration of any fraud on the Commonwealth or any state, county or municipal agency;

3. Being induced to act or refrain from acting in violation of their official duties;

4. Being influenced in either giving testimony under oath, or in the alternative, to refuse or avoid giving testimony before any court, legislative committee or any agency, commission or officer of the Commonwealth authorized to take such testimony.

For a violation of the terms contained in this section, the State Ethics Commission has determined that there must be a finding that the public official acted with a "corrupt intent."

● "Corrupt intent" exists when the public official and the private party agree that official action (or inaction) will result from the receipt of anything of value.

● "Official action" includes any decision or action in a particular matter or in the enactment of legislation.

● "Anything of value" includes not only money, but any type of service or consideration given for the benefit of the public official or for the benefit of another person or entity.

Section 3 — Additional compensation or gratuities for official acts

Section 3, like Section 2, deals with the solicitation or receipt of anything of substantial value in exchange for the interference in the performance of official acts. Section 3 is more loosely interpretive, however, because "corrupt intent" is not required on the part of the elected official. Hence, conduct not *overtly* corrupt is still covered by the conflict of interest law.

Section 3 prohibits elected officials from seeking or receiving anything of "substantial value" given for or because of their official acts or acts to be performed. The receipt of such compensation will violate this

Source: Commonwealth of Massachusetts, House of Representatives Committee on Ethics, *A Guide to Ethics*, 1986.

section even if it is given by a private party merely out of a sense of gratitude with no intent whatsoever to influence the official in the performance of his or her duties. Although the exact dollar amount of "substantial value" is not defined in the statute, the courts have interpreted it to mean anything of $50 or over. As in Section 2, the compensation need not be monetary.

Example: A public official violates Section 3 if he/she accepts an honorarium for a speaking engagement if circumstances indicate that the compensation was actually an improper gratuity. Such circumstances would include:

1. That the speaking engagement wasn't legitimate;

2. That the honorarium was excessive for the nature of the engagement;

3. That the organization has a clear interest in pending legislation that the official would be in a position to affect.

Section 23 — Standards of Conduct

Section 23 of Chapter 268A is known as the "Standards of Conduct" section which attempts to tie up any loose ends created by the preceding sections. This section deals with some of the most basic principles and guidelines appropriate to public officials; hence, it essentially serves as a statutory code of ethics. Section 23 does not merely enumerate specific actions which are considered conflicts of interest, but is designed to cover actions which would give the appearance or impression of a conflict of interest while executing one's official duties.

As applied to members of the General Court [State Legislature] §23 dictates that no legislator shall knowingly, or with reason to know:

1. Accept additional employment involving a salary compensation of substantial value if the responsibilities of that employment conflict with those of his/her public office;

2. use or attempt to use his/her official position to secure unwarranted privileges or exemptions of substantial value not otherwise properly available for himself, herself or others; or

3. by his/her conduct cause a reasonable person, having knowledge of the relevant circumstances, to conclude that any person can improperly influence or unduly enjoy his/her official duties, or that he/she is unduly affected by the kinship, rank, position, or influence of any party or person.

Such a conclusion will be considered unreasonable if said legislator has disclosed in a manner which is public in nature the facts which would otherwise lead to such a conclusion.

The Case of Edwin Meese III

A Law-and-Order Look at Ed Meese

Editorial, New York Times   September 14, 1988

Among the most visible cases of alleged unethical behavior in the 1980s were those involving Edwin Meese III, who served as Counselor to President Reagan (1981-84) and as Attorney General of the United States (1984-88). After investigating some of these allegations, Independent Counsel James McKay concluded that Meese should not be subjected to criminal prosecution, and Meese responded that he had been "vindicated" by the McKay report. However, the Office of Government Ethics then conducted its own review and in September 1988, the Director of that office, former judge Frank Nebeker, released a memorandum in response to the report on the allegations. Excerpts are reproduced here, with a New York Times editorial prompted by the memorandum. We have also appended a brief note at the end of the report, referring to some important issues involved in the controversy.

QUESTIONS TO START THE DISCUSSION

1. Are the requirements of Executive Order 11222 too vague?

2. Are the positions set forth by Senators Rudman and Cohen appropriate and on target?

Edwin Meese, who resigned as Attorney General in a hail of criticism over his ethics, blamed his troubles on political partisans, disloyal and ambitious underlings and an overzealous special prosecutor who said he probably committed crimes. He took comfort from President Reagan's constant support. Now from a law-and-order appointee of the same President comes yet another condemnation of Mr. Meese's behavior in office.

Frank Nebeker, director of the Office of Government Ethics, has sent a memorandum to Federal departments warning that Mr. Meese is a perfect illustration of how not to behave. Mr. Nebeker says that Mr. Meese not only flouted standards set more than 20 years ago but violated his own promises to the ethics agency. The agency was created by Congress to help officials comply with the rules.

Mr. Nebeker is not some political foe out to get Ed Meese and hurt Ronald Reagan. Appointed by President Nixon to the D.C. Court of Appeals, he earned a reputation as a prosecution-oriented judge in 18 years on the bench. Now he may be transforming a lapdog agency into a genuine watchdog.

Using the same Independent Counsel's report that Mr. Meese claimed as "vindication," Mr. Nebeker finds that Mr. Meese's ownership of telephone stock and favoritism for his friend and attorney Robert Wallach violated pledges he made to the Administration's ethics officials.

Three years ago the director of the ethics office, David Martin, found no ethical violation when Mr. Meese gave a job to an accountant who had arranged $60,000 in loans. The injunction to avoid the appearance of impropriety was only "aspirational," Mr. Martin said. Mr. Nebeker takes the rules more seriously and cautions officials not to raise suspicions about their ethical behavior. It's a welcome lesson in good government.

Memorandum

United States Office of Government Ethics
September 12, 1988

MEMORANDUM

TO: Designated Agency Ethics Officials, General Counsels,
             Inspectors General and Other Interested Persons

FROM: Frank Q. Nebeker, Director

SUBJECT: Guidance on ethics program issues raised in the Report of the
             Independent Counsel dated July 5, 1988

On July 5, 1988, Independent Counsel McKay submitted his report on his investigation of Edwin Meese III. . . . That same day, Mr. Meese stated to the press that he had been vindicated by the report. . . .

Because this matter has been the subject of much public comment, some highly incorrect, and a lengthy Independent Counsel's report, I believe this memorandum can best serve as an important and valuable vehicle for providing guidance on a number of issues to ethics officials, counselors and investigators. . . .

Financial Disclosure Requirements

The Act established public financial disclosure requirements for persons in high level positions so that the public along with an agency can review the reports and be assured that conflicts of interest do not exist, have not occurred, or will not occur. The issue of Mr. Meese's failure to disclose properly the assets of Meese Partners (initially reported by him as Financial Management, Inc.) has already been the subject of one Senate hearing, a lengthy statement by his counsel and lengthy correspondence from this Office regarding the requirements of disclosure. Mr. Meese's lack of attention to the requirements of properly reporting his assets outside of Meese Partners and the assets of Meese Partners was a contributing factor in the ultimate referral of the possible . . . violation by Mr. Meese. Had he reported the retention of some interest in the . . . stocks or properly reported his limited partnership or properly reported his other assets and gifts on the annual report he filed for calendar year 1985, corrective steps could have been taken prior to his acting in his official capacity in matters affecting the RBOCs [Regional Bell Operating Company stock shares, owned by Meese], and his recusal statement could have been amended to reflect his actual disqualifying interests.

Failure to pay close attention to filing a public financial disclosure report has not only caused Mr. Meese much public criticism, but many others as well. Mr. Meese's situation, however, because of his high visibility, should be a very constructive, albeit unfortunate, example for others in the future. This Office and agency ethics officials owe employees of or nominees to positions within their agencies a careful and thorough review of their reports in order not only to ensure that no conflicts or potential conflicts exist but, in addition, to assist filers in completing the form properly when a reviewer sees some indication that there may have not been a complete understanding by the filer of the reporting requirements. Filers may believe the filing requirements onerous and imposing but the price for being careless about or actually ignoring the requirements, as demonstrated by this case, is very high indeed. One can see what damage to reputation alone can result.

Standards of Conduct Issues

. . .Because Mr. Meese's statements regarding his vindication have been made in such a public manner so as to cause real confusion on the role of the standards of conduct, I believe it would be inappropriate for this Office to stay silent on these issues. . . .It is important to remember that the policy of Executive Order 11222 [first issued in 1965] as stated in section 101 of that Order is as follows:

> Where government is based on the consent of the governed, every citizen is entitled to have complete confidence in the integrity of his government. Each individual officer, employee, or adviser of government must help to earn and must honor that trust by his own integrity and conduct in all official actions.

In accordance with that announced policy, section 201 (c) states that employees should "avoid any action. . .which might result in or create the appearance of —

(1) using public office for private gain;

(2) giving preferential treatment to any organization or person;

(3) impeding government efficiency or economy;

(4) losing complete independence or impartiality of action;

(5) making a government decision outside official channels; or

(6) affecting adversely the confidence of the public in the integrity of the Government."

The most troublesome aspect of the information in the Independent Counsel's report is the extent to which Mr. Meese or Mr. Meese's official position was used for the benefit of Mr. Wallach. The standard against using public office for private gain includes the private gain of others, not simply the personal gain of the employee. Assisting a friend is not in and of itself prohibited by the Executive Order. But, assisting a friend in a manner which misuses official position for the friend's private benefit, which gives that friend preferential treatment not properly afforded, which causes a government decision to be made outside official channels, which affects the public's confidence in the integrity of its government, or which leads an informed and reasonable person to believe that any of these things have occurred, is what this section was in part intended to prohibit. This section, as well, requires that an executive branch employee take some positive steps to stop any other individual from using the official position of the employee, assuming the employee knows his position is being used or that it might be used. This is true for no other reason than to avoid the appearance that the employee is in fact misusing his position or that he is making government decisions outside official channels.

. . .The information in the Independent Counsel's report indicates that in two significant instances Mr. Meese's activities on behalf of Mr. Wallach's private endeavors bring his personal use of official position into question. While in both instances Mr. Meese appears not to have personally participated in any extended manner, his acts were crucial to the subsequent acts of others simply by virtue of the offices he held.

First, Mr. Meese asked his staff at the White House to check into what was actually a procurement matter (i.e. the attempt by Welbilt, later Wedtech, to secure a contract with the Army through the SBA's 8(a) program for minority-owned companies). This was done at the behest of and on behalf of his friend Mr. Wallach when it was the White House policy for staff not to become involved in procurement matters involving personal interests or those of friends without seeking guidance from the White House Counsel's Office.

The second was Mr. Meese's late May or early June 1985 telephone call as Attorney General to the National Security Advisor, Mr. McFarlane, asking him to meet with Mr. Wallach about the Aqaba pipeline project. This was at a time when Mr. Meese knew Mr. Wallach had been retained by Mr. Rappaport to assist him in securing a political risk insurance package for this project and at a time when Mr. Meese's recusal agreement, if followed, would require that he not take any official action involving a matter in which Mr. Wallach was representing a client. Had Mr. Wallach simply sought information from his friend Mr. Meese regarding which was the proper office in the government to contact, this same issue would not have arisen.

It is simply a fact that care must be taken, especially when acting outside one's usual official responsibilities to see that the acts are not misinterpreted, and that these considerations should be a part of any counseling provided an official who seeks assistance with a standards of conduct question.

. . .In addition, Mr. Meese seems to have used Mr. Wallach significantly in his personnel selections within the Department of Justice, having him interview prospective candidates for positions. While individuals in the government can occasionally seek advice from private parties, when the use of that advice becomes "institutionalized," the appearance that normal government decisions are being made by non-government individuals is clearly at issue. . . .

There is no more clarion standard at issue in this matter than that which exhorts an employee to avoid any action that adversely affects the confidence of the public in the integrity of the Government. While Mr. Meese's personal reputation could not but have suffered as a result of this investigation, the public's confidence in the Department of Justice has also suffered. One need only look at the well-publicized personnel resignations in the Department to see why this standard is at issue. . . .

Section 201(a) states that employees may not "solicit or accept, directly or indirectly, any gift, gratuity, favor, entertainment, loan or any other thing of monetary value from any person, corporation, or group which —

(1) has, or is seeking to obtain, contractual or other business or financial relationships with his agency;

(2) conducts operation or activities which are regulated by his agency; or

(3) has interests which may be substantially affected by the performance or nonperformance of his official duty."

. . .Gifts to government officials have always been a subject of high interest because a gift brings into play the appearance of a number of improprieties. The standard simply states that if the offeror of a gift to an executive branch official falls within one of the categories of organizations or individuals outlined in the standard, then the public official is not to accept anything directly or indirectly from that individual. Therefore, there will be no question of the integrity of the individual involved.

. . .Mr. Wallach, who sought Mr. Meese's personal actions on matters in which he was involved, is reported by the Independent Counsel to have given Mr. Meese a number of items and benefits while he served in the White House and as Attorney General. These gifts raised the spector of a possible bribe. . . .

The benefits specifically addressed by the report include Mr. Wallach's discharge of the difference between the Court's award to Mr. Wallach for representation of Mr. Meese during the investigation by Independent Counsel Stein, his free legal counsel during Mr. Meese's confirmation hearing, his facilitation of funding by the Benders of Mrs. Meese's job with the Washington Chapter of the Multiple Sclerosis Society, his facilitation of a same-day unsecured loan from a local bank for the Meeses, his assistance in securing a trip to Israel for the Meeses for the dedication of a grove of trees in memory of their son Scott, and the facilitation of the refinancing of the Meeses' home mortgage.

. . .Section 206 states "[a]n employee is expected to meet all just financial obligations, especially those — such as Federal, State, or local taxes — which are imposed by law."

The standard requires that an employee is expected to meet all just financial obligations including his Federal taxes. The report indicates that Mr. Meese initially did not meet his obligations and that his efforts at doing so were at best tardy. His failure to meet these obligations was not because of a disagreement with the Government on the extent of the obligation. It was a failure to report income. He has, however, now apparently met the obligations, but an issue arising under this standard remains as to whether the manner in which he handled his tax obligations has affected adversely the confidence of the public in the integrity of the Government. It is reasonably easy to assume that the public's confidence in the integrity of the fairness of the tax collection process will be affected when it becomes publicly known that the chief law enforcement official fails to declare income for tax purposes until after his records for the appropriate period are requested by a prosecutor.

Conclusion

A major purpose of this memorandum is to remind and inform that simply avoiding criminal conduct is not the mark of public service. The duties imposed by non-criminal standards are far harder to discharge. They may even be strange and seem overly restrictive to some joining government for the first time. But, they must not be ignored under the real pressures of other official duties. This Office strongly believes, and I hope you will assist in conveying the thought, that problems such as these are not widespread in the executive branch and that the vast majority of officers and employees are hard working and loyal individuals who make every effort to adhere to the high ethical standards the public has a right to expect from them and that they expect from themselves.

During the Meese controversy, members of Congress and other observers commented on a variety of issues raised by the case. Some Republican leaders viewed the criticisms directed at the Attorney General as partisan and strident, particularly since more than a dozen ethics cases involving members of Congress — including several prominent Democrats — were not being given equal attention by Meese's critics. However, Senator Warren B. Rudman (R-New Hampshire) thought that Meese had shown "a decided lack of sensitivity to certain situations and associations," but that a more basic problem was the tendency of a President to choose friends as senior executives, which made it difficult to remove them in the face of allegations of misbehavior. "The President would be very well served to appoint a cabinet mainly of people that he hardly knew but of absolute unimpeachable integrity and competence," Rudman concluded. "And then if somebody did something, then there would not be that friendship." Senator William S. Cohen (R-Maine) emphasized the role of the President in setting ethical standards for his Administration: "You have to have a tone that is of the highest standards and to insist that those who serve your Administration abide by that," Cohen argued, "and frankly there has not been that kind of commitment." (New York Times, April 17, 1988)

ASPA Workbook: Conflicts of Interest

Although conflicts of interest characterize all professions, they are particularly accentuated in public administration, where the need to maintain the public trust is crucial. Public administrators frequently find themselves in situations in which public objectives and private goals, as well as the means to attain them, are in conflict. So, too, must public administrators deal with conflicts in their loyalties to supervisors and subordinates, immediate unit and agency, and individual programs and broad organizational missions.

These conflicts may be minimized if there is a close match between the personal codes of the public administrator and the mission and practices of her or his organization. But given the high degree of individuality evident among public administrators, the usual case is one of some conflict and lack of matching.

Public management responsibilities also extend well beyond simply determining matters that might be considered technically legal or illegal. Involved are such concerns as:

1. Reflecting on actions of yours that result in personal gains as opposed to organizational benefits.

2. Examining the impact of your personal belief system on organizational programs and practices.

3. Considering the numerous forms of offering or accepting favors.

4. Reflecting on your use of personal power and influence in the organization and the conflicts that may result.

5. Observing and possibly intervening in conflict of interest situations involving colleagues.

6. Considering the dilemmas created for you by responsibilities imposed by agency missions, citizenship, and codes of conduct.

7. Dealing with the potential conflicts between your organization's goals and tactics and pursuing the general welfare within the political subdivision involved.

Some Self-Diagnostic Questions Concerning Conflicts of Interest

1. Do I know the provisions of conflicts of interest laws that apply to my position?

2. How do I resolve conflicts among what I think might be good for my agency, client group, or society?

3. Do I seek personal gain from "inside" knowledge or privileged information?

4. How do I reconcile my personal belief system with the tasks that I am required to perform?

5. Do I systematically examine potential sources of conflict involving my role in public management? When I identify such conflicts of interest, do I remove myself from decision making about the situation? Do I proceed in some other way?

6. Do I consult with others about potential conflicts of interest?

7. How do I react to conflicts of interest that I observe in the behavior of colleagues? Do I support the actions of others who call attention to conflicts of interest?

8. Do I accept favors from those who can be affected by my decisions?

9. When I perform the role of a consultant, adviser, or "neutral third party," what kinds of considerations influence my recommendations?

Source: Mertins and Hennigan, *Applying Professional Standards and Ethics in the Eighties*, pp. 17-18.

Case 7: The New Manager Wants to Shoot Santa Claus

This case illustrates the problems facing a new executive when his personal and professional standards conflict with an organizational tradition or the preferences of superiors.

David Graham, the young, new Wessex County Manager, did not really want to shoot Santa Claus. At least that was not the way he saw the issue. However, that was apparently the way many county employees viewed his comments at last week's staff meeting. He had voiced his concern regarding the acceptance of Christmas presents by the staff and the holding of Christmas parties in county office buildings. It looked as if he might be off to a bad start in his new job — for which he had had such high hopes. In considering this question, he recognized that it could not be separated from the broader issues of county traditions and practices, the differing concept of the manager post, and the interfaces of the personalities and roles in the leading county office.

Wessex County is a large suburban jurisdiction. Before World War II it was predominantly rural. Since then, it had grown rapidly to a population of over three hundred thousand. Wessex is, in several respects, an amalgam of contrasts. Despite urbanization, over half of the county's area remains open countryside. The picture is one of rapid suburban growth, housing developments, shopping centers, and industrial parks spread out from the neighboring central city to engulf farms, country estates, and older rural communities which have served long as identifying centers for sections of the county. Like many suburban jurisdictions the county was slow to face the need for new roads, water and sewer lines, schools, libraries, parks and recreational facilities, and other public amenities required by this rapid transformation. But for more than a decade the county had been engaged in an effort to catch up — by means of capital improvements exceeding fifty million dollars per year.

The population of Wessex is also a mixture. Many older residents maintain nostalgia for the county, thinking of the way it was in the past. Many newcomers want to keep it in the present form. Others, recognizing the lucrative opportunities presented by rapid development, have promoted growth.

Wessex County government reflects this blend. A decade earlier a new charter had been adopted as the culmination of reform efforts which had the self-serving cooperation of the entrenched political leadership. The new charter provided for a seven-member council elected at large, a full-time, elective County Executive, and an appointed Manager. The Manager is responsible for the administration of the county. By law, he selects (with the approval of the County Executive) and directs most of the department heads; he prepares and supervises the implementation of the budget; and he is responsible for the general standards and supervision of all county employees. The major aspects of county governance not subject to his control are the Department of Education, the Office of the Assessor, Zoning, and the Office of the Law. The Charter thus reflects an effort to reconcile the administrative values of council-manager and strong-mayor forms of government, yet preserves from reform control those perquisites of government from which the county politicos long had benefited and did not relish relinquishing to reform machinery.

David Graham was only the second person to hold the post of County Manager. His professional city management background contrasted strikingly with that of his predecessor, William Hall, a local boy who had worked his way up the ranks and had been promoted from the post of Budget Director when the charter had been adopted ten years earlier. Although not a college graduate and without professional ties, Hall had a detailed knowledge of Wessex County administration — but he lacked a broad grasp of the overall issues which a rapidly growing local government generated. However, he had personal charm and the ability to relate to various political factions. (He advised Graham to contribute to each of the political candidates' campaign funds.)

When David Graham had been interviewed for the managership several weeks earlier, he had been very favorably impressed with the County Executive, Carl Palmer. Palmer appeared to have a broad inter-

Source: Samuel Humes, "The New Manager Wants to Shoot Santa Claus," *The Bureaucrat*, 4:1 (April 1975).

est in county problems, a real concern for improving services, and an appreciation of Graham's education (B.A. Wesleyan, M.P.A. Syracuse) and previous city management experience. He also possessed a charming manner which some persons described as "sweetness." Carl Palmer had been elected to the post three years earlier. He was a first-generation American who had returned from World War II, attended the local law school at night, run unsuccessfully for a county-wide post, and then won the minority party's nomination for County Executive. The majority party split wide open in the September primary and the incumbent Executive had lost to what was locally called the "Old Guard." The losing side then supported Palmer in the general election (having been assured that the political appointees, including several department heads, would be retained). Palmer's tenure had not been tranquil; he failed in his efforts to start an urban renewal project and he was frustrated in almost all his other efforts by the council which was controlled 6-to-1 by the other party — two of whom already had announced their candidacy for Executive in next fall's election.

Graham found that it was difficult to avoid being caught in the crossfire between the two institutions. The council appeared to view Graham as the "Executive's man," and the Executive suspected any efforts Graham made to keep council members informed.

Graham had accepted the offer of the Manager's post and had been confirmed for the office early in November. He looked forward to working with the moderate, energetic County Executive who was already attracting favorable state-wide attention. Within several days, Graham found that the situation was somewhat different than he expected from his initial impressions.

Palmer soon told Graham that he intended to run for governor (he would rather lose a gubernatorial race than a County Executive one). Consequently, Palmer had limited remaining interest in county affairs. Graham was told to handle administration of the county and make the minimum demands on Palmer's time and judgment. (In effect, Graham was told to administer the county with the least possible "rocking of the boat.")

Graham also began to have second thoughts regarding the depth of Palmer's appreciation of governmental issues and professional administrative expertise. For example, Palmer had superficially dismissed Graham's efforts to discuss a proposal for subcounty offices, the need for local open-housing legislation, and the desirability of relinquishing county control of sewer development to a proposed metropolitan-wide sewer authority. In this and other ways Palmer did not appear to appreciate Graham's professional judgment. This was confirmed when Palmer objected to Graham's plans to attend a forthcoming professional association meeting. Graham also was surprised to be asked to substitute for Palmer as a speaker at a meeting which was essentially political. It was evident that there was a difference of opinion between Palmer and Graham whether the Manager [should] act as a political deputy or professional associate. And the interface between them already was becoming strained as a result. Judging by Palmer's comments regarding county department heads, Graham began to wonder if Palmer valued personal loyalty more than professional expertise.

Graham had resolved when he first took office to go slow in proposing any changes. He had been advised by one of his city manager colleagues, "Remember the importance of staying in office to battle to accomplish any of your goals. Choose your issues carefully." However, with the approach of the Christmas season, he was concerned with the reported prevalence and obvious nature of Christmas gift-giving. Most of those doing substantial business with the county (suppliers, contractors, construction companies, engineering firms, and so forth) by long-standing custom delivered presents to the leading officials with whom they dealt. Graham learned that not only were presents sent to homes, but many were delivered directly to public offices. Many firms delivered cases of liquor and other substantial gifts to the principal county offices (e.g., Purchasing, Planning, Public Works, Licenses, and Inspection). Some of these presents provided the basis for office parties which began the morning of Christmas Eve and continued throughout the day. Several of the parties adjourned in mid-afternoon to various clubs and restaurants in the county where the employees, politicians, and other well-wishers made the rounds visiting and exchanging season's greetings.

During an early December staff meeting, the County Manager raised the question of whether the observation of the gift-giving and office partying might give a poor impression to some of the citizens who were transacting business in the county at the time these presents were distributed or when the parties were held on the county premises. He raised with department heads the question of whether a new policy should be considered — one in which no presents would be received in county offices and no office parties held on county premises. He had suggested that perhaps the county office building should be closed at noon on Christmas Eve so that the various offices of the county could schedule Christmas parties outside the county limits. No decision was made at the staff meeting, but the matter was to be considered again at the next.

During the week before the meeting, Graham heard from several sources that many of the department heads were disgruntled with the proposed policy despite the fact that they had raised no protest at the staff meeting. Among the reported comments: "But we have always received Christmas presents" — "Private businessmen receive presents, why can't we?" — "Nobody expects to influence our judgment" — "It would be embarrassing to return the presents" — "What the hell is bugging him?" — "What does he want to do, shoot Santa Claus?" The professional Planning Director reportedly had commented, "Let's see if the young manager can carry this off."

While the County Manager had anticipated some opposition at the coming staff meeting, he had not foreseen what would occur. He had not expected that his Administrative Assistant (a local lawyer who had been selected by Palmer two years previously) would come into his office only a few minutes before the staff meeting to inform him that the County Executive was offended that the proposed new policy had even been considered without being previously discussed with him. It was reported that in the discussion of the issue, the County Executive had commented that, "If anybody thinks that I can be bought with a case of liquor — ."

In reflecting, the County Manager realized his position was somewhat precarious. His options appeared limited. He had been appointed only the previous month and he had not yet developed a strong network of acquaintances within the county to defend his position. He also suspected that the County Executive's assessment of him was that he, as County Manager, was politically naive.

After his Administrative Assistant left the office Graham attempted to call the County Executive — but found that he was not available. He had to make a decision before the staff meeting convened in a few minutes. To go ahead and propose his new policy regarding gifts and parties as he initially had intended might permanently estrange him from Palmer and other county officials. Was this the issue to choose to "go down with colors flying?" On the other hand, to drop it altogether might denote weakness. He was aware that there would be serious consequences not only immediately, but also in the long run on either stand he adopted. He wondered if there was any way he could avoid scuttling his concern completely — or was the issue already closed and the damage already done? Was this question part of a broader problem he needed to consider? He was still pondering his dilemma as he walked into the staff meeting and exchanged pleasantries with the department heads.

QUESTION TO START DISCUSSION

1. How important was it to preserve his image as the effective head of the county's administration?

POSTSCRIPT

Five minutes later. David Graham stated in the staff meeting that after considering the reactions and comments of numerous county officials to the proposed changes in policy regarding Christmas gifts and parties for county employees, he had arrived at the conclusion that any change in policy should be deferred until the following year. At that time there would be more opportunity to assess the existing practices and the implications of proposed changes.

One year later. In the November election of the following year Palmer is elected governor (again the majority party had split; many of those who had supported one of the losers in the primary had then supported Palmer rather than their party nominee). One member of the county council had defeated Palmer's choice (the County Attorney) in the general election for County Executive. Even before taking office the new County Executive-elect called on Graham to tell him he was to be replaced by Hall, who was a long-time friend and associate. Graham was terminated in January — a month after the new County Executive took office. Palmer did not offer Graham a post in the state government, although several members of the administration, including Graham's Technical Assistant, accepted top posts. Graham was told by those whose judgment he trusted that his principal mistake had been to raise the Christmas present and party issue. Graham spent several months finding a job.

Eight years later. Hall, Palmer, and Palmer's successor were indicted for criminal conduct in office and each was sentenced. Graham has left the field of municipal administration.

QUESTIONS TO START DISCUSSION

1. Did the county manager act precipitously when he learned about the nature and extent of Christmas gift-giving? What should he do at the second meeting?

2. Is there really a conflict of interest here? Is there an appearance of a conflict of interest?

7. Lying and Deception/Secrecy and Confidentiality

Lies for the Public Good
Sissela Bok

Three circumstances have seemed to liars to provide the strongest excuse for their behavior — a crisis where overwhelming harm can be averted only through deceit; complete harmlessness and triviality to the point where it seems absurd to quibble about whether a lie has been told; and the duty to particular individuals to protect their secrets. I have shown how lies in times of crisis can expand into vast practices where the harm to be averted is less obvious and the crisis less and less immediate; how white lies can shade into equally vast practices no longer so harmless, with immense cumulative costs; and how lies to protect individuals and to cover up their secrets can be told for increasingly dubious purposes to the detriment of all.

When these three expanding streams flow together and mingle with yet another — a desire to advance the public good — they form the most dangerous body of deceit of all. These lies may not be justified by an immediate crisis nor by complete triviality nor by duty to any one person; rather, liars tend to consider them as right and unavoidable because of the altruism that motivates them. . . .

Sissela Bok's book examines a wide range of moral issues raised by lying and other forms of deception in both public and private life. In this chapter she explores, with examples, some of the questions we have already encountered: Where does one draw the line between acceptable and unacceptable behavior? Can we justify otherwise unethical behavior, such as deceit, if it is a means to larger goals?

Naturally, there will be large areas of overlap between these lies and those considered earlier. But the most characteristic defense for these lies is a separate one, based on the benefits they may confer and the long-range harm they can avoid. The intention may be broadly paternalistic, as when citizens are deceived "for their own good," or a few may be lied to for the benefit of the community at large. Error and self-deception mingle with these altruistic purposes and blur them; the filters through which we must try to peer at lying are thicker and more distorting than ever in these practices. But I shall try to single out, among these lies, the elements that are consciously and purposely intended to benefit society.

A long tradition in political philosophy endorses some lies for the sake of the public. Plato . . . first used the expression "noble lie" for the fanciful story that might be told to people in order to persuade them to accept class distinctions and thereby safeguard social harmony. According to this story, God Himself mingled gold, silver, iron, and brass in fashioning rulers, auxiliaries, farmers, and craftsmen, intending these groups for separate tasks in a harmonious hierarchy.

The Greek adjective which Plato used to characterize this falsehood expresses a most important fact about lies by those in power: this adjective is "gennaion," which means "noble" in the sense of both "high-minded" and "well-bred." The same assumption of nobility, good breeding, and superiority to those

Source: S. Bok, *Lying: Moral Choice in Public and Private Life* (New York: Pantheon, 1978), Ch. 12.

deceived is also present in Disraeli's statement that a gentleman is one who knows when to tell the truth and when not to. In other words, lying is excusable when undertaken for "noble" ends by those trained to discern these purposes.

Rulers, both temporal and spiritual, have seen their deceits in the benign light of such social purposes. They have propagated and maintained myths, played on the gullibility of the ignorant, and sought stability in shared beliefs. They have seen themselves as high-minded and well-bred — whether by birth or by training — and as superior to those they deceive. Some have gone so far as to claim that those who govern have a *right* to lie. The powerful tell lies believing that they have greater than ordinary understanding of what is at stake; very often, they regard their dupes as having inadequate judgement, or as likely to respond in the wrong way to truthful information.

At times, those who govern also regard particular circumstances as too uncomfortable, too painful, for most people to be able to cope with rationally. They may believe, for instance, that their country must prepare for long term challenges of great importance, such as war, an epidemic, or a belt-tightening in the face of future shortages. Yet they may fear that citizens will be able to respond only to short-range dangers. Deception at such times may seem to the government leaders as the only means of attaining the necessary results.

The perspective of the liar is paramount in all such decisions to tell "noble" lies. If the liar considers the responses of the deceived at all, he assumes that they will, once the deceit comes to light and its benefits are understood, be uncomplaining if not positively grateful. . . .

Some experienced public officials are impatient with any effort to question the ethics of such deceptive practices (except actions obviously taken for private ends). They argue that vital objectives in the national interest require a measure of deception to succeed in the face of powerful obstacles. Negotiations must be carried on that are best left hidden from public view; bargains must be struck that simply cannot be comprehended by a politically unsophisticated electorate. A certain amount of illusion is needed in order for public servants to be effective. Every government, therefore, has to deceive people to some extent in order to lead them.

These officials view the public's concern for ethics as understandable but hardly realistic. Such "moralistic" concerns, put forth without any understanding of practical exigencies, may lead to the setting of impossible standards; these could seriously hamper work without actually changing the underlining practices. Government officials could then feel so beleaguered that some of them might quit their jobs; inefficiency and incompetence would then increasingly afflict the work of the rest.

If we assume the perspective of the deceived — those who experience the consequences of government deception — such arguments are not persuasive. We cannot take for granted either the altruism or good judgment of those who lie to us, no matter how much they intend to benefit us. We have learned that much deceit for private gains masquerades as being in the public interest. We know how deception, even for the most unselfish motive, corrupts and spreads. And we have lived through the consequences of lies told for what were believed to be noble purposes.

Equally unpersuasive is the argument that there always has been government deception, and always will be, and that efforts to draw lines and set standards are therefore useless annoyances. It is certainly true that deception can never be completely absent from most human practices. But there are great differences among societies in the kinds of deceit that exist and the extent to which they are practiced, differences also among individuals in the same government and among successive governments within the same society. This strongly suggests that it is worthwhile trying to discover why such differences exist and to seek ways of raising the standards of truthfulness.

The argument that those who raise moral concerns are ignorant of political realities, finally, ought to lead, not to a dismissal of such inquiries, but to a more articulate description of what these realities are, so that a more careful and informed debate could begin. We have every reason to regard government as more profoundly injured by a dismissal of criticism and a failure to consider standards than by efforts to discuss them openly. If duplicity is to be allowed in exceptional cases, the criteria for these exceptions should themselves be openly debated and publicly chosen. Otherwise government leaders will have free rein to manipulate and distort the facts and thus escape accountability to the public.

The effort to question political deception cannot be ruled out so summarily. The disparagement of inquiries into such practices has to be seen as the defense of unwarranted power — power bypassing the consent of the governed. In the pages to come I shall take up just a few cases to illustrate both the clear breaches of trust that no group of citizens could desire, and circumstances where it is more difficult to render a judgment.

Examples of Political Deception

In September 1964, a State Department official, reflecting a growing administration consensus, wrote a memorandum advocating a momentous deceit of the American public.[1] He outlined possible courses of action to cope with the deteriorating military situation in South Vietnam. These included a stepping up of American participation in the "pacification" in South Vietnam and a "crescendo" of military action against North Vietnam, involving heavy bombing by the United States. But an election campaign was going on; the President's Republican opponent, Senator Goldwater, was suspected by the electorate of favoring escalation of the war in Vietnam and of brandishing nuclear threats to the communist world. In keeping with President Johnson's efforts to portray Senator Goldwater as an irresponsible war hawk, the memorandum ended with a paragraph entitled "Special considerations during the next two months," holding that:

> During the next two months, because of the lack of "rebuttal time" before the election to justify particular actions which may be distorted to the U.S. public, we must act with special care — signaling to. . . [the South Vietnamese] that we are behaving energetically despite the restraints of our political season, and to the U.S. public that we are behaving with good purpose and restraint.

As the campaign wore on, President Johnson increasingly professed to be the candidate of peace. He gave no indication of the growing pressure for escalation from high administrative officials who would remain in office should he win; no hint of the hard choice he knew he would face if elected. Rather he repeated over and over again that:

> [T]he first responsibility, the only real issue in this campaign, the only thing you ought to be concerned about at all, is: Who can best keep the peace?[2]

The stratagem succeeded; the election was won; the war escalated. Under the name of Operation Rolling Thunder, the United States launched massive bombing raids over North Vietnam early in 1965. In suppressing genuine debate about these plans during the election campaign and masquerading as the party of peace, government members privy to the maneuver believed that they knew what was best for the country and that history would vindicate them. They meant to benefit the nation and the world by keeping the danger of a communist victory at bay. If a sense of crisis was needed for added justification, the Domino Theory strained for it: one regime after another was seen as toppling should the first domino be pushed over.

But why the deceit, if the purposes were so altruistic? Why not espouse these purposes openly before the election? The reason must have been that the government could not count on popular support for the scheme. In the first place, the sense of crisis and threat from North Vietnam would have been far from universally shared. To be forthright about the likelihood of escalation might lose many votes; it certainly could not fit with the campaign to portray President Johnson as the candidate most likely to keep the peace. Second, the government feared that its explanations might be "distorted" in the election campaign, so that the voters would not have the correct information before them. Third, time was lacking for the government to make an effort at educating the people about all that was at issue. Finally, the plans were not definitive; changes were possible, and the Vietnamese situation itself very unstable. For all these reasons, it seemed best to campaign for negotiation and restraint and let the Republican opponent be the target for the fear of United States belligerence.

President Johnson thus denied the electorate any chance to give or to refuse consent to the escalation of the war in Vietnam. Believing they had voted for the candidate of peace, American citizens were, within months, deeply embroiled in one of the cruelest wars in their history. Deception of this kind strikes at the very essence of democratic government. It allows those in power to override or nullify the right vested in the people to cast an informed vote in critical elections. Deceiving the people for the sake of the people is a self-contradictory notion in a democracy, unless it can be shown that there has been genuine consent to deceit. The actions of President Johnson were therefore inconsistent with the most basic principle of our political system.

What if all government officials felt similarly free to deceive provided they believed the deception genuinely necessary to achieve some important public end? The trouble is that those who make such calculations are always susceptible to bias. They overestimate the likelihood that the benefit will occur and that the harm will be averted; they underestimate the chances that the deceit will be discovered and ignore the effects of such a discovery on trust; they underrate the comprehension of the deceived citizens, as well as their ability and their right to make a reasonable choice. And, most important, such a benevolent self-righteousness disguises the many motives for political lying which could not serve as moral excuses: the need to cover up past mistakes; the vindictiveness; the desire to stay in power. These self-serving ends provide the impetus for countless lies that are rationalized as "necessary" for the public good.

As political leaders become accustomed to making such excuses, they grow insensitive to fairness and to veracity. Some come to believe that any lie can be told so long as they can convince themselves that people will be better off in the long run. From there, it is a short step to the conclusion that, even if people will not be better off from a particular lie, they will benefit from all maneuvers to keep the right people in office. Once public servants lose their bearings in this way, all the shabby deceits of Watergate — the fake telegrams, the erased tapes, the elaborate cover-ups, the bribing of witnesses to make them lie, the televised pleas for trust — become possible.

While Watergate may be unusual in its scope, most observers would agree that deception is part and parcel of many everyday decisions in government. Statistics may be presented in such a way as to diminish the gravity of embarrassing problems. Civil servants may lie to members of Congress in order to protect programs they judge important, or to guard secrets they have been ordered not to divulge. If asked, members of Congress who make deals with one another to vote for measures they would otherwise oppose deny having made such deals. False rumors may be leaked by subordinates who believe that unwise executive action is about to be taken. Or the leak may be correct, but falsely attributed in order to protect the source.

Consider the following situation and imagine all the variations on this theme being played in campaigns all over the United States, at the local, state, or federal level:

A big-city mayor is running for reelection. He has read a report recommending that he remove rent controls after his reelection. He intends to do so, but believes he will lose the election if his intention is known. When asked, at a news conference two days before his election, about the existence of such a report, he denies knowledge of it and reaffirms his strong support of rent control.

In the mayor's view, his reelection is very much in the public interest, and the lie concerns questions which he believes the voters are unable to evaluate properly, especially on such short notice. In all similar situations, the sizable bias resulting from the self-serving element (the desire to be elected, to stay in office, to exercise power) is often clearer to onlookers than to the liars themselves. This bias inflates the alleged justifications for the lie — the worthiness, superiority, altruism of the liar, the rightness of his cause, and the inability of those deceived to respond "appropriately" to hearing the truth.

These common lies are now so widely suspected that voters are at a loss to know when they can and cannot believe what a candidate says in campaigning. The damage to trust has been immense. I have already referred to the poll which found 69 percent of Americans agreeing, both in 1975 and 1976, that the country's leaders had consistently lied to the American people over the past ten years. Over 40 percent of the respondents also agreed that:

> Most politicians are so similar that it doesn't really make much difference who gets elected.[3]

Many refuse to vote under such circumstances. Others look to appearance or personality factors for clues as to which candidate might be more honest than the others. Voters and candidates alike are the losers when a political system has reached such a low level of trust. Once elected, officials find that their warnings and their calls to common sacrifice meet with disbelief and apathy, even when cooperation is most urgently needed. Lawsuits and investigations multiply. And the fact that the candidates, should they win, are not expected to have meant what they said while campaigning, nor held accountable for discrepancies, only reinforces the incentives for them to bend the truth the next time, thus adding further to the distrust of the voters.

Political lies, so often assumed to be trivial by those who tell them, rarely are. They cannot be trivial when they affect so many people and when they are so peculiarly likely to be imitated, used to retaliate, and spread from a few to many. When political representatives or entire governments arrogate to themselves the right to lie, they take power from the public that would not have been given up voluntarily.

Deception and Consent

Can there be exceptions to the well-founded distrust of deception in public life? Are there times when the public itself might truly not care about possible lies, or might even prefer to be deceived? Are some white lies so trivial or so transparent that they can be ignored? And can we envisage public discussion of more seriously misleading government statements such that reasonable persons could consent to them in advance?

White lies, first of all, are as common to political and diplomatic affairs as they are to the private lives of most people. Feigning enjoyment of an embassy gathering or a political rally, toasting the longevity of a dubious regime or an unimpressive candidate for office — these are forms of politeness that mislead few. It is difficult to regard them as threats to either individuals or communities. As with all white lies, however, the problem is that they spread so easily, and that lines are very hard to draw. Is it still a white lie for a secretary of state to announce that he is going to one country when in reality he travels to another? Or for a president to issue a "cover story" to the effect that a cold is forcing him to return to the White House, when in reality an international crisis made him cancel the rest of his campaign trip? Is it a white lie to issue a letter of praise for a public servant one has just fired? Given the vulnerability of public trust, it is never more important than in public life to keep the deceptive element of white lies to an absolute minimum, and to hold down the danger of their turning into more widespread deceitful practices.

A great deal of deception believed not only innocent but highly justified by public figures concerns their private lives. Information about their marriages, their children, their opinions about others — information about their personal plans and about their motives for personal decisions — all are theirs to keep private if they wish to do so. Refusing to give information under these circumstances is justifiable — but the right to withhold information is not the right to lie about it. Lying under such circumstances bodes ill for conduct in other matters.

Certain additional forms of deception may be debated and authorized in advance by elected representatives of the public. The use of unmarked police cars to discourage speeding by drivers is an example of such a practice. Various forms of unannounced, sometimes covert, auditing of business and government operations are others. Whenever these practices are publicly regulated, they can be limited so that abuses are avoided. But they must be openly debated and agreed to in advance, with every precaution against abuses in privacy and the rights of individuals, and against the spread of such covert activities. It is not enough that a public official assumes that consent would be given to such practices.

Another type of deceit has no consent in advance: the temporizing or the lie when truthful information at a particular time might do great damage. Say that a government is making careful plans for announcing the devaluation of its currency. If the news leaks out to some before it can be announced to all, unfair profits for speculators might result. Or take the decision to make sharp increases in taxes on imported goods in order to rescue a tottering economy. To announce the decision beforehand would lead to hoarding and to exactly the results that the taxes are meant to combat. Thus, government officials will typically seek to avoid any premature announcement and will refuse to comment if asked whether devaluation or higher taxes are imminent. At times, however, official spokesmen will go further and falsely deny that that the actions in question will in fact take place.

Such lies may well be uttered in good faith in an effort to avoid harmful speculation and hoarding. Nevertheless, if false statements are made to the public only to be exposed as soon as the devaluation or the new tax is announced, great damage to trust will result. It is like telling a patient that an operation will be painless — the swifter the disproof, the more likely the loss of trust. In addition, these lies are subject to all the dangers of spread and mistake and deterioration of standards that accompany all deception.

For these reasons, it is far better to refuse comment than to lie in such situations. The objection may be made, however, that a refusal to comment will be interpreted by the press as tantamount to an admission that devaluation or higher taxes are very near. Such an objection has force only if a government has not only established credibility by letting it be known earlier that it would never comment on such matters, and by strictly adhering to this policy at all times. Since lies in these cases are so egregious, it is worth taking care to establish such credibility in advance, so that a refusal to comment is not taken as an invitation to monetary speculation.

Another form of deception takes place when the government regards the public as frightened, or hostile, and highly volatile. In order not to create a panic, information about early signs of an epidemic may be suppressed or distorted. And a lie to a mob seeking its victim is like lying to the murderer asking where the person he is pursuing has gone. It can be acknowledged and defended as soon as the threat is over. In such cases, one may at times be justified in withholding information; perhaps, on rare occasions, even in lying. But such cases are so rare that they hardly exist for practical purposes.

The fact that rare circumstances exist where the justification for government lying seems powerful creates a difficulty — these same excuses will often be made to serve a great many more purposes. For some governments or public officials, the information they wish to conceal is almost never of the requisite certainty, the time never the right one, and the public never sufficiently dispassionate. For these reasons, it is hard to see how a practice of lying to the public about devaluation or changes in taxation or epidemics could be consented to in advance, and therefore justified.

Are there any exceptionally dangerous circumstances where the state of crisis is such as to justify lies to the public for its own protection? We have already discussed lying to enemies in an acute crisis. Sometimes the domestic public is then also deceived, at least temporarily. . . . Whenever there is a threat — from a future enemy, as before World War II, or from a shortage of energy — the temptation to draw upon the excuses for deceiving citizens is very strong. The government may sincerely doubt that the electorate is capable of making the immediate sacrifices needed to confront the growing danger. (Or one branch of the government may lack confidence in another, for similar reasons, as when the administration mistrusts Congress.) The public may seem too emotional, the time not yet right for disclosure. Are there crises so exceptional that deceptive strategies are justifiable?

Compare, for instance, what was said and left unsaid by two United States presidents confronted by a popular unwillingness to enter a war: President Lyndon Johnson, in escalating the war in Vietnam, and President Franklin D. Roosevelt, in moving the country closer to participating in World War II, while making statements such as the following in his 1940 campaign to be reelected:

> I have said this before, but I shall say it again and again and again: Your boys are not going to be sent into any foreign wars.[4]

By the standards set forth in this chapter, President Johnson's escalation and his failure to consult the electorate concerning the undeclared war in Vietnam was clearly unjustifiable. Consent was bypassed; there was no immediate danger to the nation which could even begin to excuse deceiving the public in a national election on the grounds of an acute crisis.

The crisis looming before World War II, on the other hand, was doubtless much greater. Certainly this case is a difficult one, and one on which reasonable persons might not be able to agree. The threat was unprecedented; the need for preparations and support of allies great; yet the difficulties of alerting the American public seemed insuperable. Would this crisis, then, justify proceeding through deceit?

To consent even to such deception would, I believe, be to take a frightening step. Do we want to live in a society where public officials can resort to deceit and manipulation whenever they decide that an exceptional crisis has arisen? Would we not, on balance, prefer to run the risk of failing to rise to a crisis honestly explained to us, from which the government might have saved us through manipulation? And what protection from abuse do we foresee should we surrender this choice?

In considering answers to these questions, we must take into account more than the short-run effects of government manipulation. President Roosevelt's manner of bringing the American people to accept first the possibility, then the likelihood, of war was used as an example by those who wanted to justify President Johnson's acts of dissimulation. And these acts in turn were pointed to by those who resorted to so many forms of duplicity in the Nixon administration. Secrecy and deceit grew at least in part because of existing precedents.[5]

The consequences of spreading deception, alienation, and lack of trust could not have been documented for us more concretely than they have in the past decades. We have had a very vivid illustration of how lies undermine our political system. While deception under the circumstances confronting President Roosevelt may in hindsight be more excusable than much that followed, we could no more consent to it in advance than to all that came later.

Wherever lies to the public have become routine, then, very special safeguards should be required. The test of public justification of deceptive practices is more needed than ever. It will be a hard test to satisfy, the more so the more trust is invested in those who lie and the more power they wield. Those in government and other positions of trust should be held to the highest standards. Their lies are not ennobled by their positions; quite the contrary. Some lies — notably minor white lies and emergency white lies rapidly acknowledged — may be more excusable than others, but only those deceptive practices which can be openly debated and consented to in advance are justifiable in a democracy.[6]

Endnotes

1. The Senator Gravel Edition, *The Pentagon Papers* (Boston: Beacon Press, 1971), 3: 556-59.
2. Theodore H. White, *The Making of the President 1964* (New York: Arbeneum, 1965), p. 373.
3. *Cambridge Survey Research,* 1975, 1976.
4. *The Public Papers and Addresses of Franklin D. Roosevelt,* 1940, vol. 8, p. 507 (October 30, 1940).
5. See Arthur M. Schlesinger, Jr., *The Imperial Presidency* (Boston: Houghton Miflin, 1973, p. 356. "The power to withhold and the power to leak led on inexorably to the power to lie . . . uncontrolled secrecy made it easy for lying to become routine." See also David Wise, *The Politics of Lying* (New York: Random House, 1973).
6. For discussions of lying and moral choice in politics, see Plato, *The Republic;* Machievelli, *The Prince;* Max Weber, "Politics as a Vocation," in *Essays in Sociology,* trans. H.H. Gerth and C. Wright Mills (New York: Oxford University Press, 1946), pp. 77-128; and Michael Walzer, "Political Action: The Problem of Dirty Hands," *Philosophy and Public Affairs 2* (Winter 1973): 160-80.

Is it Lying or 'the Politics of Living'?
Darrell Sifford

PHILADELPHIA — Not long ago, in a conversation with psychiatrist Harold A. Rashkis, I recounted to him a story about my younger son, Grant, 22, who felt that he had lost a job opportunity by giving the accountant who was interviewing him a true answer rather than the answer that the accountant wanted and probably expected.

Public attitudes on lying are perhaps as diverse as on any other ethical issue, as this newspaper article illustrates. Some of the comments echo Sissela Bok, but others could as easily have been drawn from the pages of Machiavelli's Prince.

The interviewer, a member of a small public accounting firm in the South, had asked Grant how he felt about going after his CPA. Grant told him: "Yes, I hope someday to get my CPA, but that's not the most important thing for me right now."

The interview, which Grant thought had gone well to that point, suddenly turned icy. Later, Grant told me: "He wanted me to tell him that accounting and getting my CPA are the most important things in my life. I know what he wanted to hear, but accounting never is going to be the biggest thing in my life. I couldn't lie to him, could I?"

No, I told him, he'd done the right thing. I took this position not necessarily because of the moral consideration but because in the long run lies often seem to come back to haunt us and we find ourselves on a merry-go-round that spins so rapidly that we can't seem to get off.

As I completed the story to Rashkis, a Philadelphia psychiatrist, I remarked that Grant seemed to have been penalized for his honesty — he really wanted the job — and I asked if Rashkis could imagine a circumstance in which it would be OK to tell a lie.

His response: "OK? It's not only OK; it's what we have to teach young people." After all, Rashkis said, it wasn't really lying. Rather it was engaging in "the politics of living," and the truth was that Grant wanted the job, not that Grant was less than 100 percent enthusiastic about immediately pointing toward his CPA.

Said Rashkis: "If I'd been Grant, I would have looked straight into his lying eyes with my lying eyes and told him: 'Sir, there is nothing I could want more than to get my CPA and eventually become a senior partner in your firm.' That would damage nobody," Rashkis said, "The interviewer has no concern about Grant's ultimate destiny on earth. He just wants to hire somebody who's going to work."

Source: Darrell Sifford, "Is it Lying or 'the Politics of Living'?" *Boston Globe,* October 9, 1982.

"Truth," said Rashkis, "has to be defined in the context in which it is spoken."

At the end of the column that I wrote about our conversation I asked readers what they thought about it. Today I'm sharing with you some of the comments.

From a partner in the Philadelphia office of a "big-eight" accounting firm:

"I have interviewed many young men and women seeking employment with a major accounting firm. . . . I also have had to counsel a few who were not performing to the level of their capabilities in public accounting because their interests were elsewhere. I don't believe that all accounting majors can become, nor perhaps will want to become, partners in an accounting firm. However, the formal continuing education programs provided by all of the major accounting firms are expensive to run and are intended for those who believe that they may have an interest in a career in public accounting.

". . . Our office will hire approximately 50 accountants this year. . . . To hire 50 we will have made offers to approximately 100. . . . I don't mind making an offer of employment to an individual who may be uncertain as to long-term career goals at age 21 or 22 since I recognize that those goals frequently change anyway. I do object to advocates of lying in order to obtain employment (and one reason is that) it may preclude employment for an individual who is also qualified and more interested in a career in public accounting."

From a woman:

"The psychiatrist who condones a small amount of lying to achieve a short-term goal is unbelievable. . . .The small 'acceptable' lie is the beginning of bigger lies; the little dishonest act is the beginning of a bigger crime. The lowering of standards has to be the major problem of our degenerating society."

From another woman:

"I wasn't even going to finish reading your column because it disgusted me so. I realized that all that really matters to me is that I know lying is wrong. This is a crazy, mixed-up world with its situational ethics, its moral relativism, its humanistic approaches — and the people who practice these things ultimately will get their just rewards: anguish, fear, sick hearts, stabs in the back . . . even as they embrace their status and money. I wouldn't want to be one of them."

From a businessman:

"If the object of your column was to get a response, I suspect that you have succeeded gloriously. My guess is that those who accept your invitation to comment will flail lying and liars, but my experience tells me that all of them will, themselves, be liars. Why do I say this? Because I have yet to meet the person who hasn't lied. At our company we give new-hires a lie-detector test, and one of the first questions is: 'Have you ever told a lie?' You'd be amazed at how many flunk out at this point by denying that they've ever lied."

From a man who identified himself as a corporate executive:

"It would be nice to think that we always tell the truth. It also would be naive. Years ago, when I made my first job move, they asked me how much I made. I inflated my salary by $3000 because I knew that it was the company's policy to offer you about a $2000 increase. So my lie enabled me to move with a $5000 increase. I've followed this practice ever since, in many moves, and I'm sure that I'd do it — or the equivalent — again if the situation seemed to demand it. To me this is called not lying but advancing."

From a college faculty member:

"In my lengthy academic career, I have been reinforced for telling lies. Or, let's say, when I tell the truth. I find out that I would have done better if I had made up some reasonable story."

From a retired man:

"Yes, I have lied. When the Gestapo knocked on my door in the middle of the night so many years ago and asked if I were Jewish, what was I supposed to say? Would God reward me in heaven for telling the truth?"

From the mother of three small children:

"To say that lying is engaging in the politics of living is a cop-out that I hope my children will avoid. Sometimes the truth hurts us, yes; but the truth never hurts ultimately like the falsehoods."

From a man:

"My life would be a lie if I did not write to disagree strongly with the psychiatrist. . . . A lie is a lie is a lie. That's what I believe and that's how I have lived my life."

From another man:

". . . The psychiatrist you interviewed has a very good point. In my own case, after many years of psychiatric treatment, I've learned the hard way to answer the question, 'Have you had psychiatric treatment?' with a firm 'no.' I'm good at my job, conscientious, hard-working, and I am doing nobody a favor by giving an honest answer. The same applies to questions about medication. . . .

"It's a matter of situational ethics — a term that much of the clergy hates. When to lie, when to be truthful is a hard thing to learn, and hard to teach."

The Iran-Contra Hearings: Lying and Deception

Oliver L. North: "Not an Easy Thing to Do"

Mr. Nields: And there came a time, did there not, when you had an interview with members of the House Intelligence Committee?

Mr. North: I did.

Mr. Nields: And staff?

Mr. North: I don't remember if there was any staff there or not. I defer to Chairman Hamilton. He convened his group in the White House Situation Room and I met with them there. . . .It was on instructions of the National Security Advisor. I was instructed to meet with Chairman Hamilton and I believe many of the members of the committee.

Mr. Nields: And they were interested in finding out the answers to the questions raised by the resolution of inquiry.

Mr. North: Exactly.

Mr. Nields: Your fundraising activities?

Mr. North: Precisely.

Mr. Nields: Military support for the Contras?

Mr. North: That's right.

Mr. Nields: Questions about Mr. Owen, General Singlaub and John Hull?

[Witness confers with his attorney.]

Mr. North: Yes.

Mr. Nields: The beginning of this memorandum that appears to be a description of what you said during that meeting. It says from Boland Amendment on, North explained strictures to Contras.

Is it true, did you explain the strictures to the Contras?

Mr. North: I explained to them that there was no U.S. Government money until more was appropriated, yes.

In the later years of the Reagan presidency, Administration officials arranged to sell arms secretly to the Government of Iran, and some of the proceeds were then used to provide funds for the rebels (the Contras) fighting against the government of Nicaragua. Diversion of the funds violated the Boland Amendment, which prohibited assistance from the U.S. Government to the contras during several periods in the 1980s. These Iran-Contra connections were made public in the fall of 1986, and Congressional hearings followed in the summer of 1987.

Like the Watergate scandal in the 1970s, the Iran-Contra affair focused public attention on a variety of ethical concerns, including the use of deception and its impact on future relationships among public officials. In this portion of the hearings, Oliver North (a major participant in the diversion scheme) attempts to justify his lying to Congress, and John Poindexter (North's supervisor and Reagan's National Security Advisor) tries to draw a moral distinction between lying and deception. Are their arguments persuasive? In addition to the issue of lying, this testimony also displays serious problems in the realm of authority, responsibility and accountability. If both North and Poindexter were telling the truth in the statements quoted here, who should be held responsible for North's earlier deceits?

Mr. Nields: And it says never violated stricture, gave advice on human rights, civic action program.

Mr. North: I did do that.

Mr. Nields: But I take it you did considerably more which you did not tell the committee about?

Mr. North: I have admitted that here before you today, knowing full well what I told the committee then. I think — and I think we can abbreviate this in hopes we can move on so that I can finish this week. I will tell you right now, counsel, and all the members here gathered, that I misled Congress. I misled —

Mr. Nields: At that meeting?

Mr. North: At that meeting.

Mr. Nields: Face to face?

Mr. North: Face to face.

Mr. Nields: You made false statements to them about your activities in support of the Contras?

Mr. North: I did.

Furthermore, I did so with a purpose, and I did so with a purpose of hopefully avoiding the very kind of thing that we have before us now, and avoiding a shut-off of help for the Nicaraguan Resistance, and avoiding an elimination of the Resistance facilities in three Central American countries wherein we had promised those heads of state on my specific orders, on specific orders to me — I had gone down there and assured them of our absolute and total discretion. . . . And I am admitting to you that I participated in preparation of documents for the Congress that were erroneous, misleading, evasive, and wrong, and I did it again here when I appeared before that committee convened in the White House Situation Room, and I make no excuses for what I did.

I will tell you now that I am under oath and I was not then.

Mr. Nields: We do live in a democracy, don't we?

Mr. North: We do sir, thank God.

Mr. Nields: In which it is the people, not one Marine lieutenant colonel, that get to decide the important policy decisions for the nation?

[Witness confers with his attorney.]

Mr. North: Yes.

Mr. Nields: And part of that democratic process —

Mr. North: And I would like to point out that part of that answer is that this Marine lieutenant colonel was not making all of those decisions on his own. As I indicated yesterday in my testimony, Mr. Nields, I sought approval for everything that I did.

Mr. Nields: But you denied Congress the facts.

Mr. North: I did.

Mr. Nields: You denied the elected representatives of our people the facts upon which they needed to make a very important decision for this nation?

Mr. North: I did because of what I have just described to you as our concerns. And I did it because we have had incredible leaks from discussions with closed committees of the Congress. I was a part of, as people now know, the coordination for the mining of the harbors in Nicaragua. When that one leaked, there were American lives at stake and it leaked from a member of one of the committees, who eventually admitted it.

When there was a leak on the sensitive intelligence methods that we used to help capture the Achille Lauro terrorists, it almost wiped out that whole channel of communications.

Those kinds of things are devastating. They are devastating to the national security of the United States and I desperately hope that one of the things that can derive from all of this ordeal is that we can find a better way by which we can communicate those things properly with the Congress.

Source: Iran-Contra Investigation: Testimony of Oliver L. North (Questioning by Counsels) Joint Hearings before the Senate Select Committee on Secret Military Assistance to Iran and the Nicaraguan Opposition and the House Select Committee to Investigate Covert Arms Transactions with Iran, One Hundredth Congress First Session 100-7 Part I July 7, 8, 9, and 10, 1987).

I am not admitting that what happened in this is proper. I am not admitting — or claiming, rather — that what I did and my role in it in communicating was proper.

Mr. Nields: Were you instructed to do it?

Mr. North: I was not specifically instructed, no.

Mr. Nields: Were you generally instructed?

Mr. North: Yes.

Mr. Nields: By whom?

Mr. North: My superiors. I prepared —

Mr. Nields: Who?

Mr. North: I prepared draft answers that they signed and sent. I would also point out —

Mr. Nields: What superior?

Mr. North: Well, look who signed — I didn't sign those letters to the — to this body.

Mr. Nields: I am talking about the last — I'm talking about oral meeting in August of 1986.

Mr. North: I went down to that oral meeting with the same kind of understanding that I had prepared those memos in 1985 and other communications.

Mr. Nields: Well you had a different boss, and in fairness, you ought to tell us whether he instructed you to do it, understood you did it, knew about it afterwards, or none of those.

Mr. North: He did not specifically go down and say, "Ollie, lie to the committee." I told him what I had said afterwards, and he sent me a note saying, "Well done." Now, I would also like to point out one other thing. I deeply believe that the President of the United States is also an elected official of this land, and by the Constitution, as I understand it, he is the person charged with making and carrying out the foreign policy of this country. I believed from the moment I was engaged in this activity in 1984 that this was in furtherance of the foreign policy established by the President. I still believe that.

Mr. Nields: Even —

Mr. North: I am not saying that what I did here was right. And I have placed myself, as you know, counsel, in a great jeopardy.

Mr. Nields: Even the President —

[Witness confers with his attorney.]

Mr. Nields: Even the President is elected by the people.

Mr. North: I just said that.

Mr. Nields: And the people have the right to vote him out of office if they don't like his policies.

Mr. North: That is true.

Mr. Nields: And they can't exercise that function if the policies of the President are hidden from them?

Mr. North: Wait a second. I mean, yesterday we talked about the need for this nation, which is a country at risk in a dangerous world, having the need to conduct covert operations and secret diplomacy and carry out secret programs. I mean, we talked at some length about that, and that can certainly be the subject of great debate, and this great institution can pass laws that say no such activities can ever be conducted again. But that would be wrong, and you and I know that.

The fact is that this country does need to be able to conduct those kinds of activities, and the President ought not to be in a position, in my humble opinion, of having to go out and explain to the American people on a bi-weekly basis or any other kind that I, the President, am carrying out the following secret operations. It just can't be done. No nation in the world will ever help us again, and we desperately need that kind of help if we are to survive given our adversaries.

And what I am saying to you, Mr. Nields, is the American people, I think, trust that the President will indeed be conducting these kinds of activities. They trust that he will do so with a good purpose and good intent. I will also admit to you that I believe there has to be a way of consulting with the Congress. There must be.

I would also point out to you, Mr. Nields, that in June of 1986, not the Tower Commission, I gave a speech before the American Bar Association on very short notice, I stood on the podium with Senator Moynihan, and I advocated the formation of a small discreet joint intelligence committee with a very professional small staff in which the administration would feel comfortable confiding in planning and conducting and funding these kinds of activities. I still believe that to be a good and thoughtful thing to do. There has to be that kind of proposal that allows the administration to talk straightforward with the Congress. . . . I want you to know lying does not come easy to me. I want you to know that it doesn't come easy to anybody, but I think we all had to weigh in the balance the difference between lives and lies. I had to do that on a number of occasions in both these operations, and it is not an easy thing to do.

John M. Poindexter: Lying No, Evasiveness Yes

Mr. Nields: Now, you, I take it, arranged for Colonel North to have a face-to-face meeting with members of the House Intelligence Committee in connection with this Resolution of Inquiry?. . .

Mr. Poindexter: I did arrange it.

Mr. Nields: Now, Colonel North, as you undoubtedly know, has testified about what he said during that face to face meeting?

Mr. Poindexter: I understand that.

Mr. Nields: And he said . . . this is his testimony — "I will tell you right now, counsel, and all the members here gathered, that I misled Congress. I misled — " and then there is a question, "At that meeting?"

And the answer "At that meeting."

Question, "Face-to-face?"

Answer, "Face-to-face."

Question, "You made false statements to them about your activities in support of the Contras?"

Answer, "I did."

Now my question to you is, did you authorize Colonel North to do that?

Mr. Poindexter: I did not authorize him to make false statements. I did think that he would withhold information and be evasive, frankly, in answering questions. My objective all along was to withhold from Congress exactly what the NSC staff was doing in carrying out the President's policy.

I felt that, as I have testified before, that the Boland Amendment did not apply to the NSC staff.

The Government, the U.S. Government, was complying with the letter and spirit of Boland, and I thought that was sufficient.

Source: Iran-Contra Investigation: Testimony of John M. Poindexter (Joint Hearings before the Select Committee to Investigate Covert Arms Transactions with Iran and the Senate Military Assistance to Iran and the Nicaraguan Opposition, One Hundredth Congress First Session 100-8 July 15, 16, 17, 20, and 21, 1987).

Don't misunderstand me. I thought that Colonel North would withhold information. There was no doubt about that in my mind. There were a lot of stories in the press that had appeared that I had talked to Colonel North about periodically.

Most of the stories were patently false and in error. I thought most of the questions would be about these rather outrageous stories in the press, and I felt that Colonel North could knock those stories down by answering the questions truthfully.

Mr. Nields: My question to you is, didn't you put Colonel North in an absolutely impossible position? How could he answer the questions raised by the Resolution of Inquiry truthfully and still withhold information?

[Counsel conferring with witness.]. . .

Mr. Poindexter: First of all, Mr. Nields, as I testified a few moments ago, I don't believe I had actually read the Resolution of Inquiry as to the kinds of questions that were being raised there. I knew, in general, the issue was what was Colonel North doing to help the Contras. As I testified before, I felt that Colonel North was a very capable officer. I did not micromanage him, and when I called him after discussing the matter on the telephone with Chairman Hamilton, I simply told him that the House Intelligence Committee wanted to talk to him, and would he be prepared, or would he be willing to talk to them?

And he indicated that he would. There was no discussion then or later as to what the likely questions would be or how he would answer them.

Obviously with hindsight, it would have been prudent to have sat down and talked to him about that before he did it to provide more detailed guidance, but that was not the manner in which I was managing and directing Colonel North at the time.

Mr. Nields: You have testified that you were aware that the Resolution of Inquiry, among other things, wanted to know about funding. Now, how did you understand Colonel North should answer a question such as the following one: Have the Contras received money from any foreign governments in 1985 or 1986? How should he respond to that question?

[Counsel conferring with witness.]. . .

Mr. Poindexter: As I said earlier, Mr. Nields, I didn't provide any guidance to Colonel North on how to answer the question. I did not know what the questions would be. I knew in general that they were going to ask about his involvement with support of the Contras. I didn't — you know, he was not there as a spokesman for the entire U.S. Government on the United States' relationship with the Contras. He was there to talk about his particular involvement.

Mr. Nields: You testified that he was supposed to withhold information.

Mr. Poindexter: That is correct. I did not —

Mr. Nields: Was he authorized to disclose, in response to a direct question, that he had met with representatives of Country Three and as a result Country Three contributed $2 million to the Contras in the last year?

Mr. Poindexter: I would have expected him to withhold that information. . . .

Mr. Nields: Was he authorized to disclose, in response to a direct question, that the Contras had received funding from the arms sales to Iran?

Mr. Poindexter: He should have withheld that information. . . .

Mr. Nields: . . . [W]as it the general understanding between you and Colonel North that he was supposed to withhold information even if a member of the House Intelligence Committee asked him a direct question calling for it?

Mr. Poindexter: Colonel North was a very competent individual, as I think you have observed. He had been in much tougher situations. I was sure. Colonel North is very resourceful. I thought he could handle it some way.

The analysis as to exactly how he would do it did not enter my mind.

Mr. Nields: Well, he has testified here that he was unable to do that, that he was put in a position where he either had to give up the information that you didn't want him to or he had to lie.

Now, assume that he faced and was faced with that choice. Which choice did you want him to make?

[Counsel conferring with witness.]

Mr. Poindexter: As I've said before, I did not expect him to lie to the committee. I expected him to be evasive, say that he didn't want to answer the question, be uncooperative, if necessary, but I rather think that with his resourcefulness, I thought he could handle it. . . .

Officers and Gentlemen and Situational Lying

Richard Halloran

Richard Halloran describes several situations in which military officers have lied and otherwise used deception. Can his examples be grouped into clusters, in terms of the seriousness of the violations of ethical standards? What kinds of remedies should be considered?

WASHINGTON, Aug. 5 — The testimony of Lieut. Col. Oliver L. North of the marine Corps and Rear Adm. John M. Poindexter of the Navy in the Iran-Contra hearings has raised a fundamental question of military ethics: May an officer lie?

Just after the two officers had testified before the Congressional committees, the six members of the Joint Chiefs of Staff were asked through staff aides:

"Is it permissible for a military officer to lie? If so, under what circumstances, to whom and about what? If not, why not?"

After considerable deliberation, the nation's top military officers declined to reply to the query, thus underscoring the ambivalence that runs through the officer corps of all services on a critical issue of military ethics and integrity.

Those in training to be officers are taught, from the moment they raise their right hands to swear allegiance to the Constitution, that officers do not lie, cheat or steal and will not tolerate those who do. That stricture is basic to the honor codes of the military academies and officer training schools.

But in recent years the practice of what military officers refer to as "situational ethics" has become pervasive. That view of ethics says that a higher end, such as national security, justifies such means as lying and deception.

In his testimony at the Iran-Contra hearings, Colonel North admitted lying to Congress, to other Government officials and to American associates in his venture.

Later, when Senator Paul S. Trible Jr., Republican of Virginia, accused Admiral Poindexter of an "unapologetic embrace of untruth," the former national security advisor to President Reagan did not deny it. But he justified his position by saying, "I think the actions that I took were in the longterm interests of the country."

Early in the Reagan Administration, Secretary of Defense Caspar W. Weinberger ordered members of the Joint Chiefs then to take polygraph, or lie detector, tests as he sought to discover who had divulged budget information to the press.

In session after session at the war colleges in recent years, many officers have risen to assert in no uncertain terms that it would be permissible to lie through the press to the American public in an effort to deceive an enemy.

The Hasenfus Incident

A military officer lied to a reporter in saying that Maj. Gen. John K. Singlaub, a retired Army officer, had arranged a flight to deliver weapons to the Nicaraguan Contras. After the plane was shot down, a crewman, Eugene Hasenfus, was captured and later released by the Sandinista Government.

In another case, a general said he was stunned to find that some lieutenants believed they had to lie on readiness reports on vehicles. "Sir," he said a lieutenant told him, "you put so much emphasis on operating rates that we feel obligated to lie about what we're doing." The general said it took him a year to get that practice stopped.

Lying, in this context, is distinct from deception of an enemy, which has been a principle of war since the Chinese statesman Sun Tzu wrote his treatise on strategy 2,500 years ago. "In war, it is legitimate to deceive an enemy," said a former officer, Lewis S. Sorley 3d, who has written on military ethics. "But we never lie to our own people."

Even in covert operations, where deception can be an art form, American officers should not lie to American officials or the public. Secretary of State George P. Shultz, once a marine, alluded to that when he told the Congressional committees: "Everybody in the Government, certainly anybody who works for me, should know they must not lie and they must not mislead." At the same time, Mr. Shultz said, it is acceptable to decline to discuss sensitive information in public.

Source: Richard Halloran, "The Armed Services: Officers and Gentlemen and Situational Lying," *The New York Times,* August 6, 1987, p. A24.

Mr. Weinberger agreed, saying that the principles of the honor codes at the military academies "are applicable at all times." He told the Iran-Contra committees: "I don't see how you can leave aside situational or other ethics."

Or, as a former Chief of Staff of the Army, Gen. William C. Westmoreland once put it: "I want to make it clear beyond any question that absolute integrity of an officer's word, deed and signature is a matter than permits no compromise."

That philosophy, while rooted in the Judeo-Christian tradition, rests on a pragmatic proposition: If an officer lies, a vital mission might not be accomplished and men could needlessly die in battle.

Disaster and Death

A senior officer who lies to subordinates about the dangers of their mission may condemn them to death.

A junior officer who lies about his unit's readiness can mislead a superior into a disastrous decision.

Ship captains must be able to trust one another to follow their battleplan, or they will see their ships exposed to the enemy.

In combat, moreover, soldiers should be able immediately to count on the integrity of a new commander replacing a slain leader.

A commander taking part in the ethics discussion said that if soldiers believe that some officers always tell the truth but that others lie, the soldiers will hesitate to follow the new leader's orders. "Then we're in big trouble," the officer said. "That's the importance of ethics."

Those principles hold true in any armed force, but particularly in a democracy where the military services are constitutionally subordinate to civilian authority. Mr. Shultz said at the hearings, "I don't think that desirable ends justify the means of lying, of deceiving, of doing things that are outside our constitutional processes."

Some military officers agree. Harry G. Summers Jr., a retired Army colonel who writes about military affairs, wrote recently: "Tampering with civilian control of the military by the President or by the Congress is a slippery slope, indeed, for at the bottom of that slope is military dictatorship."

The situational ethics in the officer corps today appears to be a vestige of the corruption that spread through the armed forces during the conflict in Vietnam. Political leaders in Washington, notably President Johnson, demanded a gauge of progress in that guerrilla war. Since the classic measure of captured territory did not work, counting dead enemy bodies became the signpost.

An obsession with numbers led to a body-count syndrome and inflation of statistics to keep headquarters happy. That in turn fostered false reports to win combat decorations and promotions. Paradoxically, the body-count syndrome flourished under General Westmoreland when he was the commander in Vietnam, which may have caused him later to order a study of military professionalism and ethics.

Even today, however, the effects of Vietnam are debilitating.

Mr. Sorely said that they had caused "the erosion of trust upon which professional relationships, lifelong friendships and loyalties of comrades in arms and the honorable perception of military service have been based."

'These Are the Rules'

Despite the widespread practice of situational ethics, many officers in each service have said that such behavior will not be tolerated under their command. The demand for integrity appears to increase as officers get farther from the flagpole in Washington.

On his first day, a new battalion commander in Texas told his officers he expected them to speak the truth. "These are the rules," he said. "If you violate them, that will be a catastrophic failure from which you cannot recover."

Similarly, a general told officers in his division: "There is no room to negotiate one's integrity. Anyone who violates his integrity will be dealt with severely and I will do my damndest to get him eliminated from the service."

ASPA Workbook: Secrecy

This area covers two elements of the administrator's role that sometimes move in opposite directions.

On the one hand, he or she must be cognizant of the public's right to know about the actions of government agencies, except when information sharing would be harmful to the security and welfare of the nation or its citizens. Thus, new emphasis has been placed on openness, full participation, and disclosure in the conduct of public business. These goals are buttressed by the Freedom of Information Act; the underlying theme suggests that we all would be better served if governance were exposed to open scrutiny.

"Sunshine laws" provide an example of the application of disclosure to various agencies and units of government. On the personal level, one finds increasing expectations for full financial disclosure by public officials who seek elective or high policy-making posts in government.

On the other hand, a countervailing force exists. Each person, whether a citizen-at-large or a public administrator, has rights of privacy to be safeguarded. Included are protections against illegal domestic surveillance, unauthorized sharing of credit information, unauthorized access to confidential personal files, and the like.

The coexistence of these two thrusts presents obvious dilemmas for the public administrator.

Some Self-Diagnostic Questions Concerning Public Disclosure and Confidentiality

1. How do I resolve conflicts between the public's right to know and the need for confidentiality, as they affect individuals, as well as my organization?

2. Am I aware of how the Freedom of Information Act and associated laws and regulations relate to me?

3. Are meetings for which I have responsibility announced publicly? Are they conducted in an open way? Are transcripts or minutes of meetings made available to the public? Are requests for public records honored?

4. When I take part in decisions that affect the public welfare, are the issues presented to the public in sufficient time and in a way that questions can be raised?

5. Am I aware of how the Privacy Act of 1974 and associated laws and regulations relate to me?

6. As a public administrator, what safeguards do I take to assure that the rights of individual privacy are not abused?

7. Do I use informal techniques and procedures to circumvent the spirit or specific requirement of freedom of information or right to privacy legislation? Under what circumstances, if any, could such behavior be justified?

Source: Mertins and Hennigan, *Applying Professional Standards and Ethics in the Eighties,* pp. 20-21.

POSTSCRIPT

We do not devote much attention in this volume to the wide range of ethical issues raised by public officials' tendency to restrict public information on their activities. For an extended discussion of these issues, see Sissela Bok, *Secrets: On the Ethics of Concealment and Revelation* (New York: Vintage Books, 1984), especially Chapter 12.

Case 8: Executive Morale

Carrying out an objective study on an issue with significant political overtones is sometimes hazardous, as this case illustrates. Does the concept of "ethics as responsibility" (Part I essay) provide a useful way to resolve the problem facing the Assistant Director? What does the case suggest about the role of the media?

You are the Assistant Director of the State Civil Service Department, which was created years ago and modeled after the U.S. Civil Service Commission. During the past decade, and in keeping with general trends in the field, the Department has taken on a more executive-centered cast, reducing its emphasis on the rigidities of the independent personnel agency, and acting as an executive arm of state government. This change was consistent with the views of the past three state governors, and it has had the general backing of the state's personnel community. The present Civil Service Board, composed of three appointees, now functions primarily as a general merit review board, and the Department's management largely rests with the Executive Director, who during the last session of the legislature became an appointee of the governor. Your position is at Level I (the top level) in the career Executive Personnel System; you were appointed two years ago after a national search.

When you assumed your position, you discovered that the Department had performed a statewide survey of the attitudes of middle- and upper-level state executives toward their jobs, toward the general work environment, and on several other aspects of state executive employment. The survey was professionally done, and the results provided the impetus for a number of new personnel initiatives in training, equal employment, reorganization, and organizational development. It has been five years since that survey was completed, so you discussed with the Executive Director the possibility of replicating the study. In addition to providing an updated view of executive attitudes, a new survey could measure the improvements that have been made as a result of the findings of the old survey.

The Executive Director agreed to your proposal. There were enough funds in the department's budget to cover the study's expenses, and the Executive Director thought the project would help the governor's reputation. He gave you the responsibility for directing the study and writing the final report.

You assembled a team of consultants from universities in the state and a private firm, and 3300 state executives were surveyed. There was a minimal amount of press interest, and the governor periodically mentioned this effort as part of her general concern for management improvement in the state. She stated that she would implement whatever recommendations were forthcoming from the study.

As the results began to come in, you detected some dissatisfaction by executives with their work environment. Once the questionnaires have been tabulated, and your consultants have prepared a preliminary report on the findings, your initial impressions are confirmed: with the exception of training opportunities, it appears the state has slipped, rather than improved, in the past five years. One out of every four executives who responded (98.2 percent did respond) was highly critical of management and policy direction; almost 45 percent of the executives were planning to retire as soon as they could; 40 percent of the mid-level executives were looking for jobs in the private sector or with other levels of government; over 60 percent of the respondents would not recommend careers in state government to their children.

You mention these findings to the Executive Director. He does not show a great deal of concern. He tells you that "you know how to write a report to make things seem all right" and dismisses the subject. You know what he is saying, but you are concerned about doing it. You decide that you should do a comprehensive analysis with recommendations. Your consulting team then devotes time to assembling a detailed analysis of the results. The picture is a bleak one. It appears that almost all the efforts of the past five years have done little to alleviate the concerns of the executive service, despite the expenditure of a great deal of time and energy. You decide to prepare your own summary of the findings, emphasizing the advances in training as positive results of the Department's efforts, and including recommendations to meet the many problems identified by the survey. You then give a preliminary draft of your summary, together with the consultants' report, to the Executive Director.

Three days later, the morning paper carries a one-column story on the front page, with a headline that reads, "STATE EXECUTIVE SERVICE HIGHLY CRITICAL OF WORKING CONDITIONS." Somehow the press has obtained your report and has emphasized all the negative aspects. That afternoon the Executive Director calls you in and says that he has had a long session with the governor, who is not very happy and wants some quick action. The director suggests that you do everything you can to "make things right." Among his suggestions are discrediting the instrument, erasing the computer tape with the results (the questionnaires have already been destroyed to guarantee confidentiality), or hiring another consultant to review and discredit the work done by the team you had assembled.

You ask for a few hours to consider what to do. What are your options, and what alternative would you be inclined to take?

8. Abuse of Authority

The Malek Manual

. . .The best politics is still good government. *But you cannot achieve management, policy or program control unless you have established political control.* The record is quite replete with instances of the failures of program, policy and management goals because of sabotage by employees of the Executive Branch who engage in the frustration of those efforts because of their political persuasion and their loyalty to the majority party of Congress rather than the executive that supervises them. And yet, in their own eyes, they are sincere and loyal to their government.

The above facts were not lost on John and Robert Kennedy. Shortly after Kennedy's nomination the Kennedy campaign reportedly hired a management consulting firm which made a survey of the Executive Branch of government. In that survey they pointed out every position, regardless of grade, regardless of whether it was career or noncareer, which was thought to be an important pressure point in the Executive Branch. They did a thorough research job on the incumbents occupying those positions. After Kennedy's inauguration, they put Larry O'Brien in charge of the effort to "clean out the executive branch" of all incumbents of those positions whom they felt they could not rely upon politically. Larry O'Brien, with the assistance of the department and agencies, reportedly, boasted that he accomplished the task in 180 days.

. . . Lyndon Johnson went a step further. He appointed John Macy to two positions simultaneously. He was the special assistant to the president for personnel matters directly in charge of the recruitment of ranking Administration officials, the political clearance system at the White House, and the Johnson White House political control over the personnel in the executive branch. He was also appointed chairman of the Civil Service Commission, the "guardian of the civil service and the merit system." Ludwig Andolsek, formerly administrative assistant to Rep. John Blatnik (D-Minn.), and the staff man in charge of Democratic patronage matters for the House of Representatives Democratic Caucus, was the vice chairman of the Civil Service Commission and "vice guardian of the civil service and the merit system." Together they formed the two-man majority on the three-man commission. Naturally, there wasn't a ripple of concern from a Democratic Congress, only the covert clapping of hands and salivation at the opportunities that now were theirs.

Any government career system is caught between two contending goals. On the one hand, career officials should be protected from narrow partisan pressures and encouraged to carry out their jobs using objective, professional criteria. On the other hand, effective leadership by elected officials requires that they have some measure of control over their subordinates, including the ability to select, promote, and remove important members of their program staffs. The first orientation carries with it the risk that the civil-service system will become rigid, protecting staff members who have limited competence or policy views strongly opposed to those of their elected superiors. However, if elected officials and their aides act vigorously to achieve policy and political control, their efforts may undermine the quality of professional competence in public service and make careers in government less attractive to able people in the future.

The "Malek Manual" provides a detailed example of the political-control perspective. The Manual was prepared by Frederic V. Malek, a member of the White House staff during the Nixon Administration, and distributed widely to top agency officials. Malek's commentary illustrates the concern for loyalty and effective control found in many new administrations (at state and local levels as well as in national government). His suggested strategies, Machiavellian in tone, offer a range of ways that Cabinet members and agency heads might violate the spirit and perhaps the letter of career personnel systems.

The Malek Manual is reprinted in U.S. Senate, Select Committee on Presidential Campaign Activities of 1972, Executive Session Hearings, 93d Cong. 2d Session (1974), pp. 8903-9041.

Of course, Congress proceeded to more than double the number of super-grade positions and Executive Level positions in the government. And naturally the White House did a thorough job of insuring that those appointed to those positions were politically reliable. Documents left behind reveal that even nominees for *career* positions at the supergrade level, and the equivalents, were cleared and interviewed at the White House.

. . . A final objective of the Johnson Administration was to insure the continued loyalty of the bureaucracy to the Democratic programs and the Johnson policies after the takeover by the Nixon Administration. They did this by several reorganizational processes in 1968 which allowed them to freeze in both the people and the positions they had created into the career service.

Organization

The ideal organization to plan, implement and operate the political personnel program necessary is headed by a Special Assistant to the head of the department, or agency, or to the assistant head of the department, or agency, for Administration.

. . . The overriding goal to be achieved is to insure placement in all key positions of substantively qualified and politically reliable officials with a minimum burden on line managers in achieving that goal. The objective of that goal is firm political control of the department, or agency, while at the same time effecting good management and good programs.

Another function is to insure that personnel, which is a resource of the government, is utilized in such a way that it not only produces better government, but [also] creates maximum political benefit for the president and the party . . . [The] office must then study and know the suitability of whatever incumbents occupy those positions. Where an unsuitable incumbent does occupy one of those positions, that office must effect his removal or devise a plan to organize the critical responsibilities he administers from without his control.

Appointment, Tenure, Promotions, Demotions, Reassignments (By Type of Appointment)

. . . Believe it or not the Civil Service rules and regulations, as complex and restrictive as we think they are, do not cause most of the problems. The bureaucrats, not satisfied with the unprecedented protection and job security given them by the Civil Service Commission (CSC) have, in various departments and agencies, piled a maze of departmental regulations on top of the CSC regulations. The Civil Service Commission will require an agency to follow its own regulations even though they may be far more restrictive and far more excessive than the CSC regulations. Some examples: in HEW career rights were extended to all attorneys though by CSC rules they are excepted employees. Some departments have extended the notification procedures of the Veterans Preference Act to all employees. A few agencies allowed formal hearings and appeals if a person was transferred to a post outside a fifty-mile radius from his present geographical location. . . . .

Techniques for Removal Through Organizational or Management Procedures

The Civil Service system creates many hardships in trying to remove undesirable employees from their positions. Because of the rape of the career service by the Kennedy and Johnson Administrations, as described in the Introduction, this Administration has been left a legacy of finding disloyalty and obstruction at high levels while those incumbents rest comfortably on career civil service status. Political disloyalty and insimpatico relationships with the Administration, unfortunately, are not grounds for the removal or suspension of an employee. Career employees . . . can only be dismissed or otherwise punished for direct disobedience of lawful orders, actions which are tantamount to the commission of a crime, and well- documented and provable incompetence (see FPM Section 752). Even if you follow the time-consuming process of documenting a case to proceed with an adverse action, the administrative and legal process is slow and lengthy and great damage can accrue to the department prior to your successful conclusion of your case. However, there are several techniques which can be designed, carefully, to skirt around

Source: White House Personnel Office, *The Malek Manual.*

the adverse action proceedings. One must always bear in mind the following rules. The reduction of a person to a position of lower status and/or grade is considered an adverse action which necessitates formal proceedings. Secondly, an administrative or management decision cannot be based on the political background or persuasion of an individual, his race, sex, religion or national origin.

Individual Techniques

Frontal Assault. You simply call an individual in and tell him he is no longer wanted, that you'll assist him in finding another job and will keep him around until such time as he finds other employment. But you do expect him to immediately relinquish his duties, accept reassignment to a make-shift position at his current grade and then quietly resign for the good of the service. Of course, you promise him that he will leave with honor and with the finest recommendations, a farewell luncheon, and perhaps even a departmental award. You, naturally, point out that should he not accept such an offer, and he later is forced to resign or retire through regular process or his own volition, that his employment references from the department and his permanent personnel record may not look the same as if he accepted your offer. There should be no witnesses in the room at the time. *Caution*: this technique should only be used for the timid at heart with a giant ego. This is an extremely dangerous technique and the very fact of your conversation can be used against the department in any subsequent adverse action proceedings. It should never be used with that fervent, zealous employee committed to Democratic policies and programs, or to the bureaucracy, who might relish the opportunity to be martyred on the cross of his cause.

Transfer Technique. By carefully researching the background of the proposed employee-victim, one can always establish that geographical part of the country and/or organizational unit to which the employee would rather resign than obey and accept transfer orders. For example, if you have an employee in your Boston regional office, and his record shows reluctance to move far from that location (he may have family and financial commitments not easily severed), a transfer accompanied by a promotion to an existing or newly created position in Dallas, Texas might just fill the bill. It is always suggested that a transfer be accompanied by a promotion, if possible. Since a promotion is, *per se,* beneficial to the employee, it immediately forecloses any claim that the transfer is an adverse action. It also reduces the possibility of a claim that the transfer was motivated for prohibited purposes since, again, the transfer resulted in a beneficial action for the employee and the word "discrimination" implies some adversity to have been suffered. . . . The technical assistance of your personnel office is indispensable in prosecuting such transfers. But there is no reason why they cannot artfully find, or create, the necessary position that will satisfy the transfer requirements necessary to cause the prospective transferee to be confronted with the choice of being transferred to a position he does not want or resigning. Of course, one can sweeten the potion by privately assuring the proposed transferee, upon delivery of his transfer notification, that should he refuse the transfer, and resign, that his resignation will be accepted without prejudice. Further, he may remain for a period until he finds other employment and leave with the highest honors and references.

Special Assistant Technique (The Traveling Salesman). This technique is especially useful for the family man and those who do not enjoy traveling. What you do is to suddenly recognize the outstanding abilities of your employee-victim and immediately seize upon his competence and talent to assign him to a special research and evaluation project. This is best explained by way of example. Let us assume that our employee is a program analyst with the Department of Transportation. You immediately discover the high-level interest and policy requirements for creating a program to meet the transportation needs of all U.S. cities and towns with a population of 20,000 and under. Nothing is more revealing than first hand inspections and consultation with town officials. And so you hand your chosen expert a promotion and his new assignment. (Again, a promotion is desirable to diminish any possible claim of adversity.) Along with his promotion and assignment your expert is given extensive travel orders criss-crossing him across the country to towns (hopefully with the worst accommodations possible) of a population of 20,000 or under. Until his wife threatens him with divorce unless he quits, you have him out of town and out of the way. When he finally asks for relief you tearfully reiterate the importance of the project and state that he must continue to obey travel orders or resign. Failure to obey travel orders is a grounds for immediate separation. . . .

New Activity Technique

[One] organizational technique for the wholesale isolation and disposition of undesirable employee-victims is the creation of an apparently meaningful, but essentially meaningless, new activity to which they are all transferred. This technique, unlike the shifting responsibilities and isolation technique designed to immobilize a group of people in a single organizational entity, is designed to provide a single barrel into which you can dump a large number of widely located bad apples. Again let us use an example to illustrate this technique. Let us apply this to the Department of Health, Education, and Welfare. A startling new thrust to HEW's participation in the Model Cities Program might be a new research and development Model Cities Laboratory. With the concurrence of the governor of Alabama, one might choose Alabama, or a region thereof, to be a "model state" or "model region" like we now have sections of cities designated as "model cities." For office facilities the Department of the Army might be prevailed upon to provide surplus buildings at Fort Rucker, Alabama. The Alabama State Department of Education, would, I am sure, be more than happy to provide school buses to bus HEW employees between their offices and the nearest town where they would live. Naturally, to such a high priority and high visibility project as a "model state" lab you would want to assign some of the most "qualified" employees and administrators you could find throughout the department, both in Washington and in the field. By carefully looking at the personnel jackets of your selected employee-victims, you can easily design an organization chart for the project that would create positions to which these employee-victims can be transferred that meet the necessary job description requirements, offer promotional opportunities in grade, and by having the project report directly into the secretary's office provide for promotions in status.

Conclusion

Malek's suggestions were carried out with varying degrees of enthusiasm and success by Nixon's agency heads. As Hugh Heclo suggested in his 1977 book, the consensus among close observers is that during the years 1969-1974 "staffing and examining processes had been subject to manipulation in a way inconsistent with merit principles," and "political intrusions into the civil service had become more systematic and widespread than ever before." (Hugh Heclo, A Government of Strangers (Brookings Institution, 1977), pp. 28, 74) These patterns illustrate continuing tensions and dangers, however, which are found in state and local agencies as well as in national governments here and abroad.

There is no substitute in the beginning of any Administration for a very active political personnel operation. Whatever investment is made in positions, salaries, systems, training and intelligent work in this area will yield a return tenfold. Conversely, the failure to invest what is necessary to a political personnel program will cost the Administration and the department or agency fiftyfold what they might otherwise have invested. These estimates are borne out by experience. Where departments and agencies, and Administrations, have failed to invest the manpower and other necessary aforementioned items into an effective political personnel program — blindly paying lip service to such a function and proceeding immediately to invest heavily in the management and program functions — they have only been plagued by such folly. The time consumed of high level Administration appointees, and the manpower and expenses involved in the creation of firefighting forces, caused by acts in an attempt to frustrate the Administration's policies, program objectives and management objectives, as well as to embarrass the Administration, engaged in by unloyal employees of the Executive Branch, has far exceeded the investment a political personnel operation would have required. In those few organizations where an effective political personnel office was the forerunner of "new directions" in policy, program objectives, and management objectives, the ease and low visibility with which they were accomplished was markedly contrasted to the rest of the Administration. There is no question that the effective activities of a political personnel office will invoke a one-shot furor in the hostile press and Congress. But there is no question that these costs are far less than the costs of the frequent crescendos of bad publicity that are sure to occur frequently and indefinitely if you do not. In short, it is far better and healthier to swallow a large bitter pill in the beginning, and then run rigorously toward your objectives, than to run toward your objectives stopping so frequently for small bitter pills that you become drained of the endurance, the will and the ability to ever reach your objectives. As one of the ranking members of this Administration once put it: "You cannot hope to achieve policy, program or management control until you have achieved political control. That is the difference between ruling and reigning."

Abuse of Authority

Sexual Harassment: The Personnel Problem That Won't Go Away

Judith Havemann

A woman complained that a man in her federal laboratory couldn't talk to her without putting his hand on the back of her neck. She said it gave her the creeps and she looked for reasons to be out of the lab when he was there.

"This costs the government money and it hurts the woman's career," says Nancy Brown, president of Nancy Brown Associates, a Cincinnati management consultant firm. "It hurts her productivity and it has a long-term effect on her chances for promotions and raises."

A survey released recently by the Merit Systems Protection Board (MSPB) found that 42 percent of all women working for the federal government said they had been sexually harassed in the past two years. The survey found that the level had not decreased a single percentage point since 1981, when a landmark study of the problem was completed.

Sexual harassment "remains a widespread problem in the federal workplace," says Daniel R. Levinson, chairman of the board, which estimated the practice cost $267 million over two years in lost productivity and turnover.

The survey of 8,523 federal workers found the most severe forms of sexual harassment — actual or attempted rape or assault — occurred rarely, affecting 0.8 percent of the female respondents. The survey said 12 percent received letters or calls, 9 percent came under pressure for sexual favors, 26 percent experienced "deliberate touching," 28 percent received "suggestive looks" and 35 percent heard "sexual remarks."

"Apparently most people didn't take it seriously enough to report it," says James Laferty, spokesman for the Office of Personnel Management. "We have received only three complaints in the past seven years" from OPM's 6,365 employees, he says, "and we could substantiate only one."

The Equal Employment Opportunity Commission reported receiving only 436 official complaints of sexual harassment from the government's 2.1 million workers in 1985, the most recent year for which figures are available.

The survey said about 5 percent of those harassed filed complaints. Most said they believed filing a complaint would do little good and would make the office atmosphere more unpleasant. Those who did file said the process is slow and burdensome, and in many cases the harasser had the responsibility to investigate the complaint.

By contrast, 44 percent simply took matters into their own hands, told the offender to stop and said this frequently "made things better."

In probably the most celebrated federal sexual-harassment case, a federal judge ruled in May that a female attorney at the Securities and Exchange Commission was sexually harassed and discriminated against. The woman was awarded eight years of back pay and a promotion and the agency said it would call in outside experts to review its personnel practices.

The problem appears to be most wide-spread at the State Department, where 52 percent of women surveyed reported sexual harassment in the last 24 months. The lowest level, 29 percent, was reported at the Department of Health and Human Services.

The most likely victims are single or divorced college-educated women between the ages of 20 and 44 who work in predominantly male environments or have an immediate supervisor who is male, according to the survey.

Sexual harassment is a wide-ranging problem in American society and in many cultures abroad. It is especially serious when the offender has a significant degree of authority over the individual harassed, as in supervisor/employee and teacher/student relationships. The first article below summarizes the general nature of the problem in federal agencies, while the second selection focuses on the abuse of managerial power.

We have also included, as a third reading on this problem, the EEOC guidelines on sexual harassment. Note in particular Paragraphs c-f, which place a strong affirmative obligation on employers — and presumably on senior supervisors — to prevent and correct situations in which harassment might occur or has occurred. Questions: does the language of these paragraphs seem to go too far in placing responsibility on employers? Are the patterns of harassment described in these articles found in organizations with which you are familiar? If so, have senior officials taken appropriate steps, or is there more they should and could have done?

Source: Judith Havemann, "Sexual Harassment: The Personnel Problem That Won't Go Away," *Washington Post Weekly Edition,* July 11-17, 1988.

Although women are more likely to be the recipients of unwanted sexual attention, 14 percent of men reported sexual harassment. When the last survey was tabulated that figure was 15 percent.

The most likely male victims were 20 to 44 years old, divorced or separated, held office/clerical or trainee positions, worked in a predominately female work group or had a female supervisor.

Since the last survey was taken seven years ago, the government has launched a program to try to discourage sexual harassment.

The average federal employee has received about one to two hours of training on sexual harassment during the past seven years, according to the MSPB survey.

"Agencies respond to perceived or real problems in this area," says Richard J. Indelicato, chief of the training systems division of the Office of Personnel Management (OPM), "and commonly assign personnel specialists and equal employment opportunity officers to two-day seminars it offers."

"Very few if any employees receive any training in this area," he says. "It is a low priority item because training is time and resources, and agencies have limited budgets."

"They know skills are directly linked to productivity, and skills training is very high [in priority]. Agencies look at the training dollar and tend to give low priority to all of the concerns such as equal employment, minority treatment, women's treatment, Hispanic treatment," Indelicato says.

Preventing Sexual Harassment of School Employees
Joyce Kaser and Marlene Ross

It began when he said, "This is going to be our year. I plan on going to bed with you, so think about when and where." Although she told him she found his behavior objectionable, he continued.

One day she found a note on her desk listing the qualifications necessary to be his secretary; one was "willing to go to bed with Supt." He often showed her a note that read, "Smile if you would like to get laid now." And on several occasions he grabbed and forcibly kissed her, attempted to touch her breasts, or tried to put his hand under her skirt.

She continued to resist. He tried to defame her character, accusing her of having a "foul mouth" and of dress that was "in bad taste and most suggestive." She sued him and the board of education; the board fired her.[1]

Is this New Jersey (Kittatinny Regional Board of Education) case a fluke, or is it an example of a problem many schools now face?

Source: Joyce Kaser and Marlene Ross, "Preventing Sexual Harassment of School Employees," *Educational Leadership*, November, 1983, pp. 53-54.

Consider the Pinellas County, Florida, incident. The facts are similar, only the characters change. According to a *Today's Education* article, an elementary teacher complained to her local education association that the principal of her school was harassing her. After that, some 14 other teachers came forward with similar charges against the man. A local newspaper reported that the principal had "fondled a teacher's breasts; written a critical evaluation of a teacher who rejected his advances; showed a teacher a magazine photograph of a nude woman, saying, 'She reminds me of you'; and suggestively held a pair of girl's underpants in front of another female teacher." The article reports that the principal testified that he was "a man first, a principal second."[2]

Several years ago these incidents would have been considered personal or private. Now such behavior is termed sexual harassment, a form of sex discrimination prohibited by federal law as well as by statutes in many states. The resolutions of these cases illustrate that such behaviors are no longer personal proclivities, and that the cases are not flukes. The New Jersey secretary received $14,000 from the board of education and the superintendent. In addition, the superintendent had to write her a letter of apology. In both instances the administrators were relieved of their duties, and the Florida principal had his certificate revoked.[3] These actions point out that what once had been considered a private matter is now clearly "another dimension of the public order."[4]

Endnotes

1. *Peter v. Aiken,* Amended and Supplemental Complaint, Superior Court, New Jersey (January, 1979).
2. Barbara Stein, "Sexual Harassment on the Job," *Today's Education* (February-March 1981): 82GS.
3. Telephone conversation with plaintiff Peter and her attorney, Naomi F. Eber, June 1981; and telephone conversation with Lou Kubler, ex-president of the Pinellas Classroom Teachers Association, August 1981.
4. Catherine A. MacKinnon, *Sexual Harassment of Working Women* (New Haven: Yale University Press, 1979), p. 58.

Federal Equal Employment Guidelines

The Equal Employment Opportunity Commission (EEOC) has issued official guidelines which define sexual harassment as a form of sex discrimination under Title VII of the Civil Rights Act of 1964. They are (official text):

Section 1604.11 Sexual Harassment.

a) Harassment on the basis of sex is a violation of Sec. 703 of Title VII.* Unwelcome sexual advances, requests for sexual favors and other verbal or physical conduct of a sexual nature constitute sexual harassment when (1) submission to such conduct is made either explicitly or implicitly a term or condition of an individual's employment, (2) submission to or rejection of such conduct by an individual is used as the basis for employment decisions affecting such individual, or (3) such conduct has the purpose or effect of unreasonably interfering with an individual's work performance or creating an intimidating, hostile, or offensive working environment.

b) In determining whether alleged conduct constitutes sexual harassment, the Commission will look at the record as a whole and at the totality of the circumstances, such as the nature of the sexual advances and the context in which the alleged incidents occurred. The determination of the legality of a particular action will be made from the facts on a case-by-case basis.

c) Applying general Title VII principles an employer, employment agency, joint apprenticeship committee or labor organization (hereinafter collectively referred to as "employer") is responsible for its acts and those of its agents and supervisory employees with respect to sexual harassment regardless of whether the specific acts complained of were authorized or even forbidden by the employer and regardless of whether the employer knew or should have known of their occurrence. The Commission will examine the circumstances of the particular employment relationship and the job functions performed by the individual in determining whether an individual acts in either a supervisory or agency capacity.

d) With respect to conduct between fellow employees an employer is responsible for acts of sexual harassment in the workplace where the employer (its agency or supervisory employees) knows or should have known of the conduct unless it can show that it took immediate and appropriate corrective action.

e) An employer may also be responsible for the acts of non-employees with respect to sexual harassment of employees in the work place where the employer (its agents or supervisory employees) knows or should have known of the conduct and fails to take immediate and appropriate corrective action. In reviewing these cases the Commission will consider the extent of the employer's control and any other legal responsibility which the employer may have with respect to the conduct of such non-employees.

f) Prevention is the best tool for the elimination of sexual harassment. An employer should take all steps necessary to prevent sexual harassment from occurring such as affirmatively raising the subject, expressing strong disapproval, developing appropriate sanctions, informing employees of their right to raise and how to raise the issue of harassment under Title VII, and developing methods to sensitize all concerned.

g) Other related practices: Where employment opportunities or benefits are granted because of an individual's submission to the employer's sexual advances or requests for sexual favors the employer may be held liable for unlawful sex discrimination against other persons who were qualified for but denied that employment opportunity or benefit.

*The principles involved here continue to apply to race, color, religion or national origin.

Iran-Contra Hearings:
John M. Poindexter on Responsibility and "Plausible Deniability"

Mr. Nields: I think you have already testified to this, that over the 5 1/2 years that you worked for this President, that you came to know him and what his policies were?

Mr. Poindexter: Yes. That is correct.

Mr. Nields: And when the issue of what has been referred to as the diversion was brought to you, I think you testified that in your 5 1/2 years, you knew how he would want that decision to be made?

Mr. Poindexter: Yes. That is correct.

Mr. Nields: And you felt therefore, that you could make the decision yourself without bringing it to him?

Mr. Poindexter: And, more importantly, I think — well, as importantly, I thought I had the authority to do that.

Mr. Nields: Because this was an implementation you felt of a policy that you — of his that you already knew about?

Mr. Poindexter: Yes. That is right.

Mr. Nields: But, admiral, didn't the diversion proposal raise two issues: One of them was what did the President favor? And that I think you have already testified you believed he would favor the diversion and, therefore — and that you felt confident you knew that? But didn't it raise a second issue? And that is — are you still with me?

Mr. Poindexter: Yes. I am still listening.

Mr. Nields: That is the question of whether he would want to be told or whether he would want to be shielded from responsibility for a political embarrassing decision? Didn't it present that second issue too?

Mr. Poindexter: I suppose it did.

Mr. Nields: And my question is this: Based on your 5 1/2 years of experience with him, what led you to believe that he would want deniability as opposed to responsibility for an embarrassing political decision?

Mr. Poindexter: That was a personal judgment on my part.

Mr. Nields: Did you believe it was what he would do?

Source: Testimony of John M. Poindexter, former National Security Advisor to President Reagan, at the Joint Hearings of the Senate and House of Representatives committees investigating the Iran-Contra activities, July, 1987.

Abuse of Authority

Mr. Poindexter: The situation I think was very clear in my mind. As I have testified, I felt confident that he would want to do this. He was very secure in his belief that it was the only way that we could bring about a democratic change to the government in Nicaragua; that it was the only way that we could keep from at some point in the future having to use U.S. soldiers on the ground in Central America.

He felt confident that unless we brought about a change to this government, at some future point, some future President would have to make the decision to send U.S. troops down to Central America.

He wanted to avoid that. He was willing, by my assessment, to take unilateral action.

In other words, the President exercising his constitutional authority without necessarily getting the agreement from the Congress. Later on, I had a specific discussion with him on that subject, which I referenced briefly the other day and you have it as one of the exhibits in your book. . . . It was [sent] back to my staff in Washington. It reads "Next, yesterday in a meeting that I had with the President, he started the conversation with 'I am really serious.'"

And the rest — this is also a quote,

> "If we can't move the Contra package before June 9, I want
> to figure out a way to take action unilaterally to provide
> assistance."

In other words he does not buy the concept of taking actions or talking about pulling out as described in the package. He has been reading Netanyahu's book on terrorism, and he was taken with the examples of Presidential actions in the past without congressional approval. He also read an op-ed piece on the same subject. I believe that was the one by Dick Pipes' son. The President is recalling the 506(a) action we took on Honduras. I told him that I didn't think that that particular provision would apply here, since we are not dealing with a government. But the fact remains that the President is ready to confront the Congress on the Constitutional question of who controls foreign policy. . . .

Mr. Nields: He is talking there about special powers that may or may not exist, but he is talking about special powers of the President of the United States?

Mr. Poindexter: That is correct.

Mr. Nields: Not powers of the National Security Adviser who has never been elected by anybody? Isn't that true?

Mr. Poindexter: Obviously — say that again.

Mr. Nields: I think that is just a yes or no question. You can expand if you wish. He was not talking about powers of the National Security Adviser?

Mr. Poindexter: He was talking about his powers.

Mr. Nields: Now my question to you is: What was it that made you believe that he wanted those special powers exercised by you with deniability rather than responsibility on his part?

Mr. Poindexter: That was a judgment call on my part based on a long time in government and a long time working with the President.

Mr. Nields: Are you saying that there is something that you learned from working with the President that led you to believe that he did not want responsibility for an embarrassing political decision, but wanted deniability?

In an earlier selection in this volume, drawn from these hearings, Oliver North and John Poindexter admitted that they had deceived or lied to members of Congress, and they attempted to justify their behavior. Later in the hearings, Poindexter discussed with Committee counsels Nields and Leon, and with several members of Congress, his views regarding the accountability of government officials and the concept of Presidential "deniability," as well as the meaning of "dealing in good faith." Excerpts from the testimony are included in this section. Questions: (1) How valid is Poindexter's defense of his actions? (2) In an essay in the New York Times, William Safire wrote that the U.S. Naval Academy "graduated John Poindexter first in his class apparently without inculcating in him the democratic value of truthfulness in office and accountability to superior officers" (May 2, 1987). Do the excerpts below support Safire's criticism? (3) Under what conditions is it defensible for subordinates not to inform elected executives of their actions, in order to protect the executives from damage to their powers and reputation? Under what conditions is it defensible for subordinates to deny that they informed their elected superiors, even though in fact they have kept them informed?

Mr. Poindexter: The President never indicated in any way to me that he did not want to be responsible for his decisions or that I should have provided deniability to him, if that is what you are getting at. This was an integration of a lot of experience that I had that made me conclude that this was the way we should go.

Mr. Nields: The same issue was raised — and I will ask you the same question — about the destruction of the Finding. What was it, if anything, that made you believe that your President would want you to destroy a Presidential document in order to avoid embarrassment to him?

Mr. Poindexter: I didn't analyze, when I saw that Finding on the 21st of November, what the President would want, one way or the other.

Mr. Nields: The same issue was presented, and I will ask you the same question, about sending Oliver North to brief the Congress and at the same time withholding information. What, if anything, led you to believe that . . . our President would want Colonel North to go to the members of the House Intelligence Committee, who were asking him questions about his support of the Contras, and withhold information?

Mr. Poindexter: That was a personal decision on my part, as I have testified. The President didn't enter into that matter. . . .

Mr. Leon: Now, with regard to the Boland Amendment, Admiral, just a few questions in that regard.

You have testified that your position was, and still is, I believe, that the NSC is not covered by the Boland Amendment?

Mr. Poindexter: That's correct. That's what I believe. . . .

Mr. Rudman [Republican Senator]: One part of your testimony I have a hard time understanding, and you said that you could say that you were complying with the spirit and the letter of Boland because you knew in your heart that it didn't apply to you: is that basically what you said?

Mr. Poindexter: Yes, that is correct.

Mr. Rudman: Well, on another law that I am interested in, is that like if I had come down to you a year ago and said to you, "Admiral, are you complying with the spirit and the letter of Gramm-Rudman-Hollings," would you have said to me, "Yes sir, I am," because in your heart of hearts you thought it was unconstitutional? That is what you are saying.

Mr. Poindexter: I have some problems with your piece of legislation.

Mr. Rudman: Lots of people do. You join a lot of folks, Admiral. I am simply saying to you that I don't understand — and I will tell you why I don't understand it. In all the dealings that I had with you heretofore in committee, I believe you would agree with me that government must operate in good faith.

Mr. Poindexter: I agree.

Mr. Rudman: And it is trust that we put in each other in government that makes it work. You would agree with that?

Mr. Poindexter: I would agree with that.

Mr. Rudman: And I would simply ask you if it didn't trouble you a bit at least to have to look people in the eye and say to them, "I am complying with the letter and the spirit of your law" because essentially you said to yourself the law doesn't apply. That really isn't dealing in good faith, is it?

Mr. Poindexter: As I have testified before, I was clearly withholding information, and unless it is for a very good reason, I think that that is a difficult thing to do. I would much have preferred if we had had another way to do it.

As I have testified before, often you don't have good options or solutions. You have got to make do with what you have. I did the best I thought I could under the circumstances. . . .

Mr. Hyde [Republican, House of Representatives]: I have a limited time, Admiral, so I won't tarry too long on the same obligatory, but nonetheless sincere, condemnations of some of the things that went on here.

I want a more comprehensive record than otherwise we might have, and so I have several issues I want to discuss with you.

Abuse of Authority

But I do want the record to be clear that I find very difficult to defend the lies and the deception — the letter of compliance, that said you have complied with the letter and the spirit of the law when you really meant to say it didn't apply. . . .

Now there is nothing more deadly dull — oh, I can think of a couple of things, but I won't — nothing more deadly dull than reading from a book. However, I think you will find this utterly fascinating, as I did. It is written by Bill Gulley with Mary Ellen Reese called *Breaking Cover.*

> The former Director of the White House Military Office reveals the shocking abuse of resources and power that has been the custom in the last four administrations.

Now, Bill Gulley and Mary Ellen Reese were writing about the Johnson administration, the Nixon administration, the Ford administration, and the Carter administration. It was written in 1980. And I am going to tell you the question I am going to ask you before I read the book. It is kind of an open exam. I am going to ask you if this doesn't seem familiar, a little deja vu?

Let me read this:

> The White House is a world apart. It's a palace, an ivory tower, an ego trip for its inhabitants. One of the elements that makes that world so special is the feeling of importance that pervades it. Whatever work is being done takes on a heightened significance; there's an urgency about everything. It's heady stuff. This sense of the critical quality of everything that's done in the White House interacts with the nature of those in it. Most are personally ambitious, have a tendency to be impressed with power, and are goal-oriented achievers.

> So you have a small, special, isolated world revolving around truly awesome power, in which there are ambitious men and women who are doing, and feel they have a better grasp of significant issues than those removed from the seat of all that power. But that's not all. If it were the White House could be a think tank, and it's not. On the contrary, the White House is the hub of the Executive Branch of the government, where decisions of government are implemented. The Hill is the talk-about-it place; the White House is the do-it-place.

> All this doesn't necessarily lead to abuse; it just makes abuse easier. If you are convinced that what you are doing is right, important and urgent, you may well be impatient with anything that might slow you down or bring you to a halt.

> The scene is set, the players are in place to take that next step, which will carry them over the line into abuse of power. When getting things done becomes the goal, value judgments about the means become blurred; more and more the standard becomes 'Will it work?' Almost imperceptibly, expediency begins to outrank principle, and when that happens, 'bending the law' becomes breaking it, and secrecy enters the picture.

The White House that Gulley saw was a palace of pragmatism where dishonesty flourished. It is a pragmatic palace because it is dedicated to the work of getting things done, not to debating the fine points. "To be efficient you have to circumvent the bureaucracy," Gulley says. "If you don't circumvent the bureaucracy you're a toothless tiger. Literally, you're a toothless tiger. Because you know if you go to Congress they're going to talk it to death, politics is going to get into it, nothing's ever going to happen. But in the White House you can get things done. You make things happen."

Richard Nixon posed the crucial question in his memoirs: "What is the law and how is it to be applied with respect to the President in fulfilling the duties of his office?" To expand: What is the law and how is it to be applied with respect to those who are trying to fulfill their duties to the President as they, and he, see those duties? It is a knotty question, which, Gulley says, hardly brushed the consciousness, let alone the conscience of those in the White House during his 11 years there.

In the White House, he says,

> You never worry about the law. I never worried about the law, about breaking the law. This never entered my mind, and I doubt it ever entered the minds of people who asked me to do things — maybe for a little bit after Nixon resigned, but it evaporated almost immediately. My thinking was, if the President wants it done, it's right. I never questioned it. It never occurred to me that some sheriff might show up . . . with a warrant. . . .

Case 9: Legislators and Professionals

This brief case illustrates a common problem in executive agencies: how to respond to pressure from legislators who have the power to help or hurt agency programs. The case also illustrates an important issue for legislators: when is it justifiable to communicate directly and forcefully on a problem important to the legislator? Can the four standards for ethical behavior (Part I essay) be used to clarify these two sets of issues?

I work in a local rehabilitation program for teenage drug abusers. Our goal is to return a client to the community when our professional teams are convinced the individual can remain "drug free." Recently a treatment team's decision to discharge a young woman from the program was strongly objected to by her parents. Adamant about continuing program treatment for the young woman, the parents used influence with a legislator on the appropriations committee to bring pressure on the agency head. I am the intermediary between the agency head and the treatment teams. The agency head has asked me to intervene and halt discharge plans.

III. Combating Unethical Behavior:
What to do When the Angels are Missing

Introductory Essay

In this final part of the book, we describe, through a selection of essays and cases, a wide range of approaches and strategies that can be used to combat unethical practices and to encourage ethical behavior. This introductory essay provides us with an opportunity to introduce some general perspectives that should be useful in thinking about deterrence, and to note briefly the themes of the readings that follow.

One obvious starting point in attacking problems of corruption and other abuses is to identify the kinds of agency programs and positions which are most likely to be vulnerable to abuse. As the President's Council on Integrity and Efficiency noted in a recent report, procurement contracts, programs involving loans and grants, and computer operations (especially those concerned with contracts and with personnel files) are prime areas for "fraud, waste, abuse and mismanagement."[1] Employees responsible for fire safety inspection, for monitoring restaurants in relation to the sanitary code, and for processing licenses and permits in a wide range of areas may also be unusually vulnerable to bribery and extortion.[2]

To target programs and positions is only a starting point, however. Any program area which is allowed to drift — without clear leadership from the top and without an active and continuous effort to monitor how division heads and lower staff members use their discretion — will in time fall prey to corruption and other forms of abuse. Some of these abuses will be initiated by officials within the government agency. Others arise from business agents and clients of government agencies, who are glad to provide large speaking fees, free vacations and other benefits to an individual public official in return for special opportunities to drain off the taxpayer's dollar.

When we frame the problem in this broad way, we may seem to imply that unethical behavior is rampant throughout the public service, and in the many connections between government and the private sector. In fact, our own view is that most public employees demonstrate high levels of personal integrity and responsibility. We think it likely that most business officials and others in the private domain also behave, and prefer to behave, ethically and responsibly. But that is not the end of wisdom. As James Madison observed 200 years ago in *Federalist* No. 51,

> If men were angels, no government would be necessary. If angels were to govern men, neither external nor internal controls on government would be necessary.

Since the power of government in this world is held only by men and women, a thoughtful approach to providing external and internal controls seems essential. Such controls will increase the difficulties and risks for those who are hungry for greater power and prestige. Moreover, a range of vigorous controls will protect the greater number of employees — who are honest and responsible — from the pressures and blandishments of their less savory compatriots and "friends."

The various approaches and strategies discussed in Part III are divided into six major sections: organizational structures that improve the monitoring of agency programs and individual behavior; the issue of whistle blowing; strategies to encourage greater "openness" in government programs and bureaucracies; the contribution of professional codes of ethics and professionalism; the role of education in encouraging ethical behavior; and, finally, the responsibility of leaders and others in bringing about an ethical culture.

Organizational Strategies

Several examples of innovation and implementation strategies to deter corruption are provided in the fifty-state summary discussed by Keon Chi and in the excerpts from the New York State report. These describe the use of internal accounting controls to identify areas vulnerable to corruption and to increase compliance. Each program targets a potential population for fraud control: taxpayers, welfare recipients, vendors and contractors.

Integrated into the procedures designed for administrative and accounting control is the idea of public trust. Public employees are encouraged to apply their specialized knowledge to the project at hand, whether it is in reliable record keeping in the case of accountants or in the design of safer O-rings in the case of engineers. Risk management is added to the tools available to public managers to strengthen ethical responses, as suggested in the Caroline Whitbeck article.

Whatever the level of government, the last several decades have witnessed the introduction of structures of government which are intended to bar illegal and unethical practices. Deterrence, through organizational units with stronger accountability measures, was targeted by the establishment of the United States Offices of the Inspectors General beginning in 1978; by the Office of Government Ethics the same year; and via the President's Council on Integrity and Efficiency set up by Executive Order in 1981. The system of Inspectors General, created to improve efficiency and effectiveness of government programs, was strengthened when reauthorized in 1988.

On the state and local levels, governmental units fostering accountability were set up with independent oversight mechanisms covering several sensitive functions such as personnel, capital planning and electoral reporting. The Burke and Messinger selections highlight a variety of accountability techniques: rigorous monitoring of state construction projects, stronger local fiscal reporting, and establishment of independent ethics commissions.

Whistle Blowing and Professional Integrity

If a staff member believes that violations of law, ethics or approved policy have occurred, and that senior officials are reluctant to take remedial action, the individual faces an important ethical issue. If one "blows the whistle," collegial relationships may be broken beyond repair, and the risk of losing one's job may be very real, as the Vandivier case in Part II illustrates. Yet to permit the pattern of corruption or abuse to continue will — for many people — be an uncomfortable, and sometimes an unacceptable, choice.

A number of professional organizations have, in recent years, begun to encourage their members to recognize the tensions involved in deciding whether to release information regarding illegal and other abusive activities within their agencies, and to "go public" when they believe doing so is the appropriate ethical action. In 1979 ASPA developed a position statement on whistle blowing which noted the division in public opinion:

> To some, whistle blowing is considered to be an ultimate expression of accountability.
> To others, whistle blowing is the spiteful behavior of disgruntled employees and an act
> of organizational disloyalty.

The ASPA statement went further, however, both in encouraging government officials to "blow the whistle" under certain circumstances, and in encouraging ASPA chapters around the country to provide counsel and support to their members when the issue of whistle blowing arises.

While professional organizations such as ASPA were developing a whistle-blowing policy during the late seventies, statutory protection for dissenters was also being formulated. A major change was the inclusion of whistle-blowing provisions in the Civil Service Reform Act of 1978. Two new national units were created, the Office of the Special Counsel and the Merit Systems Protection Board, each to prevent reprisals against whistle blowers and to combat any serious economic losses suffered by dissenters. Similarly, many states have enacted whistle-blower protection legislation. An increasing number of states and many local governments also have initiated ethics commissions, corruption investigatory units and offices of professional integrity.[3]

Whether one can be more effective in dissenting while still employed or after resigning is examined by Dobel; how to test complaint channels and still exercise personal and professional integrity is reviewed by Rowe; and the costs and benefits of whistle blowing are analyzed by Bowman. Harsh treatment of those who go public is the norm, yet is always depicted as justified by the organization, according to the Truelson study. Her research reports that "organizational retaliation" is common and concludes that "systemic corruption may be endemic to American governmental institutions."

The careers of whistle blowers have more often suffered than benefited from their efforts to call attention to illegal and other unethical activities in their own organizations.   In the field of governmental contracting, however, changes in federal law, combined with recent court decisions, suggest that this balance may be shifting. One former employee of a defense contractor, having called the Defense Department's attention to overcharging by his own corporation, was instrumental in the government's recovery of $14.3 million from the contractor; under the federal False Claims Act, he was then awarded $l.4 million. Other suits against major contractors have been initiated by employees and former employees, with the prospects of large settlements. More important, perhaps, the new incentives for employees with detailed inside knowledge to "blow the whistle" may well lead contractors to become "more diligent in policing themselves."[4]

Styles and Strategies of Managing Openness

Efforts in the 1960s and 1970s to increase citizen participation in government lent encouragement to the development of sunshine laws, ombudsmen offices, access channels, hot lines and other similar units. This participatory push led to laws, rules, and procedures governing open meetings, open documents, and open records as well as openly posted information about public sector operations. The principle espoused is that the public, the media, and interest groups will more actively monitor the actions of government if those actions are open for all to see; moreover, visible program decisions are less likely to be abusive or otherwise unethical. Harlan Cleveland put it succinctly: "The best antidote to irresponsibility is openness." His classic query for each manager is "If this action is held up to public scrutiny, will I still feel that it is what I should have done, and how I should have done it?"[5]

Several examples of the effective opening of management channels in the public sector include:

- The practice of listening in the field and directly reporting to the central office, as in the "Shriver Prescription" discussed in Richard Loverd's essay;

- The use of dissent channels in the U.S. Department of State, designed to encourage airing of independent views on foreign policy to an Open Forum Office; and

- New Jersey's effort, described in the Sinding selection, with its objective to create a department charged with representing "the public interest."

Each of these special units has a unique character which stresses strengthened informal communication channels for open reporting. These offer those who may be reluctant to speak out through traditional channels the opportunity to make a responsible presentation in a less threatening environment.

In addition to the opportunities for openness noted above, recent decades have brought a spate of conflict of interest laws, and fiscal disclosure enactments, along with campaign and political finance legislation. These latter efforts are directed at governing the conduct of elected and appointed officials by making information more readily available. John Rohr's article on financial disclosure reminds us that there may be tradeoffs between full disclosure of personal assets and the preservation of a person's right to privacy.

Establishing Standards of Professionalism

Recent years have featured a nation wide effort to establish and promulgate standards of professionalism. Professional organizations such as the International City Management Association, the American Society for Public Administration, and the National Contract Management Association have sought both to deter corrupt practices among their membership and to strengthen the public trust. Two approaches have been taken to achieve the dual goals: 1) visible standards for quality curriculum or for educational program accreditation have been established; and 2) principles of ethical conduct in the form of Codes of Ethics have been promulgated.

The National Association of Schools of Public Affairs and Administration, encouraged by the cooperation of ASPA, provided leadership to the accreditation route. Objectives were also set for implementing the second approach, the Codes of Ethics. The three main objectives for a code are to set high ethical standards, to increase public confidence, and to aid in determining appropriate action in the "gray areas" of ethical concerns.

The professional association of city managers, the International City Management Association (ICMA), has had a strong and sustained dedication to basic ethical principles since 1924, as the Tranter selection indicates. The more recent ASPA code of 1983 urges its 16,000 members to apply the principles behind the Code not merely to "prevent wrong, but to pursue right through timely and energetic execution of responsibilities." The code of contract managers (NCMA) stresses that their organization urges its members "to abide by the letter and spirit of the ethical standards of the Association." Yet support for a professional ethics code is not universal, as the selection by John Ladd vigorously attests.

During the same period, the Ethics in Government Act of 1978, for the first time, established standards for fiscal disclosure and conflict of interest situations. J. Jackson Walter's review of federal ethics legislation identifies the various barriers to executive recruitment and retention. These include concern for personal privacy (discussed earlier by John Rohr), the individual costs of financial divestiture, and the effects on employment after governmental service. The "chilling effect" on recruitment and retention has again been raised with the passage of the Federal Procurement Policy Act of 1988 and the signing by the President of Executive Order 12674. All of these efforts are directed towards achieving a "single, comprehensive, and clear set of executive branch standards of conduct that are objective, reasonable and enforceable."[7] The procurement legislation, for example, requires a "Certificate of Integrity" which attests to the fact that a government employee "understands the law." The person must also obtain certifications from all personnel, both inside and out of government, who have passed on a contract at the pre-contractual stage that they, too, understand the law. As "chilling" as these new requirements may seem to some, others agree with Senator Strom Thurmond (R-S.C.) that "It is time that public service be just that — not merely a stepping stone for future employment or profit."[8]

Encouraging Ethics Through Education and Discussion

In America, education is the characteristic mode of reform. As Lawrence Cremins notes, "In other countries, they stage revolutions. In the United States, we devise new curricula." Yet despite increasing ethical concern, there continues to be a reluctance to reform education through the introduction of ethics courses. Less than one-third (31.4%) of the member institutions of the National Association of Schools of Public Affairs and Administration in 1987 offered a separate course in ethics within their Masters programs. A recent poll on this question by the American Assembly of Collegiate Schools of Business noted that only one-third of Masters of Business Administration programs offered a separate non-required course in ethics. Yet, despite the chaotic state of ethics content, curriculum *is* being developed.

The essay by Derek Bok presents a set of recommendations supportive of teaching ethics courses which explore the reasons for "acting morally." This approach challenges the position that improving ethical behavior is not appropriate in our college classrooms. A recent project of ASPA and NASPAA to document ethics education across the nation culminated in a three-part Resolution on Ethics Education. The product of the Working Group on Ethics Education cochaired by Bayard Catron and Kathryn Denhardt, the Resolution is being circulated for adoption by professional organizations and others interested in encouraging ethics through education and discussion.

Leadership and Individual Responsibility

Throughout the readings of this book, reference is made to the importance of guidance from "the top" on questions of public trust. Ethics is no exception to the general rule of management that the success of any strategy, technique or process depends on the strength of the signals from the leader. Daily ethical problems are more easily resolved with reinforcement from one's supervisor that one is "doing right."

We may be able to agree on the importance of leadership to the encouragement of an ethical climate. However, then, the questions turn on "who is a leader?" John Gardner has suggested a possible response. Leaders "put heavy emphasis on the intangibles of vision, values and motivation. . . ."[9]

Combating Unethical Behavior: What to do When the Angels are Missing

We conclude with three selections, focused on these questions. The first — the Kennedy speech — provides a description of the characteristics of visionary leadership in which "integrity" is one of the four qualities of public servants. The Doig and Stewart selections provide guidance for identifying where responsibility resides, what is the scope of individual and collective ethical responsibility, and why "ignorance" of the ethical path is not acceptable at the top, or lower in the organization.

George Walden in *The Shoeblack and the Sovereign* commented perceptively that "In the ethics industry . . . there are too many people gesticulating from the bridge and too few left seeing what is going on in the engine room."[10] By encouraging ethics education and discussions on leadership and individual responsibility, both on the bridge — to policy makers — and especially in the engine room — to those who implement policy — university programs, professional organizations and other training units are endeavoring to minimize the chaos and encourage diversity of constructive approaches to excellence in ethical public management.

Endnotes

1. The listing was developed, according to the President's Council on Integrity and Efficiency to "enhance Government employee, general public, and audit and investigative community awareness of what constitutes unethical behavior. . ." See *Compendium of Publications on Fraud, Waste and Abuse Indicators,* June 30, 1988, p. i.
2. *The Ethics Factor Handbook,* International City Management Association, 1988, p. 14.
3. See the *Campaign Finance, Ethics and Lobby Law Blue Book 1988-1989,* Council of State Governments, edited by Joyce Bullock with Dinker I. Patel, policy analyst, 1988.
4. See Richard W. Stevenson, "Workers Who Turn in Bosses Use Law to Seek Big Rewards," *New York Times,* July 10, 1989, p. 1. The False Claims Act was originally enacted in 1863, but it was infrequently used until strengthened by a set of amendments in 1986.
5. Harlan Cleveland, "How do You Get Everyone in on the Act, and Still Get Some Action?" *Educational Record,* Vol. 55, No. 3, Summer 1974, pp. 177-182.
6. The EO12674 is referenced as the "Principles of Ethical Conduct for Government Officers and Employees."
7. "Stricter Ethical Standards Established for Executive Branch," *Frontline,* the newsletter of the President's Council on Integrity and Efficiency (PCIE), June 1989.
8. Kimberley A. Mattingly, "The Ethical Noose," *Government Executive,* February, 1989, p. 40.
9. John W. Gardner, "Mastering the Fine Art of Leadership," in Top Management Section, *Business Month,* May, 1989, p. 77.
10. George Walden, *The Shoeblack and the Sovereign: Reflections on Ethics and Foreign Policy,*(NY: St. Martin's Press, 1989), p. 8.

9. Organizational Strategies

Fraud Control in State Human Services Programs: Innovations and New Strategies

Keon S. Chi

The issue of fraud, waste and abuse has played a major role in recent welfare debates, and three major targets of critics have been the Food Stamp, Aid to Families with Dependent Children (AFDC) and Medicaid programs. In fiscal 1981, more than 22 million people received Food Stamp benefits, totaling $11.3 billion; 3.8 million families were recipients of the AFDC program, costing $12.5 billion; and 22.5 million recipients received Medicaid services at a cost of $22.8 billion.

It is difficult to calculate the exact amounts of fraud and abuse in these programs, but studies indicate that several billion dollars are lost every year through erroneously issued payments and fraud and abuse. One obvious result of fraud has been an unsympathetic public perception of the government benefits programs as illustrated by recent taxpayer revolts. Another result has been

Three elements necessary to combat fraud in State human service programs, according to Keon Chi, are administrative incentives coupled with increased authority and strengthened political leadership. Several state management programs currently in use to deter fraud and abuse are also identified.

the impact of mismanagement on needy recipients. Although nominal benefits have risen in these programs, real benefits, adjusted after inflation, have not increased significantly. Recent state revenue shortfalls during severe recession forced state governments to tighten their budgets and accelerate fraud control efforts. Many state governments, with or without federal assistance, have experimented with innovative fraud reduction programs, often using computer technology.

This report first highlights four specific innovations attempted by three states to reduce either provider or recipient fraud in Medicaid, Food Stamp and AFDC programs. All but one of these programs were chosen in 1983 by the Southern Legislative conference of The Council of State Governments as innovative state programs. The second section of the report discusses underlying issues and problems in fraud control, such as re-affirming states' roles, problems in defining fraud and abuse, computer matching, and practical strategies states may consider. And, in the last section, a list of suggestions, based on fraud control studies, interviews and workshops, is presented regarding future courses of action by the federal and state governments.

Source: Keon S. Chi, "Fraud Control in State Human Services Programs: Innovations and New Strategies," *Innovations*, August 1984, pp. 1-8.

Innovative Programs

Case 1. Termination of Medical Providers

In 1979, Pennsylvania's Office of Medical Assistance (OMA) instituted a program to identify and eliminate providers who abuse the Medicaid program. The provider enforcement program, run by the OMA's Bureau of Utilization Review with 17 professional staff and 30 part-time contract practitioners, is organized according to provider types, such as physicians, dentists or pharmacists. Practitioners providing excessive or unnecessary diagnostic tests and ancillary services are identified through computer-aided and manual analysis. OMA's physicians, licensed nurses or other practitioners check medical records against the provider's invoices to determine the integrity of treatment. When necessary, peer review committees of appropriate practitioners review the suspected treatment and hold meetings with practitioners. Names of persons terminated from the medical assistance program are released to the media.

The results of Pennsylvania's Medicaid provider fraud control program are encouraging: the numbers of terminations in all types of providers have steadily increased, from 34 in 1979 to 67 in 1981 and to 105 in 1983. Stopped payments to the 105 medical providers in 1983 were estimated to be $6 million. And average annual savings in the state's Medicaid program have been some $5 million at an administrative cost of less than $500,000 per year. Seventy-five percent of the program cost comes from federal funds.

Case 2. Recoupment of Overissued Food Stamp Benefits

South Carolina was one of the many states with low recoupment rates. Overissued Food Stamp benefits accounted for 8 percent of the total costs ($200 million) of the program, or approximately $15 million a year. The state's low recovery rate (1.4 percent) was due to several factors including: little support in federal regulations for establishing and enforcing collection of claims; cumbersome state procedures; and inadequate staffing, particularly at the county level. Encouraged by recent changes in federal Food Stamp regulations providing incentives for overissuance control, South Carolina initiated in 1983 a statewide program known as Fighting Abuse Through Investigation and Recoupment, or Project FAIR for short, to improve its recoupment rates.

Under the current federal regulations, a portion of repayments is retained by the states as an incentive: 50 percent of fraud collections and 25 percent of non-fraud collections. Food Stamp staff investigating fraud now are on 75 percent federal funding. Under Project FAIR, South Carolina returns up to 62.5 percent of the recouped funds to its counties that provide workers, and the county's share is then earmarked for an emergency welfare fund and non-recurring expenditures. This is a new monetary incentive for county officials.

Various methods are used to detect Food Stamp overissuance or fraud, ranging from quality control to anonymous reports and audits. County eligibility workers assist in identifying suspicious cases. In addition, the South Carolina Department of Social Services has recently developed a statistical model to identify Food Stamp cases that are likely to contain errors. This "Error Prone Profile" has proven to be effective. Most work, however, is done manually, not by computers. The state expects to save about $2.5 million annually through Project FAIR, which was designed not only to deter fraud but also keep abusers from imprisonment while making them repay government benefits to which they are not entitled.

Case 3. Income Verification System

Florida has been one of the nation's leaders in the detection and investigation of fraud in government benefit programs. The state's Division of Public Assistance Fraud within the Office of the Auditor General has identified welfare abusers and recovered millions of dollars and deterred potential cheaters through the Income Verification System (IVS), which checks the incomes of recipients in the Food Stamp and AFDC programs by matching Social Security numbers.

Begun as a state-funded program the IVS was first used in 1973 on AFDC, and Food Stamp cases were added in 1980. In both programs, Florida was two or three years ahead of most other states in verifying recipient incomes. Florida uses the state Department of Labor's salary and wage files as part of its match system. The IVS also uses several other income files, including Unemployment Compensation Benefit payments, Workers' Compensation Benefit payments, state retirement benefits and Supplemental Security Income. The wage matching is a starting point for investigators, who then determine whether the income was knowingly and intentionally not reported.

The results of the IVS have been impressive. Through June 1982, for example, convictions were obtained in more than 10,000 cases, nearly $23 million in fraud was uncovered, and over $12 million was ordered paid back by the courts. From the program's inception through March 1983, more than 21,000 fraud cases were referred for prosecution; of those, 17,200 persons were charged with welfare fraud. A major additional benefit has been the deterrent effect of the program. In 1973, one study concluded that potential fraud existed in 25.1 percent of the AFDC cases in Florida. By 1980, the probable AFDC recipient fraud rate was 5.7 percent. Since IVS matching began, a similar effect has been noted in the Food Stamp program. The Food Stamp caseload declined by 17.6 percent between October 1980 and February 1983. Although other factors played a part, IVS contributed to the decline.

Case 4. Computer Matching

Florida has also been a leader in intra- and interjurisdictional computer matching. The states initiative in using income matching to screen abusers in the AFDC and Food Stamp programs preceded federal mandates. Following up a match project with Illinois' Unemployment Compensation Benefit Files, Florida has been pursuing interstate computer matches to ferret out Food Stamp fraud throughout eight Southeastern states — Alabama, Georgia, Kentucky, Mississippi, North Carolina, South Carolina, Tennessee and Florida. The first phase involved computer matching by comparing the Social Security numbers between states of persons receiving Food Stamps. A primary purpose was to see if recipients were crossing state lines to simultaneously receive benefits. Out of a total of 3,394,875 Social Security numbers compared in November 1983, the number of raw matches — numbers from one state matched with numbers on another state's active Food Stamp list — was 6,557, of which 1,845 were found in Florida. Printouts of the matches were distributed to the states so that they could check their records and verify data.

A second phase of the interstate matching would involve uncovering people who may be working in one state, but not reporting the employment, and receiving Food Stamps in another state. Although each state now matches its Food Stamp rolls against its own wage data, under Florida's program individual states will be able to match income data against the other states. Following completion to the Food Stamp program matches, Florida plans to conduct a similar eight-state jurisdictional computer match for the AFDC program in the U.S. Department of Health and Human Services Southeastern district (Region IV).

These innovative approaches put states' fraud control strategies in perspective and raise pertinent questions. Can these strategies be transferred to other states? What more can states do to further reduce fraud and abuse in the human service programs? And, what are the major issues and problems in considering innovative strategies?

Two underlying issues must first be briefly discussed. What is the nature and extent of fraud and abuse in the three largest human services programs — Food Stamp, AFDC and Medicaid? And, what have the federal government and states done to control fraud and abuse in these programs?

How Much Fraud and Abuse? And, What Has Been Done?

No one knows how widespread the problem of fraud and abuse in the human services programs really is. According to the U.S. House of Representatives Select Committee on Aging's "Report on Medicaid Fraud Enforcement" (1982), estimates of fraud in Medicaid run from 10 to 25 percent of the program or between $2.5 billion and $6.2 billion at a 1981 level. A 1983 General Accounting Office report shows that about $1 billion a year in Food Stamp benefits is being illegally siphoned from the program. And, a 1983 report prepared by the National Institute of Justice for the U.S. Department of Justice estimates that AFDC fraud may range from a minimum of $376 million to a maximum of $3.2 billion. Altogether fraud consumes billions of tax dollars at the federal level and millions of dollars from state and local agencies. In addition, error rates in these three largest benefit programs add $1 or $2 billion more nationwide.

In an effort to control Medicaid fraud, Congress created in 1976 the Office of the Inspector General in the U.S. Department of Health and Human Services (HHS, then Health, Education and Welfare) and, in 1977, authorized 90 percent federal funding for the states to establish Medicaid Fraud Units (MFUs) within the offices of the state attorneys general. The Office of Inspector General in HHS assumed responsibility for supervising the MFUs in 1979. By 1980, at least 30 states took advantage of the 90 percent federal matching funds to establish their MFUs, but recovered only $3 million. According to the Select Committee on Aging's report, all the 50 states spent some $40 million in the detection of Medicaid fraud in 1980 and obtained only 228 convictions, spending an average of $175,438 per conviction. In 1980, 18 states did not convict a single Medicaid provider. The 1974-1980 average for all 50 states was 1.5 convictions per state per year.

Under the 1981 Agriculture and Food Act and the Omnibus Reconciliation Act, states are now required to match Social Security numbers of Food Stamp recipients with computerized wage data. The federal law also contains stiffened penalties for felony and misdemeanor convictions with fines ranging up to $10,000 and jail terms up to five years. The federal government pays 75 percent of the cost of the fraud investigations and prosecutions. As in the case of Food Stamps, efforts to control fraud in AFDC have been mostly centered around recipient eligibility. The 1981 amendment to the Social Security Act encourages the states to recoup more of the falsely filed AFDC benefits. Under the amendment, the federal government can sue illegal recipients. And, the law calls for civil penalties of up to $2,000 for each claim.

The Reagan administration has taken several steps to combat fraud, abuse and waste in government operations. In 1981, President Reagan created the Council on Integrity and Efficiency, strengthening the powers of inspectors general in several federal agencies to enhance integrity of federal programs. The Council was charged with developing plans to coordinate activities which attack fraud and waste in government programs. One of the projects established by the Council is the Long-Term Computer Matching Project, which in turn established a clearinghouse to maintain current information about federal computer matching activities.

Studies show that states have not done as much as they should or could have in spite of federal initiatives and continued funding. Findings of these studies point out three broad reasons for slow progress:

(1) Lack of incentives. Neither benefit program administrators nor criminal justice agencies have much incentive to control fraud. Welfare administrators at the state level lack incentives because fraud control strategies tend to interfere with routine case management processes. Reducing management costs and administrative errors are more important than fraud control, and fraud control is not likely to be among high priorities unless scandals or investigations make headlines. Recovered overpayments in benefit programs are often returned to the general treasury, not to the agencies or counties whose efforts brought about the recoupment. And, to criminal justice agencies, the fraud control issue is less significant than other forms of crimes since most, if not all, recipient cases involve small dollar amounts.

(2) Lack of authority or tools. Some states have hampered the full operation of fraud control agencies by not giving them the authority they need. For instance, Medicaid Fraud Units in many states cannot investigate fraud because they do not have authority to bring civil recovery proceedings, have no independent subpoena power, no power to arrest, and no authority to seize evidence of Medicaid fraud. In the AFDC program, state administrators face difficulties since they have little control over the daily work of local caseworkers and cannot force them to spend more time in preference to routine administration of the program. Control agencies also lack such basic tools as cost and performance data, work measurement and operations analysis and adequate staff and training.

(3) Lack of political leadership. "Since they usually wish to avoid tax increases and since other programs and lobbies are competing for funds," one study for the National Institute of Justice concluded, "governors and legislators often wish to avoid close involvement with welfare and fraud issues, letting the welfare system and criminal justice agencies take the heat for low benefit levels, high costs, and any fraud or abuse which become known." In some states, lobbying and pressure by industry groups on state Medicaid officials and legislators are also blamed for the resistance to the Medicaid Fraud Unit program, according to a recent Congressional staff report.

For these and other reasons, states lack comprehensive fraud control programs. Instead, they tend to initiate ad hoc task forces or special projects dealing with specific programs involving a limited number of agencies. Findings and implications of several recent studies on fraud control in the human service programs also suggest that both the federal government and states have placed much emphasis on identifying and prosecuting violators, but not necessarily on preventive strategies. In the past few years, most states have enacted laws to stiffen penalties for violators specifically in the Medicaid, Food Stamp and AFDC programs. Tougher penalties are provided in statutory provisions in such states as: Alaska, Arkansas, Florida, Indiana, Maryland, Mississippi, Nevada, New Mexico, North Carolina, Oregon, South Carolina, Tennessee, Utah, Vermont and Wisconsin. The Wisconsin law appears to be representative of these states: "Any person who, with intent to secure public assistance . . . whether for himself or for some other person, willfully makes any false representations may . . . if the value of such assistance exceeds $500, be imprisoned not more than five years. . . ."

Issues in State Fraud Control

There are four basic issues that states must consider in initiating or reviewing fraud control strategies in the human services programs:

- Re-affirming their roles and responsibilities.
- Defining the nature of fraud and abuse as well as major targets of fraud control.
- The extent of computer matching.
- Directions of future fraud control efforts.

States' Roles

States have important roles to play in reducing fraud and abuse in the Medicaid, Food Stamp and AFDC programs. In all cases, the federal government requires states to develop plans to reduce errors, fraud and abuse, yet basic decisions about these plans must be made by states, not federal agencies.

Under Medicaid, for instance, each state's medical plan specifies how providers will be reimbursed. Federal regulations require that hospitals and nursing homes be reimbursed on some reasonable cost basis, but the states can establish their own systems to reimburse other providers. The federal Health Care Finance Administration (HCFA) pays 50 percent of each state's administrative costs and between 50 and 78 percent of benefits costs, depending on the state's per capita income. HCFA also pays 90 percent of the costs of developing automated claims processing and managing information systems and 75 percent of their operating costs.

State agencies, through their local offices, are responsible under individual state operation plans for certifying households as eligible to participate in the Food Stamp program and issuing coupons to those households. States are required to establish claims for all identified over-issuances and initiate collection procedures for those meeting a minimum collection criteria. Additionally, regulations encourage states to pursue potential fraud either administratively or judicially. State agencies administer the program directly through state welfare agencies or supervise its administration by county or city welfare agencies. State agencies also have program monitoring responsibilities. Each state is required to establish a quality control review of a statistically selected sample of Food Stamp cases. These reviews are made continuously by each state's quality control review branch to assess whether only those who are eligible participate and whether they receive the proper amount of benefits.

Under the AFDC program, states are given substantial latitude to define who is eligible for benefits, what level of benefits will be offered, and how the programs will be administered. The amount paid to an AFDC family is determined by the state. The states are required to review each case at least once every six months to determine if the recipient is still eligible and should receive the same level of benefits. Apart from certain monitoring efforts, the federal government plays no role in AFDC program administration. Thirty-six states have "state-administered" systems, in which local offices of the state welfare department process applications and issue checks; 18 states have "state-supervised" systems, in which the state only supervises the operations of local (usually county) welfare agencies. In both systems, local welfare offices process Food Stamp and Medicaid as well as AFDC applications.

Definitions and Targets

Labeling a case (usually overpayment) as fraud, abuse or error is clouded both by the issue of intent, and ambiguities and complications in applicable rules. Compounding these difficulties are problems of bias that welfare administrators and investigators (and sometimes the public) tend to have.

Fraud involves intentional deception or illegal manipulation of government programs for personal benefit. Fraud usually refers to a violation of a civil or criminal law and involves misrepresentation of facts. On the other hand, *abuse* involves an improper use of program resources for personal benefits but without the criminal intent. Abuse usually refers to situations in which questionable benefits are obtained by recipients but which are not specifically prohibited by applicable laws and regulations.

Who should be major targets of fraud control? While it is difficult to generalize about abusers or cheaters in the government benefit programs, there is a general consensus among investigators regarding potential targets of fraud control. The fraud is perpetrated in the Medicaid program most often, if not exclusively, by providers, not by recipients. The Select Committee's study quoted previously shows that in 1980 nursing home operators lead the conviction list, followed by physicians and pharmacists, while there were no convictions against health maintenance organizations, home health agencies, Medicaid clinics or clinical laboratories. The amount of recipient fraud by comparison has been reported to be minuscule. One major reason for Medicaid provider fraud, according to the Select Committee Study, is the fact that Medicaid is a bifurcated program in which the federal government pays most of the money but leaves enforcement and program integrity efforts to states. The Pennsylvania program highlighted above seems to be headed in the right direction.

Yet, in the case of the Food Stamp and AFDC programs, agency and recipient mistakes account for the largest portion of incorrect payments — errors, fraud and abuse. The biggest losses in Food Stamps have been reported in the smallest claims, and the overpayments have been due to either recipient misunderstanding of rules or dishonesty in reporting their income. The efforts made by South Carolina and Florida illustrate the nature of the problem.

A recent report prepared by the New Jersey Legislative Oversight Committee describes targets of fraud control in the AFDC program in this way:

> The myth of welfare fraud portrays the culprit as having collected tens of thousands of dollars under several assumed names while fully employed. Another common perception pictures the supposedly absent male living with the welfare family and hiding from the caseworker. Public anger is also directed at welfare recipients who have neither the interest nor desire to work. The actual facts portray a far different scenario. Seven out of 10 recipients of AFDC are children. The adults are predominantly women. They live in families headed by women who are often unable to work for lack of day care for the children. They live on a welfare budget that is considered inadequate by virtually all observers and an inducement to commit a fraudulent act to obtain some extra assistance dollars.

Thus, fraud in AFDC is a crime committed mostly by the poor; this fact should be considered in defining targets of fraud control efforts. Stories on welfare queens, poverty pimps and Medicaid mills do not depict the real targets.

Computer Matching

Computer matching has become a buzzword in the administration of government benefit programs. Since the FBI used a computer to match the names of government employees with welfare files in 1976, over 200 matching programs have been reported.

In 1977, a federal program known as Project Match was launched during the Carter administration to compare AFDC and Medicaid files. Since 1979, federal law has required state welfare agencies to use income information in determining AFDC eligibility and payment amounts. Congress passed a law in 1983 mandating wage matches for the Food Stamp program as well. And, since January 1983, states have been required to match Food Stamp recipient files with wage information from state employment security agency files or Social Security files.

Computer matching is a type of auditing technique used to "purify" a data base by screening, editing and scanning between lists or files. Computer matching is done usually by checking benefit recipients' names, Social Security numbers, addresses or other personal identification. Computer matching used at the state level may be grouped into two broad types: intrajurisdictional (statewide) matches, and interjurisdictional (interstate) matches. Currently, all the states are conducting matches to detect unreported incomes of beneficiaries. Fourteen states conduct front-end matching to verify applicants' eligibility for benefits. Matches within a state involve comparison of beneficiaries' files from one area (usually a county) with another. Twenty states, as in the Southeastern region, are currently conducting interjurisdictional matches between two or more states. . . .

One of the most publicized computer matches is the Massachusetts bank match program, which uncovered a large amount of liquid assets owned by recipients in excess of the limits within the AFDC, Food Stamp, Medicaid, General Relief and Supplemental Security Income programs. Based on the initial test in 1982 and 1983, Massachusetts officials estimated that computer matching, if all banks in the state were matched, could generate a savings of between $136 million [and] $306 million for the state, and a minimum of 6,000 cases could be removed from the state welfare rolls. Yet, the bank match program, as in other cases, raised some queries regarding potential abuse of computer matching.

In fact, computer matching, despite its proven effectiveness, has not been without critics. Critics usually give four major reasons for objecting to the use of computer matching — all relating to its impact on individual rights: (1) computer matching violates the Fourth Amendment to the U.S. Constitution, which protects against unreasonable searches and seizures, since computer matching involves "fishing expeditions," hoping something will show up; (2) once a computer match has taken place, any person whose names appears as a "hit" is presumed to be guilty of the wrongdoing, thus violating the presumption of the innocence principle; (3) computer matching denies due process of law by not giving beneficiaries notices of their situation and an adequate opportunity to contest the results of the matches; and (4) the Privacy Act of 1974 and Tax Reform Act of 1976 restrict disclosure of matching certain data to protect the privacy rights of the individual.

Yet, there is no question that computer matching is a very attractive tool for detecting fraud, abuse and error in government benefit programs. The question is how to maintain a balance between benefits of computer matching and protection of the privacy rights. Computer matching at the federal level is regulated by guidelines issued by the Office of Management and Budget. State officials might want to consider additional measures to help state agencies regarding operational requirements of computer matching.

Strategies

Although it is difficult to say how effective federal incentives have been in securing innovations in the area of fraud control, state officials have been more receptive to federal strategies based on financial incentives than strategies based on threatened penalties. Congress has provided funding for innovations in fraud control in all of the three programs. As a result of federal financial incentives, many states have tried to implement new methods in the administration of the human services programs. Since Wisconsin adopted an innovative welfare information system known as the Computer Reporting Network (CRN), which uses common eligibility determination mechanisms and a single combined application form for the three programs, similar innovative systems have been implemented in Georgia (PARIS), Illinois (CIS), Louisiana (WIS), Michigan (CIS), Maryland (AIMS), New Hampshire (EMS), New Jersey (CODES), Oklahoma (CIS) and Texas (SAVERR).

As one 1982 survey by The Council of State Governments shows, many other states have implemented various welfare information systems. In 1980, the federal government introduced the Family Assistance Management Information System (FAMIS) to promote computerized information systems for the states. By 1983, a majority of the states either had applied or received FAMIS funds. Continued financial incentives, such as the 90 percent funding formula in FAMIS, from the federal government can encourage more states to improve their administration of the human services programs.

Which way should fraud control strategies be directed? Most studies call for a change in the direction, from reactive approaches to preventive approaches. "By actively trying to identify fraud problems, agencies can not only uncover a higher proportion of existing fraud cases but also locate and correct problems in program design and implementation which facilitate frauds in the first place," an NIJ [National Institute of Justice] report suggests. "Proactive fraud prevention makes eminently more sense than reactive approaches relying on investigation, detection, and recovery of funds." Also, current computer matches are primarily post-payment matches to detect fraud and abuse after it has occurred. More front-end computer matching is encouraged.

Finally, measuring the effectiveness of a comprehensive fraud control plan is difficult; the most common method [of] evaluating such a plan is use of cost-benefit ratio. Table 2 presents useful information for state and local officials who are planning an effective fraud control effort or reviewing existing programs in the human services programs. . . .

What Needs To Be Done?

Improving fraud control efforts in the human services programs will require concerted efforts by the federal government and states. The federal government should consider revising legislation to provide enhanced funding for fraud control programs and to allocate recovered overpayments to the control agencies. At the same time, states may consider the following suggestions:

- Provide more administrative incentives for fraud control.
- Create special administrative units with trained staff and necessary funds for fraud control.
- Provide fraud control agencies with needed authority to conduct investigations and pursue civil and criminal prosecution.
- Establish stiffened penalties for recipient and provider fraud.
- Initiate more preventive fraud control measures.
- Enact legislation providing that a share of recovered overpayments be returned to local agencies.
- Improve computer matching.

In 1983, The Council of State Governments and U.S. Office of Management and Budget co-sponsored a series of regional conferences on fraud, waste and abuse in government benefit programs. These conferences set a new tone and atmosphere for federal-state cooperation on fraud control and demonstrated the value of links among program areas and government levels. The OMB called for three plans: a central repository for information on "best practices;" a national network of federal, state and local officials to receive such information; and a permanent, nationwide partnership of government officials to tackle fraud, waste and abuse. And, the Council, in its appraisal of the jointly sponsored workshops, identified specific follow-up initiatives:

- A bibliographic and document exchange; an inquiry unit to respond to questions generated by the conferences and other activities; software package exchange; a series of newsletters (legislative, technical); model legislation for the Council's *Suggested State Legislation;* and a database on programs, laws and regulations, and speakers.
- A means for on-site technical assistance by creating a talent bank of state and federal officials who are willing and capable of providing on-site assistance, and creating teams of state officials who would exchange information on issues they have selected.
- A continuation of the regional outreach activities through additional conferences and seminars for specialists as well as for policy-makers, and training packages and seminars for legislators and staff and technical specialists.
- An applied research effort capable of case studies of innovative programs and procedures, research monographs on particular subjects, survey on specialized topics, and demonstration projects.

In conclusion, the future of fraud control in the human services programs depends upon three factors: continuing collaborative efforts by the federal government and states; political will of governors and legislators; and innovative strategies implemented by program administrators.

Vulnerability Assessment: A Three-Letter Word

Eileen Siedman

Vulnerability assessment. Is it just another catch phrase — or something new? Well — relatively new, if it provides a fresh opportunity to focus on accountability and dig around for the "real" reasons why government doesn't always function as well as it should. And isn't it interesting that those defense-related "windows of vulnerability" have now spawned civilian vulnerabilities? In the old days, we called them problems and looked for solutions. We also assumed that one had to know what caused the problems in order to solve them. No instant answers or quick fixes — only the slow, painstaking, unglamorous digging for irrefutable facts followed by rational, logical human judgment. Subjectivity was not a dirty word, common sense was a high compliment, and quantification was a useful tool, not a driving force.

Now it seems altogether possible that we've come full circle in the search for accountability and finally begun again to use that three letter word — *Why* — in looking for systemic soft spots.

Efforts to detect how vulnerable governmental agencies are to fraud, waste and mismanagement have spawned several new, popular and sophisticated approaches. However, Siedman suggests that strengthened accountability can more readily be assessed and achieved by probing generic causes through the application of the simple, but powerful three-letter word, WHY? Is Siedman's back-to-basics test applicable?

A Variety of "New" Approaches

Let's put this phenomenon in historical perspective. For example, we know that the never-ending search for governmental accountability inevitably generates "new" approaches—each perceived by its promoters as a shortcut to truth. Close examination, however, reveals that each approach is a warmed over version of an old technique with a new name such as planning, programming, budgeting system (PPBS); program evaluation; management by objectives (MBO); policy analysis; zero-based budgeting (ZBB); or the new kid on the block, vulnerability assessment.

Why Sunset Has Set

Sunset legislation, which enjoyed a short-lived popularity in the 1970s, became passé when few answers were found for the important questions, such as: who will determine whether a program has achieved legislative intent? why criteria will be used to evaluate success or failure? how much weight will political factors carry *vis a vis* available resources and program success?

The 1982 Financial Integrity Act (PL 97-255, September 8, 1982) amended the Budget and Accounting Procedures Act of 1950 by requiring ". . . ongoing evaluations and reports on the adequacy of the systems of internal accounting and administrative control of each executive agency. . . ."

The act complements OMB Circular A-123 (October 28, 1981), which is based on an inherent assumption that accountability and management improvement can be achieved through internal controls and a superficial problem-identification process called "vulnerability assessments."

Inspectors General Established

Congressional creation of offices of inspector general (OIG) in 1978 (PL 95-452, October 12, 1978) added still another dimension by establishing within the executive branch "independent" offices which report to the Congress semiannually. Viewed as a change agent with a tremendous capability for influencing organizational behavior, the OIG is not just another agency component. Under the statute, the inspector general (IG) has a special independence that prevents anyone, even the head of the establishment, from interfering in the work or changing anything in any reports. And no one in the agency, including the highest official, is immune from OIG scrutiny. With this kind of independence however, comes a heavy responsibility for accuracy, veracity, and good judgment. In addition, work of the IG is scrutinized, in turn, by the General Accounting Office (GAO), congressional members and staff, Office of Management and Budget (OMB), investigative news reporters, special interest groups, and the public; in short, by everyone.

Source: Eileen Siedman, "Vulnerability Assessment: A Three-Letter Word," *The Bureaucrat*, 12:1 (Spring 1983), pp. 32-34.

The IG Act specifically requires that certain information be reported to the Congress semiannually.

Sec. 5. (a) Each Inspector General shall, not later than April 30 and October 31 of each year, prepare semiannual reports summarizing the activities of the Office during the immediately preceding six-month periods ending March 31 and September 30. Such reports shall include, but need not be limited to —

(1) a description of significant problems, abuses, and deficiencies relating to the administration of programs and operations of such establishment disclosed by such activities during the reporting period;

(2) a description of the recommendations for corrective action made by the Office during the reporting period with respect to significant problems, abuses, or deficiencies identified pursuant to paragraph (1);

(3) an identification of each significant recommendation described in previous semiannual reports on which corrective action has been completed:

(4) a summary of matters referred to prosecutive authorities and the prosecutions and convictions which have resulted;

(5) a summary of each report made to the head of the establishment under section 6 (b) (2) during the reporting period; and

(6) a listing of each audit report completed by the Office during the reporting period.

Inspectors general also review and comment on legislation, regulations, policies, and procedures which affect their areas of concern, and provide advice and counsel on efficiency, economy, and effectiveness to their respective agency heads.

OIGs Coordinate

President Reagan's Council on Integrity and Efficiency (PCIE), established by executive order on March 26, 1981, is the successor to President Carter's Executive Group on Fraud, Waste, and Abuse. PCIE information is shared at meetings and through committees which conduct studies and projects on areas of specialized interest to the inspectors general.

Offices of inspector general exchange newsletters and bulletins, and share other information about their activities through OMB desk officer reports. OMB staff consolidate the OIG semiannual reports and prepare comprehensive reports to the president. Press conferences held in conjunction with cabinet meetings have generated considerable press coverage.

Although much attention has been focused on dollar amounts saved or recovered and indictments and convictions, the IGs are moving toward more preventive activities, such as vulnerability assessments. As a result, there may be fewer indictments and convictions eventually, if the inspectors general are successful in reducing wrongdoing and encouraging sucessful management practices. Another factor is the reallocation of OIG resources to preventive activities.

In the process of searching for information to detect, correct, and prevent fraud, waste, abuse and mismanagement, OIGs use a wide variety of techniques and methods. Audits, criminal investigations, and risk analyses or vulnerability assessments require a combination of budget, program, management, financial, legal, policy and systems analysis, research methods, and gumshoe detective work. In that respect, one of the virtues of the Inspector General Act of 1978 has been the coalescence of often fragmented analytical efforts. The act also calls for empirical evidence for conclusions and the development of pragmatic recommendations to managers.

OIG information and data generally fall into three categories: primarily financial audit information; investigative information which includes evidence to prove or disprove allegations of criminal or administrative misbehavior; and inspections, evaluations, or vulnerability assessments which attempt to identify systemic causes of actual or potential problems.

Accountability Overriding Objective

Identification of accountability remains the overriding objective of all analytical efforts, irrespective of their packaging. It is the analysts without vested interests in outcomes who must pursue the hard questions, such as:

- Who's getting the money and what are they doing with it?
- Do the regulations implement or defeat legislative intent?
- Is the law flawed so that it permits or encourages fraud, waste, abuse or mismanagement?
- Who's in charge?
- Who's responsible?
- What are the problems — and whose problems are they?

Answers to these and other questions, however well documented or described, provide only partial assistance to the managers who make the decisions and take the actions. Too often, analytical reports either contain generalized recommendations or focus on fragments of problems without recommending corrective or preventive action.

Blaming the Computer

Attributing errors to the computer, for example, is as meaningless as blaming an automobile that won't start. Both are machines which require human understanding and ingenuity to keep them running and neither can be made functional without knowing *why* it became dysfunctional. To uncover systematically the sources of computer error, people must track computerized information to discover flaws in the input and output processes (human and mechanical); errors in classifying computer-related jobs; inadequacies in staff training and supervision; and flaws in the organizational policies, procedures, and practices which are supposed to detect and correct errors.

Reorganization, centralization, and decentralization can be costly ego-tripping exercises unless they are the result of careful analysis which produces evidence that the organization and its mission will benefit from the changes.

In the name of expediency and economy, systems and organizations continue to be integrated on the basis of erroneous assumptions of compatibility. This too often leads to subsequent enormous expenditures of resources to correct problems which could have been anticipated and prevented by persistently demanding to know why — followed by how, what, who, where, and when as well as how much.

Identify Generic Causes

Although identifying each of these factors contributes to a description of the problems, vulnerability analysis — by asking *why* — serves to elicit the generic causes and, ultimately, to produce useful recommendations.

Despite the best of intentions, zealous hard work, and tons of talent in both the executive and legislative branches of government, problem resolution remains elusive. As each approach appears to fall eventually of its own weight, the time has come to remember a self-evident truth: there is no way to solve a problem without knowing what caused it.

In the human organism, headache medicine can be dangerous if taken without knowing whether the source of the pain is stress, constipation, eyestrain, fatigue, or a brain tumor. Similarly, tinkering with organizational symptoms may achieve temporary relief, but the problems become compounded and inevitably fester unless their generic causes are rectified or removed.

The current popularity of the phrase "vulnerability assessment" provides an opportunity for the kind of problem-solving which probes for generic causes of problems and is not satisfied with superficial assumptions or generalized findings. Recommending that a manager "should do something" about a problem already well-known is worse than useless. What the manager wants from the analyst are specifics about causes so that action having a reasonable chance for success can be taken.

Even though asking *why?* requires hard-nosed probing of a depth and breadth not ordinarily found in traditional organizational analysis or auditing, analysts have several options. We can ignore why, never get to the bottom line and continue to make excuses for management's failure to take our advice. We can invent "new" labels for the same tired old techniques. We can begin to add *why* to our lists of questions. Or we can conduct studies to discover root causes of problems — and call them all vulnerability assessments.

Regardless of politics, policies, bloated budgets, lean budgets, or programmatic musical chairs among federal, state, and local governments, results and consequences remain the ultimate destination. I say, let's follow the *why* to get there.

Internal Control Reform in New York State Government

New York State's approach to 'economy and efficiency in government' relies on administrative and accounting controls which are outmoded and do not establish an effective system of internal controls. The following report urges the State to adopt a systemic approach which includes prevention controls to influence ethical behavior and detection controls which focus on fiscal reporting responsibility and management systems.

Significant reduction of the probability of the occurrence of fraud, waste, abuse and error over the long run requires a system of control to ensure that information on the status of an organization's assets is reliable, that accounting of its financial transactions is accurate and complete and that procedures for detecting malfunctions are effective. A system of internal control is that set of procedures and actions taken by the management of an organization to assure that its policies are carried out with a minimum of fraud, waste, abuse and error. Appropriate organizational structures foster the development of proper controls. The American Institute of Certified Public Accountants (AICPA), which sets accounting standards for the profession, recognizes two basic elements of internal control:

- **Administrative control**, which includes procedures and records that are used to ensure that management decisions are being carried out and the objectives of the organization are being achieved.

- **Accounting control**, which encompasses procedures concerned with the safeguarding of assets and the reliability of financial records.

Source: New York State Legislative Commission on Economy and Efficiency of Government, "Preventing Fraud, Waste, Abuse, and Error: Internal Control Reform in New York State Government," 2nd. ed. 1983.

A system of internal control must also include means for keeping it reliable. An internal audit program, which checks the internal control system and audits performance, provides management with this necessary feedback. The final component of a modern system of internal control is an external check on the entire process. This is accomplished by an independent audit.

While an effective internal control system must include administrative controls that ensure effective and efficient implementation of management policies, administrative control does not receive detailed treatment in this paper. The commission has chosen to concentrate first on accounting control for two principal reasons:

1. The passage of the "Accounting, Financial Reporting and Budget Accountability Reform Act of 1981" (the GAAP bill) and the associated redesign of the accounting system now underway have focused attention on accounting issues. It is a good time to consider the topic of accounting control, which is the logical next step in a program of financial management reform for New York State.

2. Accounting control rests on an extensive and well-established body of technical literature and generally accepted standards developed by accountants and auditors. These are applicable to profit and nonprofit organizations alike.

A workable and pragmatic approach for New York State in establishing a system for preventing fraud, waste, abuse and error begins with redesigning and modernizing the accounting system to meet generally accepted accounting principles (GAAP) and to establishing a proper system of internal accounting control which will provide the foundation for a broader system of internal control. An effort to improve administrative control would follow naturally.

It is a legitimate requirement of all organizations, including governments, to demonstrate that their procedures are sound for avoiding errors, such as duplicating checks, undercounting inventories, and over- or underestimating revenues and expenditures. With respect to government, two recent events serve to underscore the necessity for effective accounting procedures. First, the New York City fiscal crisis demonstrated the disastrous consequences of letting accounting control practices become grossly out of conformity with professional standards. The Securities Exchange Commission (SEC) found that New York City's accounting and reporting practices, which led to unreliable information about the City's financial condition, were "essentially a product of its defective system of internal accounting control." Second, in 1977, Congress recognized the importance of internal accounting control in the Foreign Corrupt Practices Act, which requires all firms under SEC jurisdiction to implement strong internal accounting control systems. In this Act, Congress recognized that the best prevention against illegal activities is to assure a reliable and complete set of accounting records. New York State's efforts in this direction also should be predicated on the growing recognition that a modern and effective system of internal accounting control is the basis of effective efforts to minimize fraud, waste, abuse and error.

State-of-the-Art Internal Accounting Control and Audit Systems

Internal accounting control has three major objectives: (1) proper authorization of transactions, (2) proper accounting of financial transactions, and (3) asset safeguarding. A system developed to meet these objectives puts into place a network of checks and balances that make improper conduct unlikely.

Professional accounting literature contains hundreds of specific procedures for preventing fraud, waste, abuse and error, covering every kind of financial transaction. An effective set of internal accounting controls can be established by choosing procedures designed to meet the requirements of the specific situation.

Applying state-of-the-art internal accounting control and audit principles means adopting a systems concept. Prevention controls designed to influence behavior must interact with detection controls, such as internal audits, in order to ensure reliable financial statements and compliance with management policies. Concentrating on a single element, such as prosecution of cheaters, will not achieve the desired end. A complete system is needed for satisfactory results.

Another important consideration is the need to balance costs and benefits. Procedures that control fraud, waste, abuse and error can generate costs that must be weighed against expected benefits.

Internal Accounting Control and Audit: Current Government Law and Practice

Federal and state governments utilize a wide variety of internal accounting control and audit practices. At the federal level, inspectors general represent an innovation in the intenal audit component of internal control. In addition, Congress is considering legislation, "The Financial Integrity Act of 1981" and the

"Federal Managers Accountability Act of 1981," which would fix responsibility for adequate internal control on department heads and require them to report on the subject. Several federal departments have altered traditional preaudit practices in recent years by using statistical sampling techniques in audit selection and instituting processes to pay vouchers faster. Federal practice is moving clearly in the directions of establishing stronger detection controls, improving accountability through external reporting requirements and processing financial transactions more efficiently.

State internal accounting control and audit practices vary considerably. Hawaii is the only state with statutes that recognize internal control as a system. State laws usually treat internal accounting control through statutes defining preaudit powers, which are generally given to a comptroller. North Carolina and Georgia are exceptions to this practice of centralizing preaudits. The technical level of preaudit practices ranges from a centralized manual system of checking all vouchers before payment (New York) to computerized preaudit checks with in-depth audit of samples (Wisconsin). State internal audit practices are also mixed. Illinois statutes clearly define internal audit objectives while most other states, including New York, have statutes without reference to internal audit standards and objectives.

New York State's Current Internal Accounting Control and Audit Practice

New York State's system of internal accounting control and audit is rooted in the Constitution, which requires the Comptroller to (1) audit all vouchers before payment, (2) audit the accrual and collection of all revenues and receipts and (3) prescribe such methods of accounting as are necessary for the performance of the foregoing duties. This reflects an outmoded philosophy of control that is carried over into law and practice. The State Finance Law on this topic focuses solely on the preaudit responsibility of the Comptroller, which is only one part of an overall system of internal control. New York's preaudit practice — a manual "desk" audit that causes delay in payment — is not a cost-effective way of detecting or preventing fraud, waste, abuse and error. The Comptroller's Office, without explicit statutory direction, has recognized the need for an internal auditing component and has instituted a postaudit program which emphasizes performance and compliance audits rather than financial audits. This auditing function is essential, but overall effectiveness could be improved by establishing an explicit statutory framework for auditing and transferring emphasis to internal auditing, with its attention to the internal control system.

As a consequence of its outmoded approach to internal control, New York State government is exposed to higher than necessary risk of fraud, waste, abuse and error. The Comptroller's audits show repeated and widespread violations of important internal accounting control standards in State agencies. There are weaknesses in the ability of the Comptroller and the Legislature to follow up on findings of internal accounting control violations. Also, there are no statutory reporting requirements designed to focus attention on internal control and thereby encourage decisionmakers to act to improve it. A major weakness is the lack of periodic, independent evaluation of the internal accounting control and audit practices of the agencies and the Comptroller. Without it, the effectiveness of New York State's efforts to produce reliable financial statements and to reduce the risk of loss cannot be properly assessed.

Internal Accounting Control and Audit Alternatives For New York State

The shortcomings in the State's current approach to internal accounting control and audit suggest that a review of alternatives to modernize and increase the effectiveness of such controls is in order. Each alternative needs to be evaluated in cost/benefit terms and reviewed for constitutionality. Choices include the following:

1. Maintain the existing system.
2. Improve the preaudit process through computerization and more extensive agency participation.
3. Improve internal audit efficiency and effectiveness by specifying internal audit objectives and standards in law.
4. Modernize the legal framework for combating fraud, waste, abuse and error by either amending the Constitution or amending the law to prescribe modern standards for internal control.

5. Improve the evaluation and review of the system of internal accounting control and audit practices by creating a legislative review process and by requiring an independent evaluation of New York's system of internal accounting control and audit.

Recommendations

Designing an effective system of control over State financial transactions will require a thorough analysis or preaudit and other internal accounting control practices of the Comptroller and State agencies, internal audit practices and the costs and benefits of improvements. To stimulate action on this task, the following steps are recommended:

1. Legislation should be enacted that clarifies the internal control responsibilities of the Comptroller, the agency heads and others in the system and that permits modernization of the State's internal control procedures.

2. Each agency head should be required to adopt an internal control plan subject to approval by the Comptroller.

3. The implementation of the internal control plans adopted by agency heads should be checked on both (a) a "spot-check" basis by the Comptroller at his discretion; and (b) through regular, periodic internal control audits.

4. Annual legislative hearings should be held to review internal control practices and policies to ensure that they are in compliance with the state-of-the-art for preventing and detecting fraud, waste, abuse and error in government programs.

The Professional Responsibility for Risk Assessment
Caroline Whitbeck

The Engineer's Responsibility for Safety

Accidents in high risk systems such as the space shuttle, the chemical plant at Bhopal, and nuclear power plants at Three-Mile Island and Chernobyl have attracted public attention. These events have highlighted the importance to society at large of the engineer's responsibility to recognize and assess the risks that are posed by technology and to either eliminate such risks or reduce them to acceptable limits.

For the sake of simplicity, I shall concentrate on those risks that are *direct* risks to health and safety. This is not to discount the potential harm to individuals and the public at large from other risks, from breaches of confidentiality to economic disruption that may result from errors in software systems, but if we understand the scope of the engineer's responsibility for health and safety and what is required of the engineer to identify and reduce risks to health and safety we will have an important start on understanding the engineer's professional responsibility for other consequences of technology.

Rapidly expanding technology poses serious risks and conflicts between personal and professional responsibilities which need to be resolved. One can never identify all of the risks since the range of recognizable risks continues to expand. Citing the lessons from the Biosjoly case, Caroline Whitbeck summarizes several steps to ethical risk management using individual and professional approaches.

The engineer's responsibility for safety is emphasized in the codes of ethics or ethical guidelines of many engineering societies. Five of these societies — the American Society of Civil Engineers (ASCE), American Society of Mechanical Engineers (ASME), American Institute for Chemical Engineering (AIChe), National Society of Professional Engineers (NSPE), and National Council for Engineering Examiners (NCEE) — state that the responsibility for public health and safety is the engineer's foremost responsibility; that is, it takes precedence over other responsibilities and obligations such as to keep confidential the business affairs of an employer or client. Seven societies, including

IEEE, enjoin the engineer to report or otherwise speak out on risks to health and safety (Middleton, 1986). There is a growing consensus that whereas engineers have a right to force attention to many types of error and misconduct — such as waste and misrepresentation in work done under government contract — engineers have not only a right but a moral obligation to bring the matter to light when human life or health are at risk.

Professional Responsibility as Distinguished From Official Responsibility

It is important to distinguish professional responsibility from official responsibility. An official responsibility is whatever is part of one's job. Although it is often morally praiseworthy or at least morally permissible to do one's job it need not be. "I was just doing my job" is not a blanket moral justification. One's official responsibility might conflict with one's moral responsibility, for example if one's job were to cover up wrong doing. In contrast, a professional responsibility, in particular the engineer's responsibility for safety, is a *moral* responsibility that derives from the body of specialized knowledge that the professional possesses. In the case of the engineer's responsibility for safety, engineering knowledge enables the engineer to recognize risks, foresee dangers that others would not see. In some cases foreseeing those dangers are a part of the engineer's *official* responsibilities and may be specified in the engineer's job description, but they need not be official responsibilities in order to be moral responsibilities. In many ways the engineer's responsibility for safety is analogous to the physician's responsibility to give emergency aid to the victim of an accident. Just as the accident victim need not be a patient of the physician, the engineer's job description may not include overseeing the particular matter of safety in question, but each has been entrusted by society with the knowledge to act to prevent harm. Just as a society has had to institute so-called "good Samaritan laws" to protect medical personnel who render emergency aid to strangers, we may need more social supports for the engineer who is safeguarding public health and safety.

Of course, in discharging moral responsibility for safety it is important to *take account* of where the official responsibilities lie, because this will be relevant to the question of how to most effectively bring risks to light, but official responsibilities do not determine professional responsibilities.

Foresight and Responsibility

The responsibility to ensure some future *state of affairs* should be distinguished from the *obligation* to perform some particular *act,* (although the term "responsibility" is sometimes used loosely so as to be synonymous with "obligation"). In order to behave responsibly, an agent must decide what acts are required to attain the desired state of affairs. As I have just argued, the special body of knowledge that defines a profession enables the practitioners of that profession to design a combination of actions that will produce the desired ends which fall within their responsibility. Engineering knowledge, both theoretical and practical, enables engineers to design devices or constructions that perform as required and are safe in foreseeable modes of operation and under foreseeable conditions. The range of factors that an engineer is expected to consider expands as more is learned about the consequences of previous design decisions and of the application of technology to new problems and in new environments. Experience increases foresight and raises the standard of safety that the engineer is expected to attain. Therefore, the complexity of the engineer's task and the scope of the engineer's responsibility increases over time.

The risks that engineers are expected to recognize and control have several different sources. Risks that a device, construction or software package will fail in its intended operation and under normal conditions are only the beginning. Engineers are charged with foreseeing risks that may occur when technology is subject to extreme conditions, e.g., of temperature or humidity. Furthermore, accidental events such as automobile accidents and power surges happen frequently enough so that designers must add safeguards to prevent automobiles or software from becoming dangerous in or after such accidents.

In addition to the requirement that the engineer foresee the risks that may be posed when the technology is subject to extreme conditions or common accidents, engineers are expected to foresee risks that may occur if the technology is *misused*. Misuse of technology can range from an inadvertent error in the operation of the technology, for example, errors in keying in data, to gross misuses of the technology, as in the

Source: Caroline Whitbeck, "The Professional Responsibility for Risk Assessment," Professional Program Session Record, Institute of Electrical and Electronics Engineers, Boston, May 1988.

infamous case of a consumer who picked up his lawn mower to use it as a hedge clipper. The issue of misuse is a very subtle issue in the case of software designed to provide information to support critical decisions such as medical diagnosis and treatment or the management of accidents in power plants. Here uncritical overreliance on the system, a blind faith in the comprehensiveness of the "judgments" of the system are a common though subtle misuse of which software designers are becoming aware.

In the wake of the Kansas City Hyatt Regency disaster when a walkway collapsed, there has been new attention to the possibility that design which may be safe if fabricated, constructed and maintained as specified, may nonetheless create incentives to take unsafe shortcuts in maintenance, fabrication, construction or production.

Experience with the limits of software reliability has led to a heightened awareness of the risks resulting from errors in software and development of methods and the means to anticipate, recognize, and avoid or reduce these risks (Enfield, 1987).

These examples illustrate how the experience with technological risk has produced a rapid increase not only in the number of risks that the engineer is expected to recognize and control, but in the types and sources of risk that the engineer is expected to consider. The recognition of new risks and sources of risk has two important consequences. It has led both to better methods for identifying and reducing or eliminating risk and to the awareness that when catastrophic risks cannot be eliminated, it is foolhardy to develop the technology in question.

It is likely that the sources as well as the kinds and number of potential risks that we recognize will continue to rise. Therefore, however comprehensive our methods for risk identification, risk assessment and risk reduction, there is likely to continue to be a frontier of risks and sources of risk that we are just coming to recognize. What are the implications of such a continually expanding domain of risks for the moral situation of the working engineer?

If the domain of recognizable risks is continually expanding then it is inevitable that some engineers will recognize sources of risk before their fellow engineers, let alone before managers, corporate legal staff, etc.

Therefore, engineers must be prepared not only to conscientiously employ existing methods of risk assessment and risk reduction, but also to act constructively when they are the first to recognize some risks. What I shall now argue is that because of the continuing expansion of recognizable risks, the skills and virtues that engineers have demonstrated in attempting to raise safety and other ethical concerns to an unresponsive management are likely to be important for engineers to possess even when working with managers who are more sensitive and perspicacious.

The Biosjoly Model of Engineering Responsibility

This February [1988] Roger Biosjoly received an ethics award from the American Association for the Advancement of Science for his attempts to avert the Challenger disaster. Because of the tendency of the media to construe all issues of engineering ethics as issues of whistleblowing it is worth emphasizing that Roger Biosjoly received the award for his attempt to avert the disaster rather than for his whistleblowing activity in bringing all the facts of the case to the attention of the Rodgers Commission that investigated the disaster (although these reporting activities also seem to have been fully justified).

Furthermore, Biosjoly received this award even though he was not successful in dissuading Morton Thiokol and NASA management from proceeding with the flight in January of 1986 in spite of record low temperatures. What these facts illustrate is that a major component of engineering responsibility is the responsibility to raise ethical concerns effectively and persistently but that even when the engineer does this in an exemplary way, a good outcome is not guaranteed.

Indeed, when we review the facts of the Biosjoly case many people tend to be so distracted by the issue of why Morton Thiokol management and NASA officials failed to heed the warnings of Biosjoly and some of his engineering colleagues that they fail to notice the features of Biosjoly's behavior that made it exemplary. The problem they say was with management. When Biosjoly spoke last year about the Challenger disaster one of the MIT engineering school deans took issue with Biosjoly's expressed interest in increasing the attention given to ethics in the engineering school curriculum. The dean said that it was the managers who needed the course in ethics. Of course, if we are to reduce the risks posed by our technology everyone must act responsibly. However, if, as I have been arguing, there is likely to continue to be an increase in both the kinds and sources of risks that engineers will be able to recognize, engineers who are the *first* to see such risks will be in a position much like Roger Biosjoly's *even if he or she works with responsive managers.*

What is striking about the mistake of Morton Thiokol managers is that they reversed the recommendation against launching when they saw that this recommendation was extremely displeasing to NASA officials; that is, they recognized the risks but then convinced themselves to ignore those risks when they realized that cancelling the launch might severely compromise the business interests of Morton Thiokol. If the upper management of Morton Thiokol had been more intelligent, let alone responsible, they would not have chosen to ignore the evidence that it was unsafe to launch. Suppose we have a new breed of manager who have gotten more control over the natural human tendency to want to ignore or deny bad news so that these managers would never ignore risks that they are able to recognize. Would that mean that it would be unnecessary for engineers to have the sorts of skills and virtues demonstrated by Roger Biosjoly? No, not if the range of recognizable risks keeps expanding, because it is engineers who have the knowledge to foresee new risks and sources of risk. Even if we do make major strides in the receptivity of management to hear about risks, it will be engineers who will be on the frontier in recognizing those risks and who will be in the position of having to educate others in their organizations and in society at large to recognize those risks.

I have discussed the Biosjoly case in detail elsewhere (Whitbeck 1987). Here I will just summarize a few of the lessons that we learn from Biosjoly's example:

1. The engineer often begins with a suspicion that there is danger rather, than firm knowledge of the extent of the risk and so the engineer's first responsibility is often to raise the possibility of risk to get the expenditure of resources necessary to learn the extent of the problem. (At least some of the time when there is good reason to suspect a risk it will turn out that there is no appreciable danger.)

2. When the engineer is firmly convinced of the danger it is important to state the matter as forthrightly as possible but at the same time to avoid insulting or alienating colleagues who have not yet recognized or are not yet willing to speak out on the issue. In Roger Biosjoly's case, when he and several of his concerned colleagues were unable to get attention to the problem with the O-ring seals, he wrote directly to the Vice President of Engineering stating the danger of loss of life if the problems were not corrected. Before sending the memo, Biosjoly showed a copy to his immediate supervisor so that he would not feel slighted by Biosjoly's action.

3. When there is a matter of unusual delicacy or gravity it is frequently useful to keep a written record as an objective check on the progress of events. Although he had not kept a diary previously, Biosjoly began keeping a record of progress and lack of progress on the problem with the O-ring seals. This was in addition to the usual reports which were passed on to his superiors and in which he continued to chronicle the problems encountered in trying to improve the O-ring seals.

4. It is important to build colleague support for one's ethical concerns. Biosjoly and several of his engineering colleagues went to the Vice-President of Engineering the day before the Challenger was to fly and convinced the Vice-President that in the predicted low temperatures it would be unsafe to launch.

The honesty, courage and persistence demonstrated by Roger Biosjoly in attempting to avert the Challenger disaster, as well as his considerable skills in communication, will continue to be essential virtues for the responsible engineer as long as we live in a period of rapidly expanding technology in which new risks and sources of risk are coming to light.

The Role of Engineering Societies Like IEEE

Elsewhere (Whitbeck, 1987) I have described the efforts that we are making at MIT to better prepare engineering students to effectively raise their concerns on ethical matters within the corporate environment using an ethics project as a component of courses in engineering design. Briefly stated, this ethics project requires that students develop a case involving professional ethics that might arise for an engineer on the job. Students then take the case to a company that frequently hires MIT graduates to discover the options that an engineer would actually have in the corporation in question, and the resources, such as safety hot line numbers, ombudspeople etc. that the company might have to help engineers resolve such problems. Our purpose is both to acquaint students with the variety of supports that corporations offer and the variety of corporate cultures and how these influence the most effective means for raising or resolving ethical concerns, and to give them practical experience in raising ethical issues and seeking constructive solutions.

Engineering societies like the IEEE are in a good position to pursue similar and related goals on behalf of their members. The representation of whistleblowing as the paradigmatic ethical issue for the engineer has misled people into thinking that extremely polarized situations in which the ethical engineer is pitted against insensitive management is the normal situation. It is clearly in the long-range interest of everyone — engineers, managers, stockholders and the public at large — for there to be timely attention to risks and that matters do not proceed a point where whistleblowing becomes an issue. Many corporations realize this and have instituted measures to insure that there are channels of communication open to the engineer to air his or her ethical concerns and concerns about risk in particular. Engineering societies like the IEEE could hasten this process by surveying the companies that employ its members, cataloguing the methods that are in place, grouping companies by their general characteristics (size, geographical dispersion, type of management structure, type of projects, status as a defense contractor, etc.) providing general discussions of the pros and cons of different mechanisms more effectively and giving engineers detailed information on which to base constructive suggestions to companies as to how to install, augment or improve their procedures.

Engineering societies might make several different kinds of services available to their members who are working for companies with procedures which are inadequate or unknown to the engineers. Such services would have the explicitly stated purpose of improving the communication about ethical concerns rather than the fixing of blame for wrong doing. By adopting a facilitator role rather than a role of judge, the societies are likely to elicit the cooperation of companies. Companies may even try to develop resources to perform the function filled by the engineering society service. Some chapters of engineering societies already try to perform such a function. The function could be performed in several different ways. On the one hand there might be a designated ombudsperson on whom the engineer could call (I leave it open whether it would be most effective to make the office a paid position in the national office or a volunteer position in chapter offices). A rather different model is a clearness committee model. In this model a small group of engineers with relevant experience are convened at the request of an engineer facing an ethical problem. This committee would help the engineer to sort out the personality conflicts and the differences of opinion from any matter of intentional wrong doing to help the engineer to deal constructively with the situation.

It seems to me that the exact nature of the mechanism is best decided by interested members of the engineering societies, but the need exists, and the methods that I have suggested by which engineering societies might support their members in fulfilling their responsibility for identifying and assessing risks does not run the risk of legal liability that has in recent years dissuaded the IEEE from forming a Legal Defense Service.

References

Enfield, Ronald, "The Limits of Software Reliability," *Technology Review*, (April 1987).

Whitbeck, Carolyn, "The Engineer's Responsibility for Safety: Integrating Ethics Teaching Into Courses in Engineering Design," presented at the Winter Annual Meeting of the ASME (American Society of Mechanical Engineers, December 1987).

Massachusetts: Commission Investigates Construction Abuses

Frances Burke

Reorganizing the administration of Massachusetts construction and creating the first Office of Inspector General at the state level to oversee the complex procurement process are documented in the article by Fran Burke. Identifying decision making responsibilities was a high priority of the Special Commission's work. Accountability is often another concept aimed at during reorganization.

On April 12, 1978 the Special Commission to Investigate Corruption and Maladministration in State and County Buildings in the Commonwealth of Massachusetts was created. The seven members were empowered to:

1. Investigate all construction contracts from 1968-78 for the "existence and extent of corrupt practices and maladministration" and specifically to examine the "awarding, implementation and subsequent events" relative to the University of Massachusetts, Boston Campus contract; and

2. To recommend legislative and other reforms to improve the management and administration of public construction and practice within the state.

The special commission completed its work on December 31, 1980. Its product: three enactments, plus four months of public hearings and a 12-volume final report designed to inform the legislature and the public of its findings and proposed changes. The legislation enacted included: commercial bribery statutes, the establishment of the Massachusetts Inspector General Office and the complete overhaul of the state's management of construction. The special commission ended with a State House news conference at 4 p.m. on New Year's Eve attended by over 200 media from throughout the United States. The following article describes the commission's work.

On January 1, 1981 from coast to coast, newspapers headlined the "sad and sordid" tale of widespread pervasive corruption in the Commonwealth of Massachusetts' political scene. The *San Diego Union* highlighted that the "State Was For Sale"; *The New York Times* quoted "Venality a 'Way of Life' in 60s and 70s Governments"; and *The Boston Globe* printed a 24-page insert on the special commission's findings that "Where money and power came together, the system has been rotten."

The catchy headlines provided a sharp contrast to Massachusetts' current well-touted upbeat slogan: "Make It In Massachusetts." Certainly, the 12-volume final report of the Massachusetts Special Commission to Investigate Corruption and Maladministration in State and County Buildings (MSC) found that many had been successfully "making it" during the Peabody, Sargent and Volpe administrations in the sixties and seventies:

- Corruption was a "way of life" in the commonwealth's building and maintenance practices;

- Political influence, not professional performance, was the prime criteria for contracting with the state;

- Shoddy work and debased standards of construction were the norm;

- The "system" of state construction operations was "inchoate and inferior";

- Across Democratic and Republican administrations, the way to get contracts was to buy them;

- State construction administration was a "system" of discrete parts, so diffuse and incomprehensible that it was easy to manipulate and corrupt; accountability was nil.

The national publicity highlighting these findings hides substantial progress towards reform and change already made by the commonwealth to alter its image and construction practices: The MSC report identified four areas it previously had addressed and partially remedied by its work: corrupt practices, political influences, shoddy construction and weak administration. A major product was not just the usual study and recommendations of a commission, but was the enactment during 1980, before its demise, of three of the four MSC legislative proposals.

The commission began its work in 1978 in an election-year environment. Prior to its establishment five government offices (the U.S. Attorney, Governor, State Attorney General, State Auditor, and the Legislature's Committee of Post Audit and Oversight) each had individual probes into questions arising out of

Source: Frances Burke, "Massachusetts: Commission Investigates Construction Abuses," *Public Administration Times*, 4:8 (April 15, 1981), pp. 1, 4-5.

the federal extortion trial and conviction appeals of two state senators. These diverse investigations focused on allegations of bribery, maladministration and extortion of the largest state construction contract ever issued, $130 million, for the University of Massachusetts Boston Campus. Information from these investigations was turned over to the MSC.

Members of the commission were appointed by state constitution officers and served *Pro Bono Publico*. By the establishing Resolve, the legislature required that several professions be involved, a decision which proved to be a source of strength and continued expertise during the life of the investigatory commission. The governor appointed the chairman, John William Ward, former president of Amherst College, and Daniel O. Mahoney, president-elect of the Massachusetts Bar Association. An architect and engineer, Peter Forbes and Walter McCarthy, were named by the state auditor. The secretary of state appointed Lewis Weinstein, a Boston attorney, and myself. State Attorney General Francis X. Bellotti also served. From the formation, the seven commissioners met weekly as a group and individually worked with the staff daily in areas of their expertise.

Chairman Ward often compared the operation of the commission to the "running of a seminar, trying to keep the group focused." One of the problems with the seminar model is that it seldom makes decisions; and decisions of scope, substance, and output projections were made early by the commissioners. The story of the management and operations of this commission will be reported elsewhere; it is important to note that the MSC early established goals and objectives. One of the most important goals was the emphasis by the commissioners of its second mandate, its reform proposals, over the first charge of identifying corruption and maladministration.

Much of the MSC resources at the beginning were devoted to collecting information and analyzing the universe of construction contracts awarded since January 1, 1968. Eventually, over 3,000 contracts during the 10-year period were identified. This early effort to collect and computerize data indicated that the Commonwealth lacked rudiments of:

- A count or simple inventory of contracts let or even of buildings built;
- Any requirement for needs analyses or programs for authorized design or construction contracts;
- A space or facility management system.

Later research reinforced the early findings that the Commonwealth system of construction was not a system but a series of "discrete operations" uncoordinated with little oversight. This non-system, diffuse and incomprehensible to most, permitted easy manipulation, hidden access to corrupt practices and no accountability.

The MSC had broad powers to investigate and correct identified problems: they could issue summons, hold private and public hearings, apply to the courts for immunity for witnesses, and refer evidence to law enforcement agencies for possible prosecution. The two mandated goals of investigating corruption and specifying reform were related. Information from the corruption investigations provided the MSC with understanding of where accountability was needed; and, construction process analysis identified the areas of mismanagement or maladministration which weakened the system of public construction.

In addition to developing a data base for its deliberations and recommendations, the commission along with other efforts:

- gathered information on Massachusetts design construction and maintenance practices and procedures;
- analyzed the state procurement laws and regulations as well as those of other states and the federal government;
- examined fiscal management from sources such as the capital outlay budget and appropriations — treasurer and auditors reports;
- held weekly meetings with architects, engineers public managers to review building and construction operations from beginning to end;
- sent teams of technical experts into field to survey buildings for construction defects.

In addition to exploring the construction system processes and practices, the MSC conducted simultaneously a series of corrupt practices investigations. The first interim report of the MSC of January 15, 1979 gave notice to the general court of the time and cost involved in such complex investigations: "The books and records for ten years of any single representative private firm or governmental unit engaged in design and construction fill many file cabinets. An attorney or auditor can easily spend months merely obtaining, inventorying, and analyzing thoroughly the financial records of one firm. Thorough study of these records also requires substantial effort by engineers, public managers and financial investigators. Only after records have been carefully reviewed . . . is the commission actually sufficiently knowledgeable to conduct interviews of person involved in the firms, projects, or agencies under study."

The same broad outreach for data, information and understanding applied to the system operation was used for investigating and identifying patterns of corrupt practices. Additionally, a hot line was set up. Meetings were held with industry and business leaders and elected and appointed officials. Cooperative agreements were established with all law enforcement agencies, as permitted by the law of disclosure.

The commission's findings were publicly revealed during one month of system operation public hearings, three months straight of public hearings on corrupt practices and systemic flaws as well as in the final report released on New Year's Eve of 1980. Each of the four areas identified early by the commission — corruption and maladministration — has brought forth the development of commission reform legislation. The enactments cover the following:

1. *The Management of Construction:* Effective July 1, 1981 the chaotic, unaccountable "non-system" of building buildings in the commonwealth should yield to the implementation of a new management system in which the citizens of Massachusetts can take pride. The 142-page enactment, entitled Chapter 579 of the Act of 1980, makes sweeping changes in the way the state designs, builds, allocates funds, manages and maintains space. The change establishes high standards of management and oversight, and identifies responsibility for decisions and actions as well as sets up time, cost and information management systems.

2. *The Office of the Inspector General:* Massachusetts became the first state to legislate an independent, professional Office of Inspector General, which is established to prevent and detect the potential for fraud, waste and abuse in the procurement system. The office was given subpoena power, the power to institute civil suits and to refer cases for criminal prosecution. Signed by the governor on July 5, 1980 with an emergency preamble, the appointing officials (governor, attorney general and auditor) are still unable — 10 months later — to agree on an appointee. It is also regretful that the legislature removed themselves from the IG jurisdiction and expanded the IG Review Council to eight members before passing the bill. (New legislation was filed by the commission to break the appointment deadlock, to expand the IG jurisdiction and return confidentiality to the office — the likelihood of passage is dim.)

3. *Law Enforcement Statutes:* It was surprising to find statutes so weak or nonexistent that the state was not protected against fraudulent applications by vendors or false record keeping with the intent to mask cash generation for illegal payments. The commission legislation instituted strong civil and criminal penalties against commercial bribery (e.g. extortion of money from one firm by another) and against false record keeping.

4. *Comprehensive Campaign Reform*, including fiscal disclosure, a strong Office of Campaign Finance and application of the reform to the legislative branch. The incremental public hearings had clearly identified the pervasive pattern of political influence fostered by current campaign practices. Designers in the Commonwealth testified that "It was virtually impossible to get contracts without making a political contribution." "Simple favoritism" towards one's contributing friends was an administration and finance secretary's guideline for contract awards; former administrative officials directly approached "certain categories of people in line to get appointments and contracts" in exchange for political contributions. The commission was told to "wait 'til next year."

POSTSCRIPT

There is no "next year" for commissions. The work of the Special Commission to Investigate Corruption and Maladministration in State and County Buildings is ended . . . as well it should be. Temporary — ad hoc commissions should be just that — temporary, established to support and strengthen the operations of government, not substitute for the regular political processes.

A recurring question to all the commissioners is "Was the effort worth doing?" My answer is that the time, energy and expertise which went into the almost three years of commission work was an incredible cooperative venture which did the job it was mandated to do, and provided each one of us with the satisfaction of a job well done. The full value of the effort can only be judged by the citizens of the Commonwealth as they use the buildings yet to be built and repaired and by the elected and appointed officials who daily must work in these same buildings.

The special commission final report states that "There are, to be sure, honest and hard working administrators in state agencies, underpaid at best, struggling to do their work well." If our work and product has made their work less of a struggle, it was worth it.

TEN YEARS LATER: Two former commissioners, Architect Peter Forbes and Public Management Professor Fran Burke, participated in a six-month review of the MSC reform legislation passed in 1980. With the current staff of the Commonwealth's Division of Capital Planning and Operations (DCPO), the commissioners did a step-by-step analysis of the structures, functions and operations in place since 1981. Minor tinkering might be needed, but in the commissioners' judgment Chapter 579, the omnibus construction enactment, was serving the Commonwealth well. Buildings were being planned, built, leased and inventoried with dispatch and under conditions which helped combat corruption and encourage ethical management.

Toward a New Vision of Government Service: Structural Antidotes to Corruption

Ruth Messinger

Nearly two full years have passed since municipal corruption scandals first exploded in New York City headlines, but hardly a week goes by without some new disclosures of wrongdoing in public life. Old problems are uncovered, new problems emerge, and new agencies are involved. Corruption is endemic and epidemic in our public life.

Clearly the problem is not just New York's. There are similar crises in city halls throughout the nation, major revelations of corruption at the federal and state levels, and serious scandals in the private sector. We are a nation awash in corruption, with public morals at their lowest ebb since the 1920s.

Still, the problem is worse here and it is *our* problem, poisoning *our* public life. When New York, which touts itself as a city with controls in place to protect against such disasters, is revealed to be rife with corruption, we must respond.

The electoral system and the governmental system continue to present barriers to sound public sector operations, according to Ruth Messinger. Are the reforms advocated by Koch earlier and Messinger here possible as well as probable? What are the elements of 'a new concept of public service and a different vision of government for the future' to which she refers?

Just as we analyze a major air disaster to assign fault to either pilot or plane (or both), so here we have to examine not only individual wrongdoing but the flaws in the system that allow corruption to flourish on this scale. We have to acknowledge how few structural reforms have been made since the scandals broke, how much better the mayor has been at bewailing the treachery of friends and at posturing for reform than securing real change.

We have to understand the costs and identify the short-range and long-range changes that must be made to improve the system. We have to convince the legislature, the City Council, and the current Charter Revision Commission to make these changes. Then, most important, we have to promote a new concept of public service and a different vision of government for the future.

The Costs of Corruption

Corruption exacts a huge toll from the body politic. It threatens the stability of our society. Only if its costs are understood is there likely to be enough determination to revise the system thoroughly and make it possible for all of us to again take pride in how our city is run.

Corruption has a direct fiscal impact, accounting for revenues wasted or forgone. When an illegal deal is made for a contract, we pay. More money is spent for lower quality service so a few can line their pockets with our dollars. When a developer makes a generous campaign donation and secures a zoning variance or tax abatement, we pay. Residents and businesses are displaced, people lose light and air, and neighborhoods are destroyed. The city agrees not to collect the full taxes we could otherwise use for services. We funnel money to private developers that could otherwise pay for nurses or building inspectors or pothole-filling.

Corruption also exacts a high cost from municipal personnel. Because of cronyism and patronage the city does not get the best possible staff. The image of public service is tarnished when government employment is seen as a finishing school for young lawyers. The public assumes people go into government for what they can get out of it, accepts revolving-door departure from government to the private sector, and is not surprised to see those who leave government using their contacts to get city contracts.

People who choose government or elective office for its public service opportunities are tainted by the scandals and wounded by the public response. They choose increasingly to leave public service rather than be seen as secretly corrupt or as white-collar welfare recipients, holding jobs at public expense in a system that commands no respect.

And those public servants — and there are many — who stay, but who raise questions about contracts or complain of mismanagement, suffer. They encounter threats or experience negative actions affecting their employment or actually lose their jobs.

Finally, there is an immense political cost to corruption. Good people are precluded from running for offices that can only be won with gigantic sums of money. Candidates spend too much time raising funds. Incumbent officials raise money all the time, throughout their term, from people who do business with the city.

People have a growing sense that the real decisions of government are not made at the polls or in public hearings, but in secret and for money. They lose interest in participating. Powerlessness grows and voter turnout declines. What flourishes is cynicism and apathy. There is no greater danger for a democracy and, therefore, no better reason for acting.

Campaign Finance and Election Reform

The single most critical change we can make in our government is to take the "For Sale" sign off City Hall and end the actual and apparent corruption of large contributions.

Source: Ruth Messinger, "Toward a New Vision of Government Service: Structural Antidotes to Corruption," City Almanac, 20:1-2 (1987), pp. 17-19.

Our current campaign finance system is the shame of our city. A donor can give any candidate for city-wide office up to $100,000. In 1985, 160 developers gave more than $4 million to the campaigns of the eight members of the Board of Estimate — at the same time as these developers were seeking benefits from the board. Our political contests are so costly that effective participation is limited to those with huge personal wealth or tight connections to special interests.

The report of the Sovern Commission, appointed in response to the first wave of scandal revelations, is instructive:

A society that asks its public officials to behave honorably sends a conflicting message when its electoral process is awash in money, much of it provided by those seeking something from government. The huge sums involved create vast opportunities for abuse, influence peddling, and other improprieties. And they give rise to a substantial appearance of impropriety, a belief that large contributions receive a quid pro quo from those they support. The erosion of trust in our political processes contributes to the general loss of faith in the integrity of government and creates a climate for other abuses.

We must fulfill the commission's mandate. We need campaign finance reform, drastically limiting the maximum amount that can be contributed to a candidate, setting a cap on campaign spending, and providing public funds to match donations to those candidates who accept the limits. We should support this program to the City Council, which has a reform bill pending, and to the Charter Revision Commission which has made campaign finance a priority concern.

We need, as well, to promote serious reform of our election process. It should be easier for candidates to get on the ballot. Voter registration should be possible in every city agency, school, and community facility. More should be done to bring information about races, candidates, and election procedures to New Yorkers.

Reforms in Government Employment

In addition to changing the rules by which people gain elected office, we have to amend the structure of appointed office and alter how people enter the bureaucracy, whether or not they stay and whatever their work experience.

We must end the appearance of government as a revolving door for would-be real estate entrepreneurs, attorneys, and bankers, as an apprenticeship to the private sector. We need both to impose limits on the possibility of people leaving city government to then do business with the agencies where they had previously worked and to make careers in public service more attractive and satisfying.

We need to recognize that many of the people who might consider a position in civil service find that option untenable. They must pass tests that do not test for the skills they need on the job. The pay for many of these positions is too low to attract and retain the people we most want to keep; minorities and women, particularly, are concentrated in lower-salaried titles.

There is often too little opportunity for advancement into better paying managerial and supervisory jobs. The promotion structures do not seem to work or appear to reward those who do not make waves. Too many city workers suffer the indignity of having others regularly brought in over them to take the jobs they hoped to get.

In addition, government employees are often burdened and demeaned by the work situations they confront. They have large jurisdictions and too much paperwork. Opportunities for innovation are limited, there is little sense of reward for a job well done, and too much of the more challenging work is contracted out to private businesses.

The public treats its civil servants with contempt. If city workers hear often enough that their work is unproductive and unimaginative, that they constitute a drain on progress, they will meet that expectation. If too many people believe that there is little that government can do, that cutting taxes is a higher priority than providing service, those who enter government to be of service and make change will lose interest in their jobs, perform less well, or leave, creating vacancies to be filled by those who have no notion of public service as a calling.

We need to make a variety of reforms in our employment systems. We can set guidelines for the contracting-out of city business, overhaul our personnel system, limit patronage abuses, adjust salaries, and adopt a system of pay equity. We can seek to provide additional rewards for quality work and more opportunity for advancement.

Whistle-blower Protection

Against all odds, and despite the prevailing atmosphere of lowered expectations and distrust, a large number of government employees continue to do quality work. Some go further and report possible mismanagement, fraud, or abuse. These whistle-blowers are like bell buoys in the harbor before a storm. They give us early warnings of corruption — if we would only listen. They need not only our attention, but our help.

Virtually every major scandal of the Koch administration was reported into the system by a whistle-blower in a timely fashion. Whether the issue was foster care, fake taxi medallions, faulty personnel examinations, or the so-called Bess Mess, it was identified to the proper authorities long before it exploded onto the public consciousness.

What happened? The administration denied allegations, bungled investigations, and shelved them when they became politically sensitive. Even worse, it subjected the whistle-blowers to abuse, harassment, and, in some instances, to severe personnel sanctions, including demotions, wage cuts, and firings. Its actions were duly noted by those others in government who had thought to come forward to report problems.

Although laws have been passed to protect whistle-blowers, they have been accorded little respect by this administration. More action is needed. We must again be guided by the Sovern Commission:

> Honest and dedicated employees who find it necessary to disclose evidence of an employer's illegal conduct fill an essential function in the discovery, prosecution, and conviction of corruption. The protection of such whistle-blowers is doubly justified because it buttresses the integrity of government and protects the honest citizen who has taken personal risks in the public interest.

The commission recommended that the law be extended to cover private-sector employees who disclose instances of public corruption and that it protect government workers who refuse to participate in illegal activity. We must give those who see wrongs in government a place to go where they will be treated with respect, have their jobs protected, and their complaints investigated. We must give them appropriate recognition when their diligence contributes to improved governmental functioning.

In addition, we need to overhaul our monitoring agencies so they will function more like watchdogs than lapdogs. In the last decade, the city's Department of Investigation has not operated in an independent or rapid fashion. It has not forestalled the spread of corruption or protected whistle-blowers, so it has not protected us. The department can no longer be allowed to operate as a wholly owned subsidiary of the mayor, responsible only to him. It must be established with some independence from the administration it is charged to investigate, able to respond more fully to complaints and provide better support to whistle-blowers.

Other structural reforms must also be made. We need strengthened financial disclosure and conflict-of-interest laws, tougher prohibitions against commissioners going directly to work for the private interests they were regulating, and additional limits on the right of elected officials to practice before public agencies for a fee while they are in office. We need an ethics commission with independent power to monitor compliance, investigate violations, and enforce these provisions of the law.

Conclusion

The crisis of public confidence in government is acute. We need to use this crisis as an opportunity to rally against corruption and to return government to the people of New York City.

The steps outlined here are essential to enhance the possibility for ethics in government. The administration, the City Council and, most particularly, the Charter Revision Commission should be lobbied to limit campaign contributions, provide for public financing of elections, improve management and fiscal audits, protect whistle-blowers, restructure key units of government, elevate the status of civil service, and enhance accountability.

Such measures are necessary in the short run, but they are not sufficient. We also need to move toward a vision of government as a place to make a difference and toward the notion of public service as a calling. We need leaders in government prepared to do more than stop wrongdoing: they should be ready to set a new agenda and to introduce plans that will matter to those they represent.

Those who seek elected or line positions should be people with a desire to serve and a commitment to make change. They should encounter a government that demonstrates care for its citizenry, that is committed to results, that is prepared to innovate and test solutions to our most intractable problems, that is concerned about more than just dollars and paperwork.

If we continue to allow government to do little and do it badly, it will continue to diminish its own worth and to generate bad feeling with citizens who get insufficient return on their tax investment. If we make these broader changes, we will attract new people to public service and give them the tools and the incentives to do quality work. Immediately, they will generate a new interest in and respect for government and greater attention to keeping it honest and productive. Only if government is relevant to people's lives will they focus enough attention on it to keep it clean.

Time is our enemy. The longer we delay, the more people in and out of government will be convinced that corruption is the norm. They will consider their cynicism merited and their lack of involvement respectable. Our opportunity is at hand. We must act, beseech others to act with us, and hold accountable those who do not join this effort.

Case 10:
An Equal Chance?

Managers are often called upon to examine the organization's need to standardize or to modernize its operations and to weigh that against the investment in equipment or structure already in place. Issues of organizational inflexibility ("It's always been this way") as well as the costs in human, institutional and ethical terms must be considered. What changes in rules, enforcement, training, or other means might reduce or remove the ethical problem?

Characters:
Mike Smith — Chief Procurement Officer
Tom Drake — Procurement Specialist
Kathy Kline — Communications Staff Member

You are Mike Smith, the Chief Procurement Officer for a major university. Work generated by your staff of 20 procurement specialists includes writing proposals sent to vendors, and evaluating the vendors' bids. In order to write those bids, the procurement specialist works with someone from the university agency most knowledgeable about the project. Tom Drake, a procurement specialist, is currently working with Kathy Kline of the Communications Department to develop a bid proposal to purchase a new campus-wide telephone system that includes a quick-dial feature. The University's current telephone system was installed 15 years ago by Regional Telephone and over the last few years Regional and one other vendor have sold add-on equipment to five of the University's fifteen departments. This equipment allows the caller to quick-dial calls. This add-on equipment is expensive and represents a major investment by those five departments, one of which is the Communications Department. The departments that have the quick-dial equipment are very pleased with the results; the departments that do not have quick-dial cannot afford it and are unhappy with Regional.

Tom came to you to provide an update on the status of the proposal. The Communications office has insisted throughout the proposal process that the new phone system must be capable of using the existing quick-dial equipment. Tom tells you that if that is the case, only Regional and two or three other vendors would be able to bid on the system. Six other vendors with their own quick-dial equipment would not be able to respond to the bid. Tom goes on to explain that there have been cases where a whole new system was less expensive than one of Regional's systems that hooked up to existing quick-dial equipment. Tom also tells you he heard that several staff members from the Communications Department have threatened to quit if the bid goes to a company other than Regional. After 15 years, they feel Regional is the best and only qualified vendor. Tom wants to know how he should proceed to satisfy both the University's needs and the vendors' right to a fair bid process.

1. How should Tom proceed? Should he ensure that all bidders have an equal chance to participate in the bid process?

2. How can the practice of vendors helping buyers write a bid proposal be avoided?

3. What about Tom's responsibility to the taxpayers? Several thousands of dollars would be wasted if the quick-dial equipment already purchased were scrapped.

Source:
James Pyle,
Kansas City,
Missouri.

10. Whistle Blowing

Whistle Blowing:
A Time to Listen . . . A Time to Hear
American Society for Public Administration

The American Society for Public Administration endorses the growing public demand for improved accountability of government employees in order to achieve more efficient, effective, and ethical enforcement of the laws, and more competent conduct of the public business, recognizing that most whistle blowing results from different perceptions of accountability.

Therefore, in order to improve accountability at all levels of government — ASPA recommends that federal, state and local governments take the following actions:

1. *Establish and enforce policies and procedures that clearly describe the ethical bases for public employment and the penalties for violating them.*

   Adherence to such codes would result in improved accountability by public employees, especially managers, for their decisions and actions. This should result in a concomitant decrease in the need for whistle blowing aimed at exposing criminal activity, abuse of process, waste, withholding or distortion of information, and other unethical or illegal behavior.

2. *Establish and enforce policies and procedures for more adequately communicating to each public employee the expectations of the governmental employer with respect to job performance, ethics, accountability, rewards, penalties, and regulations.*

   Since well-informed and well-supervised employees reflect good management practices, individual employees who know what is expected of them may be more likely to meet accountability standards and less likely to refuse responsibility for their performance — or to choose *nonlegitimate* whistle blowing as a vehicle for communicating. Workshops and other forms of training programs are useful in helping managers and their employees cope with dissent and change.

The seven recommendations to strengthen the position of responsible dissenters in public organizations offer an opportunity to debate the merits of whistle-blowing as an expression of accountability versus an act of organizational disloyalty. By a vote of the American Society for Public Administration's National Council, the 16,000 member professional organization gave support to the proposal dedicated to strengthening the integrity of all public servants.

Source: Policy Issues Committee, Revised November 30, 1979, Adopted by the National Council on December 2, 1979.

3. *Establish and enforce policies and procedures for internally reporting, investigating, assessing, and acting on allegations of illegality, mismanagement, waste, or unethical behavior.*

Complaint handling offices such as inspectors general and other appropriate mechanisms should be created and adequately supported to receive, and promptly and objectively investigate, internal allegations of wrong doing in order to diminish the need for the public gesture of whistle blowing. To be effective as well as efficient, such offices must inspire the trust and confidence of both managers and employees to avoid the aura of police-state intimidation by tending first to accuse or impugn the motives of the person making the allegation.

4. *Establish and enforce policies and procedures that permit and encourage legitimate dissent and constructive criticism and protect dissenters from retaliation.*

Many public employees take an oath of office to uphold, obey, and enforce the law in accordance with their sworn responsibilities. Therefore, perceived violations of that oath which result in differences of opinion about wrongdoing should be viewed as manifestations of accountability, rather than as rejections of supervisory authority unless proven otherwise.

5. *Create and support dissent channels to permit contrary or alternative views on policy issues to be reviewed at a higher level.*

Where disaffection grows not from allegations of wrongdoing but from honest professional disagreement over policy decisions, what converts the grieved dissenter into an angry whistle blower is often the lack of any channel for additional senior review of the policy dispute. Good public administration in any institution includes provision for such open review at higher levels. Equating productive dissent or constructive criticism with disloyalty violates democratic principles of free speech and tends to discourage accountability, creativity and standards of excellence.

6. *Establish and enforce policies and procedures that require management to focus on the message rather than the messenger when an employee expresses either substantive dissent as a professional difference of opinion or makes an allegation of wrongdoing.*

In most instances, whistle blowing may be averted by giving serious consideration to the merits of the message and by taking appropriate and timely action. By focusing only on the assumed motivations of dissenters or whistle blowers, attention is diverted from the substance of their dissent or the merits of their allegations, to the detriment of the organization, its mission, and the general public.

7. *Create and use program evaluation, monitoring and other oversight methods to increase and improve the availability of reliable information for decision making.*

Top management needs accurate and timely information produced by competent staff who are encouraged to make recommendations and to energetically advocate them without fear of reprisal. Since an organizational pattern of absent, distorted, or unnecessarily suppressed information tends to produce demands for such information on the grounds of accountability, the systematic collection, analysis, dissemination, and use of verified facts should help to diminish or eliminate the motivation to blow the whistle.

Background

The American Society for Public Administration seeks to improve the quality of human life through more effective, efficient, compassionate, and trustworthy public service. Throughout its history, ASPA has supported improved management and program performance in all branches and among all levels of government. ASPA's commitment to excellence in government acknowledges the principle that any organization should be subject to an appeal to determine the fairness of its actions and that ultimate accountability rests with the citizenry. As such, ASPA supports the intergovernmental and institutionalized due process system which provides accountability through evaluation and oversight of the actions of public organizations and employees.

At times, however, these institutional oversight mechanisms may provide inadequate protection for the public, particularly in cases of certain types of hidden corruption, criminal activities, discrimination, or administrative excess.

Sometimes, public employees who become aware of organizational or employee activities which have potentially harmful consequences to the public face a moral dilemma. What should they do? Should they ignore the situation? Should they bring the situation to the attention of an appropriate source within the organization? Or should they bring the situation to the attention of a third party? Employees who choose to disclose previously hidden aspects of organizational and public employee activities have been called whistle blowers.

The American Society for Public Administration selected whistle blowing as a subject of study because the debate over this growing phenomenon more often than not has centered on whether or not one is either for or against whistle blowing and external processes rather than focusing on its causes and remedies.

To some, whistle blowing is considered to be an ultimate expression of accountability. To others, whistle blowing is the spiteful behavior of disgruntled employees and an act of organizational disloyalty.

ASPA focused on factors which tend to produce whistle blowing and the need to establish standards of accountability for whistle blowers, organizations, and the third parties which assist the whistle blowers.

Responsibilities of Public Agencies to Maintain Accountability to the Public

Federal, state, and local governments as well as all public institutions should recognize the need to be accountable to the public by creating responsive administrative environments. All public agencies should establish and enforce policies and procedures to encourage internal reporting by employees and to assure the investigation of responsible and reasonable criticisms from employees without recrimination.

In addition, organizations should protect from retaliation responsible and conscientious public employees who, after much forethought, disclose information about situations potentially harmful to the public interest. Agencies should focus on the message rather than the messenger.

Some Obligations of Public Employees

Public employees have a serious obligation to themselves to exercise their conscience in a responsible and judicious manner. Public employees must also remember their ultimate accountability to the public. Because of the serious consequences of their actions, public employees should avoid frivolous, irresponsible, or false criticism of government.

Doing Good by Staying In?

J. Patrick Dobel

Dobel explores the many assumptions which arise from the ethical justification or moral rationalization for not resigning a position of power when disagreements arise in government. Components of his 'minimum democratic humanism' provide a checklist for assessing our own ethical commitment to political service.

I can do more good by staying in than by getting out, has been a classic justification for public servants suffering from crises of conscience. Although this is a standard justification, it has not really been explored in all its ramifications.[1] As a moral defense, it presumes a number of ethical and empirical assumptions which must be satisfied to make the argument a legitimate justification. Experience, however, suggests that these very assumptions are often invalidated by the act of dissent. Most of the time, the argument that begins with a strong ethical justification for continued participation in government ends up as a simple rationalization for staying in power.

Political biographies, the revelations of whistleblowers, and the apologiae of Watergate and Vietnam participants chronicle numerous episodes of persons, sometimes remarkably ethically unreflective, who come to an awareness of their own moral responsibility in unacceptable policies or abuses of power. Once a person has become a dissenter, he or she holds a minority position from other policy makers who are at least publicly committed to the problem policy. Bureaucratic interests and momentum, group conformity pressures, genuine commitments to the policy, and complex webs of personal loyalty lead people to defend the policy or power abuse both in government discussions and in public defenses or cover-ups.[2] The entire language of justification and "tacit knowledge" of the decision-making world presumes the validity of such policies and a commitment to their success. Nonetheless, the dissenter decides to stay in. Lawrence O'Brien provides one of the clearest statements of this case as when he defended his decision to remain in President Johnson's cabinet rather than join Robert Kennedy's anti-war candidacy. Opposed to the war, O'Brien confided to Robert McNamara: "I still hope it can be changed by pressures from within the administration." Later, speaking directly to Robert Kennedy, he argued:

> You know that I share your concern, but I can't ignore the political realities. The only hope I see is that the men around the President can ultimately change his policy, that he has to be impressed by the opposition not only from you, Bob, but from people who have worked with him and have been loyal to him. . . . If the President doesn't change his policy, I, too, will face a hard decision down the road, but until then, I will remain loyal to him.[3]

This argument presumes a large number of moral and empirical assumptions. These must be elucidated and addressed to clarify the strengths and, more importantly, the weaknesses, of this commonplace justification. Most of the time the argument reduces to a moral rationalization, because the very process of "staying in" after a disagreement emerges and fighting for change undermines the very assumptions needed to make staying in and doing good a realistic and valid moral claim. For, to raise their "voice" and accomplish good presumes "effectiveness," that staying in will make a significant difference.[4] The dissenters must present their position to relevant policymakers. They must change the opinions of leaders and either change policy or end the wrong doings. If the policy cannot be changed, a person can hope to mitigate the consequences. As Thomas More reminded Raphael Hythloday, "What you cannot turn to good you must make as little bad as you can."[5] Paradoxically, the very process of moral dissent undermines one's "effectiveness" and "access" and usually means that an individual will not influence policy to the good and may end up becoming more deeply implicated or committed to the very policy he or she abhors.

Source: J. Patrick Dobel, "Doing Good by Staying In," *Public Personnel Management Journal*, 1984, pp. 126-138.

The Moral Basis for Dissenting

People do not operate in moral vacuums. Democratic politics presumes that individuals in government respect, if not positively work for, a certain set of basic political goals and rules of the political game. Public servants should posses a general and noncontroversial set of beliefs and commitments which I will call "minimum democratic humanism." These are the moral commitments expected from liberal and democratic citizens who participate in politics. They are: first, a fidelity to democratic decision making and the constitutional process; second, a respect for the basic liberties, due process guarantees, and equality of all citizens before the law; third, a concern for the safety and survival of the political order and the integrity of the law of the land; and, fourth, an acknowledgment of one's democratic accountability to both the expressed will of the people and the principles and guarantees of the constitutional order.

Citizens must possess these, not as pristine formal beliefs, but as convictions imbedded in their own habits and disposition — their character. These values generate an activist imperative which requires concrete results from the convictions. Persons do not simply desire world peace in politics, they seek to end war or minimize bloodshed in a military regime. What Thomas More called "the duty of all good men" leads individuals in politics to seek influence, to want effectiveness, and to make a difference; they seek policies which are reasonably congruent with their convictions.

If a person in politics possesses no sincere loyalty to minimum democratic humanism, then few moral dilemmas will arise for him or her. If they ambitiously seek only self-aggrandizement, then no clear concerns for the rights of others or constitutional integrity will set boundaries to their deliberations. Likewise, if they possess consuming loyalty to a person or an ideology which admits of no compromise, then they will acknowledge no limits set by democratic rules of the game, due process, or accountability since the leader's success or the dogma of the ideology override all other ethical considerations. For such persons there will be no crises of conscience in politics, only narrow self-interested power calculations or clear-cut imperatives for action justified by infallible leaders or revealed ideologies. For such persons there are no dilemmas, only tactics.

An informed conscience in politics, however, poses its own problems. An overly scrupulous conscience can

> . . . make cowards of us all;
> And thus the native hue of resolution
> Is sicklied o'er with the pale cast of thought;
> And with enterprises of great pith and moment,
> With this regard, their currents turn awry,
> And lose the name of action.[6]

Nor is Hamlet's paralysis the only problem. Individuals can be too uncompromising and threaten the daily operations of government. Political leaders obsessively complain that dissent-inspired leaks or bureaucratic resistance unravel policy formation and disrupt policy implementation.[7] Government institutions require personnel who are willing to assent to policies with which one might disagree, especially when legitimate possibilities of debate and change exist within the institution. People who provide public services over time must be willing and able to adapt to the changing mandates of democratic politics and provide the services in good faith. Without such basic loyalty and personal compromises, enduring and professional government service would be impossible.[8]

Realistic personal compromise not only undergirds the effectiveness of public organizations but is a central moral tenet of the democratic political process. In a world where there are "no final victories," different individuals or groups not only possess diverse self-interests and varying power but many have various conceptions of the common good. Unless opponents can either be killed or coerced, a person must respect others' power and goals and must constantly persuade, bargain, and build coalitions to achieve some of one's personal goals.[9] Constitutional restraints and democratic politics guarantee that personal ideals and concrete commitments face unending attrition. No policy will ever be perfect; no implementation will be flawless. A merciless strain on personal integrity is built into the rules of politics as people enter into pre-existing universes of power and commitment where others stand ready to oppose or aid one's own efforts. As Justice Brandeis remarked, "the great difficulty" is "when and what concessions to make."

Given the beliefs of minimum democratic humanism and the realistic need for moral compromise in government, most moral compromises in government do not pose the credible moral dilemmas of staying in to do good. Rather I assume that the participant has arrived at that rare moment which Karl Jaspers would call a "limit situation." Here an individual has uncovered or is participating in policies which fall under any of the following four categories which strain or transgress bounds of acceptable ethical compromise in government: 1) egregious criminal conduct such as murder, theft, acceptance of bribes for favors, or venality or negligence in procurement of equipment upon which security and lives will depend;

2) actions which undermine democratic accountability of the system of government such as illegal campaign contributions, electoral bribery or fakery, use of government agencies or para-government groups to intimidate or hurt political opponents or deliberate actions to suppress information necessary for the public to make informed choices about vital policy choices when the suppression has no plausible national security justification;[10] 3) actions which violate the guaranteed civil liberties of individual citizens or undermine the governmental rules which make democratic decisions possible and accountable;[11] 4) actions which violate basic standards of Western justice and decency which have no clear justification or excuse. This might include contributing to the needless deaths of innocent people, or sponsoring or abetting human suffering to no legitimate moral ends.[12]

These categories are not pure and usually overlap one another. The use of the IRS to audit political opponents not only violated the opposition's civil rights, broke the law, and undermined the professional morale and loyalty of the Internal Revenue Service, but also undermined democratic accountability by trying to intimidate political opponents. Similarly, a Congressional Representative who gave pay raises and then demanded kickbacks from his employees not only violated the employees' civil liberties but gained an unfair advantage in elections by padding his total campaign chest.[13]

Finally, just as there are no dilemmas where there are no liberal and democratic convictions, the dilemmas are quite different if a person does not live in a democratic republic or a political order with some means of non-violent accountability. The following discussion assumes that the country possesses a free press, a multi-party system or its equivalent, and generally holds democratic and liberal principles in honor. The citizenry expect decisions to be democratically accountable and seek ample opportunity for popular review of decisions. If none of the above exists, then the moral responsibilities and options of a public servant are quite different. In a tyrannical or totalitarian state where dissent outside the government may be either impossible or extraordinarily dangerous, the threshold of staying in the "only game in town" will be much higher. Likewise in a world where dissent, even inside the government, might result in severe threats to one's life or to the lives of friends and relatives, the requirements of dissent must be considerably mitigated.

The Integrity Assumptions

To make a difference in the moral tone and consequences of a policy in a world where most, if not all, other policymakers and superiors are committed to the wrong actions, a person must make some strong ethical assumptions about him or herself. Individuals must first know that they possess the moral beliefs and integrity of conviction to endure and fight for their position. They may have to carry the battle alone as Bill Moyers did as the last dove among Lyndon Johnson's intimate advisors. In addition, they might also try to either create a network of dissent for support among less courageous or less visible colleagues or become a conduit for dissent which percolates from lower ranks as Moyers did when he opposed both the bombing and the escalation in Vietnam.[14]

Staying in is validated by personal moral strength. Individuals can too easily be broken for their opposition. When Hubert Humphrey openly tried to fight against the escalation in Vietnam, he was preemptorily frozen out of decision-making circles until he caved in and became both a public and private defender of the escalation and bombing.[15] The pressures for "team play," the concern for promotion and access, the webs of loyalty all pull against open consistent dissent; yet if a person changes beliefs or caves in, the whole rationale for staying in breaks down.

A more subtle danger to strong commitments based on integrity is posed by self-deception. Confronted with qualms of conscience and the cognitive dissonance which arises when they must act in ways inconsistent with their private beliefs, an individual will "persistently avoid spelling out some features of his engagement with the world," even when it would be "normally appropriate."[16] The psychological stress associated with making and following up on commitments causes even more personal distress.[17]

Calculated or unconscious self-deception can resolve the cumulative stress and qualms of conscience. Individuals might subtly change moral beliefs to justify what was once illicit; they might change their weighed evaluation of actions and intentions of others to make the world more morally consistent; they might simply discover or ignore certain aspects of reality which enable them to "rectify" past mistakes of information evaluation. Once having embarked upon a morally problematic course, a person must either live with the pangs of conscience and imperatives of action, or transform either reality or their moral beliefs to reduce the stress and calls of integrity. Self-deception then represents:

> a policy not to spell out certain activities in which the agent is involved . . . once such a policy has been adopted there is even more reason to continue it, so that a process of self-deception has been initiated. Our overall posture of sincerity demands that we make this particular policy consistent with the whole range of our engagements.[18]

While most persons strive for a consistent self-image and are vulnerable to self-deception, those most concerned with integrity are the most vulnerable:

> The less integrity, the less there is motive to enter into self-deception. The greater the integrity of the person and the more powerful the contrary inclination, the greater the temptation to self-deception.[19]

Self-deception means that individuals convince themselves that they are doing good and making a difference when they are accomplishing nothing but enjoying power or contributing to the wrongdoing, policy, or cover-up. John Dean's easy assurance to himself that he was the President's lawyer acting to "protect the President" enabled him calmly to help initiate and further the Watergate cover-up and "contain" damage for months. He had ignored, slighted and bent the law until he impulsively mentioned the "obstruction of justice" to H.R. Haldeman. Shocked, he retired to his office and pulled out dusty law books and after a "sweaty tour through the obstruction of justice laws," he saw it in "black and white. We were criminals. We had skated this far on the President's power. How had I doubted it?" Two months later while destroying the "Hermes" notebooks with lists of Howard Hunt's illegal operatives, his own self-deception broke:

> Destroying the notebooks was only a small addition to a whole string of criminal acts I had committed, but it seemed to me to be a moment of high symbolism. This direct, concrete sweaty act also shredded the last of my feeble rationalizations that I was an agent rather than a participant — a lawyer defending guilty clients, rather than a conspirator.[20]

To hold moral convictions and act upon them, to resist the pressure to cave in, and to avoid self-deception are also moral conditions of making the justification for staying in a sound one. One final condition must be met; a participant must not contribute more significant harm than possible good. Because many of the individuals possess influence due to their special competence in policy areas, this condition poses special problems since they are often directly involved in executing the abhorred policy. Albert Speer, Hitler's Minister of Armaments, prolonged the conduct of the war for almost two years due to his organizational skill and drive and vainly argued that this was to some extent offset by his ability to prevent Hitler's scorched earth policy at the end of World War II or his attempts to save European Jews from extermination by placing them in forced labor camps.[21] This condition clearly involves immense subjective judgment, but the person involved must make honest and accurate assessments and be free of self-deception. They must also avoid the temptation of the suffering servant. Suffering servants know they are guilty of more harm than good but embrace a secret martyrdom. They are doing all they can and believe their own suffering and pain both offsets the harm and expiates their guilt. Lyndon Johnson, tormented as Lady Macbeth, haunted the situation rooms of Vietnam late at night internalizing and justifying the suffering inflicted even as he strengthened his own resolve to go on through his own vicarious pain.[22]

The Paradox Of Access

Assuming an individual maintains personal integrity and avoids moral collapse, self-deception, and complicity in greater evil, the rest of this justification hinges upon personal effectiveness. A person must make a difference inside the government by influencing the opinions, decisions, and actions of relevant policymakers. Effectiveness has special moral import because the person who stays in to fight deliberately eschews other routes such as public resignation, systemic leaks to press, and working directly with the press or outside political opponents.[23] A person staying in must be able to accomplish more inside than he or she could outside by using other means to actively change the policy. Such personal effectiveness is in direct proportion to access. Access consist of the real opportunity to either make decisions which affect policy or persuade relevant policymakers of a course of action with a reasonable chance that one's opinions will make a difference. If a person has no power to act or speaks and is ignored, then all the good intentions and tortured integrity will accomplish little good and probably abet harm.

Persons maintain access with leaders and decision groups through unpredictable amalgams of proven competence, loyalty, and trustworthiness. They must also keep access amidst the constant competition from other talented persons scrambling for influence and power in a world of limited access. George Reedy captures this world in his portrayal of the White House:

> For White House assistants there is only one fixed goal in life. It is somehow to gain and maintain access to the President. . . . [T]here are few fixed rules and playing consists in laying down alternating counters in patterns that permit flexibility but seek to deny flexibility to the opponent.[24]

Individuals inside government are heeded because others believe that they are not only competent but also loyal to the leader of the group and sympathetic to their values and goals. A person of exceptional competence or one who represents a needed power base might gain initial access to power without proven trustworthiness. As Richard Nixon warily remarked about Henry Kissinger early in his administration, "I don't trust Henry, but I can use him." From that inauspicious entry, Kissinger earned Nixon's respect and trust by proving his own loyalty and shared commitment and discrediting other major competitors.[25] Many powerful individuals have suffered the fates of Secretary of State Roger's exclusion from foreign policy or Vice President Johnson's almost complete exile from influence in the Kennedy administration in spite of Johnson's proven skills, needed power base, and official position; neither could cross the intangible line of trust and access.[26]

The dangerous paradox is that the process of moral dissent undermines the access of the person and destroys the effectiveness upon which the whole justification depends, for the competition and responsibility of politics places upon personal loyalty. Leaders need individuals whom they can trust, not only for their competence, but for their concern for the leader's own well-being and plans in a world where betrayal is not uncommon. Likewise, political advancement involves finding patrons and proving loyalty and soundness to them. The patrons in turn would recommend a "sound" person for further advancement to others. Individuals who seek access most constantly prove their competence and loyalty to leaders or groups and are more constantly pressured to conform or acquiesce to the needs and will of patrons, leaders, and groups. The group nature of many decisions aggravates this tendency to conformity. Groups often impose initiation costs upon individuals to prove their own commitment to the goals of the group. Most groups possess informal rules which encourage a strong group consensus and limit comments or actions which might personally threaten or affront other group members. Almost any governmental administration over time freezes out individuals who do not "go along" or "fit in."[27] Even the Kennedy administration, supposedly noted for its openness, excluded Chester Bowles and Adlai Stevenson from significant foreign policymaking, despite their experience, position, and power bases, because they were considered too "soft."[28]

These pressures discourage overt dissent in government. The complex webs of access can distort dissent into perceived disloyalty or weakness which can disqualify one from power. When the stakes are high and moral ambiguity surrounds a policy, overt emotional coercion and threats of ostracism mute effective dissent. Individuals fall into what James Thomson describes as the "effectiveness trap":

> The inclination to remain silent or to acquiesce in the presence of great men — to live to fight another day, to give on this issue so that you can be "effective" on later issues — is overwhelming.[29]

To bring up touchy questions of conscience which might prick others' consciences could easily lead to quick banishment or gradual easing out — a process hastened by ambitious persons who will use another's expressed moral qualms as stepping stones for their own advancement into inner circles. To retain access, persons tend to be quiet. As General Earle Wheeler reminded a recusant aide before one of President Johnson's policy lunches, "You just don't go in there and piss in the President's soup."[30]

Individuals can rarely do good by staying quiet in the face of wrongdoing; but conscious moral dissent, too, often dooms access. As Robert McNamara, Secretary of Defense in the Johnson administration, increasingly began to question the Vietnam War in private with both the President and with friends, he was slowly eased out of basic decision making while committed hawks such as Walt Rostow, the National Security Advisor, pre-empted access and policy. When McNamara left the government he had lost all effective power.[31] Similarly, John Mitchell slowly lost access as Richard Nixon's oldest and most trusted advisor when he balked at the stream of aggressive and illegal suggestions emanating from the White House staff. The more Mitchell ignored or curbed the excessive zeal of the White House staff, the more Haldeman and Erlichman alienated him from the President and excluded him from the campaign and domestic policy.[32]

The slow or direct loss of access does not befall all dissenters; they may keep access but lose effectiveness on the important issues or, more insidiously, they may incur additional moral burdens as the cost of keeping access while they ineffectually dissent. These patterns of access vary but result in institutionalizing dissent so that it becomes manageable. In one variation, an individual becomes a dissent specialist who is allowed to question a specific set of concerns. Sometimes they may succeed, usually they fail to make a difference, but more importantly, they are not allowed to stray beyond the one area of allowable dissent. William Safire recounts how dissent specialization worked:

> . . . certain members of the Nixon group, their loyalty proved over the years, were indulged as iconoclasts, encouraged to have their own non-group set of assumptions in certain areas, and were expected to present their objections at meetings so that the devil would not be denied an advocate . . . but the self-censorship did take place in areas outside of one's iconoclastic "specialties;" when I volunteered a suggestion in a Vietnam speech that no more draftees be sent to fight, I was promptly taken off the speech entirely, and was less inclined to do that again.[33]

In a second, more common variation, a person becomes tagged and even accepted as the "House moralist" or "conscience" of the leaders. James Thomson describes the process as the "domestication of dissenters." The dissenters feel as if they have discharged their conscience-bound duty and the other decision makers can congratulate themselves on being open-minded and fair by listening to all sides. Bill Moyers, the last Vietnam dissenter in President Johnson's intimate circle of advisors, may have suffered such a fate. While he actively worked to cultivate a network of informed dissent he became increasingly frustrated at his inability to effectively change anyone's mind. Typically Johnson would greet him with "here comes Mr. Stop the Bombing." Other policymakers had their "favorite dove" whose ineffectual dissent assuaged their mutual consciences, accomplished little but enabled the dissenter to remain in government.[34] Such dissent, as in Safire's example, is entirely predictable and nonthreatening, almost a form of role playing. Other policymakers can prepare for it and discount it. In the most insidious variation, a person suffers the terrible irony of increasing contributions to the very policy he or she opposes. Few policymakers must pay the price of Francesco Guicciardini who executed his friends and his allies in Florence and publicly defended a tyrant he hated. With this he "proved" his renewed loyalty after he vacillated in his support of the Medici.[35] But for many the moral cost of dissenting access is high. Once persons are suspected of lukewarm loyalty and moral qualms over a policy, then they are asked to continuously prove their loyalty in order to keep access. After John Dean had helped stop Charles Colson's plan to fire-bomb the Brookings Institute, he was passed over for the job of running the "plumbers unit." Informed that he had "some little old lady in you," Dean became an ardent exponent of "toughness" and using the government apparatus to harass political opponents.[36]

During the Vietnam War a number of officials who opposed aspects of the war chose to abide by the standard political rule best articulated by Lyndon Johnson describing his relationship with President Kennedy:

> I did not always agree with everything that happened in his administration. But when I did disagree with the President, I did so in private, and man to man.[37]

Robert McNamara reserved his doubts about the war for private meetings with the President or personal discussions with friends. In return for the privilege of off-the-record dissent, McNamara felt impelled to work doubly hard to destroy internal government opponents of the war. He devastated dissenting officials in policy meetings, often with doctored statistics while privately encouraged them to keep up the bureaucratic fight against the war. He personally helped dismember all effective bureaucratic opposition to the war in order to prove his loyalty to Johnson and save his private channels.[38] After his return to the fold, Vice President Humphrey again had qualms about the war but mentioned them only in private to President Johnson. Within the government and in public, he even more avidly defended the war which he increasingly opposed in private.[39]

Some dissenters pursue vigorous internal dissent rather than confine their disagreement to private chats. George Ball, like Bill Moyers, actively tried to change the Vietnam policy within government circles. To maintain his access, even with his thwarted dissent, Ball was called upon to become a major public spokesman for the policy he opposed. At one point he was dispatched to Europe as the major public defender of American policy to skeptical allies.[40]

Whether the chosen route of dissent is private conversations or inner government battle, either tactic requires backfire actions to maintain access. These almost inevitably demand deeper complicity in the very policy or crime one opposes. The complicity is greater for many such as McNamara who possess access because of their high competence. The more skilled they are, the more disproportionately they contribute to the questionable policies.

The Attrition of Integrity

The problems of access and effectiveness insure that most attempts to do good by staying in will run afoul of loss of effectiveness or increasing complicity in morally problematic actions. The last and most subtle problems for sustained dissenting participation are the inexorable pressures towards self-deception. The cumulative strain of violating basic convictions and self-image tempts a person to change their perceptions of reality or their values. Both John Dean and Jeb Magruder recount such experiences in their ambitious climbs to power.[41] Similarly as Lyndon Johnson resolved his own doubts about the Vietnam escalation and increasingly felt himself attacked by war opponents he:

> . . . indulged more and more freely in distortion and patent falsehoods: constant references to "the progress" made in Vietnam, describing things as he wanted them to be, as if he believed that by the force of his will he could transform what was or had already happened . . . his every self-deception was repeatedly confirmed in the men round him.

The cumulative result of institutionally reinforced self-deception was a changed man and war:

> . . . the outer man, the spheres of conscious thought and actions — remained intact, for most of the time. But in many ways, increasingly obvious to his close associates, he began to crumble; the suspicions congenital to his nature became delusions; calculated deceit became self-deception, and then matters of unquestioned belief.[42]

The lure of self-deception is increased by the policy language trap and the erosion of independent moral and social contacts. To persuade others, a person must use the language and categories which opponents understand and accept as valid. Bureaucratic momentum reinforces the reliance on commonly shared notions and language and often formalizes rote justifications. As Thomas More chided Hythloday when Raphael complained that no politicians would listen to his utopian harangues:

> Deaf indeed, without doubt . . . neither . . . do I think that such an idea should be thrust on people or such advice given, as you are positive will never be listened to. What good could such novel ideas do, or how could they enter the minds of individuals who are already taken up and possessed by the opposite convictions?[43]

But once one has accepted the bureaucratic definitions of the terms of the debate, it becomes almost impossible to significantly change the policy while using the very rationales developed specifically to defend that particular policy. Robert McNamara had helped create the bureaucratic justifications for the escalation and bombing in Vietnam. His own cost analysis data had discredited the CIA and other reporting which contradicted his own estimates of the effectiveness of the war. The Pentagon Papers reveal his intense problems when he tried to change the course of the war in 1967. Forced to use his own data, he hopelessly tried to demonstrate to a skeptical House Armed Forces Committee that the past bombing had succeeded, the present bombing could do no good and that further escalation would be counterproductive. Similarly, after the massive Tet offensive by North Vietnam, the Joint Chiefs of Staff requested massive new escalation and increased troop levels to 200,000 men using McNamara's own past figures and his justifications of limited escalation to prevent Vietnam from going Communist and to prevent a humiliating United States defeat. Whip-sawed by his own logic, McNamara's "victory" lay in keeping new troop commitments to only 50,000 and limiting the increased sortie level to only 12,000. Hard victories for a man now opposed to the war.[44]

As the pressures on integrity mount, individuals find themselves isolated from friends and independent social support for their own dissenting convictions. Outside friends and contacts with possible opponents can easily undermine access and trust in tense political situations. Robert MacNamara had to circumscribe his friendship with Robert Kennedy due to President Johnson's distrust. William Safire and Henry Kissinger both found themselves mistrusted because of their connections with those Nixon regarded as "liberals;" Safire lost access several times and had to curtail his press contacts while Kissinger found it necessary not only to limit some contacts but to constantly assert his own toughness to compensate for his outsider friends. Even families find themselves under pressure to homogenize their social relations and relinquish any social or moral contact outside their closed decision circles.[45]

The strains of cognitive dissonance and nagging conscience coupled with the immersion in the bureaucratic language of justification and the steady isolation from independent moral reference groups pose a lethal combination for integrity. The end result is best summed up by Albert Speer's indictment of his own guilt in spite of marginal adjustments he made to save lives; "I did not see any moral grounds outside the system when I should have taken my stand."[46]

As is always the case, if the good do not govern, the jackals and sharks will. To preserve the minimum democratic and liberal values of Western politics requires capable and committed individuals who can act and compromise with integrity. Yet the moral eddies of politics can swamp the strongest and the murk of political twilight can confuse the best. When a public servant confronts actions which violate the basic purposes or rules or threaten the foundation of a liberal and democratic order, the choice is simple — be quiet or act. Having chosen to act, a person must choose between staying in or getting out. Staying in often involves as much courage as leaving, especially when individuals leave quietly. But to justify doing good by staying in requires a clear assessment of the moral and reality assumptions involved. No enduring good can be accomplished by individuals unless they keep their integrity, avoid self-deception and implication in greater evil, and above all, maintain effectiveness. Yet such dissent is haunted by a paradox. Active dissent all too often undermines access, relentlessly reduces effectiveness, often requires greater complicity and insidiously encourages self-deception. Doing good by staying in too often becomes done in by staying good.

Endnotes

1. Morton H. Halperin, "Why Bureaucrats Play Games," *Foreign Policy,* 2 (Spring 1971) 70-90; Albert Hirschman, *Exit, Voice and Loyalty: Responses to Decline in Firms, Organizations and States* (Cambridge, MA: Harvard University Press, Harvard Paperback, 1977) pp. 115-120; Anthony Lake, "Lying Around Washington," *Foreign Policy,* 2 (Spring 1971) 91-113; Edward Weisband and Thomas M. Frank, *Resignation in Protest: Political and Ethical Choices Between Loyalty to Team and Loyalty to Conscience in American Public Life* (New York: Grossman Publishers, 1975) *passim,* esp. Chapters 1 and 5; James C. Thomson, Jr., "How Could Vietnam Happen? An Autopsy," *The Atlantic,* April 1968: 47-53 and "Getting Out and Speaking Out," *Foreign Policy,* 13 (Winter 1973-74) 49-67. The two Thomson articles are extremely important as pathbreaking explorations of the intricate moral universe of a public official under duress.

2. Irving Janis, *Victims of Groupthink: A Psychological Study of Foreign Policy Decisions and Fiascoes* (Boston: Houghton Mifflin Company, 1972) *passim* and Irving Janis and Leon Mann, *Decision Making A Psychological Analysis of Conflict, Choice and Commitment* (New York: The Free Press, 1977) *passim,* esp. Chapters 1, 3, 4, 10, 11, 12 provide in-depth analyses of the multiple psychological pressures upon decision making participants and explore numerous case studies of the distorting effects of groups, commitment and other psychological variables. Also see Sidney Verba, *Small Groups and Political Behavior: A Study of Leadership* (Princeton: Princeton University Press, 1961) esp. pp. 26ff and 231ff.

3. Lawrence F. O'Brien, *No Final Victories: A Life in Politics From John F. Kennedy to Watergate* (Garden City: Doubleday, 1974) pp. 217-218.

4. Hirschman, *op. cit.* pp. 30-44, 106-120 argues that the use of effective "voice" and dissent both renews and makes more accountable organizations, especially political organizations. Thomson, 1968 and 1973, *op. cit.,* as well as Lake, *op. cit.,* discuss the central importance of effectiveness for any policymaker.

5. Sir Thomas More, *Utopia,* edited by Edward Surtz, S.J. (New Haven: Yale University Press, Yale Paperback, 1973) p. 50. There is a third alternative which I will not discuss in the paper although it suffers from many of the same deficiencies. This justification, used by John Gardner, Secretary of Health, Education and Welfare under Lyndon Johnson, argues that a person will stay in the government which is engaged in wrongdoing because the individual is engaged in another policy area which is accomplishing positive good and which outweighs the harm of the other policy. Weisband and Frank, *op. cit.,* pp. 79-85. Similar to this argument and often allied with it is the claim that a person has no effective power to change the problematic policy but can still accomplish good in their own program.

6. *Hamlet,* III. i.

7. In recent years Henry Kissinger has become the most articulate advocate of this position. In his memoirs, *The White House Years* (Boston: Little, Brown and Company, 1979) *passim*, he not only cites President Nixon's and his own incessant problems with recalcitrant and leak-prone dissenters but invokes both President Eisenhower and Johnson in his assault (pp. 18-20, 42-43). Roger Morris, *Uncertain Greatness: Henry Kissinger and American Foreign Policy* (New York: Harper and Row, 1977) pp. 94ff., 136ff., expands upon why Nixon and Kissinger loathe internal dissent. Doris Kearns, *Lyndon Johnson and the American Dream* (New York: Harper and Row, 1976), Chapter 11, traces Johnson's criticisms of how tender consciences decimate policy.

8. O. Glenn Stahl, "Loyalty, Dissent and Organizational Health," *The Bureaucrat* (July 1974) 162-171; Hirschman, *op. cit.,* pp. 76-106.

9. Bernard Crick, *In Defense of Politics,* Second Edition (Chicago: University of Chicago Press, 1972) provides a classic defense of this central point.

10. A discussion of the legitimate limits of national security claims is beyond the scope of this paper, but it is only too evident how easily such blanket claims can be abused to justify or protect illicit actions from public scrutiny. Jeb Stuart Magruder, *An American Life: One Man's Road to Watergate* (New York: Athenaeum, 1974) describes how "intelligence operations" were justified by the Committee to Re-elect the President in order to discover what domestic "enemies" were up to (pp. 165-168). John W. Dean III, *Blind Ambition* (New York: Simon and Schuster, 1976) explains how claims of "executive privilege" or "national security" were used to hide evidence of the ITT bribes to keep incriminating evidence out of testimony. As Richard Nixon put it, "And I don't want you talking about national security matters, or, uh, executive privilege things. Uh, those newsmen's wiretaps and things like that — those are privileged, John. Those are privileged. Not that there's anything wrong with them, understand. But they're national security. There's no doubt about that" (pp. 262, 60ff, 183ff, 199ff). One of the most critical suppressions occurred in 1964 when Lyndon Johnson ran for President on the public platform of minimizing United States' involvement in Vietnam, while seriously considering a large escalation of the conflict. Doris Kearns, *op. cit.,* Chapter 9 and David Halberstam, *The Best and the Brightest* (New York: Random House, 1969), chapters 18, 19, 20.

11. The violated rules need not be simply electoral rules. Rules designed to insure accountability through formal procedures or especially reporting rules are also vital. The Strategic Air Command reporting procedures enable government civilians to keep control over the magnitude, location and actual dropping of bombs. During the illegal and secret bombing of Cambodia, the military were ordered to falsify the reporting procedures by changing the information fed into the computers and falsely reporting flightplans and locations. The violation of these basic rules which control the integrity of the United States' nuclear arsenal led several ex-pilots to report the act to Congress. William Shawcross, *Sideshow: Kissinger, Nixon and the Destruction of Cambodia* (New York: Simon and Schuster, 1979), Chapter 1.

12. While the first three entail violations of minimum democratic humanism, this criteria invokes a broader ideal of basic respect for human life and right. These ideals are the justificatory grounds for minimum democratic humanism. Roger Morris, *op. cit.,* describes one example where the Nixon Administration publicly committed itself to helping Biafran rebels in Nigeria avoid starvation by shipping in food but privately did almost nothing to relieve the suffering (pp. 120- 131).

13. For just such an example see the story of Represenatative Charles C. Diggs, *Detroit News,* June 16-24, 1977; February 8, 1978, October 1 and 8, 1978, and November 20, 1978.

14. Patrick Anderson, *The President's Men: White House Assistants of Franklin Roosevelt, Harry S. Truman, Dwight D. Eisenhower, John F. Kennedy and Lyndon B. Johnson* (Garden City, New York: Doubleday, 1968) pp. 340-347.

15. David Halberstam, *op. cit.,* pp. 533-536 and Townsend Hoopes, *The Limits of Intervention: An Inside Account of How the Johnson Policy of Escalation in Vietnam was Reversed* (New York: David McKay, 1969), pp. 31ff.

16. Herbert Fingarett, *Self-Deception, Studies in Philisophical Psychology* (London: Routledge and Kegan Paul, 1969), p. 47; Leon Festinger, *A Theory of Cognitive Dissonance* (Palo Alto: Stanford University Press, 1957); Albert Hirschman, *op. cit.,* pp. 93ff.

17. Irving Janis, 1977, *op. cit., passim.,* esp. Chapters 8-12; Irving Janis, 1972, *op. cit., passim.;* Albert Hirschman, *op. cit.,* pp. 76-106; Bruce Buchanan, *The Presidential Experience: What the Office Does to the Man* (Englewood Cliffs, New Jersey: Prentice-Hall, Spectrum Books, 1978), pp. 76-100.

18. Stanley Hauerwas, "Self-Deception and Autobiography: Reflections on Speer's *Inside the Third Reich*," in Stanley Hauerwas, Richard Bondi and David Burell, *Truthfulness and Tragedy: Further Investigations into Christian Ethics* (Notre Dame: University of Notre Dame Press, 1977), p. 86.

19. Herbert Fingarett, *op. cit.,* p. 140.

20. John Dean, *op. cit.,* pp. 167ff and 182ff.

21. Albert Speer, *Inside the Third Reich,* Translated by Richard and Clara Winston (New York: Macmillian Company, 1970), 479ff and 565ff.

22. Doris Kearns, *op. cit.,* pp. 268-273; Michael Walzer, "Political Action: The Problem of Dirty Hands," *Philosophy and Public Affairs* (Winter 1973) 176ff.

23. Edward Wiesband and Thomas M. Franck, *op. cit., passim,* discuss the public alternatives available to a dissenter who leaves government, but they emphasize the pressures which lead individuals to stay in when nothing good can be accomplished or to

leave quietly and not publicly dissent. On the other hand, Hirschman, *op. cit.,* Chapter 9, argues that dissenters who foreswear the "exit" option fatally wound their effectiveness. When individuals are already outgunned on an issue, one of their only remaining sources of leverage in discussions is the implicit threat that they will resign and go public. If exit is ruled out, there is even less reason to take the dissenter seriously. While my analysis focuses upon the decision to stay in and actively try to change the policy, a person might decide that even if they cannot influence the policy at least they can act like "Deepthroat" during Watergate and leak critical items to outside forces arrayed against the policy or coverup. Assuming the individual can avoid taking a central role in the illicit activity, this option has considerable merit as long as the person can maintain access to the information and leak effectively without getting caught. Unfortunately, such systematic and critical leaks usually inspire extensive counter-intelligence action within the government and aggravate all of the dangers associated with secrecy fetishes. Finally, the access of leakers is extraordinarily tenuous. Once suspected of leaking, an individual can lose all access, even become a source of "disinformation" to the outside and then face all the dilemmas of trying to keep access when suspected of disloyalty. For examples, see Roger Morris, *op. cit.,* pp. 157-162, 196-199 and 249ff.

24. George E. Reedy, *The Twilight of the Presidency* (New York: New American Library, Mentor Book, 1970), p. 91.

25. Roger Morris, *op. cit.,* pp. 3, 46-94; Henry Kissinger, *op. cit.,* pp. 3-73, esp. 29-32.

26. David Halberstam, *op. cit.,* pp. 40ff, 133ff, 291ff; Doris Kearns, *op. cit.,* Chapter 6.

27. Irving Janis, 1972, *op. cit., passim.;* Sidney Verba, *op. cit.,* Chapter 2.

28. David Halberstam, *op. cit.,* Chapters 1-4, esp. 69ff.

29. James C. Thomson, Jr., 1968, *op. cit.,* p. 49.

30. Roger Morris, *op. cit.,* pp. 73-74.

31. David Halberstam, *op. cit.,* 516ff, 622-646; Townsend Hoopes, *op. cit.,* pp. 83-91, 161-166; Henry L. Trewhitt, *McNamara* (New York: Harper and Row, 1971) 236-247. Halberstam's book is especially replete with examples of individuals who criticize policy from within the government and lose all access, esp. Chapter 18.

32. Jeb Stuart Magruder, *op. cit.,* 122ff, 149ff, 168ff; John W. Dean, *op. cit.,* also describes similar experiences, pp. 27, 38, 168.

33. William Safire, *Before the Fall: An Inside View of the Pre-Watergate White House* (New York: Ballantine Books, 1977), p. 352.

34. James C. Thomson, Jr., 1968, *op. cit.,* p. 49; Patrick Anderson, *op. cit.,* pp. 339-352; Albert Hirschman, *op. cit.,* 115-118.

35. Felix Gilbert, *Machiavelli and Guicciardini: Politics and History in Sixteenth Century Florence* (Princeton: Princeton University Press, Paperback Edition, 1973), pp. 281-282.

36. John Dean, *op. cit.,* pp. 46-49; Eric F. Goldman, *The Tragedy of Lyndon Johnson* (New York: Alfred A. Knopf, 1969), recounts how Kennedy appointments such as Nicholas Katzenbach or Lawrence O'Brien had to earn their access with President Johnson with their hard line stands on Vietnam.

37. Lyndon Baines Johnson, *The Vantage Point: Perspectives of the Presidency 1963-1969* (New York: Holt, Rinehart, and Winston, 1971), p. 2.

38. David Halberstam, *op. cit.,* pp. 213-250, 516ff, 581ff, 633.

39. Eric Goldman, *op. cit.,* pp. 262ff.

40. David Halberstam, *op. cit.,* 491-498, 505ff.

41. John Dean, *op. cit.,* pp. 167-168, 182, 183; Jeb Stuart Magruder, *op. cit.,* pp. 220, 229, 317.

42. Doris Kearns, *op. cit.,* pp. 311, 317, 394.

43. Saint Thomas More, *op. cit.,* p. 48.

44. Henry Trewhitt, *op. cit.,* pp. 227-260, esp. 239-241; *The Pentagon Papers: The Defense Department History of United States Decisionmaking on Vietnam — Volume IV,* (The Senator Gravel Edition. Boston: Beacon Press), pp. 177-277.

45. Doris Kearns, *op. cit.,* 319-322; William Safire, *op. cit.,* pp. 65ff, 373ff, 399-401, 445ff; Roger Morris, *op. cit.,* 105ff; Madeline Edmondson and Alden Duer Cohen, *The Women of Watergate* (New York: Stein and Day, 1975), *passim.*

46. Albert Speer, *op. cit.,* p. 480.

Organizational Response to Assessed Risk: Complaint Channels

Mary P. Rowe

The opportunity for institutional change and for a return to civic virtue as a positive organizational response is outlined by Rowe. Strongly supporting complaint channels that work, the article profiles a whistleblower assessing the risk. How do the characteristics of Rowe's risk-taker differ from those of Truelson's whistleblowers or those of Caiden and Caiden in Part II?

Whistleblowers need complaint channels that work. And organizations need complaint channels that work. For an organization to deal effectively with assessed risk, it needs to know about the risk in timely fashion. In fact it wants to know as much as possible about the risk in order to make a good assessment. Hence the need for well-designed complaints channels.

Characteristics of Whistleblowers

Good design requires meeting the specifications of the consumer. The consumer in this case is the person with knowledge of risk, the "whistleblower." What are the typical characteristics of a potential whistleblower and what do they indicate for complaint channels?

Most people who contemplate the idea of complaining about risk:

- are very fearful of retaliation;
- are concerned about loss of privacy for themselves, possibly their families and/or co-workers;
- are fearful of being seen to be disloyal, supersensitive, cowardly or childish;
- are fearful that they lack "enough evidence" about the risk;
- have widely differing views as to whom they will trust among possible complaint-handlers or other sources of help;
- do not necessarily wish to give up control over their concern or complaint;
- feel they lack the skills they need effectively to change the situation;
- are afraid that nothing will be done if they do complain;
- just want the risk reduced or eliminated (whistleblowers are not typically looking for revenge or public vindication, at least at first).

There are of course exceptions. But most people concerned about risk fit the profile above. What happens next? In many cases the risk perceiver gears up courage and reports the risk and the problem is resolved. If this does not work, there will remain people who perceive themselves as having failed in attempts to report risk.

Those who believe they have failed in their attempts to reduce or eliminate risk will typically see only four options remaining. They will consider:

- quitting the job;
- trying to forget the risk;
- going to some public agency or new media;
- "acting out," by sabotaging the risky equipment, stealing wastes, taking pictures of the problem situation, or acting in some other covert fashion.

Implications for Complaint Channels

Source: Mary P. Rowe, "Organizational Response to Assessed Risk: Complaint Channels," Professional Program Session Record, Institute of Electrical and Electronics Engineers, Boston, May 1988.

The facts reported above suggest definite specifications for organizational response and for complaint channels. A CEO must begin with the proposition that many good people do not know how to complain effectively and are reluctant to try. The organization must have policies and training programs which stress safety and ethics as business necessities. Policies must be communicated constantly. All managers and employees must come to believe that top management insists on safe and ethical behavior.

In addition there must be complaint channels outside ordinary line management. To meet the needs of complainants, these channels must:

- be confidential and private;
- be seen as having the full confidence of the CEO;
- have redundant channels and options, so people have a chance to choose among multiple modes and access points;
- be attached to a satisfactory investigative capability;
- provide a chance for the complainant to know what has happened as a result of the complaint;
- provide complainants the sense that they *do* have the skills to complain effectively and responsibly;
- provide complainants with the belief that it *is* effective and important to report risk;
- separate effective handling of risk from punishment of offenders enough so that a complainant does not have to feel responsible for disciplinary action taken against offenders.

An Ombudsman for IEEE?

Most complaint channels (hot line, safety coordinators, ombudsman, etc.) will be *inside* the organization. However, a number of professional organizations have an ombudsman to serve all professionals who are members. The IEEE should consider establishing an Ombudsman Office to advise and counsel on risk issues. This office could also serve as safe conduit for information from IEEE members to the CEOs of organizations employing engineers, thus insuring serious consideration of ethical and safety concerns reported by professionals. Experience of the author indicates this is a swift, effective mechanism for the occasional serious case where the concerns of engineers are being ignored by lower level managers.

Whistle Blowing in the Public Sector: An Overview of the Issues

James S. Bowman

In recent years, ethical issues in politics and government have received unprecedented attention. A series of scandals involving manipulation of gasoline supplies, illegal political contributions and surveillance, excessive executive perquisites, and payoffs, bribes, and kickbacks have been reported in the national media. "Koreagate," Congressional sex scandals, the Bert Lance trial, corruption in the General Services Administration, drug abuse in the White House, "Billy-gate," "Abscam" and the conviction of Congresspeople, and the first expulsion of a member of the House of Representatives in over one hundred years are only the most prominent ethical questions in the post-Watergate era. In addition to major exposés and questionable actions on the part of high officials, studies have found widespread unethical practices in daily management, the General Accounting Office has received thousands of complaints of wrongdoing over "hotline," and the Deputy Attorney General recently testified that "wherever we look [we see] significant fraud and abuse".[1]

The costs and the benefits of speaking out from within, or whistle-blowing, about corruption and maladministration are presented by Bowman. Long-range and short-run reforms to promote the exercise of personal and professional integrity and to encourage the need to 'blow the whistle' only as a last resort are evaluated.

It should not be surprising, then, that opinion polls have shown a dramatic drop in confidence in governmental institutions; the events of the 1970s had a traumatic effect on the relationship between the public and its government. Yet, if official misconduct has crippled the credibility of authority and weakened the national political consensus, it has also revealed the strength of the foundations of the country. Survey evidence demonstrates that the people have lost faith in the way the system is operated, but have not lost confidence in the system itself.[2] Perhaps one reason why this is so is that whistle-blowers have kept alive the bond of trust between the American government and its citizens. As government becomes more pervasive in these United States, it becomes more essential to control its power. The effort to regain public confidence and restore credibility in government during the 1980s cannot overlook the role of the whistle-blower in responsible public administration.

The objective of this essay, then, is to explore the importance of dissent in bureaucracies in a democratic society. As part of a larger project,[3] and in order to obtain systematic data on this subject, previously unassembled studies were compiled and analyzed. The following pages will explore the development and institutionalization of whistle-blowing in recent years, examine the relationship between the individual and the organization, and consider long-range and short-run reforms that can promote integrity in government and reduce the need to blow the whistle.

The Emergence of Whistle Blowing

The late 1960s and the 1970s witnessed the initiation of the whistle blower.[4] It was the C-5A military transport, the New York City police Department, the Vietnam War, Watergate, and the Kerr-McGee Oklahoma nuclear plant that dramatized whistle blowing: Ernest A. Fitzgerald exposed defense contract overruns; Frank Serpico spoke out against corruption in city government; Daniel Ellsberg made the famous Pentagon Papers public; the mysterious Deep Throat was instrumental in uncovering the misdeeds of the Nixon administration; and Karen Silkwood's death represented the danger in trying to reveal information to the public. While not every conscientious employee becomes a national cause célèbre, they also have been responsible for disclosing problems such as regulatory corruption, merit system abuses, dangers to the public health, and conflicts of interest. Responsible commentators now believe that corruption is ubiquitous and systemic in American life and cannot simply be dismissed as part of "post-Watergate morality."[5]

Given pervasive group norms in organizations, whistle-blowing is, nonetheless, not a frequent occurrence. Moreover, it provides little evidence where abuse may be widespread and the whistle usually is "swallowed" rather than blown. Yet, neither is whistle-blowing merely the product of a series of isolated incidents. Instead, it may be indicative and symbolic of the problems in contemporary politics — Jimmy Carter even campaigned on a promise to defend nonconforming federal workers in 1976, and the 1978 Civil Service Reform Act contained provisions to protect them.

Although dissent at the workplace is as old as humankind, it has only recently crystallized into a movement comparable in content, if not scope, to earlier civil rights and liberation movements. By the late 1970s, whistle-blowing began to be institutionalized as public interest groups formed: professional associations sponsored symposia, universities encouraged research, unions protected members, national conferences convened, and Congress held hearings and passed laws. All of these activities suggest how far society has come in its quest for truth and justice in organizations.

The more sensational examples of official impropriety, in short, have brought into focus latent concerns about the freedom of expression in government. People today are more receptive to these concerns than ever before, perhaps the liberties of the public employee are the liberties of a substantial and growing percentage of the citizenry. Blowing the whistle will continue as government grows larger, as expectations about work rise, as more females and those with fresh perspectives on work enter the labor force, as America increasingly becomes a nation of employees, and as corruption persists in bureaucracy. Alan F. Westin writes that "many observers. . . believe . . . [that] . . . demands for new individual rights . . . will reach their mature status in the 1980s."[6]

Source: James S. Bowman, "Whistle-Blowing in the Public Sector: An Overview of the Issues," *Review of Public Personnel Administration,* 1:1 (Fall 1980), pp. 15-27.

Although it may be true that the public is becoming more sympathetic to whistle-blowers, many bureaucracies remain hostile to them. Congressman William Clay (D.-Missouri) has noted that whistle-blowers are the "new niggers" in organizational society,[7] following student anti-war protesters and civil rights activists. Once attention is focused on the employees, the bureaucracy knows how to deal with the problem. Dissenters are regularly given meaningless assignments, transferred to remote locations, forced to undergo psychiatric examination, ordered to do work for which they are not qualified, assigned to "turkey farms," fired from their jobs, and otherwise savaged by having careers destroyed. By abusing personnel procedures, bureaucracy can rid itself of abnormality. Certainly it is easier to deal with the dissenter than the object of dissent. Public officials rarely welcome challenges to their authority, as exemplified by the Nixon White House designation of John Dean as a "bottom-dwelling slug."

Yet the vast majority of these employees are not malcontents, misfits, neurotics, crusaders, nor radicals. Typically, a whistle-blower is a middle manager, a knowledgeable individual who can see policy problems, but who may have a vested interest in ensuring they are never made public. Most are ordinary Americans with no record of political activism or animosity toward government. Indeed, the act of whistle-blowing is likely to be conservative because it seeks to restore, not change, a pre-existing condition.[8] Since whistle-blowers frequently seem to have believed the good government lessons taught in schools, they expect problems to be solved when they are brought to the attention of those in positions of authority. When problems remain and corruption goes unchallenged, the conscientious employee exposes the problem.

Presidents, senators, professional associations, public interest groups, ethicists, and journalists all have attempted to define whistle-blowing. A useful definition was offered by Alan Campbell, Director of the Office of Personnel Management, during the 1980 Congressional oversight hearings on the subject:

> Quite simply, I view whistle-blowing as a popular shorthand label for disclosure of legal violations, mismanagement, a gross waste of funds, an abuse of authority, or a danger to public health or safety, whether the disclosure is made within or outside the chain of command.[9]

Thus, a whistle-blower is an employee who reveals information about illegal, inefficient, or wasteful government action that endangers the health, safety, or freedom of the American public.

The difficulties in judging whistle-blowers and the issues exposed are vividly suggested by comparing Judas Iscariot and Martin Luther. Weighing all the dilemmas in blowing the whistle as Sissela Bok suggests, is not an easy task. The ideal case — where all administrative appeals have been exhausted, where responsibility is openly accepted, and where the dissenting employee is above reproach — is unusual. She warns:

> Given the indispensable services performed by so many whistle-blowers, strong public support is often merited. But the new climate of acceptance makes it easy to overlook the dangers of whistle-blowing: of uses in error or in malice; of work and reputations unjustly lost for those falsely accused; of privacy invaded and trust undermined.[10]

Bok suggests that the different instances of whistle-blowing can be distinguished by using the rare, clear-cut cases as benchmarks to analyze more complex actions. Attorney Peter Raven-Hansen advises that such cases may be characterized by a whistle-blower who focuses on the abuse itself — not personalities — uses appropriate administrative channels before "going public," anticipates and documents retaliation and knows when to give up and move on.[11] Ultimately, the courts have maintained that a balance must be struck between the exercise of free speech and the authority of government to discharge employees for the good of the service. The difficulty in defining this balance is no excuse for permitting the kind of abuse discussed earlier. Dissent in organizations suggests that society questions the idea that management possesses superior ethical wisdom and desires a new balance between employee rights and management prerogatives.

At least two significant societal issues relate to whistle-blowing. The first involves responsibility and accountability in a system of representative democracy. In light of pervasive citizen distrust of government, this is hardly an academic or philosophical problem. Ways need to be found to introduce democratic rights into bureaucracies. The second issue states that in order to assure responsibility and accountability, due process procedures are necessary to protect employees who care about the general interest. Effective methods need to be discovered to balance an individual's duty to an employer with duty to the public. In fact, "many of the rights and privileges . . . so important to a free society that they are constitutionally protected . . . [remain] vulnerable to abuse through an employer's power."[12] Society has a right, in a word, to learn about significant problems in America politics without having those who expose them destroy their careers in the process.

It is critical, in short, that we change the "I win, you lose" approach to dissent in organizations. Responsible protest should benefit both employee and employer. When management directs efforts at the dissenter instead of the policy issue in question, the conditions that make whistle-blowing necessary will not be altered. Disclosure of waste, illegal activity, and abuse of power should be seen as a commitment to make government more worthy of public trust. Open discussion strengthens, not weakens, democracy. Despite the attention that dissent in organizations has received in recent years, whistle-blowing alone will never establish standards of public accountability and credibility that the citizenry deserves and expects. Yet, if the measures reviewed below were instituted, blowing the whistle would be less necessary than it is today. Before these measures are analyzed, however, the environment within which whistle-blowing occurs requires examination.

The Context of Whistle-Blowing: The Individual and the Organization.

It is essential to recognize that individual actions occur in an organizational context.[13] Moral judgments reflect group norms; the organization itself is a moral community, the formal expression and endorsement of these norms. One of the principal problems in bureaucracy today is that growth and diversification have diminished the sense of individual responsibility. This diffusion of accountability has meant that many people work in an environment in which nobody can be effectively in charge to set standards.[14]

Since corruption is a part of the human condition,[15] structures are needed to limit, discourage, and channel it. That is, institutions must assume at least partial responsibility for the ethical conduct of their employees. Individuals may make decisions based upon personal standards, but employers can control and define the situations in which decisions are made. It is not sufficient, in other words, for individuals to be convinced of their rectitude and integrity. Managers, as moral custodians of collective goals, are strategically placed to recognize the factors that promote and inhibit ethical behavior. Accordingly, they should be responsible for professional conduct and responsible for dissent. Without it, individual conscience can be paralyzed when rules of the organization are inadequate to support personal dignity. The pathetic plight of the whistle-blower, however, demonstrates how tenuous the balance between the individual and the organization can be.

The difficulty stems from the fact that bureaucracies resemble authoritarian states that do not permit legitimate opposition. Employees in hierarchical organizations cannot act politically, except in disloyal opposition; whistle-blowing is a political phenomenon that occurs in organizations that are not supposed to be political systems.[16] The reason for this is that the prevailing, if long discredited, administrative myth is that bureaucracy is a rational, nonpartisan, technical process, divorced from politics.[17] Whistle-blowing punctures the myth of neutrality and consensus in administration. It suggests that bureaucracy is a political system consisting of human beings as purposive actors with a sense of individual responsibility.

However, whistle-blowing occurs in the context of the administrative myth: the fear of hierarchical power and habits of obedience that originate in working etiquette and bureaucratic politeness. Bogen explains:

> There is a pervasive ethic of loyalty to the team . . . which manifests itself in the sanctity of the organization *qua* organization. The self-perpetuating propensity of organizations resulting from the teamwork ethic has been variously described . . . as organizational opportunism, bureaucratic self-maintenance, and the institutional imperative (i.e., every action or decision of an institution must be intended to keep the institution going). By whatever name, this organizational characteristic ensures that whistle-blowing will tend to be perceived as a threatening affront to an organization . . . Because an organization's behavior can be no more proper . . . than the people within the organization, the job of the internal dissenter can be expected to be an enduring one.[18]

Whistle-blowing is heroic because it requires bureaucrats "to transcend the every day world by naming abuses where none are supposed to exist, by challenging authority when obedience is required, by overcoming narrow self interests, and by inventing and creating novel ways of achieving their goals."[19]

Protecting Dissenters

If whistle-blowing has come of age, it does not automatically follow that effective plans of action are developed and implemented. Since the lack of internal procedures is frequently responsible for whistle-blowing,[20] what changes might serve to protect the rights of dissenters while assuring effective management? Robert F. Allen identifies four elements of any successful, long-range program.[21] First, in an effort to deal with the causes of behavior instead of its symptoms, administrators should ask themselves "What did we contribute to this behavior?" Second, instead of relying on simple explanations for organizational problems, thorough understanding involves: (1) analysis of the organization's cultural setting, (2) introduction of the possibility of change and employee involvement, (3) implementation of new strategies, and (4) evaluation of change and development of a continuing renewal process. Third, by creating answers to such questions as "What behavior is rewarded and penalized by the institutions?" a sound database can be established. Finally, an audit of the organization's ethical and moral results can point the way to constructive change. While this approach does not de-emphasize individual responsibility nor ignore scandals, it does address the underlying weakness that produces them. Blaming the bearer of bad tidings, after all, frees conforming employees and their organizations from complicity in what happens around them.

Whistle-blowing is not as necessary if managerial indifferences are not so pervasive and if procedures incorporate dissent into decision-making. Thus in the context of long-range, the need to resort to whistle-blowing in the short run can be reduced by providing mechanisms to ensure that managers take criticism seriously.

While some executives welcome criticism, communication techniques such as suggestion boxes and "open door" policies lack power to compel top management to examine criticisms, and can result in a trap for the employee. Since he or she objects to management policy, it is not reasonable to expect an unbiased review of the dissent or the dissenter. More systematic procedures may not entirely deal with these problems, but they may have a significant deterrent effect if employers know that their actions will be subject to review. Both internal and external checks may be useful.[22] The absence of such safeguards virtually guarantees that dissent will develop into confrontation between managers and the employee.

One internal device is an "ethical audit." Used for years in some businesses, the social audit methodically reviews a corporation's activities in the area of social responsibility (e.g., environmental pollution, affirmative action, community relations). An expanded or refocused effort could include ethical concerns in all areas of decision-making beyond those normally included in a social audit. Since audits are usually done after the fact, an ongoing technique used in some organizations is the appointment of an ethical adviser comparable to a legal or financial adviser to the chief executive officer. Such a person acts as a "devil's advocate" in policy decisions. The same staff personnel could formulate ethical impact statements, design employee bills of rights, serve as an ombudsman or inspector general, provide space on standard forms for dissenting opinions, and/or serve on review boards.

A second possibility formalizes the decision making process. Clearly specified policy objectives and means would make decision-making more visible and accountable. The organization's standards and their implementation could be part of its major reports. Bureaucratic competition in the form of overlapping jurisdictions and rival organizations may also prevent concentrations of power and guard against corruption.

Since the personnel process is frequently used to harass and remove whistle-blowers, a third internal check emphasizes the importance of ethics and employee rights throughout the personnel system. For instance, knowledge of the existence of the organization's code of conduct be required as a condition of employment. Instructors in employee orientation sessions would then explain it. The role of dissent could play an important part in management training. The subordinate and the superior could discuss ethical conduct in the organization and at the time of performance evaluation. Automatic payroll deductions could provide for legal services for conscientious employees. Leaves of absence or personnel exchanges between organizations could provide administrators opportunities to stand back from their work and refine their perspectives in organizational behavior. One product of such an experience could be a newsletter story or article for a trade magazine. In fact, measures could be taken to ensure that the personnel manager or staff librarian is aware of current books on management ethics, can obtain reprints of relevant articles, and is on the mailing list of organizations that sponsor meetings on topical issues. Finally, outplacement services for separated employees could be sponsored by the agencies.

However helpful such internal mechanisms may be in improving management and protecting individual rights, their limitations must be recognized. Kenneth T. Bogen points out that "the true protection offered by . . . [any] . . . intraorganizational procedures depends on good management, the very lack of which often produces whistle-blowing."[23]

External checks on administrative responsibility are, therefore, desirable. Employee unions, for example, can assist whistle-blowers. Historically, most unions have been more interested in the material conditions of work life than in civil liberties. In fact, union membership does not seem to affect the inclination to engage in whistle-blowing.[24] Nonetheless, as members become more sophisticated and educated, activities in this area should grow, as long as employees cannot protect themselves without the union. Many of the same comments also apply to professional societies, most of which have been reluctant to defend the independence of their members. Useful programs that might be undertaken would be to recognize leadership in professional ethics by awarding citations to deserving individuals and organizations, provide ethical consulting services, operate preferential reemployment networks for whistle-blowers, and publicize those organizations that violate professional standards.

The most popular current remedy for organizational abuse is statutory relief for whistle-blowers. Since action is ordinarily not taken against agency management, however, there is little reason not to retaliate against dissenters. Thus, a recent study of eight public laws that include employee protection sections found that such provisions have had limited success.[25] Perhaps the most innovative type of statutory relief would be to extend the illegality of discrimination on the basis of race, color, religion, sex, national origin, age and union membership to political, social, or economic views. Lawrence Blades argues that it is anomalous that the courts provide relief to an employee discharged because of race and religion but they do not provide protection for an employee discharged because of the exercise of free speech. Indeed, it has been pointed out that as long as federal law denies employees the right to engage in partisan political activities and the right to strike, their constitutional right to petition the government should be broadly construed.[26] Failing that, statutory hiring preferences for abused employees could be enacted.

The most discussed form of statutory protection in recent years has been the Civil Service Reform Act of 1978. Part of that act established the Merit Systems Protection Board and the Office of Special Counsel with the power to investigate prohibited personnel practices, including reprisals against whistle-blowers. While it may be too early for definitive judgments, initial indications are not reassuring.[27]

For example, although the Special Counsel is required to maintain the anonymity of the whistle-blower, agencies are permitted to investigate themselves. To date, such investigations have been less than satisfactory. If the Counsel determines that a prohibited personnel practice is involved, the case is referred to the Merit Systems Protection Board. In carrying out its functions, the board has adopted even more formal judicial procedures than had existed under the civil service commission, which had been called a "whistle-blower's graveyard." The initial cases before the board suggest that rights of dissenters tend to get subordinated to the hierarchy. More telling perhaps, in 1980 the Office of Special Council suffered massive budget cuts, which reduced its staff by two-thirds.

Such problems suggest the importance of both technical and substantive safeguards. As Rosemary Chalk and Frank von Hipple point out, whatever due process protections "are provided [they] will have little value unless they are embedded in a process which deals effectively with the substance of dissent."[28] The situation of the whistle-blower, in other words, will only be marginally improved unless the issues he or she raises are dealt with. If internal checks are little more than window dressing and external checks are ignored or turned into management tools, little change can be expected, and confidence in government can only be further undermined.

Indeed, Congressional hearings on the implementation of the Civil Service Reform Act consisted largely of, in the words of the subcommittee chairwomen, "blowing the whistle on the whistle-blowing protections."[29] Most testimony claimed that the safeguards were a failure, and that reforms had been transformed to where there is no more protection now (perhaps less) than under the preexisting system. In a prescient observation, Deena Weinstein remarked in 1979, that:

> All of the proposed reforms of bureaucratic abuses which work within the present system confront a basic dilemma. The ground of hierarchical administrative authority is that a specific group of officials should be held responsible for the conduct . . . of the

> organization. The presence of abuses concentrates on making officials accountable to other agencies. Such accountability, however, weakens their autonomy or, in the case of corruption, allows them to be even more abusive. . . . Reform, then, diffuses responsibility and gives officials excuses for their failures.[30]

Stated differently, devices for guaranteeing accountability often will inspire techniques for evasion. Weinstein goes on to argue that the reason for this is that there are deep social conflicts over the purposes organizations should serve. "Without the consensual loyalty and trust of the citizenry," J. Patrick Dobel writes in a treatise on corruption, "reforms will simply be shams to rationalize the continuation of corrupt practices."[31] Reassurances and denials seem to merely confirm official hypocrisy and untrustworthiness.

In short, whistle-blowing is a manifestation of serious problems concerning the legitimacy of American government. Both the long- and short-run methods to help protect dissenters may be quite useful in specific organizations and for individuals. Until more basic issues about the conduct of politics are addressed, however, such devices can never be truly effective in reducing the underlying need to blow the whistle.

Summary and Conclusions

This analysis has examined the significance of corruption in American government today, traced the emergence and institutionalization of whistle-blowing as an important social phenomenon, explored the relationship between the dissenting individual and the bureaucratic organization, and discussed reforms designed both to encourage ethical behavior and to make whistle-blowing less necessary.

Only once in American history did administration reform become part of the mainstream of the nation's politics, and that was during the Progressive Era. The increasing interest in the public employee as a productive source of information about government suggests that there is an important movement to reaffirm the basic principle that the free exchange of ideas is an integral part of democratic decision-making. Nonetheless, although civil servants have rights and protections, in reality managers successfully retaliate against whistle-blowers. The quest for more ethical government must permit public employees to fulfill their role as autonomous and responsible citizens in America democracy.

Some of the trends discussed in this article suggest that the tension between individual democratic rights and organizational authoritarianism in American life may be resolved in future years. However, until dealt with the daily interactions among employees and institutions that do not provide opportunities for the exercise of integrity will continue the corruption of democracy, and whistle-blowing will remain a dangerous, if essential, task.

Endnotes

1. See James S. Bowman, "Ethics in the Federal Service: A Post-Watergate View," *Midwest Review of Public Administration* 11 (March 1977): 3-20; "Uncle Sam's Fraud Hotline," *U.S. News and World Report* 87 (August 20, 1979): 38; testimony cited in Deena Weinstein, "Opposition to Abuse Within Organizations: Heroism and Legalism," *The ASLA Forum* 4 (Fall 1979): 19. Another indication of the depth of the problem is that a convenor of a national conference on fraud informed the author that many prominent appointed public officials accepted illegal honoraria as a condition for speaking at the conference.

2. For a summary of these data, see James L. Sundquist, "The Crisis of Competence in our National Government," *Political Science Quarterly* 95 (Summer 1980): 183-208.

3. James S. Bowman, et al., *Managerial Ethics: Whistleblowing in Organizations: An Annotated Bibliography and Resource Guide* (New York: Garland Publishing, Inc. 1982).

4. Several landmark works that emphasize ethical dilemmas in organizations prior to this period include Robert T. Golembiewski, *Men, Management, and Morality* (New York: McGraw-Hill, 1965); Albert O. Hirschman, *Exit, Voice, and Loyalty* (Cambridge, Mass.: Harvard University Press, 1970); and Edward Weisband and Thomas M. Franck, *Resignation in Protest* (New York: Grossman Publishers, 1975). The latter report that among top public officials who resigned, the percentage "going public" declined by more than two thirds in thirty years, a period when the New Deal and the Cold War bureaucratized much of public policy. Important reference materials include Ralph Nader, et. al., *Whistle-Blowing* (New York: Grossman Publishers, 1972); Government Accountability Project, *A Whistle-blower's Guide to the Federal Bureaucracy* (Washington, D.C.: The Institute for Policy Studies, 1977); *The Bureaucrat* (Winter 1977): entire issue; and Auren Uris, *Executive Dissent: How to Say No and Win* (New York: AMACOM, 1978); Louis Clark, *Blowing the Whistle: Public Service, Private Agony* (Boston: Beacon Press, forthcoming); Alan Westin, *Whistle-blowing: Loyalty and Dissent in the Corporation* (New York: McGraw-Hill, 1981); Richard T.

DeGeorge, *Business Ethics* (New York: Macmillian, 1981), Chapter 9; and Rosemary Clark, ed., *Scientists as Whistle Blowers: A Report of the AAAS Committee on Scientific Freedom and Responsibility* (Washington, D.C.: American Association for the Advancement of Sciences, 1981).

5. On these points, see Comptroller General, *Continuing and Widespread Weakness in Internal Control Results in Losses Through Fraud, Waste, and Abuse* (Washington, D.C.: General Accounting Office, 1980); Gerald E. Caiden and Naomi J. Caiden, "Administrative Corruption," *Public Administration Review* 37 (May/June 1977): esp. 308; and Amitai Etzioni, "American Ethics and the President," in *Ethical Perspectives in Business and Society,* Yerchmiel Kugel and Gladys W. Greenberg, ed. (Lexington, Mass.: D.C. Heath and Co., 1977), pp. 11-17.

6. "Introduction," *Individual Rights in the Corporation,* Alan F. Westin and Stephan Salisbury, eds. (New York: Pantheon Books, 1980): xi. A recent survey of federal employees revealed that 60 percent of the respondents say they are willing to blow the whistle. See U.S. Congress, House of Representatives, Committee on Post Office and Civil Service, *Civil Service Reform Oversight 1980 — Whistleblower,* before the subcommittee on the Civil Service, 96th Congress, 2nd Session, 1980, p. 196.

7. *Ibid.,* p. 148.

8. Deena Weinstein, *Bureaucratic Oppositions* (New York: Pergamon Press, 1979), p. 76.

9. U.S. Congress, House, *Civil Service Reform,* pp. 196-197. The etymology of the word is discussed in William Safire, *Safire's Political Dictionary,* 3rd ed. (New York: Random House, 1978), p. 790.

10. "Whistleblowing and Professional Responsibility," *New York Education Quarterly* 11 (1979): 2-11.

11. "Dos and Don'ts for Whistleblowers: Planning for Trouble," *Technology Review* 82 (May 1980): 34. For a further discussion differentiating types of whistle-blowing cases, see Kenneth D. Walters, "Your Employee's Rights to Blow the Whistle," *Harvard Business Review,* 53 (July/August 1975): 26-35. On the question of the types of information that might be disclosed, the Freedom of Information Act is suggestive. See D.R.M., "The Right of Government Employees to Furnish Information to Congress," *Virginia Law Review,* 57 (June 1971): 885-919.

12. Lawrence Blades, "Employment at Will vs. Individual Freedom: On Limiting the Abusive Exercise of Employer Power," *Columbia Law Review* 67 (December 1967): 1407. Also see David Ewing, *Freedom Inside the Organization: Bringing Civil Liberties to the Workplace* (New York: E.P. Dutton, 1977).

13. On this point, also see T. Edwin Boling, "Organizational Ethics: Rules, Creativity, and Idealism," in *Management Handbook for Public Administration,* John W. Sutherland, ed. (New York: Van Nostrand Reinhold Co., 1978), esp. pp. 251-54.

14. Indeed, individuals perceive the organizational environment to be less ethical than their own values and behavior. At least four recent surveys, for example, show that the majority of managers are under pressure to compromise personal standards of conduct to achieve organizational goals. In addition, many respondents feel that their superiors are only interested in results, and not how they are obtained. See James S. Bowman, "The Management of Ethics: Codes of Conduct in Organizations," *Public Personnel Management* 10, no. 1 (1981), references cited therein. In this environment, whistle-blowing may be seen as one means of humanizing organizations, i.e., organizations *are* people. As such, a whistle-blower is a person who acts on behalf of the citizen to blow the whistle on another individual. See Eileen Seidman, "Professional Societies and Whistleblowing: An Ethical Challenge," paper presented at the annual meeting of the American Society for Public Administration, San Francisco Hilton, San Francisco, California, April 13-15, 1980.

15. J. Patrick Dobel, "The Corruption of a State," *American Political Science Review* 72 (September 1978): 858-73.

16. For a book-length statement of this thesis, see Weinstein, *Bureaucratic Oppositions.*

17. While the politics-administration dichotomy "may have been abandoned by many scholars it continues as an ideal role for bureaucracy in democracy and as a symbol against corruption. Its popularity unites administrators and political scientists alike to support and justify their current interests. Public leaders take refuge in it in order to transfer blame for themselves to bureaucrats. Practitioners would rather not emphasize that they are influencing policy . . . Scholars prefer not to examine important normative issue since they are not readily observable and easily quantified." See James S. Bowman, "Public Administration Without Ethics: The Legacy of the Politics-Administration Dichotomy," in *Politics and Administration: The Wilsonian Influence in Public Administration,* Jack Rabin and James S. Bowman, eds. (1982).

18. Kenneth T. Bogen, "Whistle-blowing by Technical Experts," unpublished thesis, Princeton University, 1978, pp. 24, 17.

19. Deena Weinstein, "Opposition to Abuse," pp. 15-16.

20. U.S. Congress, Senate, Committee on Governmental Affairs, *The Whistle-blowers: A Report on Federal Employees Who Disclose Acts of Governmental Waste, Abuse and Corruption,* by Senator Patrick J. Leahy, Committee Print, 95th Cong., 2nd Sess. (Washington, D.C.: Government Printing Office, 1978), p. 2.

21. "The Ink in the Office," *Organizational Dynamics* 8 (Winter 1980): esp. pp. 37ff.

22. For a brief discussion of these, see Bowman, "Management of Ethics," and the references cited therein, as well as Bok, "Whistleblowing," esp. p. 8.

23. Bogen, "Whistle-blowing by Technical Experts," p. 129.

24. Weinstein, *Bureaucratic Oppositions,* p. 41.

25. Rosemary Chalk and Frank von Hipple, "Due Process for Dissenting Whistle-Blowers," *Technology Review* 81 (June/July 1979): 55.

26. See Blades, "Employment at Will," p. 1433, and D.R.M., "The Right of Government Employees," p. 904.

27. See U.S. Congress, House, *Civil Service Reform,* and Comptroller General, *First Year Activities of the Merit Systems Retention Board and the Office of Special Counsel* (Washington, D.C.: General Accounting Office, 1980).

28. Chalk and von Hipple, "Due Process for Dissenting Whistle-Blowers," p. 55.

29. U.S. Congress, House, *Civil Service Reform,* esp. p. 33. Also see Inderjit Badhwar, "Analyzing the Hoax of Hoaxes," *Federal Times,* August 25, 1980, p. 9.

30. Weinstein, *Bureaucratic Oppositions,* p. 124.

31. Dobel, "The Corruption of a State," p. 969.

Blowing the Whistle on Systematic Corruption: On Maximizing Reform and Minimizing Retaliation

Judith A. Truelson

In this, no one ought to be excluded and no idea ignored. Bureaucratic revitalization by itself is insufficient; bureaucratic habits die hard. Simple remedies will not do. Contemporary administrative problems require new approaches, new organizational designs, new laws, new commitments, new relationships, new attitudes, new techniques.[1]

Truelson describes research findings in which the main organizational goal is survival, the public trust is an exception and whistle-blowing is among the acts of first resort. Citing systemic corruption as the catalyst for bringing on severe retaliation against the whistle-blower, Truelson (as did Caiden and Caiden) suggests that the result is institutional lawlessness. What reforms would obviate the bleak picture painted by this research?

This article reports results of a study undertaken in 1984-85 on the dynamics of organizational retaliation against legitimate whistle-blowing.[2] The whistle-blowers under study protested acts of corruption, in the organizations in which they worked, which were verified by the FBI, General Accounting Office (GAO), and Congressional or criminal investigations as serious violations of law, regulations and/or professional standards. Sixteen of the protest issues involved life-threatening health or safety violations; nine other protest issues involved multi million dollar contract fraud. All of the whistle-blowers experienced retaliation, administered by individuals acting as organizational agents, which could not be explained without reference to the host organization as a social system in its own right. Retaliation against legitimate whistle-blowers is assumed in this study to be a deviant organizational act, reflective of systemic corruption in that it is contrary to societal norms and is known and supported by the dominant coalition in the organization.

This study is the first empirical analysis of retaliation as the organizational response to legitimate whistle-blowing. By studying cases of intense retaliation, this research moves beyond analysis of the whistle-blowing act itself to focus on the dynamics of the interaction among individual whistle-blowers, organizations, and their environments. As such, it addresses the critical question: how does the organizational retaliation process work? Exploration of this question can help to explain why encouragement of responsible employee protest is falling behind expectations.

Whistle-blowing increased in the United States during the 1970s out of concern for the deterioration of morality. As a result of widespread post-Watergate belief in the endemic nature of official wrong doing, Congress enacted legislation prescribing a Code of Ethics for Government Service. Besides mandating honest, loyal and efficient services in the public interest, the code also requires that the public servants "expose corruption wherever discovered."[3]

Such expectations require a definition of corruption. While most people agree that the essence of corruption is abuse of a public role or trust for primitive gain, we cannot always agree on the nature of "abuse."[4] In the interest of precision and reliability, corruption is defined in this study in the formal-legal sense — as deliberate and knowing, unsanctioned deviations from the formal duties of an elective or appointed public role, involving the private-regarding use of public resources and goods by public servants. Corruption involves the breaking or bending of laws or other formal regulations, and can include failure to act as well as outright law-breaking deeds.[5]

Although whistle-blowing is also subject to a variety of definitions, most agree that it involves a process in which an employee of an organization develops an awareness of a product or policy considered to be unethical, immoral, illegal or dangerous to the public. The employee expresses concern to the immediate supervisor, without obtaining satisfaction; expresses concern to supervisors higher up in the corporate government hierarchy — still without satisfaction — and finally takes the concern outside of the organization, to the press or other support groups.[6]

The Code of Ethics of Government Service seeks to incorporate whistle-blowing into policies designed to improve overall accountability of public agencies. But whistle-blowers frequently encounter severe

Source: Judith A. Truelson, "Blowing the Whistle on Systematic Corruption: On Maximizing Reform and Minimizing Retaliation," *Corruption and Reform*, 2 (1987), pp. 55-74.

damage to their careers and substantial economic loss as a result of exposing corruption. Congress thus concurrently enacted whistle-blower protection provisions in the Civil Service Reform Act of 1978 (CSRA), including the creation of the Office of the Special Council (OSC) and the Merit Systems Protection Board (MSPB).[7]

U.S. Government employees, however, remain reluctant to blow the whistle. Congressional and GAO investigations indicate that the establishment of the OSC has not made federal employees more secure in speaking out.[8] Both the 1980 MSPB survey on whistle-blowing and its 1983 follow-up survey show that about 70% of federal employees claiming personal knowledge of corruption did not report it.[9]. . .

Deficiencies in whistle-blower protection legislation may stem in part from assumptions that retaliation against legitimate whistle-blowing is purely an individual act. Evidence indicates, however, that such retaliation may instead be the systemic defense of a corrupt organization under attack. Most criminologists and organizational sociologists agree that organizations are real, independent, acting entities which can violate the law in their own right.[10] In order to understand government employee reluctance to blow the whistle, it is appropriate to investigate retaliation against whistle-blowers in environments of systemic corruption.

The Process of Systemic Retaliation

The basic premise of this study is that retaliation is a correlate of blowing the whistle on systemic corruption. Although whistle-blowing is threatening to any organization because it challenges the legitimacy of top management's actions, organizations would seem least likely to retaliate against the whistle-blower whose case has been determined to have merit and thus some degree of public support. Research results conflict, however, indicating that employers retaliate both against whistle-blowers whose cases lack merit and who are relatively powerless, and against legitimate whistle-blowers who have public support.[11] The nature of systemic corruption itself suggests an explanation for retaliation against whistle-blowing which may account for this apparent contradiction.

Systemic corruption denotes a situation in which the goals of organizational loyalty and survival predominate over the public interest, in which behavior stemming from the notion of public responsibility and trust has become the exception, and in which wrongdoing becomes the norm.[12] As a result, whatever the merits of a whistle-blower's issue, the very act of whistle-blowing is an intolerable breach of the organization's de facto code of conduct. It thus incurs retaliation. Such retaliatory behavior is a form of bureaucratic corruption in that it is enacted by administrators in their official capacity, not in their personal or, where applicable, political capacity.[13]

A growing body of literature suggests that such systemic corruption may be endemic to American governmental institutions.[14] When, for example, A. Ernest Fitzgerald blew the whistle on the Pentagon $2 billion cost overrun in the development of the Lockhead C5A transport plane, he exposed a prime example of systemic corruption.[15] Based on hundreds of hearings and federal reports, Hanrahan alleges that federal contracting abuses extending far beyond the Pentagon may also be described as systemic, ingrained, and immune to outside intervention.[16] Some large bureaucratized police organizations have also exemplified systemic corruption. As organizational rules become ends in themselves, the police can become an adjunct of the criminal world they are supposed to fight. Internal practices can encourage and protect violations of the external code of police practice.[17]

Dynamics of Systemic Corruption

Caiden and Caiden argue that [a] corrupt system displays the following features:
1. the organization professes an external code of ethics contradicted by internal practices;
2. internal practices encourage, aid, abet and hide violations of the external code;
3. nonviolators of the external code are penalized in that they lose the benefits of violation and offend those who indulge in violations;
4. violators are protected and when exposed, they are treated leniently;
5. nonviolators, suffocating in the venal atmosphere, find no internal relief and often meet with external disbelief;

6. prospective whistle-blowers are intimidated and terrorized into silence;

7. courageous whistle-blowers have to be protected from retaliation;

8. violators become so accustomed to their practices and to the protection afforded them that when they are exposed, their surprise is genuine as is their complaint that they have been unfairly singled out;

9. collective guilt finds expression in rationalizations of the corrupt practices; there is no serious intention of ending them;

10. those formally responsible for investigating corruption rarely act, and when forced to do so by external pressure excuse the incidents as isolated rare occurrences;

11. following exposure, the organization makes gestures toward reform and for a time gives the impression of cleansing itself, but once the publicity is over, it reverts to old practices.[18]

Once whistle-blowers expose corrupt organizations to outside sanctions, those formally responsible for investigating corruption focus on the dysfunctionality of whistle-blowers, moving to expel them from the system. Even if they are subsequently reinstated, whistle-blowers find no internal relief from recurring intimidation and retaliation.

Method

This study employs the methodology of negative case analysis. Rooted in John Stuart Mill's "method of difference," negative case analysis is based on the assumption that the perfect form of scientific knowledge is universal generalizations.[19] Using essentially the same steps in this research as Cressey used in his study of embezzlers, a rough definition and hypothetical explanation of the research problem was formulated. Each of 38 cases of whistle-blowing in large agencies plus (for purposes of proof) two cases involving intense retaliation in small organizations, was successively compared against a preliminary hypothesis. When a single negative case was found which disconfirmed the preliminary hypothesis, that hypothesis was revised to account for that case.[20] A thorough search is made for cases that might disconfirm the hypothesis. Although the search and the data collection are not routinized, nor do the data yield numbers that can be added or averaged, the procedure itself is systematic.[21]

The Sample

Aerospace engineer William Bush has become a veritable one-man whistle-blowing clearinghouse in the course of fighting his own protracted legal battles against retaliation for his revelations of age discrimination. For this study his 5,514 computerized case files were searched for cases of whistle-blowing which resulted in retaliation. The 575 cases thus selected were then scanned for cases which resulted in severe retaliation — defined as firing, forcing resignation, transfer, demotion, harassment or blacklisting. Together with 15 cases gathered through personal contacts, a total population of 320 cases was constructed for this study. From this population 42 cases involving primarily public organizations of 1,000 or more employees were drawn, plus two cases of intense retaliation in small organizations. All cases occurred in the U.S. since 1960, and all could be documented on the following criteria: merit of the issue, intensiveness of retaliation, description of the whistle-blowing process, description of the support mechanisms used by the whistle-blower, and size of the organization.

Facts on the legitimacy of the whistle-blowing and the nature of organizational retaliation were verified through multiple sources including law cases, hearings, newspaper accounts, and case studies. Criteria for inclusion in William Bush's database include verification of data as to nature of dissent, employment sector of the whistle-blower, professional status of the whistle-blower, and nature of organizational retaliation, if any. In addition to the computer database, Bush has extensive files of backup data on these cases which were available for this research. In 15 cases, documentation was supplemented by interviews modelled on pretested questionnaire items.[22]

Interviews/Questionnaire

These concerned respondents' perceptions of their organizations, of their jobs before they blew the whistle, of the whistle-blowing incidents themselves, of their reasons for reporting the incidents, of the retaliation experienced, and of their jobs after blowing the whistle. Interview information on the following variables was also documented in independent sources.

Whistle-blower's Role Influence

The role influence of a whistle-blower was assessed in terms of access to information, persons and organizational resources. The relationship of a role within its role set was used to determine the kinds of influence available to that role incumbent. Role influence was operationalized as tenure of functional expertise, tenure of boundary-spanning functions, tenure of functional independence in a role set, and tenure of auditing functions.

Merit of the Issue

A whistle blower's issue was considered meritorious if it was socially perceived as legitimate and salient. Indicators of merit of the issue included truth of the allegation, precedented grounds for legal action on the whistle-blower's issue, and public acceptance of the moral grounds upon which a whistle-blower protested violation of social policy.

Intensity of the Whistle-blowing Process

Degree and duration of publicity were used as indicators of the intensity of the whistle-blowing process. Respondents were questioned as to their protest method (i.e. written, oral or both), the frequency of protest, the number of protest channels used within the organization, and the number of protest channels used outside the organization.

Intensity of Retaliation against Whistle-blowers.

The operationalization of intensiveness of retaliation against whistle-blowers is crucial to the validity of this study. It is defined as an ongoing organizational response which is simultaneously comprehensive, involving upper management collusion and widespread collegial avoidance, threats, or refusal to support the whistle-blower; and severe retaliation, involving indirect or direct separation from the organization such as demotion, denial of promotion and dismissal. Comprehensiveness of retaliation included exclusion from staff meetings previously attended, loss of perquisites, receipt of less desirable work assignments, receipt of heavier work load, receipt of more stringent work criticisms, pressure to drop suit and co-worker avoidance of personal contact. Severity of retaliation included poor performance appraisal, suspension, transfer or reassignment to a different geographical location, demotion, denial of promotion, physical assault, or intimidation of whistle-blowers and/or their families.

Support Used by the Whistle-blowers to Combat Retaliation

Assistance to whistle-blowers was considered to be supportive in that it afforded moral, financial, advisory, legal, and/or mediating support to the complainant. Respondents identified organizations such as unions, professional societies, consumer groups, civil liberties organizations, environmental defense groups, and other public interest groups as active supporters. Other indicators of support included statutory whistle-blower protection, Congressional support and grievance and appeal procedures.

Hypothesis

Since the organization focuses on making a scapegoat of the whistle-blower in retaliation for incurring unwelcome notoriety, internal organizational procedures rarely protect whistle-blowers and even more rarely discipline those who have retaliated against whistle-blowers. Actually, appeal mechanisms and dissent channels within corrupt systems such as "open door policies" have typically been captured by the very group whose conduct they were to regulate. Since these channels are not segregated from the rest of the organization, they constitute no deterrent to organizational retaliation against whistlc-blowing.

It is therefore predicted that:

> If the whistle-blowers' issue is meritorious, the target organization is large and there is intense retaliation against the whistle-blower, there will be a positive relationship between the intensity of the whistle-blowing process, the supports used by the whistle-blower and the intensity of retaliation; there will be a negative relationship between the whistle-blower's role influence and the supports used by the whistle-blower process and the intensity of retaliation.

Corrupt systems display a preoccupation with secrecy, loyalty-security systems, and the segregation of clandestine operations. In such organization, whistle-blowers who attract mass media coverage of their protests are immediately severed from continued access to organizational intelligence. If feasible, they will be expelled from the organization. In the event that expulsion is infeasible or delayed, they will be symbolically expelled through isolation from information, people and resources. Should the whistle-blowers persist in publicizing their protests — regardless of whether they are still positioned within the organization or are expelled from it — the organization will resort to defamation and even blacklisting in order to discredit adverse publicity.

The hypothesis above suggests a preliminary model of the retaliation process, as seen in Figs 1 and 2. The model assumes interaction among the individual, organizational and extra-organizational levels of activity. Although the stages within each level of activity are presented sequentially, it is understood that the stages may occur and interact simultaneously.

When an employee initiates stage 1 of the retaliation process by blowing the whistle on a corrupt system, he or she triggers the retaliatory process. The severity of retaliation at this stage may be affected by the whistle-blower's ability to document the protest — which is a function of the extent to which a whistle-blower controls access to information, persons, and resources. Given the magnitude of the issue, a well-documented protest also threatens to attract broad media attention and significant extra-organizational support. At this initial stage, the entire bureaucracy from top to bottom closes ranks against the whistle-blower — upper management backing their subordinates' retaliatory actions; the subordinates covering up for upper management.

Demotion, expulsion and/or defamation of the whistle-blower initiates stage 2 of the retaliatory process by giving the whistle-blower grounds for appeal or legal action against the organization. Now, however, the employee is blowing the whistle on a different misdeed, that is, the alleged victimization. Invariably, appeals of retaliatory personnel actions are futile in that they are made through the chain of command to the very people who were the targets — directly or indirectly — of whistle blowing and who allegedly retaliated against the whistle-blower. Nor do statutory whistle-blower protections afford much real protection against retaliation. In this legal environment, Congressional support is the best extra-organizational ally for the whistle-blower.

Deferred and prolonged lawsuits characterize stage 3 of the retaliation process. During both stages 2 and 3, the organization may pit its massive resources against the whistle-blower. The financial burden of whistle-blowing requires substantial financial resources. Legal services and court costs for private lawsuits are beyond the financial reach of the average employee and, therefore, are a continuing deterrent to cases which must be disentangled by expensive attorneys. Even if the legal assistance is available from a support group or public interest law firm, court costs may be prohibitive.

Delays also add significantly to costs. While an employee's appeal can be dismissed if it is not filed within a limited period, no such rules ensure that an appeals system or legal system will act promptly. The already substantial delay and expense associated with any litigation in today's courts is compounded for the whistle-blower by statutory loopholes such as the awarding of immunity in damages actions to public officials who have established reasonable belief in the legality of the actions for which they were sued. It is not unusual for whistle-blower suits to linger for years in the courts only to be thrown out in the end on some pre-trial motion unrelated to the merits of the case.

Regardless of the court's decision, stage 4 in the retaliatory process can present little or no victory for the whistle-blower. An award of reinstatement into a corrupt system only assures reactivation of the retaliatory process. Reinstatement settlements, if awarded, seldom allow for reimbursement of legal and court costs. Should an employee dismissed for whistle-blowing finally be reinstated, an award of back pay does little to compensate for the out-of-pocket expenses incurred.

A case of overpricing

The following case taken from the sample of 42 cases illustrates the model.

Stage 1: In 1983, a maintenance supply man in military service first attempted to report under the "Zero Overpricing Program" that the service was paying $670.07 for an armrest which he claimed could be made on his base for less than $25. His report was ignored.

> The bottom line is that my suggestion didn't even make it past the first stage of evaluation in the base suggestion program and I never heard anything from the Zero Overpricing Program after submitting my suggestion.

He turned the suggestion in again, even supplying blueprints, yet it was still ignored. He estimated that his suggestion would save $1.5 million annually.

He then tried to report this overpricing issue to his immediate superior, the squadron commander, and even the base Inspector General (IG). He was told in that office that the suggestion had to be turned down three times before the IG would look at it.

The only person who would listen to him was the supply officer (also a case study in this research project). At the officer's suggestion, the supply man reported his overpricing concerns to a military watchdog support group — The Project for Military Procurement. He then joined the officer in answering the subpoena of the Senate Judiciary subcommittee and in testifying before it, under Congressional protection, on seven examples of excessive pricing. He also appeared on television on "The Today Show," and got press coverage from the *San Francisco Chronicle,* the *New York Times* and the *Washington Post.*

Stage 2: When he returned to base, he was called into the colonel's office. The colonel threatened to bring him up on AWOL charges and put him in another squadron — until the supply maintenance man showed the colonel the letter he had from the chairman of the Senate subcommittee, which outlined the penalties for retaliating against a Congressional witness.

Stage 3: The supply man was nonetheless severely criticized for attracting the attention of an IG investigation team, which was expected to arrive on the base within a matter of hours. The enlisted man was pressed into a crash program for cleaning up as much as possible all irregularities before the team arrived. He was interrogated by the IG team as to why he did not contact the base IG.

Stage 4: After the furor of the inspection team died down, he found himself stigmatized as a squealer and a stooge for Congress. He was finally given a cash award for his suggestion in the Zero Overpricing Program, although the suggestion was never implemented. Although he continued to do the same kind of work, he felt that he was being steered away from trouble areas. Near the end of his enlisted period at the time of the interview, he did not plan to re-enlist.

Despite strong support mechanisms and protection — an officer as co-testifier, support from a military watchdog support group, and Congressional protection — this whistle-blower still experienced comprehensive retaliation in terms of co-workers avoidance, threats and intimidation and severe retaliation in that his re-enlistment plans were affected.

The data

Review of the 40 cases, after six revisions to the preliminary hypothesis, suggests confirmation of the following:

> If the whistle-blower's issue is meritorious, if the target organization is large, and there is intense retaliation — at any point in the relationship between the whistle-blower and

the target organization — the greater the public intensity of the whistle-blowing process, the greater the potential will be for use of effective, legal tactics and supports (particularly political and statutory ones); the more simultaneously these tactics and supports occur with the whistle-blowing process and the more energetically they are used, the more likely it is that the severity of intense retaliation will be regulated; the more the severity of intense retaliation is regulated by timely and energetic use of these tactics and supports, the more negative the relationship between the role influence of the whistle-blower and the intensity of retaliation.

The findings of this research correspond to the model of the retaliation process already illustrated. Negative case analysis, however, has contributed a sense of the duration and intensity of the retaliation process.

The experiences of the whistle-blowers under study reveal the destructive societal impact of systemic corruption. . . . [O]f the 23 whistle-blowers permanently separated from their organizations due to blowing the whistle, 16 were fired, six were forced to resign, and one was forced to retire. Ten of these 23 were blacklisted; six of those blacklisted have apparently never worked since. Among the remaining 17 whistle-blowers eight were transferred to positions which denied them access to continued information about their protest issue, two were permanently refused promotions and given less desirable work assignments, and seven were excluded from communications channels, avoided by co-workers and otherwise hampered in performing their assignments.

Institutional lawlessness and misuse of institutional power act as barriers to effective ethical behavior in an environment of systemic corruption. There is no indication that any of the studied whistle-blowers caused their organizations to abandon corruption. In more than 60% of the study cases, no change at all occurred as a result of whistle-blowing. In the 13 cases where some action was taken — probably because of publicized direct evidence of statutory violation — reform was localized rather than systemic. For example, FBI exposure of systemic corruption among meat-graders resulted in removal of graders in a particular region — but not throughout the system.

Institutional Lawlessness

The organizations involved in this study attacked the whistle-blowers from every side with accusations of insubordination, disloyalty, breach of confidence, poor performance appraisal — even mental instability — culminating in disgrace, reduction in role influence, and transfer, demotion or termination.

Since the 40 whistle-blowers found so little protection from reprisals, it appears that their organizations operate according to their own standards with their activities either beyond legal restriction or little penalized. The U.S. legal structure itself helps to create an environment in which institutional lawlessness flourishes. Statutory antiretaliation provisions are both too broad and too narrow to afford protection to whistle-blowers. The law gives broad leeway to the Courts in the balancing of state and individual interests, and has thus resulted in precedents such as *Connick v. Myers* which upheld a restriction on first amendment rights in the interest of an organizaton's fulfillment of its responsibilities to the public.[23] Even if the government whistle-blower is allowed to press for damages and can prevail under the Supreme Court's balancing test, defendants may be able to assert the defense of immunity to their claims. Indeed, some officials carry out such controversial or far-reaching functions that they are accorded absolute immunity regardless of the legality of their actions. When acting in official capacity, for example, the President, judges, and prosecutors have all been accorded absolute immunity.[24] The protection of administrative policies and prerogatives so dominates the legal environment that the potential for retaliation against whistle-blowers is practically unrestricted.

The Merit Systems Protection Board, acting on behalf of whistle-blowers as an administrative court in prosecutions initiated by the Office of Special Counsel has taken an unduly technical view of its task — imposing unwarranted evidentiary burdens on whistle-blowers and expressing an unusually conservative interpretation of the First Amendment. As a result, whistle-blower reprisal complaints rarely qualify for Special Counsel protection. As of December 1984, 42% of all matters under active investigation were whistle-blower reprisal cases. Yet, an extremely small proportion of these complaints meet the legal standards required of OSC for a successful prosecution or a corrective or disciplinary action.[25]

[O]nly about half of the whistle-blowers sought formal protection. Of the appeals, less than half were successful; eight of the whistle-blowers filed two appeals — several filed both an administrative and a civil suit. In all of the cases in which public employees won an appeal, reinstatement, back pay and benefits were the only reparation required of the organization.

Institutional staying power

Although none of the whistle-blowers in this study succeeded in avoiding retaliation, some of them such as the supply maintenance man were successful in regulating retaliation by enlisting outside support and by planning the timing and energy of response, and the duration of struggle. Yet, the study organizations had such complete control of their resources that they could impose at least some retaliation on whistle-blower's and sustain it indefinitely even in the face of outside support. In every case, the whistle blower's organizational role influence, in terms of access to people, information and resources, was totally or essentially eliminated.

. . . Among the study group, 27 public employees invoked a combination of legal support and Congressional support sustained for at least two to three years. In nine cases, the struggle endured for more than five years. Despite considerable expenditures of time, money and other resources, these 27 battles resulted in only nine cases of reinstatement and one case of vindication.

Few of these reinstated whistle-blowers could attract enough support or could themselves afford the financial and psychological burden of renewed, protracted battles. Two of the nine reinstated employees are on stress-related disability leave; one resigned after five years of harassment; two others were reinstated to noncomparable jobs in which their failure was assured; one has been publicly labeled as "paranoid".

Reform Implications

In order to survive the experience of blowing the whistle on systemic corruption, statutory protections will certainly continue to be invoked. Yet, the law cannot stop systemic corruption. Unable to rely on mechanisms like conscience or threat of imprisonment or death which operate within individuals to repress or sublimate a certain amount of antisocial activity before it is even thought of, law is limited to the application of minimal organizational penalties. Prosecutors such as the MSPB and the OSC must rely on weak disciplinary actions such as letters of reprimand and admonishment, and fines. Moreover, broadly written statutes such as the Civil Service Reform Act contain many administrative and procedural deficiencies such as limited coverage of protected personnel actions. These problems are likely to persist: even if the controversial whistle-blower protection legislation which was recently proposed in the House is passed, the benefits accruing from, for example, changing the standard of proof from "preponderance of evidence" to "substantial evidence" would be minimal.[26]

The major problem in relying solely on the law as arbiter of organizational retaliation against whistle-blowers is that the law is primarily a reactive institution. Even if laws could be passed to effectively protect whistle-blowers until they are passed and enforced, a great deal of damage will be done. Blowing the whistle on systemic corruption may be better protected through increased political support generated through cultural and institutional changes.

Cultural change

Environmental social control seems to be an essential ingredient in the resocialization process. Scandal as a negative public reaction to systemic corruption can constitute a social control: a punitive sanction designed to deter further deviance. Labeling of the system as corrupt seems to hinge on public revelation of its members.[27]

Mobilization of scandal is used successfully in socialist countries, primarily in the Soviet Union and China.[28] Although mobilization of scandal may seem a return to the old predevelopment style of justice, it can be a productive means to supplement the inadequacy of whistle-blowing and formal legal systems in dealing with contemporary systemic corruption. The social reaction the constitutes scandal must be one of intense outrage and anger, rather than of mere disapproval. This outrage must be stimulated and sustained by the legislature, support group protests and intense media exposure of corruption.

Inspections and investigations are also essential to the exploration of deviant behaviors as issues of social and community development. Review by peers or by higher authorities must serve as a forum for discussion of the moral stakes involved in a particular decisions. Review procedures including those of formal complaints, hearings and appeals should also contribute to critical dialogue to revive commitment to agency ideals or personal standards of honesty.

Institutional change

The creation and support of dissent channels to permit expression of contrary views on policy issues is a critical ingredient of effective administrative reform. The concept of the ombudsman as an advocate for federal employee protest could be an innovative key to unlocking the virtually untapped reservoir of employee knowledge of corruption. Some ombudsman activities relating to employee protest might include: listening to the complaints of concerned employees and counseling them on procedures and possible outcomes for lodging protests, responding directly to some employees' complaints and referring federal employees to the proper agency official or office to lodge their complaints.[29]

Conclusions

While the number of study cases is small, the conclusions of this study are nonetheless indicative of directions for future research. The prospects for reform in the United States depend to a great extent on deepening the understanding of systemic retaliation against whistle-blowing. Continued research in the United States as well as crosscultural research on retaliation against legitimate whistle-blowing in other settings could provide valuable insights. Future comparative studies may also be in order to probe this study's assumption that although public and private organizations vary in important respects, the dynamics of retaliation against whistle-blowing are similar in both.

If we are seeking the evolution of civic virtue — the respect for publicness and community — we must endorse the mission of legitimate whistle-blowers. In addition to protection, we must guide whistle-blowers operating in an environment of systemic corruption. Codes of conduct are often too general and idealistic to be of much help. The reality of systemic corruption is relative — its subjective, political characteristics elude definition and agreement. Public servants cannot get "up to code" in corrupt systems because systemic corruption has the power to effectively insulate the corrupt from denunciation and removal. Yet, the inability to adhere to codes of conduct adds to the ceaseless criticism of the public service.

Codes of conduct miss the mark because they are directed at the wrong target — the good public servants who follow them, not the corrupt ones.[30] The real target should be corrupt conduct. A new process of socialization within the civil service and among the public seems to be the best remedy for systemic corruption.[31] Codification of corruption would serve as a social reference point. For example, the New York City Police Department has devised an administrative manual which provides for the identification of corruption, including procedures for control, enforcement policy and accountability.[32]

Clearly, to make inroads into systemic corruption, a genuine public service ideology must be cultivated. Bold and informed administrative and political initiatives and active if not violent dissent could make the prospects for administrative reform brighter than they have been for some decades.[33]

Endnotes

1. G. E. Caiden, Postscript: "Public Administration and Administrative Reform," in G.E. Caiden and H. Siedentopf (eds.), *Strategies for Administrative Reform.* (Lexington, Massachusetts: Lexington Books, 1982) 231.
2. J. A. Truelson, *Blowing the Whistle on Systematic Corruption* (PhD dissertation). Los Angeles, California: School of Public Administration, University of Southern California, 1986.
3. Code of Conduct for Government Service, Public Law 96-303, October 1, 1980.
4. For discussions on the difficulties of defining corruption, see James C. Scott, *Comparative Political Corruption.* Englewood Cliffs, New Jersey: Prentice-Hall, 1972: 3-9; Susan Rose-Ackerman, *Corruption: A Study in Political Economy.* New York: Aca-

demic Press, 1978: 6-10; Arnold J. Heidenheimer (ed.), *Political Corruption: Readings in Comparative Analysis*. New York: Holt, Reinhart and Winston, 1970: 3-64; Michael Johnston, "Systematic Origins of Fraud, Waste and Abuse,' in: J.B. McKinney and M. Johnston (eds.), *Fraud, Waste and Abuse in Government*. Philadelphia, Pennsylvania: ISHI Publications, 1986: 16-17.

5. G.E. Caiden, "Public Maladministration and Bureaucratic Corruption', in McKinney and Johnston (1986: 32); J.S. Nye, "Corruption and Political Development: A Cost-Benefit Analysis," *American Political Science Review* 61: 416.

6. F.A. Elliston, "Anonymity and Whistleblowing," *Journal of Business Ethics* 1: 168.

7. Civil Service Reform Act of 1978, 5 USC 2302, 1978.

8. U.S. Congress, House Committee on Post Office and Civil Service, *Whistleblower Protection: Hearings Before the House Subcommittee on Civil Service, 99th Congress, May 15, June 18, 26, 1985*. Washington, DC: U.S. Government Printing Office, 1985: 16-21.

9. U.S. Merit Systems Protection Board, Office of Merit Systems Review and Studies, *Blowing the Whistle in the Federal Government*. Washington, DC: U.S. Government Printing Office, 1984: 39.

10. H.C. Finney and H.R. Lesieur, "A Contingency Theory of Organizational Crime', in: S.B. Bacharach (ed.), *Research in Sociology of Organizations,* Vol. 1. Greenwich, Connecticut: JAI Press, 1982: 258.

11. M.A. Parmelee, J.P. Near and T.C. Jensen, "Correlates of Whistleblowers' Perceptions of Organizational Retaliation', *Administrative Science Quarterly* 27: 30.

12. G.E. Caiden and N.J. Caiden, "Administrative Corruption," *Public Administration Review* 37: 305-308.

13. G.E. Caiden, "Public Maladministration and Bureaucratic Corruption," in McKinney and Johnston (1986: 32).

14. See, for example, M.D. Ermann and R.J. Lundman, *Corporate and Governmental Deviance: Problems of Organizational Behavior in Contemporary Society,* (2nd ed). New York: Oxford University Press, 1982: 55-67; Rose-Ackerman (1978); L.W. Sherman, *Scandal and Reform: Controlling Police Corruption*. Berkeley, California: University of California Press, 1978.

15. R. Nader, P.J. Petkas and K. Blackwell (eds.), *Whistle-Blowing: The Report of the Conference on Professional Responsibility*. New York: Grossman Publishers, 1972: 40.

16. J.D. Hanrahan, *Government by Contract*. New York: W.W. Norton, 1983: 38-39.

17. G.E. Caiden, *Police Revitalization*. Lexington, Massachusetts: Lexington Books, 1977: 151-169.

18. G.E. Caiden and N.J. Caiden, *op. cit.* 306-307.

19. See D.R. Cressy, *Other People's Money*. Glencoe, Illinois: Free Press, 1953, for discussion of negative case analysis: see also "Method of Difference' in John Stuart Mill, *A System of Logic*. Vol. 1. London: Longmans, Green, 1975: 452.

20. Cressey (1953: 16).

21. L.H. Kidder, *Selltiz, Wrightsman and Cook's Research Methods in Social Relations* (4th ed). New York: Holt, Reinhart and Winston, 1981: 105.

22. See U.S. Merit Systems Protection Board, Office of Merit Systems Review and Studies, *Whistleblowing and the Federal Employee*. Washington, DC: U.S. Government Printing Office, 1981, Appendix A; Kane, Parsons and Associates, *Engineers Survey*. New York, 1983: 1-16.

23. *Connick v. Myers,* 461 U.S. 138 (1983).

24. P. Raven-Hansen, "Protecting Whistleblowers: Can We and Should We?' First Wednesday Lecture, George Washington University National Law Center, June 1, 1983: 16-19.

25. U.S. Government Accounting Office, *Whistleblower Complaintants Rarely Qualify for Office of the Special Counsel*. Washington, DC: U.S. Government Printing Office, GGD-85-33, May 10, 1985: 17.

26. "Whistleblower Protection Opposed by Special Counsel, Justice,' *BNA Government Employee Relations Report,* Vol. 24, February 24, 1986, no. 1151.

27. Sherman (1978: 60-61).

28. S.B. Werner, "New Directions in the Study of Administrative Corruption', *Public Administration Review* 43: 152.

29. J.A. Truelson, "Protest is Not a Four Letter Word," *Bureaucrat* 14: 24.

30. G.E. Caiden, "Public Service Ethics: What Should be Done?,' in K. Kernaghan and O.P. Dwivedi (eds.), *Ethics in the Public Service: Comparative Perspectives*. Brussels: International Institute of Administrative Sciences, 1983: 162.

31. *Ibid,* p. 168.

32. *Ibid,* p. 168-170.

33. G.E. Caiden, "Reform and Revitilization in American Bureaucracy,' in R. Miewald and M. Steinman (eds.), *Problems in Administrative Reform*. Chicago: Nelson-Hall, 1984: 264.

Whistle-Blower, GSA Settle
Former Buildings Supervisor to Receive $560,000

Bill McAllister

The federal government has agreed to pay what lawyers said is a record $560,000 to settle a dispute with a former whistle-blower who was ordered reinstated this summer, five years after he was fired from his job as maintenance supervisor for most government buildings in Washington.

Lawyers for Bertrand G. Berube, a former General Services Administration executive who angered the agency's political appointees with his repeated charges that they were allowing federal buildings to deteriorate into hazardous conditions, described the award yesterday as the largest settlement of a civil service dispute ever agreed to by the federal government.

They said it will allow Berube, the highest-ranking whistle-blower to win a legal appeal, to retire with honor.

On what basis can public managers judge whether the Berube legal judgment is a "Pyrrhic victory for whistle-blowers generally" as one of Berube's lawyers moaned? Or is it a "tremendous victory" as the Director of the Government Accountability Project in D.C. remarked?

"It's a tremendous victory, obviously," said Louis A. Clark, one of Berube's attorneys and director of the Government Accountability Project, a nonprofit group that had championed his case.

In July, the Merit Systems Protection Board ruled that GSA had failed to prove it had a valid basis for firing Berube in 1983 and ordered him reinstated.

But Berube said GSA told him that his old job as head of GSA National Capital Region was filled and instead offered him a deputy regional administrator's job in Philadelphia.

"I really had precious little choice but to retire," Berube said. ". . . It was fairly clear, obviously they were not going to give me a position that was meaningful in any way.

"A deputy's job is not too dissimilar to a vice president's job. It's a do-nothing job . . . where you want to so-call rubber room someone."

Berube also said the move to Philadelphia would take him away from Washington, where he has lived for 25 years and where "there are so many problems to solve."

When Berube refused the Philadelphia job, GSA offered him a settlement, based on accumulated back pay, leave, legal fees and interest. The settlement was first reported this week by *The Washington Times*.

In his Washington job, Berube had infuriated high GSA officials with his repeated charges that the savings they were claiming came at the cost of neglecting the condition of many major buildings. Congressional investigators say many of Berube's complaints about health and safety hazards appear to have been valid.

Paul Costello, a GSA spokesman, confirmed yesterday that the agency has agreed to give the Government Accountability Project a check for $530,000 to settle the dispute, but declined to comment on Berube's charge that GSA would not offer him a meaningful position.

Clark said that after legal fees of $180,372 are deducted, Berube, who has been operating a woodworking firm in Beltsville, will receive approximately $349,000. In addition, Berube and his lawyers said the government will pay another $24,000 into his government retirement account and give the District government $6,000 in reimbursement for unemployment funds Berube received after his firing.

Berube said he expects to have "a little over $200,000" after taxes, a sum he said he will invest for retirement. "My life isn't going to change that much," he said.

By remaining in the area, Berube said he can continue to run his woodworking firm and work with the Government Accountability Project. "I will be working every day with whistle-blowers," he said.

As a result of the July ruling, Clark said Berube's retirement pay, initially $32,500 a year, should total $440,000 more than it would have been otherwise.

Source: Bill McAllister, "Whistle-Blower, GSA Settle," *Washington Post* September 3, 1988, p. A2.

At the time of Berube's firing, Clark said then-GSA Administrator Gerald P. Carmen told associates the agency would take the dispute to the Supreme Court, if necessary. But after the July ruling, GSA lawyers "were more anxious to settle," Clark said.

"They were happy to get the Berube case behind them and the attitude toward Bert, which had existed at the office five years ago, had dissipated."

Berube wanted his old job back, but he realized that would require "a couple of years more litigation," Clark said.

Thomas Devine, another of Berube's lawyers, described the case as a "Pyrrhic victory for whistle-blowers generally" because of subsidiary rulings in the case that he said will make it difficult for other federal workers who complain about their agencies to prevail.

Case 11: Greasing the Skids and Blowing the Whistle

Discretion is an important management tool which provides flexibility which is often characterized as the 'red tape' of public administration. Yet, discretion applied promiscuously, as suggested in the following case, raises serious ethical quandaries. Does the ASPA Whistle Blowing statement assist in clarifying the questions?

This scenario presents the dilemma of a case worker who discovers that another very popular and successful case worker is violating procedures and abusing discretion. He must decide whether to "blow the whistle."

Characters
*Charlie Farah — Case Worker, State Department of Human Services
Lil Gunther — Case Worker, State Department of Human Services
Harry Hoffman — Case Worker, State Department of Human Services
Mary Kirk — Senior Case Worker, State Department of Human Services*

Scene
Charlie, Lil, and Harry are standing around Lil's desk drinking coffee from plastic cups Harry has just brought in.

Charlie: Do you mind if I talk to you people about something serious for a moment . . . ? I'm really concerned about Mary. I know she has the largest case load and the highest placement rate in the office and I hate to cause trouble, but . . .

Lil: What's the problem, Charlie? Has Mary been ribbing you again? She has to be the jolliest person I know. Always laughing and joking.

Charlie: I'm afraid this is no joke, Lil. Two weeks ago, a man by the name of Shirley Boobar came in to see me. His son Willis had been one of Mary's cases. Boobar said that Mary had treated his son shabbily. He claimed that Mary had a bias against backwoods people and had foisted his son off on some pig farmer by agreeing to inflate the boy's subsistence allowance. The father says that the boy is supposed to go to school, but instead he works all day for the farmer and Mary looks the other way to keep the placement.

Harry: The guy has got to be cracked. Mary was just named State Employee of the Year by the Governor. She has one of the finest reputations and cleanest service records in state government. She has done a lot of good for a lot of people. I hope that when I'm getting ready to retire, as she is, people think half of me what they think of her.

Charlie: Unfortunately, the guy isn't cracked, Harry. I checked it out. It looks like Boobar is right. I looked into several of Mary's other cases. She plays pretty fast and loose with procedures and the paper work doesn't always accurately reflect what's going on.

Source: Edward B. Laverty, Northeastern University.

Lil: Are you sure about this? Have you talked to Mary?

Charlie: I talked to Mary, all right. I first asked her about inflating a client's subsistence payments to pay off placements for taking her clients. She said that when I had been in the business as long as she had, I'd know all kinds of ways to "grease the skids, too." Why, she asked, did I think her placement rate was so high? "You have to learn the tricks of the trade."

Harry: Well, maybe what she's doing isn't strictly correct, but she puts a lot of people in positive living environments who might otherwise be in pretty bad situations. Like I said, she has done a lot of good for a lot of people.

Charlie: Maybe for a lot of people, Harry, but apparently not all the people. I also asked her about Boobar's claim that she was biased against backwoods people and that she looked the other way when his son was used for manual labor instead of going to school.

Lil: She denied that, didn't she?

Charlie: She said some types of people were "just plain ignorant." Others, who were smarter, had a much better chance of eventually leading socially productive lives. She felt her time and limited state resources were better spent on those with the greatest chance of success. People like the Boobar boy would learn all they needed to know working on the pig farm. So what, she said, if she was a little flexible with the rules, the state was getting its money's worth.

Harry: What are you going to do, Charlie?

Charlie: I've got to report her. What she is doing is wrong. I'm going to file a formal report and complaint.

Lil: Charlie, think about this. She's an institution. As Harry says, she has helped a lot of people. She'll be retiring in a few years. She has a spotless record. She has a lot of friends who wouldn't want to see her get hurt. People could take this as over-ambition or sour grapes on your part, Charlie. You could get hurt by this.

Harry: Listen to Lil, Charlie. Who do you think you are — the white knight, Mr. Clean? Leave it alone, Charlie, it's not your responsibility. You know what happens to whistle blowers. You've got your career to think about.

QUESTIONS TO START THE DISCUSSION

1. Is there an ethical conflict here?

2. Is flexible application of procedures and the doctoring of paper work ever justified?

3. Should Charlie "blow the whistle?"

11. Styles and Strategies of Managing Openness

Dealing With Dissent:
Learning to Listen for an Ethical Organization
Richard A. Loverd

> *Know how to listen, and you will profit*
> *even from those who talk badly.*
> Plutarch

> *He who is convinced against his will*
> *Is of the same opinion still.*
> Robert Burns

Richard Loverd argues that managerial listening in an organization can be a valuable alternative to the painful processes of whistle blowing. As he notes, however, listening and openness might also entail risks or difficulties. Should all managers opt for strategies of greater openness?

When Whistles Wail

In a recent article, a disillusioned whistle-blower recounted the following recurrent dream:

> . . . It's a dark and nasty night; I'm at one of those roadside telephone booths, with an important call to make, but the person inside won't give up the phone. When he does, I have only one quarter; I drop it, pick it up and put it into the slot; the phone malfunctions. I press the buttons futilely, sometimes garbling the number I want, sometimes getting a wrong number — but no matter what I do, my call won't go through.

> Having learned, the painful way, that there are no "right" choices for a whistle-blower — only a series of choices that are all "heads they win, tails I lose" — would I, confronted with the choice again, make the same decision? I'd like to think that I would, but I'd also like to think that, this time, someone would answer the phone.[1]

Unfortunately, in all too many instances, this sort of dream is very much the reality for whistle-blowers: *whistles wail, but no one listens.* Moreover, by the time the shrill blast sounds, the level of managerial conflict, concealment and cacophony may be so great as to limit any possible resolution of whistle-blower grievances. Instead, high level legalistic salvos of charges and countercharges may be exchanged by managers with few questions satisfactorily answered, careers ruined and little long term positive benefit.

Source: Richard A. Loverd, "Dealing with Dissent: Learning to Listen for an Ethical Organization."

What can be done to deal with dissent? Because whistle-blowing constitutes a desperation effort on the part of the dissenter and stands near the extreme end of the conflict continuum, other more preventative questions for managers suggest themselves. For example, it might be asked whether whistles are perceived as providing the only realistic recourse for those seeking to disagree with their organizations; and if this is so, this view could in turn imply that managers are proving less than effective in dealing with dissent *before* it reaches the whistle-blowing stage. Furthermore, such ineffectiveness may tend to signal a certain lack of skill, or will, on the part of managers to listen to conflict at *any* level of intensity.

In this article, the development of the managerial skill and stomach to deal with dissent before it reaches crisis proportions will be of central concern. Such a responsibility is no easy task. In fact, it will be stressed that *the courage of managers to listen is every bit as important as the courage of grievants to speak out;* for only through listening can one begin to move toward the resolution of conflicts. As Peter Drucker has observed,

> . . . it is the recipient who communicates. The so-called communicator, the person who emits the communication, does not communicate. He utters. Unless there is someone who hears, there is no communication. There is only noise.[2]

And for that matter, without effective listening, there remain people "of the same opinion still," with little inclination toward early detection and constructive resolution of problems.

Consequently, in the pages that follow, an emphasis will be placed upon the need for managers to be willing to assume the responsibility to listen to dissenters by *opening channels* so that the way is clear for grievants to raise issues; by *enhancing reception,* through proven managerial authority and accessibility; and by *turning up the volume,* through the encouragement of heightened differences of opinion which require managers to work with conflict, and make conflict work, for an ethical organization.

Opening Channels

How open is the manager's door? When employees have questions, do they hesitate to ask? Are there many or only limited ways in which to hear dissent? In short, just how willing are managers to go beyond the boilerplate and open the channels necessary to listen?

As a first step toward answering these questions, managers should investigate the array of channels currently available to grievants, and where possible, make certain to provide unorthodox as well as orthodox avenues for dissent. For example, besides listening through hierarchy, managers might consider creating independent review boards, ombudsmen, or separate investigative units. In this regard, an investigative board that has come to be known as the "Shriver Prescription" was established by Sargent Shriver during his tenure as head of the Peace Corps and the Office of Economic Opportunity. Through his "prescription," an independent reporting outfit was inaugurated, completely separate from the normal chain of command, with its mission to roam the field, find out what was going on, and report directly back to its head, Sargent Shriver. In so doing, "The chain of command could be dragged in later to argue and explain itself, but the evaluation reports wouldn't be filtered through it."[3] Thus, in a very real sense, new channels were created to gather information that might otherwise be missed or distorted through the more traditional ones.

The grapevine provides yet another useful albeit unorthodox avenue for dissent. While there are those who may wish to ignore it, they do so at their own peril; for the grapevine tends to enhance and complement some of the more formal methods of communication. Moreover, studies show it to be efficient, spreading information faster than most management communications systems,[4] and surprisingly accurate, with 75 percent of its views valid.[5] Thus, keeping an ear to the grapevine is well worth the manager's time, particularly given that some of the 25 percent of the information may require correction.

In addition to the preceding *structural* aspects of communication channels, managers should also consider their *mode* when assessing how open they tend to be. In particular, the degree of dependence placed upon written communication needs to be examined. How dependent are managers on memoranda and other more formal methods of reporting when discovering or diagnosing a problem? When one considers the golden bureaucratic dictum "Never to write if you can say it, and never say it if you can nod your head,"[6] or the similar caveat from Dean Acheson noting that "A memorandum is written not to inform the reader but to protect the writer,"[7] there tend to be gaps in this mode of written listening. In fact, most managers know this, since virtually all studies of management communication indicate a very strong preference for verbal over written communication, with estimates indicating that verbal approaches take up from 57 to 89 percent of their time.[8]

The benefits of verbal over written modes are considerable. As Henry Mintzberg notes,

> Documented communication requires the use of a formal subset of the language, and involves long feedback delays. All verbal media can transmit, in addition to the messages contained in the words used, messages sent by voice inflection and by delays in reaction. In addition, face-to-face media carry information transmitted by facial expression and by gesture.[9]

Therefore, the manager who remains in his or her office, pouring over written words for answers, may be presented with only a partial opportunity to find them. Only by seeking out verbal, and preferably face-to-face contact, can the manager begin to uncover the actions that express, or belie, the written words.

Enhancing Reception

Even with channels open, there is still no guarantee that dissenters will be inclined to use them. Therefore, to enhance reception from dissenters, managers need to demonstrate *authority* and *accessibility* through their actions.

To prove authority, managers need to legitimize their roles[10] as individuals capable of demonstrating the capacity for positive action and following through on employee requests (after all, if they cannot, or will not "deliver," why approach them?). In so doing, they should be considered able, in the sense of being technically skillful, and they should be credible, by knowing the "rules of the game," the norms and the expectations that exist in their particular workplaces. They should have a history of being able to bring back benefits and protection/autonomy for their employees, and they should be regarded as persistent in the face of adversity.

To prove accessibility, managers need to show a personal loyalty toward those they manage and create a feeling of approval[11] among them which suggests that each is valued as an individual. Each should feel that the manager is "out to help me" rather than "out to get me." Only then can the manager expect loyalty, and information, to flow toward his or her office.

This feeling of mutual loyalty and accessibility is more likely to result when managers take a personal interest in employees. They should take the time to get to know them by being equally available to *all* who seek them out, thereby expressing a *genuine* open door policy. Furthermore, they should take the initiative and seek out employees by maintaining regular and frequent contacts with them. Even in instances where these contacts consist of "small talk," they create opportunities for employees to bring up problems which are of concern to them. In so doing, the manager enhances reception by letting employees decide what subjects should be discussed and by encouraging them to speak out.

When listening to employee problems, managers should use the skills of nondirective interviewing[12] as much as possible. Such skills attempt to avoid predetermined conclusions and stress the need for the interviewee, rather than the interviewer, to direct the interview. They also recognize the need to treat the interview as a series of distinct sequential stages, starting with an acknowledgement of *feelings* followed by examination of the *facts,* and leading to suggested *solutions.* During the feelings stage, the interviewee is encouraged to let off steam and express feelings. Only after having allowed for this emotional release, does one proceed to address the facts, once again providing the interviewee the widest possible latitude in presenting them. Then, once the facts have been put forth, the interviewee is asked to suggest a series of solutions and recommend the best one.

Through these nondirective skills, ideas can be expressed without being filtered through the preconceived notions of the interviewer or the need for the interviewee to make a good impression. Also, with the employee encouraged to talk freely in front of a sympathetic listener, a greater sense of catharsis, or relief, can be obtained, even if the sources of dissent should prove insoluble. Indeed, the very willingness of the manager to "hear out" the employee may generate a great deal of goodwill. And finally, by allowing the interviewee to present thoughts on his or her own terms, the mere act of "thinking out loud" may be enough to bring the employee's problems into focus and lead to their resolution through the employee's own shift in attitudes and efforts and without any further need for managerial intervention.

Of course, the interview may also uncover a deficiency in the organization which seems to require direct intervention by the manager. At this stage, the manager must decide whether to move from listening to action. If he acts on the employee's behalf, he will probably win more goodwill and responsiveness from that individual. Then again, the employee may be wrong. Moreover, what the manager previously knows may be in direct contradiction to what the employee has said, causing a form of "cognitive dissonance." How can the manager be certain whose facts, and remedies, are correct?

Turning Up The Volume

The possibility remains that, despite open channels and enhanced reception, some dissenters may still be loath to speak out, and what is heard from others may present only a self-serving suboptimal part of the picture. As well, if there is cognitive dissonance between what the manager previously knows and what the employee is saying, there may be a very great temptation to "shoot the messenger" by discounting the employee's story, smoothing over the outcry and avoiding the issue entirely.

At base, what is needed is a willingness to hear and encourage differences of opinion, a task which is not always easy. Indeed, as Harlan Cleveland has noted,

> It is too easy to get people to cooperate. People are, if anything, too conformist. That is why the executive's most difficult task is almost precisely the reverse of inducing cooperation. It is to maintain an adequate degree of tension within the organization — enough fruitful friction among its members so that all possible points of view are weighed . . .[13]

Therefore, to counteract conformity, *conflict,* the existence of "fruitful friction," should be viewed as a way to turn up the volume and help managers hear more about the dimensions of the larger picture which can help improve the quality of their actions. In so doing, conflict can serve to improve the caliber of decisions made,[14] stimulate creativity and innovation,[15] foster a climate of self-evaluation and change, allow all points, even unusual and minority views, to be considered in important decisions, and serve as an antidote for "groupthink."

In particular, the danger of groupthink, "the deterioration of mental efficiency, reality testing and moral judgment that results from in-group pressures . . . when the members' strivings for unanimity override their motivation to realistically appraise alternative courses of action . . . and foster premature consensus,"[16] is a very real one. As Cleveland observes, "many errors of judgment can be traced to too much consensus too early in the game."[17] For example, during the Eisenhower Administration, he notes that

> . . . there were complaints that Sherman Adams, who managed the White House staff, systematically prevented disagreements from reaching the President. The technique was described to me by a participant at the time: sensing a disagreement between two Cabinet members, Adams would persuade them not to raise the subject with the President in the Cabinet meeting but instead to meet with Adams afterward. After the first ten minutes of the private meeting, it would become clear that the two officials were diametrically opposed to each other on the basic issue of public policy. Adams would then suggest going through the policy paper paragraph by paragraph. Even the most acrimonious disagreement can be effectively buried if enough double-meaning words are used . . . ("One can always get an agreed paper by increasing the vagueness and generality of its statements," said Dean Acheson. "The staff of any interdepartmental committee has a fatal weakness for this kind of agreement by exhaustion.") Adams and the Cabinet members would then go in to President Eisenhower, who would inquire whether there was agreement — which there was, on the paper if not on the buried

issue. Pleased at the signs of cooperation within the Administration and completed staff work by his assistant, the President would then approve the paper, leaving the policy untouched.[18]

Thus, the desire to quell conflicts and smooth over disputes by looking and hearing the other way can lead to a misrepresentation of reality.

Of course, such problems of groupthink are hardly unique to the Eisenhower administration; other presidencies suffered from similar instances. Included among them would be President Kennedy and the Bay of Pigs fiasco, President Johnson and the Vietnam war escalation, and Richard Nixon and the Cambodian bombing and Watergate cover-up.[19] Each of these cases provides ample evidence of a common lesson: "too much agreement from too narrow a group, makes for decisions that don't 'work.'"[20]

Therefore, wide consultation, and the differences of opinion that come with it, should be encouraged to surface, and should be heard.[21] In fact, some management observers go further and urge that conflict be "deliberately induced" to maintain "a degree of tension within the organization, enough loud and cheerful argument among its members so that all possible outcomes are analyzed, the short-term benefits are compared with the long-run costs, [and] the moral dilemmas are illuminated . . ."[22] Indeed, Stephen Robbins notes that

> Too few administrators accept, and almost none attempt to stimulate, conflict. It is true this conflict is uncomfortable and that it can be a source of problems. But additionally true, and that is what is paramount to the administrator, conflict is absolutely necessary in organizations if they are to maintain their viability and to increase the probability of their surviving. One may speculate that the reason administrators are paid the highest salaries in organizations is to compensate for their supposed acceptance of conflict. A good part of their remuneration may be viewed as "combat pay" to work in an environment that is, and must be, constantly uncomfortable.[23]

There are various ways in which one might stimulate discomfort. One means to get creative juices flowing could be through forceful, direct personal behavior, perhaps best exemplified by an encounter between U.S. Army Comptroller General William Reeder and a colonel in charge of a budget unit at an Army base who told him proudly that, "This year, for the first time I can remember, we in the field agree completely with the planning figures we have received from the Pentagon." General Reeder was not pleased. "That makes either you or the man that did the Washington estimate surplus to the Army's needs," he retorted. "Which of you shall I fire?"[24]

Of course, other less harrowing approaches to stimulating conflict and creativity exist. For example, Robbins points out that conflicts can be encouraged through alterations in communication and structure as well as through personal behavior.[25] In the instance of communication, managers can deviate from traditional channels and use more unorthodox means to send information, thereby redistributing knowledge, and power, to stir the organization. They can also selectively repress information, transmit too much information or supply ambiguous information. In this regard, the methods mastered by President Franklin Roosevelt, and related by Richard Neustadt, serve to demonstrate how managers might use information to gather and refine more:

> The essence of Roosevelt's techniques for information-gathering was competition. "He would call you in," one of his aides once told me, "and he'd ask you to get the story on some complicated business, and you'd come back after a couple of days of hard labor and present the juicy morsel you'd uncovered under a stone somewhere, and *then* you'd find out he knew all about it, along with something else you *didn't* know. Where he got his information from he wouldn't mention, usually, but after he had done this to you once or twice you got damn careful about *your* information.[26]

Structurally, conflict can also be generated through such strategies as the redefinition of jobs, the shifting of tasks and the reorganization of departments. Once again, President Roosevelt provides ample demonstration of how a manager might use structure, along with personality, to acquire information:

Not only did he keep his organizations overlapping and divide authority between them, but he also tended to put men of clashing temperaments, outlooks, ideas, in charge of them. Competitive personalities mixed with competing jurisdictions was Roosevelt's formula for putting pressure on himself, for making his subordinates push up to him the choices they could not take for themselves. It also made them advertise their punches; their quarrels provided him not only heat but information. Administrative competition gave him two rewards. He got the choices and due notice, both.[27]

Therefore, conflict, and the fruitful frictions which can accompany it, can be used to turn up the volume and broaden the manager's listening base. Indeed, as noted above, in some instances where such friction is not forthcoming, the manager should consider stimulating conflict through changes in personal behavior, communication or structure in order to keep that volume high.

Proving the Courage to Listen

While much of this article has tried to emphasize the benefits of using the listening skills of opening channels, enhancing reception and turning up the volume, there is, of course, a potential darker side. Listening is not without its risks. Channels can be poorly designed, authority and accessibility can be abused, and conflict can prove destructive to organizational health. Furthermore, if a manager listens to an unpopular person or position, he or she runs the risk of being perceived as an organizational pariah as much as the dissenter, with groupthink preferring smoothness over *any* form of dissent.

And the risks do not end there. *If* a manager takes the time to listen, the opportunity to plead ignorance as an excuse and escape responsibility for the issues discussed diminishes accordingly. Indeed, perhaps the *key question* asked during the Watergate cover-up crisis was the one posed by Senator Howard Baker when he asked, "What did the President know, and when did he know it?" a question not altogether different from the one currently being broached regarding President Reagan's possible involvement in the Iran-Contra affair.[28] If a manager knows about a problem, he can be held responsible for his knowledge *and* actions and the knowledge and actions of others responsible to him.

Thus the risks of listening are considerable, and not all managers may be up to the challenge of meeting them. Some may choose to avoid conflict and ignore dissent, while other may manage them only after they have reached crisis proportions. Still others may be more than willing to shift the responsibility to someone else in any event.

Nonetheless, there are some managers who are willing to take the risks and face the dangers because they view the costs of not knowing to be far worse, to the health of the organization and to themselves. For only by listening can one know how to improve the viability and moral fabric of one's organization and maintain some measure of self-respect. Ignorance can hardly prove a blissful guide.

Some years ago, Chester Barnard noted that "the only meaningful task of the executive is to infuse the organization with a sense of moral purpose,"[29] and listening can help achieve that. By proving the courage to listen, a manager can monitor where the organization is, where it should be going, and provide the necessary leadership to move it in the right direction. Without listening, there is no moral compass.

Be not simply good; be good for something.
Henry David Thoreau

One man with courage makes a majority.
Andrew Jackson

Styles and Strategies of
Managing Openness

Endnotes

1. Don Rosendale, "A Whistle-Blower," *New York Times Magazine,* June 7, 1987, p. 56.
2. Peter Drucker, *Management* (New York: Harper and Row, 1974), p. 483.
3. Jack Gonzales and John Rothchild, "The Shriver Prescription: How The Government Can Find Out What It's Doing," in Charles Peters and Michael Nelson, *The Culture of Bureaucracy* (New York: Holt, Rinehart and Winston, 1979), p. 119.
4. Keith Davis, *Human Relations in Business* (New York: McGraw-Hill, 1957), p. 244.
5. Keith Davis, cited in Roy Rowan, "Where Did That Rumor Come From?" *Fortune,* August 13, 1979, p. 134.
6. Esmond Wright, "Taking the Rap for Benedict Arnold," *New York Times Book Review,* July 5, 1987, p. 10.
7. James Q. Wilson, *American Government: Institutions and Policies,* 3rd Ed., (Lexington, Mass: D.C. Heath, 1986), p. 382.
8. Henry Mintzberg, *The Nature of Managerial Work* (New York: Harper and Row, 1973), p. 38.
9. *Ibid.*
10. See "Legitimating the Leadership Role" in Leonard R. Sayles, *Leadership* (New York: McGraw-Hill, 1979), pp. 37-44.
11. This section is based on a discussion in Leonard R. Sayles and George Strauss, *Human Behavior in Organizations* (New York: Prentice-Hall, 1966), pp. 186-189.
12. *Ibid.,* pp. 265-267.
13. Cited by Donald Nightingale, "Conflict and Conflict Resolution," in George Strauss, Raymond Miles, Charles Snow and Arnold Tannenbaum, *Organizational Behavior: Research and Issues* (Madison, Wisconsin: Industrial Relations Research Association Series, 1974) p. 151.
14. For more discussion of the following points, see Stephen Robbins, *Organizational Behavior* (Englewood Cliffs: Prentice-Hall, 1983), pp. 336-347.
15. See Victor Thompson, "Bureaucracy and Innovation," *Administrative Science Quarterly,* vol. 10 (1965), pp. 1-20.
16. Irving L. Janis, *Groupthink,* 2nd ed., (Boston: Houghton Mifflin, 1982), pp. 7-9.
17. Harlan Cleveland, *The Future Executive* (New York: Harper and Row, 1972), p. 17.
18. *Ibid.,* pp. 17-18.
19. See Janis, pp. 14-242, and Cleveland, pp. 17-21.
20. Cleveland, p. 21.
21. For more discussion of the need for multiple points of view, see Alexander George, "The Case for Multiple Advocacy in Making Foreign Policy," *American Political Science Review* (Sept., 1972), pp. 751-785, and "Multiple Advocacy," in Alexander George, *Presidential Decision Making in Foreign Policy: The Effective Use of Information and Advice* (Boulder, Colorado: Westview Press, 1980), pp. 191-208.
22. Cleveland, p. 22.
23. Stephen R. Robbins, *Managing Organizational Conflict,* (Englewood Cliffs: Prentice-Hall, 1974), p. 18.
24. Cleveland, p. 22.
25. Robbins, *Managing Organizational Conflict,* pp. 78-89.
26. Richard E. Neustadt, *Presidential Power* (John Wiley and Sons, 1980), pp. 115-116.
27. *Ibid.,* p. 116.
28. Stephen Pressman, "New Chief of Staff: Former Senator Baker to Succeed Regan at the White House," *Congressional Quarterly,* February 28, 1987, p. 359.
29. Cited in Laurence E. Lynn Jr., *Managing Public Policy* (Boston: Little, Brown, 1987), p. 119. See also "Executive Responsibility," in Chester Barnard, *The Functions of the Executive* (Cambridge: Harvard University Press, 1938), pp. 258-284.

Channels for Dialogue in the State Department

In the late 1970s, the U.S. Department of State devised a strategy that was consistent with Loverd's general approach. The Department sought to maximize the goals of openness and creativity by establishing several intraorganizational units dedicated to the free exchange of foreign policy ideas. Would similar openness and access work successfully in other organizations?

The increasing complexity of foreign relations requires creative thinking on the part of all who serve in foreign affairs agencies. Those who make decisions need to be presented with objective statements and analyses of problems and all responsible options for action. At all levels officers should be encouraged to consider and present valid policy alternatives, including those which may differ from established policy. This requires an environment which facilitates and promotes openness and freedom of expression, without fear of penalty.

In order to further these objectives, the Department has taken a number of official actions:

- The Secretary's Open Forum — open to members of State, AID, ICA, and ACDA — was established in 1967 to encourage the responsible presentation of independent views and to further the goals of openness and creativity.

- The Department's study of "Diplomacy for the 70s" led to a new section in the Foreign Affairs Manual (2 FAM 101) which states that "as a matter of general policy, the Chief of Mission, the Deputy Chief of Mission, and the Principal Officer of a consular post, shall encourage and support the free exchange of ideas and criticism throughout the mission."

- Another section of the Manual, 11 FAM 243, requires a principal officer to submit significant reports by subordinates on political issues even when he does not agree with the views expressed.

- At Open Forum urging, the Department also created a Dissent Channel in which any member of the foreign affairs community may address the Secretary and his Principals directly on substantive policy issues and receive a full consideration of his or her views.

- The Open Forum chairmanship was established in 1974 as a full-time elected position based in the Policy Planning Staff.

- *OPEN FORUM*, a quarterly journal, was created in 1975 to promote frank internal discussion of classified topics.

- Provisions for expression of alternative viewpoints have also appeared in instructions for regional planning systems, and new policy analyses have been encouraged by several bureaus.

The sections which follow explain the Secretary's Open Forum, the *OPEN FORUM* journal, the Dissent Channel, and other vehicles for the expression of professional opinion and dissent.

I. The Secretary's Open Forum

The Secretary's Open Forum is an internal organization open to all employees of State, ICA, AID, and ACDA. It is charged by the Secretary to serve as a direct channel for new or dissenting views — primarily on substantive foreign policy issues — to the Secretary and other senior officials. The Open Forum has one full-time position — that of Chairman. The position is located within the Policy Planning Staff, but the Chairman acts independently in carrying out his or her substantive responsibilities. In order to ensure this substantive independence, no efficiency report is prepared for the Chairman. The Chairman and Vice Chairman are elected by the members of the Open Forum and serve for one year. The Chairman appoints the Steering Group of the Open Forum and is assisted by a Program and Editorial Assistant as well as a volunteer Editor and Editorial Board.

The *OPEN FORUM* has four major functions: (1) to provide the opportunity for exchanges of views with provocative outside experts or for off-the-record discussions with government officials; (2) to provide a vehicle for the expression of employee opinion on substantive issues to the Secretary and other principal officers through the preparation and/or transmission to Principals of independent Open Forum

Source: Secretary of State, "Channels for In-House Dialogue and Creativity" (Internal State Department Memo) January 19, 1977.

position papers; (3) to provide a place for professionals to write frankly, using classified information, for their whole community in the quarterly journal of professional opinion *OPEN FORUM;* (4) to monitor the Dissent Channel.

The Chairman establishes priority policy issues for Open Forum consideration, arranges for distinguished and expert speakers in these areas to meet with the Open Forum, and chairs these sessions which concentrate on two-way exchange with the guests; organizes working groups developing Open Forum position papers for distribution or transmission to the Principals; screens other papers by individual authors and sends forward to the Principals those of sufficiently high quality to deserve their time; organizes and serves on the Editorial Board of *OPEN FORUM* (which is fully independent and elects its own new members) and, with the assistance of the volunteer Editor, handles editing and publication of the *OPEN FORUM* journal; ensures that policy proposals in the Dissent Channel receive a true reconsideration and a timely, responsible, and substantive reply; and brings to the attention of decision-makers other divergent professional opinion. The overarching responsibility of the Chairman is to help guarantee that creativity and openness are both encouraged and protected in the foreign affairs agencies.

II. The OPEN FORUM Journal

All personnel of State, AID, ICA, and ACDA are invited to submit articles suggesting, or disagreeing with, major . . . policies of the United States to *OPEN FORUM,* the quarterly professional journal of opinion on foreign policy issues published by the Secretary's Open Forum. The journal is distributed within the four agencies concerned and to posts overseas. The Editorial Board has full independence in selecting and (with the author's consent) editing articles. Articles may be classified and should be sent to room 7419, Main State.

III. The Dissent Channel

The chief objective of the Dissent Channel is to bring to light policy views which many not otherwise come to the attention of policy makers as recommendations. Top management wants to hear all ideas. The Dissent Channel neither diffuses nor brings into question the authority of middle-level managers. Ideas do not bear on rank, nor do they subvert it. Supervisors are encouraged to demonstrate their leadership by passing upward the full diversity of the professional opinion in their area. Ideally, of course, the concerned mission or office should be willing to send divergent opinion forward in the normal course of business under provisions of 2 FAM 101 and 11 FAM 243, as described above. The basic goal of the policy of openness is to encourage candid dialogue on a day-to-day basis, both within the Washington agencies and in missions abroad; the existence of the Dissent Channel should not impede that goal.

Subject matter: Use of the Dissent Channel is intended to be flexible. Messages may concern subjects that are the direct responsibility of the office or mission where the sender is located, or those policies formulated and carried out elsewhere. They may contain new ideas or suggestions as well as positions which are dissenting. The Channel should be used only if one feels that normal operating procedures will not provide for full and careful consideration of one's views by key policy makers in Washington.

Content: The chief focus of the Dissent Channel should be substantive foreign policy issues. (Contents should determine the appropriate classification.) The Channel should not be used for personal matters which may be taken up in the Director General's channel or through the Department's grievance mechanism.

Availability: The Dissent channel may be used by any employee of the Department of State, the Agency for International Development, the International Communication Agency, or the Arms Control and Disarmament Agency, in Washington or overseas.

No Clearance, No Disincentives: The spirit of the Dissent Channel is the promotion of dialogue on policy issues. Top management will not tolerate any discouragement of open policy debate in the foreign affairs agencies. Users of the Channel are encouraged to discuss issues with supervisors and to show messages to them. All traffic from a post must be authorized by the Chief of Mission or a designated subordinate. If a Dissent Channel message originating in Washington deals with the responsibility of the bureau where the employee works, the message as a general rule should be shown to the director of that bureau at the time it is transmitted. However, no clearance is required for Washington or overseas. Prompt authorization of the transmission of messages being sent as telegrams or airgrams is obligatory. It is understood that such authorization does not imply concurrence in the contents of the message. Since the chief purpose of the Dissent Channel is to encourage free expression of views, any action which may or may seem to delay or stop transmission, or to penalize the drafter for using the channel, should be reported to the Director of the Policy Planning Staff and the Chairman of the Open Forum via the Dissent Channel.

Method of Transmission: From posts abroad, a Dissent Channel message may be submitted in the form of a telegram, airgram, or memorandum:

> FROM (post)
> TO SECSTATE WASHDC
> DISSENT CHANNEL (caption line)
> SUBJECT: DISSENT CHANNEL MESSAGE: (ACTUAL SUBJECT)
>
> 1. This message transmits a Dissent Channel viewpoint of (drafter's name and office designation). Second sentence should contain drafter's wishes concerning message distribution in Washington.
> 2. Text of message.

In Washington, the following memorandum format is suggested:

> TO: S/P - Director, Policy Planning Staff
> FROM: (drafter's name)
> DISSENT CHANNEL
> SUBJECT: DISSENT CHANNEL MESSAGE: (ACTUAL SUBJECT)
>
> 1. This memorandum . . .
> 2. Text of message.

Distribution: Dissent Channel messages are distributed initially only to the Secretary of State, the Undersecretary for Political Affairs, the Executive Secretary of the Department, the Director of the Policy Planning Staff (S/P) (who has responsibility for handling and response), and the Chairman of the Secretary's Open Forum. Further distribution is determined by the Director of S/P, in consultation with the Secretary as appropriate, and as indicated by the sensitivity of the message and the desires of the drafter. *Do not mark the message NODIS,* unless you seek the wider distribution that caption produces.

Normally, in order to develop a thorough and authoritative response, further distribution could be made to the director of the regional or functional bureau with general responsibility for the issue covered, or to officers with specific expertise on the subject. Overseas posts might be consulted if deemed necessary. The Director of the concerned agency normally would be supplied with a copy. There is no other distribution outside the Department without consultation with the Secretary and the drafter of the message.

The drafter may wish a different distribution pattern from that indicated above. In some cases, the drafter may have little or no sensitivity about distribution. In other cases, it may be of importance to the drafter that information about the substance of the message, or about the fact of the message be very closely held. The drafter may prefer, for example, that direct supervisors not be informed of the message. *Such preference will be honored,* but perspective drafters should note that *the potential for impact of a Dissent Channel message may be limited* if information about the message, as well as participation in and knowledge of the content of the response, are restricted or are kept from those with specific operational responsibility. It is essential that drafters be explicit about desired distribution in the first paragraph of the message with instructions like the following:

1. Drafter does not want to restrict distribution of message (normal Dissent Channel distribution).

2. Drafter desires to limit the distribution to the Secretary only (in practice, this limits distribution to the offices of the Secretary, the Undersecretary for Political Affairs, the Executive Secretary of the Department, the Director of the Policy Planning Staff, and to the Chairman of the Open Forum.

3. Drafter suggests that distribution be made to (specific bureaus, offices or persons).

4. Drafter wishes distribution of this message to exclude (posts abroad and/or other agencies).

It is understood that the Secretary, as recipient of the message, or those acting for him may also wish to restrict the distribution it receives. Consequently, actual distribution may be more than proposed by the drafter. Persons who may have authorized access to a Dissent Channel message should not give the message further distribution.

Response: Acknowledgment of receipt and distribution of the message is sent to the drafter within one week of the message's arrival in the office of the Director of the Policy Planning Staff (S/P), and a copy is provided to the Chairman of the Open Forum. After the message has been considered, the Director of S/P, acting for the Secretary, provides the drafter with a substantive reply which addresses the policy questions, proposals, or issues presented. The response is cleared by the Chairman of the Open Forum who assures that a thorough reconsideration of policy has been made and that the issues raised have been addressed directly. Normally, the response will be in the same form (airgram, telegram, memorandum) as the original message. Distribution will be basically the same as for the incoming message: restricted according to the desires of the drafter, but if not restricted made available to the officers with relevant substantive responsibility so that they may be aware of the dialogue and of any resulting policy shifts. The goal is to reply within days of receipt of the Dissent Channel message. Complicated issues may require more time, but everything possible will be done to provide responses within a maximum of 60 days.

IV. Additional Agency Channels

All of the channels described above for promoting the free expression of views are available to all personnel of State, AID, ICA, and ACDA. *Additional* channels internal to specific agencies but also aimed at promoting creativity and openness include:

AID   Employees are encouraged to send views on policy issues directly to the Administrator. An action officer will ensure prompt response. Telegrams should be slugged "Administrator's Channel." Personal appointments are also available under the Open Door program, and there are regular Brown Bag Forum meetings on major development topics, as well as several publications that carry articles on professional services.

ICA   Employees wishing to express dissenting views to top management on ICA policy questions or ICA Program matters which they consider of major significance should utilize the cable option, "DISSENT CHANNEL" included on the envelope. In addition, Agency officers may wish to make their views known through the in-house journal, *ICA World,* or through the Young Officers Policy Panel.

ACDA   Any ACDA employee wishing to bring specific policy points to the attention of Agency senior officials may contact the Deputy Director.

V. Consultation and "Feedback"

Anyone wishing information on any of these approaches may contact, in confidence, the Chairman of the Open Forum. Use of cable and official phones [is] authorized.

The Chairman of the Open Forum and the Director of the Policy Staff welcome hearing from any member of the foreign affairs community on the specifics of the Dissent Channel procedures, and on additional means of defending internal openness or otherwise promoting foreign policy dialogue and creativity.

The Public Advocate:
A Noble Experiment That Succeeded

Rick Sinding

The New Jersey Public Advocate is charged with representing the public interest, or those interests which elected and appointed officials overlook. Does the evolution of the department from an "advocate" to more of an ombudsman negate the office's major goal of openness to the public interest?

They all seem slightly out of place, these public-interest lawyers in their faded jeans and tattered sneakers, gathering at the law library on a Saturday afternoon. It looks like it could be a reunion of The Loyal But Hopelessly Starry-Eyed Order of Quixotic Attorneys. But if it is, it is being held at the unlikeliest of locations — the stark, impersonal, and stiflingly bureaucratic setting of the Richard J. Hughes Justice Complex.

The parking lot is virtually empty, of course. This is a Saturday, after all, and this is the bureaucracy. Which makes the setting all the more unlikely for this mischievous band of rabble rousers who call themselves "the voice of the voiceless" — whose mission, in the word of one of their leaders, is to "comfort the afflicted and afflict the comfortable."

It was different when they were over on East State Street, in the Old Knights of Columbus Building. There, removed from the bureaucratic trappings of partitioned cubicles and color-coordinated carpeting, they seemed more at home. The offices were cozy, the desk tops cluttered, the ambience casual. No picture windows with views of the State House dome; no blank white walls running the length of city blocks; no fern-filled, glass-enclosed, escalatored atrium patrolled by uniformed guards. On East State Street, they wore jeans and sneakers on weekdays. It was almost as if they weren't part of government.

That's the way Brendan Byrne, then the newly elected Governor, wanted it when he proposed the creation of a Department of the Public Advocate in 1974. Byrne envisioned a cabinet-level agency answerable less to him than to the public, headed by an independent-minded commissioner who — though appointed by the Governor — would nevertheless function, in Byrne's words, as "a true spokesman for the public interest, as well as being responsive to the public will."

To that end, the Public Advocate was granted "sole discretion to represent or refrain from representing the public interest in any proceeding." The commissioner was empowered — indeed, encouraged — to initiate legal proceedings against his fellow cabinet officers if he felt their departments were not acting in their public interest.

A decade later, the purpose and mission of the Department of the Public Advocate have not changed. Nor has its resolve to take on the establishment, to pursue unpopular causes, to speak for those citizens who otherwise have no spokesman. "What's important is not to lose your sense of moral outrage," says James McGuire, who has been with the department since its founding and now serves as acting director of the Division of Citizen Complaints and Dispute Settlement. "I believe we still maintain the capability to express and exercise our moral outrage."

What has changed over the last 10 years is the means of expressing, and the method of exercising, that outrage. It is a subtle change, as subtle as the effects of the department's move from the free and easy atmosphere of East State Street to the stilted formality of the Justice Complex.

The lawyers still come in on Saturdays. But these days they are as likely to be working on consent decrees as lawsuits. The division directors and bureau chiefs are as busy as ever, but they are less likely to be preparing litigation than implementing a new set of internal policies and procedures recommended by the Governor's Management Improvement Plan. The commissioner is still challenging other departments of state government, but his approach to his cabinet colleagues is more likely to be conciliatory than confrontational.

All public agencies change over time. The novelty wears off. The public fancy is captured by something else. Attention fades, interest ebbs; what used to be unique becomes routine. "At some point," explains a high-level career state employee who has seen a half-dozen new departments created in the last two decades, "you hang up the motorcycle jackets and put on the polyester suits."

Source: Rick Sinding, "The Public Advocate: A Noble Experiment that Succeeded," *New Jersey Reporter,* July, 1984, pp. 6-11, 28-30.

That's exactly what happened at the Department of Community Affairs. After a flurry of activity in the late 1960s, it quietly sank back into the bureaucracy. The Great Society ran its course, Commissioner Paul Ylvisaker moved on, his disciples followed, and the department got a reputation as a dumping ground for political hacks.

They are not wearing polyester suits at the Department of the Public Advocate quite yet. Nor has the North Wing of the Justice Complex been overtaken by anything remotely resembling the lethargy and malaise that afflict the Community Affairs offices a few blocks away on West Street. The subtle change in the Public Advocate's manner is more one of style than of substance; it should not be mistaken for a change in policy direction.

The department and its employees remain dedicated to a set of principles — representation for the mentally ill and the handicapped, for the institutionalized and the indigent, for the accused murderer who can't afford counsel, the low-income black family that can't find decent housing in the suburbs, the middle-class white family that is denied access to the state's beaches. And since many of these principles enjoy considerably less public favor today than they did 10 years ago, the department's commitment to uphold them may be even more important in 1984 than it was in 1974.

But whether the Public Advocate can retain its unique character during the transition from a radical experiment in public-interest law to a permanent bureaucratic fixture remains to be seen. Part of the price of the department's acceptance has been its willingness in recent years to substitute conciliation for litigation, making it less an advocate than an ombudsman in the classic, Scandinavian sense. That kind of ombudsman serves as a government watchdog. The difference is that the ombudsman can only bark; the advocate can bite.

Now, on the occasion of its 10th birthday, the Public Advocate must decide whether to bark or bite. If the department resumes its aggressive posture, bringing the same kinds of controversial lawsuits against state and local agencies that it has in the past, it might be digging its own political grave. But if the Public Advocate's survival rests on its inclination to dispose of cases in the conference room instead of the courtroom, it might not be worth keeping alive.

When the Department of the Public Advocate opened its doors on June 13, 1974, there were two schools of thought on its prospects for survival. One school held that it would never last beyond the Byrne administration; its unpopular stands would alienate so many government agencies and interest groups that it would ultimately be legislated out of existence. The other school held that the department would serve as a model for the nation; once the Public Advocate proved its credibility and effectiveness in New Jersey, other states would rush to create similar departments.

Somehow, it didn't turn out either way. The Public Advocate has alienated some powerful agencies and interest groups (not to mention the Legislature) over the years, but it is in no immediate danger of being put out of business. At the same time, it remains the only agency of its kind in the country; while other states have adopted bits and pieces of New Jersey's Public Advocate — a rate counsel, a mental health advocate, a citizen complaints office — none has replicated the whole package.

"It's amazing it's been around so long," says Jack Gleeson, a former director of the Division of Citizen Complaints and Dispute Settlement who has since joined the Treasury Department's Office of Management and Budget. "It's equally amazing that it hasn't been copied anywhere else."

That anomaly is explained by the unique set of circumstances that gave rise to the creation of the Public Advocate in New Jersey 10 years ago. Had it not been conceived by the Byrne administration and delivered by the Legislature within the first few months of 1974, the Public Advocate would never have been more than a glimmer in Brendan Byrne's eye.

"The climate was just right for the Public Advocate in 1974," recalls Arthur Penn, the first director of the Division of Public Interest Advocacy and later an assistant public advocate. "I have serious doubts about whether it could ever happen now, or in a different political climate."

Proposals to create a state government ombudsman had been kicking around Trenton for several years before 1974. But it was not until the Cahill administration had been riddled by scandal, the Watergate hearings were in full swing, Byrne ("the man who couldn't be bought") had arrived in the State House, and both houses of the Legislature were in the mood for reform that the idea was taken seriously.

The two men who have guided the department through its first decade — Byrne's appointee, Stanley Van Ness, from 1974 through 1981, and Governor Thomas H. Kean's appointee, Joseph Rodriguez, since early 1982 — agree that the Public Advocate might never have seen the light of day but for the peculiar climate of the times back in 1974. "It is a radical concept," says Van Ness — not one that would likely have been adopted "in more conservative times." Rodriguez believes the department was a direct response to the "trauma to public confidence" caused by Watergate.

New Jersey is one of only a few states that does not elect an attorney general, a secretary of state, a lieutenant governor, or any other executive office-holder besides the Governor. In other states, elected cabinet officers may play the role of gadfly, curmudgeon, spy, ombudsman, or general nuisance; in New Jersey, no official held an office designed to play that role until the Public Advocate was created.

"I spent a lot of time trying to sell the idea [of a Public Advocate] to other states," says Van Ness. "In Minnesota, everybody was ready to go. But the [elected] attorney general objected." In New Jersey, according to Van Ness, the proposal faced no such obstacle. "[Former Attorney General] Bill Hyland didn't have an ego problem," he notes. More important, Hyland was not elected; he was appointed by, and answerable to, a Governor whose highest priority was restoring the public's trust and confidence in government.

In New York, says Van Ness, "Mario Cuomo did a lot as lieutenant governor to pick up pieces of the public advocate concept." In Colorado, Kentucky, South Dakota, and 11 other states, citizen complaints offices have been established. At least five states have set up offices of mental health advocacy. In more than half the states in the country, independent counsel is now provided to represent the public in utility rate cases.

But in no other state have all of these pieces of the "public advocate concept" been picked up under one roof. Neither the timing nor the political circumstances have permitted it.

So the Public Advocate, in a form virtually unchanged since 1974, remains unique to New Jersey. And the Division of Public Interest Advocacy, the only one of its kind in the country, remains the scourge of local officials in Morris County, property owners in Bay Head, and the many legislators who regret not putting it out of existence when they had the chance.

Under the 1974 statute creating the Department of the Public Advocate, the Division of Public Interest Advocacy — the department's self-described "public-interest law firm" and by far its most controversial division — was scheduled to self-destruct on December 1, 1978. It did not. Despite the division's knack for irritating everyone from nuclear power plant operators to the Boy Scouts of America, a majority of legislators was never sufficiently exercised at the same time to kill it. The division was granted permanence, along with the Office of Inmate Advocacy, in October 1977.

Still, the Legislature has found ways over the years to take aim at the Public Advocate's easiest targets. Next to the tiny Division of Advocacy for the Developmentally Disabled, which has only recently been elevated to division status, the Division of Public Interest Advocacy has the smallest staff (16) and the smallest budget ($438,000) in the department. Meanwhile, the Office of Inmate Advocacy was virtually ignored by the lawmakers for eight years; from 1975 to 1983, it received no state appropriation, and operated entirely on federal money. Now it gets $50,000 in state funds — funneled through the Office of Public Defenders.

The rest of the department is decidedly less controversial. The Public Defender accounts for the lion's share of the department's resources and staff; 585 of the department's 676 budgeted positions are in this office, and it spends about 88 percent of the department's budget. Lately, in addition to the unusual caseload of trial and appellate work for indigent defendants in criminal cases, the Public Defender has assumed the added responsibility of handling death penalty trials and appeals.

The Division of Rate Counsel has become the institutional adversary of the utilities, the phone company, the insurance industry, and other businesses with rates regulated by government agencies. The divisions of Mental Health Advocacy and Advocacy for the Developmentally Disabled represent classes of citizens whose legal interests are otherwise unrepresented. The Division of Citizen Complaints and Dispute Settlement provides a place where citizens whose grievances have been ignored by the Division of Motor Vehicles, the Department of Human Services, and other bureaucracies can go for help.

That the Public Advocate remains in business today, with no substantial change in form, is largely a tribute to Van Ness and Rodriguez. Just as the timing and the circumstances had to be exactly right to allow for the creation of the department in the first place, so have the department's commissioners had to strike the proper balance between aggressiveness and patience, between combativeness and compassion, to establish and maintain the clout and credibility of the agency.

"We have been very lucky," claims former state Senator Stephen Wiley, who harbors many nagging doubts about the office but none about the two men who have filled it. "Our public advocates have done a superb job. Stan Van Ness was faultless; Joe Rodriguez is in the same mold."

Senator Gerald Stockman (D-Trenton), who accused Rodriguez of yielding to gubernatorial influence in signing a controversial cost-containment agreement with Public Service Electric & Gas Company two years ago, nevertheless praises him as "a man of integrity, with a sincere interest in the public good and empathy for the downtrodden." According to Stockman, both Rodriguez and Van Ness have been "gifted, respected, and resolute" in the role of public advocate.

Stanley Van Ness was the perfect choice to be the state's first public advocate. He was well-versed in politics, having served as counsel to Governor Richard J. Hughes in the 1960s. He was well-versed in the law, having served as the state public defender under Governor William T. Cahill in the early 1970s. He was a widely respected lawyer, if not a universally popular one; in 1972, he handled the case which led to New Jersey's death penalty law being declared unconstitutional.

Van Ness is also black — which was not an altogether unimportant qualification for the job. (Nor is it altogether coincidental that his successor, Rodriguez, is Hispanic.) Byrne wanted very much to appoint a black cabinet officer; indeed some opponents of the Public Advocate legislation accused Byrne of creating the department for just that purpose.

Van Ness was also sure enough of himself — and of his relationship with Byrne — to strike the kind of pugnacious posture the department needed to establish its credibility. "Initially, I thought it was imperative that we demonstrate an aggressiveness, a willingness to litigate," he said in a 1979 interview. In his early days as public advocate, Van Ness was fond of comparing his task to that of the farmer who has to "smack the mule a couple of times to get his attention."

"In the beginning," Van Ness noted, "I'm sure some of the other cabinet officers thought I was a wise guy. Some took it personally when we filed a suit involving their departments."

Nevertheless, Van Ness and his band of attorneys filed lawsuits with impunity — against the state Housing Finance Agency, the Board of Public Utilities, the Division of Youth and Family Services, the Violent Crimes Compensation Board, the departments of Environmental Protection, Community Affairs, and Corrections, the Camden County Board of Freeholders, the City of East Orange, the Borough of Fort Lee, the Township of Mount Laurel, the Bay Head Improvement Association, and, on at least eight separate occasions, Institutions & Agencies (later Human Services) Commissioner Ann Klein.

"It wasn't all Ann's fault," Van Ness says today. "There were any number of cases I suppose we could have resolved. I may have been less interested in trying to negotiate as time went on because I just didn't want to go through the exercise anymore." An attorney formerly with the Division of Mental Health Advocacy summed it up this way: "Ann Klein couldn't take criticism; that's why we couldn't settle with her."

One anecdote, told often by veterans of the Van Ness-Klein wars, concerns a suit in which the Public Advocate accused the Department of Institutions & Agencies of mistreating patients in state institutions. When she was named as a defendant, Klein reportedly protested, "But I never hit anybody!"

Some of the cases the Public Advocate filed against Institutions & Agencies would probably have ended up in court even if Van Ness and Klein had been on friendlier terms. These are the cases that established important legal precedents — precedents that might not have been established had the settlements been negotiated rather than litigated. "There is no institutional reform absent institutional litigation," explains Michael Perlin, director of the Division of Mental Health Advocacy under Van Ness and later special counsel to Rodriguez. "Even with the best of legislation, there is a need to go to court to effectuate it."

The passage by the Legislature of a bill of rights for mental patients, for example, did not translate into improved conditions at state institutions until the patients, represented by the Division of Mental Health

Advocacy, went to court. In one landmark case, *Rennie v. Klein,* a U.S. District judge ruled that under certain circumstances, involuntary administration of psychotropic drugs, a common practice at state psychiatric hospitals, violated the constitutional rights of patients. In another case, *Schindenwolf v. Klein,* mental patients gained the right to work in therapeutic and vocational rehabilitation programs — and to be paid a reasonable wage for their labors.

If Van Ness' relationship with Klein was icy, his relationship with the rest of the cabinet wasn't much warmer. "There was some strain between Stanley and the rest of the cabinet," recalls John Degnan, who served as assistant counsel, then as counsel, and later as attorney general in the Byrne administration. "I would call him when I was counsel and ask him to resolve a dispute. I would try to mediate, conciliate. I remember on one occasion trying to stop him from filing a suit. But Stanley, to his credit, was almost immovable."

"I always sat in the back row at cabinet meetings with my back against the wall," Van Ness relates with a smile. "You're dealing with cabinet members, with politicians, with big egos. If you sue them, or criticize them, you shouldn't be surprised if you bruise their feelings.

"But you have to remain aloof," he adds. "You have to be totally independent."

It also helps if you have a thick skin. Van Ness' lawsuits against his fellow cabinet officers made him something of an outcast in the administration. His suits against Mount Laurel Township, filed on behalf of the South Burlington County NAACP, made him a pariah in suburban towns with exclusionary zoning ordinances. His suit against 27 of Morris County's 39 municipalities, filed on behalf of the Morris County Fair Housing Council, made him a leper from Mount Olive to Montville.

The business community wasn't exactly enamored of Van Ness either. Objections by the Public Advocate helped kill a proposal by Public Service Electric & Gas to build a floating nuclear power plant off Atlantic City. Intervention by the Public Advocate in rate cases before the Board of Public Utilities and the state Insurance and Health departments resulted in lower rate increases for some of the state's commercial giants — the utilities, the insurance companies, and New Jersey Blue Cross-Blue Shield.

In 1979, the Governor's Commission on Budget Priorities — the Byrne administration's version of what the Kean administration later called its Governor's Management Improvement Plan — recommended elimination of the Division of Public Interest Advocacy. "Its selection of issues [is] generally a reflection of the personal views and objectives of the staff," the commission of businessmen concluded. "The functions [of the division] are non-essential, unpredictable, and often doubly costly to the public, which has the privilege of paying the legal costs of both plaintiff and defendant when the division chooses to bring suit."

This is the hook upon which critics today still hang their condemnation of the Public Advocate. "All this Mount Laurel stuff in Morris County," fumes Senator Walter Foran (R-Flemington). "The taxpayers end up paying for suing and for being sued. They get it both ways." Assemblyman Walter Kern (R-Ridgewood) calls the Morris County suit (from which two-thirds of the original 27 defendant municipalities have since been dropped) a "typical example of an area where the Public Advocate should not be." The Division of Public Interest Advocacy, says Kern, is "a colossal waste of money."

Senator John Dorsey (R-Boonton Township) has introduced legislation calling for a moratorium on the low- and moderate-income housing requirements established by the state Supreme Court in its *Mount Laurel I* and *Mount Laurel II* decisions. Like Kern, he maintains that the Public Advocate has overstepped its bounds. "I believe it has been an abuse of discretion," Dorsey told the *National Law Journal* in an interview last year, "in terms of how they [the Public Advocate] use their funds and employ their resources."

In arguing that way, Dorsey argues against his own financial interest. Those funds and resources have been very good for his law practice, which, for the last six years, has been representing several of the municipalities in his Morris County district against the Public Advocate's suit.

The real issue in the Morris County case, as in the Mount Laurel cases on which it rests, is not who pays for the lawsuits but what the lawsuits are seeking to accomplish. When public money is used both to prosecute and to defend indigent clients in criminal cases, nobody raises a fuss. When tax dollars are spent to support both sides of a landmark suit establishing the legal rights of mental patients or the handicapped, few object. But when a state agency challenges local governments to defend their zoning practices, striking at the very heart of home rule, all hell breaks loose.

Home-rule advocates in the Legislature are especially upset that Rodriguez has continued the Morris County case started by Van Ness. As a candidate, Tom Kean carried Morris County by 45,000 votes; as Governor, he was expected by those who helped elect him to show some sympathy for the local GOP cause — and get the Public Advocate off their backs.

Kean has shown some sympathy; in a moment of weakness, he suggested the Mount Laurel ruling smacked of "communism" — and his administration seems content to let the courts, rather than the executive and legislative branches, dictate the terms of *Mount Laurel II*. But he has not called off the Public Advocate; Rodriguez has pursued the Mount Laurel and Morris County cases as vigorously as Van Ness did.

(The cases also hold special significance for Rodriguez. In the early 1970s, he was on the board of the Camden Regional Legal Services program, which represented the South Burlington County NAACP in the original suit against Mount Laurel Township.)

Rodriguez has also pursued the controversial case against the Bay Head Improvement Association. Though it is not nearly so contentious as the Morris County suit, this is another case with home-rule overtones; it challenges the right of a private beach association, made up exclusively of local residents, to limit beach access to its members. In an earlier case, *Van Ness v. Borough of Deal,* the courts had already ruled that municipalities could not discriminate against non-residents in the "use and enjoyment of municipal beachfront property."

If Rodriguez has made enemies in Morris and Ocean Counties for continuing unpopular litigation started by Van Ness, he has raised suspicions elsewhere for failing to initiate much in the way of litigation on his own. Rodriguez is perceived as more cautious, more sensitive to political pressure, and less inclined to rock the boat than Van Ness was.

"Stanley Van Ness was willing to lose, willing to take risks," observes one of the department's veteran lawyers. "Joe Rodriguez is not willing to lose, not willing to take risks." According to a long-time department employee, "Joe is an insider. He wants acceptance in the cabinet. Unless we find an incontrovertible case against another cabinet officer, we just don't file it." Another notes, "Rodriguez is more sensitive to the Kean administration than Van Ness was to the Byrne administration."

In the Legislature, criticism of the Public Advocate — once the exclusive preserve of the political right — is starting to come from a different direction. "You don't hear the Public Advocate challenging state government as much anymore," claims Stockman, who chairs the Legislative Oversight Committee. "Maybe it's because they've accomplished a lot already. Or maybe it's because Joe Rodriguez doesn't like confrontation. Or maybe it's because the Governor and his administration are influencing him. Joe Rodriguez is a lot closer to Tom Kean than Stanley Van Ness was to Brendan Byrne."

Suspicions of undue gubernatorial influence over the Public Advocate were first raised by Stockman after the department reached its controversial cost-containment agreement with Public Service Electric & Gas in August 1982. For years, the Public Advocate had been challenging the need for nuclear power plants in general, and for PSE&G's proposed Hope Creek 1 and Hope Creek 2 plants in particular. In part because of the Public Advocate's relentless opposition, and in the face of slow growth in the demand for electricity, the utility had already abandoned Hope Creek 2.

Then, without warning, the Public Advocate and PSE&G announced their unprecedented cost-containment agreement. In return for the utility's promise to complete Hope Creek 1 for $3.8 billion or less, the Public Advocate promised not to challenge the need for the plant. Alfred Nardelli, director of the Division of Rate Counsel, accused the Kean administration of pressuring the Public Advocate into signing the agreement, and was promptly fired by Rodriguez. Stockman's Legislative Oversight Committee held hearings, and the senator was persuaded by Nardelli's charge that the Public Advocate had "caved in" to the Governor.

"I was satisfied that we found the 'smoking gun,' that the Governor had, in fact, given the Public Advocate a signal in support of this agreement," says Stockman. "There was an acknowledgement that Kean met with Rodriguez, and there was some exchange on the cost-containment agreement. The evidence was inescapable that there was involvement by the Governor that might have influenced the decision."

Rodriguez flatly denies the accusation. "The charge that there was gubernatorial influence is totally baseless," he says. Rodriguez claims — and others in the department agree — that the cost-containment agreement was "the best deal we could cut under the circumstances." Even Van Ness recalls that Hope Creek 1 "was sufficiently far along to make it unrealistic to abandon it." According to Van Ness, the most unfortunate result of the cost-containment agreement was that it "put Joe on the defensive."

Although he denies that his department has been subject to gubernatorial influence, Rodriguez, a registered Democrat, readily admits that he considers himself part of the Kean team. "I am not supposed to be totally independent," he asserts, putting him squarely at philosophical odds with Van Ness. "When they put you in the cabinet, they don't mean for you to be totally independent." Rodriguez says his cabinet status allows him "to be heard in the highest echelons of government," where he can influence decisions affecting the rights of citizens without having to resort to litigation.

"I walk in that room and everybody there knows I could sue them," Rodriguez declares. "But what's wrong with trying to resolve a problem through conversation? The chief justice of the United States Supreme Court says we're abusing litigation. The chief justice of the New Jersey Supreme Court says we're abusing litigation. The public says we're abusing litigation. The courts are not the only forum for resolving disputes."

Rodriguez also admits that he is not a risk-taker. "I don't want to lose," he says. "You don't solve anything by losing. You can't just be emotional. You've got to be a careful lawyer. If that's my weakness, then I'll bow to that weakness. You do more violence to our system of justice if your rhetoric is ahead of your preparation and your facts."

The differences in philosophy and style between Rodriguez and Van Ness are in many ways a reflection of the differences in their backgrounds — which, in turn, influence their approaches to the law. They are a reflection, too, of the degree to which the judicial environment has changed over the last 10 years.

Van Ness came up through the political ranks, and gained his courtroom experience as a public defender. His approach to the law was to follow his instincts: Identify the issue, determine the public interest, define the transgression — then use whatever legal means you can to achieve justice. If Van Ness believed the rigorous physical tests the Boy Scouts of America required of Eagle Scout candidates discriminated against the handicapped, off he went after the Boy Scouts. If he thought floating nuclear reactors posed a danger to society, off he went after the nuclear industry.

It wasn't that Van Ness "sued first and asked questions later," as his detractors so often asserted. Rather, he asked the questions, got no satisfactory answers, and then sued. To be sure, there was a certain amount of "smacking the mule to get his attention" during the first year or two. And Van Ness, by his own admission, was not particularly patient with his adversaries. But he was usually open to what he called "reasoned discourse" as an alternative to litigation. "It is always better from the lawyer's point of view to settle a dispute than to litigate it," he says.

When Van Ness *did* litigate, the courts were generally receptive to his arguments. For one thing, he was bringing cases that broke new legal ground — defining the rights of mental patients or prison inmates, establishing guidelines for municipal zoning or beach access, setting standards for Medicaid eligibility or utility fuel adjustments. Not only did Van Ness have a clear field to bring these landmark cases (his staff called them "megasuits"); he was also fortunate enough to be bringing them in an era of judicial activism.

Today, conditions have changed. "The courts, especially the United States Supreme Court, have taken a more conservative tone in recent years," says Perlin. "This has slowed down institutional reform law in terms of prisons, mental health, and other areas." Van Ness agrees. "The U.S. Supreme Court is backing away from involvement," he says. The chances for success of a "megasuit" are simply not as great as they used to be.

Nor are there as many "megasuits" to bring. "The easy 'mega-issues' have been decided already," notes Assistant Public Advocate R. William Potter. Perlin points out that early litigation in the mental health field set precedents that led to major policy changes at state institutions. Now that the precedents have been set, he says, "It's a matter of monitoring their implementation."

Moreover, the Public Advocate is required by statute to maintain every client it agrees to represent until that client's case is disposed of. The Public Advocate cannot begin a suit on behalf of prison inmates or Medicaid patients, then drop it when a monumental zoning case comes along. As the department's workload increases, without any corresponding increase in money or manpower, there is less room in its ever-expanding files for major new litigation. "We have to be more selective these days," says Potter.

With less room in the files, with fewer identifiable "mega-issues" to pursue, and in a political and judicial climate more hostile to pursuing them, it is little wonder that Rodriguez has struck a lower profile than Van Ness. The times demand caution — and Rodriguez is, by nature, a cautious man. A former chairman of the state Board of Higher Education, a former chairman of the State Commission of Investigation, his background is in trial law, with a specialty in medical malpractice. He is patient and prudent. He likes to build his cases around irrefutable expert testimony. He wants his arguments to be air-tight.

This helps explain his distinct preference for mediation and conciliation over litigation — especially when it comes to disputes involving other departments of state government. Rodriguez *will* go to court if he has to. Corrections Commissioner William Fauver found that out when he allowed "double-bunking" in state prisons; so did Governor Kean when he set up the state's temporary biennial automobile inspection program in violation of the federal Clean Air Act. But where Van Ness went after Ann Klein's department with a vengeance, Rodriguez has pointedly refused to bring suit against her successor, Human Services Commissioner George Albanese — despite a growing sense among lawyers in the Division of Mental Health Advocacy, and elsewhere in the department, that he should.

For months, representatives of the Public Advocate and Human Services have been seeking, without success, to resolve a dispute involving patients' rights at Marlboro Psychiatric Hospital. At issue is a strict set of security procedures instituted at Marlboro after local residents complained that patients were wandering off the hospital grounds and into the community. The complaint became an uproar when one patient — a Morris County man who had been found not guilty of murder by reason of insanity — was transferred from the notorious Vroom Building at Trenton Psychiatric Hospital to Marlboro.

The new security provisions at Marlboro restricted the movement of patients to their cottages and wards. The Division of Mental Health Advocacy investigated, and concluded that this violated the state law entitling mental patients to be confined "in the least restrictive setting necessary for treatment." Moreover, Marlboro was "warehousing" patients — assigning them to cottages and wards on the basis of what county they came from rather than what affliction they suffered from or what treatment they needed. The hospital had no admissions unit; it offered few therapeutic programs for patients; staff members complained that they felt more like wardens than therapists.

A formal list of demands was drawn up, signed by Rodriguez, and sent to Albanese. Human Services responded by setting up its own fact-finding panel — which, after confirming the problems identified by the Public Advocate, blamed many of them on the hospital's former chief executive officer. The panel also agreed with the major findings of the Public Advocate: that the hospital needed to be reorganized, with an admissions unit established and patients grouped by diagnosis rather than by county origin. The panel also recommended building higher fences, and beefing up border patrols, as an alternative to restricting the movement of patients.

These recommendations were presented to Albanese in late March. He promised to implement them by May 1. Yet as of mid-June, only an admissions unit was in place; Human Services was still working on a plan for changing the "catchment areas" to which patients were assigned, and patients were still limited in their movement to the immediate vicinity of their cottages and wards.

"The level of restriction is still unduly high," according to Laura LeWinn, acting director of the Division of Mental Health Advocacy. "It is having a negative and antitherapeutic impact on patients." Although LeWinn claims that "litigation is not out of the picture," others wonder why litigation hasn't been instituted already. "Stanley would have sued long ago," says one disgruntled department lawyer.

Why hasn't Rodriguez sued? "I am waiting for a report," he says. "I want to see exactly what the security situation is. I want an expert opinion. I can't simply follow my instincts. If we litigate, I want them to know we have a good chance of winning."

It is this caution — some critics call it inaction — that has come to mark the Public Advocate under Rodriguez. Another case involving the rights of deaf and hearing-impaired patients in mental hospitals has been awaiting disposition for over two years. This past spring, after the Board of Public Utilities awarded PSE&G a $289 million rate increase — six times the amount recommended by the Division of

Rate Counsel — the division did not appeal the decision. Instead, a group of private citizens, headed by former state Senator Anne Martindell, has asked the Public Advocate to represent them in an appeal. According to an attorney familiar with the case, an appeal by the Public Advocate itself "should have been automatic."

Joe Rodriguez must get awfully tired of hearing people tell him, "Stanley would have sued." It's a little like the latest center fielder for the New York Yankees being told, "Mickey would have caught the ball." Maybe so, the humbled rookie thinks to himself — but when all is said and done, I'll throw the runner out at home.

It is not altogether fair to hold Rodriguez to the same standards of performance as Van Ness. They are different people performing their jobs in different administrations under different political circumstances and different judicial climates. Van Ness molded the Department of the Public Advocate in his image — activist, independent, confrontational. That Rodriguez has chosen a more collegial, conciliatory approach does not automatically make him, or the department, any less effective.

In fact, there are some who believe Rodriguez's style is more appropriate to the office. Setting public policy, they say, is the responsibility of the Governor and the Legislature, not the Public Advocate and the courts. When the Public Advocate brings lawsuits in the name of the "public interest," asking the judiciary to provide remedies that are best left to the executive and legislative branches, it is usurping the constitutional prerogatives of those branches. Litigation becomes an accepted method of policy-making, and the Governor and the Legislature are effectively encouraged to side-step tough policy decisions.

"I find it questionable to have issues that ought to be settled by elected representatives — the Governor and the Legislature — being settled by the judiciary," says Stephen Wiley. "If I were Governor, and my public advocate were suing my commissioner of Human Services, I'd have these guys at a cabinet meeting and ask them why they can't settle it. The commissioner of Human Services being sued by the public advocate so some assignment judge can decide whether Greystone Hospital is getting enough money does not seem to me an appropriate way to make public policy."

John Degnan agrees. "The courts weren't elected," he says. "The Governor and the Legislature were." When the Public Advocate takes a dispute to court rather than settling it within the administration, Degnan claims, it invites "judicial intrusion" upon executive and legislative authority.

The former attorney general also challenges the assumption that the Public Advocate can — or even should — exercise complete independence from the Governor's office. "From my point of view," he says, "there is nothing wrong with the Governor trying to influence the Public Advocate. Unless the issue is one of constitutional protection, I have no problem with the Governor calling up the Public Advocate and offering suggestions." According to Degnan, "Where important public-policy issues are involved, it is appropriate for the Governor to be involved."

Wiley and Degnan raise insightful intellectual arguments — but their views are not widely shared in political or legal circles. While Van Ness admits, "In a balance-of-power sense, the courts probably shouldn't be deciding how many square feet a prison inmate should have," he defends the Public Advocate's pursuit of public-policy objectives through the courts. "A lot of these decisions require the expenditure of public funds, and require action and policy direction by elected officials," he says. "But when nothing is being done, or when only the majority is being represented, the minority needs representation too."

Arthur Penn offers a similar view. "Public policy *should* be shaped by elected officials," he agrees, "but there is nothing wrong with public policy being set by the courts, once it is apparent that the executive and legislative branches have failed to act." Stockman calls Wiley "naive" in his belief that the executive and legislative branches would tackle the tough policy issues if the Public Advocate and the courts didn't offer a convenient excuse to avoid them. "In the real world," says the senator, "it just doesn't work that way."

Van Ness strongly disagrees with Degnan's assertion that the Public Advocate should be responsive to gubernatorial influence. "If the Governor wants just an ombudsman or an adviser," Van Ness argues, "he's already got his counsel and his attorney general." (It's instructive to recall that Degnan served Brendan Byrne in both capacities.) "The purpose of the Public Advocate," Van Ness adds, "is to confront the administration and the Governor, to say, 'Wait a minute, maybe this is what you want to do but it still impacts on somebody in a way that's unfair.' Unless you've got that independence, there is no reason for the Public Advocate."

Which raises the ultimate question: At what point will there no longer be a reason for the Public Advocate? When the department stops pursuing its own public-policy agenda? When an embattled Governor or a frustrated Legislature start tightening the reins? When the Public Advocate stops going to court altogether, and turns into an office of dispute settlement? When politics takes over, and it becomes a mere extension of the Governor's office?

The day will eventually come when all of these points are reached. For as surely as state government is now providing a "voice for the voiceless," there will come a time when that voice does not speak so eloquently as it does today. That may happen as soon as Rodriguez leaves, or after the department celebrates a second decade of accomplishment, or maybe even three or four administrations down the road.

But it *will* happen. And when it does, the real challenge will not be to hang on for dear life like the Department of Community Affairs, or to try in vain to rekindle the fighting spirit of Stanley Van Ness or the gentle persuasion of Joseph Rodriguez. Rather, it will be to recognize the Public Advocate for what it is: a noble experiment that succeeded — in its time.

Financial Disclosure: Power in Search of Policy

John A. Rohr

> *Enslaved ourselves,*
> *we tried to enslave the others.*
> *By force subdued,*
> *we grew by force too bold.*

Bertolt Brecht

I

The purpose of this article is to attempt to contribute to the public argument over financial disclosure (FD) so that it can achieve its goal of detecting and deterring conflicts of interest without needlessly compromising the privacy of public officials. At the outset it must be acknowledged that the view presented here is that of a friendly critic of much of the current discussion in support of FD. Friendly, because I take seriously the value and, at times, the necessity of some form of FD; critic, because I object to an exaggerated righteousness that occasionally insinuates itself into the case for FD. Specifically, I object to the position or, more precisely, the attitude that presents FD as an index of civic virtue — the "tougher" a jurisdiction's FD regulations are, the stronger its opposition to corruption. This attitude will be criticized in a way that hopefully will be of interest to those who are affected by such laws as well as to those who formulate them.[1]

The article's subtitle, "Power in Search of Policy," suggests that the connection between specific provisions of FD laws and the purpose of such laws is not always as clear as the constitutional power of federal, state, and local governments to compel FD. Presumably, the primary purpose of compelling FD is to detect and deter conflicts of interest. It is the relationship between this commendable goal and specific FD mandates that is at times quite obscure. A telling symptom of this problem is the fact that the federal

Fiscal disclosure to reduce conflicts of interest to deter corrupt practices, according to John Rohr, abets an insensitivity to the value of individual privacy. Compelling individuals to disclose their finances infringes on the preservation of liberty, it is suggested. Honesty, of course, is the best policy, but protecting our First Amendment freedoms overrides this need. Or does it?

Source: John A. Rohr, "Financial Disclosure: Power in Search of Policy," *Public Personnel Management Journal*, 10:1 (1981), pp. 29-40.

"Ethics in Government Act of 1978," though in many ways a sound and sensible statute, has neither a preamble nor a statement of legislative intent.

Whatever the problems one might raise over the ends and means of FD, the power of the several levels of government to enact FD presents few serious difficulties. When the recent federal act was working its way through Congress, the House Select Committee on Ethics dismissed any constitutional scruples over compelling disclosure by simply calling attention to "the overwhelming state court and Supreme Court precedents upholding financial disclosure laws."[2]

This observation was absolutely correct; the precedents are indeed overwhelming. In the extensive litigation over FD in the 1970s, only one state supreme court has ever found an FD statute unconstitutional.[3] In *City of Carmel-by-the-Sea v. Young,*[4] the Supreme Court of California upheld a challenge to the constitutionality of a statute that required all public officials to disclose for inspection all investments over $10,000. The court balanced the right to privacy of the public officials against the state's interest in preventing corruption and found the disclosure requirement unconstitutional because of its "overbreadth." That is, the statute was overly broad in the sense that it required disclosures that were not related to one's public employment. As the court put it, the disclosure intrudes "alike into the relevant and the irrelevant private financial affairs of the numerous public officials and employees covered by the statute and is not limited to only such holdings as might be affected by the duties or functions of a particular public office."[5]

The California legislature responded with a revised statute that exempted from disclosure those financial interests "which could not be affected materially by any actions, failure to act, or decisions taken by the public official acting within the scope of his official duties."[6] This the California Supreme Court found constitutionally acceptable.

The insistence by the California Supreme Court that FD provisions be somehow related to one's official duties was unusual. Most of the other state courts that examined the constitutionality of FD laws failed to make this requirement. The Supreme Court of Illinois, for example, in a case challenging the constitutionality of a disclosure law noted that the plaintiff "questions how the disclosure of a business connection, unrelated to any activity of the State serves to avoid the conflicts of interest hoped to be disclosed and obviated by the statute."[7] The court acknowledged that a disclosure unrelated to any state activity could not help to achieve the legislative purpose. Instead of following the Supreme Court of California and demanding that compulsory disclosure be limited to matters relevant to official activities, the Supreme Court of Illinois announced a new and somewhat disconcerting line of argument:

> But who is to say whether or not there is a business connection or relation with the State? Who is to say that the business within the State which does not do business directly with the State, but which supplies another company which does, has no connection with the State? Who is to say that a capital gain from the sale of an asset to a stockholder of a company doing business with the State has no connection with the position of the public official?[8]

These rhetorical questions convinced the Illinois court that there was no practical way to restrict disclosure to job-related activities. This meant, in effect, that no financial requirements could *ever* be constitutionally overbroad. And so it came to pass that in the next Illinois disclosure case, the Supreme Court of that state upheld an executive order that required *every* employee in an executive department who earned more than $20,000 annually to file a statement disclosing *all* his assets and his net worth. In effect, the Illinois Supreme Court argued that, since the state cannot know what is or is not relevant to official duty, it may, in pursuing its efforts to prevent corruption, require every employee to disclose everything about his or her affairs.[9]

Although the executive order was subsequently modified, the blunderbuss reasoning of the Illinois Supreme Court has exerted considerable influence on the development of the constitutional law concerning the public official's privacy versus the state's interest in detecting and preventing conflict of interest.[10] It was for good reason that the House Select Committee on Ethics found the judicial precedents in favor of state power to compel disclosure "overwhelming." The mere existence of a constitutional power, however, is no guarantee of its wise use. It is the function of *policy* to direct power to its appointed ends. As

Styles and Strategies of Managing Openness

noted above, the recent federal ethics act has neither a preamble nor a statement of legislative intent. This remarkable absence is symptomatic of the problem addressed in this article and underscores the need for restraint in the use of the virtually unlimited power of federal, state, and local governments to compel disclosures.

There are good reasons for urging restraint, the most prominent of which is the familiar concern that excessive severity will weaken efforts to recruit or retain good people in government. This concern is well-founded even though, as a practical matter, discussions along these lines frequently founder on the shoals of question-begging arguments over how much severity is excessive and who the good people are.[11] Without taking anything from the importance of this familiar, utilitarian argument, I would prefer to concentrate on a different aspect of the problem — the ritualistic character of FD politics.

This ritualism was first noted by Bayless Manning, a member of President Kennedy's Advisory Panel on Ethics and Conflict of Interest in Government. Manning was concerned about an excessive zeal in the nation's efforts to eliminate conflicts of interest. The spirit of his comments can be gleaned from his pungent remark that "in an orgy of virtue, we seem to lose our grip on decency."[12] His point was that we are in danger of losing sight of the fact that conflict of interest policies are *anticipatory* measures taken to head off *potential* harms to society. To steal public funds or to take a bribe is an actual offense. To have a conflict of interest is simply to find oneself in a situation where one might be tempted — or at least appear to others to be tempted — to use one's public office for private gain. Manning sensed a moral escalation in American politics that could easily lose sight of the preventive character of conflict of interest policy. He deplored the tendency to equate conflict of interest with venality. The danger he saw was an increasing tendency to rely on coercive measures — including criminal penalties — to deter potential evils.

To illustrate his fear of an escalating "orgy of virtue," Manning suggested the image of the potlatch — a ritual found among some native Alaskans in which the participants compete in displaying generosity and bravado. The competitors in the potlatch take turns in "destroying those things that are of most value to them, the winner gaining great community prestige by reducing himself to material ruin."[13] Writing in 1964, Manning noted the helplessness of public officials in the face of demands for stricter conflict of interest standards however unrelated these standards might be to actual offenses. He showed, for example, how the moralistic tone of the 1952 Eisenhower campaign ("clean as a hound's tooth") made Nixon's Checkers performance inevitable and this in turn prompted Adlai Stevenson to respond "with objective irrelevance but symbolic political relevance by publishing a list of his personal assets."[14]

The celebrated hearings on Charles Wilson's confirmation as Secretary of Defense initiated another potlatch in which divestiture of stock by prospective DOD appointees became a staple of American politics. However desirable the divestiture of such stock might have been, the ritualistic character of the events was apparent from the fact that *only* stock, not debt securities, patent interests, or land, was discussed. Another sign of ritual was the tendency at confirmation hearings to ignore the common sense rule of *de minimis*. Distinctions were seldom made between small and large shareholders or major and minor DOD contractors. No Senator wanted to be caught on the liberal side "of anything less than Absolute Purity — however small the risks involved might be."[15]

The post-Watergate era has introduced a new potlatch. The moral escalation is unmistakably clear. *Common Cause* habitually refers to "potential conflicts of interest" — apparently unpersuaded of the redundancy in qualifying as potential a problem which by definition deals with potential evils.[16] Surpassing the standards of the Lord's prayer, our public servants are to be led not into potential temptation. Even the President has joined the potlatch. In his message to Congress in support of what eventually became the "Ethics in Government Act of 1978," President Carter called for far-reaching proposals for financial disclosure from a variety of elected, appointed, and career officials. Chief among the reasons the President gave for demanding disclosure from these people was that he had made disclosures about his own affairs and had demanded that his high-ranking appointees do the same.[17]

Ritualistic politics has its place in any well-ordered society. It is particularly expected to appear in policies — like conflict of interest in general and financial disclosure in particular — that are quite candidly and properly aimed at building public confidence in the institutions of government. A remote connection between ritual and substance is harmless as long as the ritual does not itself excessively compromise fundamental societal values. The escalating tendency to force public officials to disclose more and more about their private lives threatens to do just this.

One reason for the escalation is the link between disclosure and the public's "right to know."[18] Ritual needs incantation and the slogan about the "right to know" fills this need for the FD cause. A transitive verb without a direct object is a cannon rolling free on the deck of public argument; anything can become its target. Loose talk about an indiscriminate "right to know" can be quickly transformed into a "duty to disclose." Disclose what? Presumably, everything the public has a right to know; and who is going to say there are some things about public servants that the public should not know? Several state courts have accepted the reasoning of the Illinois Supreme Court that one must disclose *everything* about one's finances because it is too hard to distinguish between those matters that are related to the public interest and those that are not. What reason is there for limiting the principle "when in doubt, disclose" to *financial* matters? Surely favoritism, bias and corruption can be found in matters other than financial. The Supreme Court of the United States has told us that "the dichotomy between personal liberties and property rights is a false one. . . . In fact, a fundamental interdependence exists between the personal right to liberty and the personal right in property. Neither could have meaning without the other."[19] Are the civil liberties of public servants the next candidate for the potlatch? The Hatch Acts would serve as a sober reminder.

A cavalier treatment of the privacy of public servants could have an unwholesome effect on their attitude toward privacy in general. Because of the ritualistic character of disclosure politics, it is difficult for the public servant to complain without appearing to be against virtue itself. The danger here is that public servants might eventually acquiesce too graciously in governmental intrusions on their privacy. The problem with this is that we could end up with a public service dominated by people who are insensitive to the value of privacy. Because they have had to sacrifice their privacy to the public good, they might not be terribly squeamish about asking the rest of us to do the same. It is not uncommon for people who make admirable and difficult moral sacrifices to demand similar dedication from others. The military hero may grow impatient with the pacifist's scruples. The celibate cleric may see lust where others see love. The recovered alcoholic may denounce as weakness the moderation of the temperate. And as for reformed smokers . . . well, enough said!

A diminished concern for privacy would be particularly dangerous in administrative personnel who often deal more directly with the public than is customary for elected officials. The public interest would not be well served by a bureaucracy staffed with men and women insensitive to the felt needs — indeed the passion — for privacy one expects from the citizens of a liberal democracy. We do not want bureaucrats inured to these feelings through systematic violations of their own privacy. Financial disclosure must not encourage in government personnel the idea that privacy is of importance only to those who have something to hide.

II

The remainder of this article will examine the considerations that are salient in weighing the competing values of the civil servants' privacy and government's need for disclosure. The purpose is not to present a "model" FD ordinance. Sound FD policy will vary from place to place because disclosure policy, like all public policy, is a function of political culture. Instead, my purpose is to encourage discussion about FD in the trade-off language of policy formation rather than in the stern absolutes of right and wrong. What follows, then, is an effort to "structure" the public argument with an agenda of questions that might be asked and a weighing of the advantages and disadvantages of the various responses. The questions fall into three categories: (1) who must disclose? (2) what must be disclosed? (3) how is the disclosure requirement to be enforced?[20]

1. Who must disclose?

(a) Should the same FD regulations be applied across the board to elected, politically appointed, and career personnel? Probably not, if the intent is to make the disclosure provision commensurate with the degree of responsibility. If the standards are to be different, would it be suitable to have a tripartite division of elected, appointed and career personnel with a descending order of severity? Again, probably not, since many elected officials have positions that are far less significant than those of some appointed and career personnel (cf. an elected village library trustee with an appointed Director of State Revenue). Nor is it helpful to argue, as the Supreme Court of Washington did, that the elected official "voluntarily presents or thrusts himself forth as a subject of public interest and scrutiny,"[21] and therefore should be held to disclose more about himself. The public interest at stake in disclosure policy is information pertinent to public affairs regardless of the psychological disposition of the official involved. The extent of the disclosure should be determined by the official's function rather than by his temperament. Thus it would seem the best course would be to develop categories of disclosure tailored to categories of responsibility, regardless of whether a particular position is filled by one who is elected, politically appointed, or from the career service. Among the indicators that might be used to structure the categories are: scope of jurisdiction, size of budget, rank, number of persons supervised, sensitivity of specific tasks (e.g., contracting and procurement), etc.

(b) If career personnel must disclose, how far down in the bureaucracy should we reach? As we have seen, Illinois chose a $20,000 figure as a cutoff. The federal "Ethics in Government Act of 1978" drew the line in terms of grade structure — G.S. 16 and above. The literature on institutional decisionmaking would suggest these criteria are rather arbitrary if the intent is to get at those who influence policy. In the criminal statute on conflict of interest, the United States Code covers those who participate "personally and substantially" in a decision that affects their financial interests.[22] While this language avoids the arbitrariness of a salary level or grade structure, its usefulness would seem to be most apparent in determining after the fact — e.g., at a criminal trial — whether a particular person influenced a particular decision. To look for operational meaning of those who, in general, influence agency policy personally and substantially could be asking more than language can deliver.

One possible approach might be to have agency heads designate such positions, with the possibility of a right to appeal for those who object to being so designated. If such an approach were adopted, however, a further decision should be made on whether the agency head should make his designations by naming persons or offices. It is quite possible that the position of Assistant Director of Skyhook Research has significant influence on policy only as long as Mr. X holds that job. This consideration suggests that agency heads with discretion to decide who must disclose should also have discretion to change their minds.

(c) Should spouses be covered by disclosure laws, and, if so, what properties and investments should be disclosed?

It would seem that some restraint in demanding disclosures from spouses is in order if ludicrous results are to be avoided. For example, in 1977 a professor at the University of Chicago Law School pointed out the inequities of the Illinois requirement that employees in executive departments earning over $20,000 disclose not only their own income, assets, and net worth but those of their spouses as well. The professor's wife was a physician employed by the state at a salary over $20,000. Because of his wife's position, the professor, an employee of a private university, was supposed to disclose his affairs even though professors employed in state universities were exempt from the executive order on grounds of academic freedom. It made no difference that the professor published and lectured on the sensitive subject of civil liberties — an area wherein academic freedom would seem to be of considerable importance. Thus under Illinois law we had the anomalous situation wherein a professor teaching a politically sensitive subject in a private university had to disclose his financial affairs whereas another professor teaching a relatively "safe" subject in a state university had no such obligation.

If a spouse's finances must be reported, one way to limit the burden would be to require the disclosure only of those properties over which the government employee has "constructive control." Another way would be to require that only those properties related to the government employee's work need be reported. One reason for including spouses and dependent children in FD regulations is to prevent the government employee from circumventing the disclosure law by simply giving sensitive property to his or her spouse or dependent children. To safeguard against this abuse without needlessly intruding on the spouse's privacy, a regulation might exempt from disclosure those properties of the spouse which had never been owned or controlled by the reporting individual.[23]

(d) Should exceptions be made? The state of Washington allows its Public Disclosure Commission to grant waivers to those for whom disclosure would "impose undue hardship." In a recent message to the Illinois General Assembly, Governor Thompson has proposed that the disclosure of interests held exclusively by the spouse or family member be withheld from the public when "a valid objection to the disclosure" is presented.[24] These "fail-safe" provisions may perhaps be looked upon as candid acknowledgements of the difficulties involved in drafting a statute that makes a serious effort to avoid overbreadth without compromising the purposes of disclosure policy. The obvious problem with this "fail-safe" approach is the one that arises whenever government makes exceptions to general rules. The exceptions must be fair and appear to be fair. This is especially true in questions of disclosure where a major purpose of the policy is to build public confidence in the integrity of government. Heated political controversies swirling around whose applications for waivers were granted and whose were not would be counterproductive. Yet it would be easy for disappointed waiver-seekers to generate such controversies because the confidential nature of the information waived from public disclosure will necessarily preclude open and convincing explanations of why one waiver was granted and another denied. For jurisdictions that adopt "fail-safe" provisions, the wisest course would seem to be to grant the waivers generously and then make the fact of the waiver a matter of public record. Controversy over waivers denied can only weaken the objectives of disclosure policy except in cases where the request is patently outrageous.

2. What should be disclosed?

(a) Should disclosures be restricted to property within one's jurisdiction — e.g., should a high ranking education administrator in Vermont be required to tell the public about the land he holds in Arizona? Should county officials be required to disclose real estate holdings outside of their own jurisdictions but within their state? Should officials be required to disclose stock holdings in corporations not doing business within the state or county? Attention to questions of this nature will help to avoid the blunderbuss approach that requires disclosure of everything.

(b) Should disclosure be made in actual dollars or in categories such as "over ten thousand but less than fifteen thousand dollars"? If categories are selected, what should be the magnitude of the dollar intervals? The federal government requires disclosure of dividends, rents, interest and capital gains that exceed $100. The disclosure is to be made according to the following scale:

(i)   not more than $1,000;
(ii)   greater than $1,000 but not more than $2,500;
(iii)   greater than $2,500 but not more than $5,000;
(iv)   greater than $5,000 but not more than $15,000;
(v)   greater than $15,000 but not more than $50,000;
(vi)   greater than $50,000 but not more than $100,000; or
(vii)   greater than $100,000.

Quite sensibly, the federal government uses a different set of categories for reporting interests in business, real property, stocks, bonds or commodity futures. Only holdings in excess of $1,000 need be reported. The reporting categories are as follows:

(i)   not more than $5,000;
(ii)   greater than $5,000 but not more than $15,000;
(iii)   greater than $15,000 but not more than $50,000;
(iv)   greater than $50,000 but not more than $100,000;
(v)   greater than $100,000 but not more than $250,000; and
(vi)   greater than $250,000.[25]

(c) If dollar intervals are used, what should be the highest category? An early draft of the recent Federal Ethics in Government Act would have given $5,000,000 as the cut-off! Such information panders to idle speculation about who the richest man in Congress might be but would seem to have little to do with the more serious purposes of financial disclosure. Fortunately, Congress eventually settled for $250,000 as the top category.

(d) Should the disclosure be open to the public in the unqualified sense that anyone can see the financial statements simply by asking? Or should viewers be required to identify themselves? If so, should they also be required to state the reason for their request? If so, should the officials whose records are examined be notified of the identity of the examiner and the reason for the examination?

The advantage of such requirements is that they would tend to inhibit curiosity on the part of inquisitive neighbors and acquaintances. Such persons might be embarrassed if they know that public officials, known to them personally, would be given the names of those who examine their records. This might discourage frivolous inspections. The disadvantage is that such a requirement might discourage potential whistle-blowers who need some factual information on, let us say, their boss's financial interests before they can bring some irregularity to the attention of the proper authorities. A particularly difficult question is whether law enforcement officers should be required to identify themselves and state their reasons.

An early draft of the recent federal ethics act would have required prospective examiners to identify themselves and state the reasons for their inquiries. Congressman Wiggins objected to the provision on the grounds that it would have a "chilling effect" on public inspections. He contended: "If it is in the public interest to encourage disclosure of certain data, it cannot at the same time be in the public interest to discourage examination of that data."[26]

This point is not easily dismissed and undoubtedly had some influence on the congressional decision to abandon the requirement that examiners identify themselves and state their reasons. However, there is a plausible response to Wiggins' argument. If a governmental jurisdiction declines to make the effort to avoid overbreadth in its disclosure regulations, a requirement that examiners identify themselves might be a wholesome corrective. Wiggins' argument presupposes that all the data that must be disclosed are disclosed for reasons of public interest. This is not necessarily so. As we saw in the FD case decided by the Supreme Court of Illinois, a state may require an official to disclose everything because it despairs of finding a practical way to determine what is and is not relevant to the official's duties. The reasoning behind such a decision is not that everything the official owns affects the public interest but rather that something he owns might affect it. Since governments have the *power* to pass such laws and since, as we have seen, it is not easy to find language that successfully connects disclosures with responsibilities, we can expect some jurisdictions may follow Illinois down the path of least resistance and require far more information than what is relevant to public duties. When this happens, the government has actually decided that it is in the public interest to require a great deal of information that is not in the public interest! When such a decision is made, it does not seem inappropriate at all to impose "a chilling effect" upon those who would examine records that contain much information that is almost certainly of a purely private nature. It is only fair that a state or local government provide this protection to the privacy of its employees if it is unwilling to make the admittedly difficult effort to tailor disclosure requirements to public duties.

It is interesting to note that although Congressman Wiggins' objections to an identity requirement from examiners became part of the Ethics in Government Act of 1978, his victory was short-lived. In 1979, several "technical amendments" were added to the ethics act. Among them was a requirement that anyone desiring to examine a disclosure statement must state his name, address and occupation. This information itself becomes a matter of public record. While there may be something to be said for this amendment, it certainly is not merely a technical matter.[27]

(e) A final issue in the category of what should be disclosed brings us back to the finances of spouses of public servants. If the spouse makes his or her livelihood in a profession such as law, medicine, psychology, counselling, etc., and the state sees fit to require disclosure of income from this professional activity, it would probably be advisable not to require that the names of the clients be released. This could seriously and needlessly jeopardize professional relationships. One need only think of the embarrassment that might be caused by releasing the names of the clients of a noted criminal lawyer or the patients of physicians specializing in abortions.[28]

Attention should also be given to the problem of the recalcitrant spouse who simply refuses to disclose his or her affairs. In its zeal to enforce its disclosure policy, the state should be careful to avoid anything that might be interpreted as official encouragement to weaken the marital bond. It would be unconscionable to present a government employee with the Hobson's choice of divorcing her husband or losing her job. Family life is under enough stress today without the state's reneging on the traditional public policy of encouraging marital stability.

3. How to Enforce?

(a) Is the disclosed information used? If it develops that huge inventories of data are collected with hardly anyone ever looking at them, one might consider whether the state is asking for too much information. Volumes of unexamined data do little for the public and tend to demoralize its employees. A commitment to random audits might be a good indicator of a serious intent to use the information for the purposes for which it was gathered. The absence of such a commitment would give credence to complaints that disclosure policy was nothing more than ritualistic "impression management"[29] based on a sterile ideology of disclosure for its own sake.

(b) Who should enforce the law is another interesting question. Under certain circumstances, the state of Washington allows private citizens to bring suits to enforce the disclosure laws and provides a bounty for successful plaintiffs. Citizen initiatives may serve as useful checks on lazy, inept, or corrupt prosecutors but they can also serve as an incentive to frivolous and harassing lawsuits. A common safeguard against abuses from citizen suits is to require an unsuccessful plaintiff to pay court costs and attorney's fees for the defendants. This sanction, of course, would be useless against an indigent plaintiff.

(c) What sorts of penalties should be imposed for violations? Although criminal penalties for failure to comply with disclosure laws are not unknown, civil and administrative measures are far more common. This is probably as it should be because in at least some jurisdictions, a robust sense of egalitarianism might make almost irresistible the argument that if the high and mighty *can* be indicted they should be — no matter how inconsequential the offense. Reliance on criminal penalties alone would be particularly unwise. Some violations of FD regulations are so trivial that few prosecutors would seek indictments and no jury would convict. In the absence of civil or administrative penalties such offenses would not be punished at all.

(d) How should public officials be advised of their obligation to disclose in doubtful cases? Doubtful cases abound in the area of FD. A major league baseball team, for example, routinely sends a complimentary season pass to all city councilmen. Must a councilman who never uses the pass declare it as a gift and if so must he list the gift at what its value would have been had he gone to *every* home game? My favorite case is the one about the status of the puppies born of a mating between a legislator's bitch and the stud of a lobbyist. Question: must the legislator report the puppies as a gift from the lobbyist? Exquisite questions of this sort are inevitable in the area of FD.[30] Since no legislative body could ever foresee all the problems that will arise under the most enlightened ordinance, the wise course would seem to be to authorize the agency tasked with administering the FD regulations to issue advisory opinions. A more difficult question is to determine just what the legal force of these opinions should be and whether anyone other than those to whom the opinions were addressed can rely on them.[31]

Conclusion

In examining the values involved in compulsory disclosure, it is helpful to recall that at issue is a question of policy, with the tradeoffs that word connotes, rather than a struggle between the forces of good and evil. This awareness may help to save us from the potlatch discussed at the beginning of this article. In developing or modifying a disclosure policy, special attention should be paid to the political culture of the affected jurisdiction. Rather than strive for a disclosure policy as broad as is politically possible, decisionmakers should think in terms of addressing those activities within their jurisdiction that are most susceptible to abuse. It is precisely in these areas, of course, that one can expect the greatest political opposition and for this reason it is important that decisionmakers be aware of the negative aspects of financial disclosure. Otherwise, if they were to look upon disclosure as an unmitigated social good — a quasi probity calculus to measure public virtue instead of a trade-off among competing social values — there would be a serious danger that embarrassing failures to get disclosures from those who should disclose would be compensated by cheap triumphs in demanding disclosures from those whose disclosures are not needed. Far from being a useful reform, such a decision, wrapped in the rhetoric of civic virtue, would bear the mark of the moral bully.

Because of the ritualistic character of disclosure politics, it is important to keep in proper perspective the limited significance of FD and even of the corruption it is intended to prevent. President Carter surely overstated the case when, in a message to Congress in support of the Ethics in Government Act of 1978, he identified safeguards against conflict of interest with the public interest itself.[32] Although generous allowances for presidential hyperbole are always in order, it is helpful to recall that Paul Appleby was correct when, in 1952, he wrote that corruption is by no means the main problem in American government.[33] This was true in 1952 and it is true today. The main problem today is the same problem that faced the founders of the republic — the preservation of liberty. In 1787 the threat to liberty came from what the founders saw as the notorious tendency of republican institutions to succumb to the "excesses of democracy." Today's threat to liberty comes from the shift in effective governing power away from elected officials to a career bureaucracy whose technical expertise we prize and fear — just as the men of 1787 feared and prized republican institutions. It is commonplace in current social criticism to note an irresistible trend toward the accumulation of discretionary (i.e., governing) authority in our non-elected officials. This, of course, is why it is so important that these men and women be sensitive to the liberal tradition that abhors the incursions of officialdom into our private lives.

The courts have told us that there is a compelling state interest in demanding financial disclosure as a means of preventing corruption in those who govern. This may well be true but surely there is an equally compelling interest in having as those who govern us men and women who are friends of liberty. Unfortunately, there is no direct way to protect this public interest without imposing a test for political orthodoxy that would mock the very liberty we cherish.

Through our laws, however, there is an indirect way to promote this interest, especially if we recall the ancient theme that laws teach as well as govern. If our laws on financial disclosure teach those who govern us what we think about them, what lessons will they learn? Some of these laws may tell them it is too difficult to articulate a policy tailored to prevent precise and likely abuses and that we have therefore chosen instead to require them to disclose everything about their financial affairs. The lesson learned from such a law might be that honesty is very important but privacy is not — a lesson our "pupils" might learn all too well to suit the real interests of their teachers. A more wholesome lesson would be learned from a disclosure law that evidenced a serious concern to avoid overbreadth out of respect for the privacy of public servants. Such a law would teach the sound doctrine that the public interest demands not only that we prevent corruption but also that we school those who govern to cherish liberty.

Endnotes

1. In addressing remarks both to those who are affected by FD laws as well as to those who formulate them, it is realized that I have taken on a richly diverse audience. There is some overlap, of course, because many of those who formulate these laws are themselves covered by them. For those who are affected by FD laws without having had an active role in developing them, the discussion might serve a mild consciousness-raising purpose. For those called upon to develop or revise such laws, the remarks will touch on a few points that might have escaped their attention in the press of other legislative responsibilities.

    One group of potential readers to whom, it is feared, I have little to offer is the dedicated corps of women and men tasked with the challenging and often thankless job of administering FD statutes, ordinances and executive orders. Their experience has given them more insight than I could hope to offer with bookish scribbling.

2. The Ethics in Government Act of 1978 was originally reported as The Legislative Branch Disclosure Act of 1977. See *Report of the Select Committee on Ethics*. U.S. House of Representatives, 95th Congress, 1st Session. #95-574, p. 15.

3. In several instances limited provisions of an FD law have been found unconstitutional. These cases include *Hays v. Wood* 78 Cal. App. 3d 354, 144 Cal. Rptr, 456 (1978); the New Jersey case, *Lehrhaupt v. Flynn* 323 A 2d 537 (1974); the Nevada case, *Dumphy v. Sheehan* 549 P2d 332 (1976); an advisory opinion from the Supreme Court of Michigan, 242 N.W. 2d 3. The FD cases cited by the House Select Committee on Ethics include: the Washington case *Fritz v. Gorton* 517 P2d 911 (1974); the Illinois cases *Stein v. Howlett* 289 NE 2d 409 (1972) and *Illinois State Employees Association v. Walker* 419 U.S. 1058 (1974); *Klause v. Minnesota State Ethics Commission* 244 N.W. 2d 672 (1976); the Maryland case *Montgomery County v. Walsh,* 336 A 2d 97 (1975), 242 U.S. 901 (1976); the California case *County of Nevada v. MacMillen* 522 P2d 1345 (1974). The FD Act declared unconstitutional can be found in the California case, *City of Carmel-by-the-Sea v. Young* 466 P2d 225 (1970). Other FD cases include the federal cases *Plante v. Gonzales* 575 F2d 1119 (1978) and *O'Brien v. De Grazia* 544 F2d 543, *cert. denied sub nom. O'Brien v. Jordan,* 431 U.S. 914 (1977); the Alaska case *Falcon v. Alaska Public Offices Commission,* 570 P2d 469 (1977); the Florida case *Goldtrap v. Askew* 334 So. 2d 20 (1976); the Missouri case *Chamberlin v. Missouri Elections Commission* 540 S.W. 2d 876 (1976); the New York cases *Hunter v. City of New York* 391 N.Y.S. 2d 289 (1977) and *Evans v. Carey* 385 N.Y.S. 2d 965 (1976); the Wisconsin case *In re Kading* 235 N.W. 2d 409 (1975).

4. 466 P2d 225 (1970).

5. *Ibid* at 234.

6. *County of Nevada v. MacMillen* 522 P2d 1345 at 1348 (1974).

7. *Stein v. Howlett* 289 N.E. 2d 409 at 413 (1972).

8. *Ibid.*

9. *Illinois State Employees Association v. Walker* 315 N.W.2d 9 (1974). The severity of the executive order may be explained in part by the laxity of the Illinois Financial Disclosure Act. It should also be noted that Governor Walker's original executive order was considerably modified in the subsequent administration of Governor Thompson.

10. See *Fritz v. Gorton* 517 P2d 911 (1974); *Montgomery County v. Walsh* 336 A2d (1975); *Klause v. Minnesota State Ethics Commission* 244 N.W. 2d 672 (1976).

11. See, for example, the remarks of Congressmen Collins and Derwinski in *Report of the Committee on Post Office and Civil Service on H.R. 6954: Federal Employee Financial Reporting and Disclosure* (Washington D.C.: G.P.O., 1977) pp. 99-100.

12. Bayless Manning, "The Purity Potlatch: An Essay on Conflicts of Interest, American Government and Moral Escalation," *The Federal Bar Journal* 24 (1964) p. 254.

13. *Ibid.* p. 245.

14. *Ibid.*

15. *Ibid.* p. 246.

16. *Serving Two Masters: A Common Cause Study of Conflicts of Interest in the Executive Branch* (Washington, D.C.: Common Cause, 1976).

17. President Carter's Message to Congress of May 3, 1977. See House of Representatives Report No. 95-800; 95th Congress, 1st session. Judiciary Committee *Report on the Ethics in Government Act of 1977,* p. 86.

18. See *Fritz v. Gorton* 517 P 2d 911 (1974).

19. *Lynch v. Household Finance Corporation* 405 U.S. 538 (1972).

20. The effort in this article to structure the public argument over FD might well be considered as a holding action until there is a critical mass of reliable data available on the effectiveness of FD. Fortunately, there is at least one study in progress to gather empirical data on this question. The U.S. Office of Government Ethics is designing a Program Evaluation Report to present to Congress in 1982 (Memorandum: "OGE's July 1982 Program Evaluation Report"; from J. Jackson Walter, Director; June, 1980). The tentative outline of the study is an encouraging sign that serious efforts are afoot to examine critically and empirically a wide range of FD issues.

21. *Fritz v. Gorton* 517 P 2d 949 at 961 (1974).

22. 18 U.S.C. §208

23. If a decision is made to exempt from disclosure a spouse's property which had never been owned or controlled by the reporting individual, attention might also be given to the question of *benefits* the reporting individual might receive from the spouse's property. This additional consideration is associated with the term "constructive control." For example, Rule LXIX of the House of Representatives defines constructive control as follows: "The financial interests of a spouse are regarded as constructively controlled by the person reporting if enhancement of those interests would substantially benefit the person reporting."

24. Federal law is more precise in granting exemptions and waivers in its provisions for blind trusts and special government employees. See in particular Section 201 (h) of the "Ethics in Government Act of 1978."

25. "Ethics in Government Act of 1978" §202(a) and (d).

26. House of Representatives Report #95-800; 95th Congress, 1st Session, Judiciary Committee *Report on the Ethics in Government Act of 1977,* p. 100.

27. The vagaries of the question of requiring identification from those who would examine financial disclosures suggest that this issue, like many other issues related to FD, is a likely candidate for impact assessment.

28. The leading cases on FD and privileged communications are: *Falcon v. Alaska Public Offices Commission* 570 P2d 469 (1977) and *Chamberlin v. Missouri Elections Commission* 540 S.W. 2d 876.

29. Victor A. Thompson, *Modern Organization* (University of Alabama Press, 1977) p. 138.

30. Jeri McKeand, "The Political Reform Act of 1974," *Western State University Law Review* 5 (1978) pp. 269-299.

31. A recent (May 18, 1980) memorandum of agreement between the Department of Justice and the Office of Government Ethics (OGE) provides that advisory opinions rendered by the Director of OGE may be relied upon by the person involved in the specific transaction in question and "any person involved in any specific transaction or activity which is indistinguishable in all its material aspects from the transaction or activity with respect to which such advisory opinion has been rendered."

32. See Note 17.

33. Paul H. Appleby, *Morality and Administration in Democratic Government* (Baton Rouge: Louisiana State University Press, 1952), p. 56.

12. Establishing Standards of Professionalism

The Ethics in Government Act, Conflict of Interest Laws and Presidential Recruiting

J. Jackson Walter

The federal conflict of interest laws are involved in the recruiting and confirmation of the political leaders for the executive branch of our government in ways that warrant careful description and assessment. Central to the description is the Ethics in Government Act of 1978 that requires the president's nominees to disclose publicly the details of their personal financial interests, thereby creating records that the public and the press may scrutinize for potential conflicts of interest.[1] By manifesting the recent shift to "sunshine" in government that markedly distinguishes public sector posts from jobs in other parts of the economy where personal and financial privacy is carefully protected, the Ethics in Government Act may be in danger of becoming a scapegoat for all that is most difficult and frustrating in presidential recruiting. Whether the Ethics in Government Act has in fact shifted the balance too far, thereby effectively barring otherwise highly-qualified persons from serving in Washington, will be the subject of congressional oversight hearings that are scheduled to take place well before the 1984 presidential election.[2] At issue in these hearings will be the relative impact on presidential recruiting of such diverse factors as the Ethics Act, the long-standing conflict of interest statutes and the limitations on executive branch pay levels.[3] In the meantime, however, the presidential transition has focused greater attention than ever before on efforts to prevent future conflicts by identifying and resolving problems prior to the time a presidential nominee enters office.

Is the cure worse than the disease? Does ethics legislation requiring and financial reporting deter good people from governmental service? How strong is Walter's case for the laws, executive orders and other rulings as providing valuable 'rites of passage' for the entry to public service of executive appointees?

For persons who do agree to accept nomination by the president to Senate-confirmed positions, the confirmation process itself can be a most rigorous test. As evidence of how central the conflict of interest issue has become, each committee of the Senate now refrains from reporting presidential nominees to the full Senate for confirmation prior to receipt of assurance from the Office of Government Ethics that the nominees will be able to assume office legally uncompromised by their personal financial interests.

Although most of this practice regarding the identification of conflicts of interest is new, the related substantive law is not. President Reagan's administration is the first to come into office since the passage of the Ethics in Government Act which, in addition to its public financial disclosure requirements, also established the Office of Government Ethics (OGE) to provide overall direction of executive branch poli-

Source: J. Jackson Walter, "The Ethics in Government Act, Conflict of Interest Laws and Presidential Recruiting," *Public Administration Review*, 41:6 (November/December 1981), pp. 659-665.

cies related to preventing conflicts of interest.[4] OGE's judgments on the president's nominees, based exclusively on their financial disclosure reports and rendered in the form of opinion letters signed by the director of the office, are an altogether new factor. So, too, is the careful review of the financial disclosure reports by a nominee's future employing agency that serves as the basis for each opinion letter. The Senate committees, of course, long have required nominees to answer questions about personal finances and other matters. Each committee has developed its own questions and its own practices concerning standards for reviewing the answers and for releasing them to the public. Finally, it is important to note that despite the financial disclosure rules brought about by the Ethics in Government Act, nothing has changed the applicable substantive law regarding conflicts of interest. The federal conflict of interest criminal statutes (18 U.S.C. 202-209) were codified in their present form in 1962 and date back in some instances to the Civil War.

The Ethics in Government Act and the federal conflict of interest laws have consequences in three areas with respect to presidential recruiting: first, the financial disclosure requirements themselves; second, the conflict of interest laws that govern the review of the disclosed information; and third, the prospective remedies and cures for potential conflicts of interest. Although the ethics act itself may well need certain modifications,[5] the advance review and clearance process that culminates in the opinion letters of the OGE director regarding the personal financial interests of presidential nominees to Senate-confirmed positions does serve a number of important goals: protecting the president and his nominees, enhancing public confidence in the government's integrity, improving the effectiveness of public officials, and preventing the use of public office for private gain.

Public Financial Disclosure: The Report and its Review

When the president nominates someone to serve in a Senate-confirmed position, the nominee must prepare a financial disclosure report that will be made available to the public.[6] This is neither a net worth statement nor an income tax return; rather, it is a listing of income sources, assets, liabilities, and affiliations with other organizations that could be germane to a judgment regarding possible conflicts of interest. Assets held for investment need to be reported but personal property such as jewelry or private residences that do not produce rental income do not. Further, the reporting of assets, which generally may be done in reliance on a good faith estimate of value, is by six broad categories with a $1,000 threshold and an "Over $250,000" top bracket. OGE's list of some typical items of property that must be disclosed includes stocks, bonds, securities, and commodities contracts; commercial crops, whether growing or held in storage; antiques owned for resale; art held for investment; pensions and annuities; and money market mutual funds. Ownership must be disclosed for the nominee and for the nominee's spouse and dependent children. The disclosed information, which is accepted at face value for purposes of reviewing the report, is reported subject to the criminal false statement statute, 18 U.S.C. 1001.

To explain the review of a financial disclosure report, it is easiest to begin with the final work product of each review, namely, the opinion letter by the OGE director. In their least complicated form, these letters read as follows:

Dear Mr. Chairman:

In accordance with the Ethics in Government Act, I enclose a copy of the financial disclosure report filed by [the nominee]. The President has nominated [the nominee] for the position of [ ] in the Department of [ ].

We have reviewed the report and have obtained advice from the Department of [ ] concerning any possible conflict in light of the Department's functions and the nominee's proposed duties. Based thereon, we believe that [the nominee] is in compliance with applicable laws and regulations concerning conflicts of interest.

Sincerely,

Director, OGE

Keeping in mind this example of the end of the process, it should be possible to start at the beginning and fit all the pieces together into a reasonably coherent picture of how this advance review and clearance works.

The Rules. At the center of this entire topic is the distinction, and the possibility, of a clash between an official's interest in his private economic affairs and the government's (and public's) interest in the proper administration of the official's office. The scope of the conflict of interest criminal statutes is narrower than might be supposed for this formulation of the matter. For example, they reach only the executive branch of the federal government and relate only to the financial interests of government officials. Further, more serious larcenies such as bribery or fraud are not considered to be conflicts of interest.[7] Although the conflict of interest laws are criminal statutes, the regulation of conflicts of interest is concerned with potential harm and is decidedly civil and prospective in nature.

Reviewers of financial disclosure reports look to four different sets of prohibitions in the conflict of interest laws:

1. Restrictions against participation in matters in which an official has a personal financial interest. (18 U.S.C. 208)

   This, the most common and obvious type of conflict of interest, concerns those cases in which an official is called upon to act for the government in a particular matter that could result in a personal financial benefit. Awarding a contract to a company in which an official owns stock, for example. The usual test is whether an official's participation in the matter will have a direct and predictable effect upon the financial interests of the official, the official's spouse, dependent children, partner or enterprise with which the official is affiliated.

2. Restrictions against receipt of supplementation of salary from nongovernmental sources for services to the federal government. (18 U.S.C. 209)

   Some of the reviewer's most difficult problems relate to this statute because many presidential nominees receive severance payments from their former employers. The usual test is whether the payment is for past services to a former employer—in most cases, this is demonstrably true because the payment is made pursuant to a formal corporate policy and plan—or for the illegal purpose of augmenting an official's government salary. Statutory exceptions permit continued participation in a former employer's *bona fide* pension, retirement, or other welfare or benefit plan.

3. Restrictions against participation in outside matters that involve the United States. (18 U.S.C. 203 and 205)

   The basic point of these two statutes is that an official cannot be paid for or act in a representative capacity regarding activities outside his or her official duties that involve the interests of the government in a direct and substantial way. Both laws have quite complex consequences that need not be explored here. These statutes can be of particular concern to a reviewer who is analyzing, for example, a nominee's proposal to remain on the board of directors of a corporation that might use the fact of the directorship to further its interests before a government agency unrelated to the one in which the nominee is to serve.

4. Restrictions against post-employment representational activities. (18 U.S.C. 207)

   Here is the "revolving door" law, which was substantially amended by Title V of the Ethics in Government Act. Because the act vested civil jurisdiction over this statute in OGE, there are regulations that authoritatively explain the impact of this complex set of prohibitions.[8] For the reviewer, however, the "revolving door" law is not a factor because it applies only to former government officials. This statute clearly should be of major concern to presidential personnel recruiters who must be able to reassure prospective nominees that government service will not destroy their future opportunitites with non-governmental employers.

In addition to the criminal conflict of interest statutes, Executive Order 11222 prescribes comprehensive standards of ethical conduct for federal officials.[9] As a compact between the president and all employees and officers in the executive branch, the Executive Order ought to be read by reviewers as reinforcing the conflicts statutes because it is concerned directly with the elusive issue of "appearances." Its practical effect is to proffer guidance on the design and analysis of prospective cures of possible conflicts of interest, as discussed in a later part of this paper.

The Players and Possible Problems. First in time and importance among all the reviewers of public financial disclosure reports are the attorneys in the *Office of Counsel to the President.* These lawyers can work with the prospective nominees and with the staff of the assistant to the president for presidential personnel before an announcement is made of the president's intent to nominate someone. Having confidential access to a prospective nominee's personal financial situation, in much greater detail than appears on the public financial disclosure report, and to personal background information and reports by the FBI and IRS,[10] these White House attorneys can explain the applicable conflict of interest statutes and regulations to the unannounced nominees and can counsel them regarding appropriate cures and remedies prior to OGE's public review process.

The Executive Office of the President, and specifically the Office of Counsel to the President, furnishes the financial disclosure reporting forms to the nominee and forwards the completed forms to the *designated agency ethics officials* (DAEO) at the agency in which the nominee will serve. DAEOs — typically, the general counsel or deputy general counsel — are formally appointed by the head of each agency who is directly responsible for the agency's ethics in government program.[11]

The Office of Government Ethics relies upon the DAEOs to conduct a review since, as agency officials, the DAEOs know in detail the duties of the office in which the nominee is to serve, the agency's own specific conflict statues and regulations, and the particular matters that most likely could result in a conflict of interest given the nominee's disclosed financial interests. Additionally, the importance that OGE attaches to these agency reviews underscores the decentralized structure of the federal ethics in government program and the fundamental responsibility of the head of each agency for the honesty and integrity of its employees. Having completed a thorough review of the financial disclosure report, the DAEO personally must certify directly on the reporting form that it discloses no conflict of interest under applicable laws and regulations. The report is then forwarded to the Office of Government Ethics, together with an opinion letter from the DAEO to the OGE director that summarizes any problems that were encountered in reaching the conclusions on which the certification was based and any prospective cures undertaken by the nominee. OGE regulations require the agencies to complete these reviews within three days after receipt of the report.[12]

Although signature by the OGE director is the final formal step in the reviewing of a financial disclosure report, the actual staff review work by the *OGE attorneys and management analysts* proceeds in tandem with the agency reviews so that problems can be identified and resolved as rapidly as possible. The network that has grown up around the extensive "telephone practice" of the OGE attorneys has established the basis for this cooperation.

The decentralized administrative structure of the review process for financial disclosure reports enhances the ability of the OGE staff to make an informed prospective judgment regarding the potential for conflicts of interest with respect to presidential nominees. When none exists, the opinion letter of the OGE director goes forward to the Senate in the unqualified form set out above. As the following seven typical examples illustrate, however, there are instances when the review does identify possible problems.

- A nominee will be unable to make the decisions expected of the incumbent in the position in which the nominee is to serve without considering proposals advanced by firms in which the nominee has financial interests.

- A nominee owns common stock in a company, the ownership of which is prohibited by the organic act of the department in which the nominee is to serve.

- There is a remote possibility that a particular matter will come up for decision by the nominee that will involve a firm in which the nominee has a financial interest.

- The board of directors of a nominee's previous employer elects to break its tradition of not awarding severance payments in the nominee's case because of a particularly noteworthy contribution by the nominee to the firm's profitability.

- A nominee proposes to continue to serve as a paid director of a closely held family corporation whose business is unrelated to the jurisdiction of the department in which the nominee is to serve.

- A nominee is to serve in a position that develops a department's regulatory policy regarding the business of the nominee's previous employer, in which the nominee has no continuing financial interests.

- A nominee takes a leave of absence from a previous employer in order to serve in a federal executive position.

Prospective Remedies for Possible Problems

In addition to prominent press coverage and civil sanctions, alleged violations of the conflict of interest statutes by government officials may be subject to criminal prosecution.[13] In a sense, OGE's advance review and clearance process amounts to prospective enforcement of criminal laws by requiring nominees to take precautionary steps to stay out of harm's way. Authority for OGE to take the lead in seeking to prevent conflicts of interest derives from the office's grant of authority in the Ethics in Government Act and from a May 1980 Memorandum of Agreement with the Department of Justice in which OGE's authority to render advisory opinions on the conflict of interest laws was acknowledged expressly.

The tools and techniques available to fashion prospective cures generally are adequate to the task of bringing nominees into compliance with the conflict of interest laws. To illustrate, consider four approaches to remedying a possible problem under 18 U.S.C. §208, the straightforward restriction against participation in particular matters in which an official has a personal financial interest.

Disqualification or recusal. If a nominee owns stock in a firm that could have particular matters at issue before the office in which the nominee is to serve, the nominee should be put on notice regarding the relationship that is prohibited by §208. In such situations, OGE strongly prefers the nominee to agree in advance not to participate in any matters involving that firm. If the nominee honors the agreement and if the nominee's office staff screens out all related paperwork, then disqualification will prevent conflicts.[14] This remedy seems practical and recusal agreements are, in fact, "boilerplate" language in the opinion letters sent by many DAEOs to the OGE director. But this approach has less utility in those infrequent cases when the nominee has such extensive financial interests that, in order to avoid conflicts of interest, the nominee makes so many recusal agreements as to become unable to perform the duties of the office.

Waivers under 18 U.S.C. 208 (b). Federal agencies may, by regulation, adopt what amounts to a *de minimis* exemption of general applicability to the §208 restrictions by finding that certain kinds of financial interests are "too remote or too inconsequential to affect the integrity" of the services to be rendered by an official. In individual cases, the government official who appoints the nominee can make an anticipatory waiver of the §208 restrictions by determining in advance that the nominee's publicly disclosed financial interests are "not so substantial as to be deemed likely to affect the integrity of the [nominee's] services." A §208(b) waiver is an absolute statutory cure but for various reasons, including an inability to make the necessary factual determination or a political reluctance to do so, resort to the statutory cure of §208(b) anticipatory waivers has not been a regular practice.

Divestiture. If a nominee no longer owns a financial interest, it cannot pose even a possible conflict of interest. Many presidential nominees, their spouses and dependent children sell holdings that could become compromising in order to put the matters completely to rest. Divestiture is a complete remedy with respect to the asset that has been sold. Except in the case of certain departments' organic acts that expressly prohibit employees and officials from owning certain prohibited holdings,[15] it is the inescapable logic of an unavoidable conflict of interest, rather than any statute or regulation, that dictates divestiture. Because of the vagaries of the markets and the tax code, this can be a very expensive cure.[16]

Blind trusts. To prove a violation of §208, a prosecutor must show that the official knew that he or she had a financial interest in a matter that the official had acted upon. The theory of blind trusts as a cure for possible conflicts of interest is that, if an official does not know what he or she owns, then it is impossible for the official intentionally to take actions to benefit specifically the official's personal financial interests. Therefore, the general public policy goal to be achieved by the use of blind trusts is an actual "blindness" or lack of knowledge by the official with respect to the trust's holdings.[17]

Prior to enactment of the blind trust provisions of the Ethics in Government Act, there were no statutory or regulatory standards for a properly formulated blind trust. Congress suspected that many pre-act blind trusts were flawed by "20/20 vision" although there was general agreement that proper use of blind trusts could ameliorate potential conflicts of interest. The provisions of the act are extremely complex; the basic formula authorizes OGE to approve or "qualify" blind trusts provided they have a truly independent trustee, acceptable assets, and a trust instrument meeting certain minimum standards.[18] Obviously, qualified trusts are not subject to the full public financial disclosure requirements because the officials must not be allowed to discover their holdings. In certain special circumstances, therefore, establishment of a qualified trust may sidestep neatly an official's exposure to possible conflicts of interest.

These four approaches to remedying possible problems under 18 U.S.C. 208 are flexible enough to permit their adaptation to individual situations on a case-by-case basis. Executive Order 11222 is the best guide to the public policy objectives that should govern the fashioning of remedies by OGE, the nominees, DAEOs and Office of Counsel to the President. The most important part of the Executive Order counsels government officials to avoid any action that might result in, or create the appearance of:

(1) using public office for private gain;

(2) giving preferential treatment to any organization or person;

(3) impeding government efficiency or economy;

(4) losing complete independence or impartiality of action;

(5) making a government decision outside official channels; or

(6) affecting adversely the confidence of the public in the integrity of the government.[19]

In nearly all cases, it has been possible to design remedies that nominees and their families do accept. The costs associated with these remedies, particularly in terms of tax liabilities[20] and disruptions of personal and family financial planning, in specific cases can be high. The conflict of interest statutes occasionally can be characterized, therefore, as a legislative limitation on presidential recruiting because they represent fundamental standards of eligibility for federal public office-holding with which not all of the highly qualified persons in the country may choose to comply.

For presidential recruiters who are trying to persuade prospective nominees to move to Washington, possible §208 problems are the most cumbersome to resolve of all the potential conflicts of interest. Three other recurrent conflicts of interest issues, which appear in the earlier list of seven illustrative examples, deserve separate treatment.

Leaves of absence. A corporate executive who takes a leave of absence to accept a presidential nomination clearly should be disqualified from participating in decisions that will affect the corporation directly and predictably. This recusal agreement makes sense and the executive should agree readily. The presidential recruiter should [know] however, that the "revolving door" law, 18 U.S.C. 207, will concern an executive who hopes to return to a job that involves representing the corporation before the executive branch of the federal government. It is critical that the attorneys in the Office of Counsel to the President and at OGE be able to advise the executive knowledgeably and sensibly on this matter because misunderstanding the detailed impact on the conflict of interest laws frequently makes their effect seem to be more sweeping — and a much greater deterrent to serving in Washington — than is the case. (For example, a specific exemption in the "revolving door" law greatly diminishes its impact on professors who take leaves of absence from universities to accept presidential nominations.)

Severance payments. Prospective nominees often receive substantial severance payments from their former employers, thereby offsetting the personal financial sacrifices that result in some cases from limitations on executive branch pay levels. These severance payments necessarily concern reviewers of financial disclosure reports because judgments must be made with respect to the intent or motive of the former employers. Rewards for past services are of course acceptable; augmentation of an official's federal salary "as compensation for" government service is the prohibited practice under 18 U.S.C. 209 and it matters not at all that a prior employer's business has nothing to do with the office in which the prospective nominee is to serve. Paying moving expenses to Washington or guaranteeing the rental of a hometown house could be illegal payments. It is extremely difficult to document the motive or intent of the previous employer; relevant evidence that OGE's reviewers examine include resolutions of the corporate board of directors, statements by corporate officers and provisions of any corporate policy and plan regarding severance payments.[21]

Bias or prejudgment. Questions of "bias" or prejudgment on policy matters do not come within the reach of the conflict of interest laws.[22] Thus, a corporate official legally may accept without qualification nomination to a regulatory position having jurisdiction over his or her former business, as long as the official has no continuing financial interests in firms engaged in that business. Such things as vested pension rights or re-employment agreements could be financial interests that create possible §208 problems. But bias or prejudgment on policy issues is not, by itself, an issue under the conflict of interest statutes. Whether or not the record of a nominee's previous career will permit objective and impartial performance in government office is a decision to be made in the first instance by the president, who is the appointing authority, and subsequently by the Senate, which is the confirming body.

Summary

What conclusions can be drawn from this complex of laws and regulations that is intended to foster public confidence in the integrity of our government? First of all, the criticism that portrays the Ethics in Government Act as the significant barrier to presidential recruiting frequently has been imprecise and hence somewhat misleading. The prevailing executive branch salary levels and the increasingly corrosive quality of public life[23] have nothing to do directly with the ethics act but certainly do discourage many people from federal public service. In this regard, there are only three aspects of the ethics act to be considered: the financial disclosure provisions, the blind trust rules, and the "revolving door" bars. The public financial disclosure requirements certainly are stringent but very few people have turned down a presidential job offer solely because they refused to file the required report. The blind trust rules actually are intended to alleviate the impact of the conflict of interest laws. The "revolving door" bars do not appear to have been an insurmountable problem for departing Carter administration officials.[24] Apparently more serious than these three explicit ethics act topics as obstacles to presidential recruiting, however, are such closely related laws and regulations as the conflict of interest statutes themselves, the costs — particularly the tax liabilities — associated with curing problems identified by OGE's rigorous prospective enforcement system, and the prohibited financial holdings provisions of the organic acts and rules of various agencies. As stated at the outset, the ethics act may have become a popular shorthand reference to, and a scapegoat for, this entire array of barriers. This imprecision could itself create problems if one were to jump to the conclusion that the difficulties of presidential recruiting could be eased significantly by amendments to the Ethics in Government Act without corresponding attention to the other and arguably more serious obstacles.

Second, and most important, the conflict of interest review and clearance process regarding presidential nominees to Senate-confirmed positions established by OGE as a result of the Ethics in Government Act reinforces our nation's long tradition of frowning on the abuse of public office for private gain. However frequently and brazenly that tradition may have been flouted, the conviction that "public office is a public trust" does have deep roots here. It was the same fundamental public policy and popular sentiment that caused the First Congress in 1789 to prohibit the secretary of the Treasury from investing in government securities, that led to the passage of the precursor to 18 U.S.C. 208 in 1863 to curb frauds by Civil War supply contractors upon the United States, and that resulted in the issuance of Executive Order 11222 in 1965. It is the constitutional responsibility of the president to establish and maintain proper standards of personal conduct and integrity for government officials. Although advocates of advanced management techniques have tried to appropriate the provisions of Article II, Section 3, in support of their prescriptions, the original understanding of the framers of the constitutional requirement that the president "take care that the laws be faithfully executed" would be compatible with today's ethics in government program.[25]

The third and concluding point is that the conflict of interest review and clearance process not only serves lofty objectives of public policy but also contributes to the political effectiveness of a president's nominees. Succeeding in official Washington requires leaders to demonstrate not only decisiveness but also the personal strength of character to make decisions stick, once made. For many presidential nominees, preparation of the public financial disclosure report turns out to be their initiation into "government in the sunshine" and a first recognition that a myriad of people and pressures could and probably will challenge their authority by choosing to point to, as one among many possible targets, an appearance of compromising personal financial interests.[26] Because the OGE public review process is based exclusively on publicly available information, the opinions of the OGE director that the nominees are "in compliance with applicable laws and regulations concerning conflicts of interest" protect an administration by shielding a president's nominees from attacks based on alleged financial conflicts of interest. Holding the leaders of the executive departments publicly accountable to high standards of personal financial integrity must be a starting point for any presidential administration's program for governing this country.

Endnotes

1. Ethics in Government Act of 1978, Pub. L. 95-521, as amended, at Title II, "Executive Personnel Financial Disclosure Requirements"; 5 U.S.C. app. 201 *et seq.*

   This paper considers only the narrow question of the impact of the conflict of interest laws and the Ethics in Government Act on presidential recruiting for Senate-confirmed positions in the executive branch and does not attempt to discuss other topics related to the ethics act nor to review the conflict statutes in a comprehensive manner.

2. Section 405 of the Ethics in Government Act authorizes an appropriation for the Office of Government Ethics through the end of Fiscal Year 1983. It will likely be in the context of the statutorily required reauthorization process that Congress will assess the overall impact of this legislation.

3. The close interrelationship of these factors was a critical analytical and political feature of the recommendations by the Commission on Executive, Legislative and Judicial salaries, in its report of December 1976. The "Peterson Commission," as this group was popularly known, made the following recommendation: "The commission proposes — although recognizing that its only mandate is to propose certain salary increases — that these recommended increases be 'tied' to the establishment of new and stringent Codes of Public Conduct, so that the long and painful process of restoring public confidence of the governed can begin with tangible evidence that 'the era of Watergate' is finally over." (p. 2) The 1980 Report of the Commission on Executive, Legislative and Judicial Salaries, popularly known as the "Quas" [rennial] Comm, endorsed this recommendation.

4. The Office of Government Ethics was established in the Office of Personnel Management, 5 U.S.C. app. 401(a). The approach of the Office of Government Ethics to implementation of the Ethics in Government Act derives guidance from several major sources: Association of the Bar of the City of New York, Special Committee of the Federal Conflict of Interest Laws, *Conflict of Interest and Federal Service,* Harvard University Press, 1960; Robert C. Wood, "Ethics in Government as a Problem in Executive Management," *Public Administration Review* Vol. 15, (Winter 1955) p. 1; Robert C. Wood, "Caesar's Wife in the Late Twentieth Century," unpublished speech delivered at OGE's First Annual Conference, April 7, 1980, Washington, D.C.: B. Mannino, *Federal Conflict of Interest Law*, Harvard University Press, 1964; Roswell B. Perkins, "The New Federal Conflict of Interest Law," 76 *Harvard Law Review* 113 (1963).

5. The fundamental issue, of course, centers on whether or not the Ethics in Government Act of 1978 has been a significant impediment to presidential recruiting. Edwin Meese III, counselor to the president, was quoted in the *Washington Post* of June 18, 1981, as follows:

   "The problem [of recruiting conservatives] was largely one of perception rather than reality. There were lots of good people in the pipeline, *but the problems in getting them through it, which never were as much as they were made out to be,* caused some criticism." (p. A12) (author's emphasis)

   In addition to the question of whether and how to amend the ethics act in order to strike the "correct" balance, *of. infra* at p. 12, there is a general recognition within the executive branch of certain technical problems attributable to unclear language in the act, including generally when to make public the financial disclosure reports of prospective nominees and specifically the proper treatment of the reports of the intended nominees of a president-elect prior to inauguration, to which issue the act is silent; and, given the long-standing position of the Department of Justice that the holdings of a trust of which a government official, the official's spouse or dependent children are beneficiaries are deemed to be assets of the government official for the purpose of 18 U.S.C. 208, how to handle "old family trusts," i.e., trusts established by an ancestor for the benefit of his or her heirs, including a nominee, to which problem the act provides at best confusing guidance.

6. Public access to the financial disclosure reports is restricted to persons who identify themselves and any organization on whose behalf they are acting and who agree not to use the reports for such unlawful purposes as determining credit ratings or soliciting money, 5 U.S.C. app. 205.

   Regulations concerning the public financial disclosure requirements appear at 5 CFR Part 734. The requirements applicable to nominees for Senate-confirmed positions are narrower in scope than those applicable to incumbents who are required to report. *Duplantier v. United States,* 606 F.2d 654 (5th Cir. 1979), *cert. denied,* No. 79-1180 (Jan. 12, 1981). The Fifth Circuit upheld the constitutionality of the judicial branch (Title III) public financial disclosure provisions of the Ethics in Government Act.

7. The Department of Justice, of course, retains exclusive prosecutorial authority with respect to these more serious larcenies, the conflict of interest laws, and all other federal criminal statutes.

8. Regulations concerning post-employment conflicts of interest appear at 5 CFR Part 737.

9. Executive Order 11222, "Prescribing Standards of Ethical Conduct for Government Officers and Employees," Lyndon B. Johnson, May 8, 1965.

10. The Office of Counsel to the President obtains access to this otherwise confidential information as a result of various consents and waivers that each prospective nominee must execute in order to facilitate the personal background investigations.

11. Regulations concerning the responsibilities of agency heads in the ethics in government program appear at 5 CFR 738.202.

12. Regulations concerning an expedited procedure in the case of individuals appointed by the president and subject to confirmation by the Senate appear at 5 CFR 734.604 (c).

13. As provided at 28 U.S.C. 535(b), the head of a government agency shall report to the attorney general any information, allegation or complaint relating to violations of Title 18 involving government officers and employees.

14. Cf. "Chinese wall" approach to issues concerned with the imputed disqualification of attorneys adopted at Formal Opinion 342 of the Ethics Committee of the American Bar Association, 1974.

15. For example, 42 U.S.C. 7212(a), a part of the organic act for the Department of Energy, prohibits supervisory employees of the department from owning "pecuniary interests" in any "energy concerns." By way of contrast, Department of Transportation regulations prohibit employees of that department from having "a direct or indirect interest that conflicts, or appears to conflict, with [the employee's] government duties and responsibilities." 49 CFR 99.735-13.

16. Under the existing provisions of the Internal Revenue Code, no relief is available to prospective or incumbent executive branch personnel from the requirement of recognizing gain (if any) upon the divestiture of property when such action is appropriate to ensure compliance with 18 U.S.C. 208 and other federal conflict of interest statutes and regulations. At the time of this writing, preliminanry discussions of ameliorative legislation are taking place between congressional staff and executive branch persons.

17. With respect to trusts established by someone other than the federal official who is an income beneficiary, Sec. 202 (f) (2) (B) of the Ethics in Government Act provides an exemption from public financial disclosure of the details of the trust's holdings if the incumbent has "no knowledge" of the trust assets; these are called "excepted trusts."

18. Regulations concerning qualified trusts appear at 5 CFR 734, Subpart D.

19. Executive Order 11222, *supra* at note 6, §201(c).

20. Cf. *supra* at note 16.

21. Efforts to avoid the non-augmentation rule by contracting for the former executive's personal services during the official's period of government service — as an outside corporate director or consultant — also could run afoul of 5 U.S.C. app. 210 that prohibits a Senate-confirmed official from receiving earned income in excess of 15 percent of the official's federal salary.

22. Cf. Recommendations 80-4, Decisional Officials Participation in Rule-making Proceedings, Administrative Conference of the United States, June 1980.

23. Cf. Suzanne Garment, "The Ethics Act: Where Will Disclosure Stop?," *Wall Street Journal,* March 13, 1981. Garment, in part, notes:

    "The current system of bans and disclosures is working together with other things to make public service a kind of degradation ritual for businessmen. Someone supplied an example from an agency he was familiar with: 'I know a guy who would have made a wonderful commissioner. But when you put together the disclosure, the post-employment rules, the abusive congressional hearings, the salary, the press — he just wouldn't buy. The effect is cumulative.'"

    Cf. William A. Henry, III and Douglas Brew, "Molasses Pace on Appointments," *Time,* May 11, 1981, p. 19.

24. Cf. Stuart Taylor, Jr., "Those Job-Hopping Carter People," *New York Times,* May 10, 1981, p. F-1.

25. Robert C. Wood, *supra* at note 2, *Public Administration Review,* vol. 15, pp. 2-3. The Ethics in Government Act incorporates this understanding in that the director of the Office of Government Ethics is a presidential nominee in a Senate-confirmed job.

26. Cf. Hugh Heclo, *A Government of Strangers: Executive Politics in Washington,* Brookings Institution, Washington, 1977.

The Professor
Alfred S. Neely IV

Public/private partnerships include the loan of private sector personnel to the public sector and vice versa. Interchanging expertise is said to provide strength to each operation. Yet in the case that follows the academic is in a post-public employment quagmire. Would the plight of the Professor ease if he dropped out a year or two? Must professional people be penalized for contributing their expertise to the public sector? What ethical standard is being abused?

Two years ago I took a leave of absence from my faculty position at State to join the Environmental Protection Agency. I had worked with EPA under a grant several years before, and when they set up an internal task force of scientists to study toxic wastes, they called me.

My department chairperson at State agreed that it was a superb professional opportunity and saw to the details of the leave. University policy prohibits leaves of more than three years, and next semester we will be returning. The most exciting thing is that I have been named university vice president for scientific affairs. I'll miss the classroom and the laboratory, but it seemed about time to try my hand at administration.

The work at EPA has been rewarding. Don't confuse that with finances. Actually the pay here has been about what it was at State. That surprised me, but next year will be a bit better. At EPA I put in twelve or more hours a day. My family saw Washington, but I'm afraid I didn't see too much.

One thing that surprised me was that I was subject to the ethics act. I filled out my forms each year. They weren't much trouble. We've saved some, but all of it is in CDs at the bank. Nothing exotic about our family, or so my son tells me. I didn't think my job there would be high enough for that, but I guess it was.

Before I leave, the one thing I really have to investigate is what effect this job might have on my new one. I heard recently that a woman in another agency who left for an administrative position at a private university out West had some trouble in reconciling the two after she left.

The Professor's transition from the academic community to government appears to have been smooth so far as the ethics-in-government laws are concerned. There is no indication that he had engaged in activities, such as private consulting in his specialty, that could have raised issues of conflicts of interest at EPA. His personal finances were and remain uncomplicated by investments such as stock holdings, which could have the same effect. His earlier work on a government grant, perhaps as a special government employee, appears to have been his only prior nonuniversity employment. His was an easy and uneventful entry in terms of the ethics-in-government laws.

The Professor's time at EPA was similarly untroubled in this respect. He appears to have been more than a full-time employee, devoting long hours to the job. He was neither inclined nor compelled to seek outside employment, and his uncomplicated personal finances made compliance with the executive financial reporting requirements under the act a fairly routine matter.

The Professor's postemployment position in relation to conflicts of interest, however, may present him with some surprises. Universities "do business" with the government. An array of grants and subsidies make up a substantial part of the resources of almost all institutions of higher education. The outcries against current retrenchment in this support are evidence of its importance to them. Furthermore, the Professor is not simply returning to the state university as a teacher and researcher; he is returning as a high administrative official with responsibilities likely to include matters of federal support of the university's scientific research. This is sufficient reason for a closer examination of the effect of the ethics-in-government laws on his situation.

The Professor may well discover that he confronts many of the issues that would face the Industrialist, the Middle Manager, and the Entrepreneur. Since he is leaving federal employment to go to an institution that has numerous dealings with the government, the potential for conflicts does exist, especially in light of his new responsibilities at the university, which will include supervision of its research establishment. Research at such institutions customarily means work for, support from, and contacts with the federal government, and in his case EPA may be expected to be on the list.

Despite the similarities, the Professor's position with respect to EPA once he leaves will be less restricted than it would be if he were to join a different kind of organization in the private sector. This is because the ethics-in-government laws on occasion reflect a solicitous attitude toward certain kinds of postgovernment employment, including positions with educational institutions.

Source: Alfred S. Neely IV, *Ethics-in-Government Laws: Are They Too "Ethical"?* (Washington: American Enterprise Institute, 1984), pp. 42-45.

Actually this distinction may be seen in the law with respect to certain employees before their departure from government. The general prohibition of compensation or salary supplements from sources other than the United States does not apply to contributions from the treasury of a state, county, or municipality. If the Professor had taken a sabbatical leave for a year at half pay, the argument might be made that this supplement to his federal salary was not barred because the state was its source. The argument is plausible because of the statutory exemption. It would not be available if the Professor held a comparable position at a private university and received pay from the school while on sabbatical and in government service. This illustrates the distinction sometimes made under the ethics-in-government laws.

The Professor will find similar and more directly relevant distinctions after leaving and assuming his new post. In general he may not represent the university by formal or informal appearances, or oral or written communications, in particular matters in which he participated at EPA. If, however, he participated in the development of, for example, a general policy on toxic waste research for EPA, he could represent the university in seeking a grant under the program that eventually developed. The difference lies in the particular as opposed to the general.

The same prohibition would extend to any matters that had been pending under his responsibility during his EPA years, though only for two years after termination of his employment. Under another provision the Professor, as a senior employee at EPA, would also be barred for two years from lending his personal presence to informal or formal appearances of another before the agency in matters in which he participated personally and substantially.

Yet another provision generally precludes for a period of one year a senior employee's direct representation of another person with the former agency in any matter pending before the agency in which the agency has a direct and substantial interest. Prior involvement by the former employee is not required under this provision; in fact, it applies to matters that arise during that year after the employee leaves. This requirement in particular might be of great interest to the Professor if the university expects any significant dealings with EPA in the coming year. But the statute draws a distinction useful to the Professor. This limitation does not apply to, among others, persons whose principal occupation or employment is with an accredited, degree-granting institution of higher education.

Moreover, communications solely for the purposes of providing EPA with scientific or technological information are not barred, notwithstanding the other provisions of the law and the former employee's participation or responsibility in any matter. Further, the administrator of EPA could certify that the scientific or technological expertise of a former employee was necessary to the agency and in the national interest and thus justify exemption of the former employee from the otherwise applicable provisions of the law.

As this discussion suggests, the Professor will discover that he must devote more attention to ethics in government once he leaves government service that he did while he was in it. He should also find that none of the relevant legal requirements place insurmountable obstacles before him in discharging his new responsibilities for the university and that most of the restrictions on his activities with EPA will disappear in a year or two at most.

Ethical Problems Today

Revan A. F. Tranter

The International City Management Association Code of Ethics, Guidelines and Rules of Procedure have been revised six times since 1924. The latest review, according to Revan Tranter, stresses member responsibility and organizational integrity. On what basis does he claim that ICMA has "a Code of Ethics, not a Code of Law?" Is this posturing, legalese or a valid distinction for professional managers to examine?

The year was 1924. Lindbergh had yet to make his transatlantic flight. Churchill, in one of his wilderness periods, had just been defeated for a Parliamentary seat. The Australian Parliament had yet to move from Melbourne to Canberra, the new capital. Canada wasn't yet complete; Newfoundland was still a British colony. Hitler was in his jail cell writing *Mein Kampf.* Coolidge was President of the United States. Babe Ruth was in his element. And Perry Cookingham was yet to begin his career as a city manager.

It was, as they say, a different era in 1924, when ICMA's original Code of Ethics was published. As the Second Tenet put it: "No man should accept a position of City Manager unless he believes in the Council-Manager plan of Government." There were no assistants; no county administrators; no COG directors; no general management administrators; no members in Australia, Britain, or New Zealand; no consultants; and no women or minorities. Now we have them all. We also have two-career couples, public-private partnerships, and members with enough disposable income to invest in real estate.

To cope with these changes, the Code of Ethics has had to move with the times. It is now in its sixth edition (1976) and comes with Guidelines and Rules of Procedure for Enforcement. The Executive Board recently approved a series of amendments to the Guidelines and the Rules of Procedure.

The amendments accomplish two things:

- They bring the Guidelines (and therefore the Code) up to date by recognizing changes in our society and our profession.

- They streamline the Rules of Procedure for Enforcement and at the same time improve the Rules' legal protection both for members and for the Association.

In spite of the changes made necessary by time, one thing has remained constant. We have a Code of Ethics, not a Code of Law. After all, we are a profession, and in making that claim we accept and adhere to a higher standard. It is our legal right as citizens to play a vocal part in elections, to buy property in the town where we work, to proclaim in print the virtues of a commercial product, and, after a year on the job (unless otherwise restricted), to leave one position for a better-paying one. But, as true professionals, we agree not to exercise our legal rights to the limit and not to think only of our self-interest, but rather to give priority to the interest of our ultimate client — the citizens of our community.

This article presents several examples of ethical problems that confront the profession today. It is important to note that the Committee on Professional Conduct was increasingly aware of, and uncomfortable about, the unrealistic expectation that the Code in its entirety should apply to all ICMA members — even if they are, for example, elected officials, consultants, commercial vendors, or some other type of private citizen. In revising the Rules of Procedure, the Executive Board decided that affiliate members, and corporate members not in local government service, should be subject only to the First and Third Tenets.

Acceptance and Retention of Appointments

Most people assume that if they're offered a job and they accept it, they simply arrive and begin work, and that's that until at least a couple of years later. There have been cases, however, where members have applied for two positions at the same time (no problem, legally or ethically), accepted one, and then gone to the other at a higher salary. There have even been cases where a member has accepted travel or moving expenses, actually started one job, and then left for the other when it was offered. When that sort of thing occurs, the whole profession suffers.

Source: Revan A. F. Tranter, "Ethical Problems Today," *Public Management* (August 1987), pp. 2-5, 12-13.

The Committee on Professional Conduct has become tired of explanations alleging ambiguity in the terms of appointment or claiming that the acceptance had not yet been put in written form. The *Guideline on Appointment Commitment* to the Third Tenet now states that "oral acceptance of an employment offer is considered binding unless the employer makes fundamental changes in the terms of employment."

Similarly, the Committee is unlikely to be impressed by the argument, made last year by a member, that the city's financial condition was not what he had expected. Unless information has been concealed, anyone holding membership in ICMA is responsible for finding out all the circumstances basic to accepting a new position.

As the *Guideline on Length of Service* to the Fourth Tenet explains, "a minimum of two years generally is considered necessary in order to render a professional service to the municipality." It is recognized, of course, that circumstances ranging from loss of confidence in the member to refusal of the appointing authority* to honor commitments may justify a separation within less than two years. But as the Guideline puts it, "a short tenure should be the exception rather than a recurring experience." And once again it emphasizes that failure to check out fully the conditions or terms of employment is not one of the justifications for such an exception.

Endorsements

It is obvious that members don't like to see colleagues "pushing" commercial products, for they are quick to inform the Committee on Professional Conduct if they see an example of such behavior. Although the *Guideline on Endorsements* to the Twelfth Tenet makes it plain that endorsing a commercial product in a paid advertisement by quotation or the use of a picture is not acceptable — whether or not compensation is involved — times change, and the Guideline has now been amended. The amended Guideline excludes endorsements when they are for a public purpose, when they are directed by the governing body, and when the member receives no compensation. Examples might involve a new hotel whose development is the result of a partnership or agreement between a city or county and a private firm, or a training program for local officials presented by a council of governments.

There have been occasions when a commercial vendor has quoted an ICMA member in an advertisement, without the latter's prior knowledge. If this should happen to you, do what others before you have done: call the vendor and ask that the statement be withdrawn; follow up immediately with a letter; and send the Committee on Professional Conduct a copy.

Investments

Perhaps, in a way, we should be pleased that the Committee on Professional Conduct finds it necessary nowadays to be vigilant against investments that reveal or suggest a conflict of interest. When the Code was originally framed, I doubt whether many ICMA members expected to have any substantial disposable income. And if they did, the Depression soon gave their hopes an unpleasant jolt.

Six decades later, it's still true that if you sincerely want to be rich, you don't become a city or county manager, a COG director, or an assistant.** But it's also obvious that everyone's real income is far higher nowadays, and that two-career families have helped to bring about expenditure options that didn't exist a generation or two ago. We have seen, therefore, an increase in the number of complaints, and thankfully, inquiries about real estate investments and partnerships.

Neither the Twelfth Tenet of the Code nor its *Guideline on Investments in Conflict with Official Duties* flat out forbids local investments by ICMA members. But the Guideline does indicate that there should be no transaction that creates a conflict with official duties. And the *Guideline on Public Confidence* to the Third Tenet speaks of members' conduct that will "maintain public confidence in their profession, their local government, and in their performance of the public trust." It takes little imagination to see how the news media and the public would gain the wrong impression from a manager's purchase of real estate that at some point might involve the services of building inspectors or other local officials. Even the purchase of property far away from your jurisdiction can get you in trouble, for example, if you do it through a partnership involving other employees whose salaries you control or influence. When complaints are made, each case is judged on its own merits. A member would be wise to disclose to the governing body all investments, including those of a spouse. The greatest degree of safety lies in doing what many managers do: in the community where they work, they purchase only their own home.

Politics

The Association has always believed that a reputation for fairness and impartiality is the hallmark of the professional local government manager. The Seventh Tenet of the Code prohibits involvement not only in electing the member's legislative body, but also in other political activities that would impair his or her effectiveness.

Obviously you shouldn't take part in the elections for your board or council. But suppose the councilmember for whom you have the greatest respect is going to run for the state legislature or for Congress? The Seventh Tenet's *Guideline on Other Elections* makes it plain that ICMA members have the right to vote and to express their opinions on public matters. "However, in order not to impair their effectiveness on behalf of the municipalities they serve, they should not participate in election campaigns for representatives from their area to county, school, state, and federal offices." The reason is simple: as the Guideline implies, if your candidate doesn't win, the person who does may one day feel less than objective if you seek assistance on your jurisdiction's behalf. But beyond that, your involvement may permanently harm your professional reputation for impartiality. For both of these reasons, I believe the Committee on Professional Conduct would regard with disfavor even participation in the election of a state legislator from another district.

Certain kinds of election activities are in order, however, as the Seventh Tenet's *Guidelines on Elections on the Council-Manager Plan* and *on Presentation of Issues* indicate. It is acceptable to prepare or present materials on the Plan (even in another community, if requested), and to assist one's governing body in presenting referendum matters, such as annexations and bond issues.

Resumés

The problem of the inaccurate or incomplete resumé has been around for a long time — in all trades and professions — and the growing emphasis on paper qualifications has certainly done nothing to reduce it. A member may consider the school of hard knocks as good as Knox College and may award himself an appropriate degree. Or he or she may regard an experience with a particular local government as so unfortunate that no one else needs to know about it. Members whose cases were recently heard before the Committee on Professional Conduct have included one who cynically chose which parts of his background to reveal to prospective employers, and another, with an otherwise exemplary career behind him, who had awarded himself a degree many years earlier and lived with that uncomfortable knowledge for much of his life.

The *Guideline on Credentials* to the Third Tenet is pretty clear. It says: "An application for employment should be complete and accurate as to all pertinent details of education, experience, and personal history. Members should recognize that both omissions and inaccuracies must be avoided."

Travel expenses

ICMA members seem to be traveling more. Perhaps that's why attendance at the annual conference is up. Maybe it's also why there seem to be more unfortunate incidents with expense accounts. Complaints about members have involved amounts of money ranging from a few dollars to tens of thousands. Penalties have included expulsion from the Association as well as other actions imposed by courts of law.

The writers of the first Code of Ethics probably did not envision the coming of the credit card. Just as on a personal basis it has not helped the lives of those with the least self-control, so on an official basis it has occasionally proved tempting to those who consider themselves unjustly underpaid. If you belong to the latter category, I would strongly urge you not to fight your battles via an expense account. At some point everything will come to light.

After the countless hours of unpaid and unnoticed overtime you've devoted to the public service, it may seem simple — and harmless — enough to do what one member did and, on a conference visit far from home, add an extra digit or two to the stub from the hotel restaurant or bar. But if a local reporter decides to check out city hall expense accounts and make a phone call to that far-away hotel — as one reporter actually did — would you feel confident about explaining yourself to an ICMA fact-finding committee, keeping your job, appearing in court, or facing yourself in the mirror?

Two-Career Couples

The original framers of the Code of Ethics lived in a society where dad went to work and mom stayed home to look after three or four children (not to mention dad). Sixty-three years later, women manage communities of up to a million and a half people, and those who are married to managers often have careers of their own in legal or planning firms, as well as in many other professions. A typical question that arises nowadays is that posed not long ago by a city manager who asked if there were any steps he should take now that his wife had a new law practice in the city and might have a direct or indirect interest in issues before the council. The advice of the Committee on Professional Conduct was that the manager should disclose his wife's employment to the council, and that she should avoid any direct presentation of a client's interest to the council.

The Twelfth Tenet's *Guideline on Personal Relationships* recently approved by the Executive Board states explicitly that "members should disclose any personal relationship to the governing body in any instance where there could be the appearance of a conflict of interest." Although the particular example given there is that of a spouse working for a developer doing business with a local government, the Committee on Professional Conduct wishes it to be understood that "any personal relationship" would include that of a parent or son or daughter or other close relative or close friend. As the *Guideline on Impression of Influence* to the Third Tenet makes plain, "members should conduct their official and personal affairs in such a manner as to give the clear impression that they cannot be improperly influenced in the performance of their official duties." In other words, if it wouldn't look good "revealed" to the local news media, either disclose it up front or don't do it.

Allegiance to the Code

Aristotle said that people in government exercise a teaching function. A good argument can be made that the ethical tone of a community — national, state, or local — is to a substantial degree set by people in leading government positions. For two generations, ICMA's Code of Ethics has conveyed that message. As times change, the Code, the Guidelines, and the Rules of Procedure have changed too. But one thing has remained constant: the Code is a firm statement made by a proud profession. . . .

*Who, by the way, could be another member, as in the case of a manager *vis-a-vis* an assistant.

**Members with two or more children in college are asked to accept the next sentence on faith.

Codes of Ethics

How well does a Code of Ethics contribute to public confidence in public sector operations? To what extent does it reaffirm the honor and integrity of the public service? How well does it serve to detect and deter corrupt practices? The following sample of codes for generalists and specialists offers several opportunities for comparison.

ICMA Code of Ethics with Guidelines
As Adopted by the ICMA Executive Board in May 1987

1. Be dedicated to the concepts of effective and democratic local government by responsible elected officials and believe that professional general management is essential to the achievement of this objective.

2. Affirm the dignity and worth of the services rendered by government and maintain a constructive, creative, and practical attitude toward urban affairs and a deep sense of social responsibility as a trusted public servant.

Guideline

Advice to Officials of Other Municipalities. When members advise and respond to inquiries from elected or appointed officials of other municipalities, they should inform the administrators of those communities.

3. Be dedicated to the highest ideals of honor and integrity in all public and personal relationships in order that the member may merit the respect and confidence of the elected officials, of other officials and employees, and of the public.

Guidelines

Public Confidence. Members should conduct themselves so as to maintain public confidence in their profession, their local government, and in their performance of the public trust.

Impression of Influence. Members should conduct their official and personal affairs in such a manner so as to give the clear impression that they cannot be improperly influenced in the performance of their official duties.

Appointment Commitment. Members who accept an appointment to a position should not fail to report for that position. This does not preclude the possibility of a member considering several offers or seeking several positions at the same time, but once a bona fide offer of a position has been accepted, that commitment should be honored. Oral acceptance of an employment offer is considered binding unless the employer makes fundamental changes in the terms of employment.

Credentials. An application for employment should be complete and accurate as to all pertinent details of education, experience, and personal history. Members should recognize that both omissions and inaccuracies must be avoided.

Source: International City Management Association, originally adopted 1924.

Professional Respect. Members seeking a management position should show professional respect for persons formerly holding the position or for others who might be applying for the same position. Professional respect does not preclude honest differences of opinion; it does preclude attacking a person's motives or integrity in order to be appointed to a position.

Confidentiality. Members should not discuss or divulge information with anyone about pending or completed ethics cases, except as specifically authorized by the Rules of Procedure for Enforcement of the Code of Ethics.

Seeking Employment. Members should not seek employment in a community having an incumbent administrator who has not resigned or been officially informed that his or her services are to be terminated.

4. Recognize that the chief function of local government at all times is to serve the best interests of all of the people.

Guideline

Length of Service. A minimum of two years generally is considered necessary in order to render a professional service to the municipality. A short tenure should be the exception rather than a recurring experience. However, under special circumstances it may be in the best interests of the municipality and the member to separate in a shorter time. Examples of such circumstances would include refusal of the appointing authority to honor commitments concerning conditions of employment, a vote of no confidence in the member, or severe personal problems. It is the responsibility of an applicant for a position to ascertain conditions of employment. Inadequately determining terms of employment prior to arrival does not justify premature termination.

5. Submit policy proposals to elected officials; provide them with facts and advice on matters of policy as a basis for making decisions and setting community goals, and uphold and implement municipal policies adopted by elected officials.

Guideline

Conflicting Roles. Members who serve multiple roles — working as both city attorney and city manager for the same community, for example — should avoid participating in matters that create the appearance of a conflict of interest. They should disclose the potential conflict to the governing body so that other opinions may be solicited.

6. Recognize that elected representatives of the people are entitled to the credit for the establishment of municipal policies; responsibility for policy execution rests with the members.

7. Refrain from participation in the election of the members of the employing legislative body, and from all partisan political activities which would impair performance as a professional administrator.

Guidelines

Elections of the Governing Body. Members should maintain a reputation for serving equally and impartially all members of the governing body of the municipality they serve, regardless of party. To this end, they should not engage in active participation in the election campaign on behalf of or in opposition to candidates for the governing body.

Other Elections. Members share with their fellow citizens the right and responsibility to exercise their franchise and voice their opinion on public issues. However, in order not to impair their effectiveness on behalf of the municipalities they serve, they should not participate in election campaigns for representatives from their area to county, school, state, and federal offices.

Elections on the Council-Manager Plan. Members may assist in preparing and presenting materials that explain the council-manager form of government to the public prior to an election on the use of the plan. If assistance is required by another community, members may respond. All activities regarding ballot issues should be conducted within local regulations and in a professional manner.

Presentation of Issues. Members may assist the governing body in presenting issues involved in referenda such as bond issues, annexations, and similar matters.

8. Make it a duty continually to improve the member's professional ability and to develop the competence of associates in the use of management techniques.

9. Keep the community informed on municipal affairs; encourage communication between the citizens and all municipal officers; emphasize friendly and courteous service to the public; and seek to improve the quality and image of public service.

10. Resist any encroachment on professional responsibilities, believing the member should be free to carry out official policies without interference, and handle each problem without discrimination on the basis of principle and justice.

Guideline

Information Sharing. The member should openly share information with the governing body while diligently carrying out the member's responsibilities as set forth in the charter or enabling legislation.

11. Handle all matters of personnel on the basis of merit so that fairness and impartiality govern a member's decisions, pertaining to appointments, pay adjustments, promotions, and discipline.

Guideline

Equal Opportunity. Members should develop a positive program that will ensure meaningful employment opportunities for all segments of the community. All programs, practices, and operations should: (1) provide equality of opportunity in employment for all persons; (2) prohibit discrimination because of race, color, religion, sex, national origin, political affiliation, physical handicaps, age, or marital status; and (3) promote continuing programs of affirmative action at every level within the organization.

It should be the member's personal and professional responsibility to actively recruit and hire minorities and women to serve on professional staffs throughout their organization.

12. Seek no favor; believe that personal aggrandizement or profit secured by confidential information or by misuse of public time is dishonest.

Guidelines

Gifts. Members should not directly or indirectly solicit any gift or accept or receive any gift — whether it be money, services, loan, travel, entertainment, hospitality, promise, or any other form — under the following circumstances: (1) it could reasonably be inferred or expected that the gift was intended to influence them in the performance of their official duties; or (2) the gift was intended to serve as a reward for any official action on their part.

It is important that the prohibition of unsolicited gifts be limited to circumstances related to improper influence. In *de minimus* situations such as tobacco and meal checks, for example, some modest maximum dollar value should be determined by the member as a guideline. The guideline is not intended to isolate members from normal social practices where gifts among friends, associates, and relatives are appropriate for certain occasions.

Investments in Conflict with Official Duties. Members should not invest or hold any investment, directly or indirectly, in any financial business, commercial, or other private transaction that creates a conflict with their official duties.

In the case of real estate, the potential use of confidential information and knowledge to further a member's personal interest requires special consideration. This guideline recognizes that members' official actions and decisions can be influenced if there is a conflict with personal investments. Purchases and sales which might be interpreted as speculation for quick profit ought to be avoided (see the section below on "Confidential Information").

Because personal investments may prejudice or may appear to influence official actions and decisions, members may, in concert with their governing body, provide for disclosure of such investments prior to accepting their position as municipal administrator or prior to any official action by the governing body that may affect such investments.

Personal Relationships. Members should disclose any personal relationship to the governing body in any instance where there could be the appearance of a conflict of interest. For example, if the manager's spouse works for a developer doing business with the local government, that fact should be disclosed.

Confidential Information. Members should not disclose to others, or use to further their personal interest, confidential information acquired by them in the course of their official duties.

Private Employment. Members should not engage in, solicit, negotiate for, or promise to accept private employment nor should they render services for private interests or conduct a private business when such employment, service, or business creates a conflict with or impairs the proper discharge of their official duties.

Teaching, lecturing, writing, or consulting are typical activities that may not involve conflict of interest or impair the proper discharge of their official duties. Prior notification of the governing body is appropriate in all cases of outside employment.

Representation. Members should not represent any outside interest before any agency, whether public or private, except with the authorization of or at the direction of the legislative body of the governmental unit they serve.

Endorsements. Members should not endorse commercial products by agreeing to use their photograph, endorsement, or quotation in paid advertisements, unless the endorsement is for a public purpose, is directed by the governing body, and the member receives no compensation. Examples of public purposes include economic development for the local government and the sale of local government products.

Members' observations, opinions, and analyses of commercial products used or tested by their municipalities are appropriate and useful to the profession when included as part of professional articles and reports.

ASPA Code of Ethics and Guidelines

The ASPA code of ethics quite properly sets a high standard of public service performance for the members. It is, however, difficult for most of us to translate the performance requirements of the principles into rules of thumb which may help us through the decisions or actions involved in a single day in a busy government office.

The following guidelines have been developed to help public servants understand the application of the code to actual work. The principles are expected to remain largely in their present form, but the guidelines may be amended to fit with changing administrative management problems.

Most of the principles and guidelines can apply to all members of ASPA and, it is hoped, to all public servants. But it is also recognized that supervisory ethics is an important part of management which requires some roles for staff members and different roles for supervisors. In the text the Professional Standards and Ethics Committee (PSEC) has tried to give specific form to principles for supervisors and principles for staff without forgetting that the whole code is intended to help both do a better job in the public interest.

(In the following, the order of principles in the Code has been changed so that the five "Ethics" principles are grouped together, followed by the remaining seven "Quality" principles.)

1. Demonstrate the highest standards of personal integrity, truthfulness, honesty and fortitude in all our public activities in order to inspire public confidence and trust in public institutions.

Perceptions of others are critical to the reputation of an individual or a public agency. Nothing is more important to public administrators than the public's opinion about their honesty, truthfulness, and personal integrity. It overshadows competence as the premier value sought by citizens in their public officials and employees. Any individual or collective compromise with respect to these character traits can damage the ability of an agency to perform its tasks or accomplish its mission. The reputation of the administrator may be tarnished. Effectiveness may be impaired. A career or careers may be destroyed. The best insurance against loss of public confidence is adherence to the highest standards of honesty, truthfulness and fortitude.

Public administrators are obliged to develop civic virtues because of the public responsibilities they have sought and obtained. Respect for the truth, for fairly dealing with others, for sensitivity to rights and responsibilities of citizens, and for the public good must be generated and carefully nurtured and matured.

If you are responsible for the performance of others, share with them the reasons for the importance of integrity. Hold them to high ethical standards and teach them the moral as well as the financial responsibility for public funds under their care.

Source: American Society for Public Administration.

If you are responsible only for your own performance, do not compromise your honesty and integrity for advancement, honors, or personal gain. Be discreet, respectful of proper authority and your appointed or elected superiors, sensitive to the expectations and the values of the public you serve. Practice the golden rule: doing to and for others what you would have done to and for you in similar circumstances. Be modest about your talents, letting your work speak for you. Be generous in your praise of the good work of your fellow workers. Guard the public purse as if it were your own.

Whether you are an official or an employee, by your own example give testimony to your regard for the rights of others. Acknowledge their legitimate responsibilities, and don't trespass upon them. Concede gracefully, quickly, and publicly when you have erred. Be fair and sensitive to those who have not fared well in their dealings with your agency and its applications of the law, regulations, or administrative procedures.

2. **Serve in such a way that we do not realize undue personal gain from the performance of our official duties.**

The only gains you should seek from public employment are salaries, fringe benefits, respect, and recognition for your work. Your personal gains may also include the pleasure of doing a good job, helping the public, and achieving your career goals. No elected or appointed public servant should borrow or accept gifts from staff of any corporation which buys services from, or sells to, or is regulated by, his or her governmental agency. If your work brings you in frequent contact with contractors supplying the government, be sure you pay for your own expenses. Public property, funds and power should never be directed toward personal or political gain. Make it clear by your own actions that you will not tolerate any use of public funds to benefit yourself, your family, or your friends.

3. **Avoid any interest or activity which is in conflict with the conduct of our official duties.**

Public employees should not undertake any task which is in conflict or could be viewed as in conflict with job responsibilities.

This general statement addresses a fundamental principle that public employees are trustees for all the people. This means that the people have a right to expect public employees to act as surrogates for the entire people with fairness toward all the people and not a few or a limited group.

Actions or inactions which conflict with, injure, or destroy this foundation of trust between the people and their surrogates must be avoided.

Ironically, experience indicates that conflict of interest and corruption often arise not from an external affront, but as a result of interaction between persons who know each other very well. To strengthen resistance to conflict of interest, public employees should avoid frequent social contact with persons who come under their regulation or persons who wish to sell products or services to their agency or institution.

Agencies with inspectional or investigative responsibilities have a special obligation to reduce vulnerability to conflict of interest. Periodic staff rotation may be helpful to these agencies.

Individuals holding a position recognized by law or regulation as an unclassified or political appointment (e.g. Cabinet level and Governor's appointment positions) have a special obligation to behave in ways which do not suggest that official acts are driven primarily or only by partisan political concerns.

Public employees should remember that despite whatever preventive steps they might take, situations which hold the possibility for conflict of interest will always emerge. Consequently, the awareness of the potentiality of conflict of interest is important. Public employees, particularly professors in Public Administration, have a serious obligation to periodically stimulate discussion on conflicts of interest within organizations, schools, and professional associations.

4. **Support, implement, and promote merit employment and programs of affirmative action to assure equal employment opportunity by our recruitment, selection, and advancement of qualified persons from all elements of society.**

Oppose any discrimination because of race, color, religion, sex, national origin, political affiliation, physical handicaps, age, or marital status, in all aspects of personnel policy. Likewise, a person's lifestyle should not be the occasion for discrimination if it bears no reasonable relation to his or her ability to perform required tasks.

Review employment and personnel operations and statistics to identify the impact of organizational practices on "protected groups." Performance standards should apply equally to all workers. In the event of cutbacks of staff, managers should employ fair criteria for selection of employees for separation, and humane strategies for administering the program.

Any kind of sexual, racial, or religious harassment should not be allowed. Appropriate channels should be provided for harassed persons to state their problems to objective officials. In the event of a proven offense, appropriate action should be taken.

5. Eliminate all forms of illegal discrimination, fraud, and mismanagement of public funds, and support colleagues if they are in difficulty because of responsible efforts to correct such discrimination, fraud, mismanagement or abuse.

If you are a supervisor, you should not only be alert that no illegal action issues from or is sponsored by your immediate office. You should inform your subordinates at regular intervals that you will tolerate no illegalities in their offices and discuss the reasons for the position with them. Public employees who have good reason to suspect illegal action in any public agency should seek assistance in how to channel information regarding the matter to appropriate authorities.

All public servants should support authorized investigative agencies, the General Accounting Office in the federal government, auditors in the state or large local governments, C.P.A. firms or federal or state auditors in many other cases. We should support the concept of independent auditors reporting to committees independent of management. Good fiscal and management controls and inspections are important protections for supervisors, staff, and the public interest.

In both government and business, inadequate equipment, software, procedures, supervision, and poor security controls make possible both intentional and unintentional misconduct. Managers have an ethical obligation to seek adequate equipment, software, procedures and controls to reduce the agency's vulnerability to misconduct. When an agency dispenses exemptions from regulations, or abatement of taxes or fees, managers should assure periodic investigatory checks.

The "whistle blower" who appears to his/her immediate superiors to be disloyal, may actually be loyal to the higher interests of the public. If so, the whistle blower deserves support. Local, state, and federal governments should establish effective dissent channels to which whistle blowers may report their concerns without fear of identification.

Supervisors should inform their staff that constructive criticism may be brought to them without reprisal, or may be carried to an ombudsman or other designated official. As a last resort, public employees have a right to make public their criticism but it is the personal and professional responsibility of the critic to advance only well-founded criticism.

6. Serve the public with respect, concern, courtesy, and responsiveness, recognizing that service to the public is beyond service to oneself.

Be sure your answers to questions on public policy are complete, understandable and true. Try to develop in your staff a goal of courteous conduct with citizens. Devise a simple system to ensure that your staff gives helpful and pleasant service to the public. Wherever possible, show citizens how to avoid mistakes in their relations with government.

Each citizen's questions should be answered as thoughtfully and as fully as possible. If you or your staff do not know the answer to a question, an effort should be made to get an answer or to help the citizen make direct contact with the appropriate office.

Part of servicing the public responsively is to encourage citizen cooperation and to involve civic groups. Administrators have an ethical responsibility to bring citizens into work with the government as far as practical, both to secure citizen support of government, and for the economies of increased effectiveness which will result. Respect the right of the public (through the media) to know what is going on in your agency even though you know queries may be raised for partisan or other non-public purposes.

7. Strive for personal professional excellence and encourage the professional development of our associates and those seeking to enter the field of public administration.

Staff members, throughout their careers, should be encouraged to participate in professional activities and associations such as ASPA. They should also be reminded of the importance of doing a good job and their responsibility to improve the public service.

Administrators should make time to meet with students periodically and to provide a bridge between classroom studies and the realities of public jobs. Administrators should also lend their support to well planned internship programs.

8. Approach our organization and operational duties with a positive attitude and constructively support open communication, creativity, dedication and compassion.

Americans expect government to be compassionate, well organized, and operating within the law. Public employees should understand the purpose of their agency and the role they play in achieving that purpose. Dedication and creativity of staff members will flow from a sense of purpose.

ASPA members should strive to create a work environment which supports positive and constructive attitudes among workers at all levels. This open environment should permit employees to comment on work activities without fear of reprisal. In addition, managers can strengthen this open environment by establishing procedures ensuring thoughtful and objective review of employee concerns.

9. Respect and protect the privileged information to which we have access in the course of official duties.

Much information in public offices is privileged for reasons of national security, or because of laws or ordinances. If you talk with colleagues about privileged matters, be sure they need the information and you enjoin them to secrecy. If the work is important enough to be classified, learn and follow the rules set by the security agency. Special care must be taken to secure access to confidential information stored on computers. Sometimes information needs to be withheld from the individual citizen or general public to prevent disturbances of the peace. It should be withheld only if there is a possibility of dangerous or illegal or unprofessional consequences of releasing information.

Where other governmental agencies have a legitimate public service need for information possessed by an agency, do all you can to cooperate, within the limits of statute law, administrative regulations, and promises made to those who furnish the information.

10. Exercise whatever discretionary authority we have under law to promote the public interest.

If your work involves discretionary decisions you should first secure policy guidelines from your supervisor. You should then make sure that all staff who "need to know" are informed of these policies and have an opportunity to discuss the means of putting them into effect.

There are occasions when a law is unenforceable or has become obsolete; in such cases you should recommend to your superior or to the legislative body that the law be modernized. If an obsolete law remains in effect, the manager or highest official should determine if the law is or is not to be enforced, after consultation with the agency's legal advisor.

There are occasions where a lower level employee must be given considerable discretion. Try to see that such employees are adequately trained for their difficult tasks.

Tell yourself and your staff quite frequently that every decision creates a precedent, so the first decisions on a point should be ethically sound; this is the best protection for staff as well as for the public.

11. Accept as a personal duty the responsibility to keep up to date on emerging issues and to administer the public's business with professional competence, fairness, impartiality, efficiency and effectiveness.

Administrators should attend professional meetings, read books and periodicals related to their field, and talk with specialists. The goal is to keep informed about the present and future issues and problems in their professional field and organization in order to take advantage of opportunities and avoid problems.

Serious mistakes in public administration have been made by people who did their jobs conscientiously but failed to look ahead for emerging problems and issues. A long list of washed out dams, fatal mine accidents, fires in poorly inspected buildings, inadequate computer systems, or economic disasters are results of not looking ahead. ASPA members should be catalysts to stimulate discussion and reflection about improving efficiency and effectiveness of public services.

12. Respect, support, study, and when necessary, work to improve federal and state constitutions and other laws which define the relationships among public agencies, employees, clients and all citizens.

Familiarize yourself with principles of American constitutional government. As a citizen work for legislation which is in the public interest.

Teach constitutional principles of equality and fairness.

Strive for clear division of functions between different levels of government, between different bureaus or departments, and between government and its citizens. Cooperate as fully as possible with all agencies of government, especially those with overlapping responsibilities. Do not let parochial or institutional loyalty drown out considerations of wider public policy.

Approved by National Council March 27, 1985

National Contract Management Association Code of Ethics

Preamble

Each member of the National Contract Management Association accepts the obligation to uphold the purposes of the organization as set forth in the NCMA constitution, to strive for the increase of knowledge in job performance and the field of contract management, and to abide by the letter and spirit of the ethical standards of the Association.

As prescribed in Article X of the By-Laws to the Constitution of NCMA, this Code of Ethics establishes for the member a foundation of professional conduct. However, ethical conduct may require more than merely abiding by the letter of the Code. It is therefore incumbent upon each member of the association to make a commitment to honorable behavior in all aspects of work and professional activity.

Standards

Each Member of NCMA shall:

1. Strive to attain the highest professional standard of job performance, to exercise diligence in carrying out the duties of his or her employer, and to serve that employer to the best of one's ability.

2. Keep informed of acquisition developments, through academic course work and attendance at symposia, in order to increase knowledge, skill and thoroughness of work preparation.

3. Respect the confidence and trust reposed in the member by one's employer.

4. Conduct oneself in such a manner as to bring credit upon the Association, as well as to maintain trust and confidence in the integrity of the acquisition process.

5. Avoid engagement in any transaction that might conflict with the proper discharge of one's employment duties by reason of a financial interest, family relationship, or any other circumstance causing a breach of confidence in the acquisition process.

6. Not knowingly influence others to commit any act that would constitute a violation of this Code.

Source: *Contract Management* (October 1988), p. 7.

Code of Ethics for Government Service

The United States Code of Ethics of 1980 is based on guidelines developed earlier at the state level — for example, The Code of Ethics of the State of Georgia (1968), which has very similar phrasing.

Authority of Public Law 96-303, unanimously passed by the Congress of the United States on June 27, 1980, and signed into law by the President on July 3, 1980.

Agency ethics officials and the Office of Government Ethics are available to answer questions on conflicts of interest.

Any Person in Government Should:

I. Put loyalty to the highest moral principles and to country above loyalty to persons, party, or Government department.

II. Uphold the Constitution, laws, and regulations of the United States and of all governments therein and never be a party to their evasion.

III. Give a full day's labor for a full day's pay; giving earnest effort and best thought to the performance of duties.

IV. Seek to find and employ more efficient and economical ways to getting tasks accomplished.

V. Never discriminate unfairly by the dispensing of special favors or privileges to anyone, whether for remuneration or not; and never accept, for himself or herself or for family members, favors or benefits under circumstances which might be construed by reasonable persons as influencing the performance of governmental duties.

VI. Make no private promises of any kind binding upon the duties of office, since a Government employee has no private word which can be binding on public duty.

VII. Engage in no business with the Government, either directly or indirectly, which is inconsistent with the conscientious performance of governmental duties.

VIII. Never use any information gained confidentially in the performance of governmental duties as a means of making private profit.

IX. Expose corruption wherever discovered.

X. Uphold these principles, ever conscious that public office is a public trust.

The Quest for a Code of Professional Ethics: An Intellectual and Moral Confusion

John Ladd

My role as a philosopher is to act as a gadfly. If this were Athens in the fifth century B.C. you would probably throw me in prison for what I shall say, and I would be promptly condemned to death for attacking your idols. But you can't do that in this day and age; you can't even ask for your money back, since I am not being paid. All that you can do is to throw eggs at me or simply walk out!

My theme is stated in the title: it is that the whole notion of an organized professional ethics is an absurdity — intellectual and moral. Furthermore, I shall argue that there are few positive benefits to be derived from having a code and the possibility of mischievous side effects of adopting a code is substantial. Unfortunately, in the time allotted to me I can only summarize what I have to say on this topic.

Charging that codes of ethics provide a sense of complacency along with diverting attention from the "Macro-ethical problems," the Ladd article goes farther and asserts that "There is no special ethics belonging to professionals." Is Ladd's position absurd, realistic or perhaps unethical, as he proposes any professional Code of Ethics would be?

(1) To begin with, ethics itself is basically an open-ended, reflective and critical intellectual activity. It is essentially problematic and controversial, both as far as its principles are concerned and in its application. Ethics consists of issues to be examined, explored, discussed, deliberated, and argued. Ethical principles can be established only as a result of deliberation and argumentation. These principles are not the kind of thing that can be settled by fiat, by agreement, or by authority. To assume that they can be is to confuse ethics with law-making, rule-making, policy-making, and other kinds of decision-making. It follows that, ethical principles, as such, cannot be established by associations, organizations, or by a consensus of their members. To speak of codifying ethics, therefore, makes no more sense than to speak of codifying medicine, anthropology, or architecture.

(2) Even if substantial agreement could be reached on ethical principles and they could be set out in a code, the attempt to impose such principles on others in the guise of ethics contradicts the notion of ethics itself, which presumes that persons are autonomous moral agents. In Kant's terms, such an attempt makes ethics heteronomous; it confuses ethics with some kind of externally imposed set of rules such as a code of law, which, indeed, is heteronomous. To put the point in more popular language: ethics must, by its very nature, be self-directed rather than other-directed.

(3) Thus, in attaching disciplinary procedures, methods of adjudication and sanctions, formal and informal, to the principles that one calls "ethical" one automatically converts them into legal rules or some other kind of authoritative rules of conduct such as the bylaws of an organization, regulations promulgated by an official, club rules, rules of etiquette, or other sorts of social standards of conduct. To label such conventions, rules and standards "ethical" simply reflects an intellectual confusion about the status and function of these conventions, rules, and standards. Historically, it should be noted that the term "ethical" was introduced merely to indicate that the code of the Royal College of Physicians was not to be construed as a criminal code (i.e. a legal code). Here "ethical" means simply non-legal.

(4) That is not to say ethics has no relevance for projects involving the creation, certification, and enforcement of rules of conduct for members of certain groups. But logically it has the same kind of relevance as it has for the law. As with law, its role in connection with these projects is to appraise, criticize and perhaps even defend (or condemn) the projects themselves, the rules, regulations, and procedures they prescribe, and the social and political goals and institutions they represent. But although ethics can be used to judge or evaluate a disciplinary code, penal code, code of honor, or what goes by the name of a "code of ethics," it cannot be identified with any of these, for the reasons that have already been mentioned.

Source: John Ladd, "The Quest for a Code of Professional Ethics: An Intellectual and Moral Confusion," from *Professional Ethics Project: Professional Ethics Activities in the Scientific and Engineering Societies,* ed. Rosemary Chalk, Mark S. Frankel, and Sallie B. Chafer (Washington, D.C.: American Association for the Advancement of Science, 1980), pp. 154-159.

Some General Comments on Professionalism and Ethics

(5) Being a professional does not automatically make a person an expert in ethics, even in the ethics of that person's own particular profession — unless of course we decide to call the "club rules" of a profes-

sion its ethics. The reason for this is that there are no experts in ethics in the sense of expert in which professionals have a special expertise that others do not share. As Plato pointed out long ago in the *Protagoras,* knowledge of virtue is not like the technical knowledge that is possessed by an architect or shipbuilder. In a sense, everyone is, or ought to be, a teacher of virtue; there are no professional qualifications that are necessary for doing ethics.

(6) Moreover, there is no special ethics belonging to professionals. Professionals are not, simply because they are professionals, exempt from the common obligations, duties, and responsibilities that are binding on ordinary people. They do not have a special moral status that allows them to do things that no one else can. Doctors have no special right to be rude, to deceive, or to order people around like children, etc. Likewise, lawyers do not have a special right to bend the law to help their clients, to bully witnesses, or to be cruel and brutal — simply because they think that it is in the interests of their client. Professional codes cannot, therefore, confer such rights and immunities, for there is no such thing as professional ethical immunity.

(7) We might ask: do professionals, by virtue of their special professional status, have special duties and obligations over and above those they would have as ordinary people? Before we can answer this question, we must first decide what is meant by the terms "profession" and "professional," which are very loose terms that are used as labels for a variety of different occupational categories. The distinctive element in professionalism is generally held to be that professionals have undergone advanced, specialized training and that they exercise control over the nature of their job and the services they provide. In addition, the older professions, lawyers, physicians, professors, and ministers typically have clients to whom they provide services as individuals. (I use the term "client" generically as to include patients, students, and parishioners.) When professionals have individual clients, new moral relationships are created that demand special types of trust and loyalty. Thus, in order to answer the question, we need to examine the context under which special duties and obligations of professionals might arise.

(8) In discussing specific ethical issues relating to the professions, it is convenient to divide them into issues of macro-ethics and micro-ethics. The former comprise what might be called collective or social problems, that is, problems confronting members of a profession as a group in their relation to society; the latter, issues of micro-ethics, are concerned with moral aspects of personal relationships between individual professionals and other individuals who are their clients, their colleagues and their employers. Clearly the particulars in both kinds of ethics vary considerably from one profession to another. I shall make only two general comments.

(9) Micro-ethical issues concern the personal relationships between individuals. Many of these issues simply involve the application of ordinary notions of honesty, decency, civility, humanity, considerateness, respect, and responsibility. Therefore, it should not be necessary to devise a special code to tell professionals that they ought to refrain from cheating and lying, or to make them treat their clients (or patients) with respect, or to tell them that they ought to ask for informed consent for invasive actions. It is a common mistake to assume that all the extra-legal norms and conventions governing professional relationships have a moral status, for every profession has norms and conventions that have as little to do with morality as the ceremonial dress and titles that are customarily associated with the older professions.

(10) The macro-ethical problems in professionalism are more problematic and controversial. What are the social responsibilities of professionals as a group? What can and should they do to influence social policy? Here, I submit, the issue is not one of professional roles, but of professional power. For professionals as a group have a great deal of power; and power begets responsibility. Physicians as a group can, for instance, exercise a great deal of influence on the quality and cost of health care; and lawyers can have a great deal of influence on how the law is made and administered, etc.

(11) So-called "codes of professional ethics" have nothing to contribute either to micro-ethics or to macro-ethics as just outlined. It should also be obvious that they do not fit under either of these two categories. Any association, including a professional association, can, of course, adopt a code of conduct for its members and lay down disciplinary procedures and sanctions to enforce conformity with its rules. But to call such a disciplinary code a code of ethics is at once pretentious and sanctimonious. Even worse, it is to make a false and misleading claim, namely, that the profession in question has the authority or special competence to create an ethics, that it is able authoritatively to set forth what the principles of ethics are, and that it has its own brand of ethics that it can impose on its members and on society.

I have briefly stated the case against taking a code of professional ethics to be a serious ethical enterprise. It might be objected, however, that I have neglected to recognize some of the benefits that come from having professional codes of ethics. In order to discuss these possible benefits, I shall first examine what some of the objectives of codes of ethics might be, then I shall consider some possible benefits of having a code, and, finally, I shall point out some of the mischievous aspects of codes.

Objectives of Codes of Professional "Ethics"

In order to be crystal clear about the purposes and objectives of a code, we must begin by asking: to whom is the code addressed? Although ostensibly codes of ethics are addressed to the members of the profession, their true purposes and objectives are sometimes easier to ascertain if we recognize that codes are in fact often directed at other addressees than members. Accordingly, the real addressees may be any of the following: (a) members of the profession, (b) clients or buyers of the professional services, (c) other agents dealing with professionals, such as government or private institutions like universities or hospitals, or (d) the public at large. With this in mind, let us examine some possible objectives.

First, the objective of a professional code might be "inspirational," that is, it might be used to inspire members to be more "ethical" in their conduct. The assumption on which this objective is premised is that professionals are somehow likely to be amoral or submoral, perhaps, as the result of becoming professionals, and so it is necessary to exhort them to be moral, e.g. to be honest. I suppose there is nothing objectionable to having a code for this reason; it would be something like the Boy Scout's Code of Honor, something to frame and hang in one's office. I have severe reservations, however, about whether a code is really needed for this purpose and whether it will do any good; for those to whom it is addressed and who need it the most will not adhere to it anyway, and the rest of the good people in the profession will not need it because they already know what they ought to do. For this reason, many respectable members of a profession regard its code as a joke and as something not to be taken seriously. (Incidentally, for much the same kind of reasons as those just given, there are no codes in the academic or clerical professions.)

A second objective might be to alert professionals to the moral aspects of their work that they might have overlooked. In jargon, it might serve to sensitize them or to raise their consciousness. This, of course, is a worthy goal — it is the goal of moral education. Morality, after all, is not just a matter of doing or not doing, but also a matter of feeling and thinking. But, here again, it is doubtful that it is possible [to] make people have the right feelings or think rightly through enacting a code. A code is hardly the best means for teaching morality.

Thirdly, a code might, as it was traditionally, be a disciplinary code or a "penal" code used to enforce certain rules of the profession on its members in order to defend the integrity of the professional and to protect its professional standards. This kind of function is often referred to as "self-policing." It is unlikely, however, that the kind of disciplining that is in question here could be handled in a code of ethics, a code that would set forth in detail criteria for determining malpractice. On the contrary, the "ethical" code of a profession is usually used to discipline its members for other sorts of "unethical conduct," such as stealing a client away from a colleague, for making disparaging remarks about a colleague in public, or for departing from some other norm of the profession. (In the original code of the Royal College of Physicians, members who failed to attend the funeral of a colleague were subject to a fine!) It is clear that when we talk of a disciplinary code, as distinguished from an exhortatory code, a lot of new questions arise that cannot be treated here; for a disciplinary code is quasi-legal in nature, it involves adjudicative organs and processes, and it is usually connected with complicated issues relating to such things as licensing.

A fourth objective of a code might be to offer advice in cases of moral perplexity about what to do: e.g. should one report a colleague for malfeasance? Should one let a severely defective newborn die? If such cases present genuine perplexities, then they cannot and should not be solved by reference to a code. To try to solve them through a code is like trying to do surgery with a carving knife! If it is not a genuine perplexity, then the code would be unnecessary.

A fifth objective of a professional code of ethics is to alert prospective clients and employers to what they may and may not expect by way of service from a member of the profession concerned. The official code of an association, say, of engineers, provides an authoritative statement of what is proper and what is improper conduct of the professional. Thus, a code serves to protect a professional from improper demands on the part of employer or client, e.g. that he lie about or cover up defective work that constitutes a public hazard. Codes may thus serve to protect "whistle-blowers" (the real addressee in this case is the employer or client).

Secondary Objectives of Codes — Not Always Salutory

I now come to what I shall call "secondary objectives," that is, objectives that one may hesitate always to call "ethical," especially since they often provide an opportunity for abuse.

The first secondary objective is to enhance the image of the profession in the public eye. The code is supposed to communicate to the general public (the addressee) the idea that the members of the profession concerned are service oriented and that the interests of the client are always given first place over the interests of the professional himself. Because they have a code they may be expected to be trustworthy.

Another secondary objective of a code is to protect the monopoly of the profession in question. Historically, this appears to have been the principle objective of a so-called code of ethics, e.g. Percival's code of medical ethics. Its aim is to exclude from practice those who are outside the professional in-group and to regulate the conduct of the members of the profession so as to protect it from encroachment from outside. Sometimes this kind of professional monopoly is in the public interest and often it is not.

Another secondary objective of professional codes of ethics, mentioned in some of the literature, is that having a code serves as a status symbol; one of the credentials for an occupation to be considered a profession is that it have a code of ethics. If you want to make your occupation a profession, then you must frame a code of ethics for it: so there are codes for real estate agents, insurance agents, used car dealers, electricians, barbers, etc., and these codes serve, at least in the eyes of some, to raise their members to the social status of lawyers and doctors.

Mischievous Side-effects of Codes of Ethics

I now want to call attention to some of the mischievous side-effects of adopting a code of ethics:

The first and most obvious bit of mischief, is that having a code will give a sense of complacency to professionals about their conduct. "We have a code of ethics," they will say, "So everything we do is ethical." Inasmuch as a code, of necessity, prescribes what is minimal, a professional may be encouraged by the code to deliver what is minimal rather than the best that he can do. "I did everything that the code requires. . . ."

Even more mischievous than complacency and the consequent self-congratulation, is the fact that the code of ethics can be used as a cover-up for what may be called basically "unethical" or "irresponsible" conduct.

Perhaps the most mischievous side-effect of codes of ethics is that they tend to divert attention from the macro-ethical problems of a profession to its micro-ethical problems. There is a lot of talk about whistle-blowing. But it concerns individuals almost exclusively. What is really needed is a thorough scrutiny of professions as collective bodies, of their role in society and their effect on the public interest. What role should the professions play in determining the use of technology, its development and expansion, and the distribution of the costs (e.g. disposition of toxic wastes) as well as the benefits of technology? What is the significance of professionalism from the moral point of view for democracy, social equality, liberty, and justice? There are lots of ethical problems to be dealt with. To concentrate on codes of ethics as if they represented the real ethical problems connected with professionalism is to capitulate to struthianism (from the Greek word struthos = ostrich).

One final objection to codes that needs to be mentioned is that they inevitably represent what John Stuart Mill called the "tyranny of the majority" or, if not that, the "tyranny of the establishment." They serve to and are designed to discourage if not suppress the dissenter, the innovator, the critic.

By way of conclusion, let me say a few words about what an association of professionals can do about ethics. On theoretical grounds, I have argued that it cannot codify an ethics and it cannot authoritatively establish ethical principles or prescribed guidelines for the conduct of its members — as if it were *creating* an ethics! But there is still much that associations can do to promote further understanding of and sensitivity to ethical issues connected with professional activities. For example, they can fill a very useful educational function by encouraging their members to participate in extended discussions of issues of both micro-ethics and macro-ethics, e.g. questions about responsibility; for these issues obviously need to be examined and discussed much more extensively than they are at present — especially by those who are in a position to do something about them.

Are You an Ethical Public Official?

Every day, you, as a city official, face situations in which your personal and professional integrity and ethics are tested.

A recent series of workshops around the country, conducted by a nationally-known professional services company, University Research Corporation, posed 10 common "ethical dilemmas" for more than 800 mayors, city managers, county executives and other key local officials. The workshops on "Maintaining Municipal Integrity" were sponsored by the National Institute of Justice.

The International City Management Association ethics vignettes which follow offer an opportunity to test our ethical standards. Do the four Codes presented in Part III provide useful guidelines?

Each of the 10 ethical dilemmas described below can be answered with a "yes" or "no." After you have completed your answers, you can score and interpret your responses in accordance with the instructions provided.

1. The board of directors of the chamber of commerce has an annual weekend outing at a resort some miles from your city. During the weekend there is golf, tennis, swimming, card games, dinner dances with entertainment and numerous cocktail parties. During the day, there are sessions at which the chamber board reviews progress for the past year and discusses plans for the coming year. For several years, the city has contributed $100,000 annually for the support of the chamber.

You are a councilmember or the city administrator, and have been invited to the weekend outing with all expenses paid by the chamber. *Do you accept the invitation and go for the weekend?* Yes ☐ No ☐

2. You have been asked to speak to a Sunday-brunch meeting of the city council of another city some miles away. They want you to tell them about your city's cost-reduction program, in anticipation of a Proposition 13-type measure that is being proposed by the citizens of their community.

At the conclusion of your appearance, the chairman hands you an envelope containing an honorarium check for $250 and explains that "This is in appreciation of you giving up your Sunday morning." *Would you accept the honorarium?*   Yes ☐ No ☐

3. For many years, you and Frank Jordan have been close friends. You went to high school together and were college classmates. You were best man at each other's weddings. Your wives are good friends. For the past 10 years, Frank and his wife have taken you and your wife to dinner on your birthday. It is just something he insists upon doing and it has become something of a tradition. He can well afford it; Frank owns the largest plumbing supply business in the state and does more than $500,000 in business each year with the city.

You are a councilmember, and you chair the council committee which oversees procurement contracts, including plumbing supplies. Your birthday is coming up in a couple of weeks. Frank has called to remind you that he and Mrs. Jordan have a special treat for your birthday dinner this year. He had made reservations at a fancy new restaurant that everyone is talking about. *Do you accept?*   Yes ☐ No ☐

4. For some time, police officers on three adjacent beats have met each day for a coffee break at a restaurant near a point where the three beats intersect. They usually have coffee and a donut, and occasionally a piece of pie.

You are a police officer and were just assigned to one of the beats. When you go for the coffee break the first day, and you walk up to pay the check, the proprietor says, "No charge. I am glad to have you officers around." The other officers leave without paying. *Do you pay your check?*   Yes ☐ No ☐

5. Henry Settles has worked in your department for a long time. He is conscientious, in fact, maybe too conscientious, in the view of many of his fellow workers. He is always at work on time, always puts in all his hours, and works hard. But he expect others to do the same and frequently complains about others who are tardy or who take long lunch hours or call in sick when almost everyone knows they are not sick.

You are head of the department which employs Henry. Recently, Henry reported to you that some employees of the department were using city automobiles to drive to pro football games in a city about 100 miles away. You put a stop to that, but Henry has been *persona non grata* with many of the employees of the department since he "snitched" on them. Henry is a leading candidate for a new position in the department — one that would mean a promotion for him. *Do you promote Henry?*   Yes ☐ No ☐

Source: "Are You an Ethical Public Official?" *Town and Country* (Official Publication of the Arkansas Municipal League), September, 1984, pp. 14-15.

Reprinted from *Public Management*, published by the International City Management Association.

6. A new civic plaza is included in the plans to restore the downtown area of your city. The bond issue for developing the plaza which was passed three years ago is already too little to assure completion of the project, because of inflation. A developer who wants to erect a high-rise building near the plaza offers to buy a large tract of undeveloped land in the plaza area and donate it to the city, as a trade-off for permission to construct his proposed building higher than the present zoning restrictions will permit.

He has privately made this offer to you, the city administrator, and it is up to you to decide whether to communicate the offer to the city council. *Do you pass on the offer to the council?*   Yes ❐ No ❐

7. You are the city administrator. A few days before Christmas, a package arrives at your office. Inside is a card from the vice-president of a large corporation in your city. The company has never done any business with the city. The card says, "You are doing a great job for our city and we just wanted you to know that we appreciate it. We hope you will accept this token of our gratitude."

You open the package and find a beautiful crystal vase which you estimate to be worth $75 to $100. *Do you accept the vase?*   Yes ❐ No ❐

8. Your favorite brand of Scotch is Chivas Regal, but you don't buy it too often because it is so expensive. You have told this to the liquor dealer from whom you buy your booze. It's a kind of joke. "Think rich and drink cheap," you sometimes remark when you buy a less expensive brand.

The liquor dealer gets in trouble for bookmaking and his license is in jeopardy. You, as city administrator, have nothing to do with the hearing on suspension of his license, but the next time you go to buy liquor, you discover when you get home that the sack containing your liquor includes a fifth of Chivas Regal which you didn't order or pay for. *Do you keep the Scotch?*   Yes ❐ No ❐

9. A physician friend of yours asks if you would be interested in investing in a doctor's building which a group of physicians plan to erect in the city of which you are the administrator. No decisions involving your job are expected as part of the investment; the doctors are simply selling shares in their venture. It will be next to a shopping center in a rapidly growing part of town.

You stand to more than quadruple the $25,000 cost of your investment in a short time; maybe make even more than that. You have the money. *Would you invest in the doctors' building?*   Yes ❐ No ❐

10. You are a department head, and Hazel Stevens is one of your most valuable employees. She has worked for you for years and is the kind of worker you can depend upon to put in extra time and effort when it is needed. She is always there during a crisis and several times she has handled situations that would have been uncomfortable for you. You really owe her a lot.

Recently, Hazel came to you and admitted that for some time, she'd been "borrowing" money from the petty cash fund, and writing false receipts to cover it. It was never much; usually $10 or $15, and she always repaid it. But her conscience has bothered her so much that she had to confess.

Under the city's personnel policies, her action is clearly a cause for dismissal. *Do you fire her?*
Yes ❐ No ❐

An Explanation of the Answers

1. No. Not if the chamber pays your expenses. Since the city's annual donation to the chamber presumably is designed to encourage business and improve the city's tax base, it may be legitimately important for one or two city officials, such as the mayor, or city manager to attend. If so, the cost of the yearly outing should be figured into the city's annual budget. Attendance under such circumstances — where the city pays your way — would be acceptable.

2. No. The only reason you were invited was because of the knowledge and experience you possess because of your association with the city. There is an expectation that you will share your professional expertise with your municipal colleagues. You may only accept expenses, i.e., mileage, parking, etc. at the customary rates.

3. Yes. Public service does not require that you give up previous acquaintances and friendships. What is required is that at any point in the future in which your friend's business in involved, i.e., contract negotiations, bids, etc. you disqualify yourself from influencing the decision in any way. If you decide not to go with Frank, you are still ethical, but probably over-zealous.

4. Yes. Police officers and other city employees provide a service for which they are paid. Why shouldn't others — such as the postman, bus driver, etc. — receive the same benefits? It has been clearly demonstrated that small acts of corruption set the stage for, and lead to larger, more pervasive problems. In one city, a new police chief, observing a scenario similar to the above, posted an immediate order prohibiting such activity; violators to be fired. A sergeant came to him with the statement that "he hadn't realized it, but because of free coffee and donuts, he had been hesitant to report the restaurant's filthy restrooms."

5. Yes. If based on his performance, Henry should receive the promotion because: (1) he qualified for the promotion; (2) promoting Henry reinforces the fact that you expect ethical behavior on the part of your employees. And you'd better have a talk with your staff.

6. Yes. You probably have a responsibility to pass on any bona fide offer to the city council. If specific city regulations prohibit this or you feel uncomfortable in this role, you should suggest the individual make a written offer to city council.

7. No. Send it back. When a person accepts a job with the city he or she accepts the compensation that accompanies it. After all — a simple thank you letter would have accomplished the same purpose — wouldn't it?

8. No. Return the liquor immediately, for the same reasons noted above.

9. Yes. Strictly personal, private investments are fine. A prudent person would investigate the opportunity to ensure that no special considerations, zoning changes, interest rates, etc. were involved in the deal. Any special considerations: don't invest. Remember, even the appearance of your involvement in special favors could call your integrity into question. If in doubt about the investment, ask yourself: How would this look in the newspapers?

10. Yes. Strictly speaking, Hazel has committed a felony. If you excuse her, what does that say to other employees? How has she replaced the "trust and value" you placed in her? If the same situation occurred with an employee who was not Hazel, would you be lenient?

How to Score Your Answers

Points are awarded for each question on a weighted basis, as indicated below. If, for example, you answered the first question "yes," award yourself 3 points; if you answered "no," give yourself one point.

Question Number	No. of Points for	
	"Yes"	"No"
1	3	1
2	2	1
3	1	1
4	1	3
5	1	3
6	1	2
7	3	1
8	1	3
9	1	1
10	1	2

According to the ethical experts who devised this quiz, your score is "perfect" if you received one point for each of the 10 questions. If your total score is 10 to 14, indications are that you have high standards, are clearly a dedicated public servant, and set a good example for those around you.

A score of 2 for any question means that while you may not "break" the law or allow or encourage others to do so, neither do you assertively pursue wrong doing, or "marginal" practices. Probably you're more interested in keeping things smooth than in righting wrongs. If you scored 15-20, you need to do some serious reflection on your own vulnerability to unethical practices.

A score of 3 for any answer shows trouble and indicates tendency towards conduct that is based on no ethics or values and shows a real disregard for any perspective reflecting such commitment, or the impact of these acts on your community — and position. If you score 20-25, you probably need a good lawyer.

Case 12: Taking the Code of Ethics Seriously

Point number 4 of the 1980 Code of Ethics (post dating the following case) notes that government employees should "Seek to find and employ more efficient and economical ways to getting tasks accomplished." Should this guideline have been pursued before activating the guidelines on loyalty and the Constitution? In this case is the question of guideline selectivity pertinent? Concurrently, was the Appeal rejected on the basis of a technicality or on a solid ethical point? Note that the standards of professionalism are the same in 1958 as in 1980.

Robert Sullivan had been a criminal investigator in the Boston office of the General Services Administration (GSA) for over twelve years when, early in 1975, he was assigned to investigate Robert Tucker. Tucker was a GSA employee who had accused agency officials of receiving illegal contract awards and had given GSA documents to the FBI and the press. Reading the FBI reports, which had found no clear evidence of law-breaking, Sullivan believed they suggested, but had not gone far enough to prove, favoritism and collusion. After Tucker was fired, Leland, an internal GSA auditor examining the contested contracts, remarked that Tucker had been "shafted." In June, Sullivan saw Leland's audit report. It showed that over half of $9 million in construction contracts had been falsely termed "emergency situations," enabling contract officers to circumvent normal competitive bidding procedures. Contractors who had contributed to Senator Edward Brooke's 1972 election campaign might have been favored.

Nonetheless, Sullivan's superior did not even read, let alone act on, Leland's report. Much troubled by the contrast between the swift dismissal of Tucker and the inaction on the audit report, Sullivan debated what to do. During Tucker's appeal of his dismissal, GSA officials had not told the Civil Service Commission hearing officer about the audit findings. To discuss the audit report with the very officials who had disregarded it was, he decided, pointless. Albert Gammel, the Boston office head, had formerly been a campaign manager for Brooke. The FBI investigation had been inadequate; the FBI had not protected, and U.S. Attorney James Bagriel, a Brooke protege and friend of Gammel, had betrayed Tucker's identity. It was bruited that Gammel had sought and perhaps succeeded in getting Gabriel to soften the FBI report. The only recourse, Sullivan began to think, was the press. As he later stated, "Like any American citizen, I have a responsibility for taking positive action to correct wrong doing and a watchful press was the only alternative. . . ."

A deeply religious man, Sullivan discussed the situation with two priests and studied the Code of Ethics for public employees adopted by Congress in 1958, noting especially the following passages:

Any person in government service should:

1. Put loyalty to the highest moral principles and loyalty to country above loyalty to persons, party, or government department.

2. Uphold the Constitution, laws and legal regulations of the United States and of all governments therein and never be a party to their evasion.

9. Expose corruption wherever discovered.

10. Uphold these principles, ever conscious that public office is a public trust.

Source:
Harold Orlans,
Washington, D.C.

He then took three GSA audit reports and six FBI reports to the *Boston Globe,* where copies were made, and returned them to the files.

On January 18, 1976, the *Globe* ran a page one story headlined, "U.S. audit uncovers contract abuses by the Boston GSA office." Interviewed by GSA investigators, Sullivan confessed his actions, saying, "I feel that it is and was my duty to act to stop this kind of conduct within the government. . . ." In August 1976, he received a notice of proposed removal and in November, he was discharged on the grounds that he had violated regulations by removing designated documents without authorization, that he had breached the confidentiality of individuals cited therein, that he had made no attempt to report alleged irregularities to appropriate GSA officials, and that the documented irregularities did not constitute fraud or corruption. Even if his motive was "altruistic and well-intentioned," the disclosure of confidential documents, "if condoned, would certainly lead to administrative and management chaos."

Upon Sullivan's appeal to the Civil Service Commission, a three-day hearing was held in March, 1977. In his decision issued the following month, Harry Grossman, the appeals officer, noted that the Code of Ethics was a concurrent resolution, which merely expressed an opinion of Congress and did not, like a joint resolution approved by the president, have the force of law. Further the Code stated that government employees should uphold laws and regulations, which included those governing the disclosure of agency records.

> For an employee to assume authority on his own initiative to make his own private decision as to what he will elect to remove from agency records and to turn over to an outside party when he is not the custodian of the records, and when the turnover is a personal, unofficial act, smacks of anarchy regardless of his motive.

Grossman sustained Sullivan's discharge.

QUESTIONS FOR DISCUSSION

1. Did Sullivan have a responsibility to act on what he saw as evidence of improper conduct? Was his action justified?

2. Should Sullivan have communicated with his superiors and/or the FBI? What else might he have done before giving the documents to the *Globe*? Should he have mailed the documents to the *Globe* anonymously?

3. Is Grossman's view of the Code of Ethics sound?

4. Should Sullivan have been treated more leniently?

13. Encouraging Ethics Through Education and Discussion

Toward a Viable Program of Moral Education
Derek C. Bok

The current controversy over the teaching of ethics echoes an ancient dispute dating back at least to ancient Greece. In fifth century Athens, two schools of thought emerged on how to carry out the critical task of teaching ethics and civil responsibility. The traditional view relied on exhorting the young to do the proper thing and punish them when they failed. The newer way, urged by Socrates, sought to teach people to know the good by provoking them to think about fundamental moral aims and dilemmas. Socrates argued that those who had not learned to reason about such questions could not apply their principles to the shifting circumstances they would face in later life. In this, he was surely correct. Yet Socrates sometimes talked as if knowledge alone would suffice to insure virtuous action. He did not stress the

In addition to advanced knowledge and specialized skills, universities should provide an opportunity for moral education, according to Derek Bok. University rules, faculty conduct, athletic regulations, and curriculum choices, he suggests, offer guidance for the ethical development of students.

value of early habituation, positive example, and obedience to rules in giving students the desire and self-discipline to live up to their beliefs and to respect the basic norms of behavior essential to civilized communities. For this neglect, he was savagely attacked. It fell to Aristotle to see the wisdom of combining both traditions to help young people acquire not merely an ability to think clearly about ethical problems but the desire and will to put their conclusions into practice.

In the contemporary university, as in ancient Greece, the key question is how to combine education in moral reasoning with a broader effort to teach by habit, example, and exhortation. The ability to reason is essential to help us make our way through all the confusing dilemmas and conflicting arguments that abound in an era when society's consensus on issues of value have disintegrated under the weight of cultural diversity, self-serving rationalization, technological change, and other complexities of modern life. But moral reasoning alone may not be enough to cause us to *behave* ethically. How, then, can a university go further and help students to develop the desire and the will to adhere to moral precepts without resorting to forms of indoctrination inimical to the academy?

The very question will make many people uneasy. The history of higher education is studded with efforts to develop character that, in retrospect, seem quaint, ineffective, or downright objectionable. More often than not, such endeavors have degenerated into crude attempts to impose particular doctrines or petty rules of behavior. Nevertheless, moral education is too important to discard merely because of past failures. Besides, universities cannot avoid the task whether or not they relish the responsibility. Like it or not, they will affect the moral development of their students by the ways in which they administer their

Source: Derek C. Bok, "Toward a Viable Program of Moral Education," *The President's Report 1986-87* (Harvard University), pp. 13-16.

rules of conduct, by the standard they achieve in dealing with ethical issues confronting the institution, by the manner in which they counsel their students and coach their athletic teams. The only question is whether they choose to proceed deliberately and with forethought. Let us consider, then, how an institution could construct a program to help its students to enhance not only their capacity to perceive moral issues and to think about them clearly but their ability to put their ethical beliefs into practice. Having described what such a program might look like, we can then ask whether the attempt is worth making.

Early Steps. The first weeks that students spend at a university are often critical in shaping their attitude toward the institution and their expectations of what they will take away from their experience. Never again are they likely to be so attentive to what the institution says or so open to advice about what aspirations and values matter most. As a result, colleges that are concerned about moral education will need to emphasize this aspect of the undergraduate experience at the very outset in catalogues and welcoming speeches.

Much of the same applies to professional schools as well. When I came to Harvard Law School as a student, I was plunged immediately into the mysteries of early English case law. Not a word about the role of the legal profession in upholding justice. No mention of the importance of learning to reconcile the lawyer's duty to his client with his larger duty to the legal system. These were opportunities too valuable to be missed. No one should begin professional school without being reminded that to acquire professional expertise is to acquire power and that it is dangerous to wield such power without learning to use it responsibly.

Ethics and the Curriculum. Although the traditional liberal arts curriculum may not automatically provide an adequate moral education, it undoubtedly helps in many ways to develop ethical awareness and moral reasoning. The study of literature can awaken one's conscience by making more vivid the predicament of others. Traditional courses in ethics can provide a philosophical foundation for thinking precisely about moral issues. Studying the social sciences can help students to understand the causes and effects of various policies and practices and thus appreciate their moral significance more precisely. Indeed, almost any well-taught course can strengthen the capacity to think more carefully about intellectual problems, including ethical issues. Together, these experiences help to explain why several studies have found that young people continue to develop their powers of moral reasoning so long as they remain in school or university and usually cease to do so when their formal education comes to an end.

Yet by themselves, traditional courses in the liberal arts do not go far enough. Neither the classics nor history have yielded a sufficiently compelling normative vision to justify the hopes of a Jowett or a Burckhardt that studying these subjects would enable students to learn how to lead a virtuous life. Humanistic disciplines have become too preoccupied with other concerns to give close attention to ethical questions, and most professors do not feel competent to teach such material. Besides, courses in the liberal arts are deliberately nonvocational and hence are unlikely to consider the complicated moral dilemmas that arise within the professions.

These are the gaps that the new courses in applied and professional ethics seek to fill. Properly taught, they can yield important benefits. By studying problems that commonly arise in personal and professional life, students will be more likely to perceive moral dilemmas they would otherwise ignore. By finding that these dilemmas raise issues that are susceptible to careful reasoning and argument, students will be less inclined, not more, to believe that every ethical view is entitled to equal respect. By learning to analyze moral issues more rigorously, students will realize that often such problems do have reasonably clear solutions, given basic ethical premises that almost all human beings share.

Skeptics will reply that courses in moral reasoning have no effect on *behavior,* but this criticism seems overdrawn. To be sure, no instruction can suffice to turn a scoundrel into a virtuous human being. But most young people arrive at the university with decent instincts and a genuine concern for others. For them, courses that foster an ability to detect ethical issues more perceptively, to think about them more carefully, to understand more clearly the reasons for acting morally seem likely not only to train their minds but to have a positive effect on their behavior as well. Such evidence as there is seems to confirm this supposition.

In view of these benefits, there is ample reason to encourage students to take classes devoted to ethical dilemmas arising in their personal or professional lives. The question then arises whether to offer special courses on this subject or to include material on ethical dilemmas in regular courses where such issues arise naturally out of the material. Both alternatives have merit. It is undoubtedly important, at least in professional schools, to encourage faculty members in a variety of courses to discuss ethical issues arising naturally from the subject matter in their classes. Only a comprehensive effort of this kind will make the point that ethics is not simply a specialized topic confined to a separate world but a subject that is relevant to all aspects of professional life. At the same time, without courses specifically devoted to moral problems, there will be no one to teach the subject in depth, no one to carry on sustained writing in the field, no one to whom other faculty members can turn for advice on how to deal with ethical questions arising in their own courses. Under such conditions, efforts to insert ethical issues into the regular curriculum will almost certainly wither. A wise faculty, therefore, will seek to provide *both* special courses in applied ethics and opportunities to discuss moral problems as they emerge in other subjects throughout the curriculum.

Teaching Ethics, Teaching Ethically
Bayard Catron

> *Fellow Students! You come to our lectures and demand from us the qualities that of a hundred professors at least ninety-nine do not and must not claim to be football masters in the vital problems of life, or even to be "leaders" in matters of conduct.*
>
> Max Weber

Most professors are wise enough to avoid being cast as "football masters in the vital problems of life," as Weber put it. No doubt this is even more true today, given the dramatic trends toward academic specialization, than it was when Weber wrote across a broad band of disciplines. The pursuit of knowledge is now widely thought to be best served by those with the greatest technical competence in subfields of their disciplines.

Are ethical concerns a "matter of conduct?" Or of stages of moral development? Or, of professional socialization through learning the norms of the trade? Catron raises the various approaches to teaching ethics and suggests we borrow from each for guidance.

But for those who teach ethics — particularly for those who teach professional ethics — the situation is not so simple. Ethics is concerned essentially with "matters of conduct," I think, and it seems that ethics professors will tend to be cast as "leaders" in such matters whether they wish to be or not. I am uncomfortable cast in that role, and I suspect that many others are as well. The moral burden this role appears to impose might help to explain why so much has been written about the problems peculiar to teaching ethics. Academics generally are far more comfortable with the "pursuit of truth" than with the "pursuit of goodness" (or of beauty, for that matter). And this might also explain, in part, why the scholarly treatment of ethics has become so disassociated from conduct.

I do not believe that the ethics professor is an authority on good conduct in the same way that a research methods professor is an authority on good research. I also do not believe that the evaluation of student performance in an ethics course should involve a judgment of the student's ethical beliefs or moral competence. But what stance, then, *is* appropriate (ethical!) for the professor, and what standards of evaluation are justified?

I encountered these questions when I undertook several years ago to create a new course on Ethics and Public Values. I had previously designed several new courses, and I expected that it would be a rather complex process to clarify my aspirations and objectives and to create a course appropriate to them. Even so, I was surprised at the conceptual difficulties I encountered. I was perplexed for some time about my

Source: Bayard Catron, "Teaching Ethics, Teaching Ethically," *City Almanac*, 20:1-2 (Winter 1987), 32-35.

goals and then about my role in teaching such a course. I slowly came to realize that what I was trying to come to grips with was not only the teaching of ethics but also the ethics of teaching. What began as the rather familiar task of preparing a course was transformed into a larger and more fundamental reflection on my own stance and role as a professor. I came to "take it personally" and to see it as an ethical issue in itself.

While there are important ethical issues concerning teaching in general,[1] it seems to me that there is a special poignancy and perplexity about teaching ethics that does not apply to most other subjects. Here is the way I express my perplexity in a set of personal reflections on teaching ethics that I distribute to my students in the first session of an ethics class:

> While I do not want to be viewed as a moral authority, I am not indifferent to whether you learn or what you learn about ethics and right conduct. While there is a legitimate range of opinions about ethics issues, I do not believe that just any opinion is as good as any other. While each person is responsible for deciding and acting, I want to claim that some decisions and actions are better than others. While I don't want to assume the role of a preacher, it is not sufficient for me to play the role of a "values clarifier."

Although my thoughts on this issue have grown wholly out of my own experience in teaching ethics, I believe that my concerns are not merely idiosyncratic but, in fact, have important implications for two other significant questions (although I cannot explore them fully here): the *process* question of the appropriate range of pedagogical approaches to teaching ethics in a professional program and the *substantive* question of what ethical issues should be addressed in the curriculum and to what end.

Below, after critiquing the recent scholarly treatment of ethics, I address in turn several candidates for an ethical stance for teaching ethics:

- The "ethics of virtue" approach restores the connection between ethics and conduct but raises the spector of manipulation.

- The process orientation may help to break the cycle of dependency but does not itself provide an ethical stance.

- Immanuel Kant's categorical imperative supplies an adequate moral posture but lacks the vivid, concrete quality of ethical choices.

- The orientation of developmental psychology provides an intimate human scale but is burdened by a dubious objectivity and ethical naturalism.

Perhaps an adequate ethical stance for teaching ethics can be fashioned from these ingredients.

Ethics and Conduct

The crucial connection between ethics and conduct is often disguised or denied. Ethics can be taught as other subjects are often taught, as a body of knowledge — for example, by examining historical positions or a set of current issues in philosophy. The professor's goal might be to transmit *information about* ethics. The image here is of the student as consumer, and the professor as a retailer with a stock of knowledge to sell. A related but somewhat more ambitious objective would be to provide *knowledge of* ethics. In this case, the hope is that the student will be stimulated, not simply satisfied.

Both approaches might well be criticized for treating the student as the relatively passive objective of teaching, rather than as the (active) subject of learning. This criticism can be made irrespective of the subject matter. Most important for my current purposes, however, this approach to teaching ethics leaves the relationship between ethics and conduct quite obscure. Perhaps the knowledge of ethics is considered intrinsically worthwhile; or, if there are any implications for conduct, is left to the student to figure out what they may be. The student is not encouraged to "take it personally" and might conclude that ethics is academic — in the pejorative sense.

It is a sad fact that much of twentieth century ethics done by English and American philosophers has systematically obscured the relationship between ethics and conduct. The influence of logical positivism in the philosophy of science was so pervasive that, during the 1930s, A. J. Ayer argued in an influential book that ethical statements were literally meaningless.[2] Later, the emotivists like C. L. Stevenson and the prescriptivists, for example, R. M. Hare, provided partial correctives for this excessive claim but not in a way that made ethics a respectable or accessible concern in other disciplines or in the professions.[3] Hare, for example, defines ethics as the "logical study of the language of morals." The focus is thus on what people say rather than on what they do, and ethics becomes a technical enterprise reserved exclusively for philosophers.

The advent of the "good reasons" school in the 1950s and 1960s reestablished ethics as a proper field of study by emphasizing the parallel between ethical inquiry and scientific inquiry.[4] We bring reason and evidence to bear on ethical questions to establish a "warrant for action," it was argued, in more or less the same way that we marshal reason and evidence to give a "warrant for belief." This approach does not dissolve into the utter ethical relativism (or nihilism) of the earlier approaches but rather holds some promise permitting us legitimately to consider some sorts of action preferable to others. It calls upon us to reflect on our actions and to apply reason with diligence and care.

So far, so good. The upshot of this process is presumably actions that are more *defensible* from a moral point of view. Nonetheless, this again tends to divert attention away from conduct — this time by calling attention to the *reasons* people give for what they do. The traditional concerns of ethics are thus transformed into a rather peculiar subheading under epistemology. Lawrence Kohlberg provides perhaps the most flagrant example of this, although he is not self-consciously associated with the "good reasons" approach.[5] When individual moral development is assessed according to his scheme, ethical sophistication and moral maturity are determined entirely by the sorts of reasons one is able to give for or against particular resolutions of ethical dilemmas, without any reference whatever to one's actual conduct.

In an important article, Mark Lilla complains about the "good reasons" approach (although he does not call it by that name).[6] As he notes, this "modern casuistry" does not ensure moral conduct but instead tends to breed cleverness in argumentation and shrewdness in developing post hoc justifications of dubious conduct. He advocates a return to the Greek notion of the "ethics of virtue" (which Lilla calls the Aristotelian concern with ethos).[7]

Lilla's wholesale rejection of the "good reasons" approach is too extreme, I think. Although the approach is clearly subject to abuse of the sort he mentions, there is considerable merit in recognizing that ethical disputes are not hopelessly emotive and subjective but are, at least sometimes and to some extent, susceptible to reasoned discourse and intersubjective agreement. Moreover, he is somewhat cavalier in his acceptance of a "bit of 'indoctrination' in the virtues of democracy."

The "Ethics of Virtue"

The emphasis on *virtue* — on habits of moral conduct — is important because it reestablishes the crucial connection between ethics and conduct. But the greatest deficiency in Lilla's essay, in my judgment, is the lack of any apparent sensitivity to the difficulties and paradoxes in "teaching virtue." Martin Buber speaks eloquently of the difficulties in "educating the character" of young people. How much more uncertain is the attempt to instill virtue in adults? Buber is worth quoting at length.[8]

> . . . as soon as my pupils notice that I want to educate their characters, I am resisted precisely by those who show most signs of genuine independent character: They will not let themselves be educated, or rather they do not like the idea that somebody wants to educate them. And those, too, who are seriously laboring over the question of good and evil rebel when one dictates to them, as though it were some long established truth, what is good and what is bad; and they rebel just because they have experienced over and over again how hard it is to find the right way.

> . . . If I am concerned with the education of character, everything becomes problematic. I try to explain to my pupils that envy is despicable, and at once I feel the secret resistance of those who are poorer than their comrades. I try to explain that it is wicked to bully the weak, and at once I see a suppressed smile on the lips of the strong. I try to explain that lying destroys life, and something frightening happens: the worst habitual

liar of the class produces a brilliant essay on the destructive power of lying. I have made the fatal mistake of *giving instruction* in ethics.

Of course, whether it is consciously intended or not, students in a professional program acquire attitudes and beliefs about appropriate conduct just as surely as they acquire knowledge and sophistication in the use of the tools of their trade. The question is therefore not whether norms of conduct will be communicated, but what those norms are, how they are communicated, and whether professors and students are fully conscious of them.

This is commonly called professional socialization rather than the "ethics of virtue," and it is quite separable from the subject matter addressed in an ethics class. Indeed, much socialization takes place outside the classroom altogether. It occurs in advising and social situations, in casual conversations with faculty and other students, in the way faculty members treat students, secretaries, graduate assistants — and each other. This suggests that it might be more useful for a faculty to examine the ethos of its program than to fight over the specific details of which ethical issues should be addressed in the curriculum.

Not long ago, a stir was caused at the Harvard Business School when it was discovered that a student team had won a competition by using information accidentally acquired about another team's strategy. One might hazard a guess that the competitive environment of the school, the class, and the exercise contributed to the team's decision to use the information. Indeed, it is surprising that so many of those involved, students and faculty alike, were surprised and concerned. After all, the ethos was probably better characterized by "nice guys finish last" or "God helps those who help themselves" than by "the meek shall inherit the earth."

Attention to the ethos of a program and to the ways in which professional socialization may actually be occurring can be very instructive. What is far less clear, however, is the relationship between the ethos and the subsequent conduct of graduates faced with difficult ethical choices. It seems plain that students enter professional programs, for better or worse, with their characters largely formed — by the parenting they have received, their early education, and so on.

I believe that, although the program experience might be powerfully influential for particular students, there is very little chance that a concerted attempt to mold character in accordance with some preconceived notion would have the intended effect. One might even speculate that those more susceptible to the ethos of a professional degree program are more likely to be susceptible later to the ethos of their organization — and thus be excellent candidates for *petite Eichmannism.*

Process, Principle, and Personal Development

Many professors, I suspect, would be distinctly uncomfortable with Lilla's "old-fashioned stuff — preaching, witnessing, setting a good example for the children . . . " that, as he acknowledges, puts "an enormous amount of moral responsibility on *all* teachers." Certainly the notion of a systematic program to educate the character of graduate students — to indoctrinate them, to put it plainly — is not likely to win instant general acceptance, even if the "virtues" involved are generally approved as relevant and important, like public-spiritedness, honesty, and respect for law.

While agreement on a substantive program may be hard to come by — or too much to expect — agreement on process will probably be considerably easier. I believe that careful attention to the context and process of ethical discourse is very important. And I doubt that many professors would strenuously object to the first of my four course objectives for Ethics and Public Values:

> To aid in the creation of a setting in which people are encouraged to engage in the difficult and sometimes painful process of carefully reflecting on their own moral positions and conduct, and feel free to share those experiences with others in a spirit of concern and mutual learning.

Under the course description, I add the following note:

Encouraging Ethics Through Education and Discussion

Nothing significant is likely to happen without this willingness to engage personally in moral reflection and discourse. It is essential to the success of this course that participants engage fully and personally in all aspects of it. To the extent that we are individually and collectively successful in satisfying the first objective, the rest should follow.

But, while the process orientation may be a necessary condition, it is hardly a sufficient one to resolve the issue of the ethical stance of the professor. If the professor has *any goals whatever for change* in the student — whether of competence, skill, understanding, or even critical thinking — this raises the specter of manipulation (albeit well-intentioned and benign) in which the student is again treated as the object rather than as the subject (or agent) of change. If, on the other hand, the professor has no such goals — if no change is sought or if any sort of change whatever is accepted nonjudgmentally (i.e., as good as any other change) — what then is the role of the professor?

Jerry Harvey's answer to this perplexity is quite direct: the role of the professor is to profess.[9] The professor cannot have and should not accept any responsibility for the learning of the student. Harvey argues further that professors should unlearn the profession of teaching into which they have been socialized and learn instead to "not-teach."

Harvey's insight is important. To take responsibility for what another does or should learn creates a web of dependency within which little can be learned by anyone other than the "education game" most of us mastered very early on: Rewards come from figuring out what the teacher wants and giving it to him or her; avoid punishment by disguising what you don't know; appear earnest even if you don't care.

Regrettably, it is not enough to be aware that the education game is being played or to recognize the cul-de-sacs and self-defeating traps. The dependency relationship has been powerfully reinforced in all of us. And the dynamics of the game are seductive, and *some* interests of both students and teachers (although not learning) are served by it.

Perhaps it is a moral duty — or in a more fashionable modern language, a professional responsibility — for professors to do what they can to break the dependency cycle of the education game. But such a duty cannot be derived from process itself; it must emanate from some substantive source.

After considerable struggle, I resolved the issue of an ethical stance for myself through the time-honored concept of "moral autonomy." The concept, used by Jean Piaget among others,[10] is rooted in Kant's categorical imperative, one statement of which is: "Never treat others as means only, but always as ends in themselves." This principle requires, first and foremost, that people treat each other as free and responsible individuals. It entails an attitude of respect for the dignity and the worth — the personhood — of the other, and it begins to characterize and to delimit our *duty,* in Kantian language, toward each other.

Given adherence to this principle, what in other circumstances might appear as manipulation or dependency may be transformed. To me at least, having the principle as a place to stand was enormously liberating. Nonetheless, it must be conceded that the principle is abstract, and our duty in particular cases is hard to define.

For most process-oriented professors, the source of an ethical stance is perhaps some concept of personal development, usually grounded in a particular psychological theory (that of Freud of Jung, for example). The developmental approach to ethics has recently gained such favor that it might be said to rival the traditional deontological and utilitarian approaches. And it does offer considerable advantages:

- Because it is a modern form of "naturalistic" ethics, the developmental approach tends to be seen as objectivist — thus avoiding the arguments against subjectivism. At the same time, it is not seen as absolutist in ways that provoke strong disagreement. Nor, although it is relativist in a certain sense, is the developmental approach nearly as crude as the usual relativism. To the extent that "developmental ethics" is grounded in human nature, it has the undeniable advantage that it does not depend for its credibility on rhetorical force, emotional commitment, appeal to supernatural origins, divine guidance, and so on. In short, in Kohlberg's words, it allows us to commit the naturalistic fallacy and get away with it. All in all, a pretty neat trick.

- The developmental approach also provides an empirical grounding of a sort and allows a research agenda to be constructed. Much descriptive work can be done and shared with others, allowing a "community of inquirers" to form, whereas other, more purely speculative and normative approaches are perhaps necessarily more solitary enterprises. The tidy parallel between personality and behavior on the one hand and character and conduct on the other provides a rich menu of issues to pursue. For example, I think that it provides a useful modern context in which to appreciate the classic Greek concept of ethics (the "ethics of virtue") — better than any eighteenth or nineteenth century approach.

● From a personal and interpersonal point of view, I think this approach is indispensable. It is the most intimate and personal of any approach, thus squaring with our experience of ethical issues and the challenges they present. And the developmental approach provides a way of understanding the complexities of interpersonal conduct that is unavailable in the major traditional approaches.

● There is, for me, a crucial pedagogical advantage as well: I have found this by far the best place to start in trying to "teach ethics." It gives free rein to the process orientation — the emphasis on reflection and dialogue — and it avoids getting impaled too early on such thorny issues as competing principles. Finally, people engage quickly with issues of mixed motives, deception and self-deception, self-interest, and rationalization, whereas the road to these through the philosophical literature is far more difficult and uncertain.

Despite these very considerable and practical advantages, I am suspicious of the claim that the developmental approach is grounded in human nature and is "objective." It provides perhaps too convenient a cover for substantive ethical claims, which are better argued in the open, and it seems to invite misguided (and perhaps immoral) efforts to catalogue people according to their stage of moral development.

Conclusion

Perhaps an appropriate and adequate ethical stance toward teaching ethics may be fashioned from some combination of the various approaches I have sketched here. I believe that each approach individually is wanting, as I have indicated, and also that each has a distinctive contribution to make to the enterprise.

It is tempting to treat a course in ethics as a special case, requiring special attention to the ethics of teaching. Since the subject deals with issues of norms of right conduct and the "goodness" of particular values, perhaps the ethics professor bears a special burden to be sensitive to legitimate differences in opinion and to be especially careful not to impose his or her values on students. But the professor of research methods communicates norms and values no less than the ethics professor — and, it could be argued, in a more directive if less explicit fashion.

Moreover, the two professors and their other colleagues share certain ethical responsibilities to be fair-minded and even-handed; to evaluate students only on relevant criteria (whatever those may be in particular cases); to be clear, honest, and forthright about their own commitments; to know and love their subject and to give their best in communicating it; to do what they can to create an environment conducive to learning, and to bring out the best in their students.

What colleagues share is, in the end, far more important than differences in the subject matter of the courses they teach. The creation of an intellectual community, like the creation of community in general, is a moral achievement. One might hope that our academic programs as well as the public organizations in which our students will later work will come to embody more fully the ethos elegantly described by my colleague Peter Vaill:

> Ethical and moral *learning* occurs in us in the context of authentic encounter — with ourselves and with others who are important to us. The challenge to invent settings in which authentic encounter can be fostered as a precondition to the caring display of and reflection upon the choices which face us as responsible actors.

Endnotes

1. See William Griffith, "Ethics and the Academic Professional: Some Open Problems and a New Approach," *Business and Professional Ethics Journal* (1983).
2. A.J. Ayer, *Language, Truth and Logic* (New York: Dover Publications, 1936).
3. C.L. Stevenson, *Ethics and Language* (New Haven: Yale University Press, 1944); R.M. Hare, *The Language of Morals* (Oxford: Clarendon Press, 1952).
4. For example, Stephen E. Toulmin, *An Examination of the Place of Reason in Ethics* (Cambridge: Cambridge University Press, 1950); Kurt Baier, *The Moral Point of View: A Rational Basis of Ethics* (Ithica, N.Y.: Cornell University Press, 1958); Stuart Hampshire, *Thought and Action* (Chatto and Windus, 1959); Marcus Singer, *Generalization in Ethics* (New York: Alfred A, Knopf, 1961).
5. Lawrence Kohlberg, *Stages in the Development of Moral Thought and Action* (New York: Holt, Rinehart, and Winston, 1969); *Collected Papers on Moral Development and Moral Education* (Cambridge, Mass.: Harvard Center for Moral Education, 1973).
6. Mark Lilla, "Ethos, Ethics, and Public Service," *Public Interest* 63, Spring (1981). Lilla suggests that we should "send philosophers home" as a first step toward reviving an ethos of public administration. It is curious that his references do not suggest an awareness of the recent history of ethics in philosophy that I have briefly sketched. As a result, perhaps, he does not appreciate the "good reasons" approach as a notable improvement on its predecessors. Moreoever, despite his apparent enthusiasm for Aristotle, Lilla does not even mention Aristotle's fundamental concept of "practical reason," which can readily be seen as the progenitor of the "good reasons" approach.
7. See also Richard Mayer and Michael Harmon, "Teaching Moral Education in Public Administration," *Southern Review of Public Administration* 6 (2), Summer (1982).
8. Martin Buber, *Between Man and Man* (New York: Macmillan, 1965).
9. Jerry B. Harvey, "Learning to Not Teach," *Exchange: The Organizational Behavior Teaching Journal* 4 (3) (1979): 19-21.
10. Jean Piaget, *The Moral Judgement of the Child* (New York: The Free Press, 1965).

Resolution on Ethics Education
National Academy of Public Administration
Adopted by the Board of Trustees
September 16, 1988

We believe that university programs preparing people for careers in public service have a special responsibility for ethics education, training, and the encouragement of students. They should provide explicit curriculum coverage for all students that enables and encourages them to act ethically. More specifically, programs should:

In 1986, the American Society for Public Administration and the National Association of Schools of Public Affairs and Administration established a Working Group on Ethics Education, chaired by Bayard Catron and Kathryn Denhardt. The Working Group's 1988 report articulated several guidelines for ethics education. The NAPA Resolution printed here is, in effect, an endorsement of those guidelines.

• Educate students in (1) the democratic values (liberty, equality, etc.) implicit and explicit in the U.S. Constitutional history; (2) the role of government in dealing with conflicting social values; and (3) the ethical and philosophical underpinnings of public policy debates.

• Train students (1) to recognize and focus on ethical problems; (2) to develop and refine appropriate methods of moral reasoning; and (3) to be sensitive to the nuances and ambiguity of ethical situations.

• Encourage students (1) to see public service as a noble calling and a public trust, deserving commitment to the highest standards of honor and personal integrity; (2) to appreciate the ethical dimension in decision making (just as they appreciate the political and managerial dimensions); and (3) to accept the multiple and sometimes conflicting obligations of public service.

14. Leadership and Individual Responsibility

As a City upon a Hill
John F. Kennedy

During the last sixty days, I have been engaged in the task of constructing an administration. It has been a long and deliberate process. Some have counseled greater speed. Others have counseled more expedient tests. But I have been guided by the standard John Winthrop set before his shipmates on the flagship *Arabella* 331 years ago, as they, too, faced the task of building a new government on a perilous frontier. "We must always consider," he said, "that we shall be as a city upon a hill — the eyes of all people are upon us."

Today the eyes of all people are truly upon us — and our governments, in every branch, at every level, national, state and local, must be as a city upon a hill — constructed and inhabited by men aware of their grave trust and their great responsibilities.

As he prepared to assume the Presidency, Kennedy identified several criteria by which he thought his Administration should be judged. Do his four questions provide a standard for evaluation that can usefully be applied to government leaders and their aides more generally?

For we are setting out upon a voyage . . . no less hazardous than that undertaken by the *Arabella* in 1630. We are committing ourselves to tasks of statecraft no less awesome than that of governing the Massachusetts Bay Colony, beset as it was then by terror without and disorder within.

History will not judge our endeavors — and a government cannot be selected — merely on the basis of color or creed or even party affiliation. Neither will competence and loyalty and stature, while essential to the utmost, suffice in times such as these.

For of those to whom much is given, much is required. And when at some future date the high court of history sits in judgment on each one of us — recording whether in our brief span of service we fulfilled our responsibilities to the states — our success or failure, in whatever office we may hold, will be measured by the answers to four questions:

First, were we truly men of courage — with the courage to stand up to one's enemies — and the courage to stand up, when necessary, to one's associates — the courage to resist public pressure as well as private greed?

Secondly, were we truly men of judgment — with perceptive judgment of the future as well as the past — of our own mistakes as well as the mistakes of others — with enough wisdom to know what we did not know, and enough candor to admit it?

Third, were we truly men of integrity — men who never ran out on either the principles in which they believed or the people who believed in them — men whom neither financial gain nor political ambition could ever divert from the fulfillment of our sacred trust?

Finally, were we truly men of dedication — with an honor mortgaged to no single individual or group, and compromised by no private obligation or aim, but devoted solely to serving the public good and the national interest? . . .

Source: Address by John F. Kennedy before the Massachusetts Legislature, January 9, 1961.

Placing the Burden Where It Belongs

Jameson W. Doig, with
Douglas E. Phillips and Tycho Manson

Should high-level officials be held personally responsible when their subordinates act illegally? Or is it unfair to penalize top officials if they were unaware of fraud and misbehavior within their agencies?

He trespasses against his duty who sleeps upon his watch, as well as he that goes over to the enemy. —
Burke[1]

When corruption and other forms of illegal behavior are uncovered at lower levels in an organization, a common response of higher supervisors and executives is, "I didn't know." And therefore (explicitly or implicitly), "I deserve no punishment."

For high-level officials in public agencies (and in private organizations as well) ignorance is an inadequate excuse — and worse: for the belief that one can avoid responsibility (and punishment) by pleading ignorance is corrosive, undermining the capacity of these officials to monitor and manage their subordinates' activities so that the organization's operations are carried out efficiently, effectively and legally. . . .

How, then, can we reduce the tendencies of executive officials to plead ignorance, and to *be* ignorant? Stated more positively, how can we increase the incentives for leaders to educate themselves regarding the attitudes and values held by the subordinates, to locate the areas in which illegal behavior is likely to occur, to exert positive leadership in order to deter corrupt behavior, and to move quickly in order to curtail abusive and corrupt activities when they occur within their domain?

One valuable strategy is to hold the leaders of organizations *personally* responsible — and in some circumstances, criminally liable — when they fail to prevent illegal behavior by their subordinates. This approach, which we call the executive-responsibility strategy, is aimed broadly at all leaders within an organization who *could have* . . . corrected and prevented violations, including those leaders who genuinely were not direct participants. Thus, the strategy threatens sanctions against leaders in order to induce them to use their knowledge of prevailing conditions in the organization, and their authority to change those conditions, so that illegal behavior by subordinates does not occur.

As long experience reveals, executives in any organization may permit illegal behavior to thrive, simply by failing — sometimes deliberately — to make themselves aware of conditions within the organization that can encourage violation of the law.[2]

The Executive-Responsibility Strategy and the Evolving Law

In the private sector, responsibility for illegal acts (and failure to act) normally lies both with the organization and with individuals within the organization who participate *knowingly and directly* in the illegal behavior. For example, an executive who explicitly directs or authorizes subordinates to engage in illegal behavior may be considered a direct participant; the executive who says to a regional manager, "Fix the price," or "Bribe the prime minister," is liable as a participant in the violation of the Sherman Antitrust Act or the Foreign Corrupt Practices Act. Traditionally, the executive who sets requirements that can be achieved only by such means, without explicitly authorizing them — or who knows or has reason to know that such means are being used, but fails to investigate — has *not* been exposed to personal legal liability.

However, this comfortable insulation has recently been breached, when corporate activities have involved criminal violations of the Federal Food, Drug and Cosmetic Act. . . .

In 1975, the U.S. Supreme Court reviewed a lower court decision involving John R. Park, president of Acme Supermarkets, who had been found criminally liable for allowing unsanitary conditions to persist in one of his company's food warehouses — even though the building was in another city and Park had no personal, day-to-day involvement in managing the warehouse. The Court affirmed Park's conviction, stating that the Food, Drug, and Cosmetic Act "imposes not only a *positive duty to seek out and remedy violations* when they occur but also, and primarily, *a duty to implement measures that will insure that violations will not occur."*

Source: Jameson W. Doig (with Douglas E. Phillips and Tycho Manson), "Placing the Burden Where It Belongs: The Role of Senior Executives in Preventing Illegal Behavior in Complex Organizations," paper presented at the annual meeting of the American Society for Public Administration, 1983.

The duty to prevent and correct violations was imposed by the court on all officials with the authority to do so.[3]

When an executive fails to act responsibly, *criminal* liability is not the only alternative; civil sanctions may be imposed. Under the Federal Trade Commission Act, for example, "[a] manager is [civilly] liable for deceptive acts of his subordinates if he had the authority to control those acts and, with *knowledge* of the acts or practices, failed to control them." In such circumstances, the manager or executive may be required in FTC proceedings to repay funds received by his company from others because of the deceptive acts.[4] Also, civil sanctions and private damage actions may be used in cases of negligent failure by executives, when criminal liability would be rejected as inappropriate.[5] In this context, the use of innovative sanctions, such as disqualification or suspension from service as a corporate official, might be expanded.[6]

The deterrent value of an executive-responsibility perspective is also illustrated by the Foreign Corrupt Practices Act. The Act includes a provision that forbids the authorization of payments by United States corporations and their officials to "any person, while knowing or having reason to know" that all or part of the money "will be offered, given, or promised, directly or indirectly, to any foreign [government] official" or designated political figure for proscribed purposes. Violation of this provision can result in criminal penalties including fines and imprisonment for five years. Other provisions include recordkeeping and accounting requirements designed in part to elicit "reasonable assurances" that "transactions are executed in accordance with management's general or specific authorization."[7]

These provisions encourage efforts by corporate executives to prevent their subordinates and others from bribery of foreign officials and politicians, and in certain circumstances the Act effectively imposes a form of executive responsibility. For example, when executives are asked to authorize seemingly legitimate payments to foreign agents or subcontractors, they must determine whether any part of the payment is likely to be directly or indirectly relayed to foreign government officials or politicians. Otherwise, if a proscribed payment does result and a judge or jury decides that the executive had "reason to know" of that result, the executive may face criminal fines or imprisonment.

A number of steps can be taken by executives to comply with the Act. These include working with employees and auditors to plan methods of securing compliance, and being "on the lookout for 'red flags.'" Red flags include payments for goods or services, such as agents' fees, that are substantially greater than normal, payments of money without demonstrable good reasons "to persons outside the normal scope of the transaction," "[l]arge bonuses," "unusual credits granted new customers," and "[l]arge and frequent fourth quarter adjustments" as well as other signs of potential problems. These signs do not conclusively show wrongdoing but they should put management on notice, requiring investigation.[8]

According to the former federal prosecutor with principal responsibility for enforcing the Act, United States corporations doing business abroad "seem to be going to 'extraordinary lengths' to avoid violations" of the Act.[9]

The Role of Vulnerability Assessment

The objection sometimes made that an executive-responsibility strategy is impractical and unfair loses much of its force when confronted with a workable means to aid the executive in becoming aware of the internal problems. The recent development of the vulnerability-assessment strategy may meet this need. This strategy involves assigning responsibility to one or more aides for top officials (perhaps housed in a special office) to analyze areas that are especially vulnerable to corruption or other abuses. This strategy makes it possible for senior officials to identify possible areas of weakness and to devise appropriate preventive steps. Therefore, top officials of complex organizations should be expected to grasp this new instrument of managerial control, and to face the consequences when they choose ignorance.

To be more specific, if lower-level officials are charged with illegal activities (whether motivated only by "private advantage" or more broadly) it would be appropriate to ask of higher-level officials in the same organization, "Where is your specialized vulnerability-assessment office?" Such a query could be pressed not only by prosecutors and judges, but also by legislators confronting departmental officials, and by members of the board of directors in exploring the responsibility and competence of a corporation's president and other senior officials. The absence of such a unit would indicate executive laxity in a crucial area; and the existence of such a unit, with a reasonable budget and a strong reputation among professionals in the field, would be an important defense to the charge of executive irresponsibility with its exposure to civil or criminal liability.

For the organization's leaders, then, the first step is to ask the question, "In what areas is our agency vulnerable to corruption, or to other forms of illegal behavior?" For example:

Do we place a very heavy emphasis on quantitative measures in evaluating and rewarding individual performance? (If so, our staff members are under pressure to generate fraudulent statistics or otherwise to undermine the monitoring system — for example, as plant managers at times do, and police officers too, placing evidence on suspects so that drug arrests can be increased.)

Do we have extremely detailed regulations which, if fully enforced, would bring operations to a halt? (If so, each staff member learns to bend the rules in order to get the job done somehow, and — as Peter Schuck's study of meat inspectors dramatically illustrates — an atmosphere conducive to neglect and bribery is likely to be created.[10])

Do we fail to rotate our inspectors among firms or geographic regions being inspected? (If so, we can predict that some inspectors have developed profitable alliances with firms being regulated, a danger always in private corporations, in our police precincts, in our restaurant inspection systems, in our environmental protection units, and elsewhere.)

In the contracts for goods and services for our department, are most of them (for example, for truck and auto repair parts) awarded to a small number of companies? Are almost all of the firms receiving contracts from within this state? Is the reputation of our department shaky (in terms of allegations of payoffs in order to obtain contracts) among firms that provide similar services in this region?

If the answer to any of these questions is "yes," an area to probe for possible corruption has been identified. And if the answer of the senior officials in an agency is "we don't know," they are not doing their job, and only luck is protecting the organization from a future scandal.

Vulnerability assessment has been pioneered by the United States Department of Labor, which uses the approach in probing areas where "abuse of office" may have occurred.[11]

Thus, the executive-responsibility and vulnerability-assessment strategies may work to reinforce each other, with vulnerability assessment rendering executive responsibility more feasible, thereby countering objections as to its possible unfairness, and with executive responsibility increasing the likelihood that vulnerability assessment can be used effectively in deterring *all* types of illegal behavior. Since, to our knowledge, there is no case law similar to Park that is directly applicable to illegal behavior in government agencies, the potential value of an executive-responsibility strategy in the public sector needs to be explored. In the following, and final, section of this essay, we turn to that task.

The Executive-Responsibility Strategy in the Public Sector

In this section, we examine — in part through a review of two mine-safety cases — the potential use of executive responsibility in government organizations, and we comment further on the relationships between vulnerability assessment and executive responsibility.

In 1947, a mine explosion in Centralia, Illinois, killed 111 miners. The explosion was in all likelihood a chain reaction composed of several smaller explosions which produced a larger one because of the presence of large quantities of coal dust in the mine's atmosphere.[12] A procedure called rock-dusting was available that would have minimized the amount of coal dust in the air, thus guarding against the possibility of an explosion. Both the union local in Centralia and the state inspector responsible for the mine had been urging for some years that rock-dusting be maintained as a regular practice in the mine. That this dusting was not a regular practice was the responsibility of the mine's operator, the Centralia Coal Company (a subsidiary of the larger Bell and Zoller Corporation), but the Illinois Department of Mines and Minerals also played a crucial role in the events that precipitated the explosion in March of 1947.

In 1941, Governor Dwight Green of Illinois had appointed Robert Medill as Director of the Department of Mines and Minerals, and during the next five years Medill and his assistant Director, Robert Weir, received more than a dozen reports from the Department's own inspector at the Centralia mine. These reports outlined in considerable detail the Company's poor safety procedures, but Medill and Weir simply forwarded them to the Company itself, with cover letters that asked the Company to comply with proper procedures in dusting and cleaning. Generally the Company did not bother to respond to the letters at all, and it never instituted a preventive system to ensure that coal dust was kept within safe limits. Medill and Weir did not follow up on their letters to the Company.

As the Department's inspector reported that conditions grew worse, in 1943 and 1944, his criticisms were joined by letters from Centralia's local miners to Medill, to the Mining Board (which was responsible for Department policy-making), and to Governor Green. Finally, in 1945, Medill wrote to a Bell and Zoller vice president to ask for his comments on the problem. When that official responded with a letter which asserted that the demand for coal prevented his using more effective safety procedures, Medill readily accepted that letter as adequate reason to avoid taking any action. When alerted to the continuing danger in the mine by further pleas from local miners, the Mining Board also failed to conduct a careful inspection of the charges or to take any remedial or preventive steps. And when these complaints reached the Governor's Office, his aide simply forwarded them back to the Board and Medill, for their "action."

Six separate investigations followed the Centralia explosion, and a grand jury indicted both Medill and Weir for "palpable omission of duty" (and the Centralia Coal Company for "willful neglect," for its failure to comply with the mining law). Because Medill "performed an act of great political loyalty when he shouldered most of the blame" for the disaster, the assessment of direct responsibility did not reach others above him.[13] However, Medill had been appointed by the Governor and was under the supervisory authority of the Mining Board; and it was well known that he had close ties to the mine operators. Therefore, his reluctance to act vigorously against the operators, when safety procedures (which generally would reduce production rates, and company profits) were not followed, could easily have been predicted. Yet the Mining Board, and the Governor and his aide, treated signals of possible disaster with routine indifference.

Under the concept of executive responsibility, the Governor, his aide who was responsible for this area, and the Mining Board members all would have been exposed to sanctions. The severity of those sanctions would depend on degrees of responsibility; the existence of such individual exposure prior to 1947 might, we can conjecture, have led these officials to take more effective action during the several years of warnings before the explosion.

More recently, the federal Department of Labor has engaged in a vulnerability-assessment of the role of the Mine Safety and Health Administration (MSHA) in an explosion in a mine owned by Cargill, Inc., with a view to analyzing whether abuse of office, suppression of inspections, and conflict of interest occurred at MSHA. The Department's vulnerability-assessments of MSHA's general operations disclosed major programmatic weaknesses in the way that MSHA levied cash penalties (with its enforcement personnel modifying orders and citations, and reducing proposed penalties, without authorization), and in its procedures for procuring goods and services related to mine safety.[14] This kind of study makes it possible to identify — and implement — measures designed to prevent such patterns of abuse within complex public organizations. Thus vulnerability-assessment can complement and render more feasible executive-responsibility rules in areas that allow government officials broad discretion.

Conclusion

Our emphasis on situations in which organizational officials need forceful prodding to take remedial actions may create the impression that we view organizational officials in a purely negative light — as if they were, in some sense, the enemy, requiring pressure and compulsion to be brought to bear on their offices, and on their hides. Our main purpose, however, is to argue that a more *positive* conception of the role of leadership is essential, if illegal behavior in complex organizations is to be deterred.

Senior officials need to acknowledge and affirm the vital role they play in shaping their organization's overall integrity. Personally, the leaders of an organization set a moral tone which is crucial — either in persuading subordinate officials to behave legally (and, more generally, to behave ethically), or in signalling to higher and lower staff members that private advantage may be obtained with impunity and that the organization will reward those who find ways to add to its own power and profit, even if laws and public standards are violated in the process. For example, if members of the leadership group use an organization's goods and services — cars, planes, expense vouchers — improperly, for private benefit, a tone is set for subordinates; and if company memoranda announce occasionally that "thou shalt not" engage in price-fixing, toxic dumping, or other illegal acts, but promotions and other rewards for those who engage in such behavior abound, an atmosphere of duplicity and condoned illegality can be expected to pervade the organization as a whole. In part, then, an executive-responsibility strategy is an effort to promote awareness on the part of top-level officials of the immense importance of the example that they set for their subordinates, in their personal attitudes and behavior.

More broadly, the willingness of an organization's leaders to devote time and energy to understanding the incentives in their own agencies which may undermine integrity, to alter those incentives, and to reward those who behave ethically and legally is crucial to the moral and legal stance of all of their employees. The executive who turns a blind eye to illegality may be weak in moral fibre, lacking in administrative energy, or a dedicated defender of his or her own agency, "right or wrong." Here executive responsibility may wake officials from their reverie or narrow passions, with the threat of sanctions providing a needed goad.

Endnotes

1. Edmund Burke, *Thoughts on the Cause of the Present Discontents,* April 23, 1770.
2. See for example the cases described in Melvin Dalton, *Men Who Manage* (New York: John Wiley, 1960); Allan N. Kornblum, *The Moral Hazards* (Lexington, MA: Lexington Book, 1976); and Kermit Vandivier, "Why Should My Conscience Bother Me?" [reprinted in this volume].
3. *United States v. Park,* 421 U.S. 658 (1975); emphasis added.
4. *FTC v. H.N. Singer* (U.S. District Court, No. Calif., 1982).
5. A person acts negligently with respect to a material element of an offense, under the Model Penal Code, if he "should be aware of a substantial and unjustifiable risk" that the element is present or will result from his conduct. ALI Model Penal Code sec, 2.02(2) (d). "The risk must be of such a nature and degree that the actor's failure to perceive it, considering the nature and purpose of his conduct and the circumstances known to him, involves a gross deviation from the standard of care that a reasonable person would observe in the actor's situation." *Id.*
6. In a recent case involving an alleged attempt by an airline and its president (also its chief executive officer) to monopolize passenger routes, the Department of Justice sought an injunction that would prohibit the airline official from serving any airline as president, as chief executive officer or in any other pricing-related capacity for two years (*United States v. American Airlines, Inc.,* Trade Reg. Reports. March 1, 1983).
7. U.S. Code, 15, sec. 78ff.
8. Business Laws, Inc., Foreign Corrupt Practices Act 122-30 (1982), pp. 123-124.
9. In part due to the goad provided by the Act, some corporations have moved vigorously to improve their internal accounting controls. The results, according to Dean John C. Burton of the Columbia Business School (and a proponent of the Act), have been significant: "The management of many companies has been improved as a result of the steps taken. Greater data reliability, more consistent policies among companies, and better information for decision-making have resulted, as well as greater awareness on the part of boards and top management of the benefits of sound controls." *New York Times,* March 20, 1983, p. 2.
10. See Peter Schuck, "The Curious Case of the Indicted Meat Inspectors," in R.J. Stillman II *Public Administration: Concepts and Cases* (2d ed. 1980).
11. See the *Semiannual Report of the Inspector General,* U.S. Department of Labor, March, 1981.
12. This summary is based on John Bartlow Martin, "The Blast in Centralia No. 5," in R.J. Stillman II *Public Administration.*
13. *Id.,* p. 33. The quoted words are those of the case author, John Bartlow Martin.
14. *Semiannual Report of the Inspector-General,* 1981, pp. 52-57.

The Moral Responsibility of Individuals in Public Sector Organizations

Debra Stewart

The concern about the need for more attention to questions of professional ethics is expressed regularly in the pages of journals addressing public administration.[1] Most recently it served as the catalyst for a public debate in the American Society for Public Administration over the appropriateness of a proposed code of ethics in public administration.[2] The debate, however, is not limited to managers in the public sector. In virtually all the major professions today there are lively, often heated discussions about how professionals cope with the ethical quandaries they face in their work lives. Lawyers, physicians, engineers, professors, even data processing professionals are publicly examining their collective consciences to discern the proper standards of conduct.[3]

Debra Stewart argues that individuals in public organizations remain responsible for their actions and decisions regardless of whatever other administrative roles and obligations they might have. What are the practical implications of this position?

In public administration much of this reflection focuses on developing or enhancing existing jurisdictional codes of ethics and conflict of interest statutes; some explore organizational protection for whistle-blowers; still other discussions consider enhancing the power of oversight committees and other monitoring groups to ensure that missteps will be exposed or discouraged. In these discussions across professions, one concern is common: to what extent should the individual be cast as a "moral actor" in a work setting? The extent to which this particular question dominates the debate about professional ethics correlates strongly with the extent to which the profession must be practiced as part of a collective. Where the sole professional is able to deliver a service to a client directly, issues of individual responsibility pale in comparison to issues of the morality of the interaction. Should a physician lie to a dying patient about prospects for recovery? Should a lawyer maintain client confidentiality if it puts another person at risk? But in public sector organizations where large numbers of professionals are working through complex organizations to achieve broad public policy objectives, the traditional basis for "moral accountability," i.e., the relationship between the individual professional and his/her client, evaporates. (Anderson *et. al.* 1980) Hence, the first question for the public manager when faced with a moral quandary is often: "What right do I have to exercise moral judgment at all?"

Tentativeness around this question has a profoundly chilling effect on productive examination of personal moral responsibility. Such tentativeness is triggered by a perspective which sees morality as residing principally in the organization itself — its routines, its incentives, its constraints, and its opportunities. It follows that, if the organization itself is the moral agent, placing obligation on the individual is unrealistic and ultimately an inefficient strategy for enhancing the moral quality of organizational actions. To examine this proposition, it is important to clarify the meaning of individual moral obligation.

To say that people are morally responsible is to "[evaluate] their behavior relative to some principle or standard." (Flores and Johnson, 1983:538) Evaluative responsibility doesn't imply legal responsibility. But moral responsibility does mean the ability to hold an individual blameworthy for an act carried out even though that act is carried out as part of a collective. The purpose of this article is to examine those arguments against placing moral responsibility with individual actors in public sector organizations.

Three formidable arguments are marshalled against assigning significant moral responsibility to individuals in organizations: the argument from role, the argument from systems theory, and the argument from executive accountability. Each of these arguments will be presented and assessed with the objective of bringing sufficient closure to the question to permit further development in the management ethics field.

Source: Debra Stewart, "Ethics and the Profession of Public Administration: The Moral Responsibility of Individuals in Public Sector Organizations," *Public Administration Quarterly*, 8:4 (Winter 1985), pp. 487-495.

The Argument From Role

Roles are sets of sanctioned, expected behaviors in an organizational setting. (Stewart and Garson, 1983) The argument from the role suggests that, when one acts in an organizational role, "pursuing objectives and employing methods designated by it," one doesn't satisfy the necessary conditions for being held morally responsible. An individual can be morally responsible for actions only if "the action is free and the individual is himself at the time of the action." (Flores and Johnson, 1983: 541) Individuals bound by organizational roles are not free in this sense. This absence of freedom stems from the fact that they are acting as the representatives of the organizations and, as such, are obligated to carry through on past commitments and decisions as well as those dictated by their current roles. They are acting in public rather than a private capacity. Acts taken by individuals in organizational roles as distinct from private roles are, in other words, acts taken by individuals within roles they themselves did not define. (*Ibid., 541*) Hence conditions of moral responsibility cannot be met, not even in the sense of apportioning to individuals part of the collective responsibility of the group.

The counter-argument here can be summarized in four points. The first three points address role-governed behavior in any organization and the fourth point focuses on special characteristics of the public administration role. First, unless one is coerced to play a role, the fact that behavior is role-governed doesn't relieve one of the moral responsibility for actions and their consequences. While some work organizations might provide more opportunity for individuals to change, rather than escape from, an objectionable state of affairs, no organization compels individuals to stay. In A.O Hirschman's (1970) terms, both "Exit" and "Voice" remain viable options. Admittedly, the lack of another organization in which to practice one's profession might hold exit at bay. But the nature of modern work organizations is that the prohibition of the exit option doesn't exist.

Second, the distinction between public and private acts which relieve individuals of responsibility for acts undertaken in their public role fails because individuals generally gain some personal benefit from performance of their public or organizational role. While advancing organization objectives, personal goals are also served — at the minimum by compensation for time and effort. In other words, the role is one means of securing personal ends. (Flores and Johnson, 1983)

The third point is that, notwithstanding constraints implied by roles, individuals bring their own moral qualities to any position. All that is required for behavior is never totally spelled out by a role definition. Even role-constrained decisions permit individual judgments, reflecting the unique moral make-up of the decision-maker. (*Ibid.*)

All of the counter-arguments presented thus far portray a scenario where there is tension between the demands of a morally neutral role and individual judgments of right or wrong. However, this discussion of moral judgment in public sector organizational roles introduces a new factor because the very setting of the role implies a moral dimension. The historic debate in public administration over the proper mix of politics and administration highlights the central place of values in interpreting the public administrator's role. One might attribute this emphasis to historical circumstances, since the founders of our field were deeply involved with political reform movements, before, during, and after the progressive era. (Waldo, 1980:93) Or the source of the moral emphasis in the public administrator's role may simply be in the nature of the work to be done. Ralph Chandler (1983:37) notes, "Most public policy has as its declared aim some public good" and Dwight Waldo (1980:110) has identified more than a dozen sources of obligation relevant to the conduct of the public administrator's role. Whatever the reason, the role of a public administrator carries a kind of moral weight not found in private sector counterparts' roles.

The Argument From Systems Theory

The second argument against assigning significant moral responsibility to individuals in organizations relates to the nature of complex organizations. Complex organizations are systems composed of several components which interact with one another to create a whole. Component parts include people, processes, structures, and cultures. Organizations have boundaries which differentiate them from their environment, but they interact with their environment regularly. Organizations, driven by systemic imperatives, convert inputs from the environment into outputs impacting the environment. Organizations are constantly interacting with the environment, changing and adapting to develop congruence between people, processes, structures, and sectors in the external environment. (Katz and Kahn, 1966:14-29)

Thus, behavior in the organization can be understood less as the deliberate choice of specific people and more as "outputs" of large systems functioning according to standard patterns of behavior. (Allison, 1971) In order for large organizations to function, the behavior of large numbers of individuals must be coordinated. Coordination is achieved through organizational routines — a fixed set of standard operating procedures. "The behavior of these organizations . . . relevant to an issue in any particular instance is determined primarily by routines establish in that organization prior to a particular event." (*Ibid.,* 68) These routines change incrementally in response to changes in the environment.

The diverse demands on individuals shape their priorities, perceptions, and issues, but these demands emanate from position in the organization and the degree and character of interaction with sectors in the environment. Assigning responsibility for "moral reasoning" to individuals in this net of organizational system forces is inappropriate. Certainly conflicts will arise between individuals and groups within organizations as they pursue their goals along the rails of established routines. But to cast these systemic conflicts as ethical dilemmas for the participant is an error. The recent case study of whistle-blowing at the Bay Area Rapid Transit (BART) makes this case forcefully. (Anderson *et. al.,* 1980)

The counter-argument to the systems analysis rationale against holding individuals accountable has two parts. First, the systems approach to analyzing organizations is a descriptive and not a prescriptive enterprise. Systems theory is advanced to help us understand how organizations *do* behave, not how individuals *should* behave. For example, a major insight from systems theory as applied to organizations is that organizations like all systems are impelled toward survival and will adapt toward that objective. While survival makes perfect sense as a goal (i.e., we can better understand organizations by seeing them as systems striving to survive), survival is not the right objective in every situation. Some organizations should cease functioning from a public interest viewpoint. Any argument that individuals can't be held accountable because they are just part of the organizational system makes the error of confusing "system," as a description, with "system" as a prescription. System is a metaphor to describe how organizations function; it can't be used to address the question of normative judgment in organizations.

Second, even as a metaphor of organizational life, systems theory is deficient when it ignores the political process that unfolds in an organization. Organizational power holders in "dominant coalitions" decide on courses of strategic action which both establish structural forms and manipulate environmental factors. In doing so, these collections of individuals make significant value choices which advance some goals and inhibit others. Thus, even in a descriptive sense, the dominant coalition in an organization is not at the mercy of the organization as a system. (Child, 1972) Significant "outputs" are intentional. In deciding on courses of action, individuals are engaging in behavior that will help or hurt specific interests. For their contribution to such action, they are individually accountable.

The Argument From Executive Accountability

The third argument against assigning moral responsibility to organizational members is that it places emphasis on "good people" rather than on executive accountability where it belongs. The ultimate objective of the focus on management ethics is to reduce unethical behavior in organizations. In reality, unethical behavior is reduced only by strategies which place individuals in fewer compromising situations (rotation, clear guidelines, etc.) and by increasing sanctions for illegal action. (Doig, 1983)[4] Since the objective is actually to change the unethical behavior, that is where the focus should remain. To ensure that strategies for reducing opportunities for unethical action are adopted, responsibility should be placed on the top of the organization, the office of the CEO.

The response to this assertion is not so much that the analysis is wrong; it is not. Whatever steps can be taken to buffer public servants from "occasions of sin" should be taken. Efforts to induce CEOs to adopt preventative measures to ensure that their subordinates avoid unethical action are worth considering. That is particularly so where the focus is on unethical actions which constitute a violation of the law.

However, at some level we also want to "get better people." The moral quality of our public servants is important because the alternative approach, if relied on exclusively, means to tighten control in a way that makes the exercise of moral judgment on the part of individuals unnecessary or impossible. We know that "the capacity to make moral judgment is strengthened by enabling members of organizations to respond to situations, to project alternative ends-in-view to solve those problems, devise means to reach ends and test their self-generated moral judgments in use." (Spence, 1980:146) The experience in lack of opportunity to make moral judgments increases the moral degeneration of organizational life. In other words, it might be advisable to put substantial energy into reducing the occasions of sin for public administrators, particularly in those areas where sin translates into violation of civil and criminal law. But this strategy, if used exclusively, will produce the undesirable consequence of a trained incapacity for moral judgment in the large majority of public managers not occupying CEO slots.

Conclusion

Is it appropriate to consider the public administrator an ethical agent in his or her work setting? In this author's opinion, the answer is "yes." The preceding analysis of arguments to the contrary compels the conclusion that public administrators find no easy escape from the uncomfortable task of making moral judgments. Inevitably moral quandaries arise because not all claimants can be equally served, not all goods are equally compatible, and not all outcomes are equally desirable. There is no simple moral equation which political executives use to generate the "right" solution to moral quandaries. In their work lives, public administrators will be confronted by choices weighed with ethical implications.

Helping to develop the "art of voice" (Hirschman, 1970:43) is part of the task of public administration scholars. The first step is to clear the decks with respect to the question of exercising moral judgment at all. This article is an attempt to achieve that goal.

References

Allison, Graham T. (1971). *The Essence of Decision*. Boston: Little, Brown.

Anderson, Robert A., Robert Perruccci, Dan E. Schendel, and Leon E. Trachtmase (1980). *Divided Loyalties: Whistle-Blowing at BART*. West Lafayette: Purdue University.

Chandler, Ralph Clark (1983). "The Problem of Moral Reasoning in American Public Administration: The Case for a Code of Ethics." *Public Administration Review* 43 (January/February):32-39.

Child, John (1972). "Organizational Structure, Environment and Performance: The Role of Strategy Choice." *Sociology* VI (January):1-23.

Doig, Jameson W. (1983). "Placing the Burden Where It Belongs: The Role of Senior Executives in Preventing Illegal Behavior in Complex Organizations." Paper prepared for the panel on "Anti-Corruption Strategies in Public Agencies" at the National Conference on the American Society for Public Administration, New York, April 16-19.

Flores, Albert and Deborah C. Johnson (1983). "Collective Responsibility and Professional Roles." *Ethics* 93 (April):537-545.

Hirschman, Albert O. (1970). *Exit, Voice, and Loyalty*. Cambridge: Harvard University Press.

Katz, Daniel and Robert L. Kahn (1966). *The Social Psychology of Organizations*. New York: John Wiley and Sons.

Spence, Larry D. (1980). "Moral Judgment and Bureaucracy," in Richard W. Wilson and Gordon J. Schochet (eds.). *Moral Development and Politics*. New York: Praeger.

Stewart, Debra W. and G. David Garson (1983). *Organizational Behavior and Public Management*. New York: Marcel Dekker.

Waldo, Dwight (1980). *The Enterprise of Public Administration*. Novato, Cal.: Chandler and Sharp.

Endnotes

1. A recent computer search of the Public Affairs Information Service data base revealed the term "ethics" (or some variation such as ethical, etc.) appeared in the title of publications covered on an average of 39 times a year over the past six years (1977-1982). As a percentage of total citations in the PAIS data base, the number of ethics citations has grown gradually since 1981, with the percentage doubling from 1982 to 1983.

2. The Professional Standards and Ethics Committee of the American Society for Public Administration debated whether a code of ethics should be adopted for ASPA.

3. Many examples would illustrate these discussions in the various professional fields. For representative discussions in each professional field, see the following: Law, Monroe H. Freeman, *Lawyer's Ethics in an Adversary System* (Indianapolis and New York: Bobbs-Merrill Co., 1975); Medicine, S.J. Reiser, A.J. Dych, and W.J. Curran, eds., *Ethics in Medicine* (Cambridge and London: MIT Press 1977); Engineering, Rachell Hollander, "Conference Report: Engineering Ethics," *Science, Technology, and Human Values* (Winter, 1983); George M. Schorr, "Toward a Code of Ethics for Academics," *Journal of Higher Education*, Vol. 53, No. 3, (1983); "DPMA Puts Bite in New Professional Ethics Code," *Information Systems News*, p. 7.

4. Readers should note that Professor Doig's stress in advocating executive accountability is in reducing illegal behavior. This article considers behavior that may be perceived as unethical, though not necessarily illegal.

About the Editors

William L. Richter is professor and head of the department of political science, Kansas State University. He has written widely on public and international affairs in South Asia and is co-editor of *The Landon Lectures: Perspective from the First Twenty Years.* A member of ASPA's national committee on ethics since 1984 and past president of the Kansas chapter of ASPA, he also coordinates the "ASPA on Ethics" column for the *PA TIMES.*

Frances Burke is professor at Suffolk University, School of Management. She served during 1989-90 as Alice Tweed Tuohy Visiting Professor of Government and Ethics, Claremont McKenna College. A former ASPA National Council member, she chaired the committee on ethics as well as the committee on III Centuries of Public Administration commemorating the U.S. Constitutional Bicentennial. She has written on values and ethics and on the contributions of women to government.

Jameson W. Doig is professor of politics and public affairs, Princeton University. Recently he edited *Leadership and Innovation: Entrepreneurs in Government* (with Erwin C. Hargrove), and he has written on urban development, administrative behavior, and criminal justice. He has chaired ASPA's section on criminal justice administration as well as the Society's national committee on ethics.

INDEX

. . .

Other ASPA Best Selling Publications

The Wilson Influence on Public Administration: From Theory to Practice
edited by Paul P. Van Riper, Texas A&M University

Looking Back/Moving Forward:
A Half Century Celebration of Public Administration
by Darrell Pugh, San Diego State University

The Study of Administration Revisited
edited by James D. Carroll, The Brookings Institute, and
Alfred M. Zuck, National Association of Schools of
Public Affairs and Administration

Accounting and Accountability in Public Administration
PAR Classics VII
edited by Richard E. Brown, Kent State University

Program Evaluation: Patterns and Directions
PAR Classics VI
edited by Eleanor Chelimsky, U.S. Government Accounting Office

Federalism and Intergovernmental Relations
PAR Classics V
edited by Deil B. Wright, University of North Carolina-Chapel Hill, and
Harvey L. White, University of Pittsburgh

Perspectives on Budgeting
PAR Classics II, A Revised Edition
edited by Allen Schick, University of Maryland

■

For complete information and to place an order, please call or write:
American Society for Public Administration
1120 G Street, NW, Suite 500
Washington, DC 20005
(202) 393-7878/FAX (202) 638-4952

. . .